]
Translated by Maria K.

Thais of Athens

Maria K.
2468 Locust Grove Road
Hendersonville, NC 28792 USA

mariakuroshchepova.blogspot.com

Thais of Athens
Copyright ©2011 by Maria K.

Print ISBN: 978-1-463537-78-4
Digital ISBN: 978-1-458048-42-4

Cover and illustrations by Maria K.
Edited by Genevieve Graham Sawchyn

This is a work of historic fiction. While some characters are real historic figures, most names, characters, places and incidents either are the product of the authors' imaginations or are used fictitiously and any resemblance to actual persons, living or dead, business establishments, events or locales is entirely coincidental.

All rights reserved. No part of this book may be used or reproduced or transmitted in any form or by any means, electronic or mechanical, including photocopying, recording, or by any information storage and retrieval system, without written permission from the copyright owner except in the case of brief quotations embodied in critical articles and reviews.

First electronic publication by Maria K.: May 2011
First print publication: May 2011

Published in the United States of America with international distribution.

Dedication

To my Mom for introducing me to this book.
To all incredible women in my life who represent
the living proof that our era can produce strong
female characters.

Reader's Reference	8
Chapter One. Earth and Stars	12
Chapter Two. Egesikhora's Heroics	46
Chapter Three. Escape to the South	77
Chapter Four. The Power of Animal Gods	109
Chapter Five. The Muse of the Neit Temple	147
Chapter Six. The Thread of Laconian Fate	181
Chapter Seven. Hesiona's Awakening	209
Chapter Eight. The Chestnut Pacer	238
Chapter Nine. Visiting Mother of Gods	279
Chapter Ten. Waters of the Euphrates	329
Chapter Eleven. The Doom of Persepolis	364
Chapter Twelve. The Heirs of Crete	399
Chapter Thirteen. Keoss Ritual	441
Chapter Fourteen. Wisdom of Eridu	485
Chapter Fifteen. Unfulfilled Dream	520
Chapter Sixteen. The Queen of Memphis	559
Chapter Seventeen. Aphrodite Ambologera	590

Epilogue	**633**
About the Author	**634**
About the Translator	**635**
Acknowledgments	**636**
Other works by Maria K.	**637**

Reader's Reference

I. All ancient Greek words and names, with a few exceptions, should be pronounced with an emphasis on a one-before-last syllable. In two syllable words and names, the emphasis is on the first syllable: Thais, Eris. The exceptions are, for the most part, of artificial origin – they appear in Latinized words: goplit (from goplitos), Alexander (Alexandros), Menedem (Menedemos), Nearch (Nearchus), where Greek endings were removed.

II. Hellenic New Year occurs during the first full moon after the summer solstice, during the first ten days of July. The Olympic calendar begins from the first Olympiad (776 B.C.) with four years per each: the first year of the 75th Olympiad is 480 B.C. To convert the Olympic calendar to ours, one must remember that each Greek year corresponds to the second half of the same year in our system and the first half of the following year. One must multiply the number of Olympiads by 4, add the number of years of the current Olympiad minus one, and subtract the obtained number from 776, if the event occurs in the fall or winter, and from 775 if it occurs in spring or summer.

III. Greek months:

Summer

1. Hekatombeon (mid-July - mid-August)
2. Metageytnion (August - first half of September)
3. Boedromion (September - first half of October)

Fall

4. Puanepsion (October - first half of November)
5. Maymakterion (November - first half of December)
6. Posideon (December - first half of January)

Winter

7. Gamelion (January - first half of February)
8. Antesterion (February - first half of March)
9. Elafebolion (Mart - second half of April)

Spring

10. Munikhion (April - first half of May)
11. Targelion (May - first half of June)
12. Skyrophorion (June - first half of July)

IV. Some unit measures and currency.

- Long stadium: 178 meters / 584 feet
- Olympic stadium: 185 meters / 607 feet
- Egyptian skhen (equal to Persian parsang): 30 stadiums, approximately 5 kilometers / 3.1 miles
- plethor: 31 meters / 101.7 feet
- orgy: 185 centimeters / 74.8 inches
- pekis (elbow): 0.46 meter / 1.5 feet
- podes (foot): 0.3 meter / 0.93 feet
- palysta (palm): approximately 7 centimeters / 2.75 inches
- epydama (equal to three palystas): 23 centimeters / 9 inches
- condilos (equal to two dactyls – fingers): approximately 4 centimeters / 1.57 inches.
- Talant: a measure of weight approximately 26 kilograms / 57.32 pounds
- Mina: 437 grams / 0.96 pounds

- Currency units: talant – 100 minas, mina – 60 drachmas.

- Popular Greek coins: silver didrachma (2 drachmas) equal to a gold Persian daric. Tetradrachm (four drachmas) with the image of Athena's own was the main Greek silver currency (gold went into circulation during the era of Alexander the Great, when the value of talant and drachma fell steeply).

- Liquid measures – khoes (jug) – just over 3 liters – 0.79 liquid gallons; cotile (small pot) – approximately 0.3 liters – just over 10 fluid ounces.

V. Greek greeting, "Haire!" ("Rejoice!") corresponds to our "Hello!" When parting people said either "Haire!" or, when expecting a lengthy separation, "Geliaine!" ("Be well!")

Chapter One. Earth and Stars

From out of the west came the wind, strengthening with every gust. Heavy waves, oily under the evening sky, thundered against the shore. Ptolemy was heavier than the others, his swimming skills less. He tired, especially when Cape Colnad no longer protected him against the wind, and struggled behind his friends, Nearchus, Alexander and Hephaestion. He didn't dare venture farther from the shore and yet he feared the white fountains of surf spraying off the gloomy dark rocks. His friends had abandoned him, and his anger at them sucked his strength further.

Nearchus, the quiet and taciturn Cretan, was an unbeatable swimmer. He had absolutely no fear of the storm and simply could not fathom the idea that crossing the Faleron Bay from one cape to the next, especially in this weather, was dangerous for the Macedonians, who weren't quite as close to the sea. But Alexander and his faithful Athenian, Hephaestion, were both desperately stubborn, so they followed Nearchus and forgot their comrade, assuming him lost among the waves.

'Poseidon's bull', a huge wave, lifted Ptolemy on its 'horns', raising him high over the sea. From its height the Macedonian noticed a tiny lagoon nearby, surrounded by sharp boulders. At the sight of it, Ptolemy quit struggling. He lowered his tiring shoulders, covered his head with his arms and slipped under the wave, praying to Zeus the Protector to direct him into the gap between the rocks and keep him safe.

The wave scattered with a deafening roar, tossing him farther onto the sand than an ordinary wave would have. Temporarily blinded and deafened, Ptolemy wiggled and crawled a few pekises, carefully struggled to his knees, then finally stood. He rocked back and forth on unsteady legs and rubbed his aching head. The waves seemed to pummel him even here on earth.

He stood straighter, hearing a sound that did not belong. He listened carefully and heard a brief giggle needle through the noise of the surf. Ptolemy turned around so quickly that he lost his balance and fell to his knees again. The laughter rang again, quite nearby.

He looked up and saw a slender young girl of no great height standing before him. She had obviously just emerged from the sea. Water still sluiced down her smooth body, dark with a coppery tan, running in rivers off the mass of her raven black hair. The swimmer tipped her head to the side as she squeezed water out of her wavy tresses.

Ptolemy rose to his full height and set his feet firmly in the sand. He looked the girl straight in her brave and merry gray eyes, which appeared dark blue in reflection of the sea and the sky. Her long black lashes did not lower or flutter under the passionate and imperious gaze of the son of Lag, even though, at only twenty-four years of age, he was already a well known heartbreaker in Pella, the capital of Macedonia.

Ptolemy could not take his eyes off the girl. She had appeared from the foam and thunder of the sea like a goddess and her coppery face, gray eyes and raven black hair were unusual for an Athenian. Later he realized the girl's copper skin meant she did not fear the sun, the rays of which were the bane of so many Athenian ladies of fashion. Athenian women tanned too thickly, turning purplish bronze like the Ethiopians. For that reason they avoided appearing outdoors without cover. But this girl was like the copper-bodied Circe, or one of the legendary daughters of Minos with blood of sunlight, and she stood before him with all the dignity of a priestess.

No, of course she was not a goddess or a priestess, this small, young girl. In Attica, as in most of Hellas, priestesses were chosen from the tallest, fair-haired beauties. But from where did this girl's calm assurance come? She stood regally, as if she were in a temple and not standing naked before him on an empty shore. He wondered vaguely if she, too, had left her clothing at the distant Phoont Cape. Kharitas, who bestowed magical allure upon women, frequently appeared as girls, but they were an inseparable threesome. This girl was alone.

Before Ptolemy could guess any longer, a female slave in a red chiton[1] appeared, emerging from behind

---

1 A garment worn by men and women consisting of a

a rock. She deftly wrapped the girl in a sheet of coarse fabric and started drying her body and hair.

Ptolemy shivered. He had warmed up while struggling against the waves, but now he had cooled off. The wind was brisk even for a Macedonian who was hardened by stern physical upbringing.

The girl tossed the hair away from her face and suddenly whistled through her teeth as if she were a boy. The whistle surprised Ptolemy and he frowned. The sound appeared both disdainful and obnoxious, completely unfit for her feminine beauty.

Apparently in response to the whistle, a small boy appeared and glanced cautiously at Ptolemy. The Macedonian, who was observant by nature and had developed this ability further while studying under Aristotle, returned his inquiring stare. He noticed the boy's fingers clutched the hilt of a short dagger which was hidden in the folds of his clothing.

The girl said something in a voice too quiet for Ptolemy to hear over the splash of the waves, and the boy ran off. He returned and approached Ptolemy with greater trust this time, handing him a short cape. Ptolemy wrapped it around himself, then, obeying the girl's silent request, turned so he faced the sea.

As he turned, he heard the farewell "Haire!" called from behind his back. Ptolemy spun on his heel and rushed toward the stranger, who was fastening her sash after a Cretan fashion, around her waist instead of beneath her breasts. The cinched waist was just as impossibly slender as those of the ancient women of the legendary island.

He shouted, "Who are you?"

---

rectangle of cloth, wrapped around and pinned or sewn at the shoulders. A woman's chiton was ankle length, whereas a man could wear either a full length or a knee length chiton.

The merry gray eyes squinted with restrained laughter. "I recognized you right away, even though you looked like a wet bird. You are a servant of the Macedonian prince. Where did you lose him and the other companions?"

"I am not his servant, but his friend," Ptolemy said proudly, but held back from revealing anything more and possibly giving away a dangerous secret. "But how could you have seen us?"

"I saw the four of you standing in front of the wall, reading meeting requests at Ceramic. You didn't even notice me. I am Thais."

Ptolemy caught his breath. "Thais? You?"

"That surprises you so?"

"I read that one Philopatros offered Thais a talant, a cost of an entire trireme, and she still didn't inscribe the time for their meeting. I started looking for this goddess …"

She chuckled. "Tall, golden-haired , with blue eyes of a Tritonid[2], she who takes away one's heart …"

"Yes, yes. How did you know?"

"You are not the first, not at all. But farewell again, my horses are anxious to go."

"Wait!" Ptolemy exclaimed, feeling suddenly that he couldn't stand to part with the girl. "Where do you live? Can I come to you? Can I bring my friends?"

Thais studied the Macedonian. Her eyes lost their twinkle and grew darker.

"Come," she said after a pause. "You said that you know Ceramic and the Royal Market. There are big gardens between Ceramic and the Hill of Nymphs, to the east of Gamaxitos. You'll find my house at the outskirts, clearly marked by two olive trees and two cypresses." She stopped speaking abruptly and gave him a farewell nod. Then, just as suddenly, she

---

2   A sea nymph – daughter of Triton.

disappeared among the rocks, following a well-defined path that wove its way to the top.

Ptolemy leaned forward, shook sand out of his hair and slowly made his way to the road. He shortly found himself not far from the Long Walls of Munikhion. The long trail of dust from Thais' carriage floated toward the tree-covered mountain slopes, already blue with twilight. Her two-horse equipage traveled quickly; the young hetaera must have had splendid horses.

A rude exclamation from behind made Ptolemy leap to the side. Another carriage rushed past him, driven by a huge Boeotian. A fashionably dressed young man with long strands of curled hair stood next to the driver, grinning unpleasantly. He lashed Ptolemy with a long handled whip, scorching the Macedonian's barely clad body.

The offender obviously didn't know he was dealing with an experienced warrior. In a flash, Ptolemy grabbed one stone from the many on both sides of the road and tossed it after the carriage. The stone hit the Athenian in the neck just below the back of his head, and it was only the speed of the departing carriage that allowed the impact to soften. Still, the man fell and would have rolled out had his driver not grabbed him and slowed the horses.

The driver showered Ptolemy with curses, yelling that he had killed the wealthy citizen, Philopatros, and ought to be executed. The enraged Macedonian tossed away his cape and reached for a boulder. The one he chose weighed at least a talant, and he lifted it over his head and started toward the carriage. The driver, taking stock of the Macedonian's powerful muscles, lost his desire to fight and drove away, still supporting his master, who was coming around. While he drove he yelled back at Ptolemy, cursing and threatening as loudly as his booming voice would allow.

Ptolemy calmed down and tossed the boulder away. With an exasperated sigh, he picked up the cape and resumed walking along the shore path. He followed it up an overhang where it took a shortcut across a wide loop of the carriage road. As he walked, he thought about the man on the carriage. Something in his memory kept bringing back the name 'Philopatros'. That was what the driver had shouted out. Was Philopatros the one who had written an offer to Thais at Ceramic? Ptolemy grinned. Apparently he had acquired a rival in his offender.

The Macedonian could not offer a talant of silver to the hetaera for a brief liaison, that much was true. A few minas, perhaps. He had heard too much about Thais to simply give her up. Despite her seventeen years of age, Thais was considered to be an Athenian celebrity. For her skill as a dancer, her superior education and particular attractiveness, she was nicknamed 'a fourth Kharita'.

The proud Macedonian would never have asked for money from relatives. Alexander, being the son of King Philip's rejected wife, couldn't help his friend either. The trophies after the battle at Chaeronea hadn't amounted to much. Philip, who took great care of his soldiers, had split everything in such a manner that the prince's friends got no more than the last infantryman. Then Philip had sent Ptolemy and Nearchus into exile, separating them from his son. The three had only managed to meet here, in Athens, when Alexander had called them. That was after Philip dispatched him and Hephaestion to explore Athens and establish themselves there. And while the Athenian wits said "a wolf can only produce a cub", Alexander's true Hellenic beauty and remarkable intelligence made an impression with the experienced citizens of Athens, "The Eye of Hellas", "The Mother of Arts and Eloquence".

Ptolemy considered himself to be Alexander's half-brother. His mother, the famous hetaera Arsinoa, was once close to Philip, and was then married off to the tribal leader, Lag, or Hare. Lag was a man with no great accomplishments but was of noble origin. Ptolemy had remained in the Lagid family and was envious of Alexander for some time, competing with him in both childish games and military training. Once he'd grown up he couldn't help but appreciate the prince's remarkable abilities. He became even more proud of their secret blood relation, which his mother had told him about, but only after a terrible vow had been made.

And what of Thais? Well, Alexander had long since given Ptolemy supremacy in matters of Eros. As much as Ptolemy was flattered by it, he could not help but admit that had Alexander wanted, Alexander could rule among the countless swarms of Aphrodite's admirers. But Alexander wasn't at all interested in women, which worried his mother, Olympias. She was a divinely beautiful priestess of Demeter, and was considered a sorceress, a seductress and a wise ruler of sacred snakes. Despite his courage, daring and constant philandering with all manner of women, Philip had always been wary of his splendid wife, and joked that he was afraid he might someday discover a terrible serpent in bed between himself and his wife. There were persistent rumors, no doubt sustained by Olympias herself, that Alexander wasn't even a son of one-eyed Philip, but that of a deity, to whom she gave herself in a temple one night.

Philip felt stronger after his victory at Chaeronea. On the eve of his being elected a military leader of the union of all Hellenic states in Corinth, he divorced Olympias and married young Cleopatra, the niece of an important tribal leader in Macedonia. Olympias, for all her foresight and cunning, managed to make a mistake after all, and was now dealing with the consequences.

Alexander's first love occurred at sixteen, when masculinity first arose in him. She was an unknown slave from the shores of the Black Sea. The young man was a dreamer, enraptured by the adventures of Achilles and the heroic deeds of the Argonauts and Theseus. The fair-haired Amazon girl who captured his attention was barely covered by a short ecsomida, and carried her baskets proudly, as if she were not a slave but a warrior princess striding through the vast royal gardens in Pella.

Alexander's meetings could not have remained secret. Spies watched his every step on Olympias' orders. His mother, imperious and dreaming of greater power, could not allow her only son to pick his own lover. Especially when he chose one from the disobedient, barbaric Black Sea people. No. She would give him a girl who would be an obedient executor of Olympias' will, so that she could influence her son even through love of another woman. She ordered the slave caught, her long braids cut short, and had her taken to the slave market in the distant city of Meliboa in Thessaly.

Olympias did not know her son well enough. This heavy blow destroyed the temple of the dreamer's first love. The termination of that dream was far more serious than the simple first affair of a boy with an obliging slave. Alexander understood everything and asked no questions, but his mother had forever lost that opportunity for which she had ruined both his love and the girl. Her son didn't speak a single word of it to her, but ever since then neither the beautiful slaves, nor hetaerae, nor the daughters of nobility attracted the prince's attention. Olympias received no word of any partiality on her son's behalf.

Ptolemy, unafraid of Alexander's competition, decided he would come to visit Thais with his friends, including the mischievous Hephaestion, who knew all Athenian hetaerae. For Hephaestion, gambling and good wine surpassed the games of Eros. That game no longer held the former intensity of appeal for him.

It was not so for Ptolemy. Every meeting with a beautiful woman bore the desire of closeness, promising the yet unknown shades of passion, mysteries of beauty, in reality an entire world of bright and novel sensations. His expectations were not usually fulfilled, but tireless Eros pulled him into the arms of merry women again and again.

Not the talant of silver promised by Philopatros, but Ptolemy decided that he would win the contest for the famous hetaera's heart. Let Philopatros set out ten talants, he thought. Pathetic coward.

The Macedonian patted the tender mark from the lash strike, swelling across his shoulder, and looked around.

A short cape, bordered by a sandbar, swung to the left from the shore and into the troubled, white-maned sea. This was the spot to which the four Macedonians had been swimming. No, he thought, correcting himself. Only three, since he had given up the competition, but ended up arriving earlier. A good walker would always cross the same distance faster on dry ground than a swimmer at sea, especially if the waves and the wind held back the ones in their power.

Slaves had been waiting for the swimmers, holding their clothes. They were surprised by the sight of Ptolemy as he came down from the steep shore toward them. He'd rinsed off sand and dust, gotten dressed, and carefully folded the woman's cape, which had been given to him by Thais' boy servant.

Two old olive trees stood silvery under the hill, shading a small, blindingly white house. It looked small under the giant tall cypresses. The Macedonians took a short flight of stairs and entered a miniature garden filled only with roses. On a blue sign over the door were painted the three usual letters, dark in vibrant crimson: omega, ksi, and epsilon. Below them was painted the word cochleon, or spiral seashell.

Unlike at other hetaerae's houses, Thais' name was not written over the entrance, nor was there the usual fragrant dusk in the front room. Wide open shutters displayed the view of the mass of Ceramic's white houses. Mountain Licabett, shaped like a woman's breast and overgrown by wolf-infested woods, rose in the distance behind the Acropolis. Pyrean road circled the hill and descended toward the Athenian harbor like a yellow stream among the cypresses.

Thais welcomed the four friends with a pleasant smile. Nearchus, who was slender and of average height for a Helenian or a Cretan, seemed small and fragile beside the two tall Macedonian and Hephaestion, the giant.

The guests settled in fragile armchairs with legs shaped like long horns of Cretan bulls. The huge Hephaestion, fearing he might shatter the chair, opted for a massive stool, and the quiet Nearchus chose a bench with a head rest.

Thais sat next to her friend, Nannion, who was slender and dark-skinned like an Egyptian woman. Nannion's delicate Ionian chiton was covered by a blue himation[3] embroidered in gold with the traditional trim of stylized, hook-shaped waves at the bottom. After the eastern fashion, the hetaera's himation was tossed over her right shoulder, over the back and pinned with a brooch at her left side.

Thais was dressed in a chiton of pink transparent cloth from either Persia or India, gathered into soft pleats and pinned at the shoulders with five silver pins. Gray himation with a trim of blue daffodils covered her from her waist to the ankles of her small feet, which were dressed in sandals with narrow silver straps.

---

3 A heavier piece of cloth worn over a chiton as an overdress or a cloak.

Unlike Nannion, Thais' mouth and eyes were not made up. Her face, unafraid of tan, wore no traces of powder.

She listened to Alexander with interest, objecting or agreeing from time to time. Ptolemy was surprised to find that he felt slightly jealous, as this was the first time he'd seen his friend, the prince, this enraptured.

Hephaestion took hold of Nannion's thin hands, teaching her the Khalkidykian finger game: three and five. Ptolemy had trouble focusing on the conversation, so taken was he by watching Thais. He twice shrugged impatiently. Noticing that, Thais smiled and observed him with narrowed, mocking eyes.

"She will be here soon. Do not sulk, sea man."

"Who?" Ptolemy asked.

"A goddess, fair-haired and blue eyed, the one you dreamed of on the shore near Khalipedon."

Ptolemy was about to object, but just then a tall girl in a red and gold himation burst into the room, bringing with her the smell of sun-filled wind and magnolia. She moved swiftly, with purpose, a motion which the more delicate connoisseurs might have called overly strong compared to the snakelike movements of Egyptian and Asian female harp players. The men greeted her enthusiastically. To everyone's surprise, the imperturbable Nearchus left his bench in the shadow corner of the room and came closer.

"Egesikhora, the Spartan, my best friend," Thais introduced briskly, glancing sideways at Ptolemy.

"Egesikhora: a song on the road," Alexander said thoughtfully. "This is the case when Laconic pronunciation is more attractive than the Attic one."

"We don't consider the Attic dialect to be very attractive," the Spartan said. "They breathe in at the beginning of each word like the Asians do, whereas we speak openly."

"And you yourself are open and beautiful," Nearchus said smoothly.

Alexander, Ptolemy and Hephaestion exchanged glances.

"I interpret my friend's name as 'she who leads the dance'," Thais said. "It works better for a Lacedemonian."

"I like song better than dance," Alexander said.

"Then you will not be happy with us women," Thais replied.

The Macedonian prince frowned. "It is a strange friendship between a Spartan and an Athenian women," he said. "Spartans consider Athenians to be brainless dolls, half-slaves, locked in their houses like women of the East, not having a single notion of their husbands' business matters. Athenians call Lacedemonians slutty wives who act like prostitutes and bear dumb soldiers."

"Both opinions are completely wrong," Thais said, laughing.

Egesikhora smiled silently, looking much like a goddess. Her broad chest, the stretch of her shoulders and the straight setting of her strong head gave her the posture of an Erekhteyon[4] statue when she turned serious. However, her face, when filled with merriment and youthful joy, was ever changing.

To Thais' surprise, it was Nearchus, not Ptolemy, who was struck by the Laconian beauty.

The female slave served uncommonly simple food. The goblets for wine and water were decorated with black and white stripes resembling the ancient Cretan dishes, which were valued at more than their weight in gold.

---

4   One of the main temples of the ancient Athens is located at the Acropolis to the north of the Parthenon. It had an unusual asymmetrical layout due to the uneven ground on which it was built. The south side of the temple was decorated with a portico, supported by six marble statues of beautiful women.

"Do Athenians eat like Thessalians?" Nearchus asked. He splashed a little from his goblet for the gods, then handed it to Egesikhora.

"I am only half Athenian," Thais replied. "My mother was an Etheo-Cretan of an ancient family that escaped the pirates from the island of Theru in order to seek protection in Sparta. There, in Emborion, she met my father and I was born, but ..."

"There was no epigamy between the parents and the marriage was deemed illegitimate," Nearchus finished for her. "So that is why you have such an ancient name."

"And so I did not become a 'bull bringing' bride, but ended up in a school for hetaerae at the Aphrodite of Corinth temple."

"And became the glory of Athens!" Ptolemy exclaimed, raising his goblet.

"And what of Egesikhora?" Nearchus asked.

"I am older than Thais. The story of my life is like a trace of a snake and is not for the curious," the Spartan girl said, lifting her eyebrows disdainfully.

"Now I know why you are different," Ptolemy said. "A true daughter of Crete in your image."

Nearchus laughed unkindly. "What do you know of Crete, Macedonian? Crete is a nest of pirates who arrived from all corners of Hellas, Ionia, Sicily and Finikia. Scum who have destroyed and trampled the country, wiping out the ancient glory of the children of Minos."

"When I spoke of Crete, I meant the splendid people, the rulers of the sea who long since departed into the kingdom of shadows."

"And you were right, Nearchus, when you said this is Thessalian food before us," Alexander intervened. "If it is correct that the Cretans are related to Thessalians and those to the Pelasgoans, as Herodotus wrote."

"But Cretans are the rulers of the sea whereas Thessalians are horse people," Nearchus objected.

"But they are not nomads. They are horse breeding farmers," Thais said suddenly. "Poets have long since sung 'the hilly Phtia of Hellas, glorious with the beauty of women' …"

"And plains thundering with horses' hooves," Alexander added.

"I think Spartans are more likely descendants of the sea people," Nearchus said, glancing at Egesikhora.

"Only legally, Nearchus. Look at Egesikhora's golden hair. Where do you see Cretan blood?"

"As far as the sea is concerned, I have seen a Cretan woman sea bathing in a storm when no other woman would have dared," Ptolemy said.

"And he who saw Thais on horseback had seen an Amazon," Egesikhora said.

"Poet Alcman, who was a Spartan, compared Lacedemonian girls to Entheyan horses," Hephaestion said, laughing. He had already consumed a good quantity of delicious bluish black wine.

"He who praises their beauty when they go to bring a sacrifice to the goddess, nude, with dances and songs, and their hair down akin the golden red manes of Paphlagonian mares," Egesikhora replied.

"You both know a lot," Alexander exclaimed.

"It is their profession. They do not sell only Eros, but also knowledge, manners, art and beauty of senses," Hephaestion said with the air of a connoisseur. "Do you know," he teased, "what is the highest class hetaera in the most splendid city of arts and poetry in the entire Ecumene[5]? The most educated among scholars, the most skillful dancer and reader, the inspiration to artists and poets, with the irresistible allure of feminine charm? That is Egesikhora."

---

5 A term used in the ancient world to describe the known part of the inhabited Earth.

"What of Thais?" Ptolemy interrupted.

"At seventeen she is a celebrity. In Athens that is well and above many great warriors, rulers and philosophers from other countries. And you cannot become one, lest the gods gift you with an insightful heart to which senses and the essence of people are open since childhood, the delicate sensations and knowledge of true beauty, far deeper than most people possess."

"You speak of her as if she were a goddess," Nearchus said, displeased that Hephaestion set the Spartan girl below Thais. "Can't you see? She does not even view herself that way."

"That is a true mark of spiritual height," Alexander said, then fell deep into thought again. The Spartan's words of 'long manes' awoke in him the longing for the black flanked, white-faced Bucefal. "Athenians here cut their horses' manes, making them stick up like stiff brushes."

"That is to make sure the horses don't compete with the Athenian women, among whom thick hair is a rarity," Egesikhora joked.

"That's easy for you to say," Nannion said. She had been quiet to this point but now joined the conversation. "Considering the Spartan women's hair is as legendary as their freedom."

"Had forty generations of your ancestors walked around with bare hips, wearing linen peploses[6] and chitons year round, then your hair would have been just as thick."

---

6   A tubular cloth folded inside out from the top about halfway down, altering what was the top of the tube to the waist and the bottom of the tube to ankle length. The garment is then gathered about the waist and the open top (at the fold) is pinned over the shoulders. The top of the tube (now inside out) drapes over the waist, providing the appearance of a second piece of clothing.

"Why are you called phainomeris? 'Those who show their hips'?" Ptolemy asked.

"Show him how a Spartan woman is supposed to be dressed in her country," Thais said to Egesikhora. "Your old peplos has been hanging in my opistocella since we staged a scene from Cadmian folklore."

Egesikhora quietly went into an inner room of the house. Nearchus watched her until she disappeared behind a curtain.

"Fate sends us many strange gifts," Hephaestion muttered mischievously, winking at Ptolemy.

He put his arms around the shy Nannion and whispered something to her. The hetaera blushed and obediently offered her lips for a kiss. Ptolemy tried to hug Thais, moving closer to her as soon as Alexander went to the table.

"Wait till you see your goddess," she said and pushed him away.

Ptolemy obeyed without question, wondering how this young girl was able to charm and rule him at the same time.

Egesikhora did not keep them waiting long. She reappeared in a long white peplos, completely open along the sides, and held in place with a single woven tie at the waist. Strong muscles rippled under the smooth skin. The Lacedemonian's hair flowed like gold down her back, curling into thick tendrils below her knees, forcing her to lift her head higher, thus opening her strong jaw line and powerful neck. She danced the 'Hair dance', 'Cometike' for them, accompanying herself with her own singing, rising high on tiptoe and resembling the splendid statues by Callimachus, those of the Spartan dancers who undulated like fire, as if they were about to take off in their ecstasy.

A general sigh of admiration met Egesikhora, who twirled slowly, relishing the power of her own beauty.

"The poet was right," Hephaestion said, pulling away from Nannion. "There is a lot in common with the beauty and power of a thoroughbred horse."

"Andrapodysts, the kidnappers of the free people, tried capturing Egesikhora once. There were two of them – big men. But Spartan women are taught to fight and these two thought they were dealing with the delicate daughter of Attica, destined to live in the women's half of the house," Thais said. "That was their mistake."

Egesikhora, not even slightly flushed from her dance, sat next to her and hugged her friend. She paid no attention to Nearchus, who was gazing lustfully at her legs.

Alexander rose reluctantly. "Haire, Cretan. I wish I could love you and talk to you. You are uncommonly smart. But I must go to Kinosargos, the temple of Hercules. My father ordered me to Corinth, where there will be a great gathering. He is about to be elected the main warlord of Hellas, the new union of polices, without the stubborn Sparta, of course."

"Are they separating again?" Thais exclaimed.

"What do you mean again? It has happened many times."

"I was thinking about Chaeronea. Had the Spartans united with Athens, then your father ..."

"Would have lost the battle and escaped into the Macedonian mountains. And I wouldn't have met you," Alexander said with a laugh.

"What did this meeting today give you?" Thais asked.

"The memory of your beauty."

She smiled. "It's like bringing an owl to Athens. Are there not enough women in Pella?"

"You did not understand. I was speaking of it as it ought to be. The kind of beauty that brings acceptance in life, comfort and clarity. You Helenians call it 'astrophaes', or starlight-like."

Thais slipped from her chair and knelt on a cushion at Alexander's feet. "You are young yet, but you said something I shall remember all my life," she said. She lifted the prince's large hand and pressed it to her cheek.

Alexander tipped her black-haired head back and said with a tinge of sadness, "I would ask you to come to Pella, but why would you? Here you are known to the entire Attica, even though you are not in eoas, the Lists of Women. I am just a son of a divorced royal wife."

"You shall be a hero," she replied. "I can feel it."

"Well then you shall be my guest whenever you wish."

"I thank you, and I shall remember that. But you remember also: Ergos and Logos, Action and Word are one, as the wise men say."

Hephaestion withdrew from Nannion with regret, though he had already set up an evening rendezvous. Nearchus and Egesikhora disappeared. Ptolemy could not and did not wish to delay attending the Kinosargos. Unable to resist, he lifted Thais from the cushion and pulled her to him.

"You and only you have taken over me. Are you free? Do you wish me to come to you again?"

She gave him a small, intimate smile, meant only for him. "One does not settle such things on a doorstep. Come again, then we'll see. Or are you, too, going to Corinth?"

"I have nothing to do there. Alexander and Hephaestion are the only ones going."

"And what of the thousand hetaerae of the Corinthian Aphrodite? They serve the goddess and do not charge."

"I already said and can repeat myself. There is only you for me."

Thais squinted mischievously, sticking the tip of her tongue between her firm yet still childish lips.

Then the three Macedonians stepped out into the dry wind and blinding whiteness of the streets, leaving the women behind.

Thais and Nannion, left to themselves, sighed and shared their thoughts with each other.

"Such people," Nannion said. "So young and already so mature. The mighty Hephaestion is only twenty-one, and the prince is only nineteen. But how many people have they already killed?"

"Alexander is handsome," Thais agreed. "Educated and smart like an Athenian, and hardened like a Spartan, only ..." Thais paused and shook her head slightly.

"He is not like the others somehow. I do not know how to say it," Nannion mused.

"You look at him and feel his power, and yet also sense he is far away from us, thinking about things that would never occur to us. That is why he is lonely even among his close friends, even though they are not small, ordinary people either."

"Like Ptolemy? I noticed you like him."

"Yes. He is older than the prince, but closer and can be understood through and through."

As Ptolemy came around the bend, following the path that circled the Barathron hill, the giant cypresses came into view and his heart filled with an unfamiliar joy. Her house stood before him, seeming simple and plain after ten days spent in Athens. He made his way up the opposite slope so quickly it was as if a gust of wind swept him along. Feeling the need to regain composure appropriate for a warrior, he paused near the rough stone wall and listened to the rustle of silvery green olive leaves over his head.

The outskirts of the city, with its scattering of houses through the gardens, seemed deserted at this hour. Everyone, young and old, went to celebrate at Agora and Acropolis, as well at the temple of Demeter, the goddess of fertility, who was also addressed as Gaea Pandora, the All-bringing Earth.

As usual, Tesmophorias were to take place during the first night of the full moon, at the time of the fall sowing. Today people celebrated the end of plowing, one of the most ancient holidays of the farming ancestors of the Athenians, who were no longer involved in this most honorable of labors, caring for Gaea's face.

That morning Thais had passed a message to Ptolemy through Egesikhora and Nearchus. The message had stated that he was to come to her at sunset. Realizing what the invitation implied, Ptolemy became so anxious that even Nearchus was surprised, having long since acknowledged his friend's supremacy in matters of love. Nearchus had also changed since his meeting with the Spartan beauty. Glumness he had so often displayed since childhood had vanished. Playful mischief, so typical for his people, peeked from under the shield of steady self-possession he had adopted so many years before, when he had found himself a child slave in a strange country.

Cretans had a reputation of being liars and traitors because, since they worshiped the Great Goddess, they were certain of the mortality of male gods. By having shown Zeus' tomb to the Helenians, they had committed a terrible sacrilege. Nearchus said Helenians themselves had lied about Cretans, and there wasn't a more faithful or reliable man than Nearchus in all of Pella. Therefore, the message he passed from Thais could not possibly have been a joke.

The sun was setting slowly. Ptolemy felt ridiculous standing at Thais' garden gate, but he wanted to fulfill her wishes to the letter. He slowly lowered himself to the still-warm earth until he sat, leaning against the stones of the wall. He waited with the inexhaustible patience of a soldier, witnessing the last glimmer of sunset as it faded at the top of Egayleion, watching the dark trunks of the olive trees dissolve in the dusk. After a time, he glanced over the shoulder at the closed door, barely outlined under the overhang of the portico, and decided it was time. Anticipation made him shiver like a boy, as if he were sneaking to his first date with an obliging slave. Ptolemy flew up the steps, knocked on the unlocked door, then entered without waiting for an answer.

Thais stood in the doorway, lit by a double wick lantern which hung from a bronze chain. She wore a dark ecsomida, short, as an Amazon would wear. A ribbon the same color as her chiton held together the tight curls of her hair at the back of her head. Even in the faint light of the oil lamp Ptolemy noticed the young woman's cheeks were flushed, and folds of fabric over her high breasts rose and fell from breathing quickly. Her eyes, almost black in her shadowed face, looked straight at Ptolemy, freezing him on the spot.

"Like Athena Lemnia," Ptolemy thought, admiring her. Thais stood, serious and focused like a warrior before battle. With her unwavering gaze and almost threatening tip of her proud head, she really did look like the awe inspiring Lemnia.

"I am waiting for you, darling," she said simply, addressing him that way for the first time. She put so much tender meaning into the word that Ptolemy sighed with impatience and stepped closer, holding out his arms.

Thais stepped back and pulled a broad himation from behind the door, putting out the lantern with its swing. Ptolemy stopped in the darkness, puzzled, and the young woman slipped toward the exit. Her hand found the Macedonian's, clasped it firmly and pulled him after her.

"Come."

They exited through a side gate hidden in the shrubs, and headed down a path. The path led to the Ilissus River, which flowed through the gardens from Lyceum and temple of Hercules until it merged with Kephisos. A heavy half moon hung low in the sky, showing the way.

Thais walked quickly, almost ran, never looking back. He felt her intensity and followed in silence, enjoying the straight, regal posture set in the small figure before him. Her shoulders were open, her slender neck proudly supporting her head, which was crowned by a heavy, high-set knot of hair. She pulled the dark himation close around herself and it creased deeply to the left and right of her waist with each step, emphasizing her flexibility. Small feet stepped lightly and assuredly, her periscelides, ankle bracelets, jingling like silver bells.

Shadows of giant sycamore trees crossed their path and the couple ran past the wall of darkness toward where a platform of white marble, a semicircle of smooth tiles, shone in the night. Ilissus murmured quietly somewhere below.

A bronze statue of the goddess stood on a tall pedestal, her head slightly tilted. She was tossing a thin cape off her shoulders and her gaze was hypnotic, burning through eyes made of green glowing stones. A peculiar expression of both compassion and sincerity, rare for a deity, combined in the omniscient gaze, adding to its mysterious depths. It seemed as if the goddess were descending toward the mortals with the goal of telling each of them their own secret in the silence and loneliness of the starry night.

This was Aphrodite Uranus in the Gardens, famous all around Hellas. In her left hand the goddess held a large rose, a symbol of feminine essence, the flower of Aphrodite and love. Her strong body, outlined by the folds of her peplos was in a state of calm enthasis. Her garment, unusually open on one shoulder according to an ancient Asian or Cretan standard, left her breasts bare – high, closely set together and wide like wine casks. Their sensual power was in sharp contrast to the inspired mystery of the face and the restrained pose of the Heavenly Aphrodite.

Of all Hellenic artists, Alcman was the first to succeed in combining the ancient power of sensual beauty with the spiritual ascent, creating a religious image of irresistible allure and filling it with a promise of flaming happiness. The Goddess: Mother and Urania in one.

Thais approached the goddess reverently. She whispered something Ptolemy couldn't hear, then hugged the legs of Alcman's famous creation. Afterwards, she paused at the feet of the statue, then suddenly pulled back toward the motionless Ptolemy. Leaning against his powerful arm, she peered silently into his face, trying to find the right response.

Ptolemy sensed that Thais was searching for something, but could do nothing but continue to wait for her, wearing a puzzled smile.

Suddenly she leapt onto the middle of the marble platform, clapped her hands thrice, then started singing Aphrodite's anthem. She sang with an emphasized rhythm, the way it is sung in the goddess' temples before the entrance of the sacred dancers.

" ... Smile never leaves her sweet face, and the goddess' flower is lovely," she sang, approaching Ptolemy in the measured movement of the dance.

He grinned, watching her. "Goddess, accept this song and set Thais on the fire of passion!" Ptolemy thundered and grabbed the girl.

This time she didn't pull away. She wrapped her arms around his neck, pressing herself against him. The himation fell, and Thais' firm body felt warm through the thin fabric of her chiton.

"You, soldier, know Aphrodite's anthems?" she whispered, sounding surprised. "But do not ask the goddess about fire. You might burn in it."

"Then ..." Ptolemy found Thais' lips, but the young hetaera pushed against Ptolemy's broad chest, drawing away.

"Let's go further," she said, out of breath. "I purposefully waited until this day. The bulls were taken to the mountains today ..."

"So what?" Ptolemy asked, not understanding the significance.

Thais rose on tiptoe and whispered into his ear. "I want to be yours. And I want to become yours by the ancient ritual of the Athenian farmers, in a freshly plowed field."

"In a field? What for?"

"At night, on a thrice-plowed filed, to take Gaea's life-bringing power into me, to awaken it ..."

Ptolemy smiled, then squeezed the girl's shoulders, silently agreeing with her. Thais headed along the river downstream, then turned north toward the sacred Elysian road, Ptolemy right behind her.

Deep darkness settled in the Ilissus valley, as the moon vanished behind the crest of the mountain.

"How can you see the way?" Ptolemy asked. "Do you know it?"

"I do. We are going to Skiron's field. Women celebrate the holiday of Demeter the Law-bearer there at full moon."

"Are hetaerae allowed to participate in Tesmophorias? And what happens at Skiron's field? I'll try to make it there if I am still in Athens during full moon."

"No you won't. You can't. Only young women are allowed access there on the night of Tesmophorias after the torch run."

"Then how did you find a way?"

"It was before I became a hetaera. After the torch run, Demeter's priestesses picked me as one of the twelve. And when the celebration was over for the uninitiated, we ran in the nude, in the middle of the night, for thirty stadiums that separate the field from the temple."

"And then?"

"I cannot tell you. It's a female mystery and we are all under a terrible oath. But it's something I will remember for the rest of my life. And the run across the field is unforgettable. You run under the bright moon, in the silence of the night, along with swift and beautiful friends. It was like we ran while barely touching the ground, because our entire bodies are like a string waiting for the goddess' touch. The branches touch you in passing, the light wind cools your burning body. And when you pass the menacing road crossings, watched by Hecate's guardians ..." Thais stopped speaking, as if she felt to exhilarated to tell more.

"Go on. You tell it so well," Ptolemy insisted.

"It's only that there is a feeling of freedom from everything. You stop and your heart is beating fast, you spread your arms and take a deep breath and it seems as if in one more second you'll fly away, into the scent of grass, woods and sea. That you will dissolve in the moonlight, like salt dissolves in water, like chimney smoke dissolves in the sky. There is nothing separating you from Mother Earth. You are Her and She is you."

Thais picked up the pace again and turned left. A dark band of trees appeared, bordering the field from the north.

Everything around was silent, save for the rustling of the wind carrying the scent of thyme. Ptolemy could clearly see Thais, but nothing further in the distance. They stood listening to the night which wrapped around them like a black blanket, then finally descended from the path and stepped onto the field. The soil was fluffy after having been plowed many times, and their sandals pressed deeply into it. Finally Thais stopped, sighed and tossed off her himation. While Ptolemy watched, she lifted her hands to her head, loosed the ribbon and let her hair down. He came close and she went to him in silence. Her fingers dug into the thick softness of Ptolemy's hair. They clasped and unclasped among the strands, then slid over the back of his head and neck.

A strong, fresh scent rose from the moist soil. It seemed that Gaea herself, eternally young and filled with life-bringing energy, had spread herself across the field in powerful languor.

Ptolemy filled with the strength of a titan. Every muscle in his powerful body became as firm as bronze. He swept Thais up in his arms and lifted her toward the glittering stars, challenging the indifferent eternity with her beauty.

Some time passed before they returned to reality on Skiron's field. When his mind cleared so that he could think again, Ptolemy leaned over his lover's face and whispered a verse from his favorite poem. He regretted now that he knew so few compared to Alexander's vast knowledge of poetry.

"Asperos aysaugazo aster aymos." "You are looking at stars, my star."

Thais slowly turned her head, gazing at Ptolemy. Ptolemy saw her eyelashes, strands of hair on her forehead and dark circles around her eyes and wondered again at her beauty.

"You are well educated, darling. My countrymen are stupid to consider Macedonians to be barbaric mountain men. But I understand. You are removed from Urania. You would be happier with Gaea."

He looked around. The edges of the field, which had seemed endless in the dark, now seemed nearby. The long end of summer night was over.

Thais propped herself on her elbow and watched in amazement as the dawn rose from behind Gimett. Bleating of the sheep could be heard from a grove below. Thais rose slowly and stretched toward the first rays of the sun, which emphasized the reddish copper tone of her skin. Her hands rose to her hair in an eternal gesture of a woman, a guardian and bearer of beauty, exhausting and appealing, vanishing and reappearing again, as long as humanity exists. Thais wrapped her himation around herself as if she were cold, and slowly walked with her head thoughtfully lowered until she was beside the proud Ptolemy.

When they reached the Elysian road, Thais went to the temple of Aphrodite Urania directly across Ceramic.

"You are back to your heavenly queen of love," the Macedonian said, laughing. "As if you are not an Athenian. Aristotle said that the first people to worship Urania under the name of Anachita were some ancient people. Were they Assyrians, perhaps?"

Thais nodded. "They worshiped her even before that when they were on Crete, then on Citera, where Urania stands armed, then Theseus' father Aegeus set up her temple in Athens," Thais said reluctantly. "But you must not come with me. Go see your friends. No. Wait," she said urgently. "Stand to the left of me." and, not minding the passersby, Thais clung to Ptolemy and made Hecate's protective sign with her right hand.

The Macedonian looked, but saw nothing but an old, forsaken sacrificial stone that must have been richly decorated at one time, with a trim of massive dark stone.

"What is it that can frighten the brave Thais? The Thais I know is not afraid of the night, the starry sky or the gloomy road crossings ruled by Hecate?"

She shuddered. "It's a sacrificial stone of Anteros, god of anti-love, love's terrible and cruel antithesis. Even if Aphrodite herself is afraid of the powerful Eros, we, her servants, are even more afraid of Anteros. But say no more. Let us get away from here."

They climbed into the marble glow of squares and temples, above Ceramic and the market.

"Tell me more of Anteros," Ptolemy asked.

"Later. Geliaine!" Thais lifted her hand in a farewell gesture and ran up the white steps of Urania's temple.

A few weeks later, Thais sat in the garden, enjoying the last pale roses and clutching a himation around herself as protection from the brisk wind. Dry leaves rustled, sounding eerily as if ghosts stepped carefully over the couple, making their way to their unknown destinations.

Ptolemy handed Thais a simple cedar box and touched her knee. She glanced questioningly at the Macedonian.

"It is my anakalipterion," he said solemnly. He was surprised to receive a peal of laughter in response.

"You shouldn't laugh," Ptolemy said sternly.

"Why not? You brought me a present normally given by a husband to his new bride after the wedding, as he is about to undress her for the night. But you give me your anakalipterion on the day of our parting? And after you have taken off my garments many times. Is it not too late?"

"Understand, Athenian ... or Cretan," he said, frowning. "I still do not know who you really are ..."

"Does it matter? Or do you dream of a girl whose ancestors are from the eoas, the Lists of Women?"

"As I understand, any true Cretan woman is of more ancient bloodline than all Athenian foremothers taken together," Ptolemy objected. "I don't care anyway. This is different. Up until now, I haven't given you anything, and that is bad manners. But what do I have to offer compared to the piles of silver you receive from your admirers? Only this ..."

Ptolemy knelt on the floor before her and opened the box in Thais' lap. The statuette of ivory and gold was unquestionably old. In fact, no fewer than a thousand years had passed since an incomparably skillful Cretan sculptor had created this image of a Tauromachia participant, a player in a sacred, dangerous game. The game was played with a particular breed of giant bulls, bred on Crete and since extinct.

Thais carefully picked up the little statue and touched it with her fingertips. She sighed in delight then laughed so infectiously that Ptolemy smiled as well.

"Darling, this piece is worth that very pile of silver of which you dream. Where did you get this?"

"At war," Ptolemy replied.

"Why didn't you give it to your friend Nearchus, the only true son of Crete among you?"

"I wanted to. But Nearchus said that it was a woman's piece and would bring bad luck to a man. He is subject to the ancient superstitions of his country. Did you know that at one point his people considered the mother goddess to be the most important of all heavenly dwellers?"

Thais glanced at the Macedonian thoughtfully. "There are many people here who believed and still believe the same thing," she said.

"And you too, perhaps?"

Thais closed the box without answering, then rose and led Ptolemy into the inner room of the house, toward the warmth and the smell of psestions. Thais occasionally did her own cooking, and had prepared the barley buns with honey, fried in butter. They were particularly tasty.

After setting her guest down, Thais fussed around the table, putting out wine and spicy sauce for the meat. She already knew that Macedonians were not fond of fish, though the dish was so popular in Athens.

Ptolemy watched her silent movements, entranced. Dressed as she was, in a transparent silvery chiton of Aeolian cut, made of the most delicate fabric imported from Persia, and working in a room shaded with green drapes, Thais appeared to be dressed in moonlight, akin to Artemis herself. She had let her hair down, tying it in the back with a simple ribbon, like a Pyrean teenager, and looked every bit an embodiment of merry youth: daring and tireless. She carried this quality in combination with the assured wisdom of a woman, aware of her beauty and capable of avoiding the traps of fate, the ability of a famous hetaera in the most splendid city in all of Hellas. The contrast was devastatingly irresistible, and Ptolemy clutched his fist, nearly moaning at the agony of their parting. More likely than not, he was losing Thais forever.

"I cannot help leaving," he said, feeling the need to explain himself. "The prince's matters are going poorly; he had another argument with his father. After that he escaped to Epirus with his mother, and I am afraid his life might now be in danger. Alexander won't abandon his mother, and she is starved for power – a dangerous thing for a former wife."

She frowned, confused by his explanation. "Am I reproaching you?"

"No, but that is what is so hard," Ptolemy smiled sadly, feeling uncertain.

Thais felt sorry for this young, yet hardened warrior. She sat next to him, caressing his coarse wavy hair, cut short as was required by army rules. Ptolemy stretched to kiss Thais and noticed a new necklace, a thin, intricately woven chain of dark gold, connected in the center by two sparkling stars of bright yellow electron[7].

"Is that new? A gift from Philopatros?" the Macedonian asked, unable to keep ugly tone of jealousy out of his voice.

A brief, quiet giggle, so typical for Thais, was his only answer. He kept waiting, so she finally answered. "Philopatros, or any other, must earn the right to give me another star."

"I don't understand. What right? Each one gives whatever he can."

"Not in this case. Look carefully," Thais said. She took off the necklace and handed it to Ptolemy.

Each star was one dactyl across. It was decorated with ten narrow, faceted rays and a letter kappa in the middle, which also meant the number ten. Ptolemy returned the necklace and shrugged, puzzled.

"Forgive me," she said. "I forgot that you are from Macedonia and may not be familiar with hetaerae traditions, although your mother Arsinoa ..."

"Wait. I recall something. Isn't it a kind of distinction?"

"In love."

"And kappa?"

"It's not only a number, but also the name of the goddess Cotytto. She who is honored in Frakia, in Corinth, and along the southern shores of the Black Sea. You may add a third star."

"Aphrodite Migonitida! I didn't know, and I won't have time to give it to you."

She smiled. "I'll do it myself."

"No. I'll send you one from Pella, if the gods look upon Alexander and myself. Our destinies are woven together. Whether we burst into the Ecumene or go underground, we'll do it together."

---

7   Amber

"I believe in Alexander. His purpose is unknown, but he has power uncommon among ordinary people."

"And I don't?"

"Not exactly like he has, but I am glad of it. You are my strong, smart and brave warrior and you might even become a king. I shall be your queen."

"I swear by the White Hound of Hercules, you will be."

"Someday. I am ready," she purred.

Thais moved closer to Ptolemy and both stopped looking ahead into the unknown destiny. From the immeasurable distance of the future, time flowed in a slow current, unavoidably and steadily moving into the past. Their meeting came to its end. Then Thais stood in the doorway, and Ptolemy, unable to pull away from his lover, was urged ahead by the need to hurry to Gidaphineus, to Nearchus, where they had been ordered to bring their horses. He had no idea that the punctual, reliable Cretan was only just rushing along the streets of Ceramic with his head lowered after his parting from Egesikhora.

"You didn't tell me what would happen if Alexander remained alive and became a king after his father," Thais said.

"There will be a long road, then war, then road again, help us Athena Caleutia, the goddess of all roads. Alexander dreams of reaching the end of the world, the dwelling of gods where the sun rises. And Stagiritus Aristotle encourages his desire by all means necessary."

"And will you go with him?"

"To the end. Thais, would you go with me? Not as with a soldier but as with an army leader?"

"I have always dreamed of distant countries, but such travels are unachievable to us women by any means other than in a carriage of a victor. Be a victor, and if I am still dear to you ..."

Ptolemy had to leave. When he had long since disappeared behind a distant house, Thais still watched the road. It wasn't until her slave touched her, reminding her that her bath was prepared, that she returned to reality.

Ptolemy, struggling with the ache of leaving his love, walked briskly, not allowing himself to glance back at Thais. It was an ill omen to look over one's shoulder when leaving. He didn't even look at her marble copy, one of the girls on a balcony of the temple of Nika the Wingless. She was one of the statues in an ancient peplos, her head thrown eternally back as if she were about to dash forward, and she resembled his beloved. Until now, the Macedonian had never passed the temple without pausing to glance at the bas relief.

Chapter Two. Egesikhora's Heroics

Metageytnion, a month that had always been hot in Attica, turned out to be particularly scorching during the last year of the hundred and tenth Olympiad. The sky, always so clear and deep that even the foreigners marveled at it, acquired a tinge of lead. Crystal clear air that always gave the statues and structures miraculous distinction, shimmered and fluttered, as if someone had tossed a cover of uncertain and fleeting changefulness upon Athens. Like a cover of deceit and distortion, so typical for the desert countries on the distant southern shores.

Thais stopped going swimming when the road became too dusty. She only went riding at dawn from time to time so she could feel the wind from the swift gallop upon her flushed skin.

Afternoon heat settled heavily upon the city. All living things hid in shade, in the coolness of temples and colonnades, in the darkness of shuttered homes.

Only the wheels of a lazily rolling cart or the hooves of a sweaty horse with a shade-seeking rider rumbled down the pavement.

Egesikhora entered briskly as usual, then stopped, blinded by the transition from light to the dusk of the bedroom. Without a moment's hesitation, she dropped her light chiton and sat at the feet of her friend, who sprawled nude on the bed. Judging from Egesikhora's fluttering nostrils and heaving breasts, Thais surmised that the Spartan was angry.

"What is wrong?" she asked lazily.

"I don't know. I'm mad at everything. I am sick of our Athenians. They are loud, talkative, and too willing to gossip. Are they really those great builders, artists, scholars and warriors of whom so much was written in the times of Pericles? Or has everything changed since then?"

"I don't understand," Thais replied. "What's come over you? Did you get food poisoning at yesterday's symposium? The wine did taste a bit sour ..."

"Maybe it was just the wine for you, but my entire life feels sour to me. Athens is getting more and more crowded. People are snappy from being cooped up, from being deafened by the noise, the shouting, the constant lack of water and food. In this heat everyone sees everyone else as if they were an enemy. And the gineconomes are mad for no good reason. Before long, an attractive woman won't be able to show up at Agora or at the Acropolis in the evenings."

Thais nodded thoughtfully. "I agree with you on that subject. Athens is getting tight, as is the entire Attica. They say five hundred thousand people now live in Attica."

"Holy mother Demeter! There aren't more than a hundred and fifty thousand in all of Sparta. In such multitudes, people can only interfere with each other and get angry. They see luxury and beauty and become jealous, saturating the air with vapors of black bitterness."

"It's not just a lack of space, Egesikhora. There are also consequences to the recent war, especially last year's. Our handsome prince is now the king of Macedonia and essentially the ruler of Hellas. And he is not afraid to bare his wolfish teeth, glory be to the Lykean Apollo. To this day, Theban men are sold for a mere hundred drachmas at the market, and women for a hundred and fifty. The city itself has been wiped off the face of Gaea. The entire Hellas was horrified."

"Except Sparta."

"Will Sparta hold out on its own? Your king, Agis, is doing badly. He wanted to stand alone when joining forces with the Greeks would have resulted in victory. Now he is left to stand alone against a mighty enemy."

Egesikhora sighed. "Only two years have passed since the Macedonian boys came to us," she said.

"Only the Macedonian? And what about Crete?"

The Lacedemonian flushed, then continued. "Philip was murdered, Alexander became king and the main warlord of Hellas destroyed Thebes. Now …"

Thais nodded. "Now he is headed for Persia, continuing his father's mission."

"Have you heard from Ptolemy? Has it been long?"

"I have heard from him," Thais said, closing her eyes. "It was during one of the dog days of Hekatombeon. There has been nothing since then. He does send me one letter a year." She sighed. "In the beginning he used to send five."

"When did he send you this?" the Spartan asked, touching the third star that glittered against her friend's coppery skin.

Thais looked away, then spoke again after a pause. "Ptolemy writes that Alexander truly possesses a divine gift. Like Themistocles, he can instantly come up with a new maneuver, make a different decision if the first one isn't working. But Themistocles was drawn to the west, whereas Alexander is going east."

"Which one is right?"

"How would I know? The east is filled with legendary treasures, countless peoples, and limitless space. In the west there are fewer people, and Themistocles even dreamed of moving Athenians to Entoria, beyond the Ionic Sea. But he died in exile in the mountains of Thessaly. His tomb is on the western side of the Pyrean hill where he liked to sit, gazing upon the sea. I have been there. It is a secluded spot of both serenity and sadness."

"Why sadness?"

"I don't know. Can you say why deep grief, even terror overcomes people in the ruins of Mycenae? It is a menacing, forbidden place, rejected by gods. On Crete they take visitors to see Pasiphae's[8] tomb. It, too, fills travelers with fear, as if the shadow of the queen with a glorious name and terrible fame stands near them."

"You ought to be called Pantodae, my dear," Egesikhora said, then kissed her friend in delight. "Let's go to Themistocles' tomb and be melancholy together. I feel a kind of rage against this life. I need consolation but cannot find it."

"You yourself are telktera, a consoling sorceress, as the poets say," Thais objected. "It is just that we are becoming older and see life differently even as our expectations become greater."

---

8   Pasiphae was one of the daughters of the Sun, given in marriage to King Minos of Crete. Poseidon cursed her with lust for any male, and sent her a white bull. After mating with the bull, Pasiphae gave birth to Minotaur – the terrible half-man, half-bull, who dwelled in the Cretan labyrinth and killed many young men and women, until he himself was slain by Theseus. Pasiphae became a symbol of untamed bestial lust.

"What do you expect then?"

Thais shrugged. "I don't know. A change, a voyage perhaps."

"What about love? What about Ptolemy?"

"Ptolemy does not belong to me. He is a telictratus, a conqueror of women. I will not live with him like a hidden away Athenian or Macedonian wife. And I don't wish to be called a rafanide in case of an affair. I could have gone with him far, far away but I did not." She took a deep breath, then changed topic. "Let's go to the Pyrean hill today. I'll send Clonaria with a note to Olorus and Xenophilos. They are good young men, courageous and strong. Xenophilos performed at the last Olympic games in youth wrestling. They will accompany us. We'll sail in the evening, when the heat diminishes, and spend a moonlit night there."

"With two men?"

"Those two are so fond of each other they only need us as friends."

Thais returned home before the sun's rage befell the white streets of Athens. Strange musings came to her there, at the hill slope above Themistocleyon. She and Egesikhora sat together while their two companions sprawled out near the boat and discussed the upcoming trip to Parnea for the wild boar hunt.

When they were settled quietly, Egesikhora could hold her tongue no longer, and told her friend a secret. She said that Eositeus, the younger cousin of Agis, king of Sparta, was sailing to Egypt with a large detachment of soldiers, hired by the Egyptian pharaoh Hababash as his bodyguards. He was probably planning to oust the Persian envoy. Six ships were about to depart together and the leader of Lacedemonians was calling Egesikhora to come with him, promising the beautiful daughter of Sparta great glory in the country of poets and ancient art.

Egesikhora held Thais tightly against her and tried to talk her into coming with her to the legendary Egypt. She'd be able to visit Crete, and with such reliable guards she needn't fear pirates or thieves.

Thais reminded her friend of what Nearchus had told them both about the demise of the ancient beauty of Crete, the disappearance of the original population, the squalor that presently reigned on the island, decimated by uncontrolled attacks and wars of various tribes. As a result of fires and earthquakes, the palaces of Knossos and Festus had turned into piles of rubble, the natives had left and no one could read the inscriptions in the forgotten language.

However, the giant stone horns could still be seen here and there in the hills, as if the bulls of Poseidon the Earth Keeper were rising from under the ground, and broad staircases still descended to the platforms designated for sacred games. Sometimes people ran into the shards of heavy amphorae as tall as two human heights, with snakes curling around their sides. Water still splashed in clean sparkling basins, still ran down the water pipes ...

Thais pulled out the box she always carried, the box containing the Cretan statuette that had been Ptolemy's gift. She took out the precious sculpture and stretched out on the bed, examining the little figure as if she were seeing for the first time. Time and sad ponderings of recent days had given her new eyes.

A thousand years was an enormous period of time, and the statuette was older than that. The splendid Athens hadn't even been around then, and heroic Theseus had yet to travel to Knossos to slay Minotaur, and to crush the mighty sea state. From that immeasurable distance had come to her this delicately carved face with enormous eyes and a small, tragic mouth. The little figure's arms were bent at the elbows and raised with her palms up, a signal either for a pause or for attention. Her long, girlishly thin legs were stretched and slightly spread, and she stood on tiptoe, as if caught in the moment of pushing away from earth. Her clothing was made of gold leaf and appeared to wear a short, ornate apron with a broad sash, wrapped around an incredibly thin waist. A close-fitting bodice was supported by two shoulder straps, leaving her breasts open. A wide necklace lay over her collarbones at the base of her strong neck, laying rather than hanging because of her pronounced chest. A head band ran under the girl's chin, holding together a tall coneshaped hairstyle. The tauropola was young, fourteen years old, fifteen at most.

Thais suddenly realized that by calling her a tauropola, she had called the unknown Cretan girl a bull hunter, one of Artemis' titles. Gods were jealous and possessive of their rights, but what could the goddess do? She had long since vanished into the kingdom of Hades, inaccessible even to Zeus himself. Of course it was possible Artemis could become angry with the living Thais ... But what did she, the virginal huntress, have in common with a hetaera, a servant of Aphrodite?

Thais calmly resumed her examination of the statuette. There was nothing childish left in the face or figure of the watchful girl. More than ever before, Thais was moved by her tragic mouth and fearless gaze. This girl knew what was coming. Her life was to be short, having been dedicated to the deadly game, the dance with the long-horned spotted bulls, which were considered to be the embodiments of Poseidon the Earth Shaker.

The tauropola girls were the main participants in the sacred ritual. The ancient meaning had nearly been lost, but remained in the victory of the feminine beginning of the masculine one, of the earth mother over her temporary spouse. The might of the awesome beast was spent during the dance, which was a duel between it and the quick young girls and boys who were specially trained as jumpers and prepared for this deadly ballet by the connoisseurs of the complex ritual. Cretans believed that this was a way to dissipate the god's anger as it matured slowly and inevitably in the depths of earth and sea.

It was as if the dwellers of ancient Crete had sensed their sophisticated culture would perish from terrible earthquakes and tidal waves. Where had they come from, those distant ancestors of hers? Where had they come from, and where had they gone? Based on what she knew from the myths, and from what Nearchus had told his two enraptured listeners, she believed the beautiful, sophisticated people - the artists, seamen, and travelers – already lived on Crete when the surrounding lands were still inhabited by the savage ancestors of the Helenians. It was as if a magnolia tree, full of spicy, fragrant flowers, suddenly grew among the wind-beaten pines and poisonous oleanders. Such was the inexplicably delicate, poetic beauty of the Cretan culture among the coarse, war-loving nomads from the shores of the Inner Sea[9], which were only comparable to that of Egypt.

Her slave, Clonaria came in, shaking her coarse-haired , closely cropped head.

"That man is here," the girl said, and her voice shook from her deeply ingrained hatred toward the trader of human merchandise.

Thais returned to reality. "Take the money box, count out three minas worth of owls and give it to him."

The slave laughed. Thais smiled and gestured her to come closer. "Let's count together. Three minas are a hundred and eighty drachmas. Each owl is four drachmas, for the total of forty-five owls. Got it?"

---

9   Mediterranean

"Yes, kiria. Is that for the Theban? It's not much," the girl said, giving a disdainful chuckle.

"Yes, you cost me more," Thais agreed. "But do not judge quality based on price. Everyone is different, and just because you cost much, you can be sold cheaper."

Before Thais had even finished speaking, Clonaria had pressed her face to her knees.

"Kiria, don't sell me when you leave. Take me with you!"

"What are you talking about? Where am I going?" Thais asked, brushing the girl's hair off her forehead.

"We, your servants, are afraid you are going somewhere. You don't know how terrible it would be to end up with someone else, after you've been so kind and beautiful."

"Are there so few good people in the world?"

"Few people like you, Mistress. Do not sell me."

"Very well, I promise you. I'll take you with me, even though I am not going anywhere. How is the Theban girl?"

"After we gave her something to eat she washed for so long that she used up all the water in the kitchen. She is sleeping now, sleeping as if she hasn't had any sleep in a month."

Thais nodded her approval. "Now off with you. The trader is waiting. And don't bother me anymore. I want to sleep."

Clonaria quickly counted off the silver and ran out of the bedroom, a smile on her face. Thais rolled onto her back and closed her eyes, but sleep wouldn't come. She was too wide awake after the nighttime trip and the emotional discussions with her friend.

When they docked in the Pyrean harbor, the port was already full of people. Leaving their boat in the care of their two friends, Thais and Egesikhora decided to take advantage of the relative coolness of Leuconot, the "white" southern wind, and strolled along the large market, where trade was already going at full speed. The minor slave market was located at the intersection of the Faleron and Mid-wall Pyrean roads. The well packed, dusty square was bordered on one side by long low barracks that had been rented out to the slave traders. This market consisted of coarse slabs of stone and boards of the platforms, polished by the feet of countless visitors. This was in contrast to the large raised platform of pale marble which stood in the shade of a roofed colonnade within the walled-in porticos ornamenting the major slave market in Athens, fifteen stadiums from here.

Both hetaerae headed around, following the side path. Thais' attention was attracted by a group of emaciated people displayed at the edge of the market, huddled pathetically on a separate wood platform. The group included two women, barely covered by their tattered clothes. Without a doubt, they were Helenians, most likely Thebans. Most of the citizens from the decimated Thebes had been sent to the distant harbors and long since sold. This group of four men and two women had probably been brought here, to the port market, by some rich landowner with the intent of simply getting rid of them. Thais was appalled by the sight of free citizens of what had once been a famous city, dumped here with so little respect.

A tall man paused before the platform. His face was powdered and framed by a thick beard in large curls. Thais thought he was possibly a Syrian. With a careless flick of one finger, he ordered the trader to push forth the younger of the two women. She was an attractive girl of about eighteen, not tall in height as was typical for Helenian women. Her cropped hair sat at the back of her head in a thick punch, held by a narrow blue ribbon. Judging by the thickness of her hair, Thais could see what splendid braids the Theban girl would have once had.

"Price?" the Syrian asked, his chin lifted at a haughty angle.

"Five minas. That's practically free, I swear by Athena Aleya!"

"You are mad. Is she a musician or a dancer?"

"No, but she is virginal and beautiful."

The potential buyer frowned, examining her as if she were a piece of meat. "That is questionable. She is a war trophy. Look at the outlines of her hips and breasts. I'll give you a mina, or two. That is my last offer. A slave like that won't be sold in Pyrea, but will be displayed in Athens. Undress her."

The trader didn't move, so the buyer himself yanked off the slave girl's last covering. Mortified, she clung to the shred of worn out fabric and turned sideways. The Syrian buyer gasped and the passersby burst out laughing. The girl's round bottom was ornamented with swollen stripes from a lash. They were fresh and red, crisscrossed by previously healed scars.

"You scoundrel!" the Syrian yelled, showing good mastery of the Attic dialect.

Grabbing the girl by the hand, he found the marks of leather straps that had been used to tie her hands. He then lifted the cheap necklace dangling around her neck and uncovered a scar from a leash.

The trader jumped forward, placing himself between the Syrian and the girl.

"Five minas for a stubborn bit of a girl, who has to be kept on a leash?" the Syrian demanded. "You can't trick me. She is only good to be a maid or to carry water. After the destruction of the Hundred-gated Thebes the girls here have become cheaper. Even the beautiful ones. Houses all around the Inner Sea ports are filled with them."

"Let it be three minas. A real bargain," the subdued trader tried.

"No." The Syrian frowned at the Thebans, thought it over, then said, "I'll give you half: ninety drachmas total. I'll take her to entertain my sailors on the way back. That is my last offer." To show he was serious, the Syrian stepped decisively toward another group of slaves sitting on a stone platform a few paces away.

The trader hesitated, and the exhausted girl paled, or rather grayed through the layer of dust and sunburn covering her face.

Thais approached the platform. She lifted the light gauze scarf that was commonly worn by wealthy Athenian women to protect against dust, so that it slid off her raven black hair. The golden-haired Egesikhora stood next to her, and even the eyes of the slaves being sold shifted toward the two beautiful women.

While Thais watched, the dark, stubborn eyes of the young Theban widened, the fire of troubled hatred went out of them. Thais recognized before her the face of a person taught to read, appreciate art and comprehend life. Teonoa, the divine understanding, had left its trace on this proud face. The Theban saw the same reflected in Thais' face, and her eyelashes fluttered, barely able to contain the insane sense of hope that suddenly flared within her. Thais couldn't look away. It was as if an invisible thread stretched between the two women.

The trader glanced around, looking for the carriage which had brought the two beauties. When he saw none, a smug grin touched his lips, but it was immediately replaced by a look of respect when he noticed Thais' two male companions just catching up. They were well-dressed and shaved according to the latest fashion, both striding imperiously through the parting crowds.

"I am offering two minas," Thais said.

"No. I was here first," the Syrian exclaimed. At the appearance of Thais, he had returned to stare at the two Athenian women. Now he already regretted, as would most people, that someone else might walk away with his potential purchase.

"You were only offering a mina and a half," the trader objected.

"I'll give you two." He turned to Thais. "What do you need this girl for? You won't be able to manage her."

"Let us not argue," she replied and faced the trader. "I'll pay three, as you wanted. Send someone for the money or come to the house of Thais between the hill of Nymphs and Ceramic."

"Thais!" exclaimed a man standing nearby, and a few more voices echoed, "Thais, Thais!"

The Athenian held out her hand to the Theban slave girl both to help her off the platform, and as the sign of her ownership. The girl clutched at it like a drowning person at a rope and hopped down, still holding Thais' hand.

"What is your name?" Thais asked.

"Hesiona," the Theban said proudly.

"It is a noble name," Thais said. "Little Isis."

The girl stood straighter. "I am the daughter of Astiochus, a philosopher of the ancient family," the slave girl replied.

Thais was so weary she didn't even realize she'd fallen asleep. She woke only when the window shutters were being opened toward Not, the southern wind from the sea that lifted the heavy heat from the Athenian streets this time of year. Scorching temperatures weakened the passions of Aphrodite's admirers, and not a single symposium was scheduled over the next few days. In any case, Thais had at least two or three free evenings. She realized it had been many days since she'd last gone to read proposals at the Ceramic wall, and thought she might do that later on.

Thais, feeling fresh and rested, decided to dine alone. She knocked on the table twice and ordered Hesiona to be brought to her. The girl entered, smelling healthy and clean. Thais could see she was embarrassed by her dirty himation. Keeping her eyes lowered, she knelt at the hetaera's feet with an awkward mix of shyness and grace. She had apparently gotten used to rudeness and beatings, and clearly did not know how to behave with the sweet, gentle Thais.

Thais asked her to toss off her cape, then examined the flawless body of her purchase and picked out a modest linen chiton from her own wardrobe. A dark blue himation she normally wore for her evening outings completed Hesiona's outfit.

"You do not need the mastodetona, the breast binding, I do not wear it either. I gave you this old stuff."

"To avoid distinguishing me from others," the Theban said quietly. "But it's not old at all, Mistress."

The slave girl dressed quickly, skillfully arranging the folds of her chiton and straightening the ties at her shoulders. She was instantly transformed into the very picture of a dignified young lady from the educated upper classes of society. Looking at her, Thais realized that the beautiful Hesiona had caused inevitable hatred among her former mistresses, since they would have been devoid of all the qualities with which their slave was endowed. Education must have been at the top of that list. That was a thing no longer possessed by the Attic housewives, who were forced to lead a secluded life poisoned by bitter jealousy.

Thais chuckled inadvertently. They would have been jealous in their ignorance of every facet of Hesiona's life, not realizing how defenseless and easily hurt a tender young woman could be when she found herself in the power of someone who acted like a pig.

Hesiona misinterpreted Thais' chuckle. She flushed and hurriedly smoothed her clothes with her hands, looking for flaws and not daring to look in the mirror.

Thais smiled. "Everything is fine," she said to the girl. "I was just thinking. But I forgot -" She leaned to the side and picked up a pretty silver belt, then wrappe it around the slave girl.

Hesiona flushed again, this time with pleasure.

"How can I thank you, Mistress? What can I give you for your kindness?"

Thais wrinkled her nose merrily, her eyes twinkling with mischief, and the Theban became wary again.

"Much time will pass," Thais thought, saying nothing out loud, "before this young creature will acquire the human dignity and calm possessed by all free Helenians. Was this not the main difference between us and the barbarians who were destined for slavery? That they were in complete power of the free? The worse they are treated, the worse the slaves become, and in response, their owners turn beastly."

It was strange, pondering these thoughts for the first time. For a long time she had simply accepted the world as it was. What if Thais and her mother had been kidnapped by the pirates, of whose cruelty and cunning she'd heard so much? Then it could have been her, standing on a platform covered by lash scars, being groped by some fat trader.

Thais hopped up and gazed into the hard, pale yellow, bronze mirror which had been brought by the Finikians from a country whose name they kept secret. Frowning slightly, she tried to make the expression of a proud and menacing Lemnia, but couldn't do it because of the merry twinkle in her eyes.

She wanted to send Hesiona away and return to her own private thoughts, but her mind was taken up by one question, and she couldn't let the girl leave without an answer. Thais began asking her new slave girl about the terrible days of the siege of Thebes and of her capture. She tried to hide her puzzlement, but couldn't help wondering why this proud and well-bred girl hadn't killed herself, instead opting for the pitiful fate of a slave?

Hesiona immediately understood what is was Thais wanted to know.

"Yes, I remained alive, Mistress. At first it was from sheer shock and the sudden fall of the great city. Our house, open and defenseless, was invaded by insane hordes who trampled, robbed and murdered. We were unarmed people who had grown up in honor and glory, well-respected citizens only moments prior. We were shoved into a crowd like a herd, beaten mercilessly if we lagged behind or were stubborn. They knocked us out with blunt ends of spears and shoved us behind a fence like sheep. It is impossible to think in this situation. It is as if a strange paralysis overcomes the people from such sudden turn of fate."

Hesiona shivered and sniffed, but forced herself to continue. She explained that the place where they had been held was a livestock market. Before her eyes, Hesiona's mother, still a young and beautiful woman, was dragged off by two shield bearers, despite desperate resistance. She vanished forever. Then somebody took Hesiona's little sister away. Hesiona, hidden under a trough, decided to make her way to the walls and look for her father and brother. She hadn't even been two plethors away from the fence when she was grabbed by a soldier who had only just dismounted from his horse. The man wished to have her right there and then, at the door of some empty house. Anger and desperation gave Hesiona such strength that the Macedonian couldn't subdue her at first. He moved with experience, however. He must have raped and pillaged in many an invaded city, and had soon tied

Hesiona up and tethered a horse's harness on her so she couldn't even bite back. After this, the Macedonian and one of his companions took turns raping the girl till late night. At dawn the dishonored and exhausted Hesiona was taken to the slave traders who followed the Macedonian army like vultures. One of them sold her to a Brauron noble, who in his turn sent her to the Pyrean market after unsuccessful attempts to get her to obey. He had been concerned that the girl might lose value from the constant beatings she was receiving.

Hesiona hung her head, shamed. "I was dedicated to the goddess Biris, and I was not to be with a man before I was twenty-two."

"I do not know this goddess," Thais said. "Does she rule in Boeotia?"

"Everywhere. She has a temple here in Athens, but I no longer have access to it. The Minians, our ancestors, who were a seashore people from before the Doric invasion, considered her to be a goddess of peace. Those who serve her are against war. I was already a wife to two soldiers and hadn't killed either of them. I would have killed myself had I not felt obligated to find out what happened to my father and brother. If they are alive and in slavery, I shall become a port prostitute and will rob scoundrels until I have enough money to buy out my father. He is the wisest and kindest man in all of Hellas. That was the only reason I stayed alive."

"How old are you, Hesiona?"

"Eighteen, almost nineteen, Mistress."

"Do not call me Mistress," Thais said, rising to her feet in the grip of sudden inspiration. "You shall not be my slave. I am setting you free."

"Mistress!" the girl exclaimed. It was a moment before she could find her voice, then it was almost lost in her sobs. "You must be from the family of gods. Who else in Hellas would do such a thing? But allow me to remain at your house and serve you. Since I came here I have eaten and slept a lot, but I am not always like that. It's was just after all the hungry days and the long standing at the slave trader's platform ..."

Thais fell into thought again, not listening to the girl, whose passionate plea momentarily left Thais as aloof as a goddess. Hesiona shrank away, then opened like a bloom at the sight of the hetaera's attentive and mischievous gaze.

"You said your father was a famous philosopher? Is he famous enough to be known around Hellas and not only in the Hundred-gated Thebes?"

"Former Thebes," Hesiona said bitterly. "But yes. The entire Hellas knows philosopher Astiochus. Not as a poet, perhaps. Have you not heard of him, Mistress?"

"I have not. But I am not a connoisseur, so let's leave it be. Here is what I came up with." Thais shared her plan with Hesiona, making the Theban shake with impatience.

After Philip of Macedonia was killed, his guest Aristotle left Pella and moved to Athens. Alexander provided him with money, and the philosopher from Stagira founded a school in Lycea, the sacred grove of Apollo the Wolf. The school held a collection of rarities and was a home for his students, who explored the laws of nature under his guidance. Aristotle's establishment was dubbed Lyceum after the name of the grove.

Using her connection with Ptolemy and Alexander, Thais decided she could turn to Stagiritus. If Hesiona's father were alive, then wherever he was, word of such a famous slave would have reached the philosophers and scientists of Lyceum.

A walk of a mere fifteen Olympic stadiums separated Thais' house from Lyceum, but Thais decided to take her carriage so she would make the right impression. She ordered Hesiona to put a slave's bracelet on her left arm and carry a box containing a rare jewel, a green chrysolite with yellow sparkles brought from a distant island in the Eritrean Sea. Thais had received it as a gift from the Egyptian merchants. Ptolemy had told her of Stagiritus' great greed for rarities from distant lands, and was hoping to open his heart with this key.

Thais had wanted to eat her dinner with Hesiona that night, but the girl convinced her not to do that. She feared the role of a servant, which she honestly wished to uphold in Thais' household, would become false and deprive her of a good opinion of the hetaera's servants and other slaves. So Thais ate alone again, since Egesikhora had not appeared for dinner for some unknown reason.

The sacred pines silently and motionlessly soared into the scorched sky. Thais and Hesiona slowly approached a gallery dwarfed by ancient columns, where the old scholar studied with his students. Stagiritus was out of sorts when he met the hetaera on the broad steps of crooked stone slabs. Construction of new buildings was only just beginning.

"What brings here the pride of Athenian whores?" Aristotle asked haltingly.

Thais made a sign, Hesiona handed over the open box, and the chrysolite, the symbol of Cretan Crown, sparkled against the box' black fabric. The philosopher's disdainful mouth drew up into a grin. He picked up the stone with two fingers and examined it in the sunlight. Finally, he looked up and studied Thais, who waited quietly for his attention.

"So you are Ptolemy's lover? I must say, he wasn't a gifted student. His mind is too occupied with war and women. So. Now you have come. You need to find something out from me?" he asked, throwing a sharp, piercing glance at Thais.

The hetaera met his eyes calmly, then dropped her head modestly and asked whether he knew anything of the Theban philosopher's fate. Aristotle pondered briefly.

"I heard that he either died of wounds or was captured and became a slave. But why does he interest you, hetaera?"

"And why does he not interest you, great philosopher? Does the fate of your brother, famous in Hellas, not concern you?" Thais demanded, then flushed when he frowned at her.

"You are becoming disrespectful, girl."

"Have mercy, great Stagiritus. Due to my ignorance, I was surprised by your indifference to the fate of a great philosopher and poet. Is the life of such man not precious? Perhaps you could save him."

"What for? Who dares to cross the path of fate, the will of gods? The defeated Boeotian fell to the level of a barbarian, a mere slave. You can consider that philosopher Astiochus no longer exists and forget about him. I do not care whether he was thrown into silver mines or is milling the grain for Carian bakers. Each free person chooses his fate. The Boeotian made his choice, and even the gods dare not interfere."

The famous teacher turned away. Continuing his examination of the jewel sitting on his palm, he indicated that the conversation was over.

"You have a long way to go to Anaxagoras and Antiphontus, Stagiritus!" Hesiona shouted, beside herself with anger. "You are simply jealous of Astiochus' glory as the singer of peace and beauty. Peace and beauty are alien to you, philosopher, and you know it."

Aristotle spun angrily toward her. One of his students stood nearby, and when he heard the conversation he slapped Hesiona across the face. She shrieked and leaped forward, wanting to attack the muscular, bearded offender, but Thais grabbed her by the hand.

"Scum, slave girl, how dare you?" the student exclaimed. "Get out, pornodions!"

"Philosophers are dropping all pretenses," Thais said mischievously. "Let us depart from this abode of wisdom."

With these words, Thais snatched the chrysolite from the dismayed Aristotle, picked up the hem of her himation and sprinted down the wide path between the pines, headed toward the main road and followed by Hesiona. Several men, either overly devoted students or servant, rushed after them. Thais and Hesiona hopped into the waiting carriage, but the boy driver didn't have time to start the horses before they were grabbed by the bridle, and three huge middle-aged men dashed toward the open back of the carriage to drag both women out of it.

"You won't escape, whores! We've got you, you sluts!" yelled a man with a broad, untrimmed beard as he reached for Thais.

Hesiona grabbed the whip from the driver and shoved the handle into the man's wide open, screaming mouth as hard as she could. The attacker collapsed on the ground.

Thais, now free, opened her bag, which hung on the side of the carriage, and snatched a box of powder, which she tossed into another man's eyes. A short delay didn't give them much. The carriage could not move and they could not get out of it.

Matters were turning serious. There were no other travelers on the road, and the angry philosophers could easily overwhelm the helpless girls. The boy driver, who Thais had taken with her that day instead of her regular, elderly stableman, gazed around helplessly, not knowing what to do. He was trapped behind a wall of people.

But Aphrodite was merciful toward Thais. A thunder of wheels and hooves suddenly sounded from the road and a foursome of madly running horses, harnessed into a racing carriage, appeared from around the corner. They were driven by a woman whose golden hair flew in the wind like a cape: Egesikhora!

"Thais, malakion (little friend), hold on!" she cried.

Knowing the Spartan was about to do something incredible, Thais grabbed the side of the carriage and shouted to Hesiona to hold on with all her might. Egesikhora turned sharply without slowing down, circled Thais' carriage and suddenly yanked the horses to the right, hooking her axle into that of Thais' wheel. The bearded men holding the horses ran away screaming, trying to dodge the wheels and hooves. Someone rolled in the dust right under the horses' feet and screamed in pain. Thais' horses pulled forward, and Egesikhora, holding the foursome back with unwomanly force, unhooked the two undamaged carriages.

"Go! Don't wait!" Thais shouted, smacking the boy firmly. The driver came to his senses, and the bay pair ran forth at full speed, followed by Egesikhora's foursome.

Yells, curses and threats could be heard from within the clouds of dust billowing behind. Hesiona, feeling relief surge through her, started laughing hysterically until Thais yelled at the girl to stop. Thais' nerves were not well after all her trials.

They passed the intersection, crossing the Akharna road before they knew it. Holding back their horses, they turned back and to the right, descending toward Ilissus, then riding along the river toward the gardens.

Only when they reached the shadow of the giant cypresses did Egesikhora stop and jump off the carriage. Thais ran toward her, pulled her into an embrace and kissed her.

"Wasn't it a nice amatrochia? It's very dangerous to hook the axles like that in a competition."

Thais laughed. "You really are Kiniska's heiress, Egesikhora. But how did you end up on the road, thank the gods?"

"I came for you so we could go riding, but you'd gone to Lyceum. It wasn't difficult to figure out that you went to look for Hesiona's father, and that worried me. You must remember that we cannot talk properly to the scholars, and they are not fond of hetaerae. Especially if the latter are beautiful and smart. In their opinion, the combination of these qualities in a woman is unnatural and dangerous," the Spartan said, laughing out loud.

"How did you make it just in time?"

"I rode from the Lykean grove up into the mountains, stopped there with the horses, and asked my driver to stand at the turn and watch for you to pass. He ran back with the news that the philosophers were about to beat you up. I barely made it. I actually left him there on the road."

"What are we going to do? We have to hide in order to avoid punishment. You have crippled my enemies."

"I'll go to Seven Bronzes, where Dioreus lives and let him watch my carriage. Then we'll go swimming at our favorite spot. Tell your driver boy to follow me to the turn, then wait."

Then the brave Spartan rushed off with her mad foursome.

The women swam and dove in a secluded lagoon until evening. It was the same lagoon where Ptolemy had landed two years prior, after having been thrown by the waves.

When they grew tired, Thais and Egesikhora stretched out on the sand, which was like a sheet of bronze on the floor of a temple. Pebbles rolled down from a rocky overhang, dipping underwater, screeching and chafing as they went. A lovely breeze touched their bodies, exhausted by heat. Hesiona sat at the edge of the water, hugging her knees and resting her chin on them. Thais heard her humming something quiet amidst the noise of the waves.

"The angry Stagiritus will file a complaint against you to the gineconomes," Thais said. "He'll never forgive us."

"He doesn't know me," the Spartan teased. "But you did give him your name. Most likely, he'll send a dozen of his students to destroy your house."

"I'll have to ask some friends to sleep in my garden. Or maybe hire two or three armed guards, perhaps. That would be simpler. I only have to find people who are brave enough," Thais said thoughtfully. "I am a little sick of them, my Athenian friends."

"I am not afraid of Stagiritus, even if they do find out who ran over the philosophers," Egesikhora declared. "I have already decided to sail to Egypt with the Spartans. That was what I wanted to tell you when we went riding earlier today."

"Then why didn't you say anything?" Thais sat up, then, realizing the ridiculousness of her reproach, burst out laughing. When she was calm again, she frowned.

"Then you are leaving me in Athens alone?"

"No. Why alone?" Egesikhora replied calmly. "You are coming with me."

"I never said that."

"Ah well. No matter. The Gods have decided. I went to a fortuneteller - the one whose name is not uttered, nor is that of the goddess he serves."

Thais shuddered and paled, curling up her toes. "Why did you do that? Why?"

Egesikhora's eyes were dark on Thais. "I cannot bear to part with you. Also, I had to give an answer to Eositeus Euriponidos."

"Is he from the ancient line of Laconian kings?"

"Yes."

"And what did he-who-can-see-forward say to you?"

"That you will have a path in a loop for many years. And me, too, but my path will be short, although you will be with me to the end."

Thais gazed silently into the scattering of pebbles on the slope before her, at the blades of grass fluttering in the wind. Egesikhora was watching her, a strange sadness deepening the corners of the Spartan's full, sensual mouth.

"When are they sailing?"

"On the twentieth day of Boedromion. From Gitius."

"How are they getting there?"

"A week prior to that we must sail from the Pyrean harbor. His ship will pick us up with all our possessions."

"There isn't much time left," Thais said, rising and brushing the sand off her belly, hips and elbows.

Egesikhora rose as well, dividing her heavy hair into strands with her fingers. Hesiona ran up to Thais with a piece of cloth for wiping off the salt and rubbed her down. The women set off, managing to reach Thais' house with barely a sound. Egesikhora covered her face with a veil and went home in the dusk, accompanied by a strong groom.

The next day the entire Agora buzzed with excited discussion about the incident at the Lykean grove. Athenians, who were fond of gossip, tried to outdo each other in describing the details. The number of "victims" grew steadily and reached fifteen by noon. Thais' name was repeated either with admiration or with outrage, depending on the age and gender of those who were discussing her. All respectable women agreed that "ta metroten Kressa", that Cretan on her mother's side, had to be taught a lesson for being so audacious as to disturb the peace of the great scholar's abode.

Gineconomes had already dispatched their representative to Thais to summon her to court for testifying. And while Thais herself was not accused of any serious crime, and had nothing to be afraid of save a monetary fine, even if the court decided against her, her friend could be severely punished. Witnesses had seen a woman riding in a carriage, and the entire city knew that only hetaera Egesikhora could drive a tetrippa, four horses at once. Her benefactors managed to delay the case, but it became known that the son of a wealthy and influential citizen, Aristodem, had been crippled by wheels and hooves. Three more of Stagiritus' students demanded satisfaction for broken ribs, an arm and a leg.

During the "heavy days" of Megateynion, the last three days of each month, dedicated to the dead and the underground gods, Egesikhora suddenly appeared at Thais' house, accompanied by her slaves and an entire detachment of young men who carried bundles of her most precious possessions.

"It is over," the Spartan announced. "I sold everything else."

"What of the horses?' Thais exclaimed.

Her friend's glower suddenly lightened. "They are already on the ship, at Munikhion. I will be there before dawn. So. Was the fortune teller wrong? Are we to be parted by the will of gods?"

"No," Thais said passionately. "I decided, too."

"When?"

"Just now."

The Lacedemonian squeezed her friend in her arms, wiping tears of joy against her hair.

"But I need time to get ready. I won't sell the house, I'll just leave it to my faithful Akesius. The gardener and his wife will stay, too. The others, Clonaria, Hesiona and the stableman, are coming with me. I need three days."

"Let it be so. We are sailing to Aegina and will come back for you in three days."

"No. Don't come back. Wait for me in Herculea. I will find sailors who will transport me willingly and without attracting anyone's attention. Hurry, we have decided everything."

"Thais, my darling," Egesikhora said, beaming. She hugged her again. "You took a stone off my liver."

At that, the Spartan led her improvised little army toward Pyrean road, humming a tune.

"I took off, and you put on," Thais thought, looking after her friend.

Beloved constellation shone over the black tips of cypresses, having heard so many of Thais' silent prayers to Aphrodite Urania. The hetaera sensed an unusual longing, as if she were forever leaving the great city, the focus of powerful beauty, created by dozens of generations of Helenian artists.

She sent Clonaria to get Talmid, a powerful athlete living nearby. Armed with a dagger and a copper bat, he had often accompanied the hetaera when she'd wanted to wander around at night. Thais paid well, and Talmid stepped after her silently, not interfering with the girl's simple enjoyment of the night, stars and statues of gods and heroes.

That night Thais meandered toward Pelasgicon, the wall of enormous stones erected by the distant ancestors at the foot of Acropolis. Perhaps it had been built by the mighty people, whose blood flowed through the veins of the half-Cretan. These stones had always attracted Thais. Even now she touched one slab and pressed her entire body against it, feeling its timeless hardness and warmth through her thin chiton.

The darkness of the moonless night was akin to translucent black fabric. Such a sensation could only be experienced in the clear, light-bearing air of Hellas. The night dressed everything in a delicate veil, akin to that on a statue of the nude Anachita in Corinth, hiding, yet simultaneously revealing the unknown depths of mysterious sensations.

Thais quietly ascended the worn steps toward the temple of Victory. A distant light flashed from behind Pnix, a lantern over Barathron the terrible abyss, reminding Athenians of the wrath of Poseidon the Earth Keeper. Sacrifices to the menacing underground gods and Erinias were thrown there. Thais wasn't thinking about Hades yet, and she hadn't done anything to anger the goddesses of retribution.

Gods were jealous, that much was true. Remarkable beauty, happiness, success and admiration, all things Thais had enjoyed in abundance since the age of fifteen, could bring on the anger of the gods. Disasters would surely follow. Wise people wanted success and failures to follow each other in equal measure, happiness mixed with sadness, hoping that by approaching life this way they would be protected from the more devastating blows of fate.

Thais thought it ridiculous. How could one buy happiness by groveling before gods and begging them to send you misfortune? The cunning goddesses could inflict a blow so painful that any happiness would feel bitter after it. No. It was better to ascend to the top of the mountain like Nika, and if a fall were to follow, then let it be forever.

Thais drew her eyes from the little light over Barathron, thinking she ought to bake a magis tomorrow, a sacrificial pie for Hecate, the goddess of road crossings. Hecate was the goddess who struck far and never granted passage to the late night travelers. She should also make a sacrifice to Athena Caleutia, the goddess of roads. Oh, and she shouldn't forget Aphrodite Euploa, the goddess of trouble-free sailing. No trouble there. Egesikhora would take care of that.

Thais' light footsteps resonated under the colonnade of her favorite temple to Nika Apteros. There, she sat on the steps for awhile, gazing upon the tiny lights that twinkled on the streets of her beloved city like fireflies scattered in the wind as well as at the

Pyrean lighthouse and two low lanterns of Munikhia. With a sigh, she realized Egesikhora's ship would have already entered the Saron Gulf and turned south to the nearby Aegina.

Thais descended toward Agora. As she passed the old, deserted temple of Night, Niktoon, two "night ravens" (owls) flew by her right side: a double good omen. Many of these sacred birds of the goddess Athena flew around the city, but such coincidence was the first one for Thais. Sighing with relief, she sped toward the massive, glum walls of the ancient sanctuary of Mother Goddess. After the decline of the ancient Minian religion, the sanctuary had become a municipal archive of Athens; however, those who continued to believe in the might of Rhea and the feminine beginning in the world, came here at night to press their forehead against the corner stone and receive a warning of any upcoming danger.

Thais did so, pressing both her forehead and her temples to the time-polished stone, but didn't hear either a light hum or the barely-there shaking of the wall. Rhea-Kibela knew nothing, and therefore nothing threatened the hetaera in the near future. Thais rose, then almost ran toward Ceramic and her house, moving so swiftly that Talmid grumbled behind her. Laughing, the hetaera waited for the athlete, threw her arms around his neck and rewarded him with a kiss. Slightly overwhelmed, the big man snatched her up in his arms and carried her home, despite her laughing protests.

On the day Thais designated for her departure, the weather changed. Gray clouds piled up in the mountains and hung low over the city, powdering the golden marble of statues, walls and columns with a tinge of ash.

Euriclidion, a strong northeast wind, justified its nickname of "the one rising broad waves" and swiftly propelled Thais' little ship toward the island of Aegina.

Thais stood at the stern, turning her back to the departing shore of Attica, and giving herself up to the soothing roll of the ship over the swell. She couldn't shake off the memory of a stranger she had met the day prior, a warrior with scars on his arm and face, which he'd half-covered with a beard. The stranger had stopped her at the Tripod Street, near the statue of Satire Periboeton, by Praxiteles.

Clear perceptive eyes had stared at her, and the hetaera felt deep in her soul that she could never lie to this man.

"You are Thais," he said in a deep low voice. "And you are leaving our Athens to follow Chrisocoma the Spartan."

Thais nodded, silent with awe.

"Athenian state must be doing poorly, if beauty is abandoning it," he said. "Beauty of women, arts and crafts, all things beautiful used to converge here. Now they run away from us."

She felt a need to defend herself. "I feel, stranger, that my compatriots are more occupied these days with cheating their competitors in war and trade, instead of admiring that which their ancestors and their land has created."

"You are right, oh young one. I am a friend of Lysippus the sculptor, and a sculptor myself. Soon we shall be off to Asia to meet with Alexander. You are headed the same way. Sooner or later, we shall meet there."

"I do not know. It is unlikely. My fate draws me in the other direction."

"No," he said calmly, shaking his head. "It shall be so. Lysippus is there. He has long wanted to meet you, and so have I. But he has his own desires, and I – my own …"

"It is too late," the hetaera said, genuinely sorry. Attention of one of the greatest artists in Hellas was flattering to her. There were beautiful legends told of love between Praxiteles and Frina, Phidias and Aspasia.

He smiled. "I didn't say now. You are too young. We require maturity of body for our purposes, not fame. But time will come, and you will not refuse me then. Geliaine!"

The stranger departed without naming himself, taking broad dignified strides. The bewildered hetaera returned home with the memory of their meeting imprinted on her mind.

Chapter Three. Escape to the South

Thais thought of the stranger as she stood on the deck of her small ship. Could it be that when the life force of the people and the country weakened, the beauty became scarce as well, and those seeking that beauty went off into the distant lands? That was what had happened to Crete and to Egypt. Was it the turn of the Hellas? Her heart ached at the mere memory of the divine City of the Maiden. Corinth, Argos and now-demolished Thebes were nothing compared to Athens.

Clonaria approached Thais, stepping awkwardly across the rocking deck. "Do you wish to eat, Mistress?"

"Not yet."

"The helmsman says Herculea is coming up soon. See? Aegina is already rising from the sea."

"Where is Hesiona?"

"The Daughter of the Snake[10] sleeps like her foremother."

Thais laughed and patted the girl's cheek. "Don't be jealous. Go wake up the Daughter of the Snake."

Hesiona appeared before her mistress, having quickly splashed some seawater over her face. Thais asked the Theban of her further intentions. Hesiona had begged her to take her with her, the hetaera had argued, feeling Hesiona was making a mistake by leaving Attica. In Attica she had a greater chance of finding her father because the largest slave market in Hellas was in Athens. Several hundred people were sold off its platform every day. There was a possibility she might find something about philosopher Astiochus through the traders, connected with all cities of Hellas and lands surrounding the Inner sea. Hesiona admitted that she had gone to a fortuneteller after Egesikhora's nighttime visit. The man had asked her to give him something that had belonged to her father. Not without trepidation, the Theban had handed him a small cameo on a thin chain, which she carried in the knot of her hair. It carried the profile a skillful carver had created of her father on the surface of a greenish "sea stone", beryllium. Her father had given it to her on her nymphean day, the day she had become old enough to be a bride. That had been only three years prior. The fortuneteller held the cameo briefly in his strange, square-tipped fingers. He had sighed and stated with certainty that the philosopher was dead, and in all likelihood the same fate had befallen Hesiona's brother.

"You are all I have now, Mistress," Hesiona said, stubbornly continuing to call Thais by that title, despite Thais' objections. "How can I not follow you and share your fate? Do not turn me away. Please?" the girl begged, clinging to Thais' knees.

---

10 Reference to Isis who was frequently portrayed with a snake and, according to legend, had power over serpents.

"Must be fate," Thais agreed. "But I am not a wife. Nor am I a daughter of an aristocrat, or of royal blood. I am but a hetaera, a plaything of fate, entirely dependent on accidents."

"I shall never leave you, Mistress, no matter what happens."

Thais glanced at the Theban, her knowing eyes twinkling with mischief. She stuck out the tip of her tongue, and the girl blushed.

"Yes, yes. Aphrodite herself fears the power of Eros, to speak nothing of us mere mortals."

"I do not love men," Hesiona said with disgust. "And if I fall in love, I shall kill him and myself."

"You are much more a child than I thought judging by your body," the hetaera said slowly, squinting her eyes at the Herculean harbor.

The little ship was expected in Herculea, since they had correctly calculated the length of their trip. Thais saw Egesikhora, surrounded by a group of soldiers, her mighty stature noticeable from afar. She waited for Thais on board the same ship that had taken her away from Athens. They departed for a three day voyage to Gitius, not far from the delta of the river Eurot. Gitius was in the heart of the Laconian harbor, where Spartan ships were constructed and equipped. Had Euriclidion continued to push them on, the journey could have been as short as two days, but southeast winds were not steady this time of year.

Egesikhora's friend was in Gitius, assembling his big detachment. His hecatontarchus, squadron leader, was in charge of the ship. Thais didn't like him because of his overt ogling. He was constantly trying to see through her himation. Egesikhora ordered the soldier around as she wished, not at all bothered by the sincere adoration of smaller commanders, simple spear-bearers who also served as rowers, or of the old one-eyed helmsman, whose only eye – round like that of a Cyclops – noticed everything around him. The man seemed to be everywhere. The slightest imperfection in the strike of an oar, a delay in the turn of the tiller causing a slight loss in their speed, everything caused an abrupt shout from the one-eyed helmsman, followed by a sarcastic joke. The soldiers nicknamed the man a Finikian for his wicked temper, but treated him with respect.

The waters of the Laconian gulf, smooth as the blue mirror Aphrodite had given the Swan's daughter[11], seemed to slow the ship as if it were sailing through thick wine. Halfway through their journey, across the Cyprus Cape, the sea turned grassy green in color. Waters of Eurot fell into the sea not far from there. It was a large river housing Sparta, the capital of Lacedemonia, at its origins, two hundred and forty stadiums from the harbor. Rocky and menacing Tyget ridge loomed on the left, a spot famous in the Hellas. This was where the Spartan elders sent newborn children in whom they found imperfections of body and health.

Thais' ship approached the delta of Smenos with its Las pier, filled with numerous small ships. The ship passed around the wide cape, behind Gitius, the main harbor of Lacedemonia. They docked at the sound end of the harbor where the steep slope of the cape veered to the north, locking in the inner part of the harbor. Deep waters were as still as a dark mirror, even though Not, the south wind carrying rain clouds, came down in gusts and crashed against the opposite edge of the gulf. The ship's deck ended up about four elbows lower than the pier. The scuffed logs of its edge hovered just over Thais' and Egesikhora's heads as they stood at the stern.

---

11 Helen of Troy. According to the legend, Helen's mother Leda was seduced by Zeus who came to her in the shape of a swan.

Both hetaerae were noticed instantly, dressed as they were in stunning chitons. Thais wore one that glowed yellow, and the Spartan wore black, setting off the incredible golden redness of her hair. Several soldiers ran toward them shouting, "Eleleu! Eleleu!", led by the bearded giant Eositeus, who held out his massive arms to Egesikhora. She declined Eositeus' assistance and pointed at the bow of the ship where four horses waited impatiently under a reed tent. The Spartans were obviously delighted when solders and two stablemen carefully led the stallions forward. The shaft pair was of that rare, snow white color called leukophaes by the Athenians, while the outrunners were leukopyrrian or reddish gold to match their mistress. All the powerful beasts rolled their eyes and twitched their ears. The combination of white and gold was considered particularly lucky since the ancient Cretans had initiated the art of making chryselephantine (gold and ivory) statues of gods.

The gangway was lowered from the pier. The first stallion in line refused to step on the bowing wood, choosing instead to leap straight across to the pier. The ship tilted from the powerful push and the second white stallion, who had tried to follow his brother, had failed to complete the jump off the deck. He was now stuck, reared up, with his front hooves hooked on the edge of the pier.

The ship began pushing away from the pier so that the gap between the pier and the side of the ship widened. In the stallion's desperate effort to hang on, all of his muscles strained, and a large vein swelled on the side of his belly. The Spartan flew to her horse, but was beaten to it by a soldier who jumped down from the pier. When he landed on the deck, the ship tilted again and the horse's hooves started slipping off the log, but the warrior shoved the stallion from behind with incredible courage and force, literally tossing the animal to the pier. He moved away, but couldn't avoid the hind hooves and stumbled back to the unsteady deck. Fortunately, he rose immediately, unharmed.

"Hurray for Menedem!" the leader of Spartan's shouted, and Egesikhora rewarded the hero with a deep kiss.

"Ha, ha! Look out Eositeus, or you might lose your chrisocoma!"

"No, that is not to be." The leader of Lacedemonians jumped down to the deck, grabbed Egesikhora and was back on the pier with her in an instant.

The gold colored stallions were taken up the gangway and Thais remained on the deck, laughing at her friend's attempts to free herself from the powerful arms of her lover. Menedem froze before Thais in admiration, struck by the black-haired Athenian. Her coppery tan and gray eyes were set off perfectly by her yellow chiton. The Spartan youth was dressed only in an epoxida, a short chiton fastened over one shoulder. The only sign that he was a soldier was his wide belt.

During his struggle with the horse, the chiton had fallen off Menedem's shoulder, leaving the Spartan nude to the waist. Thais admired him openly, recalling the statue of a Spear-bearer by Polycleitus, who had also used a Lacedemonian youth as a model. Menedem's torso, neck and legs were equally powerful as those of the famous statue. Over his extremely broad, conves chest rested solid slabs of chest muscles, barely missing the perfect arch at the edge of his ribcage. His stomach muscles were so thick that instead of narrowing at his waist, they overhung his thighs. His thigh and calf muscles bulged above and below the knees. The narrowest part of his body was at the top of his hips. Such muscular armor had easily withstood the impact of the hind hooves of the panicked horse, suffering no damage.

Thais looked into the embarrassed athlete's face. He blushed so hotly that his small ears and childishly round cheeks turned into one crimson spot.

"Well, Menedem," Egesikhora teased from the dock. "I doubt you can lift Thais. She is pantashilioboyon, worth five thousand bull," she said, hinting at the price set by Philopatros on the Ceramic wall. The ancient Athenian silver coins, originally minted by Theseus, carried an image of a bull. Each coin used to equal the cost of a bull and was also called a bull. A bride in the ancient farming Athens was always paid for in bulls, which was why a daughter in the family was called "bull-bringing". The largest ransom was one hundred bulls, hekatonboyon, approximately two minas, which was why the monstrous size of Thais' "ransom" caused a series of surprised exclamations in the group of soldiers.

Even Menedem took a step back, and Thais burst out laughing. "Catch!" she shouted.

Instinctively, the soldier lifted his arms and the girl jumped off the stern. He caught her deftly, and she settled comfortably against his broad shoulder. But Hesiona ran after her, clutching at her leg. "Do not leave me alone with the soldiers, Mistress!"

"Take her too, Menedem," Thais said. This was accompanied by general laughter. The athlete shrugged, then effortlessly carried both women to the pier.

Egesikhora and Eositeus spent the next day walking and exercising the horses, who were now clean and brushed despite the frequent gusts of wind and rain. As soon as the weather improved and the sun dried the slippery mud, the Spartan asked Thais to go with her to visit the capital of Lacedemonia.

The long road across the Eurot valley was famous for its easy horse travel, and two hundred and forty stadiums split into two stages weren't much of a challenge for Egesikhora's runners. The carriage holding Eositeus and Menedem constantly lagged behind the mad foursome. Thais was so caught up in the lightning ride to the capital, holding on tight when they roared around turns, that she almost didn't look around.

The closer they came to the city, the more people greeted Egesikhora. At first Thais thought the exclamations and gestures of greeting were addressed toward Eositeus, a strategist and a nephew to king Agis. But people ran enthusiastically toward their carriage even when the soldiers' carriage fell far behind. They entered a grove of mighty oaks whose crowns converged so thickly that the grove was wrapped in twilight. Dry soil had been covered by a thick layer of leaves accumulated over hundreds of years. The place had a grim feeling to it, as if it were a desert, and was called Scotita by the Spartans.

Once they had passed through the grove, the carriage headed to the city. Egesikhora stopped only once, near the statue of Dioskures, at the beginning of a straight street or alley called Dromos: Run. Spartan young men frequently used Dromos to race against each other. Passersby gazed upon the carriage in amazement, appreciating the four splendid horses and two beautiful women. While in Athens such a sight would have assembled a crowd of a thousand people, in Sparta the visitors were surrounded only by a few dozen soldiers and youths, enchanted by the beauty of the women and horses. When their companions caught up with them, they rode together into a broad alley shaded by giant sycamore trees. Shouts and greetings followed them along the way.

Eositeus stopped near a small sanctuary, built at the end of the sycamore grove. Kneeling, Egesikhora poured oil and wine for the gods and lit a piece of fragrant resin from a sacred shrub. Menedem explained to Thais that this temple was dedicated to the memory of Kiniska, the daughter of Archidemos, who was a king of Sparta. Kiniska was also the first woman in the entire Hellas and all of Ecumene to win the tetrippa race during the Olympic games. This was a dangerous competition which required great skill with horses.

"Was she a sister of Agis? The sanctuary looks ancient," Thais asked.

The Spartan soldier smiled childishly and a bit naïvely. "It's not the same Archidemos who was the father of our current king, but the one from the ancient times. This was a long time ago."

The Spartans must have seen an heiress to their heroine in Egesikhora, because they brought her flowers and showered her with invitations to their homes. Eositeus declined all invitations and led his beautiful companions into a large house with a sprawling garden. Numerous slaves of all ages ran out to tend the horses while the Spartan captain took his lover and her friend into the modestly appointed inner rooms. The girls were left alone in the female portion of the house, which was not nearly as strictly separated from the male portion as it would have been in Athens.

Thais watched her friend. "Tell me, why do you not stay here in Sparta, where you are treated like a daughter and everyone loves you?"

"That will only last as long as I have my foursome, my beauty and my youth. Then what? Spartans are poor. Even the king's nephew has to hire himself out as a mercenary into a strange country. That is why I am an Athenian hetaera. My compatriots, it seems, became too carried away with physical perfection and military upbringing, and that is no longer enough to be successful in this world. It used to be different in the ancient times."

"Are you saying that the Laconians traded education and mental development for physical prowess?"

"Even worse. They gave up their world of feelings and intelligence for military supremacy and immediately fell under brutal oligarchy. During endless wars they brought death and destruction to other people, never willing to give in to anyone. And now there are a lot fewer of my compatriots in Sparta than there are Athenians in Attica. Spartan women even give themselves to their slaves just for the sake of bearing more boys, but fewer and fewer are born."

"I'm so sorry to learn of this. Now I understand why you do not wish to stay here. Forgive me for my ignorance," Thais said. She hugged Egesikhora, and the other clung to her, the way Hesiona had before.

The Spartans didn't want to let their charming guests go so quickly. They made them postpone their departure day after day. Finally, Thais told them her people would run off and that she needed to sort through her possessions, assembled so hurriedly before the road.

Their return trip was much longer. Thais wanted to take a good look at the strange country. Egesikhora and Eositeus took the foursome and rode ahead, leaving Menedem as Thais' driver. They traveled slowly, sometimes turning off the main road to look at a legendary spot or an old temple. Thais was struck by the great number of temples of Aphrodite, Artemis and the nymphs. Temples of modest size were hidden in sacred groves, scattered all over Lacedemonia. The worshiping of female deities in Sparta made sense in light of the high position of Spartan women in society.

The women of Sparta were able to travel and walk alone wherever they wanted, without male chaperones. They could even take distant trips on their own. The participation of young women in gymnastic exercises, athletic competitions and public celebrations, competing alongside young men did not surprise the hetaera. She had heard about it before. She watched as local celebrations assembled not only nude young men to demonstrate their athletic skills, but also girls, walking proudly past the crowds of admiring spectators to perform sacrifices and sacred dances in temples.

All hetaerae of the highest Corinthian school considered themselves dance experts. They frequently mentored young students, or auletridae. Aristocles' ancient thesis on dance was memorized by each of them. However, it was only in the Laconian capital that Thais saw fantastic dance performances by large groups of people right in the streets. Completely nude girls and youths danced Cariotis, a proud and imperious dance in order of Artemis, considered there to be the goddess of flawless health. She also saw them dance Lamprotera, the dance of purity and clarity. Dance Gormos was also performed, this time by slightly older people. Nude men and women spun in a circle, holding hands, representing a necklace.

The hetaera was completely enraptured by Yalkade, a children's dance that included goblets of water. Through tears of delight she watched the rows of lovely Spartan children, full of health and self-possession. All this revived traditions of ancient Crete in Thais' eyes, as well as the legends of celebrations in honor of Britomartis, Cretan Artemis.

The influence of the ancient religion, with its female deity supremacy, could be felt more strongly here than in Attica. In Sparta there were fewer people, but more land. Laconians could set aside more space for meadows and groves. Thais saw more herds of livestock along the way than she would have in the same space on the way from Athens from Sounion, which was the cape at the tip of Attica where they were erecting a new temple of the Blue eyed Maiden on top of the terrifying shore cliff.

Menedem and Thais reached Giteyon after sunset. They were met with wishes of long life and many children, customary wishes made during a nymphius, a marriage celebration. For some reason, Menedem became upset by them. He was about to leave the circle of his merry comrades when a small Messenian man, a hunter, appeared and declared that all was ready for the next day's hunt. The officers cheered, from strategist Eositeus himself to the last decearchos.

A herd of huge wild boars made its home in the thicket of reeds between the Eurot and the Hellas. Their nighttime outings often inflicted significant damage upon the nearby fields and even in the sacred grove. The grove had been plowed through and through by the hungry pigs.

Hunting boars in the reeds was considered to be particularly dangerous. Because of the height of the reeds, a hunter couldn't see anything except for the narrow paths made by the animals. The reeds stood like tall walls, seven elbows high, covering half the sky. At any time the reeds could part, admitting an enraged male boar with fangs sharp as daggers, or a furious female. The animals moved lightning fast. Frequently a dismayed hunter found himself on the ground, his legs cut by a strike of those fangs before he even realized what was happening. But a male boar wasn't the worst. It struck and kept on running. A female pig was far more terrifying. Having overturned a hunter, she trampled him with sharp hooves and tore at him with teeth, pulling out pieces of flesh and skin. The wounds took years to heal. But something about the short, violent struggle, the unexpected excitement attracted many a brave man wishing to test his courage.

The soldiers became so carried away while discussing the hunt that both hetaerae felt abandoned. Egesikhora decided she would take the opportunity to remind them of her splendid self. Eositeus, distracted by her efforts, interrupted the discussion, pondered briefly, then made up his mind.

"Let our guests take part in the hunt," he said "Let us be together everywhere, be it Egypt or the reeds of the Eurot."

Menedem supported him with ardor, but the older soldiers laughed.

"It is impossible, master," a Messenian objected. "We will only put the beautiful women at deadly risk."

"Wait." Eositeus lifted his hand. "You are saying that here," he said, pointing at the map of their hunting site which had been drawn on the ground, "there is an ancient Eurot temple. It would be set on a hill, would it not?"

"It is a small bump with only a few rocks and columns left over from the temple," the hunter said.

"Even better. And here, there is a clearing because the reeds do not grow on hills?"

The Messenian nodded and the captain immediately ordered them to change the direction of the hunt. The main hunting party would now hide at the edge of the reed thicket in front of the clearing, while both hetaerae hid in the ruins of the temple. The other group of soldiers would accompany the chasers in case the animals decided to attack. The brave men were armed with nothing more than small shields and spears. The more experienced hunters also took long daggers.

Clutching pale, reed colored himations around them, Egesikhora and Thais did their best to get comfortable. The two friends lay on the broad slabs of crossbeams which still sat upon the six low columns of the Eurot temple, with a perfect view of the clearing. They had been told in no uncertain terms that they were not to get up, not to even move when the chasers drove the boars toward the river.

They spied Eositeus, Menedem and two more hunters hiding behind bunches of dry reeds, clearly visible near the tall wall of reeds to the west of the clearing. To show their disdain for danger, the Lacedemonians were without clothes, as they would be during military exercises, and only wore greaves. Death held no fear for a professional soldier. Every

Helenian was brought up with a wise and calm attitude toward death. Tombstones in Attica, in Laconia, and in Boeotia spoke of thoughtful parting, of sweet and sad memories of the departed without protest, desperation or fear. Injury, however, was worse than death to a Spartan warrior, as it deprived him of the ability to fight alongside his compatriots, the only thing a free Lacedemonian would ever want.

They heard the reeds crackle, and a huge male boar appeared in the clearing. The two women froze, reflexively pressing themselves into the stone. The beast sniffed suspiciously, turning its thick body this way and that. The boar's inflexible neck made it impossible for him to turn his head. It was this peculiarity that had saved many hunters' lives.

Menedem rose slowly from behind a reed-covered hummock. Lowering his left arm so that his shield covered the bottom portion of his stomach and hip, he gave a quiet whistle. The boar turned instantly and received a spear strike deep in its right side. The spear shaft snapped with a loud crack, and the boar charged. Its wicked yellow fangs snapped over the shield, and Menedem lost his balance. Stumbling backward, the Spartan fell over his head into a shallow pit. Eositeus shouted and the boar turned its left side toward him. All was over in seconds. Menedem, embarrassed and confused, reproached his commander for interfering. It would have been much more interesting to finish the animal off on his own.

Within a few minutes, the yells and clattering from the chasers attracted no fewer than a dozen large boars. The animals burst into the clearing and overturned two soldiers standing near the right corner of the clearing. They rushed toward the river, then turned and attacked Eositeus and Menedem. Menedem beat away an enraged pig; Eositeus was knocked down by a particularly large male. Gray hair bristled along its spine, spit and foam flew from its snapping, footlong fangs. Eositeus, whose shield had been knocked out of his hands by the animal's strike, had tossed down his spear and now pressed himself into the ground, clutching a long Persian knife in his hand. The boar's next move would be to try and toss him up with its snout in order to gore him. He pressing his huge head over the Spartan's back and, bending its front legs, attempted to hook him with fangs. Eositeus kept shifting back, watching the monster carefully, but not getting an opportunity to deal the deadly blow.

Egesikhora and Thais watched the struggle with bated breath, having forgotten about Menedem, who was still fighting off the old, experienced pig. Suddenly Egesikhora clutched at Thais' shoulder. The boar was pushing Eositeus toward a bump in the hummocky soil, and there was only a small distance left. Then the strategist would have nowhere to go …

"Ai-i-i-i-i-i!" Thais screeched, her voice piercing like that of a witch. She clapping her hands and leaned forward from the stone slab.

The boar dashed to the side to seek out its new enemy. That instant was sufficient for Eositeus to grab the boar's rear leg and bury the knife in its side. The boar broke free – only Hercules or Theseus could have held such giant in place – and charged Thais.

The famous dancer possessed the reaction of an Amazon and managed to roll backward, falling on the other side of the stone slab. The boar slammed against the stone, making two deep, bloody tracks in the colorful lichen. Eositeus picked up his spear and hopped over to the beast, already dying from the wound. He struck one more blow, finishing the fight.

Victorious shouts came from the left. Eositeus' and Menedem's comrades had finally subdued their animals, and Menedem had managed to kill the pig. The Spartans gathered together, wiping off sweat and dirt, and praising Thais, who had escaped with nothing more than two large bruises after her rocky fall.

The chasers had already passed the thicket in front of the clearing, and the drive headed to the north, toward the junior officers. Four hunters from the group in the clearing decided to go toward the Eurot in order to wash up and swim after the battle while the servants pared the meat and cooked it for the evening feast. Eositeus lifted Thais onto his broad and scratched shoulder and carried her to the river, accompanied by a playfully jealous Egesikhora and a sincerely glum Menedem.

"Watch out, Eositeus. Have you warned our beauties of the Eurot's dangerous properties?" Menedem shouted to his captain, as the latter walked briskly with his lovely cargo. Helenians loved to carry women they admired. It was a sign of respect and noble intentions. The strategist didn't reply until he had lowered Thais to the ground at the riverbank.

"Egesikhora knows that the Eurot originates from under the ground," Eositeus said. "At its upper reaches, near Phenius in Arcadia where the Nine Peaks are, there are ruins of the city called in honor of pelasgus Licaon, son of Callisto. There is a chasm of terrifying depth at the foot of the nine peak mountain Aroania, where snow lies even in summer. The river Styx falls from the chasm in a small waterfall and crashes on the rocks. Its waters are deadly to all living things and can dissolve iron, bronze, lead, tin and silver, even gold. The Styx's black waters run through the black rocks, then turn bright blue where the rocks become colored with black and red stripes: colors of death. The Styx falls into the Cretos, then into our river, where it dissolves and becomes harmless. However, on certain days known only to the oracles, the waters of the Styx do not mix with those of the Eurot. They say you can see the difference. On those days the Styx water shimmers with rainbow colors, like old glass. He who spends time in that water will meet aoria, untimely death. That is why swimming in our river can cause trouble sometimes."

"And what of you all? Do you dare?"

"I swear by the killer of Argos, we do not even think of it," Menedem said, catching up with them. "For if we did, we should all meet aorotanatos, early death."

"Then why do you frighten us?" Thais reproached the Spartans. She untied a ribbon under the heavy knot of her hair and the black waves fell across her back and shoulders. As if in response, Egesikhora let her golden tresses down and Eositeus slapped his hips in delight.

"Look, Menedem, how lovely they are side by side. Gold and black. They should always be together."

"And so we shall be!" Egesikhora exclaimed.

Thais shook her head slowly. "I don't know. I have yet to arrange my naulon, the price of my journey to Egypt, with Eositeus. I don't have nearly as much silver as they gossiped about in Athens. My house there was quite expensive."

"Serves you right, settling near Pelargicon," Egesikhora scolded. "I told you …"

"What did you call it?" Thais chuckled.

"Pelargicon. A slope of cranes. That is what Lacedemonians jokingly call your Pelasgicon at the Acropolis. Let us go up the stream. I see a willow grove there."

Willows were particularly revered by hetaerae as they were trees dedicated to such powerful and deadly goddesses as Hecate, Hera, Circe and Persephone. Willows played an important role during the mysterious moonlit rituals of Mother Goddess. The trunks of the old trees hung low over the water, bathing their branches in the light swift stream, as if surrounding the deep backwater with a curtain.

Thais, having tied her hair back into a tight knot, swam toward the opposite shore, leaving her friend behind. Egesikhora wasn't as good a swimmer, so she was more careful around water.

White water lilies, nenufars, covered the deep pool near the shore, their leaves flooded with noon sun. Thais had loved nenufar thickets ever since childhood. She thought they seemed to be hiding some kind of a secret in the dark deep waters. Perhaps a dwelling of the beautiful river nymphs, a delicate precious vase, or a sparkling shell. Thais had taught herself how to dive and oh, how she loved to go deep down under the lilies and admire the small columns of sunlight piercing the dusky water. Then she would suddenly burst through the water into the blinding heat, surfacing amidst the floating leaves and flowers, laughing at the rainbow winged dragonflies hovering above them.

Now, as she had in her childhood, Thais came up among the lilies. She found a crooked tree trunk at the bottom with her foot and stood on its slippery bark with her arms spread wide over the leaves. She looked around, enjoying the quiet. The babbling of the stream over the pebbles and branches was the only sound breaking the scorching silence of Boedromion, the last month of summer. The pretty green and gold birds had long since had their babies and taught them how to fly. Black bee-eater nests could be seen in the overhang of the riverbank. The bee-eaters themselves, swift, colorful and sharp-nosed, sat in a row on a dry branch, warming themselves after the nighttime chill.

"Soon, very soon, they will fly south, to Libya, where they come from every year," Thais thought. "And I shall sail there even sooner."

She glanced around the quiet pool, warm in the beating sun, admiring the silvery green leaves of the old willows. She noticed two halcyons, or kingfishers, their bright blue wings fluttering over a fallen tree.

As a child, Thais had lived near a small river. Sweet memories came to her, ran through in a bittersweet wave of sad joy, then flew away. Bright and dark life experiences. She had come to know the limitless sea, its power and might, as well as the sea of human life. But the young hetaera was not intimidated by it. Instead, filled with energy and confidence, she was drawn further away to Egypt, the ancient country of wisdom and mystery to all Helenians.

It took her awhile to find Egesikhora. She swam along a channel that looked like a dusky corridor made of trees, their arm-like branches woven tightly above and found the Spartan settled comfortably in a curve of a thick tree. Her beautiful hair hung on both sides of the tree like a cover of golden silk. Her white skin, so carefully protected from tan, had a milky opal glow to it, possessed only by the true chriseides, the gold-haired women. Thais, who was tanned in the face in the Attica fashion, and had the Cretan raven black hair, climbed out of the water on the dark shade of the channel, looking like a sun scorched dweller of southern countries.

"Enough laying around. They are calling us, can't you hear?" Thais said. She started crawling toward her friend's feet, her fingers curled like claws.

"I am not scared," the Spartan said. She shoved Thais with her foot so that Thais tumbled off the tree and into the water. Egesikhora, too, rolled off the trunk with an indignant yelp.

"My hair! I was drying it!" she cried, and fell into the deep pool.

Both hetaerae swam to the shore, got dressed and helped brush out each other's hair.

The swim, having brought back childhood memories for Thais, had also prompted a surge of sadness. No matter how alluring the distant lands may seem, leaving her home country was difficult.

The Athenian turned to her friend. "Tell me. Would you want to return to Athens now, without any delay?"

Egesikhora squinted one eye in amusement. "Are you mad? I'll be captured as soon as I am seen."

"We could dock at Freato and ask for the judges to come there," Thais said, reminding the Spartan of an ancient Athenian tradition. Every exile or fugitive could dock near Pyrean harbor, where there was a well, and there he could defend himself from his ship. The place was considered sacred, and even if the fugitive was found guilty, he could not be captured as long as he stayed on his ship.

"I do not believe in the sacredness of this tradition. Your compatriots became traitorous over the last few centuries, after Pericles," Egesikhora replied. "I am not planning to go back anyway. And you have nothing to worry about. My Spartans will take you as far as it takes."

Thais' concerns that she would not have enough silver to pay for her journey turned out to be groundless. After Egesikhora intervened, Eositeus allowed her to take all her servants and promised to deliver her not to Naucratis, but to Memphis, where the detachment of Spartan mercenaries was to settle in the former Tyrrean stratopedon, a military camp.

Thais had absolutely no problems with sea sickness. She would remember enate phtinontos, the ninth day of the departing Boedromion, for the rest of her life. It was the day when the ship of strategist and sea captain Eositeus came to the shores of Crete. They sailed without stopping at Citera, directly across the Ionic Sea, taking advantage of the last few weeks of the pre-fall calm and steady west wind. Lacedemonians have always been excellent seafarers, and the sight of their vessels struck terror into the hearts of all pirates of the Cretan Sea. The ships passed the western edge of Crete and sailed around the Cold Cape, also known as Ram's Forehead, at the southwest of the island, where ancient demons were still rumored to dwell in the dark woods. The woods covered the entire island, which seemed to consist solely of mountains looming nearly black in the distance, dotted white from lime outcroppings near the shores.

Eositeus' ship entered the wide Midland Gulf, open to all south and west winds. Not one, but three ancient cities were situated above it, and the oldest one, Phestes, could rival Knossos, with its foundations sinking into the darkness of ancient times. Before sailing to the Beautiful Harbors where they would stock up on water before the long voyage to Egypt, the ships docked at Matala. They would remain there for several days.

Dark, rounded ledges on tree-covered mountain slopes descended toward the water. They were separated by moon-shaped cut-outs of sunny harbors filled with glittering foam and rolling mirrors of transparent water. The glorious blue of the open sea turned purple near the shores of Crete, then to green at the edge, where it splashed indifferently over the black lime pits and caves.

Blue mist of the plateaus hid the ruins of huge structures of unimaginable age. Giant, thousand year old olive trees grew through cracks in foundations and between staircases shattered by earthquakes, seeming to emerge from out of the gigantic slabs of stone. Powerful pillars, widening toward the top, still supported porticos and loggias; the entrances of long forsaken palaces stood gloomy and menacing. Sycamores and cypresses rose high above everything, overshadowing the remains of the walls, where the surviving crossbeams protected the frescoes. There, human figures were still visible in bright and delicate colors.

When she was near one of the better preserved buildings, Thais followed a vague feeling and ran up the still-intact steps of the upper platform. There, in a circle of cracked columns with dark stains was traces of a long-extinguished fire. Under the roof slabs, which were arranged like steps, was a round basin. Beautifully set slabs of marble lined by green veins made up the upper edge of the deep pool. Water trickled through porous lime, blocking the outlet of a spring, thus becoming filtered and acquiring a particular transparency. It then flowed down a pipe which had sustained a consistent water level in the pool for many centuries. The bright blue of the sky was visible through an opening in the center of the roof, turning the sacred water blue as well. This basin had been intended for the ritual cleansing of priests and priestesses before approaching the images of the awe inspiring deities: the Great Mother and the Earth Shaker, Poseidon, who had destroyed the Cretan kingdom and its great people.

Thais thought she sensed a strange smell. Perhaps the stones of the basin still held the aroma of the healing herbs and oils for which Crete was once so famous. The walls of the pool had absorbed forever the fragrance of the sacred cleansings, performed here for millennia. Thais dropped her clothes and lowered herself into the barely rustling water, as if to get in touch with sensations once experienced by her distant ancestors.

Egesikhora's worried exclamation returned her to reality. The Spartan girl found herself overcome by a vague fear, brought on by the imperious ruins of unclear and unknown purpose. Thais got dressed and hurried to meet her friend.

Egesikhora paused, then beckoned her companions. She stood before an image of a woman in a pale blue dress, her thickly curled black hair flying in the wind. Her large eyes held an open and mischievous expression beneath thin lines of proud eyebrows. She had a straight nose, slightly longer than a typical Hellenic one and with a somewhat lower bridge. Her peculiarly shaped mouth combined sensuality with a childish outline of a short upper lip, protruding slightly over the lower portion of her face.

Egesikhora looked from the fresco to Thais, then hugged her friend's unusually slender waist with her hands and pulled back the folds of her chiton. The Spartans clapped their hands in delight. If not a sister, then certainly a close relative of the woman in the fresco stood before them, incarnated in Thais.

A strange feeling of worry penetrated Thais' heart. Death, from which this Cretan woman had temporarily escaped in a fresco, was too ancient. Those who had built these palaces, painted portraits of beautiful women, danced with bulls and sailed the seas had long since descended into the underground kingdom. Thais hurried back into the sunlight, towing her quiet companions and Egesikhora behind her, feeling as if she had had a glimpse into something forbidden.

On the southern shore of Crete sun showered the earth with bright, blinding light, but the air did not possess the divine transparency it did in Hellas. Bluish mist overshadowed the distant horizon, and the heat seemed meaner and stronger than at the shores of Attica.

A band of stone tiles, sunk into the soil and half overgrown with dry grass and lichen, stretched from the ruins across a gently rolling plateau. At the end of that ancient road, where it vanished into a valley, stood an enormous boulder with tall bull horns carved into it, as if one of Poseidon's underground bulls tried climbing to the surface. It reminded people they were but temporary dwellers of Gaea. They walked over the shifting soil, while invisible forces nested beneath their feet, strengthening and preparing for terrible cataclysms.

Long shadows fell from the horns and stretched toward Thais, as if trying to grab her between their tips. This was probably how the sacred spotted bulls of Crete had aimed their horns at the young girls during a performance of the ritual dance. The hetaera quickly walked between the two strips of shadow, heading to the sunlit top of the second hill. There she halted and looked around.

Her entire being was overwhelmed by the realization that the land of her ancestors was the world of the dead. Their souls had been wiped away by time, taking their knowledge, skill, feeling of beauty, faith in gods, songs and dances, myths and fairy tales into the dark kingdom of Hades. They hadn't left behind a single tombstone, the way Helenians would have, asking the best sculptors to capture the lifelike enchantment, dignity and nobility of the departed. Looking at them, their descendants attempted to emulate their ancestors or even surpass them. Thais could never forget the marvelous tombstones of Ceramic, dedicated to young women much like herself. She remembered the hundred year old monument of Gegeso, capturing the image of the young woman and her slave. But there were no Necropoli here. Closed in on their island, inaccessible to anyone in those days, Cretans did not pass their spiritual treasures onto other people.

Godlike children of the sea, they had hidden their island behind the curtain of naval might, never fearing the attack of barbaric nomads. Thais did not see any reinforcements, and none were ever described by travelers. Beautiful palaces were built right near the harbors. Rich cities and warehouses that were both wide open to the sea and unprotected from the land spoke clearly of the power of the sea people.

The impossibly beautiful Cretan art never portrayed military heroics. Images of victorious kings, tortured victims, tied and humiliated prisoners of war were absent from these palaces and temples.

Instead, the art was of nature: animals, flowers, sea waves, trees, and people walking among them, primarily women. Ritual sacrifices and bull games, strange animals never seen either in Hellas or on the shores of Finikia were all portrayed in these frescoes. The sophistication of their taste and perception of beauty amazed Helenians, who considered themselves to be above all people in the Ecumene.

The delicate paintings were full of joy, light and purity of color. There were statues of women, animals and domestic pets, amazing seashells made of ceramic, but no mighty heroes, swinging swords or raising heavy shields and spears.

Where else in the world was there a country that dedicated all of its art to the harmonious connection between people and nature, and above all to women? Powerful, ancient, existing for millennia ... Did they not know of the simple law of gods and destiny? They ought not to have been tempted by a lengthy period of flourishing, for it would surely be followed by retribution, the terrible interference of underground gods. So the gods punished the children of Minos for forgetting the sort of world in which they lived. The splendid palaces crumbled, the writing remained unread, and the delicately painted frescoes lost their meaning. Alien tribes had moved to the island, warring among themselves and all others. They felt the same toward the true dwellers of Crete as the barbarians from Hyperborean woods felt toward Helenians and their Pelasgoan ancestors.

The Spartans walked behind the thoughtful Thais, not daring to break her reverie.

Could it be that the sun-filled beauty, created and assembled in Hellas, would vanish in Erebus, like a glittering flow into an unknown chasm? And what of the Egypt she tried so hard to reach? Would it too become a kingdom of shadows, dissolving in the new life like a memory of the past? Did she act rashly by leaving Hellas? Well, the way to Athens was not yet closed. She still had her house there and ...

Thais never finished the thought. With a careless toss of her head, she ran down a small path, weaving between rocky outcroppings, not heeding her surprised companions. She stopped only when she saw the harbor with its peacefully rocking ships. Soon the great sea would separate her from all things beloved that were left in Hellas. The person closest to her would be Egesikhora, the friend of her half-childish dreams and grownup disappointments, the companion in her success.

The helmsman said there were four thousand stadiums to the shores of Libya. Then they were to sail another thousand along the shore to Naucratis. With good wind that would make a ten day trip. The Egyptians would transport them on a different set of ships, sending them up from the great delta of the Nile. There was no fewer than a thousand stadiums from Memphis up the river.

Aphrodite Euploa, the goddess of sailors, was unusually merciful to Thais. Weather akin to the clear halcyon days preceding autumn equinox was rare for the end of Boedromion. The ships were in the middle of the broad and noisy sea when suddenly the stillness was replaced by a weak and scorching Not. The rowers were exhausted because of having to row against the wind, and Eositeus ordered a respite till evening, saving the energy of his warriors. He purposely hadn't brought slaves with them, ensuring the ships could carry his entire large detachment.

Smooth waves rippled over the blue surface of the sea, dissolving into a blue mist in the distance, rocking the motionless ships like ducks on a windy lake. A hot wind, weak but steady, blew from Libyan shores, bringing the breath of savage desserts two thousand stadiums away to this place in the middle of the sea. The same distance separated the ships from Cretan shores.

Egesikhora was terrified, peering into the midnight gaps between waves, trying to imagine the terrible, unmeasured chasm of the sea depths below. Thais glanced at her friend mischievously, the latter feeling so hot she had lost her usual look of a victorious goddess. People sprawled lazily under a tent on the deck. The stronger and more impatient ones stood under the woven willow mats fastened above the sides of the ship, trying to find some coolness in the breath of the Libyan Not, under whose light push the ships slowly retreated to the north.

Eositeus sat in his armchair at the stern, grim and unhappy about the delay. His assistants lay around him on reed mats, like simple soldiers.

Thais beckoned quietly to Menedem. "Can you hold an oar for me?" she asked, then explained to the puzzled athlete what she wanted to do.

Menedem pulled the huge oar deeper into the rowlock so the paddle was perpendicular to the board. Under the surprised glances of everyone on deck, Thais shed her clothes and walked along the external trim. She held onto the woven mats, then stepped onto the oar and paused there as she got used to the rhythm of the waves. Then she suddenly pushed away from the board. With the skill of a Finikian tightrope walker, Thais balanced on the oar, ran to the end with small steps and jumped into the sea, vanishing into the depths of a slick dark wave.

"She is mad!" Eositeus shouted, while Hesiona dashed to the board with a desperate scream.

Thais' black head, tightly wrapped in a traditional ribbon of a Lemnian hairstyle, appeared at the top of the way. Rising from the water, the hetaera blew a kiss to the Spartans and burst out laughing.

Eositeus, forgetting everything, rose up in amazement and went to the board, accompanied by Egesikhora. "What is this?" he cried. "Is your black-haired Athenian a daughter of Poseidon himself? But her eyes are not blue."

"There is no need to seek descendants of gods among us mortals," the Spartan girl said with a laugh. "You saw her mysterious likeness with those who abandoned Cretan palaces a thousand years ago. Her ancestral blood came alive in her through the Cretan mother. Cretan Nearchus told me they weren't at all afraid of the sea."

"We Spartans are skilled in the art of the sea beyond all other people."

"But not beyond Cretans. We fight the sea, are wary of it, avoiding its cunning arms at all costs. Cretans are friends with the sea and are always ready to be with it, whether in joy or in sadness. They understand the sea like a lover instead of studying it like an enemy."

"And Nearchus told you all this? I heard rumors that you two have exchanged the oath of the Three-faced Goddess. He discarded you like a useless toy and sailed off into the sea while you were left to weep on the shore. If he and I ever meet …"

The chief of soldiers didn't finish, his words frozen by the hetaera's darkened gaze. She lifted her chin, her nostrils flaring, and suddenly ripped off her head wrap, tossing the mass of her golden hair over her back. The moment she lifted her hands to the fastenings of her chiton, Eositeus knew her intentions and tried to stop her.

"What are you doing, mad woman? You swim worse than Thais."

"But I will still follow her, trusting the Cretan instincts, considering that none of my brave compatriots seem to overcome their fears. They seem to prefer gossip, much like the Athenians."

Eositeus flinched as if from a whip, cast a furious gaze upon his lover and barreled overboard without another word. The Spartan's huge body fell awkwardly into the gap between waves, making a dull and loud splash. Thais, who had observed the scene between her friend and the chief, glided under the waves to help Eositeus. She realized that the Laconian chief, while he was an excellent swimmer, didn't know how to jump from a great height into the rolling sea.

Eositeus, stunned and rolled over by a wave, felt someone nudge him from the depths. Once on the surface, he found himself on the crest of a rising wave. He breathed in, then saw Thais' merry face bobbing nearby. Annoyed by his own clumsiness, and stung even more by the thought of the great swimmer Nearchus, the Spartan pushed away the hand offered by the Athenian hetaera. He finally regained his confidence and started swimming away with increasingly powerful strokes. With a battle cry, dozens of soldiers followed their chief from his and other ships.

"Get her!" the soldiers shouted. They gathered into a chain and surrounded Thais like a legendary Nereid. The Athenian swam farther and farther away, gliding lightly while the soldiers chased awkwardly after her.

Eositeus, having cooled down in the sea, became an energetic leader once again. "Stop her! The imp will drown all my warriors!" he yelled, rising above water and making energetic gestures signaling Thais to return.

She understood and turned back, swimming directly into the semicircle of Spartans trying to catch her. Accompanied by their victorious cries, Thais found herself in a tight circle of her pursuers. Dozens of arms reached for her from all directions.

Suddenly, the hetaera vanished. The soldiers dashed this way and that, diving after her here and there, but Thais, who dove the deepest, managed to swim a quarter of a stadium underwater and appeared far beyond the line of her pursuers. While they turned and gained speed, the Athenian was already near the ship, clutching at the rope tossed to her from above.

Menedem pulled her up to the deck, much to the disappointment of the "hunters". To add to their embarrassment, many of the swimmers were so exhausted by the chase and the struggle with the waves that they too had to be lifted up to the ships. Eositeus, tired and out of breath, but no longer angry, climbed up a rope ladder and walked to Thais. She was being wrapped and dried by Hesiona, using an Egyptian sheet.

"I ought to have left you in the middle of the sea," the Lacedemonian exclaimed. "I swear by Poseidon, I will give him this sacrifice next time."

"Are you not afraid of a revolt?" Egesikhora asked, defending her friend. "Although I am quite certain she will ride there on a dolphin and get there faster than we. Ah, there they are," the Spartan said. She pointed at the spots of foam accompanying the glistening black bodies of the dolphins. They had been attracted by the game of their human brothers.

"Where did she learn to swim like that?" Eositeus grumbled. "And to walk the oar in the wind? That is harder than tightrope walking."

"We were all taught the art of balance at the hetaerae school in Corinth. You can't perform the dance of sacred triangles without it. As for the swimming, you cannot learn that. You have to be born a Nereid."

Hesiona carefully massaged her mistress' head and gently reproached Thais for tempting the fates. "How is it that you weren't afraid to appear nude in front of such assembly of soldiers, Mistress? They were chasing after you as if you were a dolphin!" the girl declared, glancing around as if afraid of another attack.

"When you are surrounded by so many genuinely strong and brave men, you may rest assured that you are perfectly safe," the hetaera replied with a laugh.

"They are, after all, Helenians and Spartans to boot. Remember that. It will come in useful. And besides, remember that men are usually more shy than we are. We are much braver when following tradition, while they become embarrassed."

"Why Spartans in particular?"

"Because Spartans are hymnophiles. They love nudity, like Thessalians. That is in contrast to hymnophobes like you, the Boeotians and the Macedonians. In this case, Spartans are as much in contrast with my fellow Athenians as Aeolians are to Lydians in Ionia."

"I have read about Aeolians. They even refer to the month of Munikhion as Pornopion."

"In fairness, most Helenians do not consider clothes to be a sign of good manners. And Spartans and Thessalians have adopted the laws and tradition of ancient Cretans. In their case, appearing nude at feasts and celebrations was a privilege of the highest aristocracy."

"That must be where the legend about tekhinas comes from. The legend of the demons of seduction that still live on Crete and in the wilder corners of Ionia."

"Perhaps. I think that in Egypt, nudity was initially the lot of servants and slaves. In Ionia it was the right of the strong. On Crete it was the privilege of royalty and aristocrats, and in Hellas of gods. Let's go into our cubbyhole. I want to rest after my swim. Clonaria shall rub me down."

"Me, Mistress, let me!"

Thais shrugged and nodded. Still wrapped in a sheet, she headed to a tiny compartment under the deck designated for her, Egesikhora and their female slaves.

While rubbing Thais down with fragrant oil, Hesiona returned to the earlier topic. "Who are Egyptians? Are they hymnophiles or not?"

"They are hymnophiles, and the most ancient ones of all people. Have you heard of Aphrodite of Knid?"

"The one sculpted by your compatriot Praxiteles?"

Thais nodded against her pillow. "He created two statues of Aphrodite from the same model, hetaera Frina. One was dressed in a peplos and the other was nude. He displayed them both for sale at the same time. The dressed one was purchased by the stern rulers of the island of Cos, and the nude one was bought for the same price by citizens of Knid. They placed her in an open alter, in the glow of yellowish pink marble of her body. They said that Aphrodite herself descended to the temple from Olympus and, upon seeing the statue, exclaimed, 'When did Praxiteles see me naked?'

"The transparent surface of the statue gave it a peculiar glow, surrounding the goddess with a sacred aura. For many years poets, artists, military commanders, craftsmen and farmers filled the ships going to Knid. Aphrodite of Knid is revered more than that of Cos, and her image is minted on coins. One king offered to forgive all debts of the island in exchange for the statue, but the citizens refused.

"Praxiteles' fame was shared by his model, hetaera Frina. The grateful Helenians placed a statue of her made of bronze and covered with gold leaf, at the staircase leading to the temple of Apollo in Delphi. Such is the power of divinely beautiful nudity. You need never be afraid of hymnophiles. They are true people."

Chapter Four. The Power of Animal Gods

There were many Helenians in Memphis, which the Egyptians called a Scale of Both Lands. Thais came to love the city. It was one of the oldest ones in the ancient land, located at the boundary between Delta and the Upper Egypt. Memphis was far enough away from the rainy winters typical down the Nile, as well as from the scorching summers of the southern part of the country.

Memphis Greeks, especially the young ones, were excited by the arrival of two beautiful women from Athens. Poets, artists and musicians tried to capture Thais' heart, dedicating poems and songs to her or begging her to become their model, but the Athenian appeared everywhere either with Egesikhora or accompanied by the shy warrior, whose appearance discouraged any potential challengers.

The regal Spartan hetaera tied her destiny firmly to that of the chief of the Laconian mercenaries, and was interested in nothing but him and her incredibly swift horses. A woman driving a tetrippa had never before been seen in Memphis. Young Egyptian women revered Egesikhora almost as if she were a goddess, seeing in her the embodiment of the freedom they themselves didn't possess even if they lived in the most aristocratic of households.

Thais sometimes agreed to perform at symposiums as a dancer, but she usually left as soon as the company turned rambunctious from the sweet Abydos wine. More often than not she left Memphis to visit other famous cities and temples, rushing to acquaint herself with the country, whose many legends and tales had attracted Helenians since childhood. Thais surprised both Egesikhora and Hesiona, who continued to consider herself Thais' slave, by not being in a hurry to acquire a wealthy lover. She preferred to spend money on trips instead.

Mnema, mother of all muses, added wonderful memory to the gifts bestowed upon Thais by Aphrodite. Memory, which absorbed all details of the world, inevitably bred curiosity akin to that possessed by Hellenic philosophers. No matter what new and unusual things Thais encountered in Egypt, so different from the Greek world, her first impression acquired during the voyage up the river and during the first days in Memphis didn't change.

One of the brightest memories of her childhood kept returning to Thais. Her mother had taken her to Corinth to dedicate her to the temple of Aphrodite, and bring her to the hetaerae school. Weather had been hot in the city, which sprawled at the foot of a huge mountain. Little Thais became thirsty while she and her mother climbed to the top portion of Corinth. She remembered the long, narrow gallery leading to a sacred spring, famous in all of Hellas. A light breeze blew inside the shaded gallery, while the noonday sun showered everything outside of it with a sea of light and heat. Cool, clear water burbled gently ahead, under a round roof supported by double columns. Further away, beyond the water basins, a reflected line blinded the eye at the foot of a steep slope. Heat and the smell of scorching rock surface was stronger than the moist breath of the spring.

The gallery of water and greenery that was Egypt stretched between two flaming deserts for tens of thousands of stadiums – a colossal distance compared to the small Hellenic states. It was all gardens and temples, temples and gardens, fields near water, and endless necropoli along the outside edge of this band of life. Like cities of the dead with countless tombs. There were no tombstones here, but rather homes for the departed. For the wealthy and important citizens, the homes were the size of a regular house, while those for the poor and the slaves were the size of a dog house.

Three royal tombs were utterly striking: the pyramids with their titanic Sphinx, seventy stadiums down from Memphis. Thais had heard much about the pharaohs' tombs, but until she saw them, she could never have imagined their true magnitude. The pyramids were geometrically perfect mountains dressed in mirror smooth stone tiles, set together so tightly that seams between the stones were barely noticeable. During the morning hours each of the large pyramids reflected a vertical pillar of rose colored light into the gray sky. As the sun rose, the mirror sides of the stone giants burned brighter, until each pyramid turned into a star – a focus of four blinding streams of light stretched across the desert to the four points of the world. At sunset broad columns of red fire stood above the tombs of the pharaohs, piercing the purple evening sky. Below them, the outlines of the god kings of the

Black Earth (as Egyptians called their country) burned like sharp fiery blades. These incomparable structures seemed to be the work of titans, although knowledgeable people assured Thais that the pyramids had been built by common slaves.

"If a man is frequently and severely beaten," a priest from Heliopolis told her, grinning cynically, "he will do anything that might seem incomprehensible to his descendants."

"These are the largest structures in Egypt. That means people here were beaten harder than anywhere else," Thais said, her voice lowered with menace.

The priest glanced at her sharply then pursed his lips.

"Do Helenians not beat their slaves?"

"Of course they do. But those who do have a bad reputation."

"Are you trying to say, woman ..." the priest started.

"I am not trying to say anything," Thais objected quickly. "Each country has its own tradition, and one must live there a long time in order to understand them."

"Then what don't you understand?"

"The great complexity of power. In my country everything is simple. You are either free or a slave. If you are free, then you are rich or poor, famous for arts, or knowledge, or military and athletic prowess. And here, every free person is a tiny step higher or lower than the next. One is allowed something, the other less, and the third person nothing at all. Everyone is filled with jealousy, everyone bears a grudge. It seems that everyone is a slave locked in a big cage between two deserts. I haven't met many people here who have visited other countries of the Ecumene. Although, it is fair to say I haven't been here very long."

"You are observant, Helenian. Even too much so," the priest. He spoke Greek with light clicking, allowed a threat to slip into his words. "I will leave you now."

Egyptian temples struck Thais by their sharp contrast with those of Hellas. Each Greek temple, with the exception of perhaps the most ancient ones, stood in an elevated spot, open, graceful and light, as if it were about to take off into space, sea and sky. Statues of goddesses, gods and heroes drew admirers to themselves with their miraculous beauty. The boundary separating gods from mortals seemed thin, almost unnoticeable. One could believe that gods leaned forth in order to better hear the prayers addressed to them, and were about to step off their pedestals, as they did in those legendary times, when they bestowed their attention upon all people – from farmers to warriors, instead of just priests.

Temples of Egypt were gloomy, squeezed between thick walls and rows of massive columns. They were covered by inscriptions and a multitude of pictures and signs. Each sanctuary hid its visitors from the vastness of earth and sky, from wind and clouds, flowing creeks and splashing waves, from human songs and voices. Dead, menacing silence reigned in the temples, as they descended unnoticeably underground. Dying light faded with each step, and gloom grew thicker. It was as if a visitor descended into the darkness of past centuries. While only a thin boundary separated mortals from the dwellers of the light-filled peak of Olympus in Hellenic temples, here one felt but a step away from the kingdom of Hades, where the souls of the dead have long since wandered in the dark.

This sensation of the endless night of death oppressed the young woman. Thais hurried away, toward light and life. Temples and palaces were guarded by frighteningly identical statues of lions with human or ram heads. The image of the Sphinx, a terrible female strangler from Hellenic myths, took on a male gender in Egypt and became a favorite symbol of strength and power. Not only the Sphinx, but all Egyptian deities, including the most important ones, wore animal and bird guises, combining human and animalistic features. Thais had seen Egyptian amulets, statuettes and jewelry before, but had always thought Egyptians used the images of animals only to express a particular purpose of a talisman or a knickknack. As it turned out, it was rare for the gods to wear fully human guise. More often the faithful bowed before half-people, half-beasts and birds, sometimes grotesquely ugly, like the hippopotamus-like Tueris.

Hippopotami and crocodiles disgusted and frightened Thais. Revering them as deities seemed unworthy to the Athenian. The others were just as unattractive: Anubis with the head of a jackal, Tot with a long beak of an ibis, mean lioness Sekhmet, Hathor the cow, and Khnum the ram. Huge statues of birds of prey: kite Ra and hawk Horus, looked much more imperious as they were portrayed in the ancient times.

The complex hierarchy of gods remained just as confusing to the Athenian, as did the multitude of honors and titles and the complicated ladder of Egyptian societal relations. Each moderately sizable city was overseen by its own god. Large temples which owned wide lands and multitudes of slaves also gave their preference to one of a score of gods. Deities changed and lost their supremacy many times over the millennia.

The thing that continued to surprise Thais the most was the animal likeness of the gods revered by people, whose wisdom and secret sciences were so admired by Helenians. She knew that the great scholars of Hellas: Solon, Pythagoras and Plato, all studied in Sais. Herodotus, too, acquired a wealth of knowledge in Egypt. If this were so, then how could citizens of Egypt bow before monsters like crocodiles, which were senseless and disgusting creatures? Could they not express the essence of a deity by some other means rather than setting the head of a jackal or a kite onto a human body? Had the Egyptians not been such skilled artists, one might think they didn't know of other ways to express the divine spirit.

Soon Thais saw a living god: sacred bull Apis, the embodiment of Ptah. He was the main god of Memphis. Using twenty-nine signs, priests had found Apis among thousands of bulls, grazing peacefully in the meadows of the country, and honored it like a god till death. Then they found a new embodiment, while the dead one was embalmed akin to the other living god, the Pharaoh. Mummies of sacred bulls were buried in a huge temple named Serapeyon, which was guarded by hundreds of stone sphinxes.

One could trace many generations of bulls by the tables inscribed on the walls of their burial chambers. There were so many bulls from ancient times that Serapeyon was already half-filled with sand.

Adoration of a black bull with a white spot on its forehead still flourished in Memphis. Local Greeks tried to humanize the cult of Apis by merging it with Osiris, under the name of Serapis.

Hellenic religion had long since departed from the primeval animal worship. Even on Crete, whose age was almost equal to that of Egypt, the giant sacred bulls were only honored as symbols of Poseidon. They were killed as sacrifices at the altars and on game platforms. In Egypt, however, Apis was considered a real god, just like the loathsome crocodile or the reed cat howling in the night.

None of this sat well with the deep faith that was such a huge part of the particular wisdom of Egyptians. The Athenian had dared to express her doubts to the high priest of Ptah during a feast by the Helenian admirers of Serapis. In the heat of argument she hadexpressed her disgust rather harshly toward Sebek, the crocodile god. In Corinth, she had been brought up in the spirit of respect toward religions of eastern countries. But the years of living in Athens had left in her the disdain to all things alien and incomprehensible to Helenians.

Thais had no idea how dearly she would have to pay for the uncharacteristic expression of Athenian supremacy over the rest of Ecumene.

She convinced Egesikhora to go to the White Antelope settlement up the Nile, so that they could see the second wonder of the world described by Herodotus: the Egyptian Labyrinth. Her friend flatly refused, but Thais set off anyway, accompanied by Hesiona and her faithful Menedem, whose captain had given him permission following Egesikhora's request.

It was a brief trip, only four thousand stadiums up the river, and another hundred up a canal toward the famous lake Merida. During that time of year the canal and that branch of the river filled with silt, and the way became impassable. Thais and her companions had to leave the ship behind and make their way through shallow waters in a light boat, maneuvering between reeds. Fortunately, the true bane of Egyptian rivers and lakes – mosquitoes – were absent in the fall.

The translator they had hired specially for the trip was a Greek man from Memphis. He glanced around nervously, saying there were many zukhoses living in the vicinity of Crocodilopolis since time immemorial. These were the huge, living embodiments of the god Sebek, some of them as long as thirty elbows.

Naïvely, Menedem asked why the dreadful monsters hadn't been killed off in all that time. This was when he discovered that if crocodiles, especially young ones, get stuck in the silt and die during sudden decreases in water levels, their bodies were embalmed. Scores of crocodile mummies were stored in special rooms of the Sebek temple in Crocodilopolis, in the ancient Hetep-Senusert, and even in the Labyrinth.

Despite the oarsmen's best efforts to deliver the visitors to the Labyrinth sooner so they could examine it before dark, they arrived there only at midday. Foreigners were not allowed to spend the night here, on sacred land. Instead, they could stay at xenon, an inn eight stadiums to the north, on the same strip of land which connected the river and the swamp housing the Labyrinth and two pyramids.

A learned priest from Herculeopolis told Thais the Labyrinth had been constructed by Amnemkhet the Third as a burial temple for himself. Based on the priest's calculations, the great pharaoh had died four hundred years before the destruction of Knossos and the reign of Theseus in Athens. That was six centuries before the Trojan war and fifteen hundred years prior to the birth of Thais herself.

The usually bold hetaera entered the endless suite of rooms of the Labyrinth with some trepidation, even though the white pyramid to which it was attached was only half the size of those in Memphis. A huge corridor divided the Labyrinth into two halves. Its walls were decorated with marvelous frescoes whose bright colors hadn't faded a bit after fifteen centuries. There were no usual canonical figures of gods and pharaohs accepting gifts, killing their enemies or beating their prisoners. Instead there were scenes from everyday life, painted with incredible liveliness and delicacy: hunting, fishing, bathing, grape harvesting, tending livestock, dancing and celebratory gatherings with musicians, acrobats and wrestlers.

It was as if Thais had been transported into the Egypt of that period, captured by a talented artist who was following a request from a wise king.

Though they were weary, Thais, Menedem and Hesiona wandered from one hall to the next, winding between the white columns covered with relief images in the usual Egyptian style. They strolled through ornate corridors, through rooms decorated with friezes and ornaments of incredible beauty: blue zigzags, white and purple patterns that looked like carpets woven of thick threads, and even more complex colorful frescoes. Their tired eyes refused to make out the interconnections of spirals, curlicues of wheels with twelve spokes, miraculous lotus flowers with red petals and long stems. Cleverly made cuts under the stone slabs of the ceiling let enough light into the upper rooms of the Labyrinth that they could do without torches.

According to the interpreter, exactly the same labyrinth of lower rooms corresponded to the upper portion. That was where the sacred crocodile mummies were kept, and that was where the particularly interesting ancient sanctuaries were located, painted with the images of extinct animals such as giant hyenas and unicorns. The attendant who took them around the Labyrinth did not show them the lower portion, explaining that there was an ancient rule against letting foreigners there.

Daylight was fading and the halls and corridors were beginning to darken. It was time to make their way out of the thousand-room structure. The priest led them toward the exit, and the tired visitors happily followed him. Not far from the main northern staircase, where reddish evening light trickled through the broad slots in the walls, Thais paused to examine a relief of a young woman carved in yellowish stone.

It had been done with skill unusual even for Egypt. Dressed in a delicate, transparent garment which was tied in a knot under her bare breasts, the woman held an unknown musical instrument. Her face, surrounded by a thick net of schematically drawn hair, bore unquestionably Ethiopian features as well as a sense of nobility the likes of which Thais had not seen even among the most aristocratic Egyptian women.

While the hetaera pondered to which people the ancient musician might have belonged, her companions walked ahead. A light touch to her bare arm startled her from her reverie. A woman in a common white linen stole, a long dress of sorts, stepped out of a dark portal.

Behind her stood a priest in a necklace of blue ceramic and golden beads. He nodded his closely-cropped head and whispered in broken Greek, "Down, you can go, I'll lead."

Thais approached the woman, nodded and turned around to call Menedem and Hesiona because they were already at the end of the gallery. But she wasn't able to raise her voice before strong hands grabbed her from behind, shoved a rag into her mouth to stifle her shouts, and carried her off. Thais fought desperately, but more hands grabbed at her and tied her with strips of her own torn clothing. Eventually she gave up, letting them drag her along without resistance.

The kidnappers must have known the way well. They ran swiftly into the pitch dark, not needing the torches. Weak light scattered the gloom ahead. She detected the scent of wet grass and water. The kidnappers finally pulled the suffocating rag from her mouth and dragged her to the stone wall. Dark, still water glistened in the last rays of sunset, no further than half a plethor away. Having regained her ability to talk, Thais demanded to know what her kidnappers wanted of her, asking in both Greek and broken Egyptian. But the six male figures, whose faces she couldn't distinguish in poor light, remained stubbornly silent. The woman who had lured Thais in was gone.

The Athenian was propped against the wall, freed of ropes and whatever had been left of her clothes. Thais tried to defend herself, but when she did, she received a punch in the stomach that left her breathless. The kidnappers untangled the jingling object they'd brought with them: thin but strong belts with buckles similar to horse tack. They tied Thais' wrists to the rings that were built into the wall at chest level, wound the belts around her waist and ran one of them between her legs to a bracket behind her back.

Not understanding, the hetaera started asking again, demanding to know what they were planning to do with her. One of the people came closer to her. By his voice, Thais recognized the priest who had been with the woman and spoke some Greek.

"My brothers ordered to place you – you who spoke heresy in a public forum – before the face of our god. We will let you know his might and bow before him during your last hour."

She was aghast. "What god? What do you speak of, scoundrel?"

The priest did not reply. He turned his back on her and said a few words to his companions. All six approached the water, knelt and raised their arms. Thais understood only one thing from their loud incantations, pronounced in a singing fashion, like an anthem, "Oh, Sebek ... come and take ..." but that was enough.

Sudden realization made her go numb. She panicked, yelling hoarsely and weakly, then stronger and louder, screaming for Menedem, or anyone outside of the influence of these dark figures who knelt at the edge of water in a solemn prayer.

The priests rose. The one who spoke Greek said, "Yell louder so Sebek will hear. He'll come sooner. You will not be tormented by a long wait."

There was no mocking in the priest's words, no gloating. Thais was overcome by utter hopelessness. It would be just as useless to beg for mercy, threaten or try to reason with these people, as it would be to ask the same of the frightful beast they served, half-animal, half-fish with absolutely no feelings. The priest studied his victim one more time then made a sign to his companions and all six departed without a sound. Thais was left alone.

She pulled forward, felt the unbreakable strength of the belts and bowed her head in desperation. Her hair covered her body and Thais was startled by its warm touch. For the first time in her life she experienced the terror of death. The closeness of her unavoidable demise turned her entire world into a tiny cluster of hope. Menedem! Menedem! He was an experienced and fearless warrior, and a passionate lover. Surely he wouldn't leave her to the fates.

Thais could see fairly well in the dark. She looked around carefully and realized she was tied at the foot of some statue in a semicircular opening at the end of an underground hallway which led to a lake or a small arm of the river. Another giant statue was visible on the right, one of two colossal, seated statues, rising thirty elbows above water, not far from the pyramid. Thais realized that the gallery opened to the northwest, not far from the northern entrance. A small fire of hope sparked in her heart, then grew brighter and warmed her up. It was immediately dulled by the weight of terrible danger as soon as the Athenian realized there were three thousand rooms in the Labyrinth. While it might have been possible for Menedem to find where she was, it would take a lot of time. By that time the monstrous zukhoses would have ripped her into pieces and vanished in the reeds.

Thais pushed and pulled, trying to break free of the bonds, all of her young flesh protesting against her upcoming death. The tightly buckled belts sobered her, cutting painfully into her skin. Clenching her teeth, she swallowed back her sobs and started looking around again, searching for a way out.

The floor of the wider portion of the gallery sloped gently toward the narrow band of wet shore. Two thin pillars supported the overhang of the roof, making it impossible to see the sky. Apparently the portico was open to the water, but why were there no steps?

Suddenly primeval terror shot through Thais as he realized what this sloping floor at water's edge was for.

"Menedem! Menedem!" Thais screamed as loudly as she could. "Menedem!"

She grew cold, remembering that the creature to whom she was intended would also be attracted by her cries. She stilled, hanging against the belts. The stone was icy against her back, and her legs grew numb.

When the last glint of sunset died in the black water, Thais lost track of time.

She thought she heard a weak splash in the pitch blackness of the reeds, somewhere at the edge of the shimmering reflection of the stars. A dull roar, similar to a cow's mooing, sounded over the swamp. Distant and not loud, still it was revolting with its peculiar hidden threat, sounding different from any other animal sound to which humans were accustomed. Shivering and clenching her fists, Thais summoned all her power to keep the dark fear from overcoming her. The courage of her bull-fighting ancestors was limitless, as was that of the Amazons, untamed by wounds. She thought of the Athenian women who were as strong as Leanna, the lover of a famous Athenian revolutionary and tyrant slayer, Aristogeyton.

Except they had all fought with their hands free, in an honest battle. All except for Leanna, who had been tied like Thais, but did not give in to people who abused and misrepresented the law.

But here in the loneliness and cold silence of the swamp, waiting for a monster, Thais struggled against her bonds, fighting until she felt defeated. She leaned against the cold stone in a near faint.

The night was silent. No more splashes could be heard from the swamp.

Thais came awake from a cramp in her numb legs. How much more time had passed? If only she could see the sky above, the movement of constellations. Shifting and flexing, she managed to restore circulation, then froze in position when she thought she heard careful, slow steps in the underground gallery behind her.

Blood rushed into her head and joyous hope flushed through her. Menedem? But no. Would Menedem slink around, pausing after each step? No. He would rush in like an enraged bull, crushing everything in his way.

Not knowing what else to do, Thais let out another loud scream over the nighttime swamp, then listened again.

What was that? A barely audible response? Thais held her breath.

No, nothing.

And what of the steps from behind? The lower portion of the statue concealed the gallery entrance. Thais listened again and realized there was no one in the passageway: the sounds came from the swamp and echoed in the dungeon.

Oh, the great Aphrodite and Zeus-protector. It was a footfall of heavy paws over silty earth, beyond the pillars of the portico leading to the lake.

Slow and uneven slurping was interrupted by long pauses. Then a crested back came up next to the shore, its huge tail still in the water. Two eyes, sunken under the bony eyebrow bulges, lit up like dull red lights. The endlessly long body, undulating left and right in rhythm with the steps of its widely spread feet, crawled upon the narrow bank so slowly that sometimes the monster seemed motionless. There was a peculiar hissing sound, the sliding of a heavy body over damp soil or wet stone. The little red lights vanished, obscured by the opening maw almost three elbows wide, and framed by mighty white teeth.

Despite her terror, Thais noticed the crocodile didn't open its lower jaw, as most animals did when opening their mouths, but lifted the top portion of its head instead, obstructing its own field of view. That was why the red lights of its eyes vanished for a moment. Oh, if only the belts hadn't been holding her in place, she would have known exactly how to slip away from the giant zukhos.

The crocodile snapped its mouth shut and the red eyes returned, their cold, indifferent gaze upon her. The crocodile didn't rush as it peered into the gallery, but seemed almost to pause as if it were studying Thais. Many times in its life it had devoured victims at this spot, tied and helpless. The zukhos pulled its belly up from the silt with a loud squelch, rising slightly on its powerful, stubby legs. Thais knew the disgusting creatures moved quickly on solid ground. All it had to do was cross a short distance now, only slightly longer than its own body.

Thais screeched at such a pitch that the monster settled back onto its belly and suddenly turned right. Just then Thais heard a sound that almost made her sob. It was the smacking of running feet on dirt, overshadowed by a menacing man's voice.

"Thais, I am here!"

"Menedem!"

For a moment his silhouette flickered in front of the entrance between the puzzled monster and its intended prey. Menedem peered into the dungeon. Thais called to him, her voice sounding as if it came from a nightmare. In the blink of an eye the Lacedemonian was at the foot of the statue, yanking at Thais' belts with all his might. After the first, the belt on her left hand popped apart. At the second powerful tug, the right belt pulled the ancient bronze ring out of the wall but managed to stay whole. Menedem became even more enraged and tore the third belt like a bit of thread.

Thais was free. She fell to her knees with a sudden rush of weakness while Menedem spun toward his monstrous enemy. He had no weapon and was covered in mud head to toe, having left his clothes behind so he could run faster. The soldier's rage was so great that he took two steps toward the monster with his bare hands spread out, as if he were about to strangle a mad dog.

Another pair of feet splashed over the mud and a reddish band of light spread over the water along the bank. The light became brighter, and Hesiona, half-dead from the mad dash and terror, froze at the portico, holding up her torch. Seeing the monster, the girl screamed in horror. The crocodile paid no attention to her, having now focused its gaze upon Menedem. The torch in Hesiona's hand shook and she fell to her knees, just like her mistress.

"Light!" Menedem barked.

In the flickering light of the torch Thais saw the bulging muscles on the Spartan's broad back, his stubbornly tipped head and his feet firmly set against the stone floor as he glanced around, looking for something with which to meet the monster.

Suddenly Menedem made a decision. In one jump he pulled the torch out of Hesiona's hands and shoved it at the zukhos, causing it to back away. Menedem tossed the torch back to Hesiona, but Thais, who had risen to her feet by then, caught it. Menedem yanked at the wooden pillar of the portico, causing it to crack, then pushed as hard as he could. Finally, the old, dry wood gave in and everything happened all at once.

The crocodile moved at Menedem, who struck it in the snout, but the monster didn't back down. Instead, it opened its jaws and rushed at the soldier. That was exactly what Menedem was waiting for. He shoved the pillar into the giant reptile's maw with all his might, not even noticing as he ripped the skin off his palms. He fell, not able to remain standing while he stopped a twenty-five elbow zukhos, but managed to push the free end of the log toward the pedestal. The crocodile rammed the pillar into the immovable stone, thus shoving the wood even further into its own mouth. Terrible strikes of its tail shook the gallery, thrashing close enough to crush Hesiona. One strike broke the second pillar of the portico and the roof came crashing down, saving Hesiona from certain death. The crocodile fell on its side, convulsing, then dragged itself back to its feet and slithered back into the swamp, creating an entire fountain of mud with its tail.

Menedem and Thais stood shivering, unable to speak. Then Thais remembered and ran to Hesiona, lying prone at the entrance to the dungeon. She was covered in sticky mud, shielding her face and ears with her arms. The moment Thais touched her, Hesiona leaped up with a scream, but when she saw it was her mistress, and that Thais was unharmed, she threw herself into Thais' arms.

Menedem took their hands. "Let's go," he said. "This is an evil place. The zukhos might return, or another one might come in its place. Or the priests ..."

"Where do we go? How do we get out of here?"

"The same way I got here: along the shore, around the temple."

All three walked quickly over the mud and under the Labyrinth's wall. Soon the strip of shore widened, the soil turned dry and made for better footing. But Thais' strength was exhausted, and Hesiona wasn't much better off. Realizing it would be dangerous to stay there, Menedem put out the torch and picked up both women. He tossed them lightly over his shoulders and, in a steady trot, ran away from the menacing bulk of the Labyrinth, heading toward the glimmering light of the House of Pilgrims, which had long since been converted into a xenon, or an inn.

They had to wash before arriving at the xenon. To avoid attracting attention, Thais, dressed in nothing but her sandals and a mane of her long hair, hid behind palm trees. Menedem and Hesiona washed quickly near a wall and brought her clothes from the luggage delivered to the xenon in advance by their guides. The

Greek interpreter vanished, frightened both by Thais' disappearance and by Menedem's rage.

While Hesiona smoothed medicinal ointment over Thais' wounds, she told Thais how they had come to find her in that horrible state. After a fruitless search in the upper rooms of the Labyrinth, the Spartan had grabbed a priest. He had smacked the man against the column and promised to cripple him for good if he didn't explain how the Helenian woman could have disappeared. He demanded to know where he should search for her, and was able to extract a suggestion that Thais had been taken by those who served Sebek. Those worshippers left the intended sacrificial offerings in the dungeons which had access to the lake, in the western part of the sanctuary. If one circled the Labyrinth from the lake and went left from the main entrance, he could find the passageways into the lower level galleries.

Without losing a moment, Menedem had torn off his clothes to make it easier to run through water and rushed along the massive walls of the temple. There was nowhere for him to get any weapons, and had left his with their boatmen to avoid violating the rules of the temple. Someone shouted that he ought to take a lantern, but Menedem was long gone. Behind him, Hesiona grabbed two torches in their bronze holders, touched one to the flame of a niche lantern and dashed after Menedem, running as light and swift as an antelope. She ran in the gathering dark, finding her way by the gloomy wall on the left turning from west to south.

Thais kissed her faithful Hesiona. Menedem received an even more tender reward. Bunches of medicinal herbs were tied to his bleeding palms, making his hands look like claws of the same zukhos that nearly killed Thais.

The Spartan soldier kept glancing with concern at the Labyrinth. It stood tall in the distance glowing in the first rays of sunrise. Guessing his thoughts, Thais said, "There is no need, darling. Who can find the scoundrels amidst three thousand rooms, passages and dungeons?"

"And what if we bring Eositeus' entire detachment?" he snarled. "We shall smoke them out of there like desert foxes out of their dens."

"What for? We foreigners who eat beef are unclean in the eyes of the Egyptian people. We will do nothing but commit a great sacrilege at their sanctuary. Those who are guilty will run away, if they haven't already. The punishment, as always, will befall those who don't know anything and had nothing to do with this. I am the first to blame. I ought not to have argued with the priests, expressing Hellenic disdain toward foreigners and their religion. I should also be more careful traveling around temples filled with traps, mean people, and terrible deities that still demand human sacrifices."

Menedem touched her arm gently, his gaze tender. "I am finally hearing words of sense. I wish you'd said this earlier, my beloved. You haven't danced for us in over a month and have abandoned horseback riding since we got here."

"You are right, Menedem. Dancing and riding demand constant exercise, otherwise I'll turn as bulky as Tueris."

"Tueris!"

Menedem imagined Tueris, an obese Egyptian goddess, sitting on her fat hind legs with an impossibly huge flabby belly and an ugly hippopotamus head. He laughed for a long time, wiping tears from his face with the back side of his bandaged hand.

In Memphis Thais was greeted by news from the east. A battle between Alexander and Darius had taken place at the Issus River on the Finikian side, and the Macedonians had emerged victorious. The great king of the Persians turned out to be a coward, running away from the front lines, leaving behind all his possessions, his tents and his wives.

Alexander continued to head south across Finikia, taking one city after another. Everything and everyone fell before the victorious hero, the son of gods.

Rumors flew ahead of the Macedonian army. Wealthy merchants who escaped the seaside cities appeared in Lower Egypt. They formed a union and bought ships to sail to the distant Carthage. The Egyptian envoy, Mazakhes, is terrified, and the impostor pharaoh, Hababash, ordered the Spartan mercenaries to be ready. A squadron was dispatched to Bubastis, where there was unrest among the Syrian soldiers.

The admirers of the young Macedonian king saw in him deliverance from the Persian rule. They hoped he would offer his powerful arm to support the weak son of the rightful pharaoh, Nektaneb, who had been crushed by Darius some years prior.

Egesikhora, flushed with excitement, told Thais in secret that Nearchus was in charge of Alexander's fleet, and that his ships were at Tyre. The ancient Byblos, with its famous temple of Lebanese Aphrodite or Anachita, gave up almost without delay, as did Sidon. Everyone said Alexander was bound for Egypt. Eositeus was glum and held long meetings with his associates, after which he dispatched a messenger to Sparta.

Thais glanced at her friend inquiringly.

"Yes, I love Nearchus," Egesikhora answered the unspoken question. "He is one of a kind, the only one among others."

"And what of Eositeus?"

Egesikhora formed a finger gesture, used by hetaerae to indicate indifference toward an admirer. "This one is no better than others."

"Are you waiting for him?"

"Yes," Egesikhora admitted.

Thais thought about that. Alexander would be accompanied by Ptolemy. According to the rumors, Ptolemy was now among the best army commanders of the Macedonian king, and nearly the closest of his associates, save for Hephaestion. Ptolemy! Thais' heart beat faster. Her friend, watching her expression, was no less observant.

"What of Menedem?"

Thais didn't answer, trying to understand her own feelings. She was bewildered by memories of the past, the confusion of the last year in Athens, and something altogether new that came with the selfless love of the Laconian athlete, trusting as a child and courageous as a mythical hero.

"You can't decide?" Egesikhora teased.

"I can't. I know only one thing: it's either one or the other. I could never lie."

"You have always been that way. That is why you shall never have great wealth, like Frina or Thero. You don't need it anyway. You simply don't know how to spend money. You don't have enough whims or imagination."

"That much is true. I can't seem to come up with things to impress my competitors or admirers. But it's easier when -"

"Yes, Menedem is not rich. As a matter of fact, to put it simply, he is poor."

Thais was faced with her lack of wealth and its difficulties, when she decided to buy a horse. A rare dappled gray mare was up for sale. She was from Azira, and of a Libyan horse breed supposedly brought in by the Hicsos. The horses from Azira were renowned for their stamina against heat and lack of water. The horse's name was Salmaakh and no one could claim she was beautiful. Her coat was ash gray and while her front pasterns were overly long, her hind quarters sagged. However, that would mean a softer gait for a rider. Not even a hint of white in the corners of her eyes - a sign of mean temper - deterred the prospective buyers. When it became known that Salmaakh was a triabema, meaning she possessed a peculiar "three footed" trot, she was immediately purchased by a Tanisian merchant for a good price.

Thais liked the slightly wild Libyan, and Salmaakh must have recognized in the Athenian woman that strong, calm and kind will to which animals are so sensitive, especially horses. Thais was able to get the horse in exchange for the chrysolite, the very same that was intended for Aristotle to help fine Hesiona's father.

Menedem found a panther's hide to cover up the horse's flanks, blanketing the small sweat pad used by the riders who wore greaves, or narrow Asian pants. This she rode barelegged, like ancient women of Thermodont. Without the hide, riding Salmaakh would have inevitably ruined her calves. When riding in hot weather, horse sweat could cause inflammation and ulcers on human skin.

The soft hide of a predatory cat was pleasant to the touch but made riding difficult. Thais' Amazonian posture, riding with bent knees and heels resting nearly over the horse's kidneys, demanded great knee strength. The rider stayed in the saddle by squeezing the upper portion of the horse's torso between her legs.

The slippery panther hide forced her to double her efforts during a gallop, but Thais didn't mind that. In fact she was rather pleased about it. After two weeks of agony, the iron grip of her knees had returned, for which her Paphlagonian riding teacher called her a true daughter of Thermodont.

While it was true that Salmaakh's trot was soft, Thais preferred to dash about at a gallop, competing against Egesikhora's frenzied foursome, flourishing in the dry Egyptian climate. The main roads around Memphis were always crowded by slow donkeys, carts, processions of pilgrims, and slaves carrying heavy baskets. The women were fortunate enough to discover a sacred road leading south along the Nile, only barely covered by sand here and there. The sand-free sections stretched for hundreds of stadiums, and Egesikhora reveled in mad speed rides. When Thais opted to ride her Salmaakh, Egesikhora took Hesiona into the carriage with her.

The fourth year of the hundred and tenth Olympiad was drawing to a close. The season of fifty day west wind came to Egypt, the breath of ferocious Set, drying the earth and alienating the people.

Previously unfamiliar with the wind of Set, the Helenians continued their rides. Once they were caught in a red cloud, as hot as a furnace. Sand devils twirled and danced around them. When it grew dark, Egesikhora's frightened horses reared up against the wind. The women barely managed to subdue the stallions. It was only after Hesiona jumped off the carriage and bravely grabbed the two pole horses by the reins, helping Egesikhora turn them north toward the city that they were all right. Salmaakh remained completely calm, obediently turning her back to the storm and trotting softly next to the carriage, its bushing screeching from the sand.

The horses gradually calmed and ran more smoothly. Egesikhora rode amidst the noise and whistling of the wind, passing through dust clouds like Athena the warrior maiden. They reached the spot where they frequently stopped, by a half-ruined memorial temple, where the road went around a dark chasm. Thais was the first to notice an elderly man lying against the white steps, wearing a long, linen Egyptian garment. He hid his face within the bend of his right elbow and covered his head with his left arm, breathing heavily. The Athenian hopped off her horse and leaned over the old man with concern. They gave him a bit of wine with water, and he was able to sit up. Much to the two friends' surprise, the old man explained in a perfect Attic dialect that he became ill from the dust storm and, not knowing where to get help, he decided to wait it out.

"Most likely I was waiting for my own demise, considering that Set's wind always blows with all the stubbornness of its god," the old man said.

Three pairs of strong female hands managed to get him into the carriage, Hesiona mounted Salmaakh behind Thais, and all four made it to Memphis safely.

The old man asked them to take him to the temple of Neit near the large park on the river bank.

"Are you a priest at the temple?" Egesikhora asked. "But you are a Helenian, despite your Egyptian garb."

"I am a guest here," the old man said and beckoned Thais to him with an imperious gesture. The Athenian obediently rode up to the steps.

"Are you the Athenian hetaera who was thrown to the crocodiles but escaped? What are you looking for in the temples of Black Earth?"

"Nothing. Not anymore. I was hoping to find wisdom, much more satisfying to the soul than philosophizing about politics, war and knowledge of things. I heard all that back in Attica, but I am not seeking to wage war or found a polis."

"And you found nothing here?"

Thais laughed disdainfully. "They revere animals. What can one expect from people whose gods have yet to become human?"

The old man suddenly straightened his back and the expression in his eyes changed. Thais felt as if the stranger's gaze penetrated the depths of her soul, ruthlessly uncovering secret thoughts, hopes and dreams she had thought to be well hidden. But though she was startled, the Athenian was not afraid. Despite the multitude of impressions and acquaintances, there was nothing shameful or unworthy in her short life, no underhanded actions or mean thoughts. There was only

Eros, the joy of knowing she was always beautiful and desirable, and an acute curiosity.

She returned the old man's piercing gaze, her gray eyes fearless. He smiled for the first time.

"According to your own understanding, you deserve a little more knowledge than Egyptian priests could give you. Be thankful to your name that they even stooped to talking with you."

"My name?" the hetaera exclaimed, "Why?"

"Do you not know that you bear an ancient name for a daughter of Hellas? It is Egyptian and means 'the land of Isis', but came by way of ancient Crete. Have you heard of Britomartis, the daughter of Zeus and Karma? You remind me of her portrait."

"You speak so well, Father. Who are you and where are you from?"

"I am from Delos, a Helenian, a philosopher. But look, your friend is barely holding back the horses, and Salmaakh is dancing on the spot."

"You even know the name of my horse?"

"Do not be naïve, child. I have not yet lost my hearing, and you have addressed her at least twenty times."

Thais blushed, laughed and said, "I would like to see you again."

"I also feel that is necessary. Come any day early in the morning, when Set's ferocity weakens. Come in under the portico, clap your hands thrice, and I shall come to meet you. Haire!"

Gold and white horses raced along the endless palm alley toward the north part of the city. Salmaakh, relieved of her double load, galloped merrily along. Thais gazed upon the lead colored water of the great river, sensing that the meeting with the old philosopher would be an important one for her."

Egesikhora was curious as to why her friend had become so interested in a weak and insignificant old man. Hearing of Thais' intentions to resume her "temple wandering", as the Spartan called it, she stated that Thais was asking for trouble and would get it eventually. She asked Thais if she should complain to Menedem to keep her from going to the temples, or ask him to stop rescuing her the next time she is thrown to a lion, a hippopotamus, a giant hyena or some other deified monster? But that wouldn't help. Despite his menacing appearance, the athlete was but soft clay in the hands of his beautiful lover.

Egesikhora was right, but meeting the philosopher peaked Thais' curiosity. She went to the temple of Neit the next day, as soon as the red tinges of dawn appeared in the lead colored sky.

The philosopher, or priest as may be, appeared as soon as the claps of her little hands sounded in the shade of the portico. He was dressed in the same white linen garment that distinguished Egyptian men and women from all other city dwellers.

For some reason, he was glad of Thais' visit. He signaled for her to follow him, and she did without question. They headed down a passageway on the left, the thick wall of which was made of enormous stone slabs and lit by no more than a narrow crack up above. The tiresome howling of the wind was inaudible here, and Thais walked amidst calm and seclusion. She noticed bright light ahead, and eventually they entered a square room with window openings as narrow as slits. There wasn't even a taste of dust in the air, as there was in the rest of the city. The high ceiling was painted with dark colors, creating an impression of a night sky.

Thais looked around. "Egyptians build so strangely," she said.

"Built," the philosopher said, correcting her. "It was a long time ago. They weren't aiming for perfection, but took great pains to create the mystery of seclusion, the enigma of silence and the secret of the unexpected."

"Our temples, wide open and bright, are a hundred times more beautiful," the Athenian objected.

"You are mistaken. There is a mystery there too, but not the same as the one that descends into the dark of past pages. That is the one of being one with heaven. It is with the sun during the day, and with stars and moon at night. Have you never felt enlightenment and joy among the columns of Parthenon or under the porticos of Delphi and Corinth?"

"Yes, yes."

Rolls of papyrus and parchment sat atop massive boxes, along with writing slates. The center of the room was occupied by a large, wide table. Five point stars and spirals were painted in bright blue against the gray stone table top. The Delos philosopher led the Athenian to the table and sat her down on an uncomfortable Egyptian stool across from himself. The philosopher was silent for awhile, his intense gaze focused upon Thais. Strangely, a sense of calm filled her entire body. Thais felt so well that her entire heart was drawn to the serious, unsmiling and reticent old man.

"You surprised me by your remarks about the animal gods of Egypt," the philosopher said. 'What do you know of religion? Have you been initiated into any mysteries?"

"Never. I don't know anything," Thais said, wanting to be modest before this man. "I have been a hetaera since I was young and haven't served at any temple other than that of Corinthian Aphrodite."

"Then how do you know that gods become elevated along with man? That means that one searches for the divine within himself, and such statements could put you into much danger."

"You shouldn't consider me so smart, wise man. I am simply -"

"Continue, my daughter. I do not have children, but I feel drawn to call you that. This means there is closeness between our souls."

"As I studied the myths, I noticed how the gods of Hellas gradually became kinder and better from the ancient times through to our days. Artemis, the huntress and assassin, became a healer. Her brother Apollo, who began as a ruthless executioner, a jealous killer and a greedy man, is now a glorious giver of life, revered in gladness. My goddess, Aphrodite, used to stand with a spear in ancient temples, like in Athena. Now Urania brings sacred, heavenly love to people," Thais said and her cheeks flushed.

The philosopher-priest gazed upon her even more gently, and Thais grew bold.

"I have also read Anaxagoras: his teachings about Nus, the universal intelligence, the eternal struggle between the two opposing forces of evil and good, the closeness and the enmity. And Antiphontus, who taught that all people were equal and warned Helenians against disdain toward other people ..." Thais hesitated, recalling her own mistakes, for which she had nearly paid with her life.

The philosopher guessed what she was thinking about. "And you yourself couldn't overcome that disdain," he said. "And for that you ended up with the crocodiles."

"I could not and will not accept the ridiculous worship of gods in animal shape: the hideous hippopotami, the disgusting zukhoses, the stupid cows and senseless birds. How can wise people and good people with common sense -"

"You have forgotten, or rather may not know, that the Egyptian religion is several millennia older than the Hellenic one. The deeper you go into the ages, the darker things were around man and his soul. This darkness was reflected in all of his feelings and thoughts. Countless beasts threatened him. He didn't even understand destiny the way we Helenians do. He believed his every moment could be his last. The animal gods, trees, rocks, creeks and rivers passed before him in an endless parade. Some of them vanished, but others survived to our days. Has it been long since we, Helenians, worshiped rivers, so important in our water-poor country?"

"But not animals."

"Trees and animals, too."

Much to Thais' surprise, the philosopher-priest told her about the cult of sacred cypresses on Crete, related to Aphrodite. She was struck most by the ancient worship of the goddesses in the shape of horses. Demeter herself, or Cretan Rhea, was portrayed with a horse's head in the temple of Figaly near the river Neda in Arcadia. The sacred mare possessed particular powers at night and was considered an omen of death.

Neither the philosopher nor Thais could suspect that more than two thousand years after their meeting, a scary dream would still be referred to as a "night mare" in one of the most widely spread languages in the world.

The mare goddess morphed into a three-faced goddess-muse. Her three guises corresponded to Thought, Memory and Song. Only later, when female deities retreated before the male ones, that the three-faced Muse became Hecate. When that happened, the maiden muses increased in number to nine and became a retinue of Apollo, lord over the muses.

Thais stared at her teacher, mesmerized. "Now I understand why the ancient names of nymphs and Amazons were Leukippa the white mare, Melanippa the black mare, Nikippa the victorious mare and Ainiippa the mercifully killing mare."

The philosopher nodded. "And later, when the animal deities lost their meaning, the names changed. There was Hippolita during the time of Theseus, and Hippodamia, the mistress and tamer of horses. They were heroic women, not nymphs in animal guise. So the evolution of religion took place here as well, as you rightly noticed."

"But then ..." Thais hesitated.

"Go ahead. You can say anything to me."

"Then why is the image of Mother Goddess, the Great Goddess, tender and gentle, even though it is much older than that of the murderous male gods?"

"You are mistaken again, thinking of her as only the goddess of love and fertility. Have you not heard of the bassarids, the half-mad women of Thessaly and Frakia? They were intoxicated by sacred leaves, and in their ferocity they ripped apart lambs, goats, children and even men. The women ran wild and carried branches of fir trees, wrapped with ivy, symbols of Artemis and Hecate. The same took place in Athens during Leneas, the celebrations of 'wild women' in the days of winter solstice of the month of Posideon. The face of the goddess-destroyer, goddess of death, was a counterbalance to that of the mother. The image of love was the only link between them, and that is the only one you know."

Thais touched her temples with her fingertips. "It is all too wise for me. Could it be that in the dark ancient times even the female deities were as ferocious as the male ones were later on?"

"Ferocious? No. Ruthless? Yes, like life itself. For what else could they be but the reflection of life, the higher powers of fate, ruling over gods and people alike? They were ruthless and merciful at the same time."

Thais sat there, quiet and confused. The philosopher rose and placed his big warm hand over the stray curls of hair dangling over her forehead. Incredible calm poured through the hetaera's body, as well as a sense of complete safety. She found she understood better.

"Listen carefully, Thais of Athens. If you understand what I tell you, you'll become my spiritual daughter. One can believe in anything, but faith only becomes religion when it is interwoven with the rules of life, the evaluation of deeds, the wisdom of behavior and the consideration of the future. We, Helenians, are still immature. We do not possess the morality and understanding of human feelings as they do in the far East. The Egyptian faith will never evolve into religion, but we too have a few philosophers, of whom you named two, forgetting Plato and a few other wise men."

"I haven't forgotten Plato. But the great scholar forgot about women and their love when creating his plan for an ideal state. I think he only recognized love between men, which was why I do not consider him a normal person, even though he was a famous philosopher, an Olympian wrestler and a man of state. But you are right, I did leave out Aristotle, even though I have met him personally." Thais smiled mysteriously.

The Delos philosopher winced. "No. This scholar of natural phenomena is as barbaric in the moral questions as the Egyptians. You may exclude him. What is important is that any religion lives and has true power over people only at the beginning of its existence, and that includes the smartest and strongest ones. Then faith becomes replaced by interpretation, and righteous living is replaced by ritual, and everything ends in the hypocrisy of priests as they struggle for a well-fed and honored life."

"What are you saying, Father?"

"What you are hearing, Thais? Does it matter whether it is a female deity or Apollo, Artemis or Aesculapius? Life on earth without fear, life that is beautiful, spreading far and wide, like a bright marble road, that is what has become my dream and care."

"So you came from Delos to Egypt ..."

" ...In order to discover the roots of our faith, the origins of our gods. To understand why Helenians are still living without understanding the duties and purposes of men among other people and in the surrounding Ecumene. You already understand that there is no sense in looking for the moral laws in Egypt. There are none in the religion of the ancient hunters, still maintained by the farmers of the Nile. But there are other people ..." The philosopher paused, then wiped his forehead with his hand.

"You are tired, Father," Thais said softly. She rose, then touched his knees as she bowed.

"You understand. My strength is waning. I sense that shall not see my Delos again and shall not write everything I saw in Egypt."

"Do not trouble yourself. Rest, eat the local pink grapes and the tasty fruit of the prickly palm trees," the hetaera said sweetly, making the old man smile. "Yes, yes, I shall bring you some next time. When can I visit you again?"

When she didn't receive an answer, she looked at the slack lines of his face and realized the old man had fallen asleep. She left him and navigated the dark passageways alone, recalling with a shudder what she had gone through at the Labyrinth.

Light and the heat of noon struck her with a hot wave. The dull hum of the fifty day wind seemed almost pleasant after the cool tunnel. But in the evening, while she sat in her drafty house, surrounded by the troubled rush of shadows from the wind-swayed lanterns, Thais felt drawn into the darkness of the temple again, to the strange old Helenian. He had given her the serenity of detachment for the first time in her life.

As a young girl, Thais had dreamed of Aphrodite Urania. The dream had come back several times over the last few years. In it, Thais, barefoot and nude, ascended an incredibly wide ladder, climbing toward a green wall of thick myrtle trees. She slipped between their tangled branches then stepped out into the light. It was bright but not harsh, warm but not scorching. Once there, she approached the statue of Aphrodite Urania. The goddess, made of translucent pink Rhodes marble, was saturated by heavenly light. She descended from the pedestal and put her unimaginably beautiful arm around Thais' shoulders, then gazed into Thais' face. A feeling of amazing delight and serenity filled the young hetaera's heart.

But she didn't like that dream. With time, the contrast grew sharper between the pure serenity of love emitted by Urania, and the frenzied art and labor of the kind of life for which Thais became famous. She was an educated hetaera and a famous dancer among the most knowledgeable Athenians in the world. The same joyous serenity Thais had experienced in those half-childish dreams of Urania had returned to Thais during her meeting with the philosopher.

Rumors of the godlike son of Philip, the Macedonian king, continued to spread through Memphis. Alexander laid siege to Tyre. Its citizens were stubborn, but the skilled Macedonian mechanics decided to create a link between the island upon which the city stood, and the mainland. The demise of the ancient Finikian port was inevitable. When Tyre fell, there would be nothing but Giza left to resist the victorious Alexander.

After that, he could be expected in Egypt any day.

Alexander's fleet cut off Tyre, then continued further and further south. A Hellenic ship traveling to Naucratis had recently met five ships which had supposedly been commanded by Nearchus himself.

Egesikhora became belligerent and restless, which had never happened to the Lacedemonian before. Perhaps it was the unrelenting hot Libyan wind that penetrated people's souls, making them impatient, quick to punish, insensitive and rude. Thais had long since noticed that she tolerated the heat better than Egesikhora did. The wind of Set influenced Thais less, and she tried to meet with her friend less frequently to avoid arguments. Instead, Thais went to the river bank with her faithful Hesiona or with Menedem. There she sat on a floating pier for a long time. The slow flowing water hypnotized the Helenians and each became absorbed in his or her own thoughts: deep, secret, and vague.

One day Thais received an invitation from the Delos priest, delivered to her verbally by a boy, a servant from the Neit temple. Thais dressed modestly and was ready at dawn of the following day, anxious for the meeting.

The Delos philosopher sat on the temple steps which descended toward the Nile. He was absorbed in contemplation of the surprisingly quiet dawn.

"Have you been to the Thebes we Helenians call Diospolis?" he asked, meeting the Athenian with a question. He continued in response to her affirmative nod. "Have you seen the base of a golden circle, stolen by Kambis two centuries ago during the invasion of Egypt?"

'I have. It was explained to me that the original circle was made of pure gold and was thirty elbows across and one elbow thick. Could that be?"

"Yes. The circle weighed approximately thirty thousand talants. Kambis used five thousand camels to transport it to Persia, after cutting it into ten thousand pieces."

"Why would anyone cast such a senseless mass of gold?"

"It was silly, but not senseless. The greatest pharaoh-conqueror wanted to prove to the entire Ecumene the eternity of Egypt, his power, and his faith in the great circle of things. The ascent to power of male rulers brought on a desperate desire to be eternalized. Women know how fragile life is, how near death can be, but men dream of immortality. They kill endlessly, and for any reason. Such ancient contradiction has no solution. And if a man can create a closed circle for himself, for others and for an entire country, it would be with him in the center and an omnipotent and menacing god above."

"What would be the purpose of this?"

"Solidity of power and wellbeing for kings and nobles, strength of faith for priests, stability of thinking among people, and unquestioning obedience of slaves."

"Is that why Egypt carried its faith through millennia?"

"Not only Egypt. There are countries completely closed upon themselves for the purpose of preserving their kings, gods, traditions and way of life for millennia. I call them circular. Such is Egypt, as well as Persia and Syria. There is Rome in the west, and far to the west there is the Middle country of yellow - skinned , slant-eyed people."

"And what of us Hellas? Do we not have the understanding that everything flows?"

"Starting with Crete, the entire Hellas, Ionia, and Finikia are open countries. There is no life-locking circle for us. It is replaced by a spiral."

"I have heard of a silver spiral."

"You have? It is not time to speak of that yet. The heritage of the vanished children of Minos covers a vast territory. It spreads to the west, into Libya and even further to the east, where ancient cities stand tens of thousands of stadiums beyond Hircania. It continues all the way beyond Parapamizes, beyond the desert Arakhozia to the river called the Ind. They say there is not much left of them but ruins, akin to Crete, but the open spirit of these people lives in others thousands of years later."

"Why do you open this knowledge to me, Father? How can I, a servant of Aphroditem, help you?"

"You serve Eros, and there is no mightier force in our Hellenic world. Meetings, conversations, secret exchanges are in your power. You are intelligent, strong, curious, and dream of spiritual enlightenment."

"How do you know that, Father?"

"Much is open to me in the hearts of people. And I think you will soon follow Alexander to the east, into the vast expanses of the Asian plain. Every intelligent woman is a poet in her heart. You are not a philosopher, or a historian, or an artist. Each of them is blinded by his own purpose. And you are not a woman-warrior, for all you have from an Amazon is the art of horseback riding and courage. You are not a killer by your nature. That is why you are more free than any other person in Alexander's army, and I choose you to be my eyes. You shall see that which I never will. Near death awaits me."

"Then how will I tell you?"

"Not me. The others. Intelligent, important people will always be near you. Poets and artists will be attracted to your essence. And it will be even better than if I could tell them. If it comes from your mouth it will remain in the memory of people, become a part of the poets' songs and the writings of historians, will spread through Ecumene in legends and reach those who need to know."

Thais regarded him anxiously. "I am afraid you are making a mistake, Father. I am not the one you need. I am not wise, I am ignorant. Eros turns my head, as do dance, song, admiration of men, envy of women and a fast ride."

He held up his hands as if to hold her back. "Those are only transitional signs of your power. I shall initiate you, teach you the inner meaning of things. I shall free you from fear."

"What must I do?"

"Come tomorrow in the evening, dressed in a new linostolia, accompanied by the one I send. Wait on the steps until Niktur, the Guardian of Heaven, is reflected in the waters of the Nile. Arrange your affairs so you could be absent for nine days."

"Yes, Father. But who will you send?"

"He will appear at the appointed time. Are your periods in correspondence with the Moon?"

"Yes," Thais admitted, suddenly shy.

"Do not be ashamed. There is no mystery or anything unworthy about a woman's healthy body. Give me your left hand."

Thais obeyed. The Delos philosopher placed it on the table, spread her fingers and ruffled through a small ivory box for a few seconds. He produced a ring made of electron with a red hyacinth of incredible deep pink shade. An isosceles triangle, one with a broad base and its tip pointing down, was carved into the flat stone.

Slipping it on Thais' index finger, the philosopher said, "This is the sign of power of the great female goddess. Now go."

Chapter Five. The Muse of the Neit Temple

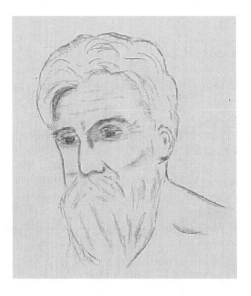

Having returned from the temple early, Thais sprawled out, facedown, on her wide bed. Her arms were under her head, and she swung her heels in the air while Clonaria rubbed walnut oil into her back. Hesiona, offended it had not been she given the honor, rustled in the corner, fitting the newly purchased linen garment, the linostolia.

As always, Egesikhora didn't just enter, but burst in, spreading the scent of rose oil and sweet Arabian resin.

"You've been to the Neit temple again," she challenged her friend. "When will it end? I can't wait for the Macedonians to get here and straighten you out."

"Why? Because the Spartans failed?" Thais teased.

"Helenian artists and poets of Memphis are having a symposium tonight," Egesikhora announced, ignoring her friend's jibe. "I dare you not to be there."

"Then what?"

"Then I don't envy you. They can embarrass you in songs and drawings. You won't forget it."

Thais grew serious. "You are right. I'll go."

"Good for you. And we'll have to dance, so we'd better rest."

Egesikhora stretched out next to Thais and beckoned Hesiona. The latter perked up, tossed away the linen dress and started massaging the Spartan thoroughly, pouring generous doses of oil over her. Both friends relaxed became drowsy under the caring hands. They fell asleep, covered by a blanket of soft Cappadocian yarn.

The symposium took place in a large house with a sprawling garden, owned by the wealthiest Greek merchant in Memphis. Considering this was not the best time of year, the number of guests was unprecedented. Haughty Persian nobles, who had despised Helenians until recently, stayed away from them after Alexander's invasion and the battle of Granic. Now they sought the company of influential Greeks after the king of kings had sustained a brutal defeat at Issus. Thais and Egesikhora had earned the nicknames Chrisosphira and Argiropesa ("Gold-footed" and "Silver-legged"), by their poetic admirers, and their arrival caused shouts of admiration. Both friends showed up accompanied by Spartan captains, led by the strategist Eositeus himself.

The wine servers diluted both the thick purple wine from the Upper Egypt vineyards and the bright pink one from Syria using water from glass goblets decorated with fanciful spirals of various colors. Music played quietly, combining the sadness of Helenian double flutes and the sharp moans of the Egyptian ones, the seemingly distant ringing of sistras, the humming of sitar, lyre and a large harp. A choir of Egyptian mandolins with long necks and bells joined in from time to time, overpowered by tambourines. Following a skillful conductor, the collection of such different instruments created a sad rhythmic chorus interspersed with bright, lively splashes of high notes and slightly rough ringing strikes. To all of this, the dancers of Hellas, Egypt and Finikia danced well.

Both famous hetaerae wore transparent silvery white chitons. They were identical except for the different jewelry emphasizing Thais' tanned darkness and Egesikhora's divinely gold coif. A necklace of fiery red garnets (pyrope or Nophek), the stone of spring equinox, circled the Athenian's long neck. The dangling earrings of large amethysts, amulets against intoxication, glittered on each side of her lively round face. Egesikhora had the same earrings but made of beryllium, the sea stone, while her wide Egyptian necklace of lapis lazuli and white Syrian agate signified the coming of summer to those who understood the language of jewels.

The Symposium started, as was customary in Hellas, with a light dinner, followed by dancing, performances by singers, poets and storytellers, eventually deteriorating into drunkenness and debauchery. That was when respectable hetaerae and actresses left the overly enthusiastic male company.

However, for now there was still a long way to go before the crossing of limits and loss of the sense of beauty. The enraptured guests listened and watched, forgetting to drain their goblets. Helenians despised gluttony, and considered themselves to be above barbarians, which included all foreigners. The Greeks considered it uncivilized and ridiculous to follow the Syrian and Persian customs of constantly eating or drinking something, snacking on nuts or seeds, making coarse jokes, talking incessantly, and hugging strange women. They preferred calm contemplation, self-pondering and joyous admiration of beauty.

A star dance performed by Egyptian girls unraveled slowly, accompanied by the ringing of bells and sistras. The girls were draped in long garments of the finest linen and wore red wreaths over their wavy hair. They walked in a line, slender like blades of grass, focused and haughty. Their row turned to the right, by the sun or strophe, showing the movement of stars. Breaking the line, a group of swifter girls moved antistrophe, or to the left. Their entire outfit consisted of a belt made of colorful glass beads. The dancers in white leaned forward, touching the floor with outstretched hands, while the dark-skinned bodies undulated between them in smooth, snakelike movements, their clasped hands raised above their heads. The Egyptian dances were performed carefully and reverently with no unattractive, awkward or unfitting movements. Nothing violated the charm of these streaming and bending young bodies. The Helenians froze in numb and respectful admiration.

Then the Egyptian girls were replaced by auletridae, accompanied by the fast trills of strings and beat of tambourines. They twirled, spun and shook their hips in the movements of apokinnis, the hetaerae's favorite dance of erotic courage and bravery. The Helenians were set on fire by the power of Eros. Delighted shouts were heard, goblets were raised higher and wine was splashed to honor Aphrodite.

"The Greek girls dance wonderfully here," Eositeus exclaimed. "But I am waiting for your performance," he said, and put his arm possessively around Egesikhora.

She obligingly leaned against his shoulder. "Thais has to go first. And you are mistaken thinking the auletridae dance well. Look, along with the perfect movement they have quite a few coarse, unattractive poses. The pattern of the dance is disorderly and excessively varied. It is not the highest art, like the Egyptians showed. Those were beyond all praise."

"I don't know," Eositeus grumbled. "I just don't like dance if there is no Eros in it."

"There was Eros, just not in the form you understand," Thais interrupted.

A group of male poets appeared before the guests, their garb flamboyant. Eositeus reclined on his settee and covered his eyes with his hand. Thais and Egesikhora left their seats and moved to the outer edge of the table. The poets belonged to kikliks, dedicated to the circle of Homer-like epic tellers. They gathered in a circular choir and sang a poem of Nauzikaya, accompanied by two lyres. Akin to Leskh of Mitilena, the poets strictly followed the smooth flow of hexametric form and drew the listeners in with the power of the poem. They told about Odyssey's heroics, something every autochthon, or natural-born Helenian, could relate to as they'd heard the stories since childhood.

As soon as the last verse of the rhythmic declamation was sung, a jolly young man stepped before the audience. He was dressed in gray blue garb and his black sandals sported high, 'feminine' crisscrossing of straps around his ankles. He turned out to be a rhapsody poet or an improvisational singer, accompanying himself on a sitar.

The poet approached Thais, then bowed, touching her knees. Afterwards he straightened solemnly. A thickly-bearded lyre player in a dark chiton came to stand behind him. After the young man's nod, he struck the strings. The rhapsodian's strong voice sounded through the banquet hall, constructed with the knowledge of laws of acoustics. The poem, the anthem to Thais' charms, caused a humorous excitement among the guests. People started singing along with the rhapsodian, and the kiklik poets gathered into a circle again, serving as a vocal accompaniment. New epithets placed at the end of each verse of the improvised anthem was picked up by dozens of strong throats and thundered through the hall. Anaitis, the fiery one; Targotelea, Anedomasta, the proud-breasted one; Kiklotomerion, round-hipped one; Telgorion, the charmer; Panthorpa, she who gives the greatest bliss; Tolmeropis, daring-eyed one …

Eositeus listened and frowned, glancing at Egesikhora for direction. The Spartan hetaera laughed and clapped her hands in delight.

"Thais' hair," the poet continued, "is deca oymon melanos kianoyo, ten strips of black steel on Agamemnon's armor. Oh, sphayropigeon telkterion, she who is full of charm, Kikloterezone …"

"Oh, my chrisocoma Egesikhora," Eositeus interrupted in a mighty bass. "Leukopoloa, she who rides the white horses! Oh, Filethor eunekhis, beloved of the beautiful shoulders. Meliboa, the sweetness of life."

Thunderous applause, laughter and encouraging exclamations drowned them both out. The dismayed rhapsodian froze, letting his mouth hang open. Thais jumped up, laughing, and held out her arms both to the poet and to his accompanist, then kissed each one.

The bearded lyre player held her hand and pointed at the ring given to her by the Delos philosopher. "You will be at the Neit temple tomorrow night."

"How do you know?"

"I shall accompany you. When shall I come for you, and where?"

"We can speak later. I must dance for them now."

"No, you mustn't," the bearded accompanist stated firmly.

"You speak nonsense. How can I not? I must thank them for the rhapsody and show the poets and the guests that they didn't sing in vain. They'll make me dance, anyway."

"I can spare you. Nobody will ask or force you."

She grinned. "I'd like to see the impossible."

"Then step outside, as if to change and wait in the garden. Don't bother changing your dress, though. Nobody will want you to dance. I'll call you."

Persistent cries of "Thais! Thais!" grew louder. Mad with curiosity, the Athenian ran out through the side door, which was covered by a heavy curtain. Against the bearded man's advice she didn't take the steps into the garden but stayed to watch, shifting the heavy fabric off to the side a little.

The bearded man handed his lyre off to someone and made a sign to his assistants.

"While Thais is getting ready, I will show you some miracles from the eastern lands," he announced.

Two glass globes were placed near the tables and round mirrors reflected beams of light upon them from the bright luminaries. Glowing with golden light, the globes began revolving, helped along by leather straps that were moved by the assistants. Light striking at the metal mirrors filled the hall with long, even vibrations, ringing as if from afar.

The bearded man spread his arms, and his assistants placed two enormous censers to his left and right. He gazed upon the guests with his bright eyes. "Those who wish to see Tihe, the goddess of happiness, and ask her to fulfill their dreams," he said, "must look into either of the globes and repeat her name in rhythm with the sound of the mirrors."

Soon the entire room was chanting "Tihe! Tihe!" in unison. The globes revolved faster. Suddenly the bearded man stuck both hands into his leather sash and poured two handfuls of herbs over the coals. Sharply scented smoke, picked up by a light draft, spread rapidly through the hall. The bearded man stepped back, examined the crowd of partygoers and exclaimed, "Tihe is before you in her silver dress, wearing a sharp golden crown over her red hair. Do you see her?"

"We do!"

The powerful choir of voices indicated that all guests were now participating in the strange game.

"What would you rather have?" he asked. "Thais' dance or Tihe's mercy?"

"Tihe, Tihe!" the guests roared as one, reaching for something Thais couldn't see.

The bearded man tossed more herbs over the coals, made a few strange gestures and people suddenly appeared to freeze on the spot. Then he turned and stepped behind the curtain. Thais barely managed to step aside in time.

The bearded man said briskly, "Let's go."

"What about them?" she whispered to the mysterious stranger.

"They will soon come back to their senses. And those who watched from the distance will testify that you were rejected in favor of Tihe."

"Did she really appear to them?"

"They saw what I told them to see."

"Where did you learn the art of ruling the crowd like that?"

"Satep-sa has been known in Egypt for a long time, and I have also been to India, where people are even more skilled at this art."

"Who are you?"

"A friend of the one who waits for you tomorrow after sunset. Come, I shall escort you home. It is improper for Thais to walk around alone at night."

"What am I to be afraid of next to such a ruler over people?"

"It is not as you think, but you won't understand it now. My power is in my well-developed lema (will), and it can be used only at appropriate and carefully prepared moments."

"Now I understand. Your magic is but an art that is unknown to us. And here I thought you were a son of Hecate, the goddess of night illusions."

The bearded man chuckled. Without another word, he escorted Thais to her house. Once they arrived, they arranged a meeting time and place for the next day, left.

All the servants were asleep except Hesiona, who sat next to a lantern with her sewing and waited for her mistress. She had fully expected Thais to show up at dawn, accompanied by torch bearers and a noisy crowd of admirers. Hearing her voice in the silence of the night, Hesiona ran out to meet her, concerned and dismayed. Thais reassured her voluntary slave, had some honey drink and went to bed. Then she called Hesiona, informed her that she would be going away for ten days, and gave the Theban instructions for the duration of her absence. The girl begged to come with Thais, and her mistress' refusal caused Hesiona to despair.

"You reject me, Mistress, and leave me alone. I don't have anyone else in the world except you, and now you don't need me. What am I to do if I love you more than life? I will kill myself."

Hesiona had cried rarely till now. Reserved and somewhat stern, she absolutely refused to participate in dances or symposiums and rejected the men who attempted to pursue her.

Thais told Hesiona to climb into bed with her, patted her head and face and when her sobs subsided, explained to the Theban the reason why she couldn't take her along either the previous time or this one. Hesiona calmed down and sat up on the bed, looking at her mistress with admiration and a bit of fear.

"Do not be afraid. I shall not change," Thais said with a laugh. "And you will be with me, as before. But not forever. Your turn will come, and the one will appear for whom you'll follow to the ends of the world.

You will know the sweetness and the bitterness of a man's love."

"Never! I hate them!"

"Perhaps, but only until you recover from the war-induced trauma. Love will take what's due. You are healthy, beautiful, and courageous. You cannot avoid Aphrodite's traps."

"I shall love only you, Mistress."

Thais laughed and kissed her. "I am not a tribada. The goddess did not bestow the gift of double love upon me, or upon you. That is why the Eros of male love is unavoidable for both of us. It divides women, and fate pulls them apart. Be ready for it. However, both our names mean servants of Isis. Perhaps we are destined to be together."

Hesiona slipped to the floor, frowning stubbornly, but relieved in the knowledge that Thais was not rejecting her. Her mistress fell asleep almost immediately, tired by the many events of a long day.

Thais and the poet-magician from the day before sat on the steps of the Neit temple in the twilight, above the dark river, waiting for the Sky Sentinel to rise.

The bearded poet said that the Delos philosopher forbade her to ask his name. He was a great scholar, but was only known to those who were initiated in the ways of the Orphics, Pythagoreans and gymnosophists. For several years he had lived in the west of the Libyan desert, where he discovered the empty ruins of ancient Cretan sanctuaries.

That was where the cult of the triple goddess Hecate, the snake goddess of Crete and Libya, had spread from all other Hellenic countries. Her beautiful, seductive priestesses, or Lamias, became the terrible night demons in Hellas. The owl-goddess turned into a demon too, becoming Lilith, the first wife of the first man, in Syria. The Syrian moon goddess was sometimes portrayed with a snake's body, and sometimes with a lion's head when she was pictured in Egypt. Neit was essentially the same three-faced snake, the goddess of Libya. The main goddess of Attica, Athena the Wise, was born on the shores of the lake Triton in Libya as a triple snake goddess. The triple goddess of Love dominated all ancient religions, and that was where three Muses or Nymphs came from. In the later myths, she was always defeated by a male god or a hero, like Perseus.

The Delos philosopher said that goddesses and gods of the ancient religions always transformed into evil demons when they were transferred to new people. It was necessary to soil the old in order to establish the new. That was just the way people were, unfortunately.

The great Mother Goddess, or Ana, who united the faces of Wisdom, Love and Fertility, turned her other side toward people. She became the goddess of Evil, Destruction and Death. But the intuitive memory was stronger than that, and the ancient beliefs constantly floated up from under the mass of the new ones. The image of Ana divided and became the goddesses of Hellas: Ur-Ana, Aphrodite; Di-Ana, Artemis; At-Ana, Athena. The moon goddess, Artemis, the most ancient one of all, preserved her triple image and became Hecate, the goddess of evil enchantment and night illusions, the leader of the night demons. Her brother, Apollo the Assassin, became the glorious god of the sun and healing.

"Are you not afraid to speak of gods as if they were people?" Thais asked with concern, having listened to the bearded man without interrupting.

"The Delos teacher have already told you. And besides, I am a poet, and all poets revere the female goddess. There is no poet without her, he only addresses her. She must succumb to the power of his words. For a poet always seeks the truth, and comes to know things that do not interest Muse or Love. She is a goddess, but she is a woman, too."

"You are speaking to me as if I were -"

"That is why he is a poet," a weak but clear voice sounded behind them.

They both jumped up and bowed to the Delos priest.

"You have even forgotten that Nikturos have already reflected in the waters of the river," he said.

The bearded man, having instantly lost his solemnity, mumbled something to justify himself, but the Delos philosopher signed for him to stop.

"A poet should always be ahead of a man," the philosopher said, "for such is his essence. If something mighty became overripe or dead, it must be destroyed, and the poet becomes a destroyer, directing the strike of humiliation. If something sweet is still weak, not fully grown or even destroyed, it needs to be created anew, and have new power poured into it. This is where a poet is dreamer, exalter and creator. That is why he always has two faces, or better yet, three, like the Muse. But woe for him and the people if he only has one face. Then he is a spreader of harm and poison."

"I would like to object, Delos scholar," the bearded man said, lifting his head. "Why do you only speak about a poet? Are the philosophers not equally responsible for their words?"

"I am not talking about the limits that are equal for all. You know how the magic of word and sound is much stronger than the quiet voices of the sophists. The power of a poet over people is much greater, which is why -"

"I understand, teacher, and I bow again before your wisdom. Do not waste any more words."

"No, I see you have not yet reached all of the depth of a poet's power, even though you are initiated by the

Five Petals of Lotus. The notion of a poem originates from the root of the word 'struggle', but a poet in his other guise always stops the warring parties. He is a peacemaker, and has been since ancient times. Why is that?"

The bearded man spread his fingers to indicate that he was at a loss, betraying by this gesture that he was from Mitilena, and the Delos philosopher smiled.

"Then you listen too, Thais, for this will help you understand many things. After the establishment of male gods, the arrogant male spirit replaced the order and peace, associated with female dominance. These male gods came from the north with Achaeans, Danaians and Aeolians, the tribes that had enslaved the Pelasgoans, 'People of the Sea', fifteen centuries ago. Warrior-heroes replaced the splendid female rulers of love and death and the priests declared war on the female beginning. But a poet serves the Great Goddess and is, therefore, a woman's ally, even though a woman herself is not a poet, but a Muse.

"New people separated the Sun and the Moon, the male god from Anatkha-Ishtar, bestowing upon him the greatest power and considering him to be the beginning and the end of all existence. You were just telling Thais, and correctly so, that the gods of old religions become demons of the new one. I will add to this that the goddesses, as the rulers of evil magic, are being increasingly pushed away. This is happening in the east, in the west and in Hellas. Along with the goddesses, poetry is leaving as well, the number and the power of poets decreases. I foresee trouble from this far in the future."

"Why trouble, Father?" Thais asked quietly.

"The essence of a person is being torn in half. A poet-thinker is becoming increasingly rare. Nus and Fronema, the mind more typical among men, becomes more dominant, rather than that of Mnema, Estesis and Timos, memory, feeling, heart and soul. And men, as they lose the poetic force, become akin to the Pythagorean number-crunchers, or to the vengeful and calculating deities of Syrian and western peoples. They declare war to the female beginning, and with it lose the spiritual interaction with the world and gods. When they pay their debt to a deity, they count their honors and sins like money, and instead of a cleansing they receive a fateful feeling of guilt and helplessness."

"When did it start, Father? Why did it happen?"

"A long time ago. When a man first picked up a tool or a weapon, invented a wheel, he lost faith in himself and started relying on the tools he invented, increasingly departing from nature and weakening his inner strength. A woman lived differently and preserved herself better, becoming spiritually stronger than men in love and in the knowledge of her essence. That is what the Orphics believe. But enough discussion, night has fallen, it is time to go."

Anxiety hastened Thais' breath. She followed the men through a small courtyard which led to a stone pylon. The pylon was erected over a gallery, which led into the slope of a hill. For some time they walked silently, stepping carefully in the dark.

Then Thais heard the bearded poet ask the Delos philosopher, "Must we understand from what you said, that we Helenians, despite enormous knowledge and great art, purposely avoid creating new tools and machines so we can avoid parting from the feelings of Eros, beauty and poetry?"

"I think yes, although it is possible we do not even realize we are doing it."

"Is it wise?"

"If the entire world is going toward the separation of a poet and a philosopher, feeling and mind, toward the acceptance of the all-intelligent and all-powerful, toward a punishing god and away from living nature to polises, under the protection of walls and machines, then our way will lead to destruction."

"But it will be a glorious demise. We shall be sung about for centuries."

"You are right. For thousands of future years Hellas will remain a beautiful dream for at least somewhat worthy people, despite all our shortcomings and mistakes. Here we are."

The Delos philosopher stopped and turned to Thais. The hetaera froze. The philosopher smiled encouragement to her and took her hand, having whispered something to the poet. The latter vanished in a side passageway, while the philosopher led Thais into a high, round space lit by smoking torches and made of aromatic wood. He raised his arm, and invisible drums thundered from somewhere. They beat loudly, increasing the tempo, and soon the thundering cascades of sounds crashing over Thais made her entire body shiver, drawing her into the rhythm and power.

The philosopher leaned toward the Athenian and, raising his voice, ordered, "Take off everything. Sandals too."

Thais obeyed without question. The Delos philosopher patted her hair approvingly and told her to take out the comb and ribbons.

"The blood of the Great Goddess is obvious in you. Stand in the center of the circle."

Thais stood in the center, still shuddering from the thunder, and the Delos philosopher disappeared. Suddenly, nine women appeared, seeming to come out of walls themselves. They wore wreaths over their hair, and were otherwise nude, like Thais. They were not Egyptians but not Helenians, either. She thought they belonged to some people unknown to Thais. One of them, she appeared to be the eldest, was stout and broad-chested, with dark bronze skin. An entire mane of fine curly hair surrounded her face. She ran up to Thais while the rest formed a circle.

"Do as we do," she ordered in good Greek, taking the Athenian by the hand.

The women moved in a line, lifting their knees high and holding each other's long hair. The tempo increased and transformed into a run. Disconnecting, they spun like a top, strobilus, then froze and began undulating in a wild dance of the Trojan goddess, rotating their hips madly. They ran again, tossing back their heads and spreading their arms, as if they were ready to hug the entire Ecumene. The thunder of the drums turned into solid roar, the dancers performed complex moves, sometimes shouting something out with dry mouths. One after another, the women fell on the floor and rolled to the wall, away from the other dancers' feet.

Thais, having given herself up to the wild ritual, didn't notice that she was alone with the eldest dancer. The other eight lay on the floor, exhausted. The eldest continued to dance, sheathed in sweat, looking at Thais in amazement, as the latter kept up with her and only flushed brighter and brighter.

Suddenly the dancer stopped, her arms raised high. The music, if one could call the deafening thunder music, stopped just as silently. The eldest dancer bowed to Thais, then wailed sharply, summoning the other dancers up from the floor. The Athenian remained alone, still fluttering with excitement.

The voice of the Delos philosopher sounded from somewhere above. "Wake up. Go to the right."

Thais noticed a narrow, crack-like exit from the round hall and went that way, weaving slightly, as if she were in a fog. A door clanged closed behind her and she found herself in complete darkness. Thais reached out with her arms and took several cautious steps.

Suddenly, a mass of sea water washed over her from above. The stunned Athenian stepped back, but remembered the closed door behind her and went forward instead. The passage turned at a right angle once, then again. After the second turn, a barely noticeable light flickered in the corner. Wet from head to toe, but still not completely cooled from the dance, Thais rushed forward with relief, then stopped in terror.

She stood in a tall hall without a roof, its walls rising into the starry night sky like those of a well. The entire floor was taken up by a pool of water. A narrow strip of beach pebbles sloped toward the water from where Thais stood and water splashed carefully over the pebbles. A breeze came from somewhere, trying to put out the only torch, throwing red glints over the black water. Thais' teeth chattered and she moved her shoulders trying to stop shivering, but the oppressive feeling of strange and mysterious fear refused to go away.

"Do not be afraid, my daughter. I am with you," the Delos philosopher said, appearing on the opposite side of the pool. She waited as he walked slowly along the granite edge toward her.

"According to the ritual, we must chain you to the rock to be devoured by a sea monster. But you have already undergone a much more frightening test at the Labyrinth, and we decided to drop the first stage. I shall spread the coal from three sacred trees here: oak, walnut and willow. They are used for burial pyres and symbolize power, wisdom and charm. You shall spend the night on the coals, like on a death bed." The philosopher turned and gathered an armful of black sheep fleece from a niche in the wall which he handed it to Thais. "Take this," he said. "You shall spend the night here, lying prone till the first signs of dawn. At dawn, go back to the gallery, turn left to follow the light of a luminary, and enter the dark cave, where you shall spend the day. When you hear a bell, go back to the pebbles till the next dawn. This time, lie on your back, look at the sky and recite the ancient anthem to Gaea. You will pass two more nights in this manner. Then I shall come for you. You will have to fast. The drinking water is in the cave, in an amphora near the bed. Haire!"

Thais, shivering from the chill, spread some of the fleece over the rocks. She tried unsuccessfully to get comfortable on this unusual bed, tried to cover herself with the other half. Fortunately, the barely audible splash of the waves soothed her and she drifted to sleep.

She woke up shaking from the cold and hurting from the pain of the pebbles sticking to her body. The fleece smelled of sheep, the dark water in the pool seemed unclean, and her hair was in disarray, stuck together from the salt water shower the night before. Thais raised her head and saw the sky had lost its velvety blackness and was turning gray. Recalling the teacher's orders, she gathered the fleece in a pile, rubbed her numb limbs and went into the underground passage.

She felt hungry, her mouth was dry and she felt dirty. Thais was puzzled. Could it be that such simple inconveniences constituted the trials of initiation? And what kind of initiation was this? Suddenly, the Athenian remembered that the philosopher had never said anything about it, and she hadn't asked, having felt childlike trust toward the strange old man. If he considered it necessary to initiate her, then she assumed that's what was needed. But the night's inconveniences, followed by nothing but discomfort made her skeptical. She had simply slept, albeit on a dreadful bed, in an odd gloomy well. Why? What had changed about her if anything?

To her surprise, in the cave the Athenian found a wash basin and everything necessary to complete her toilette. Having washed and brushed out her thick hair, Thais drank some water and felt much better, despite the hunger. The luminary faded and went out, leaving the cave completely dark. Thais found the bed, which was covered with soft cloth, by touch and lay there deep in thought until sleep came upon her. She woke at the ringing strike of a copper bell, went back to the pool, spread the fleece to make it as comfortable as possible, then settled down on the crackling pebbles, gazing into the bright starry sky.

Having gotten plenty of sleep during the day, she didn't sleep all night, and never took her eyes away from the stars. She didn't notice the strange sensation of flight when it came to her. Along with Thais, Earth itself was reaching for the sky, ready to embrace it.

"Rejoice, mother of gods, oh, the wife of the many-starred sky," she said, remembering the newly understood words of the ancient anthem.

In that moment, Thais felt as if she merged with the broad, generous Gaea, waiting to unite with the black infinity that sparkled with stars. The great mystery of the world was just out of her reach. Thais spread her arms, her entire body straining, and a moan of torturous impatience escaped her lips. But the black veil of the night still hung over her like an abyss, and the mysterious flickering of celestial bodies was not coming any closer.

All at once she saw herself lying there: pitiful, small, and naked at the bottom of the well, enclosed by an inescapable circle of tall, smooth stone walls. Her perceived merging with Gaea had been nothing but an arrogant sacrilege, and all things incomprehensible still remained so, while the future did not promise anything great or glorious. Thais wanted to jump up and run away, like an impostor who had entered forbidden territory, then realized her own insignificance. Something, perhaps the will of her Delos teacher, held her in place.

Gradually, Thais obeyed the calm of the starry night, letting a feeling of self-confidence replace her earlier dismay. However, when she returned to the cave to fall into a fretful slumber, her restlessness returned, exacerbated by hunger and puzzlement.

The third night alone with the stars on the shore of a symbolic sea started differently. After two days spent in the dark, the stars appeared particularly bright. One of them attracted Thais' attention. Its sharp beam penetrated her eyes, continuing through them to her heart, and spreading through her body in a blue fire of magical power. With her gaze fixed upon the star, she remembered the magical chants of ritual dances meant to help focus physical and emotional energies, and started repeating, "Gaea – Thais, Gaea – Thais, Gaea – Thais …" The disorderly flow of her thoughts slowed, the soil under Thais rocked a little and she was carried forth smoothly, like a ship in the night sea.

Thais finally understood the purpose and the meaning of her trials. There, on the islands of the Inner Sea, a man left alone with the sea in the middle of the night had an easier time becoming absorbed in a primal connection with the natural forces of Gaea, dissolving himself in the eternal splashing of the waves.

The understated symbolism did not allow her to dramatically assume the right mood and enter the flow of time, akin to the Akheloy-Argirodines, the river in ancient Sparta which flowed and disappeared underground, rolling its silvery waves from the unknown future into the dark caverns of the past. Had her intentions been sincere and strong from the beginning, the focus and the spiritual rise could have been achieved, even in this almost theatrical setting.

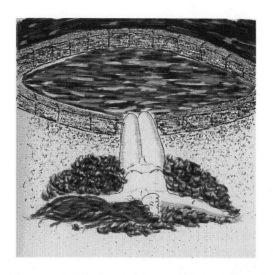

The seemingly short night passed quickly, and the colorful multitude of stars began growing cooler, tinged with the silver of dawn. Obeying a sudden urge, Thais rose, stretched her entire body, then dove into the deep dark water. She was at once enveloped in surprising warmth. The water that had seemed stale and unclean to her before was as clear as sea water. An almost imperceptible current caressed her with a gentle hand, soothing her irritated skin. Thais rolled over onto her back and gazed into the sky again. Dawn was rolling in from the eastern desert, but Thais did not know whether she was to go back into the darkness of the cave or wait for a sign here.

Her puzzlement was interrupted by a familiar coppery strike and the old philosopher appeared on the strip of pebbles. "Come to me, daughter. It is time for the ritual."

Almost simultaneously with his words the vibrant dawn of a clear day rose into the gloomy sky and reflected in the smooth wall of the well. Thais saw herself in the crystal clear water of the pool made of dark, polished granite. Rolling over, she swam quickly to the strip of pebbles. Blinded by so much light after spending such a the long time in the cave and in the nighttime darkness, she came out of the water, covering herself with wavy strands of her hair.

The bearded poet appeared behind the Delos philosopher, carrying some kind of black stone in his hand.

"You must be symbolically struck down and purified," the philosopher said. "He will strike you with the stone that fell from the sky. Push your hair back and bow your head."

Thais obeyed without question, so great was her trust in the old philosopher.

The strike never took place. Instead, the poet stepped back with a sigh, covering his face with his free hand.

"What is the matter, Mitilenian?" the old man asked, raising his voice.

"I cannot, Father. This creation of Gaea's formative powers is too beautiful. Look at her perfection. I feared I might leave a scar and my hand fell."

"I understand your feelings, but the ritual must be completed. Think of where a scar would be least noticeable."

Seeing the poet's hesitation, the Delos priest took the stone himself.

"Put your hands behind your head," he ordered Thais, then struck her quickly with a sharp edge of the stone over the inner side of the arm, just above the armpit. Thais cried out slightly as blood trickled out of the wound. The priest collected a little bit of blood and mixed it in with the water in the pool. Bandaging the Athenian's arm with a linen band, he said with satisfaction, "See? Only she and the two of us will know about this scar."

The Poet bowed and handed Thais a cup of goat milk with honey, the drink fed by the divine goat

Amalthea to baby Zeus in a Cretan cave. Thais carefully drank it all and felt her hunger fade away.

"This is a sign of rebirth," the philosopher said.

The poet placed a wreath of fragrant five-petal flowers over Thais' head, then brought her a light blue stola, hemmed not with the usual fringe but with a pattern of hooked crosses. The design seemed sinister to the Athenian, but the Delos philosopher guessed her thoughts, as always.

"This is a sign of a fire wheel that came to us from India. See? The ends of the crosses are bent anti-solon. Such a wheel can only roll solon, with the sun, and symbolizes kindness and benevolence. But if you see similar hooked crosses with ends bent solon, so that the wheel can only roll against the sun, know that you are dealing with people who chose the path of evil and unhappiness."

"Like a dance of black magic, danced anti-solon at night around that which they want to harm?" Thais asked, and the philosopher nodded.

"Here are the three colors of the three-faced goddess-muse," the poet said, putting a sash of striped white, blue and red cloth around Thais. He made another deep Egyptian bow to the Athenian, touched his right knee with his palm, and left silently.

The Delos priest led Thais out of the dungeon, through the brightly lit courtyard, and into the top floor of the pylon above the gates.

The following seven days and nights were filled with strange exercises for focus and relaxation, effort and rest, taken in turns with the philosopher's disclosure of such things of which the well-educated Thais had no idea.

A large change seemed to have taken place in her. She could not yet tell whether it was for the better or for the worse. All she knew that a different Thais was to leave the Neit temple, and it would be a calmer and wiser one.

She would never tell anyone of the difficult days and unusual feelings that had flared up like fire, consuming the worn remains of her childish faith. She wouldn't mention her pain from the declining charm of new successes that seemed so important once, nor the gradual establishment of new hopes and goals she could only tell a daughter who was like her. Life no longer lay before her in fanciful twists of a road, passing from light to shadow in its endless turns, from groves to rivers, from hills to the shores of the sea.

All things had become unknown, new and tempting, waiting everywhere. Her life path now appeared straight as the flight of an arrow to Thais. It cut through the valleys of life, broad and clear at the beginning, narrow and indistinct in the distance, until it finally vanished beyond the horizon. But it was astonishingly uniform all along the way, like an open gallery with identical pillars, stretching into the distance till the end of Thais' life.

Deira, the knowledgeable one, as Persephone was secretly called, had stepped into her soul, where only Aphrodite and her mischievous son had ruled until then. This feeling, unusual for a young, healthy woman, never left the Athenian during her stay at the Neit temple, and strangely enhanced her comprehension of the Delos philosopher's teachings. The old man uncovered to her the teaching of the Orphics, called such because they considered it possible to leave the underground kingdom of Hades, akin to Orpheus who rescued his Eurydice.

The teaching sprang from the depth of past centuries of the combined wisdom of Crete and India, uniting the belief in reincarnation with the rejection of the hopelessness of the circles of life and fate. The great principle: "all things flow, change and pass", reflected in the name of the great Cretan goddess Kibela-Rhea, ran into a question: would there be a return to the past?"

"Yes, there always will be," the scholars of Syria and Pythagoras stated, the latter being the most famous student of the Orphics. They were the Pelasgoan from the island of Samos, who had led the Orphics away from ancient wisdom, succumbing to the game of numbers and symbols under the influence of the scholars of Ur-Salim.

"No, there will not be," the philosophers of the old-Orphic type disagreed. "It is not the Wheel that constantly makes one circle after another, but a Spiral. That is the true flow of changing things, and that is our salvation from the Wheel.

"Gods did not create the Universe," taught the Orphics. "It came to be from the natural physical powers of the world. Cosmos is order, first and foremost. The egg of the Universe formed from Chaos, Chronos (time) and Ether (space). The egg started growing until one half of it formed the sky and the other one formed the earth. Between them Bios – life – was born."

Satisfying the needs of thinkers in their own era, the Orphics could not have suspected, of course, that twenty-six centuries later the greatest minds of the hugely increased humankind would accept a similar concept of the origins of Cosmos, with the exception of excluding Earth from the dominance over the Universe.

In Gaza, the Cretan colony on the shores of Syria which had been founded twelve centuries before Thais' birth, a myth of Samson was born. He was a blind warrior, chained to a mill and doomed to eternally revolve its wheel. He escaped due to his tremendous strength, having broken the columns and crashed the temple roof on everyone. The meaning of the hero's deed was in the fact that the entire world would have to be destroyed. All people would have to be killed in order to escape the eternal circle.

The Orphics solved that problem in their own way. Their instructions could still be found on the gold medallions they put on their dead. As each thirst-tormented departed soul stumbled its way through the underground kingdom through the fields of white lilies, or asphodels, it had to remember not to drink from the river Leta. Its water, dark from the tall cypresses shading its shores, made everyone forget his previous life. Thus the soul became helpless material for a new cycle of birth, destruction and death without an end. However, if a soul were to drink from Persephone's sacred spring hidden in a grove, then the soul could preserve its memory and knowledge, escape the endless Wheel, and become the ruler over the dead.

Along with the teachings of reincarnation from Asia, the Orphics preserved the ancient local rituals.

"From you," the Delos philosopher said. "The Orphics teaching requires us to remember that a man's spiritual future is in his hands, and not entirely dependent on gods and fate, as everyone from Egypt to Carthage believes. One cannot compromise along this path. They cannot deviate, otherwise, akin a sip of water from the Leta, you will drink the poison of evil, envy and greed, and be tossed into the distant abyss of Erebus.

"We, the Orphics of Ionia, teach that all people are the same on the path of the good and are equal in their search for knowledge. The difference between people at birth is enormous. There is only one way to overcome it, to unite everyone as well as to conquer the differences between them, and that is the way of knowledge. But one must understand what sort of a path unites different nations. Woe be upon us if it does not lead to the good or, even worse, if one people considers itself above all others, chosen by gods and destined to rule. Such people will make others suffer and feel the general hatred, wasting their energies on reaching insignificant goals rather than the breadth of life. We Helenians have only recently stepped onto this savage and evil path, while the Egyptians and the people of Syria arrived at it sooner. Now an even worse supremacy of Rome is growing in the west. It will achieve terrible power. And this power will be worse than all others because the Romans are not of the Helenian mindset. They are ignorant and reach for the military invasions and wealthy living accompanied by bloody spectacles.

"But let us return to you," the old philosopher said, interrupting himself. "One cannot be an Orphic of our kind if he remembers the goal but forgets the price at which people came to possess things. I am not talking about simple things made by the hands of craftsmen, but of large structures: temples, cities, harbors, ships, just about everything that requires the effort of many people. You must not be captivated even by the most beautiful temple if it has been erected upon torment and bones of thousands of slaves. No grandeur is worthy if people were killed, starved or enslaved for the sake of achieving it. And not only people, but animals as well, for their suffering also weighs down the scale. That is why many Orphics do not eat meat."

"Father, why do gods demand bloody sacrifices?" Thais asked, then pulled away, seeing a flash of anger in her teacher's eyes.

He paused, and when he spoke again his voice was hoarse, his words halting, completely unlike his usual calm manner. "Only murderers offer savage sacrifices to savage gods."

Thais became embarrassed. This wasn't the first time during their talks when she had felt as if she were getting into forbidden territory, sacrilegiously pushing away the curtain separating people from gods.

Sensing this, the Delos philosopher dismissed the subject. "Let us not speak of something you are not ready for yet." And he let Thais go for the day.

In the subsequent days he taught her proper breathing and development of particular flexibility of the body, allowing her to assume poses for concentration and quick rest. Trained since childhood, beautifully developed and moderate in food and drink, Thais turned out to be such a capable student that the old man slapped his knee with delight, encouraging the Athenian.

"I can teach you only the basics. You may continue on your own if you wish and if you can, although this path takes more than one year," he said over and over again, making sure Thais remembered it well.

On the sixth day, the symbolic number of life among the Pythagoreans, the old man told Thais in greater detail about the foremother of all religions, the Great Goddess. He taught her the preachers had lied trying to prove that the male deity began it all. Thousands of years ago, all people worshiped the Great Goddess, and women were heads of households and families. The path had split when men became dominant. Ancient religions were wiped off the face of Gaea, or were preached against, and women were called the source of all things evil and impure.

In the east, in the immeasurable distance, there lay an enormous Middle Empire[12] that was contemporary to the demolished Cretan civilization. The yellow - skinned, slant-eyed people living there considered the male Yang to be the essence of light, and the female Ying to be that of darkness in heaven and on earth.

In the scorched valleys of Syria there lived another people, just as ancient and wise, who initially worshiped Rhea-Kibela, as the Cretans did. Then the goddess' female name turned into a male one: Jehovah. Recently in Egypt, there had been a cult of Jehovah and two goddesses, his wives: Ashima-Betkhil and Anatkha-Betkhil. When the wives disappeared, the god remained alone. In the east, the combined worship of the great goddess Ashtoreth or Ishtar and Jehovah split

---

12 China

into two separate faiths. The former borrowed much from Crete, where women were deified, from the Cretan colony of Gaza, and from the ancient city of wisdom Byblos. The famous temple of Solomon was constructed to resemble Cretan palaces with the help of the builders from Gebal-Byblos.

The faith of the Jehovah worshipers declared a woman impure and evil. They accused her of causing the eviction of people from the primeval paradise by her sins. A woman who dared enter a temple, or appeared nude, even before her husband, was punishable by death. The more awkward the faith, the more the ignorant people clutched at it. Once they believed in this, their souls darkened and they became more fanatical. Endless wars, including bloodshed between closely related people, all resulted from men's ascent to the thrones of gods and kings. All things poetic associated with the Muse, vanished. Poets became the court singers of a menacing god, while the philosophers justified his actions as the mechanics created new weapons.

And if a king became a poet and worshiped the Muse in the guise of a beautiful lover, then she was murdered. Such was the story of the Comagen king, Solomon and Sulamyth. She was also killed because she violated the taboo and did not hide her nudity.

"But there are so many poets and artists in Hellas who glorify the beauty of women," Thais said.

"Yes, our female and male gods have not parted too much. That is good luck for Helenians and provides eternal envy for other people. In Hellas, the world is open to women, and that is why they are not as ignorant as those of other peoples, and their children do not grow up to be barbarians. Those who pose before artists and sculptors in all of their splendor are not killed, but celebrated, because we believe that to give one's beauty to people is no less honorable than for a master to depict it in a fresco or in marble. Helenians have always understood the power of Eros and the importance of poetry for evolving the senses. We did not reach a point where women embody all their qualities in one incarnation, but at least we created two kinds of women in two most important guises: the lady of the house and a hetaera-friend."

"Which one is more important?"

"They are both important. And both united in the Great Goddess Mother, the Mistress of Wild Animals and Plants. But remember, the Great Goddess does not live in cities. Her dwellings are among hills and groves, valleys and mountains, inhabited by animals. She is also in the sea, for she is a sea goddess as well. The prophets of Syria considered the sea to be the homeland of all things sinful. Rahab, the seductress and heiress of the Babylonian goddess Tiamat, is connected with the sea. They have an exclamation: 'There will be no more sea'. The Egyptians too are afraid of the sea."

"How strange. I think I couldn't live without the sea," Thais said. "But I am not afraid of a city if it stands on the seashore."

"Do you not know which guise to follow?" the philosopher asked, then chuckled. "Don't think about it too much. Fate itself made you a hetaera while you are young. When you are older, you'll become a mother and much will change about you, but for now you are Circe and must fulfill your purpose."

To Thais' question as to what exactly her purpose was, the Delos priest explained that the female goddess, the Muse, while not being bloodthirsty, was still not as kind as her admiring poets saw her. There was a saying among people that to be a poet, to love a poet, or to ridicule him – all were equally deadly. The ancient moon goddesses of Crete and Syria were decorated with snakes as a reminder that their beautiful images concealed death, as lions guard their victims at their feet. Such are their sisters: the owl goddess with her wisdom-burning eyes, flying at night, announcing death. She is akin to the "night mare" Demeter, or the ruthless hawk Circe, the omen of peril, or to the mistress of the island of Tears, Ea, in the north of the Inner Sea. Circe was the enchantress of love, turning men into animals according to their worth: pigs, wolves or lions. Artemis Elate, the Huntress, watched over the health of all wild animals and people, destroying the feeble, the sick, the weak of mind and the ugly.

The great goddess Muse was always portrayed in the nude, as the giver of truth, unattached to any place or time. She could not be a housewife. She would always counter that guise. Therefore, women could not play her role for any length of time.

"I know," Thais said with sadness and concern, "how many maenadae commit suicide during the love festivals."

"I am increasingly pleased with you," the philosopher exclaimed. "I shall add to your statements that she who was born to be a muse, but is forced to be a housewife, always lives with the temptation of suicide. Your role in life is to be a muse to artists and poets, charming and merciful, gentle but ruthless in all things pertaining to Truth, Love and Beauty. You ought to be an inspiring beginning that awakens the best aspirations of the sons of men, distracting them from gluttony, wine and fighting, stupid competition, miserly jealousy and humiliating slavery. Through poets and artists, you, the Muse, must not let the stream of knowledge turn into a dead swamp.

"I am warning you: it is not an easy path for a mortal woman. But it will not be long, for only young women full of strength can stand it."

"And what then? Death?"

"If gods are merciful to you and allow you to die young. But if not, then you shall turn a different feminine face to the world, that of an instructor, a teacher of children, a gardener of those sparks of light in children's souls that can later become torches. Wherever you are and whatever happens to you, remember you are a bearer of the Great Goddess' face. When you lose your dignity, you humiliate all women, both Mothers and Muses. You allow the dark forces of the soul, especially the male soul, to be victorious instead of winning over them yourself. You are a warrior, which is why you must never fall before a man. Do not let the power of Eros do what you see as disgusting, allowing things that humiliate you. Better Anteros than such love."

"You said Anteros, Father?"

"You grew pale. What are you afraid of?"

"We were taught since childhood that unrequited love was the worst misfortune, feared by Aphrodite herself. It dooms a man to intolerable suffering, the world becomes like the Nesses' clothes[13] to him. Anteros, God of unrequited love, invents new misfortunes and torment. And I cannot overcome my childhood fear."

"Now that you are initiated into the knowledge of the Orphics and the three-faced goddess, you shall overcome this fear. Have you seen people who, like our poet, had the gift of subjecting others to their will? There are more of them than you think. They include tyrants, demagogues and strategists. It is great trouble when they serve the forces of evil, causing suffering. One must avoid all contact with such people for they spread around themselves the harmful breath of dark magic, also called black magic. You must know that there are ways to influence people through physical love, through attraction of genders, through beauty, music and dance. Obeying the purposes and knowledge

---

[13] Poisoned clothes of centaur Nesses. Hercules put them on and could not take them off, suffering cruelly as the clothes stuck to his body.

of a black mage, a woman possessing beauty increases her power over men several fold, and a man does the same over women. And woe be upon those who will crawl at their feet, despised and willing to do anything for one word or glance. All this constitutes true Anteros. People and their lives are endlessly varied. But you possess the power not to obey blindly either people, or love, or deceptive words, whether they be they spoken or written. Why then would you be scared of unrequited love? It can only strengthen you on your way, bringing out your hidden powers. That was why I taught you."

"And what about the terrible companions of Anteros, revenge and payback?"

"Why should you follow them? You must not humiliate and torture a man just as you must not humiliate yourself. Keep to the thin line of wise behavior or else you shall fall to the position of the one you humiliated, and both of you shall drown in the mud of lowly life.

"Remember the people who consider themselves to be "chosen". They oppressed others by military force, by hunger or by deprivation of knowledge. Invariably, a sense of guilt grew in their souls, strange, blind and even more terrible because of it. That is why they rush about in search of a deity that could remove their guilt. Not finding such among the male gods, they rush toward the ancient female goddesses. And the others store the guilt within themselves. Becoming even more angry, they become torturers and executors of others, trampling over dignity and beauty of men, dragging them into mud and drowning there themselves. Such people are the most dangerous ones. Once upon a time the Orphics employed nemetors, the secret priests of Zeus Metron, Zeus the Measurer, whose duty was to eliminate such evil people quickly with the aid of poison. But the cult of Zeus the Measurer is no more, nor are his secret priests. And the number of tormentors grows in the Ecumene. Sometimes I feel that the daughter of Night, Nemesis, has fallen asleep, intoxicated by her own wreath of the daffodils which feed forgetfulness."

"Do you know the secret of the poison?"

"No. And even if I did, I wouldn't tell you. Your purpose is different. One cannot overlap different paths. This leads to errors."

"You taught me yourself: the Orphics do not kill people. I would like to know, in case -"

"There are no cases. All things require Understanding and Discovery, two great components of Justice. No matter what you encounter in life, never step onto the dark path, and always do your best to dissuade other people from it. You are sufficiently armed for that. You may go home. I am tired, my daughter. Geliaine!"

Thais fell to her knees before her teacher, filled with gratitude. The Delos philosopher became serene when she kissed his hand.

"If you learned modesty here ... But no, you were born with this gift of fate. I am glad for you, beautiful Thais," the philosopher said, rising from the chair with difficulty.

Desperate longing, the anxious anticipation of a long separation from her beloved mentor, made Thais stall with her departure. She went to the main entrance, but stopped when she remembered her strange and colorful outfit. She couldn't possibly walk down the street in it. Perhaps this clothing was only given to her temporarily. As if in response to her thoughts, a servant boy of the empty temple ran across the courtyard toward her. He bowed and took her into a side room, where she had gone in the beginning. There she found her clothes and sandals.

The boy said, "I shall take you home."

Chapter Six. The Thread of Laconian Fate

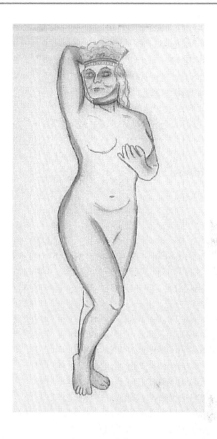

After nine days of cramped and dark temple rooms, her head spun slightly in the open space. The wind of Set was over. The air had become so clear that the giant pyramids could be seen eighty stadiums to the north. The two shallow lakes behind the temple had almost completely dried out. Thais pulled up the hem of her linen stola, walked across the well-trampled clay between the ponds, and headed to the large park, avoiding the noisy street. After so much quiet, she felt uncomfortable in the midst of a large crowd.

As soon as she stepped outside the wall which surrounded the park, and turned toward the pier, she heard the swift footfalls of a soldier behind her. She recognized the sound of Menedem without even looking.

"Where are you coming from, darling?" she gently greeted the Spartan.

"I was loitering around the temple. Today is the tenth day and the end of your captivity. I didn't guess right away that you would go across the ponds. Oh Thais. I missed you so. I didn't even have a chance to say goodbye before you left because the damn sorcerer clouded all of our brains during the symposium. Thank gods for your Theban. She explained everything to me, or else I would have broken that Mitilenian's every bone."

Thais placed her hand on the warrior's huge shoulder. "Don't be jealous."

"Oh no, not at all. I know now who you are, Mistress."

Thais stopped walking, staring at him inquisitively.

"Yes, yes," the Spartan continued. "Here." He took her hand, bowed and kissed the ring with the triangular symbol on her finger.

"You are an Orphic?" Thais exclaimed in surprise. "Have you been initiated too?"

"Oh no. My elder brother is a priest of Rhea. From him I learned mysteries I am unable to comprehend. But they draw me, the way the curtain between life and death does, between love and beauty. And I can feel them, even though I do not understand, because I am but a simple soldier brought up for battles and death. A true Orphic doesn't even kill animals and birds. He doesn't eat meat."

Thais suddenly felt a surge of tenderness toward this mighty man, who was as sensitive and gentle as a boy in the matters of gods and love.

"Come with me," Menedem said. "I want to celebrate your initiation."

"Very well," Thais agreed. She smiled warmly at him. "I am glad you came to meet me."

For his meetings with Thais, Menedem had rented a small adobe house on the western edge of the city, surrounded by scarce palm trees and vegetable gardens. The river valley narrowed here and the house stood not far from the third main alley. Thais was always touched at the sight of Menedem's home, furnished plainly even for a Spartan. She kept forgetting that from the Laconian standpoint, Menedem was still not of age, was not an andros since he was not yet thirty years old. He still obeyed the army discipline, which was far more severe than even the society rules applied to free Spartan women.

Two or three lovely vases and several animal skins were all the decoration the modest soldier could afford. During Thais' absence, a bronze tripod of ancient workmanship had appeared in the house.

Menedem offered Thais to take off her long linostolia, then lifted her up and set her on the tripod, as if she were an oracle priestess or a goddess. The surprised Athenian obeyed, curious as to what would happen next.

The Spartan brought some burning coals from the kitchen and poured them into two incense burners standing to the sides, and the fragrance of precious Arabian gums rose next to Thais in two smoky streams.

Menedem took her hand again and pressed his lips to the ring with the triangle. Bowing his head, he knelt slowly and remained in this position for so long that Thais started feeling awkward, both from his solemnity and from the uncomfortable seat on the tall tripod. She moved carefully, afraid to offend him.

The Spartan spoke. "You are so intelligent and beautiful. I believe you are not a mere mortal. Thank you for the divine joy you bring to me. I cannot express my great happiness, my tongue does not obey me, but even in my sleep I see the gentle smile of Aphrodite. I have nothing to give you except my life. But it is so little, the life of a soldier, destined for death."

"Oh, you are the best for me, my Soter, my savior. I rejoice under the wing of your strength and I love you," Thais leaned toward the Spartan and placed both hands on his curly head. "Get up, please."

Menedem lifted his eyes and Thais sensed the adoration and joy of his pure and courageous soul. Embarrassed but happy, the Athenian tried to be cheerful and push away her worry that came from someplace unknown. She was concerned over the great responsibility of her lover, for whom she had become a goddess and the apple of his eye.

The day passed so quickly for them that Menedem barely managed to get ready for his night duty in stratopedon.

Ignoring her objections, Menedem sat her on his shoulder and ran down to the pier, then hired a boatman there and ordered him to transport her to the north side of the city. Only after that did he run to the camp. He was a tireless runner, and he always managed to make it on time.

A tired Thais sat in the boat, gazing sadly upon the clear cool water. The Nile was particularly clear this time of year. Perhaps the melancholy had been brought on by Menedem's words about their approaching separation. He had been subdued when he'd told Thais about a letter, received by Eositeus from king Agis, in which he was ordering the detachment back to Sparta. The arrival of the Macedonian king, Alexander, to Egypt and his conquering of the country were inevitable. It would be senseless for a handful of Spartans to oppose the one who had beaten the

Persians. Thus, their presence in Egypt was no longer required.

The pharaoh was a servant of priests. He departed for Elephantine and his treasury had already hinted to Eositeus that their payments might soon stop. Darius' envoy hadn't issued any orders either. Presently, the country was in the hands of priests.

"And so you must go with your people?" Thais asked, feeling panic race through her body.

"It is unavoidable. But how can I part with you? A goblet of coneyon[14] would be better."

Thais placed her fingers over the warrior's lips. "Don't say that. Would you like me to come with you? Come back to Hellas?"

"That would be beyond my greatest dreams. But …" The Spartan hesitated.

"What?"

"Had I been going home after the end of war, but now … Don't tell anyone, but I think there will be a war."

"Against the Hellenic union and Alexander?"

"Who else?"

"You, Spartans, are desperately brave and stupidly stubborn. You will end badly. But can't you stay here with me?"

"As who? Salmaakh's stableboy? Or to make flower wreaths?"

"Why so harsh? We'll think about it, we'll find a way. There is still time. Eositeus is not sailing anytime soon, is he?"

"No sooner than Alexander's arrival."

"It is too bad that you cannot join Alexander."

"Ah, you understand. Yes, being a Spartan, of whom he is not fond … You know, he even rejected Sparta's name on a trophy."

"This can be resolved. He is my friend."

---

14 Very strong poison

"Your friend? Yes, of course, I forgot about Ptolemy. But I must be with my men either way, both in glory and in death."

"I understand. This is why I do not think you'll go into service for the Macedonians."

Thais spent the entire trip home trying to come up with something for Menedem, but failed. She felt helpless and sadness overcame her more and more.

As soon as Thais appeared among the Persian apple trees of her little garden, Hesiona ran to her with a joyous squeal, then hugged the Theban like a sister. Clonaria ran over too, regarding the "Daughter of the Snake" jealously and trying to push her away from the mistress.

Without further ado, they made Thais lie down on a rough massage bench. Both girls fussed over her, reproaching her for completely letting herself go.

"We'll have to work all night to get the mistress' body into proper shape," the slave girl said, deftly wielding a pair of bronze tweezers and a sponge which had been soaked in a solution of bryony root for eliminating skin hair and restoring the smoothness.

At the same time, Hesiona was preparing a fragrant liquid using Thais' favorite scent: iris and neuron. Delicately feathered leaves of neuron with their sharp fragrance of slightly bitter freshness were available aplenty here in Egypt. In Hellas they only blossomed for a short time in the month of Elafebolion.

Thais' transformation into a priestess of Aphrodite, fragrant and smooth as a statue, was interrupted by the arrival of a triumphant Egesikhora. She kissed her friend in greeting, but her horses were waiting so she was forced to rush off after promising to come and spend the night.

That night the friends relaxed in the dimly lit bedroom. The flame of lucnoses[15], subdued by the tiles

---

15 Luminaries in the shape of goblets or jugs.

of yellow onyx, lit the room with a soft golden flickering. A nightlight was set near the bed, and Egesikhora thought that Thais' clear profile looked carved out of some dark stone against its backdrop. Thais raised her hand and the sparkling ring attracted the Spartan's attention.

"You started wearing that recently. Tell me, whose gift is it?" Egesikhora asked, examining the carved stone.

"It's not a gift but a sign," Thais objected.

The Spartan snorted mockingly. "We all wore such signs as auletridae. It was convenient. If you turn the tip of the triangle away from you everyone knows you are taken. If you turn the tip toward you, you are free. But the rings were bronze and the stone was blue glass."

"Was the pattern the same as this?" Thais smiled mischievously.

"Yes, the triangle of the great goddess. No, wait. Ours were narrower, sharper. The triangle on your ring has its sides widely spread, like Astarte's. And the background is a circle. Do you understand the meaning of this sign?"

"Not entirely," Thais replied reluctantly, but Egesikhora lifted her head, distracted. Faint sounds could be heard from somewhere in the house, as if someone was composing a sad melody.

"It's Hesiona," the Athenian explained. "She made a siringa[16] from reeds."

"She is an odd one. Why don't you marry her off if you don't intend to teach her as a hetaera?"

"She needs to recover from all the horror, rape and slavery."

"How long is she going to be recovering? It's time."

---

16 A kind of flute

"Different people heal differently. What's the rush? When Hesiona becomes a real woman and falls in love, a new star of beauty will rise. Beware then, gold-haired one."

Egesikhora chuckled in disdain. "Your miserable Theban is going to compete with me, is she?"

"Anything is possible. Just wait till Alexander's army gets here."

Egesikhora's expression suddenly turned serious. "Lie next to me, cheek to cheek, so that no one can hear us."

The Spartan told her friend what she already knew: Eositeus was getting ready to leave Egypt. The Spartan strategist had demanded that Egesikhora come with him. He did not wish to part with her, thought he could not do it.

"What about you?" Thais asked.

Egisikhora shook her head. "I am sick of his jealousy. I don't want to part with you and would rather wait for Nearchus."

"What if Nearchus has long since forgotten you? Then what?"

"Then ..." the Lacedemonian said, then smiled mysteriously. She hopped off the bed and returned with a small basket, woven from the leaves of a date palm.

Wealthy shoppers usually took such baskets to buy cosmetics. Egesikhora sat on the edge of the bed with one leg curled under her (the leg celebrated by the Memphis poets as a "silver-sculpted" one), and pulled out a box made of wood Thais hadn't seen before. Interested, she sat up and touched the smooth, grayish cover with her fingertips.

"This is narthex wood in whose trunk Prometheus brought fire from heaven to the people of earth. Alexander has an entire chest made of narthex. He keeps a copy of the Iliad in it, edited by your friend Aristotle." Egesikhora burst out laughing.

"And who ran away from Athens because of this friend?" Thais replied, flicking an eyebrow at her friend. "But how do you know such details about Alexander?"

The Spartan silently opened the box and pulled out a sheet of papyrus, covered on both sides with Nearchus' small, tidy handwriting.

"Nearchus, the son of Merion, sends wishes of health to Egesikhora and encloses all this." The Spartan poured a handful of precious stones onto the bed, as well as two bottles of sparkly tiger's eye set in gold.

High class hetaerae knew as much about precious stones as would a professional jeweler. Thais pulled one of the lanterns out of the onyx shade and the friends leaned over the gift. There were fiery red pyropes ("flaming eyes"), a huge ruby with a six point star inside, deep blue "royal" beryllium, several bright violet hyacinths, two large pink pearls, a flat pale purple stone with metallic sheen with which the hetaerae were not familiar, and the golden chrysolites of the Eritrean Sea. Nearchus knew his gems well and had made a truly royal gift to his lover, from whom he had been separated for so long.

Egesikhora, flushed with pride, lifted the jewels in her hand, reveling in their sparkle. Thais hugged and kissed her with congratulations.

"Oh, I almost forgot. Forgive me, I lose myself at the sight of the gift."

The Spartan unrolled a piece of red leather and handed Thais a tiny statuette of Anaitis or Anachita, skillfully carved out of a large sapphire. It was approximately the size of a pinky finger. The goddess stood in a lifelike pose, different from the usual solemn, motionless one, with one arm behind her head and the other supporting a heavy spherical breast. The dark blue stone shimmered like silk around her curves.

"Nearchus sent this to you and asked to remember him."

The Athenian picked up the precious knickknack with mixed feelings of irritation and relief. Ptolemy also could have sent something as a sign of remembrance, but considering he hadn't sent anything, she thought he must have forgotten her. Thank Migonitida. If Alexander and his captains showed up here, she wouldn't have to solve a problem of getting rid of a former lover who was now an army leader of a mighty conqueror.

"Are you thinking about Ptolemy?" the Spartan asked. She pressed a warm hand to her friend's cheek, perceptive like all women are.

"No." Thais shook her head, dismissing the subject. "What are you going to do?"

"Wait for Nearchus," Egesikhora replied with certainty.

"What about Eositeus?"

"Let him go to Sparta, to Macedonia, even to Erebus itself."

"Are you not afraid of his jealousy?"

"I am afraid of nothing."

"I know you are timoleaina, as courageous as a lioness, but take my advice. Keep this box at my house."

"Your advice is sound."

At the end of the last Attica spring month, Skyrophorion, the entire land of Egypt became unusually restless. Alexander's mechanics built a huge pier and finally took the invincible Tyre after a seven month siege. Eight thousand defenders of the city were killed, thirty thousand citizens were sold into slavery. Three thousand of them were now building a slope of sand at the walls of Gaza, suffering greatly from a lack of water, an abundance of beatings and the cruel sun. The city decided to resist, despite the lesson of the mighty Tyre. They had been deceived by the assurances of Darius' messengers that the king of Persia was coming with an innumerable army.

Darius didn't come to the walls of Gaza, rather they met with a wall of sand taller than its towers. From this wall the Macedonians struck the defenders as if they were in a valley. The cleverness of the mechanics didn't stop there. Protected by the sand walls, the Macedonians dug under the walls of Gaza, causing them to crumble.

In the last cruel battle, Alexander was badly wounded. Aristander the seer warned the king that he would be in grave danger if he decided to participate in the battle, but Alexander's hot blood kept him from heeding the warning. A boulder from an "apparatus", as they called the war machines for throwing stones, pierced his shield and struck his left shoulder, breaking a rib and a collar bone. As he was carried away from the battlefield, accompanied by the dismayed cries of his army, Alexander smiled and greeted his soldiers by raising his right hand.

All male defenders of Gaza were slaughtered, all women and children were sold into slavery. Alexander ordered his men to destroy all temples. In Tyre he stopped and placed a military siege machine at the main temple of Bel, and left Nearchus' ship in the main square of the city.

The way to Egypt lay open before him, and Alexander was expected in Memphis by the end of summer. In Boedromion, in fact, as soon as he recovered from the wound. Many wealthy people escaped across the sea. Beautiful houses with large gardens in the northern part of Memphis were sold at half price.

The Spartans were getting ready to leave. Two ships of the strategist Eositeus arrived from Naucratis. They waited at the pier, ready to take on a hundred goplits of the guards, the strategist's possessions and Egesikhora's horses.

The Spartan hetaera walked around as if lost, having learned of her friend's decision to return to Hellas. After two sleepless nights, Thais came up with a job for her Spartan in Athens. Thais' house was still intact with all the furnishings. She invited Egesikhora to stay with her. The term of punishment for crippling Aristotle's philosophers had ended in Megateynion of the same year.

The Lacedemonian begged Thais and Menedem not to abandon her in Memphis.

"Why do you want to stay?" the Athenian asked. "Let us sail with Eositeus on the Spartan ships."

"I can't. Your clarity of mind has abandoned you because of your love for Menedem," Egesikhora objected. "Once we are in Sparta, I shall never break free of Eositeus. And he has plans for a big war."

"Again? Haven't your compatriots had enough? I am so sick of their war mongering cruelty. Young Spartans learn how to hunt slaves since a tender age."

"What is so bad about that? They are taught manly toughness in handling the slaves in order to suppress the mere thought of freedom in them."

"A slave owner is a slave himself, even worse than his servants."

Egesikhora shrugged her shoulders. "I have long since gotten used to the Athenian frivolity in such things, but you shall pay for it."

"Sparta will fall sooner, like an elderly lion that becomes food for vile hyenas."

"We are arguing about superficial things, as if we were men," Egesikhora said impatiently. "You are avoiding my request. Why won't you and Menedem stay with me until the Macedonians arrive. They won't harm your lover, I swear."

"I can protect him myself."

"Then do it for me."

"Very well, I'll talk to Menedem."

The Lacedemonian clasped her friend in her arms and covered her dark cheeks with kisses of gratitude.

But disaster fell upon them, unexpectedly as always, akin to a lightning strike. Both friends were walking along the pier, already accustomed to the shouts of admiration of the passing citizens both male and female. They were enjoying the river during the gentle Egyptian late summer evening.

At the height of its water level, the Nile flows faster. Its darkened waters carry fewer boats than during the shallow water period.

Menedem was on duty at the Spartan camp. Instead of him, Hesiona followed Thais, always walking a step behind, hiding her face behind a silk scarf from overly inviting glances. The endless procession of pedestrians moved slowly in both directions as they watched the Memphis celebrities. People here dressed much more modestly than in Athens, and especially more in wealthy cities of Asia Minor and Syrian coast. Further behind the two friends came Eositeus who attracted everyone's attention with his height, which was over four elbows, and three enormous lokhagosi, or detachment captains. The Spartans, wearing battle sashes, capes and helms crowned by tall brushlike crests of horse hair, towered over the crowd like menacing gods. The Egyptian and Persian soldiers were nowhere to be seen.

In the spot where the Nile circled the ancient dam, used for setting a floating bridge, the pier widened into a large square, surrounded by huge trees. Two palm alleys spread in a fork, away from the west side of the square, decorated with two brightly polished obelisks.

A cloud of dust moved down the right alley toward them, coming from a rider in a blue cape of angareyon, Persian horseback mail. A bunch of hair similar to the tip of a lion's tail hung from his spear, meaning that he had been dispatched with a special assignment. The rider halted his horse between the obelisks and searched the crowd of pedestrians. His experienced eyes quickly located that whom he sought. He dismounted and strode across the stream of people, walking in the awkward gait of someone who spent his life in the saddle. He shoved aside the curious and stopped before the hetaerae.

Egesikhora grew so pale that Thais became worried about her and hugged her, pulling her closer in the eternal feminine gesture of protection.

The rider in blue bowed. "I have ridden from your house, Mistress. They told me that I could find you walking along the river. Who could be mistaken, seeing you? You are Egesikhora the Spartan."

The hetaera nodded silently, licking her lips.

The messenger pulled out a packet of thin red leather from behind his belt.

"Nearchus, the Cretan and the fleet leader of the divine Alexander, sends you this letter and requests an immediate answer."

Egesikhora grabbed the small packet, clasping it in her delicate fingers.

Thais came to her aid. "Where can we find you in the evening for reply and reward?"

The messenger named a xenon of the mail station, where he was staying, and Egesikhora waved him away. She did so just in time. Eositeus made an attempt to grab the letter, but Egesikhora evaded him and hid the leather bundle under the sash of her chiton.

"Hey, come here!" the strategist yelled at the departing messenger.

The man in blue turned around and Eositeus grabbed him.

"Tell me, where is the letter from? Who sent you? Tell me, or else you shall be detained and answer to the whistling of a whip."

The messenger flushed and wiped his dusty face with a corner of his cape.

"Captain, you threaten me against tradition and law. The letter came from afar, and from a powerful man. All I know are the words I was to say when I handed in the packet. You would have to ride for many parsangs through tens of mail statmoses (stations), before you find out where the gold-haired one's letter came from."

Eositeus came to his senses, released the messenger and approached Egesikhora. He scowled at her. "Gods are clearing my mind. Your reluctance to leave ... Give me the letter. It is important for my military purposes."

The hetaera lifted her chin higher. "I shall read it myself first. Step aside."

Egesikhora's tone was firm. Eositeus stepped away and the hetaera instantly opened the packet. Thais, who was watching her, saw that the stern wrinkle between her friend's eyebrows disappeared. A light, carefree smile of the former Egesikhora of the Athenian days touched her lips. She whispered something to Hesiona. The girl stepped to the side, bent over, then handed a heavy stone to the Spartan. Before the strategist realized what was happening, Egesikhora wrapped the letter around the stone and tossed it deftly into the river with unfeminine force. The packet vanished in the depths of the river.

"You shall pay for this!" the strategist roared. The Memphis citizens who observed this scene laughed and joked.

Eositeus wanted to grab her hand, but Egesikhora twisted away and vanished in the crowd. The military captain considered it beneath his dignity to pursue a woman, and turned arrogantly toward his camp, accompanied by his associates.

Thais and Hesiona ran and caught up with the flushed Egesikhora. Overjoyed, her eyes shining with excitement, she looked so beautiful that everyone turned around to look at her.

"What was in the letter?" the Athenian asked briskly.

"Nearchus is in Naucratis. He offers to sail to meet him or to wait in Memphis. Alexander is to arrive here even sooner than planned," Egesikhora said, slightly out of breath.

Thais was silent, regarding her friend as if she were a stranger. The sun was setting beyond the cliffs of the Libyan desert, and the soft light of pre-twilight calm clearly outlined Egesikhora's entire figure. While she watched, Thais thought she saw a strange shadow tossing a veil of doom over the Spartan's face. Black circles appeared around her eyes, dark grooves undercut her delicate nostrils and overshadowed the clear lines of her mouth. It was if her friend became instantly strange and distant, aged by dozens of years.

Thais sighed and reached out to touch a strand of the Lacedemonian's golden hair, realizing it was only a play of shadows of the fast Egyptian sunset. Egesikhora laughed, not understanding her friend's mood. But the vague foreboding had darkened Thais' mood.

"You must disappear for a little bit, my friend," Thais said, grabbing her friend's arm. "Just until the Spartan detachment leaves."

"No one will dare, especially now. Not as I am under the protection of the invincible one," Egesikhora objected.

Thais could not agree with her. "Eositeus and his Spartans are people of particular courage. They are not afraid either of death or of fate. If you do not want to sail from Egypt tied up in a ship's hold, I suggest that you think about it. I can find you such a hiding place, one so well hidden that even his spies wouldn't know where to look."

Egesikhora laughed again. "I cannot imagine that the chief strategist, a seasoned soldier, a king's relative, would bother with a woman, a hetaera at such a time. Even if it is a woman as splendid as myself."

"You are mistaken. He wants to own you. It is precisely because you are as beautiful as a goddess and are surrounded by everyone's attention and admiration. To part from you, and especially to give you up to someone else, be it the killer of Argos himself, that is a humiliation worse than death. His death or yours, and I fear it will be yours first. But as soon as you drink the cup of humiliation, he shall reward you with your power over him and your disobedience."

Thais paused. Egesikhora was silent as well, not noticing the passersby or the torches being lit at the pier.

"Let's go to your place," she said, rousing herself. "I must write an answer."

"Which is?"

"I shall wait here. I am afraid of ships. My compatriots might trap me anywhere above Naucratis. I am also afraid to leave the horses behind. Where would I hide them? Especially considering that you agreed to stay here with me for a time," she said, and wrapped her arms around her faithful childhood friend.

The Spartan asked Thais to write a short reply filled with love in her neat handwriting, then sealed it using a signet ring sent by Nearchus. She borrowed two gold darics from her friend to dispatch the messenger to the next station immediately.

The slave gardener hid the letter in his loincloth and ran to the xenon of the mail station, not far from the oldest step pyramid of pharaoh Josser. Egesikhora waited for the slave to return, staying until late at night. Only after having confirmed that the messenger agreed to leave in the morning, did she go home with torches and two strong companions.

It was unlikely that anyone in Memphis would dare touch the lover of the strategist himself, but all nikteridae (bats) looked the same at night.

Having fallen asleep late, Thais slept longer than usual. She was awakened by Clonaria, who burst in screaming, "Mistress! Mistress!"

"What happened?" Thais jumped out of bed.

"We are just back from the market," the slave girl rushed to tell her, "and all anyone can speak of is the murder of the messenger who arrived yesterday from Delta. He was found at dawn near the station gates."

"Go get Hesiona," the Athenian said, interrupting Clonaria.

Hesiona ran in from the garden and was immediately dispatched with the order to bring Egesikhora. Thais ordered them to prepare broad white Egyptian capes and to saddle Salmaakh. Having put on a short chiton for horseback riding, she paced impatiently in front of her terrace, waiting for her friend. Finally, alarmed by the delay, she told Clonaria to run and check on Egesikhora. A distance of a quarter skhen was nothing for the healthy girl. When the slave girl returned, out of breath but alone, Thais realized that her concerns were coming true.

"Chrisocoma and the 'Daughter of the Snake' rode off together on the tetrippa," Clonaria said.

"Where?"

"Nobody knows. Down that road." The slave girl pointed south.

Thais realized Egesikhora must have decided to hide her precious horses in the gardens, near the tombs of the ancient kings by the Blunt Pyramid. The owner of the gardens was a Helenian on his father's side, and one of the most fervent of Egesikhora's admirers.

Thais jumped into the saddle and disappeared in a cloud of dust before the slave girl could say another word. The western cliffs ran close to the river. Having circled them, Thais reined in Salmaakh. Egesikhora's tetrippa appeared from behind the shrubs, approaching slowly. One glance was enough to confirm that something terrible had happened.

Hesiona stood leaning against arbila, the front wall of the carriage, with her head bowed. Her hair was tangled by the wind, her chiton slid off one shoulder. Pressing Salmaakh forward, Thais realized with piercing clarity that the fan of dusty golden strands fluttering in the wind through the cutouts in the right side of the carriage was her friend's hair. Riding closer, she saw Hesiona's bloodstained chiton, the dark stains on the yellow paint and slow terrible drops falling into dust behind the horses.

Hesiona, who was whiter than the walls of Athens, wrapped the reins around the ledge in the arbila, supporting the top harness pole. The girl was not guiding the horses, but rather holding them back. Salmaakh backed away from the carriage, sensing blood and death. Thais jumped off her mare, tossed the reins to the side and caught up with the carriage at a run. Egesikhora leaned on the arbila sideways, her lifeless head hanging low under the burden of heavy hair. Stepping over the Spartan's legs, Thais put her arms around the semiconscious Hesiona, took the reins away from her and stopped the tetrippa.

Hesiona came to her senses. Opening her mouth with difficulty, she whispered, "We can't. There are murderers behind."

Thais didn't answer, but leaned over her beloved friend. She lifted her head and saw the gray lips and the whites of her eyes visible through half-closed lids. A wide wound below her left collarbone, inflicted from above with a military dart, had been deadly. Thais turned the still warm and flexible body of her friend to the side and settled it at the bottom of the carriage.

For a moment she imagined that Egesikhora, alive and well, had simply curled up and fallen asleep along the way, but reality brought Thais back to the moment. A sob shook the Athenian's entire body. Trying to overcome her grief, Thais busied herself with Hesiona. There was a long wound along the girl's right side from yet another strike. The killer had missed and only sliced through the skin and the surface muscles; however, blood still flowed in a wide band over her hip. Thais used her head wrap to bind the wound, then started the horses, whistling to Salmaakh, who trotted nearby.

She reached a small clear creek, still not saying a word to Hesiona. After giving the girl some water to drink and washing her face and blood-covered hands, Thais froze in thought. Hesiona, kept quiet. She had tried to say something but the hetaera's expression frightened her into silence. It was distorted by grief and desperation, and turned increasingly menacing, yet was strangely filled with light at the same time.

Suddenly Thais dashed toward the carriage and examined it, fixing the crooked krinon, a ring on the harness pole. Hesiona followed her, but Thais shook her head and silently pointed at Salmaakh. Hesiona came out of her bewildered state and hopped into saddle with unexpected ease. As she sorted out the reins, Thais observed the Theban and felt confident the girl could stay in the saddle.

Suspicious figures in white Egyptian capes trotted up the straight portion of the road behind them. Thais smiled ominously, then emitted a piercing screech that sent the horses dashing forward like mad. The startled Salmaakh leaped sideways, almost tossing Hesiona off the saddle, but the Theban spread out on the horse's back, clutching at her mane. Thais rushed forward headlong, driving the four horses as her friend had taught her. She have never before done that, not even with Egesikhora by her side.

Egesikhora, the gold-haired one, the silver-legged one, she of the beautiful shoulders ... her inseparable friend, the confidant of all secrets, the companion of all travels ... Thais shook with sobs. But the thought of the murderer and revenge, anger and rage overcame all other feelings. She flew forward like an Erinia herself, focused on nothing but reaching her goal.

She hadn't had enough time to learn from Egesikhora the musical work of the fingers required to coordinate all four horses, but remembered that reins of the pole pair were held between the thumbs and the index fingers of the right and left hands, whereas the middle and ring fingers held the reins woven through the harness rings at the withers of the outrunners. The turns of tetrippa at her hands were awkward, so Thais rode in a straight line as much as she could, barely avoiding obstacles.

Thais' urge transferred to Hesiona, who rode Salmaakh next to the carriage. The mare caught up with the carriage, rode ahead, then lagged behind when the road became straight and even, like a stadium field.

Whenever she caught up with Thais, Hesiona tried telling her what had happened. Thais didn't need any explanations. What had happened was the one thing she had been most afraid of, and she rushed at full speed to the one she knew to be guilty of Egesikhora's death.

From Hesiona's halting, unconnected exclamations Thais understood that her friend was trapped on the way to the gardens, which were three skhens away from the center of Memphis. Egesikhora had asked Hesiona to accompany her and help handle the horses, in case her friend wasn't home. Thais realized that Egesikhora must have sensed the approaching danger and didn't want to be alone.

After covering more than two skhens, they reached a small grove, its trees leaning over the road. Two men with spears blocked their way. Egesikhora rode straight at them. The men jumped to the side, but someone hiding in the branches of a large tree threw a spear at Egesikhora. She collapsed instantly, dead on the spot.

Hesiona had no clear memory of what happened next. She could think of only one thing: to take

Egesikhora to the city, to the mistress. She must have been forced to stop the running foursome and turn around on the narrow road when the murderers appeared again. That was when someone had thrown a knife and wounded her.

She rode away despite her bleeding wound. Having left her pursuers far behind, she slowed the horses and wrapped the reins around the arbila ledge in order to pull the spear out of Egesikhora's body. With great effort she managed to yank the weapon out before she felt faint.

That was when Thais had found her. She claimed the gods themselves must have brought the mistress there, otherwise the assassins would have caught up with the carriage.

They rode through the crowded streets at a mad gallop, accompanied by the frightened screams and threats of the scattering pedestrians and porters. The foursome flew up to the gates of stratopedon like a storm.

The soldier on guard, sleepy from the heat, didn't move initially, having recognized Egesikhora's foursome. Then he noticed that something was wrong and reluctantly tipped his spear, blocking their way. Thais didn't even bother slowing down the enraged horses. The shield flew to the side with a thud, the spear crunched under the wheels. The Spartan was tossed toward a pillar. He screamed, raising the alarm.

The carriage barreled through the wide yard for military exercises, heading toward a tent, which was surrounded by a grated barrier. This is where strategist Eositeus usually sat. His house was located further back, under the tent. Attracted by the shouts, Eositeus ran out from under the tent. Thais wasn't strong enough to stop the tetrippa, so she made it swerve and hooked an axle through the grate. Pieces of dry wood flew everywhere as the carriage destroyed the fence. Having run the tetrippa into a pillar, the horses were stopped. They reared up, swinging their front hooves and tossing their heads.

Worried captains ran in from everywhere. A group of goplits, the soldiers in metal armor, rushed out of the barracks and lined up. Hesiona snuck through the gates, following the carriage, and rode up to Thais' aid.

The Athenian jumped off the carriage, landing at the shocked strategist's feet.

"Murderer! Miserable coward!" she shouted, straightening as tall as she could. She stood in front of the giant, pointing her finger at him. "Go, look at your handiwork," Thais snarled, then pointed at the carriage.

After hitting the pillar, Egesikhora's body had rolled back and slid toward the carriage step. With her head resting over the mass of golden hair and her arms spread wide, the Spartan appeared asleep after a long trip, albeit in an awkward pose. Her life path had turned out to be short, only twenty-five years, so her incredible beauty hadn't been able to delight people for long.

"How dare you accuse me, the descendant of Spartan kings, the famous warrior?"

"Have you heard this hyena's deceitful words?" Thais turned to the shocked soldiers who had gathered near the broken grate. She let out a disdainful laugh. "The assassins he sent have already been caught and admitted everything."

Thais spoke with such unshakable conviction that Eositeus turned gray with anger.

"Be quiet, you vile whore!" he roared, covering Thais' mouth with his huge hand.

Hetaera bit his fingers, and the strategist screamed in pain, yanking away his hand.

"The gold-haired one didn't want to be with him anymore, and you were leaving Egypt," Thais explained hurriedly. "So he bribed three ..."

The Athenian barely managed to dodge an enormous fist. Then Hesiona, half-naked, jumped over Eositeus' shoulders with a scream.

"I am a witness!" she screamed, clawing at his eyes.

The strategist pulled her off as if she were a cat, tossing her into a corner. He bore down upon Thais, pulling out a broad Kilian knife. Thais realized in that moment that she was about to be killed. Feeling no fear, she stood before the giant, looking him straight in the eye.

At the last moment Thais was defended by Menedem, who appeared out of nowhere.

Eositeus roared at him. "Away with you, cub, slave of a slut. Hey, someone grab the damn woman!"

None of the soldiers moved, despite the famous Spartan discipline. Everyone loved Egesikhora and Thais, and the accusation sounded too much like truth.

Eositeus realized hesitation would mean his downfall. Pushing Menedem aside, he grabbed Thais by her chiton and pulled her toward him, tearing the fabric. That was when Menedem struck him so hard in the chest that the strategist flew off by several steps and fell, hitting his head on the wall. When Eositeus jumped up, there was neither fear nor anger in his face, just determination. He was a skillful fighter, and deceived the unarmed young warrior with a side swipe of a knife. Then he turned suddenly, leaned over a bent knee and dealt a terrible blow into Menedem's liver from underneath.

As if in a terrible dream, Thais saw the powerful muscles of her faithful athlete sag. As if he broke in half. Clasping his hands over the wound, Menedem fell to his knees, dark blood rushing out of his mouth. Eositeus leaned forward, trying to free the deeply set weapon, and at that moment, Menedem gathered the last of his strength and struck Eositeus over the top of the head with the edges of both hands. There was enough power left in the dying athlete to make the strategist's neck crunch, causing him to fall at Thais' feet with his arm reaching out, as for one last strike, still clutching the bloody knife.

Thais leaned over Menedem and the warrior managed to smile at her. Every true Helenian died with a smile, which always struck foreigners. Menedem's lips moved, but Thais could not hear him. Light went out for her and she fainted over Menedem's broad chest.

The Spartan captains silently lifted Thais, leaving her in the care of Hesiona. Menedem was dead, and Eositeus hummed dully, turning his head, unable to move his paralyzed arms and legs.

The strategist's second in command, a Spartan of a noble family, approached Eositeus. He pulled out a sword and showed it to Eositeus. According to the sacred tradition, Laconians always finished off their deadly wounded with their consent, if they were conscious. The strategist asked for death with his eyes, and in a moment he was no more.

Hesiona managed to wake up her mistress. She begged her to wait till the strategist's second provided a cart. The hetaera pushed the Theban away and jumped up.

"We must go. Bring Salmaakh," she replied, ignoring Hesiona's frightened gaze. "I must bury Egesikhora and Menedem, like ancient heroes of Hellas. And I must do it immediately, while they are still beautiful." Thais looked around, then whispered, "Where is Archimachus, the strategist's second?"

Hesiona managed to delay her mistress just long enough that she could brush out her hair a little bit and pin up her chiton.

Thais knew Archimachus well. She sought him out in the crowd of excited captains, seeking the stern, elderly warrior, and arranged the burial with him. Then she went back to the city with two junior officers, having sent Hesiona to Egesikhora's house with a covered cart. Inside it, Egesikhora's and Menedem's bodies had been placed on a pile of capes. Archimachus provided an entire detachment, and a lumber merchant sent thirty slaves with sixty carts of fragrant cedar logs. Thais paid for the logs as well as for five trunks of fragrant Arabian trees with all of her remaining money, half of her jewelry and her bed of iron wood with ivory.

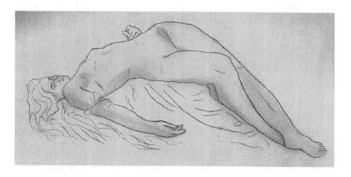

When the Athenian's two most beloved people lay dressed in holiday garments, united in death on a giant pyre, decomposition hadn't yet touched them. Their heads pointed north, and the golden red horses, killed, like in ancient times, to accompany Egesikhora on her way across the asphodel fields of Hades, lay on the left. Their manes and bright hides matched the Spartan hetaera's long braids, flowing almost to her bare feet. The white pole horses were laid out on the right side, and the carriage was set at their feet.

The pyre towered on the ledge under the wall of the western cliff, almost exactly across from Egesikhora's house. Thais climbed up to the corner of the pyre at the height of five elbows, and paused in her farewell grief, gazing for the last time at the beautiful faces of the two people most precious to her, taken away too soon.

Menedem's comrades stood around in full armor, silent and glum, their spears tipped forward. Only an hour prior they had buried their strategist behind the wall of a small Helenian cemetery on the eastern bank of the Nile. Slaves of both hetaerae wept, but did not scream, as was appropriate in Hellas. Two servants who started wailing after the Egyptian fashion were quickly asked to leave. Only the sharp screams of the wooden burial gingras (flutes) violated the heavy silence.

A priest prepared to carry out the last pouring, and quietly prayed to the master of the underground world. A huge crowd of Memphis citizens stood respectfully at a distance, the admirers of the gold-haired horse tamer as well as simple onlookers.

Egesikhora's and Menedem's faces seemed calm and beautiful. The Spartan hetaera's slightly lifted eyebrows gave her face an expression of sweet puzzlement, unusual for her. Menedem smiled with the same weak smile he'd sent Thais with his last breath.

Thais had no time to realize the depth of her loss. At the present she felt only the departing beauty of her loved ones, lying on a common burial pyre, akin to the ancient heroes of Hellas.

Thais looked around. The rows of Spartans still stood motionless, the soldiers regarded the dead. The Athenian jumped off the pyre and someone handed her a burning torch, which she raised high above her head. Every second soldier handed his spear to a friend, then picked up resin-covered sticks and lit them in the braziers which smoked at four corners of the pyre.

Thais circled the pyre until she stood at the north end, then shoved the torch under a pile of thin cedar shavings. The flame, almost invisible in the sunlight, breathed hotly and crawled to the top edge of the pyre. Thin blue smoke rose into the sky as the Laconian soldiers set fire to the entire pyre. The manes and tails of the horses crackled, and one could smell the sharp scent of burning hair. Thais glanced at the dead for the last time through the dancing flames. She imagined Menedem moved his hand in farewell, and the Athenian turned away. Lowering a light Egyptian scarf over her face, Thais went home with Hesiona, never looking back.

The next day, after the enormous fire had cooled, the Spartans would gather Egesikhora's and Menedem's ashes, mix them with the ashes of the horses, and scatter them in the middle of the Nile. From there they would flow to the Inner Sea, on whose shores they had both grown up. A day later the Spartans themselves would sail down the river to Naucratis, and from there the route would take them back to Lacedemonia.

The Spartans insisted that Thais leave with them, but the hetaera refused. She could not bear to leave Memphis right away. It no longer made sense to leave Hellas. Troubling gossip from Athens spoke of the riots caused by Demosthenes' speeches, and the entire Hellenic world, excited by the incredible victories of the Macedonian king, seemed ready to move east, into the lands considered forbidden until then.

Chapter Seven. Hesiona's Awakening

Thais spent five days locked away indoors. She lay face down in the gloom of her bedroom and allowed no one to see her but Hesiona, who tried to convince her mistress to eat something. Thais' strong feelings of friendship toward the Theban had strengthened gradually, despite Hesiona's persistent attempts to keep to the role of a servant. Now, during these bitter days, these feelings increased and developed into true attachment. It was hard not to love the courageous, pure and beautiful daughter of Boeotia.

On the sixth evening Thais finally left her home to go to the Neit temple. Much to her disappointment, she discovered that the Delos philosopher and his student the poet had left for Hellas before the last full moon. The Spartans were gone, too. Memphis, excited by the triple murder for a time, had already forgotten it all.

New events related to Alexander's approach occupied Helenians and Egyptians alike.

Thais hired a horse for Hesiona, and every day after that the two of them took long rides together. Thais was training Salmaakh, and Hesiona marveled. She had never thought such stunts were possible or that such a complete understanding could be possible between a rider and a horse.

Thais discovered she liked to descend down the impossibly steep, sandy slopes of the Nile shores. Salmaakh would slide with her hind legs bent while her rider leaned back, the back of Thais' head touching the horse's croup, her knees closed over the high withers. It seemed as if the horse would flip over at any moment and go crashing down, breaking her rider's bones.

Going along with Hesiona's pleas for safety, Thais found a smooth, comfortable clearing and used it for dancing. Hesiona secured her own horse's reins around a rock, then stood at the edge of the clearing, singing a flowing Thessalian melody, accompanying her voice with a small tambourine. Salmaakh was stubborn at first, until a few days later, when she finally figured out what was required of her. All thoroughbred horses have an innate sense of rhythm, the result of millions of years of keeping a proper pace. No horse can trot for any length of time without a clear sense of rhythm. Hoofbeats of a good runner are expected to be akin to the measured drops of water in a clepsydra, a water clock. A good, well-defined rhythm is required for human runners as well. It is necessary whenever a living creature has to sustain longterm strain and demonstrate endurance.

Soon enough, Salmaakh tapped away to Hesiona's tambourine like a real dancer, which was no great surprise. After all, she was being educated by the "fourth Kharita" of Hellas herself. According to legend, the ancient dance of a woman on a horse, hippoginnes, was created by the Amazons. The legendary women of Thermodont performed in the valley of Temiskira[17] at the Paphlagonian coast of the Black Sea. It always happened on a full moon, under its bright light, during the days of ellotias, celebrations in honor of Artemis. Presently, hippoginnes was nearly gone, performed only rarely by the brave Thessalian women, who were professional horse acrobats and performed it in Attica or in Sparta when invited by the wealthy feast hosts.

Through doing these exercises, Thais unsuccessfully tried to find oblivion and fill the emptiness in her life, which not only remained but seemed to grow bigger each day. Helenians had no faith in the trouble-free life after death that filled meager lives of people of other faiths, who expected rewards and meetings with the loved ones on the other side of death. The dignity with which sons and daughters of Hellas met their end was founded on the feeling of a fully drunk cup of one's own life, the passionate love of land and sea, body and passion, beauty and intelligence.

The Spartans' incredible courage and physical perfection, the Cretan's amazingly sophisticated connection with the sea, the Athenian's inventiveness, initiative and eternal thirst to discover new things became legendary in all of Ecumene.

But Thais no longer possessed either joy or fulfillment. Her formerly lively spirit had faded, giving way to the sad thoughts of her future path. Hesiona too started thinking of how to heal her mistress' and friend's heart-deep wound. She even regretted the departure of Thais' mysterious teacher, of whom she used to be so jealous. The Delos philosopher would have done something to speed up the mistress'

---

17 Presently the Turkish coast of the Black Sea in the vicinity of Sinop.

recovery after having been wounded so badly by the unseen weapon of fate and gods.

But Hesiona, with her feminine intuition, sensed the inevitability of Thais' rebirth. There was too much strength in that young body, and too much active interest toward everything in the world, inherited from her Athenian ancestors.

Waters of the great river receded, and the Nile became slow and transparent as it would be in winter. Thais shared her time between Salmaakh and a light narrow boat, boating with Clonaria and "the Daughter of the Snake". She did not respond to any of her increasingly persistent admirers. Hesiona still rejected all things male, and when Clonaria fell in love with a middle-aged Greek merchant who offered to buy her from Thais, the slave girl herself refused out of fear of leaving Thais' home, where she felt safe and was used to gentle treatment.

Thais invited the merchant to come over and stated that she would release Clonaria without a payment, but only under the condition of legal marriage. The merchant promised to think about it. He was a widower, but there was not epigamy between his native Lydia and Rhodes, where Clonaria was from. However, there was nothing to prevent an arrangement of a special agreement for Clonaria's "taking", and Thais decided to insist.

Thais had to let go of her house. Its owner wanted to raise the already unaffordable rent. Only the uncertain situation in Egypt on the eve of Alexander's arrival kept the landlord from trading Thais for wealthier tenants.

Hesiona watched anxiously as the mistress' jewels disappeared from the large box one after another. Even during her wealthiest times Thais had lived modestly compared to the unguarded spending of other famous hetaerae.

Egesikhora's death had taken half of her heart and Menedem's demise had deprived her of love and safe haven. Thais lost sight of her path, like a horse that stumbled at full gallop, and now twirled in a circle of slow days, having lost all aspirations. She saw no sense to living in Egypt and had no idea where to go in order to fill the emptiness in her soul. Only the horse races and dangerous feats with Salmaakh managed to bring back the old Thais, the flushed cheeks and shining eyes that were mischievous and serious at the same time, the combination of inspired dignity and girlish liveliness which gave Thais irresistible allure.

During the last three days of the month, the days of the dead, also known as the "heavy days" of Puanepsion, Thais felt particularly lost. The calm and trouble-free life, her confident expectation of better and more beautiful things, the divine certainty of her own beauty, those things were gone, never to return. Along with those went the feeling of health and the hope for a fortunate future that only happens at the height of one's youth. Thais turned twenty-three years old, full prime for a Helenian woman, yet she felt her beauty was leaving along with her youth. She believed she was losing her irresistible charms and had no desire to try them on anyone again. This absence of desires frightened Thais. It was like a ghost of the future aging most of all. If only the scholar from Delos were here. She would have found herself sooner and revived, sought a new life. How much she needed her teacher-friend.

Thais left the house in Hesiona's care and went back into the seclusion of the Neit temple. The priests accepted her benevolently, probably informed in advance by the Delos philosopher.

The hetaera settled in a library-like room in the top story of the pylon and sought out Plato's Gorgius among the Greek books. She remembered the ironic chuckle of the Delos teacher in response to her dismissive attitude toward Plato. She felt that she may have made a mistake and decided right away to reread the works of the great philosopher. Indeed, in his dialogs Thais discovered his deep concern about the people of Athens, which she had not understood before. She read of his attempts to elevate the Helenians of Attica so that each lived in harmony with the spirit of the city of the Maid. She sensed the wise man's nostalgia corresponded to her own present mood. He pined for the past of Athens, which had become an empty vessel of former splendor after the war with Sparta.

Where in the past she saw only boring admonitions, she now discovered his firm belief that high moral code and people's spiritual attitude toward each other could create a true arche, or state. The task of people's improvement was the most important one, in Plato's opinion. The rulers who plunged Helenians into lawlessness and taught their people nothing but anger and betrayal never achieved anything except for shame and infamy.

It would be interesting to know what Alexander was trying to achieve. Where was he going to direct his mighty army? Where was he going to apply his great wisdom and the constant benevolence of the gods? Then again, why would Thais bother with such things? Where was she to go to rediscover her own love of adventure and travel?

It was time to leave Memphis if only to separate herself from the loss of Egesikhora and Menedem. Over the last few days she had been persistently approached by one Stemlos, the only son of one of the wealthiest merchants in Memphis. He had only just come out of the age of epheb[18] and probably was no older than Thais herself. He felt as if a boy before a goddess. But, she recalled, the mighty Menedem had

---

18 A teenage boy or very young man

often been like a boy as well. Kind, trusting, fearless. Should she accept Stemlos' offer? Oh, no. She didn't want anyone.

While reading Plato's seventh letter, Thais sensed that the wise man revered the ancient and sacred, as he called it, religion of the Orphics. Still she retained some of her old dislike toward Plato's teachings. Perhaps it was because he preached suppressing the physical, natural essence in a person. She was put off by his ancient mindset and the feelings of a devout slave owner, since she had developed a broader outlook upon people and the world in general. Thais stayed at the temple for several days, thinking and reading, until she became overwhelmed and gave up trying to guess her own future. She felt some relief at that decision, and some of her former lively confidence regarding health and strength returned.

That was when she heard a servant's call, announcing that "a beautiful girl in a pink chiton was asking Thais to come to the gates of the inner courtyard."

"The beautiful girl" turned out to be Hesiona. She wore a bright garment, not typical for the stern Theban. Hesiona had changed significantly and grown lovelier since she had come to Thais' household from the slave market.

Hesiona noticed her mistress' amazement and blushed, then told her, "All citizens of Memphis are ordered to dress in their best garb."

"What? Why? Alexander?"

"Yes."

Thais clapped her hands, summoning the servant boy. "Tell the honorable priests that I thank them for their hospitality, but I must go. I shall be back soon."

Thais had no idea how mistaken she was. She would once again cross the threshold of the Neit temple nine years later – as the queen of Egypt.

It had been a long time since Memphis streets were so filled with life. Thais and Hesiona slowly made their way home through the excited throngs. The normally restrained and polite Egyptians, the one aspect in which they resembled Spartans, could not be recognized. They did not give way to women and elders, but instead pushed each other around like Athenians at Agora.

Thais was not recognized and was even insulted several times because of her worn and dull colored dress. She did not respond, but chose to bow her head and cover her face with a scarf.

The people of Memphis greeted Alexander with delight and wanted to hold a general celebration in his honor. The great conqueror, however, vanished as suddenly as he arrived, as soon as he received the admission of surrender from the envoy and the priests, who announced the pharaoh's resignation.

Thais did not wish to see Alexander, and fate accommodated her. Late in the evening, two days after Thais returned from the temple, she received a visit from Nearchus. The Athenian recognized the seafarer immediately, even though he had changed noticeably and acquired sharp and commanding tones in his speech. His beard stuck out arrogantly, against the fashion of the rest of Alexander's captains. The Cretan did not seem to be surprised to see his old friend. When he stepped toward Thais, she ran out to greet him. He took her hand firmly and spoke a single word, "Egesikhora?"

The hetaera's lips trembled, and her eyes filled with tears. She hung her head, holding her breath. They stood before each other silently. Nearchus' hands squeezed the soft gold bracelets around her wrists. Finally Thais caught herself and called Hesiona.

"Sit. Have some wine."

Nearchus obediently lowered himself into a heavy carved armchair, moving with a slowness that was unusual for him. Without even noticing, he poured himself some undiluted wine.

Hesiona came in shyly with her gaze lowered, carrying Egesikhora's jewelry box, which had ended up staying at Thais' house as Thais had originally suggested.

The Cretan flinched at the sight of his gift. Thais grabbed Hesiona, who was about to leave, and pushed her toward Nearchus.

"She is the witness of Egesikhora's last hour. Talk!"

Hesiona burst into tears and knelt on the carpet, then quickly took hold of herself and related to Nearchus what he wanted to know, speaking in a relatively coherent narrative.

Several tears rolled from under the young fleet leader's lids. The Cretan remained motionless, only his hand shook over the armrest and his thin fingers squeezed the neck of a carved lion. Following a sudden urge, Hesiona rose from the carpet and pressed her cheek to his hand. Nearchus didn't take it away but lifted his other hand and started patting the Theban's hair, as he listened to Thais adding details to her story.

"And my Menedem went to accompany Egesikhora into the dungeons of Hades," Thais said between sobs.

"And the damn Eositeus is there, too. Oh, Spartans!" Nearchus said with dull hatred and threat as he rose.

"Egesikhora was a Lacedemonian, too," Thais objected quietly, and the Cretan had no answer to that.

"Tomorrow at dawn I shall make a sacrifice in her memory. I invite you," Nearchus said after a pause, then turned to Hesiona, "and you. I shall send a carriage or a palanquin."

"Very well," Thais answered for them both. "But you are forgetting this." She held out Egesikhora's jewelry box.

Nearchus stepped back, pushing away the small box. "No. I am giving it to the one who took Egesikhora away from the assassins. To your friend."

Hesiona was so shocked and anxious that she turned crimson. "What is the matter with you, navarchus[19]? How can you give such expensive things to a penniless girl? After all, I am not a slave only by the mistress' mercy. I cannot take this."

"Take it. As a memory of the terrible hours you went through with my golden beloved. And let me judge your virtues for myself."

Hesiona glanced at Thais with hesitation. The hetaera raised her eyebrows, signaling that she had to take it. The Theban made a low bow as she accepted the box under the Cretan's gloomy gaze.

Nearchus stopped at the threshold. "I have word from Ptolemy," he said to Thais. "He was looking for you on the first day, but he had to sail with Alexander toward the sea. He hasn't forgotten you. If you want to see him, Alexander and Hephaestion, then come sail with me. I am waiting for a messenger from the Harbor of Heroes where I must join Alexander. Our divine leader and friend wishes to found a new city, possibly the future capital of his kingdom. There is a suitable spot where a Cretan port used to be a thousand years ago."

"Where is that?" Thais inquired.

"On the shore. You would have to sail to Naucratis, then further to Canopus, then along the seashore to the west. You know the place from Homer. It is a dwelling of the old man of the sea Proteus."

"There's an island that lies near Egypt in turbulent surf. The people who live there call their settlement Pharos," Thais instantly remembered and recited.

---

19 Akin do an admiral of the fleet, which was essentially Nearchus' role in Alexander's army.

"Yes, Pharos. Alexander is particularly fond of this spot. You know how much he loves Homer. Will you come?"

Thais flushed, feeling embarrassed. "How big is your ship?"

Nearchus chuckled for the first time of the entire evening. "My biggest ship stands in Tyre, in the square before the main temple. As the sign of victory. Just as Deiad's siege machine was set in the temple in Gaza. Deiad is, by the way, Alexander's chief mechanic." Thais threw up her hands with delight and Nearchus frowned. "Why do you need to know the size of my ship?" the Cretan asked. "I'll give you a separate ship, or two, or three. As many as you want."

This was the first time the Athenian truly felt the power of the young Macedonian king and his equally young associates.

"Do you agree to sail to Pharos? But why do you need a big ship? You have less stuff here than you had in Athens," Nearchus said, then glanced around the less than luxurious furnishings of Thais' home.

"I need to take my horse with me," Thais replied shyly. "I can't part with her for a long time."

"I understand. Is that all? What else?"

"Also my stableman and two women in addition to myself."

Nearch said proudly, "You shall have an entire ship with an experienced crew at your disposal. I expect my messenger in two days. Then we'll sail to Eshmun and Small Hermopolis, past Naucratis. You have been there, haven't you?"

Thais recalled the dull plains with their numerous salt lakes, sand dunes and immeasurable thickets of reeds, the entire Delta barrier that separated Egypt from the glorious blue sea.

Mistaking the Athenian's silence for hesitation, Nearchus said, "Ptolemy told me to give you as many darics as you want. I'll send the money tomorrow."

Thais shook her head thoughtfully.

"No, don't. I haven't seen Ptolemy yet. And he hasn't seen me."

Nearchus chuckled. "You need not doubt. Ptolemy shall be at your knees the moment he sees you."

"I doubt myself. But I shall borrow three hundred darics from you."

"Certainly. Take it. I brought a lot of money."

As soon as the clanging of the swords and armor died in the distance, Hesiona dashed toward Thais and slid to the floor, hugging her knees.

"Mistress, if you love me, please take this royal gift from me," she pointed at Egesikhora's jewelry box.

"I do love you, Daughter of the Snake," Thais replied gently. "But I cannot take what was given to you. By the will of fate and gods it belongs to you."

"I have no place to keep jewelry."

"Then hide them in my room. By the way, I think it is time for you to get your own room. Would you like to have the small bedroom?"

"Oh mistress, I want to sleep on the rug at your bed."

"I shall strike you every time you call me that," Thais decided, then planted a firm smack on Hesiona's behind. "It is not proper for us to sleep in the same room. I feel you shall wake up soon."

The sad ritual of a memorial sacrifice, accompanied by mournful Greek songs, was brief. Everyone left, even Thais. Only Nearchus remained, standing at the place of Egesikhora's burial pyre for a long time.

The Cretan showed up at Thais' house two days later. "Alexander's messenger is here," Nearchus informed her right away. "Apparently, there is no need to rush to Pharos. Foundations of Alexandria have been laid already, and the great strategist himself, along with Ptolemy, Hephaestion and other associates is headed for the Libyan desert, toward the oasis where the famous oracle and oak of Ammon are located."

"Is that far?"

"More than three thousand stadiums across the desert."

"And three thousand back? That will take a whole month."

"Alexander will take less than that."

"Then why should be sail to Pharos?"

"You don't have to. Alexander ordered me to look over the spot for a harbor. I'll go. For a short while."

"Would you take me with you? On your ship? Without the horse, just me and Hesiona?"

"Certainly. But why?"

"I want to see Pharos. I want a chance to see the sea, and not Ptolemy. The horse will stay here with my slave girl."

Clonaria told her merchant about the imminent departure and he hurried to "take" her into his house and sign the marriage contract. The merchant had enough room in his household for Salmaakh as well.

The swift ship of the fleet leader carried Thais and Hesiona down the western arm of the Nile. Nearchus sailed forth with warlike speed, not dallying anywhere, and stopping only to get provisions. Thais spent most of the trip on deck, sitting under the stern tent next to Nearchus. She clutched around herself a blue cape of fine wool which Nearchus had initially intended for Egesikhora. Hesiona sat nearby in her favorite pose on three layers of carpets, her legs curled up. It was a kind of luxury that was unheard of even in Athens at the time. In Egypt it was only available to the noblemen and the highest-ranking priests. Three slaves, two tall Mizian men and a slender, mean-tempered Finikian girl, waited off to the side, ready to carry out any order.

Nearchus told them about the adventures during Alexander's campaign. Being more of an explorer and seafarer at heart than a military man, he remembered more about the places along the Ionian and Finikian coasts than about the battles. There were mountains and harbors which closely resembled Crete and Hellas, but were more spacious and less populated, with vast, untouched pine and cedar woods, light and pure, cleansed by the mountain winds. The hills below were akin to the gardens of gods, with chestnuts, mighty walnuts and pomegranate trees, and groves of sakuras, with their round crowns bubbling up like green clouds. Even lower, right near the coast, were thickets of almonds, hazelnut bushes as big as houses, fragrant myrtle and laurel, pistachios and carob trees with black pods, as sweet as dates.

All this wealth of food, barely touched by men even in close proximity of the cities, allowed people to live in spacious solitude. Had it not been for the constant pirate attacks, life there would have been much easier than on the shores of the native Peloponnese and Crete. But the cities demanded more and more new slaves for construction and taking care of the households, and the Asian shores became deserted, emptied by the "living tool" hunters.

Nearchus recalled the harbors surrounded by cliffs of white lime, saying they were like marble goblets filled with blue, crystal clear water. Deep gulfs among red mountains hid mysterious black underwater rocks, covered with huge sea sponges and blood red corals.

The shores, overgrown with thyme, lavender and myrrh, emitted a sharp fragrance during the hot, calm days, diluted only by the fresh scent of the sea. Further to the south, in Cilicia, the narrow mountain valleys, shaded by the enormous sakuras, were saturated by the poisonous fumes of oleanders and magnolias. Woe befell those who lingered near the bubbling rivers at the bottoms of those valleys. Cypresses sixty elbows tall, a height unheard of in Hellas, framed the approach to the sea like burial columns.

Entire islands of silvery gray olive foliage spread around cities and large villages.

Finikian shores, which were drier and had poorer soil, had many oaks and shrubs, but its mountains were home to the same titans as in Cilicia and Caria, the cedars and firs.

Nearchus told them about the cities. Some of them had opened their gates to the victorious Macedonians, welcoming them gladly. Others fought desperately, and for that they had been pillaged and all their men murdered. Those others had included Millet, Galicarnass, Tyre and especially Gaza.

Each time he spoke of the conquered cities and battles, Nearchus mentioned Alexander. The friend of his childhood games and youthful adventures, the exiled prince in the eyes of his closest friends, not to mention the cream of Macedonian cavalry from the noble families to his devoted getaerosi (comrades), had grown from an inexperienced soldier into a divine army leader. Alexander accomplished things that no Helenian could even dream of, not even his father Philip, who had long since considered a war against Persia.

Against the advice of men experienced in politics, Alexander rejected his father's underhanded tricks. He always acted straightforwardly, kept his word, and fulfilled his promises to the letter. His ability to make lightning fast decisions surpassed even that of Themistocles. He never gave up on his goals and acted with such confidence in successful outcome that his captains considered it divine foresight.

During the first large battle at Granic, the senior officers could still reproach him for carelessness. But after the giant battle at Issus, when Alexander and thirty-five thousand Macedonians and Thessalian horsemen decimated hundreds of thousands of Darius' soldiers with minimal casualties, his associates started treating Alexander with reverent fear. The old simplicity, even familiarity, in their attitude was replaced by something akin to worship. Alexander's habit of suddenly throwing himself into the most dangerous spots in the battle, and fighting with a godlike rage, made him like Achilles, whom Alexander counted among his ancestors. Over a short period of time he received two serious wounds: one to the hip and another one in the shoulder, from which he recovered inhumanly fast.

"He must be surrounded by the greatest beauties of Ionia, Syria and Egypt," Thais said.

Nearchus burst out in a kindly laughter. "You'd be surprised. Imagine this: Alexander doesn't have anyone, unless you count some plain-looking widow he took into his tent after his senior officers advised him not to inspire gossip among his soldiers and take a lover. Tens of thousands of young women have been sold into slavery. He could have had his pick. During the battle of Issus he took in all of Darius' possessions, as well as his family. That included his mother, wife and two daughters. Darius' wife, Stateira, was considered the first beauty of Asia, and the princesses are beautiful as well."

"And he didn't take her?"

"No. And wouldn't let anyone else have them, telling everyone that the women were to be his hostages."

Thais picked up a handful of Carian almonds from a clay platter. They were a common Helenian treat which she missed greatly during her time in Egypt.

"Then he doesn't like women at all?" she asked.

"I wouldn't say that. When Ptolemy hinted that the ladies of the Persian royal family were beautiful, Alexander sounded almost anguished. 'Yes, and it is a torture to my eyes' was what he'd said. No, he senses feminine beauty keenly and reveres it."

"Then why does he avoid women?"

"I think Alexander is not an ordinary man. He is indifferent to food and drink. I have seen him disgusted by the gluttony of his comrades who wanted to have a feast after each victory. He is not greedy, even though there isn't a person in Hellas who ever possessed such treasures. His favorite occupation is to read at night and spend his days consulting with the cryptii, the people who survey the way ahead, as well as talk with the philosophers."

"What of the widow?"

"She doesn't love Alexander and is afraid of him, hiding in the back section of the tent like a mouse."

It was Thais' turn to laugh. "How well do you understand him, close friend? Or are there others, even closer? Ptolemy? Hephaestion?"

"Most likely. Hephaestion because he is Alexander's complete opposite. Ptolemy always stands for himself, although Alexander highly values his cleverness and ability to make decisions quickly. I know the sea, but he is distant from it. We, his closest friends, have become more distant from him lately. Alexander's decisions are difficult to foresee, and his actions are frequently inexplicable."

"For example?"

"Sometimes Alexander acts like a wise ruler, merciful toward those he conquered, respectful of the others' traditions and temples, filled with good intentions toward the citizens of the taken cities. But sometimes he is akin to a wild, untamed barbarian. He destroys cities to their foundations and sets off bloody massacres. When they were at Thebes, the Macedonians demonstrated what they were capable of."

"Oh yes," Hesiona exclaimed.

Nearchus glanced at her, then continued. "The same fate befell Millet and Galicarnass, to say nothing of Gaza. Resistance makes Alexander mad, and he deals with his enemy like a savage, forgetting all his beautiful words about equality between people of Asia and Hellas. Myself, I think courage and bravery deserve at least some respect. After all, courage lives in the best of people. And if that is so, how can he kill the courageous and the brave ones, leaving behind only the weak of body and spirit? Not one intelligent livestock farmer would do a thing like that with animals, let alone people."

"There is a worse side to such savagery," Hesiona said suddenly, blushing deeply. "Among those who are murdered or sold as slaves like livestock, there are irreplaceable people: artists, healers, philosophers, singers, actors. Each polis, each city-state is known for its masters and its achievements in creation of beauty, in crafts and knowledge. It is clear that all this requires centuries of gradual perfection, even millennia, like Egypt, Hellas and the lost Crete. When we annihilate a city with all its carriers of arts and knowledge, we rob ourselves and the entire Ecumene, and lose wisdom and beauty that took centuries to be created."

Nearchus raised his eyebrows, thought about it, then nodded decisively in agreement.

"Tell me, have you tried talking to Alexander about this?" Thais asked.

"I have. He listened to me at first because he knew that I rarely speak, and when I do it is only about things that are important."

"And?"

"And he forgot everything in yet another fit of Achillean rage. He is not as much like Philip as his mother, Olympias."

"What was she like?"

"Why 'was'? She is still alive. She is not much older than forty, and she is still beautiful, with a peculiar, slightly wild kind of beauty. Do you know that she is a princess of an ancient line from the mountainous Timphea, an orphan dedicated to

Dionysus who became his priestess? And, of course, she is a maenad."

"So she is subject to enraged ecstasy. Alexander must have inherited that ability. Now I understand his inexplicable behavior a little better."

"It is possible. He becomes enraged when he runs into any resistance, be it a clash with an enemy or a dispute with his friends. He tries to overcome obstacles with a savage shove, not sparing his own life or those of others. During those times he thinks nothing of human dignity, that of which he speaks so frequently during his calm moments, when he disagrees with his teacher, Aristotle."

"This happens to very fortunate people, the favorites of Tihe, the fate," Thais said thoughtfully.

The companions remained silent for a long time, listening to the bubbling of water under the steering oars. The ship moved under sails. The steady east wind shortened their voyage. The mournful shouts of the livestock herders and roaring of donkeys could be heard from the distance. Thickets of donax, or reeds, spread as far as the eye could see, rippling in the wind like a brownish green sea. More reeds with fluffy tips, fluttering in rhythm with the current, grew closer to the shores of rivers and channels.

"Have you seen that most beautiful one, Darius' wife?" the hetaera suddenly asked.

"I have. She is very beautiful."

"More beautiful than I am? And ... Egesikhora?"

He shook his head. "Not at all. Tall, slender. Gloomy black eyes under wide black eyebrows. Large, thin-lipped mouth, slightly hollow cheeks, long neck. I don't know about her legs. You can't see them under those heavy long dresses of theirs. Long black braids, thin like snakes. That is all there is to her. In my opinion, she is nothing to you or ..." Nearchus paused, then gazed at the Theban, who flushed hotly. " ...or to Hesiona."

"The Daughter of the Snake" hid her face in her hands, and Thais hopped up, hugged Nearchus and kissed him somewhere under an eye, trying to avoid his prickly beard.

"You deserve a reward. I shall dance for you. Call your musician girl. I think you have a flutist, and Hesiona can manage the sitar."

Nearchus and his companions were thrilled by the unexpected performance, for there was no greater pleasure for Helenians, Finikians and Egyptians than a dance performed by a beautiful woman.

The quiet "kingfisher" days had ended after winter solstice, but weather still remained calm, even when Nearchus' ship exited the Nile and turned along the shore to the west, propelled by the steady east wind. Two skillful helmsmen remained constantly at the steering paddles. In this wide band of yellowish water, churned by the rolling surf, sandbanks continuously changed their location. In the liquid sand, mixed with the Nile silt, the ship's bottom could get stuck so firmly that no effort of the rowers or sails could move the entrapped vessel. That was why the helmsmen didn't dare sail at night and always stopped in small harbors.

Thais and Hesiona were under Aphrodite's protection. The goddess made their trip easy and fast. Soon the ship entered clear waters outside of the sands carried by the Nile, and approached the white band of foam beyond the island of Pharos, which was visible from afar. Eight ships carrying lumber and rock were crowded around the strip of land between the Mareotide lagoon and a broad strait where a poor settlement of fishermen Racotis used to be only a month before. In this early morning hour, thick smoke rose above kitchens in the soldier's camp and in the slaves' quarters. It was picked up by the wind and carried to the west, along the deserted Libyan coast.

Alexander's architect, Dinocrates, had accomplished quite a lot. Grooves and rows of boards hammered into the ground ran through the future city, marking the outlines of temples, streets and squares yet to be built. The chief of the city construction, a middle-aged, scar-covered Macedonian, greeted Nearchus with great respect.

Two tents woven of the delicate wool of Pamphilian mountain goats were set under the protection of a wall, still smelling of damp lime. The ship of the fleet commander carried plenty of beds, cushions and curtains. Thais and Hesiona settled quite luxuriously under his omnipotent care.

Meeting with the sea brought on memories of the past for Thais. A little bit sad, she relived the unforgettable moments of her short, yet saturated life to the hum of the sea, the splash of broadly rolling waves, and the constantly changing patterns of foamy bands. There were many seagulls, their rocking flight and piercing, troublesome cries making her think of Ea, the island of tears, and the dwelling of Circe in the midst of the deserted Ionic Sea.

In order to shake off the sudden sadness, Thais asked Nearchus for a boat and some oarsmen. The Cretan volunteered to accompany his guests, and they sailed across the strait to the legendary abode of the old man of the sea Proteus.

It was after noon, and the wind suddenly faded. Heat breathed upon them from above, and sparkling light spots dappled the calm water. The boat approached the island, low, sandy and completely empty. Even the seagulls grew quiet. Nearchus turned left, to the western side of Pharos, and the bow hit the sandy bank. Nearchus jumped into the water and handed both women over to the shore.

Ordering the oarsmen to wait, he led Thais and Hesiona through heat-saturated sand dunes covered with dry brambles. Beyond the dunes the wide band of surf-packed sand was cut off by a straight stone wall. Giant boulders, even larger than those in the Athenian Pelasgicon, were set together with a thoroughness resembling Egyptian and Cretan structures.

"What is this? Who lived here in the ancient times?" Thais asked quietly.

Without a reply, Nearchus led the Athenian to the edge of the wall and pointed at the boulders which had been scattered by an earthquake and were now submerged in the clear water. A pattern in the shape of squares could be seen on the surface of the boulders, marked in regular deep grooves. Some of the squares were carved out, and some had been left even with the surface of the stone. Together they made a net-like pattern of dark and light squares.

Thais immediately remembered where she had seen something like that. "It's Crete, isn't it?" she exclaimed, her eyes shining.

Nearchus replied with a wide pleased smile. "There are ruins further down. See? That looks like a column."

"I want to see that," Thais said. She looked down at the water, considering. "The water is not cold, despite winter time, unlike in Hellas ..."

"The locals wouldn't be caught dead swimming this time of year," Nearchus said with a chuckle, then grew suddenly glum.

Thais realized that he remembered Egesikhora and gently patted his arm.

"I'll go for a dive," she said, and ran toward the sea.

Hesiona dashed after her, but both were passed by Nearchus. "In that case," he yelled over his shoulder, "I am going first. A-e-o ..." he yelled, clearing his lungs, the way sea sponge divers did.

The Cretan shed his clothes, then dove, followed by Thais and, much to Thais' surprise, Hesiona, who ended up close by. Thais knew the Theban was a decent swimmer, but had never considered her capable of more. Concerned, she signed to Hesiona to go back to the surface, but the girl shook her head stubbornly and went even deeper into the dusky shadow, to where Nearchus was beckoning.

A large image of an octopus was clearly visible, the fanciful curves of his tentacles illuminated by a ray of light on the flat surface of a large stone slab. A fallen column with a wide top narrowed toward the bottom, after a Cretan fashion. Unfortunately, they didn't have enough breath to examine it.

Thais went up, but Hesiona suddenly fell behind. The movements of her arms slowed. Nearchus dashed to her aid, shoving the Theban up and catching her at the surface just in time. As she recovered, Hesiona lowered her eyes sheepishly. She no longer tried competing with swimmers like Nearchus and Thais, who kept diving until they grew cold.

Climbing out onto a dry slab warmed by the sun, Thais was surprised for the second time. Hesiona didn't rush to get dressed, but was taking her time to dry her hair. She was not heeding Nearchus, who jumped and walked on his arms to get warm, glancing at his companions discreetly, as was appropriate for a polite hymnophile.

Thais' deep tan, that had scandalized Athenian fashionistas, had grown paler in Egypt, her coppery skin becoming lighter. Hesiona, barely gilded by the sun, looked charming even next to the famous hetaera. Her legs, which were as strong as Thais', could have looked too muscular, had they not been so beautifully outlined. Her hair became fluffed by the wind and surrounded her head in a thick mane, seemingly too heavy for the delicate, maidenly neck.

Hesiona tipped her head to the side. Deep shadows hid her large eyes and gave the girl's face an expression of tired sadness. She rested one hand on a prominent curve of her hip and used the other to brush the sand off her body with slow, smooth movements. A brief sigh of a shore wind tossed Hesiona's hair over her forehead. She started with chill and lifted her head. Suddenly embarrassed, she covered herself with her hair and ran away under the questionable protection of the tall clumps of dry grass.

Nearchus felt a strange sense of pity and attraction to the tragic, gentle and passionate Hesiona. This girl, in whom he sensed a bright and delicate spirit, seemed akin to him, a former hostage and exile since childhood.

From the glint in his eyes Thais understood the Cretan's emotions. While she dressed, Thais said quietly, "Do not rush, seafarer, and she will make a good companion for you."

"I will not rush. I understand that she needs to be awakened. Will you give Hesiona away?"

"How can I not? She is not a slave, but a free, educated woman. I love her and will be glad of her happiness. But you must watch out. One wrong step and you will be dealing with an unusual destiny and you will not be able to take her, like the others who have tried."

"Will you help me?"

"First of all, I will not interfere."

Nearchus pulled Thais to him and kissed her bare shoulder.

"Do not rush with your thanks," Thais said, laughing. Then she remembered something and pushed Nearchus away.

Calling Hesiona, Thais pulled apart the bracelet on her left arm, the sign of a slave, with one swift movement. She pulled it off and tossed it into the sea. The Theban had no time to say anything, and Nearchus clapped his hands thrice, expressing his approval.

They crossed the strait, steering at the tall pillar which marked the spot for a future breakwater, and found more remains of Cretan structures near the west end of the strait.

Nearchus said that he was repeatedly surprised by Alexander's unmistakable instinct. A port, constructed so substantially thousands of years ago, undoubtedly was an important harbor along the trade routes of the great Cretan sea state. And now it was to serve the state of Philip's son.

Thais stayed in the future Alexandria till new moon, swimming in the sea even during windy days.

Part of the Macedonian detachment, which had accompanied Alexander to the Ammon's oasis, arrived without him. Much to everyone's surprise, Alexander went from the oasis straight to Memphis, taking a difficult and dangerous path across the Libyan desert. He was accompanied by Ptolemy, Hephaestion and Cleitus, the brother of Alexander's wet nurse, and an incredibly powerful giant, nicknamed Black. The trip to Ammon's sanctuary turned out to be not hard in the winter time. They were able to find water in every large hollow. The way to the east, to Memphis, however, was more dangerous and difficult. Huge mountains of sand fumed and rustled under the wind, obstructing the entire four thousand stadiums with an endless series of hills.

It was unclear why Alexander had decided to undertake this trip, since it contributed little to his glory.

Nearchus shrugged. "It is clear to me."

"I don't understand. Explain."

"Alexander needs to follow Darius into the depths of Asia, across deserts and heat-filled plains. He wants to test and strengthen himself."

"What did the oracle of Ammon say?"

"Nobody knows. The oracle's priests and garamants, the keepers of the oak, met Alexander with the greatest of honors. In the morning, he entered the temple alone. His companions waited for him the entire day and the following night. At dawn Alexander left Ammon's sanctuary, saying that he'd found out everything he wanted, and everything he needed from the god."

"Then what are we to do?"

"Sail to Memphis. Today. Or do you want to spend more time with the sea?"

"No. I miss Salmaakh."

Again the endless plains of the Delta stretched before them, looking even more dull after the open spaces of the sea. The Cretan continued telling tales about Alexander's campaigns, except now Thais frequently went to the bow deck, leaving him alone with the Theban. She noticed that Hesiona's glances directed at Nearchus were becoming increasingly tender and dreamy. One evening Hesiona quietly slipped into their shared quarters where Thais had retired earlier, but still lay awake. Hearing that the girl could barely contain her laughter, Thais asked what had happened.

"Look," Hesiona said, and held an enormous sea sponge to the light of a lucnos.

"A gift from Nearchus," Thais said, admiring the sponge. "It is a rare thing, to match this basin."

A shallow, silver lined cleansing basin stood in the corner of their quarters, so large and heavy it could only be moved by two strong slaves.

"Shall we try it?" Hesiona suggested with a laugh. She rolled the basin out like a wheel and dropped it to the floor.

The ship shook from the basin's thunderous fall, and the helmsman's assistant ran into the room in a panic. Charmed by the women's smiles, he immediately sent two sailors to fill the basin with fresh water.

Thais lowered the sponge into the basin and watched it absorb almost all of the water. She ordered Hesiona to stand in it, then lifted the sponge with great effort and squeezed it over the Theban. A delighted squeal burst out of Hesiona, her breath caught by an entire shower of cold water.

"Make sure that Nearchus' love doesn't drown you like this sponge," Thais joked, and the girl shook her head violently.

However, on the fourth day of their trip, Hesiona did not come out to the deck. She stayed in their room instead. Thais demanded an answer from the saddened commander.

"I grew to love her. But she ... I am afraid Hesiona will never truly recover. I am afraid to ruin everything. Help me somehow. You, skillful priestess of Aphrodite, ought to know such things."

"Trust me," Thais reassured him. "While it is strange for me to be a man's ally, I am certain that you shall not harm my Hesiona."

"What more can I say?"

"No need," Thais said, then went back into her quarters and stayed there till night.

Two more days passed. The ship approached Eshmun in the midst of a dark, moonless night. Thais lay awake in her quarters, thinking about what Nearchus had said about Alexander wanting to go to the end of the world in the east. What was she going to do now?

Suddenly, Hesiona burst into the room and threw herself on the carpet in front of the bed. Hiding her face, she held her arms out over the silk throw toward Thais.

Thais pulled Hesiona to her, kissed her flushed cheeks several times then pushed her away slightly. Thais looked into the chestnut colored eyes with an unspoken question.

"Yes, yes, yes," the Theban whispered passionately. "And he gave me this bracelet and this ring. He bought them in Naucratis. These are not the other ones, not Egesikhora's."

"Are you going to him again?"

"I am. Right now."

"Wait a little. I shall teach you how to become even more beautiful, though you are not bad as is. Take off your epoxida."

Thais pulled out a set of cosmetics for the body as well as fragrant essences. She looked over her friend critically, then asked mischievously, "Is male love really that bad?"

"Oh no!" the Theban exclaimed, then blushed and added, "Except I don't know what to do to make it good for him."

"You must descend to him like a goddess to a poet, ready to give yourself to a sacred ritual without fear or impatience. Serve him as you would serve Aphrodite at a seashore, without limit or hesitation. I mean, if that is your way …"

"Yes, yes. I know that he is a fleet commander of the great Alexander, and I … But still, I am happy with whatever the fate holds. Who can argue with it?"

"Gods themselves cannot and dare not," Thais agreed. "But we mortals must be spiritually strong in order to avoid humiliation."

"What gives us strength?"

"Long preparation, demanding training, strict upbringing."

"Even for hetaerae?"

"Especially for us. Many girls gifted by Aphrodite above all others, rose up and accepted adoration like queens, but ended up being pitiful slaves of men and wine, nothing but broken flowers. Any hetaera, who becomes famous, shall perish if she is not spiritually trained in advance. That is the meaning of the teachings at the temple of Corinthian Aphrodite."

"I do not understand."

"You will soon. And when you do realize that you cannot be famous by love alone, it won't be too late to study dancing and the art of being a lively companion and storyteller."

"I would so love to become a dancer, like you."

"We'll see. I know one Finikian woman in Memphis who could teach you the mysteries."

"Oh, I need no mysteries. I love Nearchus and will not love anyone else except him."

Thais looked carefully at the Theban. "This happens too, but rarely."

Chapter Eight. The Chestnut Pacer

Ptolemy saw Thais riding her dark, ash colored horse, as he returned from a visit to the pyramids with Alexander, Hephaestion, Black Cleitus, and Leontiscus, the head of Thessalian cavalry. Alexander rode Bucefal, exercising his beloved steed during the early morning hour. Usually he rode him only into battle, trying not to overheat the black horse in long trips under the scorching sun of Asia. Bucefal lifted his smart head, displaying a broad forehead marked with white, and neighed to greet the mare. Salmaakh danced coquettishly, controlled by Thais' firm hand.

Three astonished shouts sounded almost simultaneously as the three friends recognized "the fourth Kharita". The Thessalian froze, gazing at this small, modestly dressed woman, who had stopped three powerful men in their tracks, including the divine conqueror himself.

"It is her, my dream: the Athenian!" Ptolemy exclaimed, dismounting and grabbing Salmaakh's reins.

"Such arrogance," Hephaestion noted mockingly. "Yours without you?"

"I said dream," Ptolemy repeated stubbornly, giving Thais a searching glance.

She rested both hands on the horse's withers and held her head high. But her eyes were only for Alexander, as if she were mesmerized by his gaze.

Frowning slightly, Thais threw her leg over the horse's left side and slid to the ground. She looked small in front of the three giant men on their horses. Alexander, Hephaestion and Cleitus were each an entire palysta taller than four elbows, while Thais was only three elbows, three palystas tall. Nevertheless, the hetaera hasn't lost her dignity or daring independence that had initially struck Ptolemy back in Athens. He could not take his eyes from her. Thais was in her feminine prime, having lost all things boyish, and she had become inexplicably alluring, distant and even more desirable.

Thais' horse stepped to the side, and Ptolemy had to look at her against the sun. Powerful golden light penetrated the hetaera's light garment and wrapped her entire body in a glorious fire, as if Helios himself embraced the beautiful daughter of Hellas and Crete. Thais gazed into the distance as if she saw something invisible to others, and she reminded Ptolemy of Alexander. Ptolemy shuddered at the thought and lowered his eyes to avoid betraying his feelings.

Alexander dismounted, tossed Bucefal's reins to Cleitus and approached Thais. He held his head even higher than he had during their first meeting and squinted his eyes with a proud and perceptive expression.

"Haire," Thais said, raising her hand to the army leader's chin.

"What do you wish to ask me for?"

"Nothing, my king," Thais said, addressing Alexander by the title of Persian rulers. "You have become so imperious in the last few years, that we mere mortals involuntarily pause before you with a prayer."

Alexander listened to Thais' words carefully, but no, they held no tine of flattery. He smiled. "I hope my forefather Achilles forgives me, but truly, you have become more beautiful than Helen of Troy, the daughter of Tindar."

The Macedonian king looked the hetaera over, but his curiosity was somehow different than Ptolemy's.

"Her eyes are crystal clear, like the spring of Artemis," Alexander thought. "Gray with glints of gold and blue, calm and kindly. Her lips seem to be carved out of crimson stone, and their outline is so clear, just like the long cut of her eyes under narrow eyebrows. Her skin is like pale copper, transparent and silky, like a thin cloth of fire burning on an altar at noon."

After a silence, broken only by the clanging of reins and hoofbeats, Alexander said. "Remember my promise in Athens that you may be my guest whenever you wish? Would you like to?"

"Of course I would. Especially now that you surprised me by remembering a brief meeting with a girl-hetaera."

"I have been planning to invite you for a long time," Ptolemy interrupted. "Any horses, slaves or tents are at your disposal. I have everything aplenty."

Ptolemy caught himself under Alexander's gaze. Thais thought the army leader looked at his comrade not with anger, but with pity. Then he returned his attention to Thais.

"I am but at the beginning of my path," the king said. "But you may accompany us. Not in battles and chases, but in the peaceful part of my army, with artists, philosophers and performers. Ptolemy will take care of you. He is good at that," he said, and a light smile scattered the awkwardness between the king's companions.

Thais bowed her head, revealing with a heavy knot of hair arranged in a tall updo, and childishly pursed her lips into an arch.

"I thank you, my king."

"Call me Alexander, as before. And come to the celebration I am arranging for the city. Show them the high art of Helenian women."

Alexander hopped back onto his black horse with an agility that was amazing for someone so large. The horse was covered by a sweat blanket fastened with three belts, after a Persian fashion, and wore a Persian harness of glittering gold shaped like letter xi, with gold starbursts at the intersection of the straps and under the horse's ears. Thais swiftly mounted Salmaakh, still saddled with a worn panther hide, making the horse rear up and turn deftly after the departing Macedonians. Then she turned again and slowly rode to the spot where Hesiona waited, having decided to part from Nearchus for a few days. The fleet commander had promised to come back before the big symposium, and their separation would not be long.

Memphis was swept up in a celebratory mood. People greeted the young "pharaoh" Alexander, marveling at his beauty, strength, and the feeling of supremacy and power, exuded by the deified army leader.

As always, people hoped for big changes in their destinies, something to alter their sad lives under of the will of the new king. They always hoped for immediate improvement, not understanding that the course of history is slow and difficult to change. Nothing could be changed for the people living at that moment. Military disasters, riots, fires and floods would invariably burst into the colorless existence of human mobs with stunning suddenness. Historic experience existed only for the wise.

Among those who greeted the victorious Macedonians and Helenians were a few people akin to Thais, those joyous bundles of life, with body and muscles seemingly cast out of bronze and with steadfast souls, imagining themselves to be the masters of Ecumene.

"Will you help me, Hesiona?" the hetaera asked on the eve of symposium. It had been arranged by Alexander for the Memphis nobility in the so-called Southern Gardens.

"You are very brave to perform before such a crowd of people. Won't Salmaakh be scared?"

Thais stretched lazily and took out a bottle of dark ancient glass. From it she pulled a pinch of greenish powder which emitted an unpleasant smell, and placed it in a small cup.

"I'll mix this with water and give it to Salmaakh to drink. A little bit of this Asian herb is enough for a man or an animal to shed the chains of embarrassment or fear. A bit more and the body gets out from under the heart's control. That is why, not having much experience, I shall only give her a tiny bit."

Flames burst into the dark sky within spinning columns of smoke, rising out of resin-filled stone vessels. Large tents protected the guests from the north wind. Musicians and a Greek choir with actors performed a Tragedy, "The Song of Goats", on the smooth tiles of the courtyard, an excerpt from adventures of Dionysus during his Indian voyage. Alexander was particularly fond of that legend.

The great victor half-reclined in the midst of his inebriated and arrogant companions. Only Nearchus and Leontiscus sat slightly aside from everyone, listening to a splendid Tinos singer. She was tall and dressed in a peplos that was black as night, looking much like Hecate. Instead of the mean hounds, the goddess' usual companions, she was performing with two lively female flutists, who were nude, according to tradition. They accompanied her deep voice with the power well beyond that of an army captain. A broad flow of the song washed away human disappointments, like the sea, compelling everyone to be calmer, kinder and more attentive.

Drums thundered. The steady beat of the wood drumsticks sharpened. Slaves fired up the incense burners, causing bands of heavy scented smoke to undulate around the tiles of the improvised stage.

Six nude Finikian dancers, dark and slender, with narrow hips and low breasts, twirled in the fragrant smoke. As they pulled apart and dashed madly at one another, they presented the outrageous, coarse and straightforward portrayal of the strength of the sexual desire that possessed them. These were the victims of goddess Cotytto, obsessed with one goal: to become free of her tormenting power as quickly as possible.

Hoarse shouts of approval sounded around the room, but neither Alexander nor Black Cleitus expressed any admiration. Nearchus and Leontiscus remained calm as well. The incense burners went out, the dancers' bodies glistened with sweat, and the deafening drumbeat grew silent. The Finikians vanished along with the last few fading beats.

Without any pause, a curtain of the most delicate silvery cloth fell in front of the stage, stretched between two torch pillars. Large mirrors made of silver covered copper sheets were placed behind the curtain and set to reflect the light of large oil lanterns.

String instruments rang out, flutes joined them in a melodious song, and eight more nude girls appeared in a beam of light projected from the mirrors behind the fabric. They were all small in height, muscular and busty. Their hair did not slither down their shoulders in thin, snakelike braids as had that of the Finikians', but was closely cropped, akin to the mythical Amazons.

Their small feet stepped forth in unison, in one coordinated movement. They were Thessalians, the daughters of the ancient country of witches, and their dance looked like a magical act or a secret ritual.

The silvery cloth fluttered slightly, separating the dancers from the dusk under the party tent like light fog. The Thessalians' agile bodies obeyed a different musical rhythm than what the others had followed. The dance was free and flowing. As the tempo increased, the young dancers, who were just as impassioned as the Finikians, seemed to rush through the wide, horse-running planes of Thessaly. The spectators appreciated the flight of their imagination and watched in silence, captivated by the feeling of tinoesthesis, a sensation through the heart that Helenians considered the embodiment of the soul.

A somewhat sad Leontiscus leaned toward Nearchus and murmured, "Once upon a time I saw Thessalian women performing the dance of the Amazons. It was so beautiful."

"Would you like to see that again?" the Cretan asked, smiling mysteriously. He already knew everything through Hesiona.

"I would pay a talant to her, she who could perform the Amazon dance."

"Very well, pay up," Nearchus said calmly and held out a hand.

The chief of Thessalian cavalry laughed in surprise.

Just then, the curtain was removed. Reddish glints of the resin torches scattered through the tiles of the courtyard. A girl with her hair down appeared near the left torch pillar, wearing a short ecsomida, which left her left shoulder and breast exposed. Nearchus recognized Hesiona, and no one paid attention to her at first.

The Theban raised a tambourine over her head and demanded everyone's attention with a few sharp strikes. The bells around the rim of the tambourine jingled and Thais, riding Salmaakh, burst into the bright circle of light. The horse wore nothing but a bridle, and the rider wore nothing but an Amazon's battle bracelet.

The horse jogged sideways from one pillar to the other in a graceful cross-step, then reared up, tipping her small head and swinging her front hooves in a greeting. From there Salmaakh moved in the opposite direction, following the beat of the tambourine, alternately tossing her front and hind quarters while Thais sat firmly, never moving a shoulder.

Having danced three rounds, the Athenian suddenly sent Salmaakh into a gallop. Hesiona beat the tambourine madly, while the Macedonians, all excellent horsemen, yelled in rhythm with the gait.

Imitating the legendary stiganorae[20], Thais braced herself on one knee at full speed, then turned to face the horse's tail and spread back over her back, hugging the mare's broad curvy neck. After she turned back to sit properly, she made the horse rear up again, and Salmaakh spun around swiftly and gracefully, making two full turns in each direction. Urged by the thrilled shouts of the spectators, Thais slowed the horse to a moderate trot and stood up on her back, holding on by one strand of the long mane, and balancing perfectly.

No one had noticed the slaves as they quietly covered the courtyard with heavy, palm-tree boards. Thais settled down and stopped smiling, her face growing serious as she approached the boards. Hesiona's tambourine, scattering the rhythm of the graceful dance, echoed the beat of the hooves. Obeying the hetaera's knees, Salmaakh drummed over the resonating wood with all four hooves. Two, then four beats of the front hooves, then steps backward, then

---

20 Literally – man-haters. This was an epithet frequently used for the Amazons.

more beats of the front hooves. Two, four, eight, twelve, the grouped beats sped up, as the horse either trotted forward or receded to the back. Thais bent backward, arching her back and pointing her breasts toward the dark sky.

Hesiona, unable to stand still, danced on the spot, shaking the tambourine as hard as she could. The excited horse started jumping too, as if she were in a gallop, striking with three hooves at once, tossing her hind quarters and shaking her head.

Suddenly Thais hopped off Salmaakh's back. Holding onto the horse with her right hand, she began an old ritual dance. Rising onto her right toes, the hetaera lifted her left leg high and grabbed its ankle with her outstretched left hand. Thais' coppery body, flexed like a bow, formed a triangle that looked like the letter gamma with a bar on top against the horse's dark gray hide. Then both her arms stretched out, level with her shoulders, in rhythm with the arching of the body. The right went up as the left one came down.

Another triangle appeared for a moment. Salmaakh hopped, moving slowly in a circle, ready to turn her other side. Thais flew up to the horse's back and slipped down over the other side, repeating the triangle of the strange dance.

The tent was now filled with the roaring of her admiring audience. Leontiscus, unable to control himself, dashed forward but was stopped by Nearchus. Ptolemy appeared outwardly calm. He clutched his hands firmly together, then pressed them against his chest while glancing at the Thessalian. Even Alexander rose from his seat. He almost knocked over a broad shouldered, slightly slouching man who stood next to him, watching Thais' dance as if his life depended on it.

Salmaakh jumped for the last time. Thais was on horseback again, and the horse reared and bowed to each side. Then Thais lowered the horse to her knees, with her head pointed toward Alexander. She hopped down and greeted him, and the delighted crowd went wild. Salmaakh was startled by the noise and jumped up, pressing her ears back and rolling her eyes. She backed up toward the backdrop of the "stage" and Hesiona caught her by the reins.

Alexander beckoned Thais to him, but the hetaera wrapped herself in a fringed Egyptian cape and ran off. She had to wash off the caustic horse sweat as quickly as possible, and she had to dress properly for the feast.

A few minutes later, Thais appeared under the tent, dressed in an orange chiton with three ribbons: blue, white and red, braided into the black mass of her wavy hair.

Before Ptolemy and Leontiscus had a chance to say anything, the hetaera approached Alexander. The king of the Macedonians took both her hands, kissed her and sat her down at the three legged Greek table between himself and the slouching man. The latter wore a short beard on his thin face, and a tired, intelligent gaze.

"Look at her carefully, Lysippus," Alexander said.

Thais was startled by the name. This was the first time she had ever seen the famous sculptor who had left Hellas to accompany the conqueror of the Persians. The sculptor took Thais by the shoulders and started examining her face as unceremoniously as would an artist or a doctor. The hetaera saw that he wasn't slouching at all. It only seemed that way because of his habit of leaning forward when he wanted to look at something carefully.

"Why, Majesty?" Thais could not bring herself to call the Macedonian by name, even though she knew Alexander was only twenty-four, a year older than she. Familiarity was not in her character.

"Alexander," Lysippus replied, instead of the king, "wants me to create a statue of you as the queen of the Amazons. He's been dreaming of reliving the story of

Theseus and Hippolita since his childhood, and was disappointed to discover that the female riders of Thermodont have long since vanished, leaving behind only a legend. However, you presented yourself today as their true heiress. Look at our Leontiscus devouring you with his eyes."

Thais bowed before Alexander in an exaggerated plea. "Mercy, Majesty. For the last three hundred years artists have been portraying the brave Helenian warriors conquering the Amazons, killing them or dragging them off as prisoners. Have you noticed that the Amazons are portrayed on foot for the most part, in order to avoid elevating them over the men?"

"What do you mean?" Lysippus asked curiously.

"Any amphorae, either red or black figured ones, dating to the first Olympiad or even earlier. All artists made them, both the famous and the obscure ones: Euphronius, Eukhrides, Andokides, Arkhesilaus. It's hard to remember them all. But all of their heroes: Theseus, Hercules, Achilles, are portrayed dragging the poor Amazons off by their hair, beating them with huge bats, or piercing them through with swords and spears. I have seen almost no drawings where the Amazons are portrayed on horseback, as they ought to be. And even fewer where they defeated men in battle."

"But that is the case with the amphorae, and the old ones at that," Lysippus objected.

"Not at all. Remember the scenes of Antipope's kidnapping on the bas-reliefs of the temple of Apollo. And what about our Parthenon? Have you forgotten the huge painting by Micon in the pinacotec of Athens, in the left wing of Propilea, where Helenian warriors are portrayed ruthlessly beating the Amazons? It was only painted a hundred years ago, maybe a bit more."

"What are you trying to say?" Alexander asked, frowning.

"When male pride is stung, you begin making up stories to justify yourselves. And the artists try to portray these lies as accurately as possible."

"Why would the artists do that?" Lysippus asked.

"Because they are men, too. And they too cannot tolerate the thought of female supremacy."

Leontiscus, who had approached without notice, clapped his hands.

"What are you happy about?" Ptolemy growled menacingly.

"The Amazon's intelligence. And truth."

"Do you see the truth in this?"

"I see the truth in the fact that all these defeats, portrayed so happily by Athenians, have not taken away the Amazon's courage, as they did with Boeotians and Athenians. Their capital, Temiskira, had been taken by Hercules, and some of the Amazons died in Athens, but they still came to the walls of Troy to fight against the Helenians. The descendants of those who were defeated by the Amazons cannot forgive them that, or their terror-inducing lack of sensitivity toward wounds."

Alexander laughed merrily, and Ptolemy couldn't find anything with which to object. Lysippus asked Thais, "Tell me, what made you think of performing hippoginnes in the nude?"

"First of all, the desire to match the legends. True Amazons, the girls of Thermodont dedicated to Artemis, who lived a thousand years before us, always fought in the nude and rode horses without sweat blankets. The story that they burned out one breast in order to use the bow is a ridiculous lie, because there is not a single ancient image of a single-breasted Amazon. The stiganorae shot directly in front of themselves above the horse's ears, or, as they rode by an enemy, they turned and struck over the horse's croup. True Amazons can be found on the old Clamezone vases and basins. They are shown as muscular, even stout nude girls, riding strong horses, and accompanied by bearded stablemen and dogs. Ionian and Carian women, who were accustomed to freedom, could not live with the crass Dorian invaders. The bravest, strongest and youngest of them went north to the Black Sea, where they founded the polis of Temiskira. They were not a nationality, but a group of sacred maidens of Artemis and, later, Hecate. Ignorant historians and artists confused them with Scythian women, who were also wonderful warriors and riders. That is why Amazons are frequently portrayed either fully clad in Scythian garb or in the short Cappadocian ecsomidae."

"You should teach history at the Lyceum or at the Academy," Lysippus exclaimed in amazement.

Thais' eyes twinkled merrily. "I barely got out of the Lyceum alive, after having met Aristotle."

"He never told me anything about it," Alexander interrupted.

"And he won't. For the same reason the Amazons are always portrayed defeated. But tell me, sculptor, have you ever heard of a woman teaching grown people anything but love? Only Sappho perhaps, but look what men did to her. We hetaerae-friends not only entertain and console, but also educate men so that they could see beauty in life."

Thais paused in her excitement, calming her breath. The men watched her with sincere interest, each pondering her words in his own way.

"Also," Thais said, addressing the sculptor, "You, whose name is 'he who frees horses' for a reason, will understand me. As will they," the hetaera indicated Leontiscus and the Macedonians, "who are rulers of horses. When you navigate a dangerous road on horseback or fly forward in a gallop, do you not feel as if the Persian sweat blanket or any other padding gets in the way? What if there is nothing between you and the horse? Do your muscles not merge with those of the horse, as they work together in agreement? You can respond to the smallest change in the rhythm and sense the horse's hesitation or daring, understanding what it needs. And what can hold you in place better than horse hide if there is a sudden stumble or slowing down. How in tune it is with the order of your toes or the turn of your knees."

"Praise the true Amazon!" Leontiscus exclaimed. "Hey, some wine to her health and beauty!" He lifted Thais in the crook of his arm and raised a goblet, holding the precious rose wine to her lips with his other hand. The hetaera took a sip and ran her fingers thought his closely cropped hair.

Ptolemy laughed forcefully, barely restraining his jealousy. "I speak well, I know," he said. "But you get too carried away to be truthful. I would like to know how a steed can feel these little toes at full speed," he said, carelessly touching the hetaera's foot within a light sandal.

"Take off my sandal," Thais demanded.

A puzzled Ptolemy obeyed.

"And now, Leontiscus lower me to the floor," she said, and Thais flexed her foot on the smooth floor, causing her to spin on her big toe.

"Do you understand now?" she challenged Ptolemy.

"With proper aim, she could deprive you of descendants with a toe like that," Leontiscus said. He laughed, then finished his wine.

The symposium went on till morning. The Macedonians became increasingly noisy and mannerless. Alexander sat motionless in the pharaoh's precious armchair, constructed of iron wood with gold and ivory. He gazed above the guests' heads, seeming to dream of something.

Ptolemy kept reaching for Thais with lusty arms, but the hetaera moved away from him, sliding along the bench toward Alexander's armchair until the great ruler put his heavy, protective hand on her shoulder.

"You are tired. You may go home. Lysippus shall take you."

"What about you?" Thais asked.

"I must be here, just as I must do many other things regardless of whether I love them or not," Alexander replied quietly, his voice tinged with vexation. "Though I wish for something else."

"For a queen of Amazons, for instance," Lysippus said.

"I think the Amazons, who dedicated themselves to Artemis and the sole purpose of defending their independence must have been poor lovers. And you, my king, would have found nothing but grief," the hetaera said.

"Not like if I were with you?" Alexander leaned toward Thais, who blushed like a teenage girl.

"I am not for you either. You need a queen, a female ruler, if a woman can be near you at all."

The conqueror of Persians peered at Thais and, saying nothing, dismissed her with a wave.

As soon as they were in the shadow of trees, Lysippus asked quietly, "Are you initiated in the Orphic religion? What is your initiated name? How much was disclosed to you?"

"Very little," the hetaera admitted. "My Orphic name is Tiu …"

Once she told him about the Delos philosopher, Lysippus lost his suspicions and started telling her about the Orphic-like cult of Zoroaster he had discovered in the heart of Persia. Supporters of Zoroaster revered kindness in the guise of the male deity, Ormuzd, who constantly struggled against the evil, Ariman. Ormuzd wore the same three colors of Muse: white, red and blue. Lysippus suggested that, should she go to Persia, she should wear three colored ribbons there as well.

"I must see you again, as soon as Darius is completely crushed and I have a permanent studio in Persia. You are not an easy model for an artist. There is something rare about you."

"Won't I grow old by then?" Thais teased.

"You don't know Alexander, silly," Lysippus replied. He was convinced that the final victory over the Persians would happen soon. That Alexander would be undeterred in reaching this giant goal.

Hesiona and Nearchus waited for her at home. The delighted Cretan congratulated Thais for her unprecedented success.

"The captain of cavalry is completely struck by Eros," Hesiona said, remembering with a laugh. "You have conquered the famous hero akin to Hippolita."

Thais asked Nearchus to tell her how Leontiscus had become famous. He said that during the battle at Issus, Alexander's army had ended up squeezed in a shoreside valley by the numerous Persian troops. Their cavalry, which was several times greater in number than that of the Macedonians, rushed from the hills to the shore, crossed the river and attacked Alexander's left wing, which consisted of the Thessalians' horsemen. Alexander sent the Frakian riders and the splendid Cretan archers to help them, under the leadership of Parmenius, an experienced army man.

The Thessalian cavalry managed to hold the seashore until Alexander's guard, the heavy cavalry of getaerosi-comrades and shield bearers, dealt a terrible blow at the center of the Persian troops, causing Darius to flee and securing the victory.

For their heroic battle at the seashore, the Thessalian horsemen were rewarded with the right to pillage Damascus. Damascus turned out to contain all of the equipment of the Persian army: carts, slaves, money and treasure. Thus, Leontiscus was now in possession of substantial wealth. Alexander rewarded him personally, along with the others who had distinguished themselves in that battle, splitting three thousand talants between them, which they took on the battlefield and to the Persian camp.

"Truth be told, Ptolemy is probably even wealthier. He is a wise and patient leader. He knows how to gather and wait. I think he will have you in the end, not Leontiscus, who is as passionate as Alexander," the Cretan said at the completion of his story.

Thais raised her chin under Hesiona's mischievous and loving gaze.

The first month of spring, Munikhion, had not yet started when Thais found herself on Nearchus' ship yet again, along with her friend and Salmaakh. They sailed down the east arm of the Nile, through Bubastis to the First canal constructed on Darius' orders, which connected Egypt with Eritrean Sea and Persia.

Three hundred years before, the Egyptian pharaoh, Neho, had ordered the construction of the canal. That was the same pharaoh under whom Finikian sailors carried out an incomparably heroic deed by sailing around the entire Libya, from Egypt to the Pillars of Hercules, then arriving back in Egypt.

However, the work started by the Egyptian slaves remained unfinished. Only two centuries later, Darius the First, with an enormous number of war slaves at his disposal, finished the waterway from the arm of the Nile to Succoth, located among the Bitter Lakes, not far from the Gulf of Heroes, which was a narrow branch of water between the Arabian and Sinai deserts.

In Succoth, Thais was to leave Nearchus' ship and part with Hesiona for the first time. It would be for some time, possibly forever. Nearchus would then sail to the Euphrates to construct the fleet, in order to be able to sail to Babylon if necessary.

The possibility of defeat had its place in the thoroughly thought out plans of the great army leader. In that case, Alexander did not wish to repeat the difficult Anabasis[21], the march of the Greeks toward the sea, across the mountains and plains of Cappadocia and Armenia. The Greek mercenaries were not being pursued by anyone at the time, yet they still lost many people. In this case, the huge Persian army would be right behind them. Alexander considered it the best strategy to retreat toward the Euphrates, put the army onto ships, and sail away from their pursuers. In the case of victory, Nearchus would meet them in Babylon. That was where Thais and Hesiona hoped to meet again.

They spent the last sleepless night before Succoth in Thais' quarters. Chilly Sinai wind penetrated the heavy drapes, causing the weak flame of the luminary to flutter and encouraging the two friends to snuggle closer together. Hesiona remembered all the years spent at Thais' household. They both cried aplenty, grieving for Egesikhora and for their own approaching separation.

Blinding sun rose from the dull hills in the east as the docking ropes were tossed to the pier. Ptolemy appeared in a Persian cape embroidered with silver, surrounded by a crowd of his friends. They greeted the new arrivals with loud shouts, which scared Salmaakh as much as it had during the Memphis symposium. Thais herself led the snorting and bucking mare to the pier and handed her off to the experienced stablemen. Thais and Hesiona were taken in a carriage along the north shore of a small salt lake to the east, where the camp of Alexander's top captains was located on a ledge above a valley. The inevitable symposium ended early, since Nearchus was in a hurry. Thais returned from the feast by midnight with her eyes swollen with tears. She settled in a luxurious tent that had once

---

21 A famous march of Greek mercenaries, described by Xenophontus, when the Greeks were forced to retreat from Persia taking a longer more circuitous route.

belonged to some Persian nobleman, and was now prepared for her.

The hetaera could have never imagined that the grief from being separated from her former slave girl would be this strong.

The wound from the loss of Egesikhora and Menedem had not yet fully healed, and the Athenian felt particularly lonely here, on a deserted slope, before a march into the unknown. As if guessing her state, Ptolemy came to see her, despite the late hour. He captivated Thais with stories about Persia and she again fell under the spell of his intelligence, his articulate speech and incredible observance.

Since the beginning of the campaign, the Macedonian had kept a travel journal, capturing the amazing events efficiently and precisely. While Cretan Nearchus noticed primarily the nature of seashores, Ptolemy turned out to be not only a supreme military man, but also an explorer of traditions and everyday life of the people in the conquered lands. Of course, much of Ptolemy's attention was captured by women, as well as traditions pertaining to love and marriage. These were also of great interest to Thais.

He told her about strange peoples living in the heart of Syria and Arabia. They treated women with little regard, and considered Aphrodite Pandemos to be a goddess of debauchery, since they did not understand her high gift to people. They did not understand it because they were afraid of love, which made them feel defective and apparently ugly, because they were strangely afraid of nudity.

These were the people whose women did not dare appear nude, even before their husbands. Unfulfilled in Eros, they were greedy for food and jewelry, and were afraid of death, even though their life was dull and unattractive. It was difficult to imagine that they did not understand drawings or paintings, and were unable to recognize images. It was useless to tell them about beauty created by artists. That was how they lived on the edge of the desert: without joy, in wars and riots.

"Do they completely reject women?" Thais asked, surprised.

"Not at all. They desire to have as many of them as possible. But all of it turns into crassness and rudeness. Their wives are slaves who can bring up only slaves. Such is the payback for their ignorant and frightened women."

"You are right," Thais said, becoming excited. "The Lacedemonian women enjoy much freedom, and there are no people braver than Spartans. Their heroics are legendary, as is the glory of their women."

"Perhaps," Ptolemy agreed reluctantly. He noticed the gold necklace around the hetaera's neck and frowned. "Have you added any more stars after mine?"

"Of course. But not enough. Only one. I must be growing old."

"Wouldn't we all wish to grow old like that," Ptolemy mumbled. "Show me." Not waiting for her to respond, he pulled the necklace out.

"Twelve beams on the star. And letter mu in the middle. Does that stand for number twelve as well or is it a name?"

"Both a name and he number. But it is time. Dawn is coming from the hills."

Ptolemy left without a word. Thais have never seen him this glum. She shrugged her shoulders in puzzlement as she slid under the light warm spread, and declined even a massage, which was offered to her by the new slave girl, Za-Asht, a Finikian. Za-Asht was ill-tempered and proud, with the stature of a priestess of some unknown god. She managed to win her mistress' respect and, in her turn, grew sympathetic toward her. Za-Asht's gloomy eyes warmed up considerably when they rested upon Thais, especially when her mistress couldn't see her looking.

Thais spent the entire next day in her tent. The dull valley surrounding them did not inspire her curiosity, and the entire large Macedonian cavalry was swept up in the chaos of preparation for the next campaign. Hundreds more Macedonian soldiers arrived all the time and were temporarily settled on the fertile lands around the Delta.

The army was going to Tyre, the main gathering point, following an ancient road which passed through Edom to Damascus. The first stage of the journey was four and a half thousand stadiums long, according to the experienced guides and road surveyors.

This road went through deserted plateaus, tree covered mountains, valleys and river shores. It had been witness to the campaigns of many people, many forgotten bloody battles, and tragic marches of those taken as slaves. Giskosi, Assyrians, Persians, and many others had attempted to get to the wealthy and fertile Egypt over thousands of years. Even Scythians would have passed here, moving from the Caucasian lands in the distant east to the borders of Egypt.

Infantry detachments were formed from the best soldiers, who did not wish to part with the treasures they had gathered. They sent their possessions ahead to Tyre, using hundreds of carriages captured from the Persians, and were soon to follow in the same direction.

Alexander managed to beat Ptolemy with his usual speed, and was already in Tyre.

Thais told Ptolemy that she didn't want to use a carriage. The tooth-shattering bumping of these vehicles along the rocky mountain roads would ruin the entire trip. The Macedonian agreed and ordered to bring Salmaakh, to have the mare examined by the connoisseurs before the long journey. Leontiscus showed up too, being the best horse expert in the entire army. Flax seed was added to Salmaakh's feed for several days, including the time on the ship, in order to purge her digestive system. Her dark ash hide, brushed out by a Paphlagonian stableman, glistened like dark silk.

Leontiscus ran his fingernails along Salmaakh's back, pressing hard. The horse shivered and stretched. The Thessalian hopped onto her back and sent her galloping across the valley. The even beat of her hooves made the connoisseurs nod approvingly, but the chief of Thessalian cavalry was displeased when he returned.

"Shaky trot. Look. Her front hooves are rounder than her rear ones, but not any bigger. Her pasterns are too arched. She'll wear off her hooves on the rocky roads of Syria."

Thais ran up to the mare and hugged her around the neck, ready to defend her favorite. "It's not true. She is beautiful. You yourself admired her at the feast. Look how she stands. Her legs are perfectly in line."

"Her legs are a bit long. It would be better if they were shorter."

"But look how broad her chest is."

"Yes, but her rear is too narrow. Also, look. Her groin is long and stretched out to an entire palm and two fingers. You might be light, but if we do twenty parsangs, she will run out of breath."

"I will run out of breath before she does. Or do you think I am anywhere near you?"

The Thessalian burst out laughing. A vertical wrinkle at the bridge of his nose smoothed out, his frowning eyebrows rose, and the Athenian saw a young man in this stern warrior, almost a boy. Contrary to Spartans, who considered a man mature only from the age of thirty, Macedonians began their military service from the age of fourteen or fifteen. They became seasoned veterans by the time they were twenty-five. The chief of the Thessalian cavalry must have been just such a young veteran, like many of Alexander's captains.

"Forgive me. You are attached to your horse, as a true rider should be. And Salmaakh is not at all a bad horse. Still, if you are to go to Asia with us, you ought to get another horse, and keep Salmaakh for dancing."

"Where am I supposed to get another horse?" Thais asked, offended for her mare. "And one better than my beautiful girl?"

She patted Salmaakh's curving neck as the latter threw a mean sideways glance at Leontiscus, as if she understood she was being criticized.

Leontiscus exchanged glances with Ptolemy, and the Macedonian waved at someone.

"Hey, bring a horse for mistress Thais."

The hetaera didn't get a chance to say anything before she heard clear, distinctive hoofbeats. A boy burst out of the stables atop a chestnut stallion, and barely managed to stop the spirited horse by leaning back and pulling hard on the reins.

The steed's hide was a coppery chestnut without a single spot, shiny and shimmering. His long, neatly trimmed mane and full, tight at the base tail, were black as his eyes, which made the animal that much more beautiful. The Athenian has never seen a horse of that color.

Thais immediately noticed the longer torso with its curving flanks, and legs that were shorter than Salmaakh's. His front hooves were larger than the rear ones. Long flat shoulder blades, long withers, broad croup, all these advantages were obvious. Even to a layman. The steed's raised head and proudly carried tail gave the stallion a particularly majestic posture. The horse's face seemed serious, almost mean, because of the fluttering nostrils.

But as soon as one looked into the animal's large, kind eyes, any concern vanished. Thais walked boldly up to the steed, took the reins from the boy, and patted the animal's neck. The chestnut stallion neighed briefly and quietly.

"He recognizes you!" Ptolemy exclaimed. "Very well, take ownership. I have long since been looking for an Enetian horse for you with qualities that distinguish one out of a hundred thoroughbreds."

"What is his name?"

"Boanergos, Child of Thunder. He is six years old and has been well-trained. Have a seat and try him out."

Thais tossed off the battle cape she used to protect herself against the wind, patted the chestnut stallion once more, then hopped onto his back. The steed seemed to have expected that and immediately launched into a broad trot, steadily increasing his pace.

It was odd. After Salmaakh's trot, this horse made Thais feel as if she almost weren't bouncing at all. The horse rocked from side to side, hitting with two hooves at the same time. Curious, the Athenian leaned over and noticed that the horse moved both legs on the same side simultaneously, front left with hind left, front right with hind right. He was a pacer, a kind of horse Thais has never ridden before.

Delighted by the pacer's gait, Thais turned around to send a smile to the great horse connoisseurs, which caused her to accidentally squeeze her knees a little. The sensitive steed dashed forward so quickly that the Athenian arched backward and had to use one hand to lean against the horse's croup. Her breast seemed to form one line with the pacer's outstretched neck and the strands of his long mane. The wave of her loosely tied black hair streamed in the wind above the fanned out tail of the chestnut steed. This was the image of Thais that Leontiscus would remember forever.

As if wanting to show what he was capable of doing, the chestnut pacer flew forward faster than the wind, carrying his torso evenly and rocking from side to side. The hoofbeats increased in pace, but the breadth of his gait did not grow shorter. Thais felt as if earth itself rushed under the horse's hooves. The sensitive dancer's ear could not find a single error in the precise rhythm, akin to the tempo of the maenadae's dance during the celebration of Dionysus: two strikes to one drip of a fast clepsydra, used for keeping time in dancing.

The chestnut pacer reached far with his front legs, as if trying to cover more space. Thais, filled with tenderness, patted his neck, then started gently slowing him down. Boanergos recognized the skill and strength of his rider and obeyed her without delay. When the pacer slowed to a walk, she found it less comfortable and let the pacer go back to full speed when returning to the camp. She flew up to the group of connoisseurs and stopped the horse just as they were getting ready to jump out of the way.

"How do you like Boanergos?" Ptolemy asked.

"Very much."

"Now do you understand what a proper horse for distant trips is like? He'll trot for thirty parsangs. Although," he said, scratching his head, "the Syrians do have a saying that a mare is better than a stallion, for she is akin to a snake since she gets stronger in hot weather. Yours, however, just doesn't have the right build."

"Yes. Look at the breadth of his throat, and how proudly he carries his tail. He is filled to the brim with life force," one of the connoisseurs said. "A horse like that cannot be found for an entire talant, because he is a rarity."

"Thais is a rarity, too," Leontiscus said. "By the way, did anyone notice …"

"I did," a young lokhagos said, stepping forward. "The mistress and the horse are the same color. Only the eyes are different."

"Have I earned forgiveness?" Ptolemy asked.

"What for?" the hetaera asked with surprise. "Although if you are guilty of something, you would know better. Still, you have earned it. Catch!" Thais cried, then jumped off the horse straight into Ptolemy's arms, as she had many times with Menedem. But while the mighty Spartan had stood like a rock, Ptolemy wavered despite his strength, and almost dropped the hetaera. She managed not to fall only by putting her arm firmly around his neck.

"Bad omen," Thais said, laughing. "You won't hold on to me."

"Yes I will," Ptolemy spat.

Thais freed herself from his arms and ran to the pacer. She patted him gently and kissed his soft warm nose.

Boanergos shifted from one foot to another several times, tipped his head, then lightly pushed Thais with his head, neighing softly. There was no better way he could indicate that he liked his new mistress. At Ptolemy's signal, a slave handed Thais a piece of barley bread. She unbridled the horse and gave him the treat. Having eaten it, the steed rubbed his head against her shoulder. As he was led away, Thais could have sworn he looked back and winked at her, so mischievous was his expression.

Despite all of Ptolemy's efforts, he could not seem to revive his old relationship with Thais. The spirited, mischievous and courageous girl, who had seemed like an ideal lover to the Macedonian, had given way to a woman. The woman was just as courageous, but possessed greater inner strength and was both mysterious and incomprehensible. Her interests no longer coincided with those of Ptolemy, despite the fact that he was an observant pragmatist and good strategist.

Thais' thirst for knowledge reminded him of Alexander. Ptolemy remembered one nighttime conversation when he had tried to engage Thais in politics. While pontificating on the subject of Plato, Aristotle, Athenian democracy, and Spartan military state, he talked about the need to create a new city that would be more splendid and glorious than Athens.

Lands conquered by Alexander had already formed a strong empire, including the entire Inner Sea coast from Hellespont to the Libyan shores. Not one of the previous state structures: polis (city-state), monarchy, or oligarchy suited this new country. Nothing but tyranny would do: a rule by one man in possession of military force. But tyranny was short-lived, and military luck was changeable. The life of an army leader was even more subject to chance, especially the life of one as prominent as Alexander. It was necessary to create a clear plan for structuring Alexander's empire, but the king himself hadn't even thought of the name for his new country.

Ptolemy noticed that Thais was bored, and was listening only out of courtesy. In response to his forced outrage, Thais said calmly that all these thoughts appeared immature to her. One could not fantasize about the future, but had to do what was best for the people now, at the present moment.

"People? What people?" Ptolemy asked with irritation.

"All of them."

"What do you mean, all of them?" the Macedonian asked. He stopped when he saw a patronizing smile flicker across her face, and suddenly remembered that Alexander was telling him the same thing when he discussed homonoya, the equality of all minds.

Their road took them north. Green islands of forests appeared more and more frequently, appearing in the midst of a grayish sea of shrubs which grew on the slopes of hills. Thais had been used to the rough, scratchy oak, as well as the pistachio and myrtle thickets since childhood. Large areas of black-trunk strawberry trees grew here as widely as they did in Hellas, as did the small laurel groves, where the air was stuffy even during cooler days. Thais loved the tall wide pine trees with long needles, the soft carpet of fallen needles and slanting rays of sunlight poking through the branches.

When the road passed through the crests and flat peaks of mountain ranges, the army was surrounded by the primal might of ancient cedar and fir trees. Thick and bumpy fir trunks, their straight branches hanging to the ground, obstructed the entire world, creating a quiet, dusky kingdom of silence and isolation. The powerful Syrian sun barely penetrated their short, coarse needles.

The Athenian was impressed by her first meeting with a grove of Lebanese cedars. Until then, only the oaks and tall pines growing in sacred places had filled Thais with reverence. No matter how big, the trees lost their individuality in groves and forests, becoming a crowd, from which an eye could only distinguish certain features, adding them up to build the image of a tree.

But here every cedar was a "personality", and the multitude of colossal trees did not merge into an impression of a forest. Row after row of these remarkable, incomparable giants approached, allowing one to admire every detail, then vanished behind the next turn in the road. Their trunks grew up to ten elbows thick, with coarse, scaly bark the color of Salmaakh's hide. They seemed to melt under their own weight, pouring into the rocky soil in bumps and bubbles. The cedars branched out low to the ground, their huge branches undulating into fanciful shapes. Snakes, hydras and dragons were outlined against the blinding sky. The trees reminded Thais of hecatoncheirs, hundred armed creations of Gaea, who rebelled against heaven with all of their awkward might.

More slender trees grew further down the slopes, having escaped the axes of Finikian shipbuilders and citizens of Byblos who prepared lumber for the temple of Solomon. These giants stood up straight, frequently splitting into two treetops and spreading their mighty branches to fantastic breadth. Millions of small branches with a fluff of short, dark, green or bluish needles grew horizontally, forming flat, patterned levels, one row after another, soaring up like the stairway of tree-dwellers, the dryads.

Ptolemy explained that these were leftovers of the once mighty woods. Further to the north they turned broader and more imperious, especially in the Taurus mountains of Cilicia, in Southern Cappadocia and in Phrygia. Hearing about the woods that were cut down there, Thais thought that despite her love of beautiful ships, these most important creations of human hands were not worth cutting down a giant. Destruction of a colossal tree seemed like sacrilege against Gaea's sacred rights as the all-bearing, nursing mother of all. This would unquestionably be punished by the wrath of mother Earth. In fact, punishment could already be seen in the endless rows of sun scorched mountain ranges, whose searing stones emitted suffocating heat day and night.

Having passed through the cedar grove, the road took the Macedonian army to a ledge leading through pale, craggy mountains with scant plant life, covered with dark vertical "ribs" that made them look like walls of a city. Their route was taking them closer to the sea.

"Are there any wild animals here?" Thais asked. "Do I need to worry about the horse?"

"You might run into a lion or a panther here and there in the mountains, but they've become rare because of the constant hunts. Several centuries ago a breed of small elephants lived in the valleys and hills of Syria. They were hunted by Egyptians. Finikians gathered ivory for Crete and exterminated the elephants completely."

Thais easily made daily marches of three hundred stadiums. Ptolemy did not rush, letting the last few detachments from the Delta catch up with them. Leontiscus and his Thessalians rode off ahead of everyone. Before they parted, Leontiscus taught Thais how to use the Persian sweat blanket with wide straps and a military-style chest cover. The Athenian quickly came to appreciate its conveniences, especially for a distant trip. Leontiscus gave Thais a jug of potion made of leaves and the green shells of walnuts, boiled in vinegar. It was used to wipe down the horses; its scent repelled stinging insects. The Thessalian explained to Thais the rules for rubbing down sweaty horses, and the hetaera always made sure the stablemen rubbed down her steed starting from the legs. Whenever a horse became fatigued, its ears grew cold, Leontiscus said. He told her how to massage the ears, restoring the steed's energy. Thais found out many such small and important secrets from Leontiscus during the five days the Thessalians traveled with Ptolemy's men.

At this point, after ten days on the road, approximately three thousand stadiums separated the detachment from the Egyptian border. Having crossed the low mountains, they emerged onto a plain. Ruins of massive ancient structures towered above the disorderly mass of small town homes on the eastern side. This was Armageddon, one of the "Wheel" cities of the ancient king Solomon, with stables that had housed hundreds of horses seven centuries ago.

Ptolemy told Thais about an ancient prophecy of Hebrew elders who had said the last battle between the forces of good and evil was to take place at this exact place, in the valley of Armageddon; however, the seers did not indicate the exact time of the battle. Later on Thais discovered that Indian philosophers had, in fact, predicted the time of the decisive battle between Light and Dark, but not the place. It was thought that the great contest was started by the godlike rulers in order to satisfy their arrogance and love of power. It destroyed the best of their people and gave birth to a new historic era consisting of the accumulation of anger and despotism: Kaliuga. The terrible final battle was to take place at the end of Kaliuga.

Putting the two prophecies together, Thais determined that the Armageddon battle was to take place twenty-three and a half centuries after the year of her birth, and was surprised that people could be so interested in something that might happen in the impossibly distant future. However, she remembered that Indians believed in reincarnation and a series of repeated births, and they believed in a manner even stronger than the Orphics. If someone believed in the endless duration of his life on earth, it was no wonder that he was interested in the events of such distant future.

Thais did not believe in the possibility of endless transformations. The Orphic teachings were yet to overcome the Helenian notion about the temporary nature of life, sucked in with a mother's milk. And the endless wanderings through the darkness of Hades was not attractive to anyone.

The road descended to the sea and stretched along the coast, all the way to Tyre. Ptolemy decided to increase the pace, and they crossed the remaining four hundred stadiums over a day and a part of a moonlit night. This last dash proved to be fairly easy for Thais, who was sufficiently trained by then, and had an excellent horse. Za-Asht was left in charge of Salmaakh, as well as the cart carrying Thais' possessions.

Having arrived at the huge camp near Tyre, the hetaera discovered the reason for Ptolemy's rush. Alexander had had his first large disagreement with the oldest and most experienced officers of the Macedonian army. Darius had sent a letter in which he offered peace, a huge ransom as well as the entire coastal portion of Asia and Egypt. Alexander rejected the offer, replying that until Darius showed up for the decisive battle or laid his title at Alexander's feet, he would be pursued to the ends of Ecumene.

Parmenius, the oldest of the Macedonian captains and Philip's comrade, was the first to object to such arrogant reply. "If I were Alexander, I would have accepted the Persians' conditions," Parmenius said.

"So would I," Alexander agreed, "if I were Parmenius."

Senior officers believed that one ought not constantly push their military luck, especially when the enemy still had enormous resources. Heading away from the sea and into the heart of the country, foraying into the endless plains, was dangerous. The Macedonian army could find itself cut off from their supply chains, since no one knew where Darius was gathering his troops or when he was planning to deliver the decisive strike.

While the army had a chance to rest during winter, a scorching summer still lay ahead, including a difficult march into the immeasurable distance. The army would become exhausted, especially its strongest part, the infantry: the phalanx and the shield-bearers. The latter were now referred to as Argiroaspides, or "silver shields". They had received this distinction for their unprecedented courage at Issus.

Arguments, supported by taking stock of the fantastic trophies, conquered lands and captured slaves, were so weighty that the contingent of older and more cautious officers took Parmenius' side. Younger officers, who were missing only Ptolemy, were decisively in favor of continuing the campaign, crushing Darius completely and conquering lands to the end of Ecumene.

Alexander realized that the younger ones were carried forth by the battle spirit and love of adventures more than by any other considerations. The great strategist understood the grave danger of the continuing war but, unlike the elders, he also saw the impossibility of ending it.

After the battle at Issus, the destruction of Finikian cities and the invasion of Egypt, he could not stop at this halfway point. In a few more years his splendid army, dissipated among various stations, would stop being that reliable military force with which he could resist the scores of Persians. Even if there were no new battles, thirty thousand Macedonians would dissolve in these lands like salt in water. Alexander had no choice. Most importantly, with a stubbornness inherited both from his mother and from Philip, he wanted to realize his longtime youthful dream: to go to the east, where the sun's carriage rose from the edge of earth and the waters of the ocean, to the boundaries of mortal life, to the cape Tamar of the ancient maps.

Viewed from the last mountain range, the Macedonian camp was laid out in a scattering of lights. Despite the late hour, fires still burned, lighting the circles of soldiers caught in lively discussions. The others, who had missed supper for some reason, were waiting for bread to finish baking and meat to finish roasting. All of these were provided to the army aplenty on Alexander's orders.

Ptolemy slowed his tired horse and turned back toward Thais. The hetaera rode up to him, coming as close as she could because she saw Ptolemy's intention to speak with her in secret.

"Listen, Orphian. Sometimes you possess the gift of foresight and point out correct solutions. What would you advise Alexander – to make peace with Darius or go against him?"

"The king needs no advice. Especially not from me."

"I understand that more than anyone else. The question is for you, if you were asked to make a decision, which would you choose?"

"I say forward, only forward. We must not stop. To stop means death."

"I knew it," Ptolemy exclaimed with admiration. "You are a true companion for an army leader. Perhaps for a king."

With these words, Ptolemy put his arms around Thais and pulled her to him for a kiss. Suddenly he pushed away with a yelp and his horse jumped into the darkness with a strike of his heels. Thais looked around, puzzled by the Macedonian's disappearance. When she realized what had happened, she burst into laughter. Boanergos, jealously protective of his rider, had bitten Ptolemy, who reappeared after a moment.

"Let's ride down," he said and urged his horse forward, not looking at the hetaera.

Subdued luminaries burned in a side attachment to Alexander's tent. The tired army commander lay on his wide and uncomfortable bed, listening to Thais. He had invited her over on the eve of their departure, after keeping her from dancing for his officers. Thais enjoyed the flashes of spirited curiosity in his eyes which she saw whenever he lifted his heavy head from the pillow of his arm.

The shield of Achilles hung over his bed, blackened by time. Alexander had never parted with it since the day he'd taken it from a temple at the ruins of Troy, where he'd left his own shield instead. The weight of the shield was proof of having belonged to a mighty hero, whose example had excited the Macedonian prince since childhood. However, Alexander carried in his soul the disappointment he, and many before him, had experienced at the Ilion hill. All of Iliad's heroes had fought there. That had been difficult to imagine while he'd stood in front of a small hill. Of course, nearly a thousand years had passed since the Iliad, but the giant temples of Egypt, the palaces of Crete and the cities of Finikia were even older. Alexander had reconciled himself to the loss of his childish fantasies about Troy only when he realized that the number of people inhabiting the face of Gaea grew every century, the boundaries of Ecumene broadened, and a truly great deed would have to satisfy higher standards. He had more than fulfilled the dream of his father Philip and the warlike Isocrates[22]. Now, if only he could crush Darius and conquer Persia completely.

As if guessing his thoughts, Thais asked, "What happens when you defeat Darius and open the gates to Asia?"

"To the east, to the ocean," Alexander replied easily, feeling inexplicable trust toward the Athenian hetaera.

"Is it far away?"

"Do you know of a diaphragm of mountain range separating dry land?"

"I know a little."

"There are thirty thousand stadium from here to its eastern edge. The Cape Tamar is at the distant end of land."

"Locheara[23]! To go through this, constantly fighting ..."

"It's not that much. In order to get here from Memphis, you have already traveled over four thousand stadiums. I think once we defeat Darius there won't be much of an army left to resist us. In a year, maybe a year and a half I shall reach the shores of the ocean never seen by another mortal, or even immortal, except Helios."

---

22 Helenian army leader who dreamed of payback to the Persians.
23 "Arrow-shooting" Artemis.

Alexander's perceptive gaze did not find the expected admiration in Thais' face. The hetaera appeared to be deep in thought.

"Is this really your most coveted dream?" she asked quietly, lowering her head.

"Yes. I have been obsessed with it since youth. And now I am at the threshold of realizing it."

"And how many thousands of people will die, paving your path with corpses? Is the mysterious cape really worth it? It is probably just a bare rock on the shore of a dead ocean."

The great army leader laughed. The sound was unexpected and merry. "A woman, even the smartest one, always remains shortsighted. Pericles' Aspasia was the same way."

"My mind really must be small. I do not understand you, Majesty."

"It is so simple. I will only kill those who resist the movement of my army. It will go through like a plow, equaling all people. Did you not say yourself that good people everywhere are alike? Did you not admire my disagreement with teacher Aristotle? I believe intelligent people are worthy everywhere, and homonoya, the equality of mind, must unite Persia, India, Hellas, Egypt, Italy and Finikia. This can only be achieved by military force."

"Why?"

"Because rulers and tyrants, army leaders and statesmen are afraid to lose their rights in my new state and thereby become lost within the multitude of the worthiest people. They will force their people to fight. They can only be brought to obedience by destroying their fortresses, killing their officers and taking away their wealth."

"Are you capable of doing that amidst the endlessness of Ecumene?"

"I am the only one who can. Gods made me unbeatable till my death, and the Ecumene is not all that endless, as I told you. I'll go to Parapamizes, beyond the Roof of the World[24], to the Indus and further to the south till I reach the ocean, while Nearchus outlines the coast from Babylon to our meeting point at the edges of the earth."

"When I listen to you, I start believing the teachings of Hebrew scholars," Thais exclaimed. "They have Sephiroth, or Mind, also referred to as Heart or Vina, the female beginning. Wisdom or Hokma is a male beginning. With you, I realize that if women represent considerate order, then wisdom destroying it belongs to men."

Thais' philosophic discussion was interrupted by the Black Cleitus. He glanced at the Athenian, noticed his leader's slight nod, then said, "Some wise man wants to see you. He says that he has an important apparatus (battle equipment) and can tell only you about it. You are leaving camp tomorrow?"

"Indeed. Some people find things out before I do. He really must be a wise man or a great mechanic. Let him in."

A slightly plump, short man with shifty eyes entered, bowing constantly. He observed Thais cautiously, probably decided that such a beautiful woman must undoubtedly be as stupid as a Boeotian sheep, and knelt in front of Alexander.

"What kind of apparatus do you have and where is it?" the king asked.

"Presently only here," the newcomer said, then pointed at his forehead and heart.

"How dare you?"

"Do not be angry, Majesty. The idea is so simple that the apparatus can be created in half an hour." The inventor pulled out a massive, sharp copper nail with roughened surface, about one epydama[25] in length.

---

24 Tibet
25 21 centimeters

"You need to take wide cedar boards and nail these into them. A hundred such boards scattered in front of the enemy will stop the fastest cavalry attack, and you can make many hundreds. They are light to transport and easy to use. Can you imagine how effective such a defense would be? A horse that steps on a nail with one hoof would rip its own leg off, and if it steps on a board with two feet, it will fall and throw off its rider. If the boards are spread widely enough, he would also land on the nails and it would be over, for he could never get up. He would die a terrible death. Your soldiers would only have to pick up the weapons and valuables. It is a simple and effective defense."

"It really is simple and effective," Alexander said slowly, looking at the inventor.

From the corner of his eye, the king saw disgust on Thais' face, which the Athenian wasn't even trying to hide.

"Were you the only one who came up with this? Does anyone else know?"

"No, no, great victor. I am just for you. I thought only you could appreciate the value of my invention. And maybe there would be a reward …"

"Yes. A reward," Alexander mused. His eyes suddenly flashed with anger. "There are limits that no mortal or even god is allowed to cross. True destiny is determined through an honest battle between the best with the best. Cleitus!" he shouted. The inventor, who was just rising, fell back to his knees before the king.

The giant burst into the tent.

"Take him, gag him, and kill him immediately."

The inventor's screams coming from behind the tent suddenly stopped. Thais knelt silently at Alexander's feet, gazing at him with admiration and gently running her hands over the deep scars on his knees. Alexander placed a hand on the back of her head under the heavy knot of hair, trying to lift her up for a kiss.

But just then, merry voices sounded outside the tent and Black Cleitus called out to someone. Alexander's associates entered, including Ptolemy. They brought news that a messenger had arrived from Lysimachus, saying a bridge across the Euphrates near Thapsak was ready. The leading detachment of Agrians had already crossed to the left bank. Information supplied by the cryptii-spies was confusing and contradictory, which was why the crossing had been delayed.

Alexander rose, forgetting temporarily about Thais. The hetaera slipped out of the tent and made a farewell gesture to Black Cleitus, who sat like a statue atop a massive chest in the front section of the royal tent. Then she stepped into the open air, walking under the large stars of the Syrian night. Having descended carefully down the slippery gravel path to a creek where her tent stood, Thais paused thoughtfully at the entrance until Za-Asht called her in for the evening bath. The hetaera sent the Finikian to bed, then sat on a leather cushion from Damascus, listening to the quiet bubbling of the creek and watching the sky. Over the last few weeks, she had rarely managed to be alone with the sky, which she found was necessary to restore her inner peace. Night's carriage rolled on behind the hills, and Thais heard gravel from the path crunch under Ptolemy's heavy steps.

"I came to say goodbye," the Macedonian said. "Tomorrow we'll fly ahead of everyone to Damascus, and from there to the north, across Hamat, to the Euphrates crossing."

"How far is that?"

"Three thousand stadiums."

"Artemis argotera!" Thais blurted. She always called on Artemis when she was startled.

"It's nothing, darling, compared to what we have yet to travel. I leave you in the care of the head of the detachment, who is in charge of guarding the crossing. That is where you shall wait for the next turn of fate."

"Where? In a military camp on the river?"

"No. Alexander himself advised ..." Ptolemy shrugged. "For some reason he wants to take care of you."

"Have you forgotten that he invited me back in Athens?"

"I have. He is acting as if you are ..."

"Perhaps I would like to, but that's not the way it is. So what did Alexander advise?"

"Three hundred stadiums north of the crossing, along the royal road from Ephesus to Susa, lies the city of Hierapolis. Its ancient temples of Aphrodite Militis stand amidst pine groves atop sacred hills. You shall give this silver chest with Alexander's seal to the high priestess there, and they will treat you like a messenger of the gods."

"Who hasn't heard of the Hierapolis sanctuary? I thank you. I shall set out tomorrow."

"You won't need any guards until you reach the crossing. After that you will be entrusted to the one-eyed Gigamus, who has three hundred soldiers. But enough about business. It has all been decided. You shall wait for me or my messenger, or some other news."

"I do not want 'other news'. I believe in victory." Thais put her arms around Ptolemy and pulled him close. "Potnia Teron, the mistress of animals, will be on your side. I shall make rich sacrifices to her because everyone is certain that the plains beyond the river are under her power."

"That would be good," the Macedonian said. "The unknown lies before us, frightening some, exciting others. Alexander and I remembered the time we hunted borius in the Libyan desert. It was a beast never seen by anyone in Egypt, and so feared by the Libyans that they wouldn't dare even talk about it. We never found borius. I wonder whether the same might happen with Darius."

The Macedonian left Thais at dawn, when the camp filled with the jingling of horse's bridles. Pushing a curtain aside, Ptolemy stopped at the entrance with flashing eyes and flaring nostrils.

"Kinupontai phonon halinoi!" he recited. It was a verse from a famous poem. "The horse's bridles ring of death."

Thais made a sign of protection with her fingers, the curtain fell and the Macedonian hurried toward the tent of his commander where the rest of the associates had already assembled. The hetaera spread out on her bed, thinking and listening until the noise at the camp ceased and the sound of hooves faded in the distance.

Chapter Nine. Visiting Mother of Gods

The temple of the Great, or the Highest, Goddess Ashtoreth, the Ruler of the Lower Abyss, the Feminine Triad: Ana, Belita and Daukippa, the Queen of Earth and Fertility, Kibela and Rhea All-carrying, Mother of Gods, the Mistress of Nights, was strange and slightly barbaric. It was not a temple of Aphrodite at all, as it had mistakenly been called by Alexander and consequently by Ptolemy.

At the outskirts of a grove of huge pine trees, double walls with cube-shaped towers outlined a large square courtyard containing rows of low, wide trees Thais did not recognize. Much to her astonishment, enormous spotted bulls, horses and lions walked and rested among the trees, and black eagles sat atop the walls.

The guards wore gilded armor and carried spears ten elbows long. They let Thais and Za-Asht go through, but left the hetaera's soldiers between the walls. The horses became nervous, sensing the presence of predators, but their cousins in the courtyard of the temple didn't mind the lions at all.

The aroma of Arabian incense floating from the temple doors could be felt even here. The temple itself stood on a platform of unpolished rocks. Thais hurried toward the stairs, but the strange company of animals didn't bestow a single glance upon the women or their companions.

According to legend, pillars of black granite a hundred elbows tall had been erected by Dionysus himself. They guarded the entrance to the southern part of the courtyard. The broad wings of the temple were constructed out of large green bricks. Plum and Persian apple trees grew on the roofs of secondary structures. A staircase of white stone led from the platform up to the main entrance, which was above a wide, cube-shaped threshold, covered by glazed dark red ceramic tile. The entrance, framed by massive slabs of black stone, was divided into three sections by two pillars. Seven square columns on each side supported the flat roof with a garden and a walking platform. The center of the roof was crowned by a rectangular structure with no windows or doors.

One of Thais' powerful benefactors had apparently informed the keepers of the temple of her arrival. As soon as the hetaera stepped onto the platform in front of the entrance, she was surrounded by an entire crowd of women. A man and a woman stood in the center of the group, dressed in heavy embroidered garments of identical cut, but of different colors: white for the man and black for the woman.

Thais handed over the gift chest from Alexander and received a deep bow in reply. The priestess in the black peplos took her hand and led her into the back of the temple. The doors, covered with mirror-polished electron, opened into a sanctuary with a ceiling of gold leaf.

A statue of the Great Mother, Astarte or Rhea sat atop a white rectangular stone slab. The ancient image was fairly small, just over two elbows. Legends claimed it was several thousand years old. The statue was made of terracotta, covered by pale brown glaze the color of tanned skin. The figure of a nude woman woman was kneeling, her torso turned slightly to the right and her hands pressed against her round belly. Her broad hips were much wider than her massive shoulders and served as a pedestal to the powerful torso, muscular arms and large, half-spherical breasts. Her neck was straight and long, almost the same circumference as her narrow head with its barely outlined face. It gave the statue an expression of proud alertness, or enthasis.

Woven gold chains, ornamented with purple hyacinths and emeralds, hung from the statue's shoulders, and some unknown stone shone like fire from the middle of her forehead. Thais discovered later that the stone shone just as brightly at night, lighting the sanctuary.

The statue of the male god, with a coarsely carved, shovel-like beard, sat a step behind the goddess, in the shadow of a niche atop a similar slab. Bronze wheels with wide rims supported both pedestals. During the big moon celebrations these heavy carriages were somehow transported to the temple courtyard. After that, Rhea-Astarte's carriage was drawn by the lions, and the male god, whose name Thais could not remember, was drawn by the sacred bulls.

The high priestess, who either didn't wish or didn't know how to speak Coyne[26], silently unclasped Thais' chiton and lowered it to her waist. Two groups of priestesses quickly and quietly appeared from the darkness of the sanctuary. They were young with focused, glum, almost menacing faces, and were grouped by height and hair color. They lined up to the right and to the left of the statue of Kibela-Rhea allowing for Thais to get a better look at them. Those on the right had dark red "Finikian" hair and were dressed from neck to knees in nets. The nets were similar to fishing nets, except they were made of thick red yarn, and seemingly woven to fit the girls precisely. Black chains with square links held these amazing garments at the waist. At the neck, a black strap decorated with metal secured the nets. Black bracelets held the nets at the knees and wrists. Their hair was shorter, after the fashion of slaves. It was pulled back and twisted into tight knots in the back, framing the broad low foreheads in the front and emphasizing the menacing fire in their dark eyes.

The priestesses belonged to different nationalities, but looked similar to each other, not only in hair color, but also in the regularity of their features, the perfection of their strong bodies and their height, which was no taller than an average Helenian woman.

The women on the left had dark bronze skin and black hair, and were dressed in thicker nets of black yarn with belts, bracelets and neck straps of red bronze. Their penetrating, luminous eyes shone with savage light. Gold dagger hilts could be seen in the heavy knots of their long hair. The priestesses examined the famous hetaera curiously. Thais smiled at them, but

---

26 Conversational Greek used around the entire Mediterranean.

didn't receive a hint of response in the dark gazes of the servants of Astarte-Rhea-Kibela.

The red priestesses stood with their hands held at shoulder level, their palms turned forward. The black ones rested their palms on their curvy hips with their fingers spread out.

The rightmost red priestess carefully handed a small gold vial to the high priestess. She dipped her pinky into it and rubbed some red oil with spicy fresh scent over Thais' eyebrows. The Athenian's head spun a little after that. She vaguely recalled a story she had heard somewhere about Ashtoreth's red oil. It was said one drachma of the oil was worth a fortune.

A black priestess on the left held forth a chalcedony cup. Only now did Thais notice that both the black and the red priestesses' nails were covered with sharpened bits of electron, sparkling like little mirrors. The high priestess took a little bit of dark ointment from the cup and drew a cross between Thais' breasts, then underlined the breasts and circled the nipples. The skin became bluish. Thais became worried about whether the stains would last.

Still silent, the high priestess unclasped the necklace with golden stars, examined it and smiled for the first time. She took off an incredibly beautiful necklace made of sky blue berylliums, encased in pale gold. Thais made a gesture of protest, but the priestess paid her no attention as she put the beryllium necklace around the Athenian's neck. She put her arms around the hetaera's slender torso and put the star necklace around her waist.

One more sweep of delicate fingers, and a blue arrow was drawn over Thais' belly. The priestess stepped back and clapped her hands. She was Immediately handed a wide cup with a drink of some sort. She tasted it, let Thais have some, then the cup was passed among all of the red and black priestesses. There were eighteen priestesses, nine on each side.

Thais felt awkward under the intense eyes surrounding her. They lacked judgment or approval, sympathy or animosity.

"Something remarkable has happened," the high priestess suddenly said in Helenian, with a clear Aeolian accent. "Our guest wears the ancient sign of feminine mystery and the power of letter mu," she said, pointing at the star necklace she had moved to hetaera's waist. "For that reason I initiate her at the highest level. Take her to the apartments already prepared for her in advance."

With these words the priestess kissed Thais with her hot, dry, almost feverish lips and repeated the same instructions in a language unknown to the Athenian.

Two priestesses, one black and one red, from the outer ends of their rows, approached Thais, bowed respectfully, pinned up her chiton and carefully took her arms. Thais laughed, pulled her arms out of their grasps and walked between the two women, remembering to bow to the statue of Rhea on her way out.

A long hallway cut through the thick walls sloped gently down. It reminded the hetaera of the Egyptian temples. For a moment, grief for her past, still so alive in her memory, cut through her heart.

At the end of the hallway the faint light of an oil lamp lit a massive copper grate which blocked the passageway. The black priestess made a hissing whistle. A chain clinked and a woman appeared near the grate. She looked like a black priestess, but without the net, belt or bracelets, and with her hair in disarray. Covering her face, she opened the grate and jumped back toward the wall. Thais noticed that the woman was shackled to the wall with a light chain.

"Is she a slave?" the hetaera asked, forgetting that her companions might not know the language of Helenians. "She looks like ..." Thais pointed at the black priestess.

The black one smiled slightly, but it was the red one who responded, picking out the words of Coyne with difficulty. "She is a priestess, punished."

A heavy oak door blocked the exit from the corridor. The red priestess knocked three times and the door opened, blinding them with daylight. It was opened by Za-Asht, who was nude and had her hair down.

"Forgive me, Mistress, I had no time to dress. They brought me in here through the lower temple and took my clothes."

"What for?"

"They examined me as if I were at a slave market."

As if to confirm her words, the red priestess walked over to the Finikian and felt her shoulders and arms. Thais pushed the woman indignantly, gesturing for her to leave.

All of the hetaera's possessions had already been laid out on the carpets in the second room, which opened onto a terrace. A staircase descended toward the road under the tall pines. Thais' dwelling was located on the outside of the temple walls, while the passageway with the grate apparently pierced the entire thickness.

Thais breathed in the dry air, saturated with scents of pine resin and wormwood. She felt sick. This never happened to her. She was dizzy, and her breasts and belly, where they had been anointed with the blue stuff, were burning. She could still taste the tart temple potion in her mouth. Shivers ran down her spine.

Thais returned to her rooms. Vaguely, as if in a dream, she noticed Za-Asht's strangely luminous eyes and wanted to ask whether she had been given anything to drink at the temple, but before she could say anything she was suddenly engulfed by a strange kind of languor. She fell on the bed among strangely-scented pillows and throws, falling asleep instantly.

She woke up several times in alarm, then collapsed into sleep again.

A series of visions and uncommonly strong sensations, more vivid than life itself, was torturous. The bewitching ointment or the drink or both of them combined brought forth sexual desire of unbearable power. A frightened Thais sensed her own body as something separate, filled with wild cravings, trapping her mind and willpower, and focusing all the powers and senses of the body in the essence of its feminine nature.

The deepest, hot darkness with nary a glint of light or breath of coolness, wrapped itself around Thais. She tossed, moaned and twisted in the monstrous nightmares she couldn't have imagined in her most feverish moments. The terror before the abyss that opened within her made her wake several times.

Thais didn't know of an antidote to the poison given to her by the priestess. The drug possessed her, and fire raged in her body, burning from the ointment. Thais descended lower and lower in her desires, incarnating into the primitive mythical heroines: Leda, Philarrenippa, Pasiphae ... The hetaera was exhausted under the burden of the dark forces of Anteros. Had it not been for her spiritual training, acquired from the Orphics, she would have rushed to the temple of Rhea to beg the goddess for release. During yet another period of wakefulness she stumbled to her medicine chest, rocking and shaking, and managed to crush a few bits of dried poppy flowers in some wine. Having downed an entire goblet, Thais soon fell into a foggy sleep with no memory and no visions.

Wind, pure and cold, flew in from the eastern plains, burst through the open door and windows and woke up a chilled Athenian. Thais barely contained a moan, feeling sore in every muscle as if she'd galloped for twenty parsangs without a stop. Her bitten lips were swollen, she didn't even dare touch her breasts. Thais found Za-Asht in the next room on a woven reed mat, spread out as if in a fever. When she woke the girl, Za-Asht couldn't seem to come to her senses, glancing at her mistress with either fear or rage. Thais herself was growing coldly furious. She mentally sent to the ravens[27] the temple rituals she was so interested in, and the cunning priestesses of Astarte, who had purposely given her the horrible potion in order to force the servant of Aphrodite to feel the power of the Great Mother.

She gave the Finikian something to drink and rubbed her temples with fresh scented oil. Finally Za-Asht, moving slowly, brought some warm water, bathed and rubbed Thais down, finally waking completely. A servant from the temple brought some food, fortunately of the simplest kind: honey, milk, bread, dry grapes, none of which could be mixed with poison.

Thais felt stronger after she ate, so she went down to the grove to visit her soldiers, who were settled outside of the temple boundaries. She sped up, feeling her energy returning, and finally ran, rejoicing with her entire body.

Around the bend in the road the hetaera almost ended up under the hooves of the horses. Five riders rode toward her, leading two saddled horses. One of them reared up with a loud whinny. Thais recognized Salmaakh only after the mare greeted her mistress, and was astonished at her own absentmindedness. She blamed it on the poison. Boanergos, who was running next to Salmaakh, neighed quietly, as if embarrassed to express his feelings. Salmaakh pressed her ears back and tried to kick him to prevent his approaching the mistress. The pacer let the mare go forward, then suddenly bit her on the croup. Salmaakh dashed

---

27 To hell

forward and missed her, while Boanergos stopped right in front of the Athenian.

Without further ado, Thais hopped onto his back and yanked the reins away from the stableman. Boanergos touched off at such a pace that he quickly left everyone else behind. Thais rode for nearly a skhen, going deeper into the grove, until she finally stopped the chestnut pacer. She squeezed him firmly with her knees and patted his broad neck.

The captain, lokhagos, had caught up with her. He noted sternly that she oughtn't walk or ride alone here in the strange country, though he admitted he admired her courage.

"Why?" Thais exclaimed.

"Because you'll be kidnapped or killed. Then all I'll have left is to ask my comrades to kill me and spare me the disgrace, because I was unable to take care of you. I don't even want to think of the punishment Ptolemy might come up with, or even our divine Alexander himself."

The old soldier's sincerity shamed the hetaera. She swore by the waters of Styx that she would be obedient. She would not stray far from the temple, even on horseback.

"In that case, one soldier is sufficient," the captain decided. "He can cover your retreat, while you go get help, if needed." Thais noticed that the young hestiotus, Lykophon, was as handsome as Ganymede. He swapped his horse for Salmaakh, who was compliant with her new rider, then rushed to the Macedonian's house to get his weapons. His four remaining comrades waited for his return, wished their beautiful charge the best of health, then rode to reunite with the other seven Macedonians who were busy exercising the horses to the south from the temple.

Thais knew her companion from their trip to Hierapolis and frequently caught his admiring gazes. Smiling at him, she directed the pacer to the east, where the pine trees grew thinner and faded into the sand hills covered with bunches of tamarix. A few stadiums ahead, the waves of sand dunes surrounded a large grove of trees that looked like poplars. Thais suddenly wanted to peek into this cozy grove, which seemed as if it hid something forbidden.

The horses continued on, their hooves sinking in the sand, until they came to a particularly tall hill. As soon as the riders reached its top, both exclaimed in delight. A small, crystal clear lake glittered at the foot of the hill like a blue sickle. Where the lake was deeper and shadows of tall trees fell over the water, the eye was charmed by a deep turquoise color. The eastern wind did not reach here, and the green semicircle of reeds hugging the blue water barely moved their slender tips.

The visitors saw no sign of any other people, and Thais decided she simply had to bathe in this beautiful place. The plants indicated this to be fresh water, and springs bubbled up near the northeast tip of the "sickle".

"Go on down to feed the horses, but not too far," Thais said to Lykophon. "I'll go for a swim then join you."

The young Thessalian shook his head. "Hippophont, the horse-killing herb, grows there. I should warn my friends not to let the horses graze there."

Pale green, thin-stemmed grass fluttered beyond the hills on the flat plane, interspersed by strips of wormwood and tall bunches of needle grass. The growth stretched to the edge of a distant pine forest, which marked the boundary of the oak-covered hills.

"Then watch the horses and don't let them go down to the lake. We don't know what sort of water is there."

"What about you, Mistress Thais?"

The Athenian lifted her hand to calm him. "I'll test it before diving. Perhaps you should tie the horses to a tree."

Thais slipped down the steep, sandy slope, barely managing to stop at water's edge. She threw off her sandals, tested the water, then splashed some onto her face. It was clear, cool spring water. It had been a long time since Thais had seen such water, so completely different from the cloudy Nile and the Euphrates. Like any true Helenian, she highly valued good water.

With a joyous squeal, the hetaera dove into the glassy turquoise depths and crossed the narrow lake. She jumped out to a white sand bank, splashed around some more, then swam to the northern tip. Here the ascending current of the warm underground springs tossed her up, then dragged her down, as if rolling her in huge, soft waves. Thais wasn't afraid. She swam up, rolling onto her back and sweeping wide circles with her arms. Thais played in their bubbling domes until she grew tired and returned to the deeper waters, where she floated on her back. She swam, dove and splashed, washing away all the terrors of Anteros, until the impatient whinny of the pacer reminded her of the time.

Refreshed and happy, Thais climbed the hill to where the horses and her companion waited under a tree. By his flushed cheeks and obvious signs of embarrassment, Thais realized that the young warrior was admiring her.

"You were enjoying the water as one would fine wine, Mistress," Lykophon said. "I found I wanted some, too."

"Go, and you'll see how much better it is than any wine. I'll watch the horses." The hetaera scratched Boanergos' neck and patted Salmaakh's face, while the latter threw jealous glances at the former.

The Thessalian parted with his weapons and his military belt only when he reached the bank. Thais gazed approvingly at his wonderfully built, muscular form, which complimented the beauty of his face.

"Are you married?" she asked Lykophon after the soldier had enough of swimming and climbed back to the top of the hill.

"Not yet. Our people don't marry before twenty-five. I couldn't marry before the war, and now I don't know when I'll make it home, if I make it at all …"

"Everything is in the hands of gods, but I think they ought to be merciful to you. You will make good children."

The soldier blushed like a young boy.

"But I don't wish to invite trouble," the Athenian said, then caught herself. "Gods can be jealous. Shall we go?"

Salmaakh and Boanergos dashed forward at full speed as soon as they made it out of the sands. In order to exercise the horses, Thais turned to the north when they reached the road and, having ridden almost a parsang, rode up to the ridge above the valley of one of the Euphrates' tributaries. Gnarled, sprawling oak trees surrounded a moss-covered portico with four pillars, hiding a statue of Ishtar Kutitum, which was made of smoothly polished gray stone. Greenish gold chrysolite eyes glittered in the shadow. The Scythian face had slightly high cheekbones framed by shoulder length, cropped hair, and bore a disdainful expression.

In the back of the portico, behind the statue, a narrow passageway led into a small cell. It was well lit through a wide opening in the roof. A tile of fired clay was set into a niche in the eastern wall, above the black wood altar. The tile was covered with pronounced sculptural images. The nude goddess stood on legs which ended in tightly joined owl's feet, and her hands were held at the level of her face, with palms turned outward. A rope knot was carved in detail, held in her left hand. Owl's wings, pictured behind her back, hung to the middle of her hips, and feathers were also visible above her ankles.

The goddess stood on the back of a lion, with another lion lying behind, its head turned to the side. The lower corners of the tile were taken up by the images of huge owls, much larger than the lions. Scale-like protrusions at the lower edge symbolized a mountain range. The entire sculptural group was painted with bright colors, including red for the goddess' body and black for the lions' manes. Black and red feathers were in both her wings and those of the owls.

Something about the enthasis of the goddess' perfectly straight posture, her menacing companions with their terrible paws and wings, frightened Thais. But her fear vanished before the delight of the statue's physical beauty. The goddess' strong. shapely legs and pert, semi-spherical breasts were similar to those Thais had seen on the Cretan and late Helenian sculptures. Her narrow torso and curvy hips, all combined to create a harmonious image of sensuous power. The goddess was the seductive Ashtoreth-Ishtar, aggressive in her feminine power over beasts and people, more terrible than Rhea-Kibela, more mysterious than Artemis and Aphrodite.

Thais bowed before the ancient sculpture and promised the goddess some flowers.

Later, the Athenian asked the high priestess about the strange winged goddess. She discovered that separate sanctuaries of Ishtar Kutitum, who was worshiped along with the queen of the night, goddess Lilith, have existed near the temples of the Mother of Gods since the times of the ancient kings of Mesopotamia, approximately fifteen hundred years ago. She was still considered to be one of the faces of the Great Mother: Lilith was a goddess of submission to male love, and the rope in her hand was a symbol of that duty. Thais remembered the story by Herodotus about the Babylonian tradition of service to the Great Goddess, when the most prominent women of the city went to the temples of Ashtoreth to offer themselves to strangers. As a sign of their service, they tied a thick rope around their heads. Ishtar Kutitum must have brought forth the Syrian and Finikian goddess Cotytto, who was worshiped as the mistress of uncontrolled passion.

Lilith did not come across as being particularly benevolent on this first meeting. Trying to push away a bad premonition, Thais sent the pacer down to the pine grove at a swift trot. Reveling in the speed, the warm wind and the freshness of her own clean body, Thais rode up to the temple of the Great Mother, handed the reins to Lykophon and thanked him. From the moment they had left the lake of the Waxing Moon, as Thais nicknamed it, the Thessalian kept mum as if he had given a vow of silence.

Za-Asht said that a messenger had come from the high priestess and left a bronze disk. Whenever the mistress was rested enough, she should strike it and the messenger would come to take her back to the temple. The hetaera winced. She really did not want to go back into the sanctuary of the powerful goddess. She sensed there were more trials ahead.

The light, beautiful and mischievous joy of gods and people serving Aphrodite was very different from the unflinching Mother of Gods. It was not entirely in contradiction with her, but not in agreement either. One was the depth of fruit-bearing Earth, the other like the flight of the wind in the clouds.

As usual, Thais had dinner with her slave girl. But the Finikian, who was generally fond of food, hardly touched her meal. Quiet and keeping her eyes down, she settled the hetaera down on the bed and started massaging her legs, which were tired from the ride.

Thais watched her slave girl quietly, then finally asked, "What is the matter with you, Za-Asht? You haven't been yourself since last night. Did you have too much of the poison?"

Suddenly the Finikian threw herself onto the floor and whispered passionately, clutching her mistress' knees. "Let me stay at the temple, Mistress. They say I may become a priestess after a year of trials and serve Ashtoreth-Kibela like they do."

Thais sat up in surprise. "Did the priestesses tell you of the trials? They could be such that you won't even think about the temple. It is possible that you would begin your service to Kibela from the lowest stage and offer yourself to every stranger that comes here."

"I don't care. I am not afraid of anything. If only I could stay here and serve her, whose power I experienced last night. Her power enslaved me."

The Athenian studied her slave girl carefully, remembering how sarcastic, mean and skeptical she usually was. Now she had been consumed in the fire of faith, as if she were fourteen. Perhaps Moira, the goddess of fate, had brought the Finikian here to serve at the temple. If she actually discovered herself here, it was the same as falling in love. In cases such as this, Thais never objected. If she lost her beautiful servants she would simply finding new ones just as eager to serve her.

But Thais hesitated. She was always careful when deciding the fates of her people. Besides, Za-Asht was all she had at the moment. Would she be able to find her replacement in this secluded temple town? Thais shook her head, not refusing, but not agreeing either.

"Wait. First, I shall find out what they will do with you, then I will find a replacement."

The girl's moist eyes lit up. "But you do not refuse. Oh, thank you, Mistress."

"Don't celebrate just yet. Nothing has been decided," Thais warned the Finikian, who had started massaging her with twice the energy. "Tell me, Za-

Asht," Thais asked thoughtfully, rolling over onto her back. "Do you not see any other path in life, save for the service to the Mother of Gods? You are intelligent and attractive, and while fate made you a slave, that can change. Slavery at the temple is worse, for Kibela's power is limitless."

"You don't know, Mistress, how jealous Finikians, Syrians and other local people are. We women do not like to see beauty in other women. The Great Mother makes everyone equal with her mighty hand."

"I think different people serve her in different ways," Thais objected. "Do I understand you correctly? Do you not love me at all?"

"Yes, Mistress, but you are too beautiful. I have looked and could not find a flaw in you. You are as agile as our thirteen year old dancer girls, strong as a mare, your breasts are as firm as those of the Nubian women at the dawn of their youth ..."

"It is a list worthy of a lover," the hetaera said, then laughed. "But what is it that offends you so?"

"You are better than everyone around, including me."

"And because of that you are ready to be a slave to the temple?"

"Yes, yes."

Thais shrugged her shoulders, still not understanding her slave girl. After a long pause, Za-Asht said, "The blue stones are so beautiful against your copper skin, Mistress. They make your gray eyes look even deeper. Whoever gave you this necklace understands the beauty of things."

"It was the high priestess of Kibela-Rhea, Ashtoreth, or Ishtar, the many-named Mother of Gods."

"Are you going to wear your old necklace like a belt?"

"Yes, like Hippolita, the queen of the Amazons." Thais inspected the golden chain and decided to take off all the stars, except one. Her first victories and successes had long since vanished into the past, and even the star that had been given to her by Ptolemy didn't mean anything. Only the last one with the letter mu. The priestess had said it had been a female symbol since the ancient times.

"Can you find me a jeweler to take off the stars, except the last one?" the hetaera asked.

"Let me. I am the daughter of a jeweler and know a thing or two."

The Finikian took the belt, went into the corner of the room and pulled out tiny tweezers from her bag. She worked her magic with them, then returned. She triumphantly fastened the chain with one star around Thais' waist.

"Now the balance is in the middle," she said, fixing the former necklace. She handed Thais the remaining stars.

"Put them in the jewelry box," Thais said. "You are quite a skilled woman. How can I bear to part with you?"

The Finikian's face fell, but then she realized Thais was teasing her. With a smile, she ran to get the box.

"Would you like to come with me tomorrow?" the hetaera asked, snuggling lazily into the cushions. "There is a little blue lake nearby in the shape of the moon. I bathed there today and enjoyed it more than I have enjoyed anything in a long time."

"What did you do, Mistress?" Za-Asht demanded. Her expression was filled with terror.

Thais lifted herself on one elbow and frowned. "Why are you yelling as if you are at the Syrian market? What is the matter?"

"I was told there is a sacred lake of Ishtar to the east of the temple, shaped like the moon. Cleansing of Ashtoreth takes place there in secret on the days of celebration. I think Helenians call her Artemis. Anyone who gets a glimpse of the sacred ritual is killed on the spot by the priests with long spears. I am afraid for you, Mistress. Ashtoreth is vengeful, and her servants are just as bad."

Thais pondered this. "I think I'll keep quiet about this. And I won't take you with me, although I will go swimming there again."

"Oh, Mistress ..." Za-Asht began, then she dashed to the terrace door, hearing the clanking of armor. Thais pulled a silvery throw over herself. Lykophon entered shortly.

"Forgive me, Mistress, for disturbing you at a bad time," he said with a bow.

"Is something wrong? With Boanergos or Salmaakh?"

"No, the horses are alive and well. It is only that an army messenger arrived and brought you a letter from Ptolemy the strategist. Here," the soldier said. He handed her a packet of thin leather tied with a rope. A deltorion was attached, a small slate bearing Thais' name and instructions to deliver immediately.

Thais placed the packet on a pillow and asked the soldier to sit down and have some wine. The Finikian, who had long since been enchanted by Lykophon's beauty, instantly diluted and served some pink wine, wiggling her hips and throwing brief and pointed glances at the Thessalian. The young warrior straightened and drank a goblet, and Za-Asht poured him another. Lykophon waved his hand to decline, but accidentally as he did so he knocked the bronze disk from the edge of the table to the floor.

The bronze disk rung loudly as it struck the floor tiles. Soon someone knocked on the door to the corridor leading into the temple. A priestess in black net entered the room. Raising her hand to her forehead, she straightened up and gazed at everyone present with indifference.

"Ah! What have you done?" Thais asked the soldier, frowning. "Now I have to go."

Lykophon didn't notice her reproach. He slowly rose from his seat, gazing at the black priestess as if Aphrodite herself had magically appeared before him, taking shape from sea foam and starlight.

Thais was disturbed by the feeling of alien power emitted by the incredible woman. It felt like something not altogether human. It was as if she were an oread, a mountain nymph, or a mythical changeling, a titanide. The priestess was not indifferent toward the Thessalian's admiration. She tipped her head slightly, and it was as if lightning flew out of her enormous eyes, finishing the victim. The young man blushed and lowered his eyes, pausing to look with awe upon her muscular legs and her amazingly sculpted feet. The priestess, glittering with her mirror nails, moved a strand of black hair to reveal her glum and beautiful face, as if before a battle.

Thais, who was normally far from jealous, couldn't stand seeing one of her soldiers being bent in half like a thin branch.

"Za-Asht, won't you offer Lykophon more wine? Perhaps he would like something to eat? Come," she said dismissively to the black priestess, who smiled briefly and condescendingly, but not before sending the young soldier one more long, promising glance.

Thais wanted to walk ahead, but the priestess slipped silently forward and walked along the passage without a backward glance. She paused to wait for the hetaera near the grate, blocking the corridor. She summoned the chained gatekeeper, who huddled on a pile of dry grass in a barely lit niche. The guide did not go straight into the sanctuary, but turned right into the side passage, which was brightly lit and ended in a staircase leading up. They entered the upper floor, went up another staircase, and found themselves on a verandah. Behind them was the topmost structure. It had no windows and only one single bronze door of tremendous weight and strength. Cone-shaped protrusions covered the walls and the top floor. Thais guessed that it was a treasury and thought it was rather careless to keep valuables at such a height. What if there were a fire?

"What are you looking at, my daughter?" the high priestess asked.

Thais turned and saw her sitting in an ivory armchair next to a man, probably the high priest. The Athenian walked up to her, sat down on a bench decorated with ivory, and shared her concern.

"I know that you are smart, servant of Aphrodite. But those who built this sacred place weren't fools either. The entire temple consists only of bricks, frescoes, and tiles of granite and marble that cover the ceilings. The builders made it so that even if fire were set intentionally, nothing would be lost save a few curtains and armchairs."

Thais was interested. She told them she had seen such methods of longterm construction in Egypt. The high priestess asked her several questions, then grew silent. Thais enjoyed the artful setting of the temple. In Hellas, the temples were built atop natural high points, like the tops of hills, along the edges of tall river banks, or on the crests of mountain ranges. When someone physically ascended to the temple, he also ascended spiritually, preparing to commune with the gods.

This temple, the priestess explained, was constructed according to the canons of the most ancient sanctuaries of Mesopotamia. It stood in the center of a round valley, walled by mountains on the south, west and north, leaving the east side open to the Euphrates. The treasury structure on the top and the pedestal on the bottom made the total height of the temple quite impressive. People who approached it from the valley could see the sanctuary from far away. As they came nearer, the building appeared to hang or loom over people, oppressing them so that they felt small before the mighty goddess and her servants.

Thais particularly enjoyed the view of the surrounding lands, perhaps seeing for the first time how the influence of height affected a person's consciousness. The reality of being separate from everything that was taking place down below, the feeling of one's own inaccessibility, the ability to cover great areas with one glance, all were different from just being in the mountains. A mountain climber conquering great heights was still a part of the surrounding nature. But this artificial structure protruded arrogantly in the middle of the valley, separating itself from the natural soil and bestowing feelings of superiority, purity and independence upon those who lived at the temple. Far in the east, beyond the dusty fog, lay the valley of the Euphrates. Its tributary flowed through the dark canyon in the north. The range above was home to a small temple to the Ishtar of Persia.

The silence was broken when the high priest said something, speaking in a language with which the hetaera was not familiar. In response, the priestess stretched out in her roomy armchair and asked whether their guest would like to continue familiarizing herself with the mysteries of the Mother of Gods. Thais replied that she had felt poisoned all night, and if "familiarizing" continued down the same path, she wouldn't last much longer. The priestess chuckled both sternly and approvingly, then confessed that Thais' dose of the ointment had been too strong. They hadn't realized the Helenian was unaccustomed to such things. She promised they would be more careful in the future.

To delay giving an answer, because to directly refuse the hosts of this sacred place was inconceivable, Thais asked about the meaning of the priestesses' garments and why they they were separated into two groups.

"There is no mystery in that," the high priestess said. "The red priestesses serve during the day and represent the daytime powers of Kibela, while the black ones represent nighttime. In Libya and Hellas they are called Lamias, Hecate's companions. It is thought that he who earns the love of such a priestess partakes of the powers of Kibela-Rhea, or Gaea, as you call her. He shall have good health, luck and fine offspring for the rest of his life. The skill of the priestesses, especially of the black ones, is above anything a mortal woman can give, because it is inspired by the Great Mother and strengthened by her might.

"Can any man attain that?"

The eyes of the high priestess flashed like those of a wild beast. Thais shivered, but held her gaze. "Any man," the priestess said. "As long as he is not ugly and is of good health and sufficient strength."

"How do you determine that?"

"That is what the net garment is for. It is strong, and in order to take the priestess, he must rip the net with his bare hands. Only a strong man possessed by uncontrollable passion is capable of that."

"And what if he is not capable and can't rip it?"

The high priestess leaned toward Thais and said quietly, "Then Kibela's wrath falls upon him. If he chose a red priestess of the day, she calls out and the ill-fated man is caught, castrated on the altar before Kibela, and made a temple slave if he survives. The black priestess, Lamia, calls no one. Instead, she holds the unfortunate man to her, then bestows upon him Kibela's kiss, stabbing him with a dagger here," the priestess said, placing her finger in the hollow behind her left collarbone.

"What is the sense the Great Mother places in such violence?"

"Only the strongest, most beautiful and most self-assured heroes come here to become the lovers of Day and Night. Children are born and the girls become high priestesses. The boys become guards and keepers of the sanctuary. Have you noticed how strong they are? How long their spears are, and how heavy their swords?"

"I have also noticed that your high priestesses are beautiful, not one more so than the other. But is the intention only to get offspring for the temple? One could find children that are just as beautiful among thousands of others," Thais objected.

"You are much too intelligent for someone not initiated," the priestess said with a slightly mocking smile. Like Ishtar, Thais thought. "Of course that is not the true meaning. Humankind weakens over time, and the passionate madness of Kibela-Ashtoreth-Atargatis no longer possesses people like it used to. Kibela wants the fire of sensual rage, just as Aphrodite wants love."

Thais thought of Urania and the priestess continued. "The service of our women immerses people into nature, uniting them with all living things reared by Rhea-Kibela. That is a man's happiness and destiny. Gods do not offer a better path. Men find themselves and do that for which they are destined. If they turn out to be unsuitable, the Great Mother calls them back to her, to bring them forth again for a better life. And the men go to her never knowing the bitterness of old age, in the midst of fiery youth."

"Why are you so certain that people are growing weaker?" Thais asked, hiding a smile.

The priestess suddenly laughed. "Look once again at the image of Kibela-Rhea captured in the ancient statue, and you'll realize that only insatiable desire can seek such an ideal, and only incredible strength and endurance can hope to match hers."

Thais remembered the incomparable might captured within the boundaries of that harmonious body and emitted by Rhea's statue, and couldn't find any objections.

"Where do the black ones and the red ones live?" she asked, changing the subject.

"They do not leave the temple while they are young. They frequently marry important people or travel, taking high level positions in other, less important temples of Rhea. On certain days of the month they go bathing in a sacred lake, and woe be upon those men who violate their seclusion."

"What if it is a woman?" the hetaera asked, realizing which lake the woman meant.

"Nothing would happen to her. Only if the unfortunate woman violates the purity of the sacred water would she be killed."

"Do the priestesses live there?" Thais asked quickly, pointing at the southern wing of the temple. Its flat roof was level with the floor of the main section.

"You are correct. Would you like to visit them?"

"Oh no. And what is in the northern wing?"

The priestess' eyes flashed again. "I want to take you there at sunset. But I cannot do that unless you bring a sacred vow upon the alter of Kibela-Rhea: the vow of silence. We keep the ancient mysteries of the Great Mother secret. The rituals of the ancient times, brought here thousands of years ago from Licaonia and Phrygia, give power to the servants of Ashtoreth."

Thais swore to keep the secret in the sanctuary, which was completely deserted at this hour. The mistress of the temple poured her a drink and Thais stepped back.

"Don't be afraid, it's not yesterday's potion. But you will require courage when you see the mystery. Remember that the Great Mother is a mistress of animals," she said in a strained whisper which filled the hetaera with vague fear. She downed the entire goblet at once.

"Excellent. Now accept this gift." The priestess handed Thais two vials made of milky white glass, their deep pink stoppers made of precious Indian tourmaline. A moon sickle was carved on one of the vials and an eight point star on another.

"How can I? I cannot accept such expensive things," Thais exclaimed.

"It's nothing," the high priestess replied. "The temple of the Great Mother is wealthy and can make even more precious gifts to beautiful women, for they are jewels created by Rhea for her own purposes. But you didn't ask what is in the vials. This one," she said, pointing at the vial with the star, "was in the potion you were given yesterday. If you ever wish to experience all of Ashtoreth-Kibela's power in the guise of Anaitis, put six drops into a cup of water and split between the two of you. This one with the moon will free you from the effect of the first one. If you drink it alone, it will make you as cold as the distant Moon. No more than three drops, or you might remain cold forever," the priestess said, then laughed, a sound both grating and menacing.

She led the hetaera to a niche in a side wall and pulled out a shiny black disk which Thais thought looked as if it were made of glass. In it she saw her own reflection, as clearly as in a regular mirror of silver covered bronze.

"This mirror is not made of glass but of stone," the woman informed her. "It was made when people knew only stone. Metal ores served them as permanent paints, for even then they already painted on walls. Women gazed into this mirror many thousands of years ago, before Egypt and Crete. Take this as a gift as well."

"You are giving me another priceless object. Why?" Thais asked.

"I am giving it to you along with the vials containing poison. Beauty and death are always together, since the dawn of men."

"Death for whom?"

"For the one who is beautiful, or for the one who takes it, or for both."

"Is there no other way?"

"No. Such is the way of the Mother of Gods, and it is not up to us to discuss it," the mistress of the temple said sternly. Her tone almost threatened.

"I thank you. Your gift is truly beyond all treasures."

"Are you not afraid?"

"Of what?"

"Of the mysteries of the Great Mother." She narrowed her eyes while Thais shook her head. "No? Then come."

In the north portion of the sanctuary a thick column protruded from the middle of a dark opening in the floor. A spiral stone staircase circled the column, leading down. The poorly lit passage led into a temple, decorated in a way Thais had never seen before. Broad stone benches on each side of the passage were set with real horns of huge bulls, or aurochs, curved with closely set, vertical tips. The low, square space of the sanctuary, with its coarse half-pillars of red terracotta, were decorated with beautifully-made heads of bulls constructed of stone or clay but with real horns. The bull's horns on the western wall stuck out like those of the aurochs on the northern wall: bent down. The ones on the eastern wall were spread out broadly in wavy, horizontal blades after the fashion of the ancient bulls of Mesopotamia.

This ancient sanctuary was strange, sinister, even frightening. Enormous horns were everywhere, including on the short, square pillars and long benches, making it difficult to move around the temple.

Silhouette frescoes of red ocher outlined figures of the bulls on the walls closest to the entrance.

Between the bulls' heads were women's breasts made of blood red clay, their nipples decorated with beaks of black griffons and snarling ferret skulls. The first room was followed by a smaller hall, with a sharp-cornered niche in the northern wall. Three horned bulls' heads were set vertically, one above the other, with the figure of the goddess soaring above them with her arms and legs spread. On each side of the niche, two black passages loomed black.

The horns bothered Thais for some reason she was having trouble placing. Suddenly a vivid recollection flashed in her memory. The same symbols, but made of stone and magnified to titanic dimensions, marked sacred places on Crete. In one of the frescoes the Athenian had seen the image of a sanctuary, similar to the one she was in now. Horns of different sizes had separated the fresco's sacrificial room into different segments. But here the real horns of wild bulls seemed particularly sinister. Though they were relatively small, they made just as strong an impression as the gigantic stone horns rising from the soil of Crete. Thais could clearly see the deep connection between the ancient religion of the Great Mother in Asia and the faith of her ancestors on Crete.

The sculptures of bulls in the sanctuary were particularly terrifying. They did not look like the blunt-faced Cretan giants with their tall horns pointed up. The bulls of the ancient sanctuary were portrayed with long lowered heads, their huge horns pointed forward. They either converged over the forehead with their tips curved menacingly, or were spread wide and arched like knives. This was definitely a different breed, and the Athenian thought that the sacred Cretan dance with the bulls wouldn't have been successful with these frightening creatures as they seemed hellbent on a fight.

The high priestess paused and listened. Deep, low, rhythmic sounds of gipatas, the strings on the very bottom of a sitar, could be heard in the distance, interwoven with female voices, moans and screams.

Thais' heart beat faster, expecting something terrible. The priestess silently picked up a torch from a horn-decorated pedestal, lit it from the coals simmering on the sacrificial stone, and stepped into the left passage. After passing through another dark corridor which felt more like a dungeon, Thais found herself in a spacious building, level with the temple garden.

Thais would never tell anyone about the things she saw here, but she remembered every single moment. In Egypt she had been struck by the frescoes in the dungeons of the Dead, portraying Tiau or the Path of the Night Sun. That was the Egyptian version of hell, located on the other invisible side of the Moon. But those were only images. Here at the temple that was almost as ancient as the stone mirror, the ten thousand year old rituals of the Great Mother took place in reality, and were performed by real people.

Strengthened by Rhea's potion, Thais managed to withstand the performance to the end. All four stages of the incredible ritual passed before her eyes, gradually clarifying their secret meaning. The roots of Earth-Gaea and all things living on it descended into the abyss of chaotic storms, sweeping over Tartar in the terrible darkness of Erebus. That was why the roots of the soul also rose from the darkness of primal feelings, swirling in the womb of Kibela. These feelings, the darkness and terrors had to be experienced in order to become free from their secret power. They had to be released before the eyes of the women who were simultaneously the victims and the participants of the great union with the roots of all nature in the image of Ananka, an unavoidable necessity.

Late at night, accompanied by a black priestess, Thais returned to her temporary home feeling astonished, tired and depressed. Za-Asht was awake, waiting for her mistress. The slave girl's eyes were swollen from tears, and Thais noticed nail marks in her palms. Thais had no energy to ask, and fell into bed without a bath. As a result, Ptolemy's letter remained unread.

Thais could not sleep. The Finikian also tossed and sighed until the hetaera called her over.

"Sit down and tell me what happened. Did Lykophon offend you?" Za-Asht nodded silently, and anger flashed in the dark depths of her eyes.

"I shall call him tomorrow and ask the lokhagos to punish the Thessalian."

"No, no, Mistress. He didn't do anything and I don't want to see him anymore."

"Really? What a strange young man. You are beautiful, and I saw the way he looked at you. Did you give him more wine?"

"He downed a goblet as if it were nasty desert water. He didn't touch the food and said nothing, simply stared at the door after that Lamia, daughter of the dark. This went on forever until I lost my patience and kicked him out. And then he left without a thank you or a word, as if he were drunk with millet beer."

"I had never expected this," Thais exclaimed. "Did the Lamia truly strike him with Eros? Why? He had seen you dance balarita, how agile your body is and how slender your legs are."

"You are kind to me, Mistress," the Finikian replied, barely holding back tears. "But you are a woman and won't understand the black Lamia's power. I looked at her carefully. Everything in her is contrary to what is in me."

"How so?"

"Everything that is narrow in me is wide in her: hips, ankles and eyes. Everything that is wide in me is thin in her: shoulders and waist," the Finikian said, clearly upset. "She is built like you, Mistress, but heavier, more muscular. And it drives men mad, especially those like this boy."

"So he rejected you and thinks about her?" Thais shrugged. "That is all right. We shall soon travel on and the Lamia will fade from Lykophon's memory. Oh, I forgot. Do you still want to stay here? Do you?"

"Now more than ever, Mistress. We Finikians have a teaching of Senhuniathon. It says that desire is creation. And I want to create myself anew."

"We too have desire: Pothos. That is also creation. Desperate desire either brings forth the necessary form or ends in anoya, or madness. We shall see when the time comes. Give me the letter."

Ptolemy sent his greetings and asked her to remember him. He instructed Thais absolutely not to travel further until he sent a detachment of soldiers to get her, commanded by his friend. If the news were bad, Thais should not stay at the temple, but take her soldiers and make a dash to the Issus bay. That was only fifteen parsangs away to the west, over the mountains. Three ships would be waiting there. The captain would pick up Thais and wait another half a month. If Ptolemy and Alexander did not appear by then, they should sail back to Hellas.

Thais kissed the letter tenderly. She thought Ptolemy was more noble at heart than he wanted to show among the crass Macedonian army leaders. Ptolemy wrote about the march across the hot plain, how the sea of tall grass had already faded from the summer drought. He said they rode and rode, day after day, going further beyond the horizon.

Vague premonitions had bothered everyone, even Alexander. Ptolemy could see lanterns burning late into the night in Alexander's tent. The king had consulted with his spies and read their reports. Gradually Alexander had directed the army to the left, further to the north. The guides had warned him about the greater heat yet to come. The grass would fade, and the small rivers and creeks which supplied the army with water would dry out.

Thirty-five thousand people were now following Alexander, but there in the limitless plains of Asia, the king felt for the first time that his army wasn't all that big. Hot winds blew at them with the breath of the deadly deserts which sprawled beyond the plains. Dust swirled like demons, and hot air at the horizon seemed to lift the earth above the blue lakes of ghostly water.

Ptolemy went on to say that when they turned north, the grass became taller and thicker, and yellowish rivers turned gray. There was a full Lunar eclipse.

"How did I miss that?" Thais wondered, then continued reading.

Knowledgeable people said the army was now in the country governed by the Mistress of Beasts, including those of heaven, earth and subterranean. She was called Ashtoreth, Kibela or Rhea. Helenians called her Artemis or Hecate. If she appeared riding a lion, everyone would perish.

Alexander had addressed his soldiers in a speech, asking them not to be afraid. He knew their destiny, and led them to the end of war, as well as countless treasures.

Thais read between Ptolemy's lines, realizing he was a born writer. She discovered that the Macedonians had encountered a new feeling: fear.

For the first time, the hetaera thought about how insanely brave was Alexander's mission. What divine courage one must possess in order to walk away from the sea and plunge into the depths of a strange country where they would meet the countless troops of the King of Kings. If they were defeated, Thais realized, the Macedonian army would be wiped off the face of earth. The divine army leader, Ptolemy, and Leontiscus would all cease to exist. Nearchus alone might possibly manage to save his fleet and return to his native shores.

Their countless enemies, both large and small, must be waiting for this with such wicked impatience, burning with justified revenge and the cowardly triumph of hyenas.

Her friends could not possibly rely on the mercy of others. Ptolemy was wise to leave behind two possibilities for saving Alexander and himself. The first was with Nearchus' fleet, waiting near the delta of the Euphrates in case they met Darius in the south. Ptolemy wrote about the rumors that Darius had assembled all his troops, including countless horsemen ranging from the famous Persian Immortal guards to Bactrians and Sogdians.

It was strange, but despite glimpses of anxiety she read in Ptolemy's letter, Thais was filled with the certainty of victory soon to come. She would wait for more news with even greater impatience.

The next day, instead of Lykophon, the lokhagos sent a pockmarked Macedonian with fresh scars on his shoulder and neck.

"I am here instead of the hestiotus," the soldier said, smiling. He was clearly pleased at the prospect of a ride with a famous beauty of Athens, the city of legendary elegance and wisdom.

"Where is Lykophon?"

When he said nothing, Thais clapped her hands, summoning Za-Asht, then sent the soldier to get his horse. The Finikian hopped on Salmaakh, whom she had ridden many times during the trip from the Egyptian border, and her sad face lit up with childlike joy. The two women started racing each other, leaving their guard behind and pausing only after he shouted angrily.

Having arrived at the edge of the deserted plane, both women stopped, enchanted. The plain was blooming with incredibly bright flowers unseen in Hellas. Globes the size of apples painted in a divine sky blue color fluttered on tall bare stems. They were scattered everywhere, along with the tall plants blooming with round yellow, almost gold flower clusters and sparse narrow leaves. The gold and blue pattern spread out as far as the eye could see, glorious against the background of dusty green in the transparent morning air.

"It's a miracle!" the Macedonian exclaimed, struck by the fairytale colors. They decided not to ride through, because it would be a shame to ruin all that beauty with the hooves of horses.

They turned right to go around, but were forced to stop again before the growth of even more incredible flowers. Coarse tipped plants, tall enough to reach the riders' feet, grew around them, covered with large crimson flowers and shaped like five point stars. Their petals had wide bases and sharp tips.

Thais couldn't stand it. She hopped off the pacer and picked an armful of purple flowers while the Finikian gathered gold and blue globes. The stems of the latter turned out to be much like regular chive with a sharp onion scent.

Thais rode back at full speed, ascending the northern range and heading toward the small temple of the mocking, alien Ishtar. Trying not to look at the goddess' slanted green gold eyes, Thais spread the flowers on the altar, stood for a minute, then snuck into the sanctuary with the high relief tile of the menacing Lilith. There she pulled out a hairpin and stuck it into a finger on her left hand. She smudged blood onto the altar, then walked away, licking the scratch. On the way back, her good humor deserted her. She suddenly felt sad, the way the young Thessalian had the day before. Was it the magic of the Persian goddess?

Soon Thais discovered the reason for her pensive mood. For some reason, after visiting Ishtar, she had felt concern for the handsome warrior. What if the young man decided to ask for the love of the black priestess, not knowing anything about Kibela's laws?

Would they warn the neophyte about what he was up against? If they did not, it would be not only cruel, but disgusting as well. Without waiting for an invitation, Thais decided to go and ask the high priestess; however, getting to see her turned out to be a difficult matter.

After the evening meal, the hetaera opened the inner door of her apartment. It led into the long hallway, which ascended to the sanctuary. She reached the locked grate and knocked, summoning the chained guard. The fallen priestess peeked out of her niche, pressed her finger to her lips and shook her head. Thais smiled and turned back obediently, remembering the hungry glint in the eyes of the punished woman, her hollow cheeks and belly. Thais sent the Finikian with some food for the woman, and Za-Asht was gone a long time. The guard had taken awhile to accept the food, since she had to ensure she was being neither bribed nor betrayed. After that, the Finikian or Thais herself fed the woman twice a day, having discovered a good time when there was no risk of getting caught by the servants of the temple.

Several days passed and Thais heard nothing of her hosts. The people of the temple seemed to have forgotten about their guest. Thais figured the high priestess must have been disappointed, since she had failed to captivate the hetaera and attract her into the service to Kibela-Ashtoreth, and into the mysteries of the Mother of Gods. Darkness, cruelty and torture inspired nothing but unyielding resistance in Thais' soul.

She went riding either with the old pockmarked soldier, or with the lokhagos himself. The soldier was, for some reason, nicknamed Onophorbos, or "shepherd of donkeys", by his comrades. Despite great temptation, Thais dared to swim in the wonderful little lake of the Waxing Moon only once. It was not out of fear of being caught – Boanergos' speed would have saved her from that – but because she did not wish to offend the servants of Rhea. Za-Asht always asked to accompany her mistress and grew quieter each day. Thais decided to let her slave go.

Days passed, but there was no news from the east. Alexander's army appeared to be lost somewhere in the vast planes and labyrinths of the hills. Thais consoled herself by reasoning that there simply hadn't been an opportunity to send a letter. Still, not even the rumors that had reached her before from beyond the Euphrates, had come. Thais stopped riding, didn't go to the temple and hardly ate. At night she frequently lay awake, falling asleep only at dawn.

Such strong anxiety was completely unlike the strong, healthy Athenian. She blamed it on the sinister atmosphere of Kibela's sanctuary. Had it not been for Ptolemy's warning, Thais would have long since left this "safe haven", especially considering that Rhea's temple was not really a haven for anyone. One only needed to meet her servants to realize what would be the fate of their "noble guest" should Alexander's army lose and perish. Her handful of soldiers would be killed in their sleep by the mighty guards, and Thais herself would be sent to the lower temple to earn money for the Mother of Gods. Should she resist – well, there were many places here requiring a chained guard. And that would be the better option. At worst ... Thais shuddered as she remembered the mysteries of Anaitis.

As if in response to her thoughts, there was a weak, desperate knock at her door from the temple passage. Thais jumped up and listened. She called Za-Asht, then carefully approached the door and asked, "Who is it?"

"Mistress ... open up ... in the name of ..." the voice broke off.

Thais and her slave girl recognized Lykophon. The hetaera grabbed a lantern, while the Finikian opened the door. The young warrior lay just beyond the threshold, covered in blood and too weak to lift his head. Thais dragged Lykophon into the room, and Za-Asht locked the door. On Thais' orders she took the external entrance and ran after the Macedonians as fast as she could.

Lykophon opened his eyes and smiled weakly. His dying smile cut her deeply, bringing back the pain of Menedem's death.

The familiar dagger of a night priestess stuck out of the soldier's left shoulder, having been shoved in all the way to the hilt by a firm and merciless hand. Along with his clothes, the dagger went through a wide gold necklace, becoming stuck between the links.

Like any Helenian woman, Thais knew a thing or two about wounds, and this one felt wrong. Lykophon could not possibly have survived with such a wound, let alone crawled along the long passageway, even though it sloped down. Something was different. Despite the blood still seeping from under the dagger, Thais didn't dare pull out the weapon until the arrival of the lokhagos. He was not only an experienced officer, but also a surgeon and the veterinarian of his detachment.

The soldiers didn't make her wait long. An entire decade of soldiers burst in after the Finikian, all ten with their swords and spears at the ready. The soldiers lifted the Thessalian and transferred him onto the bed. The lokhagos shook his head glumly at the sight of the wound and started examining Lykophon's shoulders. To Thais' amazement, Lykophon moaned, though his eyes remained closed. The veteran suddenly smiled.

"What? It isn't deadly?" Thais asked, gasping with shock.

The lokhagos grinned, and shrugged. "A handsome warrior is always Aphrodite's favorite. See? The dagger struck here and it would have pierced his heart, had it gone straight. But Lykophon had dressed up and put on the heavy necklace. The dagger pushed through one of the links, making it go between his ribs and his left shoulder blade. But the boy has lost too much blood. Prepare as much wine as you can, mixed with warm water. Give me some clean linen."

Without further ado, the lokhagos ordered two soldiers to hold Lykophon's shoulders down securely. He wiped the blood from the handle of the dagger, then wrapped his right hand around it so he had a good grip. While the others held Lykophon in place, the lokhagos pressed his left hand against the shoulder and pulled the weapon out in one powerful motion. The young man screamed. Despite the men holding him down, he sat straight up, his eyes bulging. Then he collapsed again on the blood-soaked bed, losing consciousness again. The lokhagos soaked his fingers in vinegar, then used them to pull the edges of the wound together. He wiped the blood from around it and bandaged it tightly with strips of linen stola, tying his comrade's arm to his torso.

The Thessalian lay quietly and indifferently, barely moving his dry, blackened lips. At the lokhagos' instruction, Za-Asht gave Lykophon water mixed with wine, which he drank one cup after another. When he had finished repairing Lykophon, the captain of the soldiers straightened up, wiped sweat from his face and accepted a goblet of wine offered by Thais.

"Who did this to him?" one of the soldiers demanded, voicing the question everyone else was thinking.

Thais tried explaining the temple rules, then told them of Lykophon's meeting with the black priestess and the young man apparently having insufficient strength. It was possible that the Thessalian had forgotten that he was only just recovering from a previous wound.

"Well, both sides are guilty, and nobody is guilty. A condition is a condition," the lokhagos said. "If you take something on, then do it. If you can't, then don't try. He is lucky to be alive, the young fool. I am glad. Lykophon is a good soldier, but has a bit of a weakness toward women. And here I thought the boy was going after her," he said, pointing at Za-Asht.

"No, no, no!" The Finikian jumped up, her eyes flashing.

He frowned at her. "Leave it be, wildcat. We all know you are into him, so be quiet," the captain said.

Za-Asht wanted to respond but was interrupted by a sharp knock from the temple door.

"Here come the pursuers," the lokhagos said. He was grinning for some reason. "Open the door, Pilemenos."

The soldier nearest to the door obeyed. An entire group of black priestesses with lit torches burst into the room, led by the high priestess, who was identifiable by her golden tiara. She was followed by the weeping black priestess who had originally come to get Thais and ended up captivating Lykophon.

"See, Kera, how much blood? I did not pity him. I struck correctly. I know not what saved him."

"You did strike correctly," the Macedonian's captain replied. "The gold necklace the young idiot put on for you is what saved him."

"I see that," the eldest agreed. "You are acquitted, Adrastea. We cannot finish him off," she said, then nodded at the Macedonians, who had grabbed their swords. "Let the great priestess be the judge of that. But Eris must be put to death for her second crime. Or, if you wish, we can send her to perform rituals in the temple of Anachita."

Only then did Thais remember the guard in the passage. She realize that had the guard not felt pity for the soldier, Lykophon would have bled to death near the locked grate and never made it to Thais' door.

Back in the dusk of the passage, one of the priestesses held the guilty woman by the hair. She was free of her chain, but her hands were tied behind her back. The eldest went back into the passage after casting an evil smile at the blood-covered, ashen young man on the bed, and an indifferent glance at the other Macedonians.

"Wait, Kera!" Thais exclaimed, having memorized the menacing name of this still-young woman. She pointed at the tied-up guard. "Give her to me."

"No. She is twice guilty and must not live."

"I will pay a ransom for her! Set the price!"

"One cannot set a price for life and death," the eldest priestess said flatly, then paused. "However, you may give one life for another," she said.

"I do not understand."

"Pity. It is simple. I shall give you Eris, and you shall give me your Finikian girl."

"Impossible. You'll kill her!"

"What for? She is not guilty of anything. I see it this way: if we are losing a priestess who fell too low to tolerate, we are acquiring another who will be suitable to begin with."

"But if you kill her, you'd lose her, even if you get another to replace her," Thais objected.

"Death and life are equal before the Great Mother."

Thais looked back at her slave, hesitating. The girl stood as pale as a whitewashed wall, leaning forward and listening to their conversation.

"Look, Za-Asht, you wanted to serve at the temple. Here is your chance, and I am letting you go. I am not exchanging you and not giving you away. You must follow only your own desires."

The Finikian dropped to her knees before Thais and kissed her hand. "Thank you, Mistress!"

Za-Asht straightened, tall and proud, then added, "I am going."

"Take your things and clothes," Thais reminded her gently.

"No need," the eldest priestess said, and nudged the Finikian toward Adrastea.

Za-Asht held back a little, but the black priestess put an arm around her waist and led her into the dark passageway. The priestesses made way and the one who was holding the tied-up girl by the hair kicked her in the back. The guard flew into Thais' room and fell facedown onto the bloodstained carpet. The door slammed shut behind her, and all became quiet.

The puzzled soldiers hesitated, then one of them picked up the fallen girl, cut the bonds around her wrists and smoothed her hair back from her face.

"Sit down, Eris," Thais said gently. "Give her some wine."

"They have such strange names," the lokhagos exclaimed. "Trouble, revenge, discourse ..."

"I heard the other two addressed as Nalia and Ata: demon and madness," Thais said. "Apparently all black priestesses have frightening Helenian names. Is that so, Eris?"

The guard nodded silently.

"Let's make a stretcher so we can carry Lykophon," the lokhagos said, breaking the silence.

"Leave him here," Thais suggested.

"No. Their patroness might change her mind. The Thessalian must be moved. But how are we to leave you alone, Mistress Thais?"

"I have a new servant girl."

"She'll stab you to death, like Lykophon, and run away."

"She has nowhere to run to. She has already saved two lives while risking her own."

"So that is how it is. Good girl. Still, I'll leave two guards on the veranda," the captain insisted, then ordered the soldiers out.

Thais locked the temple door and put both bars across, then started cleaning up the room, wiping up all the blood. Eris snapped out of her shock and helped scrub and clean.

"Clean yourself," Thais told her.

Caring nothing about her nudity, Eris ran a few times to the water cistern and furiously scrubbed off the dirt. It was layers thick since she had lived in that dirty niche near the grate.

When the dawn came, the tired hetaera closed the outside door and pulled a heavy curtain over it. She pointed Eris toward the second bed in her room, because the Finikian's bed was covered in blood.

Thais settled down and stretched out, glancing at Eris. The girl sat motionless on the edge of the bed, looking into the distance with wide open eyes. The hetaera took the chance to examine her new "acquisition".

"She appears to be a melaskhroma, black -skinned ," she thought, then changed her mind. "No, she is a melena, dark bronze with a touch of African blood."

Without her net, bracelets, belt and dagger, the black priestess was revealed as a young woman with enormous blue eyes. Those eyes were filled with the same dark stubbornness as was in the eyes of the other priestesses. Her hair fell in tight curls, and her round cheeks looked to be as delicate as a child's. Only her full, half-open lips, as well as an unspoken sensuality controlling her young, but already powerful womanly body, spoke of the fact that this young girl was actually a black servant of the Night and Great Mother.

Eris' colouring reminded Thais of Ethiopian women, who were highly valued in Egypt. They came from a distant country, beyond the origins of the Nile. The freed guard could have been a daughter of such a woman and a pale-skinned man.

The Athenian rose, then approached Eris and stroked her shoulders. The black priestess shuddered, then suddenly clung to Thais with such force that she almost fell over. She was forced to put an arm around Eris to keep her balance.

"You seem to be made of stone," Thais exclaimed in surprise. "Are you all like that?"

"Yes. Body of stone and heart of copper," the girl said in broken Coyne.

"Oh, good. You can speak. But you have the heart of a woman, not that of a Lamia," Thais said and kissed Eris.

The latter shook and sobbed. Thais whispered soothingly to her and told her to go to bed, but the girl pointed at the door and pressed a finger to her lips. It appeared the girl had to return to the grate for something important, and she had to do it before a new guard was chained there.

The hetaera and the black priestess opened the door noiselessly, and Eris slipped into the dark. She returned and carefully locked the door behind her, now holding a sacred knife of the Night priestesses. Its gold hilt glittered in her hand. Eris dropped to her knees and put the dagger at Thais' feet, then touched it to her eyes, lips and heart.

A few moments later, Eris was asleep, spread out over the coverlet with her mouth half open. Thais watched her for a bit longer, then went to sleep herself.

The captain of Thais' soldiers turned out to be right. Lykophon didn't die. The priestess' dagger had not been poisoned, as the lokhagos had feared. The deep wound was healing quickly; however, due to a great loss of blood, the soldier was weaker than a kitten.

She heard no more from her hostesses. The high priestess did not send for Thais and did not demand the soldier back so they could finish him off.

The entire town and the temple of the Great Goddess seemed to be on guard, waiting for news of Alexander. Thais ordered her detachment to get ready to march.

"Where to?" the lokhagos asked cautiously.

"To Alexander."

Everything changed in less than three days. Late one evening, when Thais was getting ready for bed and Eris was brushing out her thick, wavy hair, shouts were heard from the temple town. Torches were lit. Thais ran out to the veranda wearing only her short chiton despite the north wind, which had been blowing for several day.

A rush of hoofbeats sounded through the pine grove and a veritable avalanche of horsemen on tall Parthenian horses rode up to Thais' house, holding torches high above their heads. The Macedonians of her detachment were among them. They looked much cleaner, albeit sleepier, than the dust-covered, sun-scorched visitors.

A horseman in glittering, golden armor rode a snow white horse to the very steps of the veranda and Thais ran to him.

"Leontiscus, oh Leontiscus!" Thais cried.

The chief of the Thessalian cavalry caught her deftly and lifted her onto his horse, tossing off the smoking torch. "I am here for you, Athenian! Long live Alexander!"

"Victory, then! It's victory, isn't it, Leontiscus? I knew it!"

Unexpected tears rolled down Thais' cheeks. She put her arms around the Thessalian's neck and covered his face with kisses. Leontiscus kissed her back and, lifting her with his powerful arms, set her onto his shoulder. Elevated above everyone, Thais laughed while the soldiers yelled in delight, striking their shields and waving their torches.

A huge soldier with a fluttering mane of red hair sat atop a tall gray stallion. He spotted Eris on the veranda, looking puzzled, then rode to the railing and invited her to ride with him. Eris glanzed at her mistress, who nodded with encouragement. The girl leaped into the horseman's arms and the giant set her onto his shoulder as Leontiscus had done with Thais. The former priestess rose even higher than Thais and there was a new roar of admiration.

The Thessalians rode around the sanctuary, yelling and waving their torches. Their armor clanked and the air thundered with the sound of hooves and shields being pounded. All the temple's servants ran to the roof, including the high priestess.

Thais, joyous and triumphant, noticed the agitation among the priestesses and realized it was caused by Eris' appearance on the soldier's shoulder. The mistress of the temple made an abrupt gesture with her arms and the veranda was suddenly empty.

Thais chuckled. How disappointing for the mistress to see her former victim, who had been sentenced to humiliation, now being carried before the temple as if she were a goddess. The parade returned to Thais' house and both women were carefully carried inside, not even allowed to touch the ground. Leontiscus came in too, and the other horsemen were let go. Only two close associates stayed to wait for him.

"So, it's victory, darling?"

"Complete and final. Darius was crushed completely, his enormous army is scattered. We killed tens of thousands until we were so exhausted that we fell over the corpses with our swords and spears still in our hands. All of Persia lies open before us. Alexander is the new King of Kings, the son of immortal gods."

"I have only recently understood that only a chosen one of fate, a titan-like hero like Achilles could conquer Asia."

"I got to see it," the Thessalian said quietly and fell, exhausted, into an armchair.

"Are you tired? Will you rest here? Eris will bring some wine and some walnuts in honey with cream. It's the most nourishing food."

"I'll eat, then go to my camp. We have set up a tent at the edge of the grove where the rest of my people are."

"How many are there?"

"Sixty horsemen, one hundred and fifty horses."

"Did you come just to get me?"

"Yes. After the great battle, where my horsemen distinguished themselves yet again, I was out for two days as if in a sleep. Alexander decided I needed rest and sent me here to fetch you."

"And what of him?"

"He is going straight to Babylon with his army."

"Are we going there?"

"Certainly. I'll just let the horses rest a bit. I galloped the entire way because I wanted to see you."

"How far did you have to gallop?"

"A hundred parsangs."

Thais thanked the warrior without words, instead expressing herself with a long kiss. Then she asked, "How far does Alexander need to travel to Babylon?"

"A bit longer than I did."

Thais looked up and smiled. "Ah. Here is Eris. Eat and drink. I'll drink with you to the victory."

"Is the underground kingdom in your service now?" Leontiscus asked, sipping wine and observing her new slave girl.

"This story is interesting, but long. I hope to have time to tell it along the way and to hear your stories about the great battle."

"Definitely," the Thessalian assured her. He quickly swallowed a handful of walnuts boiled in honey and rose to go. Thais saw him to the steps of the veranda.

After taking some rest, Leontiscus appeared again. He wore such gorgeous armor that even Homer wouldn't have been able to describe it. The tanned horseman in white silk and golden armor, sitting a beautiful white horse, looked like a demigod. And while a deep wrinkle crossed his forehead between the eyebrows, and the corners of his mouth were surrounded by a double groove, his squinted eyes, light and fearless, were laughing.

"What a beautiful horse you have. Like a titanide, Leukippa the changeling. What is her name?" the hetaera exclaimed in delight.

"Melodia."

"Song? Who named her so beautifully?"

"I did. Do you remember that there is a river Melos? It sings as it flows over the ringing stones. My Melodia runs the way the river flows and bubbles."

"You are a poet, Leontiscus."

"I simply love horses. And this is for you," the Thessalian said. He unrolled a package and handed Thais the costume of a Persian princess. The hetaera declined, saying she didn't want to wear foreign togs, and decided just to put on the tiara, made of rare stones that sparkled in the sun. She kept the blue necklace of the temple of Rhea around her neck and put tinkling periscelides of electron with turquoise around her ankles, as if for a dance.

She ordered the servant to bring her Salmaakh instead of Boanergos and gasped when she saw her mare. The animal wore a golden harness, decorated with large tourmalines of the same divine pink color as the ones decorating the vials of Kibela. The sweat blanket was overlaid with the hide of a rare beast, yellowish red with black stripes, which she learned was called a tiger.

The horse's fetlocks were dressed in glittering silver bracelets with little bells. Salmaakh seemed to understand the beauty of her attire and stepped proudly, her hooves ringing in unison with Thais' anklets.

An entourage of thirty soldiers accompanied Leontiscus and Thais, who rode side by side along the wide path toward the main entrance into Kibela's sanctuary. The Thessalians were singing, and Thais asked them to strike their shields in rhythm with the battle song. The warlike cavalcade entered the first courtyard, where Thais and Leontiscus dismounted. They were met by the priests armed with spears, and went to the gate in the low fence which separated the paved yard from the cypress alley. At the end of this was an arched bridge and a staircase going over the pool, leading straight to the lower terrace. When they were on the other side of the gate, they were approached by a nude gatekeeper. She gathered her thick hair, dipped it into a silver basin of fragrant water and sprinkled it over the visitors.

Suddenly she shrieked and covered her face, but before she could hide, Thais recognized her Finikian girl.

"Oh, Leontiscus. Make them wait a minute," she said, then nodded at the stern priests. She approached Za-Asht and pulled her hands away from her crimson face.

"They have punished you already? What for? Is it bad? Tell me."

From her incoherent, rushed explanation Thais figured out that the Finikian had been forced to do something intolerable, but had refused. She was sent to the temple of Anaitis, where she revolted again. She was then sent here to be a gatekeeper, and the first treat for tired pilgrims.

"What happened at the temple of Anaitis? First stage of the mysteries?"

"Yes. They tried to force me to participate in the second one." Za-Asht covered her face again. She shook in reaction to the impatient knocking of the priests' spears as they struck sharply against the ground.

"My poor girl. You make a bad priestess. We'll have to save you."

"Oh Mistress!" The Finikian's voice was even more pleading now than when she had asked to let her stay at the temple.

Not wishing to delay the priests any longer, Thais walked on. The high priestess and priest met her on the lower veranda, not inside the temple. This was a new sign of respect. Leontiscus bowed to the priestess and, following Thais' example, accepted a smudge of fragrant oil on his forehead. He then untied a large leather sack he had carried carefully the entire way, and beckoned to a spear-bearer who carried another one. Together they poured a pile of gold and silver necklaces and bracelets, large precious stones, and skillfully-made tiaras onto the wide pedestal in front of the temple. Gold ingots fell with a heavy thud from the second sack.

"This is only a part of it," Leontiscus said. "They are bringing four more talents soon. The priests are not used to carrying such heavy loads."

The high priestess sighed deeply and her eyes flashed with greed. Alexander's gift was truly royal.

"We took good care of our beautiful guest," she said gently. "I hope she is pleased?"

"I am pleased and grateful, thank the Great Mother," the hetaera replied.

"Is there anything else I can do for you?"

"There is, Mistress of the temple. Give me back my slave, the Finikian Za-Asht."

"But you have traded her."

"Yes. But I just saw her chained at the gate. She doesn't fit in at the temple."

"That is why she is being punished."

Thais glanced at Leontiscus and he understood her without words. "Perhaps I shall call back those carrying the gold," he said, as if pondering.

"Don't," the high priestess said quickly, raising her hand. "The disobedient Finikian isn't worth even a hundredth of this. You may have your stubborn slave back."

"I thank you." Thais bowed again and, hiding a smile, said goodbye to the mistress of the famous temple.

Za-Asht, forgetting about everything else, dashed to Salmaakh with a yell. "Here you are, my beautiful girl," she cried, shedding tears all over the horse's neck. One of the soldiers gave her a beautiful robe and set her behind him. The Thessalians left the courtyard in the same formation in which they had arrived, and Thais left the dwelling of Kibela, the Great Mother and Mistress of Beasts, forever.

Chapter Ten. Waters of the Euphrates

Dusty sky hung over the scorched plain like an enormous, hot copper pot. The cavalry detachment, led by Leontiscus, crossed to the left bank of the Euphrates. They headed south across a large river valley, parallel to the ancient "royal road" from Ephesus to Susa. Eight hundred stadiums separated them from the mouth of the river which fed the Euphrates from the east. There they transferred onto large boats.

The Euphrates could carry entire ships. The only drawback of sailing there was the frequent bends in the river. This more than doubled the distance to Babylon, but they could sail without stopping for days on end, conserving the energy of the horses, who were also loaded onto the boats. Even such passionate horsemen as Thessalians agreed with their captain's plan.

Lykophon was still too weak to ride. His comrades decided to transport him all the way to Babylon and procured a cart for doing just that. Thais ordered Za-Asht to accompany the Thessalian. The Finikian glared at Eris, who had seemingly pushed her out of the mistress' heart. But Thais pulled the upset Finikian to her and whispered a few words. The girl blushed, dropped her eyes, and obligingly went to arrange a comfortable bed for the young man's transportation.

Thais was mostly worried about Eris, as she could see Kibela's priestess was a poor rider. Eris frowned at her concern and swore not to let her mistress down. After some hesitation, Thais decided to let her slave girl have Boanergos. She would take Salmaakh for herself. She advised Eris to keep her legs bent with the help of a belt slung over the shoulders and attached to both ankles. A Persian sweat blanket was covered with thin textured fabric to protect the rider's skin should it get inflamed. Athenian, cone-shaped sun hats did not work in this climate because of the wind, so the women decided to take Leontiscus' soldiers' advice and cover their heads with turbans of black cloth. The soldiers were accustomed to the heat of Mesopotamian plains.

The heat was oppressive even to the sun-loving Helenians and war-hardened Macedonians. As usual, their departure was postponed due to the extra time it took to gather troops and minor issues. The detachment started when the sun was already high in the sky, the great celestial body trying to bend the restless humans into slave-like obedience like an angered ruler.

Thais rode Salmaakh side by side with Leontiscus on his snow white Song. The hetaera's nostrils fluttered, breathing in the hot and bitter dry air.

Thais was overflowing with joy and daring, like a prisoner who had been set free. Victory! Alexander had crushed more of Darius' hordes at Gaugamela. She wanted to sing, make Salmaakh rear up and dance on her rear hooves, or do some other kind of mischief. She listened to Leontiscus, barely able to contain her laughter. The captain of cavalry started by telling her various funny adventures that had taken place during the march to Gaugamela. Then he became carried away with describing the great battle.

Initially, the Macedonian army marched across dead country. The valleys to the north of Mesopotamia were nearly deserted. The handful of shepherds who traveled this way either ran away or had already left for the mountains before the coming of summer heat.

The spies reported a gathering of the enemy troops beyond the Tigris. True to his strategy, Alexander hurried to cross the river. They passed the semi-ruined Nineveh, one of the most ancient cities in the entire Ecumene, and were observed by a small group of people from atop its tall walls. Priests of ancient gods stood among them, dressed in colorful garments.

Alexander ordered his men not to touch the city. Its minuscule population did not pose any danger, and the worst enemy was ahead. The Macedonians turned more to the north after passing Nineveh in order to be closer to the hills with good grass and creeks of fresh water. Alexander wanted to reach a river flowing from the north which would provide enough water for the entire army. The small river fed a tributary of the Tigris, which flowed from northeast. Darius had assembled his enormous army near that tributary.

The Macedonian army moved at a slow pace, since the great army leader didn't want to wear out the soldiers. When they arrived at the river near the small settlement of Gaugamela, Ptolemy noticed that the arch of low hills to the north looked like the front of a carriage, or arbila. This nickname was recorded in the chronicles of the war, and went on to confuse historians for thousands of years. Two hundred stadiums away from Gaugamela, along the southern road, stood a fortress which was also called Arbila, settled between an empty plain and rocks.

Alexander gave his army three days of rest after they'd covered several thousand stadiums. They would need the rest. Spies reported a huge gathering of the enemy cavalry only a few parsangs away, converging like a cloud. Alexander didn't rush. He wanted to deal a final blow to the entire Persian army rather than chase separate divisions around endless plains. If Darius did not understand that a decisive battle should have taken place at the Euphrates, if he were following the example of his ancestors and hoping for the multitude of his hordes, all the better for the Macedonians. Their fates would be decided in that battle. Or that was, at least, the case for the Macedonians, because defeat meant death for the entire army.

"Could they not retreat?" the hetaera asked, having listened carefully. "After all, ten thousand Helenian soldiers managed to escape from the same area in the past."

"Do you mean Anabasis by Xenophontus? At that time, the Greek mercenaries retreated without being surrounded by enemies, especially not as many of them, as there were Persians at Gaugamela."

"The danger was grave then?"

"Very grave. Defeat would have meant death or slavery to us all."

The giant number of horsemen facing the Macedonian camp surprised and frightened even the most experienced warriors. War elephants, never before seen by the Macedonians, hovered in the distance like gray ghosts. Gilded armor and spears of the "Immortals", Darius' personal guards, glittered in the sun as they rode in tight rows atop incredibly tall horses. The more experienced soldiers recognized the colorful dress of the Partheans, Sogdians, Bactrians, and even Scythians from beyond the great Asian river, Oxus. It seemed as if the horde would rush through like a storm to bring death under the hooves of countless horses. Like they waited to crush the impudent army that dared penetrate so far into the strange country at the border between the steppes and the labyrinth of mountain ranges.

The wind rose in the evening, shadowing the entire valley in red dust, and an even greater fear possessed the Macedonians. During a military council, Parmenius, the commander of the entire cavalry, sided with the other captains when they began to ask Alexander to strike at night, when the Persian cavalry would have no advantage over the Macedonian infantry. Alexander declined this suggestion. Instead, he set the battle to right after dawn, but not before the soldiers were fed.

Ptolemy supported his friend, although the great strategist would have been just as staunch even if he had stood alone.

Later on, Hephaestion told Leontiscus about Alexander's consideration. The army leader both saw and felt the fear taking greater hold of his soldiers, but did nothing to dispel it.

For the same reason, Alexander showed a calm exterior that was unusual for him. He knew that a man was most dangerous to his enemy when he was the most afraid, with years of training and military discipline keeping him in formation along with his comrades. The army knew very well what would happen in the case of defeat. Alexander used that fact in place of inspiring speeches and loud promises.

Had they attacked at night, the men would did not feel the same sense of common support and would not be able to see their captains. In that case, their fear could have assisted the Persians and ruined that desperate battle push that was used so frequently by the Macedonian infantry and cavalry.

Alexander's calculations turned out to be completely justified.

Untried in campaigns, not molded together in battles, Darius' giant army rushed at the Macedonians, creating incredible crowding and chaos in the center. Alexander's left wing, commanded by Parmenius and including Leontiscus and his Thessalians, was crumpled by the Persian cavalry, torn in half and forced to retreat behind the temporary walls of the Macedonian camp.

Parmenius asked for help twice, but Alexander did not respond. Leontiscus feared the end was near. But the Thessalian horsemen decided to not sell themselves short. They fought desperately, deflecting the push of the Persian riders. Stout, broad-chested Thessalian horses exchanged bites with valley horses, pushed them and struck them with their hooves. At the same time, the Macedonian infantry-phalanx moved forward in the center of the battle, step by step, in the midst of terrible chaos, cutting into the mass of enemies like a knife. The crowd was so dense that Darius was unable to use either the elephants or the carriages with sickle-like knives protruding from the spokes and rims, designed to cut down the enemy at speed. Alexander, too, was unable to introduce his heavy cavalry into the battle. Having mounted Bucefal, which usually indicated the start of an attack, he was forced to wait, not answering Parmenius' cries for help.

Finally, the phalanx was able to penetrate deep into the center. The light Persian cavalry was pushed to the right, and getaerosi, heavy cavalry, were able to strike through the newly-formed gap. They crushed the

"Immortals" and found themselves standing before the Persian king's personal guards, just as they had during the battle at the Issus.

The Argiroaspides, or Silver Shields, proved that they deserved their military glory by running fearlessly at the weakening rows of the Persians. The shield-bearers, chosen to include the strongest men, struck the enemy with their shields at a dead run. The Persians broke rank, opening their unprotected sides to the Macedonian swords.

Darius, seeing the break made by getaerosi, rushed away from the battle on a carriage with the "Immortals" right behind him.

The battle at the flanks continued with unrelenting rage. Alexander took some of the getaerosi and managed to make it to Parmenius from the left, immediately improving the situation for Leontiscus and his Thessalian horsemen. Side by side with the battle-fierce Alexander, Leontiscus crushed and pushed back the enemy.

Amidst the clouds of dust, nobody noticed the gradual retreat of the Persians. Suddenly, they were all running, and an army that consisted mostly of cavalry was able to retreat much faster than one dominated by infantry. Somewhere on the right, Alexander's Frakians and Agrians still fought with the Sogdians and Massagets, but the main Persian troops ran southeast, past the left wing of the Macedonian army.

Alexander ordered Parmenius and Leontiscus, the most battle-weary, to remain on the battlefield and gather the wounded and trophies. Alexander himself took some of his reserve troops in order to pursue the enemy. The warriors had been exhausted by the terrible battle, and were only able to chase them as far as the river before the army leader himself stopped the pursuit.

The chase did not eliminate the enemy, but forced the Persians to leave behind anything that was marginally burdensome to the horses. The loot turned out to be even greater than it had been at the Issus. In addition to jewels and weapons, clothes, tents and splendid fabrics, the Macedonians captured the war elephants for the first time, and took possession of both the carriages with knives and white wool tents embroidered with silver.

Alexander didn't let his men celebrate the victory. In fact, he allowed only five hours of rest, then drove the army further to the south, ordering Parmenius to follow behind with the giant parade of carts and prisoners.

That was when Leontiscus collapsed from exhaustion.

But Darius did not go south to the main cities of his kingdom. Instead, he ran away to the northeast, into the mountains. Alexander discovered Darius' abandoned carriage and weapons for a second time, but decided not to chase him through the labyrinth of ranges and chasms. Instead, he turned south to Babylon, Susa and Persepolis, distributing the loot and allowing the army to have a few days of rest. Ptolemy was sent to conduct some surveillance with a group of soldiers. That was when Ptolemy asked Leontiscus to send for Thais.

Leontiscus was only too happy to take on this chore.

"Parmenius wanted to keep me at the camp for the wounded," he told Thais. "But I decided to get you myself."

Thais rode closer to him and the riders' knees touched. She wrapped her arms around Leontiscus' mighty shoulders and pulled him to her for a kiss. The captain of the cavalry glanced around and blushed slightly, seeing the Athenian's mocking smile.

"Are you afraid of Eris?"

"It is funny, but you are right. Her gaze is so steady and merciless, that my soul fills ... not with fear, but ..."

"You could say caution," Thais suggested, laughing.

"Exactly. I am not afraid of the dagger in her hair or the elegant little knife she hides behind her bracelet which I know is used for cutting bellies open. It is not her weapons. I am afraid of her."

Thais shook her head. "I am only afraid that she will get tired on horseback, because she is not used to it."

"You always fuss over your slaves more than they fuss over you."

"How can I not? I do not want them to be strangers to me. Why would I want to be touched by evil fingers, or looked at by eyes that hate me? That would only bring illness and misfortune. After all, these people live in my house and know every hour of my life."

"You call them people. Many other Helenian women would call them barbarians and use a pin, a stick or even a whip to interact with them."

"Would you have tried a whip on Hesiona?"

"Of course not. Hesiona is a noble Helenian and very beautiful. So much so that a mistress less beautiful than you would torture her mercilessly."

"Then what do you know of the virtues of others? Eris, for example."

"She will bruise Boanergos' back, and then -"

"No, she won't. She promised to sit properly."

"She'll get tired. It's a long way."

Thais waved a dismissive hand at him. "I am watching her. But tell me more of the battle. If I understand this right, Darius' mistake was to throw all of his forces at you at once. The Persian army became so crowded that people couldn't fight properly. What if he hadn't done it? What would have happened then?"

"It probably would have been worse for us. But I am not Alexander. He would have found a way out of any situation. Although ..." Leontiscus paused.

"Were you going to say something?"

"I remembered an incident. Captive tribe leaders and army captains were always brought before Alexander. He spoke to them through translators, asking primarily about how they viewed their defeat. A young Massaget, a leader of Scythian cavalry, who was tied despite his wound, had given Alexander a short answer: the Persians paid for their inability to fight."

The conversation, he said, went like this:

"'Would you have done better?' the victor asked the Massaget curiously.

"'It would be laughable to think of that with my forces of five hundred horsemen. But if I had at least a half of the royal army, I would have finished you off in two or three months.'

"'How so?'

"'I would have armed my cavalry with heavy bows. I would have showered your infantry with arrows, never letting them close enough to use spears. Reserve forces would have deflected your cavalry, which is seven times smaller than Darius'. I know that is the number because I counted.

"'What would you have done with the shield-bearing infantry?' Alexander asked, at once serious and stern.

"'Nothing, as long as they held rank. They could be whittled at little by little, day by day, month after month. They can't hold formation forever. I don't know whether your infantry could even retreat beyond the Euphrates, never getting a chance at a major decisive battle.'

"Alexander paused. Then he became angry and asked, 'Was that how you battled the Persians two hundred years ago, when their king Cyrus was killed?'

"'I do not know. If you think that way yourself, all the better,' the Massaget replied proudly.

"Alexander looked at the Scythian carefully then said, addressing his captains, 'He is intelligent and brave, which makes him dangerous. But he is a child. Who tells an important military secret, while standing tied up before the victor? Kill him without delay.'"

"Did they?" Thais asked quietly.

"On the spot," Leontiscus replied.

They rode in silence for a long time. Thais occasionally glanced at Eris, rocking steadily atop the pacer and keeping her distance from the soldiers, of whom she was wary. Nature was benevolent to Aphrodite's favorite. By noon the sky became covered with dusky fog, too thin to threaten rain, but thick enough to keep the sun from raging and punishing the travelers for their delayed departure.

They stopped in a small grassy valley, thirteen parsangs from the river crossing, where Thais received her own light tent. The soldiers, having unsaddled and tied the horses, set up haphazardly, spreading their capes on the ground. They clearly didn't mind the scorpions or the tarantulas, which were big jumping spiders Thais had found disgusting even back in Hellas, where they were much smaller.

Taking refuge in her tent, the hetaera went to stretch after the long ride. Her legs were sore and strained after Salmaakh's shaky trot. Eris entered, bringing water for a bath. She walked so straight that Thais was reminded of the girls at the Amphorae Celebration, held in Athens on the second day of Antesterion, the Holiday of Flowers. From the posture of the girl, the sensitive Athenian suspected something was wrong, and ordered Eris to undress. She gasped at what she saw.

The delicate skin on her inner thighs was inflamed and covered with bruises, her calves and knees were swollen and her big toes bled from rubbing against the sweat blanket. The girl could barely stand. Only after a stern order from her mistress did she give up the jug of water and stretched out on a rug.

"Do not fear, Mistress. The horse's back is undamaged."

"But you are hurt," Thais said angrily. She left to find medicine and bandages among her possessions. Healing Egyptian ointment subdued the pain and Eris fell asleep almost instantly. Thais bathed and, refreshed, went to a small fire where Leontiscus, a lokhagos, and the eldest of the ten unit captains waited for the meat sizzling on the coals.

At her request, someone brought Boanergos. The Thessalians examined the steed's back carefully and saw that Eris had been right, the horse was fine. But Thais realized the girl would not be able to stand the second half of the journey. Or, considering her enormous physical and spiritual strength, she would make it but damage the precious horse. The hetaera decided to put Eris onto one of the carts that were going to catch up with the detachment at night.

When the Athenian entered her tent, Eris woke up. Thais announced that she would ride from there on a cart, along with Za-Asht. The black priestess said nothing, but declined food. The hetaera fell asleep without a care, falling into slumber as if she haven't slept in a long time. Leontiscus woke her up to invite her to breakfast: a piece of salty Syrian cheese and a handful of tasty, almost black dates.

Horses stood in the distance, already harnessed and covered by sweat blankets. People still slept near the cart, and Thais decided not to wake her Finikian. When she glanced around, looking for Eris, she was disappointed not to find her either near the horses, or the carts. She asked Leontiscus whether he had seen her slave girl, but instead of chief of cavalry, it was the lokhagos who replied, and he was smiling for some reason.

"The black one told me not to disturb you. She asked you to forgive her, but she could not tolerate the shame of having to ride in a cart with the Finikian"

"Then what did she do?" Thais asked, becoming alarmed.

"Do not worry about her, Mistress. Nothing can happen to a pharmakis, a sorceress, like her. She simply ran forward and must be some ways away by now."

"When did she tell you this?"

"Half a shift from the first night guard change. About six hours ago."

"Artemis argotera! Alone at night, on a deserted path among jackals and hyenas. Also, she was completely exhausted from the day's ride."

"Nothing will happen to your black one. How she ran! I watched her. She ran like a good horse."

Leontiscus burst out laughing. Thais bit her lip with concern, then suddenly laughed herself, certain for some reason that Eris' adventures would end well.

They caught up with the escapee only two parsangs from their destination. Thais saw her from a distance, running down a low ridge leading into the wide valley of a Euphrates tributary. Eris' only clothing, a white knee-length chiton, fluttered in the wind, and her head, wrapped with black fabric, was held high. The black priestess rocked smoothly as she ran. It was obvious she knew the means of even, lengthy running. Thais felt sorry that she hadn't seen her run at night under the late moon, akin to the fearless goddess, Artemis. Yet again, the hetaera felt slightly superstitious with respect to her new servant.

Thais and Leontiscus quickly caught up with Eris and ordered her to ride Boanergos. During the night and half a day, Eris had covered nearly fourteen parsangs. Strangely, yesterday's wounds had closed and were almost unnoticeable. She took a four hour break under a tamarix bush while she waited for the riders to catch up with her, but did not appear to be weary. Only her worn sandals showed the signs of her long journey.

Thais was so happy to see her that she hugged the black priestess, who did not respond to the gesture.

The boats waited for the riders at a designated spot. "These are not boats. They are ships," Thais thought. "Awkward, flat-bottomed structures."

Twelve horses could fit easily into the biggest boat. Leontiscus decided to take his horses with him as well as his entourage, also with horses. The lokhagos and the remaining horses rode along the river bank, much to the joy of the stern captain, who was tired of watching over the wounded. Light tents for Thais and Leontiscus were set up at the stern platform of the head boat.

"Could we set up your goddess of discourse somewhere away?" Leontiscus asked playfully, putting his arm around the Athenian's waist as they watched her horses being loaded up.

"No. She won't go to the bow with stablemen and helmsmen."

"And what if I want to kiss you? Will she kill me?"

"Not if you don't get caught," Thais advised.

For three days the boats sailed along the river banks seeing nothing but sprawling gardens. But the gardens of Babylon itself dazzled even the most experienced veterans. The trees grew on the roofs of entire districts as well as on streets and squares set far above the river. These were the famous hanging gardens of Semiramis.

Leontiscus ordered the men to dock and unload at a merchant pier outside of the five rows of city walls. The horses were tired of standing in the boats and struck out with their hooves impatiently, demanding a ride. The Athenian and the Thessalian had to ride almost a full parsang before their horses were calm enough to walk along the crowded streets.

They took the Acadian road into the city, through the double gates of Ishtar. The hetaera saw this as a lucky omen. Its towers were covered with dark blue mosaic tiles, decorated by yellow and white tiled images of dragons and long-legged wild bulls. The straight Road of Processions was fifteen elbows wide and tiled in white and red. The road led to Esagila, the former sacred inner city with the enormous temple of Marduk, the chief Babylonian god. Presently, the temple was obscured from Thais' sight by the giant Etemenanki tower, which had been damaged by time but was still famous through the entire Ecumene. It consisted of seven levels of different colors and was crowned with a small, bright blue temple. The Etimenanki tower dominated the entire city as if it reminded every citizen that the sleepless eye of the god was watching him or her from two hundred elbows above them.

To the right of the tower was a vast palace, unoccupied and crumbling. Further beyond the walls was a second palace, and to the left they could see smaller gardens of Semiramis atop tall arches, built in steps, as was almost every other structure in Babylon.

Such a large quantity of greenery this far away from the river was surprising. A deep canal flowed near the south wall of the palace, but thousands and thousands of slaves were required to water the elevated gardens of the old city. This was similar to Egypt, except those ancient gardens had long since perished under the sand. Only the large and wealthy temples that owned multitudes of slaves still had large gardens at the heights above the flood line. The rest of the greenery of the Egyptian cities grew in valleys level with the Nile. Here, in Babylon, the old rules were still in action, possibly due to the tight concentration of the city. In any case, the Etemenanki tower made a much greater impression upon the hetaera than did the gardens of the legendary queen.

The messenger who had been dispatched ahead returned on his sweat-darkened horse with the news that Ptolemy departed for Susa, while the chief officers settled in the palaces of the Old City. Leontiscus was pleased. Thais promised him she would set up a small symposium to celebrate the end of the long journey.

The Road of Processions filled with Thessalians eager to greet their chief. Surrounded by all these people, Thais and Leontiscus rode on, passing a large blue wall decorated with glazed reliefs of lions with white and red manes. They crossed several bustling streets and, turning right through the sacred city, found themselves on the bank of the Euphrates once again.

A bridge connected the eastern portion of Babylon, which was called the Old City, with its western portion, the New City. This area contained fewer temples, inner walls and reinforcements, but more greenery. As they made their way along, Thais discovered a wonderful little house in the northern part of the New City, nestled between the gates of Lugalgira and the river, and settled in.

Thais was struck, as she was in many Asian cities, by the abrupt transition from noisy, dirty streets tormented by heat and buzzing flies, to the calm coolness of shady garden yards with canals of running water behind thick walls.

Eris arrived shortly after with her possessions, followed by Za-Asht. Thais quickly found a good stableman, in addition to the gardener who already lived at the house, and a slave woman who could cook dishes to suit Helenian taste.

In the evening she danced for her Thessalians at the improvised symposium. Rumors about the famous Athenian hetaera arriving in Babylon had spread as fast as lightning, and as a result, the house near Lugalgira was surrounded by the curious. It was as if there were no war going on, and as if the victorious army from another country were not occupying the city. Leontiscus had to send soldiers to guard the gates from the annoying Babylonians.

Stories about the military might of Macedonians and the invincibility of the divine Alexander spread further and further. Cities showed their obedience by surrendering without battle and handing all keys to Alexander's messengers. This occurred in Susa, where Ptolemy had gone, and even Ecbatana, a distant summer residence of Persian kings located far in the north. It contained one of the main treasuries.

Despite the fact that it was autumn, heat was brought to Babylon by winds from the limitless plains of Persia and the rocky plateaus of Syria, Elam and the Red Sea deserts. Nights were suffocating with stuffy humidity. But that wasn't what Thais found exhausting. It was the silent and relentless struggle between her servants that wore her down. She always wished for peace and calm in her household. It was just as well that the Finikian was desperately afraid of the "sorceress" and didn't dare openly express her jealousy.

Eventually the slave girls divided their duties. Much to Za-Asht's delight, Eris let her have the personal care of Thais so that she could take on the management of the house and the horses, as well as the mistress' protection. Despite Thais' protestations, she considered the latter her primary obligation.

The Finikian eventually admitted that Lykophon, the young soldier from Leontiscus' detachment, wanted to buy her from the mistress as soon as war ended and he was able to go home. Then they would marry. Thais questioned whether there was epigamy between Finikia and Thessaly and was surprised to discover that marriage was now lawful between all Helenian polises in Alexander's new empire. The great army leader still called himself the chief strategist, but was, in fact, the king.

"You dream of leaving me," Thais reproached her slave half-jokingly. "But why are you angry at Eris?"

"I would have never thought of parting with you, Mistress, but Lykophon is beautiful and he loves me. And you have always let your slave girls go for marriage."

"I have," Thais agreed, frowning slightly. "Aphrodite won't let me keep them. It is a pity because I become attached to people."

"To me, Mistress?" Eris asked suddenly, in the midst of picking over the flowers brought in by the gardener.

"To you too, Eris."

Blue eyes suddenly lit up under the frowning eyebrows. The unusual expression completely altered the face of the black priestess, flickered and vanished.

"And you too shall abandon me for love and family." Thais smiled, wanting to tease her strange slave girl.

"No," Eris said indifferently. "I became tired of men at the temple. You are all I have in the world, Mistress. I shall not go running after love, like Za-Asht."

"I've heard that before," the Finikian said, and her black eyes flashed.

Eris shrugged her shoulders imperiously and left.

During one particularly hot night, Thais decided to take a swim in the Euphrates. She followed a path that led from the garden, through a narrow gap between clay walls to a small pier. Thais let Eris accompany her, but forbade her to swim. She feared the daughter of a southern country could catch a severe cold. Eris splashed her feet around a little, then climbed out obediently and patiently waited for her mistress. The night was silent in the sleeping city, broken only by the barking of dogs and voices of some merry party, carried by the humid river air.

When the slightly cool water took away the stupor of the hot night, Thais felt her usual energy return. She swam against the current toward the Old City and climbed out near a forgotten temple or small palace. She sat on the steps, enjoying her loneliness, securely hidden by the moonless night. She thought of Alexander, living somewhere nearby in a south palace of the Old City, and of Ptolemy, probably sleeping peacefully somewhere on his journey. Three thousand stadiums of sand and swamps separated the mysterious Susa from Babylon. Ptolemy would return soon. Thais knew from Leontiscus that the entire army was ordered to get ready for another march to somewhere.

The Athenian dreamed of getting to know Babylon, the ancient city so unlike Athens and Memphis. Soon the army would travel to the east, taking with them the soldiers who now filled Babylon. They greeted her everywhere, recognizing her as the friend of their leader, as well as Ptolemy's lover and Leontiscus' favorite "goddess". On the second day after her arrival to Babylon, when Thais was walking down the Road of Processions to the temple of Ishtar, she ran into a detachment of Argiroaspides, or Silver Shields. Their chief recognized the Athenian as did some other soldiers, who remembered her from Alexander's camp at Tyre. Before Thais could say anything, she was surrounded, lifted onto their shields and carried triumphantly down the Road of Processions, toward the temple.

The Babylonians were astonished. Eris, alarmed, dashed after them. The soldiers, singing a celebratory anthem, carried the laughing Thais to the entrance of Ishtar's sanctuary, then let her go before the frightened servants of the goddess were able to shut the gate.

Naturally, that visit to the temple turned out to be in vain. The hetaera wondered whether the goddess had become angry with her.

The next day, through sacrifices and prayers, she did her best to convince the goddess that she was not trying to compete with her. She told the goddess that men's admiration of women was customary in Hellas, where female beauty was valued above all things.

"The hilly Phtia of Hellas, glorious with the women's beauty …" she murmured, remembering the beloved poem from distant Athens.

Argest, the eastern wind, rushed over the roofs of the Old City. Nearby alleys rustled and water splashed lightly at the bottom step of the staircase.

Thais dove into the dark water of the night river. Suddenly she heard clear, measured splashes of someone who was strong and a capable swimmer. The hetaera dove, hoping to get into the middle of the river underwater, then take another dive to get to the pool with the reed pier, where she was expected by the patient and predatory Eris. The deep water turned out to be cooler. Thais swam less than she had thought, then rose to the surface.

She heard a quiet, "Stop. Who are you?"

Thais froze. The voice was quiet but deep and powerful, like a subdued roar of a lion. It couldn't be.

"Why are you quiet? Do not dare dive again."

"Is that you, Majesty? You alone in the river, in the middle of the night? That is dangerous."

"Is it not just as dangerous for you, fearless Athenian?" Alexander said.

"Who needs me? Who would look for me in the river?"

"Nobody needs you in the river, that much is true," the great Macedonian said, then laughed. "Swim here. Are we the only ones who invented this method for relaxing? It seems that way."

"Perhaps the others can't swim as well," Thais said, following the king's voice. "Or are afraid of the night demons in the strange country."

"Babylon was a city of ancient magic long before the coming of Persian kings." Alexander reached out and touched the hetaera's cool shoulder. "The last time I saw you nude was at the symposium, where you impressed everyone with the Amazon dance."

Thais rolled over onto her back and gazed at the king, barely moving her spread arms, the mass of her black hair tossed onto her chest. Alexander put his hand over her hair and it was like he emitted a warm power.

"Set herself free at least once, my king," Thais said after a pause as the current carried them toward the bridge.

"With you?" Alexander asked quickly.

"Only with me. You will understand later, why -"

"You know how to inspire curiosity," the conqueror of Asia replied with a kiss, making them both sink underwater.

"Let's swim to me," Alexander ordered.

"No, King. To me. I am a woman and must greet you dressed and coiffed. Besides, too many eyes follow you at the palace, and not all of them are kind. What I have is mystery."

"You are a mystery yourself, Athenian. You turn out to be right so often, as if you are a wise pithier and not a conqueror of men."

They pulled away from the current just in time to avoid the bridge and arrived at the quiet pool where Eris, who had been dreaming and stargazing moments before, jumped up with the speed and a hiss of a wild cat.

"Eris, this is the victorious king himself," the hetaera said quickly. The girl knelt in a respectful bow.

Alexander declined an offered cape, walked through the gap between walls and the garden, and stepped into the faintly lit front room in all the splendor of his mighty body, akin to Achilles or another beautiful ancient hero. Comfortable benches were built into the walls according to the Babylonian tradition. Thais ordered both her servants to dry and oil the king, and brush his hair, which was carried out with much anxiety.

The Athenian went into her bedroom, tossed her most precious coverlet of the soft blue wool of Taurus goats onto the wide bed, and soon appeared before the king in all the glory of her remarkable beauty. She had dressed in a transparent blue chiton, with a turquoise tiara in her tall coif, and the beryllium necklace from the temple of Kibela.

Alexander rose, pushing Za-Asht away. The hetaera gestured to both slave girls to leave.

"Are you hungry?" Thais asked, settling on the thick carpet. Alexander shook his head. Thais brought an ornate Persian goblet of wine, diluted it with water and poured it into two travel cups from green Cyprus glass. Alexander lifted his cup quickly, splashing slightly.

"To Aphrodite," he said quietly.

"Wait one moment, Majesty." Thais picked up the vial with a tourmaline stopper decorated with a star from a tray. "This is for me. Three drops," she whispered, measuring three drops into her wine. "And this is for you. Four drops."

"What is that?" the Macedonian asked. He spoke without caution, but with curiosity.

"A gift of the Mother of Gods. She will help you forget for tonight, that you are a king, a ruler and conqueror of people. She will take away the burden you have carried from the time you took the shield of Achilles from Troy."

Alexander observed Thais carefully, and she smiled at him with that fleeting tinge of superiority the king had always found so attractive. She lifted the heavy glass vial and downed the tart and burning potion without hesitation. Thais poured him more wine, and they drank again.

"Rest a bit."

Thais took Alexander to the inner room and he stretched on a bed. The mattress was made of leopard skins. Thais sat down near him, and placed a hot hand on his shoulder. They were both silent, feeling the inevitability of Ananka (fate) drawing them to each other.

Thais felt the familiar sensation of fire running up her spine and flowing through her chest and belly. Yes, this was the terrible potion of Rhea-Kibela. But this time she wasn't frightened.

The beating of her own heart resonated in the hetaera's head like tambourines of Dionysus. Her consciousness started dividing, setting free the other Thais. This Thais was not a human being at all, but a primal force, separate and at the same time inexplicably connected with every other sensation, sharpened to its limit. Thais moaned, arched her back and was caught by Alexander's strong arms.

Through the thick blanket of sleep, Thais heard a vague noise, some subdued exclamations and a distant knocking. Alexander opened his eyes and slowly propped himself onto one elbow. The voices became louder and the hetaera recognized them as belonging to Leontiscus, Hephaestion, and Black Cleitus. The king's friends and bodyguards froze in the doorway, not daring to enter the house.

"Hephaestion!" Alexander called. "Tell everyone to go to the ravens, including you. Don't you dare bother me, even if Darius himself is attacking the city."

All Thais heard in response were hurried steps down the stairs and away.

The great army leader came back to his senses only late in the evening. He stretched with a deep sigh and shook his head. Thais ran out of the room and came back with an armful of clothes, which she placed silently before the king.

"This is mine," Alexander exclaimed with surprise. "Who brought it?"

"They did," Thais replied, meaning the Macedonian's friends.

Eris and Za-Asht had managed to tell her about the terrible panic that had ensued the morning after Alexander did not come back after swimming. His friends and bodyguards had eventually arrived at Thais' home after scouring the entire city looking for their king.

"How did they manage to find me here?" Alexander wondered.

"Leontiscus figured it out. He knew I went swimming in the Euphrates at night and heard that you did the same."

Alexander chuckled quietly. "You are dangerous, Athenian. Your name and death begin with the same letter[28]. Last night I felt how easy it was to die in your arms. I still feel light and transparent, without desires or cares. Perhaps I am already a shadow in Hades."

Thais lifted the king's heavy hand and pressed it to her chest. "Oh no. You are still filled with flesh and power," she assured him, kneeling on the floor at his feet.

Alexander studied her for awhile, then said, "You are like me on the battlefield. You are filled with the same sacred power of the gods and the divine madness of the effort. You do not possess the first basis of care, which preserves life."

"Only for you, Majesty."

"So much the worse. I cannot do that. One time I allowed myself to be with you, and a day is completely ripped out of my life."

---

28 Greek god of death is Thanatos.

"I understand. Do not say anything more, beloved." This was the first time Thais had addressed the king this way. "The burden of the shield of Achilles."

"Yes. The burden of the one who decided to know the limits of Ecumene."

"I remember that, too," Thais said sadly. "I shall not ask you anymore, even though I'll be here. But then do not ask me, either. Chains of Eros are forged faster for women and hold them stronger. Promise?"

Alexander stood and picked up Thais as if she were a feather. He held her against his broad chest for a long time, then suddenly tossed her onto the bed. Thais sat up with her head lowered and started braiding her tangled hair. Alexander leaned forward and picked up the golden chain bearing a star and letter mu in the center.

"Give it to me as a memory of what took place," the king asked. The hetaera picked up her chain belt, thought about it, then kissed the ornament and held it out to Alexander.

"I shall order the best jewelers of Babylon to make you another in two days. It will be made of precious red gold with a star of fourteen rays and a letter xi."

"Why xi?" Thais lifted her long eyelashes in surprise.

"Remember. Nobody can explain this to you, except me. The ancient name of the river in which we met is Xarand. In Eros you are akin to a sword, xyphos. But for a man to be with you is epi xyron ehestai, as if on the blade of a razor. And also, xi is the fourteenth letter of the alphabet.[29]"

The Athenian's eyes dropped under the king's long gaze and her pale cheeks flushed.

"Poseidon the Earth keeper. I am so hungry," Alexander exclaimed suddenly, smiling at the quiet hetaera.

"Then come. Everything is ready," the Athenian said, perking up. "Then I'll see you to the south palace. You can take Boanergos and I'll ride Salmaakh ..."

"No. I'll take one of your Thessalian guards."

"As you wish."

Thais spend the entire day alone in her bedroom. She came out only in the evening, ordering Eris to bring kiura from the stash prepared with the unforgettable Egesikhora back in Sparta.

Eris reached out and touched the Athenian's wrist with her warm fingers. "Do not poison yourself, Mistress," the black priestess said.

---

29 Ivan Yefremov does not provide an explanation as to the significance of this statement. The number fourteen could be associated with the fourteen gods of Olympus. The letter xi is also associated with bearing fruit – Alexander could be implying that Thais might become pregnant by him.

"What do you know about this?" the hetaera asked sadly, but with conviction. "When something like this happens, Gaea is unstoppable. And I do not have the right to allow myself to have a child of the future ruler of the Ecumene."

"Why, Mistress?"

"Who am I to make my son an heir to the great empire? He will get nothing from the fate except slavery and early death, because it plays with all people that harbor thoughts of the future, be they dark or light."

"And what if it is a girl?"

"Alexander's divine blood must not experience the cruel destiny of a woman."

"But a daughter would be as beautiful as Aphrodite herself."

"All the worse for her."

"Do not fear, Mistress," Eris said firmly, changing her tone. "You won't have anything. Don't drink kiura."

"How can you know this?"

"I can and I do. We are all initiated in the ancient knowledge of Kibela about the mysteries of the moon's influence upon a person. Everything in a woman's body depends on it. You won't have anything. You met with the king at such a time when all is allowed."

"Why are we, who are taught all the wisdom of feminine art, not taught this?" Thais asked with astonishment.

"Because this knowledge is secret. A woman must not be free from the power of Gaea-Kibela. Otherwise humankind will vanish."

"Would you perhaps tell me this secret?"

"Yes. You serve another goddess, but her purposes are the same as those of the Great Mother. And while I am with you, I will always tell you which days will have no consequences."

"While you are with me. But when you are not …"

"I shall be with you till death, Mistress. I shall tell you everything before I die."

"Who is getting ready to die here?" a merry voice rang out.

Thais squealed with joy and dashed to meet Hesiona. The two women hugged and held each other for a long time. Both of them had waited for this reunion ever since Thais had gone one way on horseback and Hesiona had headed in the opposite direction aboard a ship.

The Athenian dragged her friend out to the veranda where there was still some sunlight left.

"The Daughter of the Snake", as she had once been nicknamed by a jealous Clonaria, had lost a lot of weight. Her face and hands were wind-bitten and her hair was cut short, as if she were a fugitive slave or a wife punished for being unfaithful.

"You look awful," Thais exclaimed. "Nearchus will find someone else. There are plenty of seductresses here in Babylon."

"No, he won't," the Theban replied. There was so much certainty and calm in her voice that the hetaera felt he really wouldn't.

"Are you here for long?" Thais asked, gently patting her friend's coarse hand.

"Yes. After the victory at Gaugamela, Nearchus is planning to build a dock and a port here. He will sail to Arabia, but not for long and without me. It is so wonderful, my star. The final victory."

"Not so. Not everything is over with Persia yet. And then, as far as I understand Alexander, there is still the long march to the edges of Ecumene. You and I probably won't get to go there. We will remain behind."

"I don't like Babylon. It is a decaying city of former glory. I have yet to find a home here."

"With Nearchus?"

"Nearchus is going to live near the ships and come here to visit."

"Then stay with me. There is plenty of room."

"Thais, phile[30]," Hesiona said, smiling gratefully. "This is the best I could think of, to find you and stay with you. I don't even have a servant."

"We'll find someone. Mine are not from Babylon but from far away."

"This black one is interesting. What is her name?"

"Eris."

"What a terrible name: the goddess of discourse from the dark world."

"They all have names like that where she is from. She is a former priestess, like you, but a fallen one, not enslaved. She served the menacing Mother of Gods. I shall tell you about her later. First I want to hear about your voyage."

"Very well." Hesiona frowned, looking uncertain. "You know, Eris has strange eyes."

"Ah, you noticed."

"She seems to contain all of feminine depth, as dark as described in the ancient myths, and at the same time she appears hungry for all things new and beautiful."

Thais shook her head. "But enough about the slave girl. Tell me about yourself."

Hesiona's story was brief. Her journey had been much simpler than that of Thais. At first she had accompanied Nearchus up the Euphrates, where lumber was being prepared in a hurry for the construction of ships. Then they traveled around several Syrian cities to look for older, properly dried lumber. Countless carts brought the lumber to the "royal road" before it was floated downriver to the lower Euphrates crossing. That was where Nearchus had set up the docks for navy ships.

---

30 Friend

"Just think of it. I sailed past them at night," Thais exclaimed. "And didn't even think of you."

"I wasn't there. After the news of the great victory, Nearchus sailed down the river and we visited the place where both of them come together, where swamps take up enormous areas. We will probably have to go back there again, and it is an inhospitable place."

"Who directed you here, to Lugalgira?"

"Your hero, Leontiscus the Thessalian. He is so in love with you, my darling Thais."

"I know," Thais looked despondent. "And I cannot respond in kind. But he would agree to anything as long as he could be near me."

"Thousands of other men would accept the same conditions. You are growing lovelier by the day and have never looked more beautiful."

Much to Hesiona's surprise, Thais burst into tears.

In a large throne hall of the Southern palace, constructed of dark blue glazed bricks with a pattern of yellow bars, Alexander presided over the council of his army officers. Ptolemy, who had only just arrived and barely managed to wash off the sweat and dust from the sun-scorched trip, reported treasures captured at Susa, a city which had surrendered without battle. Aside from silver, gold, and ornate armor and weapons, Susa contained scores of statues. These had been stolen by Xerxes from the pillaged Hellas, including the bronze group of Harmodius and Aristogeyton, the two assassins of tyrants. Alexander immediately ordered the sculpture to be sent to Athens. This pair of powerful warriors, stepping forward in unison with their swords raised, would inspire sculptors for centuries to come. It was a symbol of brotherhood and inspired purposefulness.

Ptolemy left all the treasures where they were under the protection of his soldiers, whose numbers were too small to fight in an open battle, but sufficient to protect the loot in a fortified city. Fifty thousand talents were kept in Susa. Silver mines of Alexander's homeland couldn't have produced that much in fifty years. According to the information gathered from Persians, the main gazaphilakia, or Persian state treasury, was located in Parsa, in the capital of kings of the Akhimenes dynasty. It was called Persepolis by the Greek geographers. There were no large armies at Parsa, as Darius was still in the north.

Alexander acted as swiftly as ever. In seven days he gathered the best of his cavalry, and his infantry was ordered to prepare to march toward Susa in three days. Provision carts were dispatched immediately. The main forces and the entire provision train was expected to travel slowly under Parmenius' command.

Cool winter reigned in the valleys of Susa and Parsa, making this the best time for the march. There was plenty of food and water for the horses. Alexander gave strict orders for the thousands of actors, artists, women, servants and merchants accompanying the army to stay in Babylon. Nobody dared follow the lead detachment. Only after Parmenius' troops and provision carts left would the inevitable army companions receive permission to travel toward Susa and Persepolis.

After the counsel, Alexander went to the temple of Marduk, where the priests serving the ancient gods of Babylon held a sacred ritual in his honor. The great conqueror sat on a throne in a place of honor next to the high priest. The priest was middle-aged, but not yet old man. He had a long, narrow, carefully arranged beard.

A procession of priestesses carried golden vessels on their heads, and fragrant blue smoke rose above them in small streams. They were adorned in red garments so light that the slightest breeze caused them to rise and flutter, akin to flashes of transparent fire.

Alexander looked tired and glum. The high priest beckoned a young temple servant who spoke good Coyne and served as a translator.

"Conqueror of kings, please turn your benevolent gaze upon the woman up front carrying the silver mirror. She is the daughter of the noblest family, more noble than even the Akhimenides. She is portraying Sharan, the one close to goddess Ishtar."

Alexander had already noticed the tall girl. She had amazingly white skin and snakelike thin black braids which hung almost to the floor. He abandoned his thoughts and nodded to the priest, who smiled with insinuation. "Say but a word of desire, oh conqueror and ruler. She will expect you this very night at the hour of bat on a splendid bed of glorious Ishtar in the upper rooms of the temple. You will be taken there," the priest said, then paused, seeing Alexander's gesture of refusal.

"Does the love of a noble servant of Ishtar not attract you?" the priest said, clearly disappointed.

"It does not," the Macedonian replied.

"Forgive me, oh ruler, if I dare ask of the forbidden as I am ignorant of your divine ways," the priest said, then paused again. The interpreter stopped abruptly, as if having stumbled.

"Continue," Alexander said. "I do not punish for awkward words. You and I are from different people, so it is important that we understand each other."

"They say the only woman you've chosen here is an Athenian whore. Do nobility and virtue blessed by a deity mean nothing to you?"

"The one of whom you speak is not a whore as you understand it. That is, she is not a woman available to anyone for a certain price. In Hellas, all free women are divided into wives, ladies of the house and mothers and, on the other side, the hetaerae, female friends and companions. Hetaerae know many different arts: dance, ability to dress well, to entertain with a conversation or poetry, they know how to host a party-symposium. Hetaerae are surrounded by artists and poets, who draw inspiration from their beauty. In other words, hetaerae give a man the opportunity to enjoy the beauty of life, shaking off the monotony of everyday things."

"But they offer themselves for money."

"Yes, and great money at that. Art and long education are worth a lot, and natural talent even more. We understand that well. A hetaera is free in her choice of men. She may give herself for a great price, she may refuse, or she may take no money at all. In any case, Thais cannot be simply obtained on a divine bed the way you are offering your 'virtuous' Sharan."

The priest quickly dropped his eyes to avoid betraying his anger. The conversation was over, and Alexander remained glum and indifferent through the remainder of the ritual ceremony.

Thais spent the entire week trying to convince Ptolemy to take her along for the march. Ptolemy warned the hetaera of the incredible dangers of the journey through the unknown mountains, populated by savage tribes, as well as the difficulties of a march under the speed set by Alexander. She needn't experience all these hardships, though, since she could travel comfortably within one of Parmenius' carts. Thais believed that at least one Athenian woman had to be present during the conquering of the sacred and, until now, invincible capital of the Persians. These were the same people who had decimated Hellas and sold tens of thousands of its daughters into slavery. Men could stand for themselves, but she was the only woman capable of making this journey, having hardened along the way and owning a splendid steed.

"Why else did you give me such a wonderful pacer?" she asked Ptolemy mischievously.

"That was not what I dreamed of," Ptolemy fumed. "Everything is turning out differently. I don't see the end to this journey."

"Is Alexander not going to spend the winter in the warm Parsa?"

"Winter is only two months long around here," Ptolemy grumbled.

"You have become completely unreasonable. Why don't you just say you are afraid of Alexander's wrath?"

"It is a small pleasure when he becomes enraged."

Thais paused to think, then suddenly perked up. "I shall go with the Thessalian horsemen," she said. "I have friends there, and they will hide me from Alexander. Leontiscus, their leader, is a soldier, not an army leader, and he is unafraid of anyone or anything. There. It's decided. You don't know anything, and I'll take care of the meeting with Alexander in Persepolis."

Ptolemy finally agreed. Thais' greater challenge was convincing Eris to stay in Babylon without her. Hesiona came to her rescue. The two former priestesses found something in common in each other and Eris' resistance was finally overcome with the Theban's help. Hesiona promised to join her friend should she stay in Persepolis, and bring both their slaves and Salmaakh.

Thais had only a few days to prepare for the journey, and she had to consider many things. She would have failed had it not been for Leontiscus and her old friend the lokhagos, who rejoined the ranks of the same detachment with which Thais was planning to travel.

A march this long and at this great speed would have frightened her in the past. But now, having covered an even greater distance on her pacer, Thais didn't feel the slightest bit of hesitation and was not at all worried. Finally, one morning in the late fall, she kissed Hesiona goodbye, hugged the silent Eris, and sent Boanergos along the deserted streets of Babylon, his black tail flowing in the wind. She was to meet the detachment of Thessalians beyond the Urash gates, along the road to Nippur.

Chapter Eleven. The Doom of Persepolis

Susa was built on a series of hills, with a high central area similar to the Athenian Acropolis. It reminded Thais of her homeland. She wished she could spend at least one day breathing the blessed air of Hellas, ascending the marble staircases of temples, hiding from the sun in Athenian galleries aired by the clean breath of the sea. She was further reminded of the past during a celebration and a run with torches. It had been allowed by Alexander, despite his impatience to continue moving further south toward Persepolis, where the main treasury of the Persian state was located. Alexander had to arrive to Persepolis before

Darius managed to gather and bring his troops there. The army commander set the example of tirelessness, both in the saddle and on foot, abandoning his horse from time to time and walking a parsang or two with his infantry men.

When snow-covered peaks appeared in the east and the valleys became steeper and rockier, the Macedonians ran into strong resistance from Persian troops. On a mountain range known as the Gates of Parsa, which squeezed between steep slopes on both sides, Alexander's army was obstructed by a hastily built rock wall. There, the Persians deflected one Macedonian attack after another until Alexander eventually stopped. The shorter mountain route turned out to be impassable.

The great army leader dispatched Philotas and Kenos with a part of the army. He sent them down the lower road to capture the crossing and build bridges across the river Araks, the last big obstacle on the way to Persepolis. Alexander himself traveled down the mountain paths with getaerosi, Thessalian horsemen, Silver Shields and Cretan archers, and with the assistance of local mountain tribes, whom he spared. He even forgave their initial attacks on the Macedonians. Alexander ended up at the back of the detachment, guarding the Gates of Parsa. Attacked from two sides, the Persians retreated, which meant the way to the river was open.

Thais and two hundred Thessalian horsemen traveled in Philotas' detachment, which was attacked by a horde of Asian riders that appeared seemingly from nowhere. Initially, the Macedonians didn't even realize with whom they were dealing.

In predawn twilight, Thais rode up to the top of a hill, accompanied by the lokhagos and another officer, where they paused to survey the valley laid before them. Suddenly both officers vanished, riding swiftly down, calling on their soldiers at the foot of the hill.

The Athenian could barely see a bunch of half-naked horsemen, rushing at full tilt across the dusky gray valley. The horses flew through fluttering grasses, running side by side in a solid wave. Their gray outline looked like waves in a river of tall, dry grass, rising during a flood.

Fear crept into the hetaera's courageous heart. The ghostly horde looked like something out of Hades, resurrected by the sorcery of local mages-priests.

Alexander's riders charged toward the menacing flood. A wild roar rose into the sky, sobering Thais. As if in response to the shouts, rays of dawn sprung out from behind the mountains, shedding light over a real battle. The Thessalians went to the left, cutting the horde from the mountains, the Agrians struck from the right. The infantry, carrying giant, fourteen elbow-long spears headed directly for the center. The fight was over quickly, like all horsemen clashes. The attackers, or rather what was left of them, turned back with shouts of anger and cries of horror. The Macedonians got to keep many of the splendid, although poorly tamed, valley horses.

The detachment met no one else all the way to the Araks. The bridges were being constructed with utmost speed because everyone knew Alexander would be there as soon as he was finished with the Persian detachment at the ridge.

The delay turned out to be longer than Philotas and Kenos had expected. The bridges were ready, but Alexander and his army still hadn't arrived. It turned out that the battle along the mountain path had turned into a massacre. Chased by their ruthless enemy, the Persians fell down sheer drops, crashing into rocky mountain rivers. Some of them jumped off willingly, preferring a free death to slavery or a torturous death from swords and spears.

Alexander did not expect such persistence from the Persians, and he became enraged, but calmed down when he saw everything was ready for the crossing. The bridges were lit by torches and the head detachment waited for his orders on the opposite bank. He ordered the getaerosi, Thessalians and Agrians to cross over to the other side immediately.

Alexander himself rode up the steep bank of the Araks on his faithful Bucefal, whom he hadn't used in the mountain battle, having opted instead for a lighter horse accustomed to steep mountain paths. From there he observed the crossing and lineup of his troops. Suddenly Alexander noticed a caped rider of small stature atop a long-tailed, long-maned horse. The figure sat without moving, also watching the soldiers as they crossed the river.

Curious as usual, Alexander rode up to the rider and demanded, "Who are you?"

The rider pulled back the cape, revealing a woman with black braids wrapped around her head, though her features were barely visible in the dusk. Alexander peered into her face with astonishment, trying to guess, what woman could end up here, five thousand stadiums away from Babylon and three thousand stadiums from Susa.

"Do you not recognize me, Majesty?"

"Thais!" Alexander exclaimed. "How? I ordered all women to stay in Babylon!"

"All women, but not me. I am your guest, Majesty. Have you forgotten that you thrice invited me: in Athens, in Egypt and in Tyre?"

Alexander remained silent. Understanding him, the Athenian added, "Do not think badly of me. I have no wish to use our meeting at the Euphrates and I am not running after you to beg for some favor."

"Then why did you go on such difficult and dangerous journey?"

"Forgive me, Majesty. I wanted at least one Helenian woman to enter the heart of Persia along with the victorious warriors, instead of being delivered by a cart along with trophies, provisions and slaves. I have a splendid horse, and you know I am a good rider. Accept me. I am only here with one goal."

Not seeing Alexander's face, Thais sensed a change in his mood. She imagined that the king was smiling.

"Very well, guest," he said in a different tone. "Come. It is time."

Bucefal and Boanergos descended from the ridge. Thais rode next to Alexander till dawn. The king sent Bucefal into a broad trot, ignoring the fatigue of his soldiers. They were not surprised, since many of them thought the divine army leader was not subject to human weakness.

The mountains grew lower once they'd traveled away from the river, and sloped into a wide valley in the southeast. Legendary Parsa spread under the hooves of the Macedonian cavalry. Leophoros, as Helenians called the comfortable road designed for heavy carts, led to the coveted Persepolis. This was the largest gazaphilakia, or treasury of Persia, the sacred place of both coronations and royal visits of the Akhimenide dynasty.

At dawn, when they were only a few hours away from Persepolis, the Macedonians saw a huge crowd on the road. When they drew nearer, they realized middle-aged people, carrying green branches as a sign of peace and submission, were walking toward them. They were Helenians who had been captured or tricked into working at the capital of Persia. Skillful craftsmen and artists, they were all cruelly and purposefully disfigured. Some were missing feet, some hands, yet others their noses or ears. These people have been purposefully crippled so that they could still perform their work, but could not escape and go home in such pitiful or terrible state.

Alexander's eyes filled with tears of outrage. The cripples fell to their knees before his horse, begging for his help. Alexander dismounted and called over a few noseless leaders of the crowd. He promised to help them return home.

The leaders discussed this among themselves and came back to the patiently waiting Alexander, begging him not to send them to their homeland, where they would be subject to mockery and pity. Instead, they asked that he let them settle together in a place of their choice. Alexander approved their decision and ordered them to walk toward Parmenius' provisions train, then further to Susa, where each one of them would be given three thousand drachmas, five new garments, two pairs of buffalo, fifty sheep and fifty measures of wheat. The cripples moved on with joyous shouts, glorifying the king. Then Alexander rushed toward the most hated city in Asia, as he called Persepolis.

Ptolemy, clearly moved, rode up to Alexander and Thais. She rode slightly behind, shocked by what she had just seen.

"How could they destroy the beautiful Athens? Its temples, galleries, fountains? What for?" Thais asked.

Alexander glanced at Ptolemy. "What would my best observer of countries and states say?"

"It is very simple, great king."

The hetaera noticed the unusually formal address.

"It is very simple," Ptolemy repeated. "Beauty serves as support for the spirit of the people. When we break it, shatter it and tear it to pieces, we break traditions that cause people to fight and give their lives for their homeland. Love of your people, your past, military valor and civilian courage cannot grow in a polluted, decimated place. When people forget their glorious past, they turn into a crowd of vagrants, wishing only to fill their bellies and drink wine."

"Excellent, my friend," Alexander exclaimed, then turned to Thais. "Do you not agree?"

"Ptolemy is right, as usual, but not in everything. Xerxes went through the entire Attica with destructions and fires, and burned down Acropolis. The next year, his envoy Mardonius came to Athens and burned down whatever was left after Xerxes. Ptolemy is right. Mardonius burned and destroyed primarily temples, galleries and collections of sculptures and paintings. But my compatriots did not restore anything. They left the shattered walls, blackened columns, broken statues, and even the charcoals left from the fires. They all remained until the Persians were pushed out of Hellas. The black wounds marking our beautiful land strengthened the Greeks' hatred and rage during the battles against Asian conquerors. They crushed them in the battle of Plataea, thirty long years later. Then came Pericles, Aspasia, Phidias, and Parthenon was created."

"Are you saying that not only the most beautiful things, but also the sight of their destruction strengthens the people's spirit?" Alexander asked.

"Precisely so, Majesty," Thais replied. "But only if the people, who created the beauty of their land and sublimated it, realize what they have lost."

Alexander grew silent.

As if sensing the approaching end to their journey, the horses perked up and ran swiftly down the road, ascending into thick forest. The thickness of the ancient oak trees indicated that this forest had been sacred since the ancient times, protecting the Persepolis valley from north winds. The forest was followed by plowed fields, carefully irrigated by mountain creeks. Peaceful farmers, most likely slaves of the royal land owners, plowed the fields, aided by mighty black bulls, apathetic and slow, with horns curved to the inside. Macedonians were already familiar with these animals, as well as with their unusually fatty milk and tasty meat.

Far ahead, the white palaces of Persepolis seemed to float above the flat plane. Their roofs of pure silver glittered blindingly in the sunlight even at the great distance.

Infantry and archers switched to a run, using the last of their energy to keep up with the cavalry. The army opened up into a broad front. Having divided into small groups, the Macedonians crept through the gardens, along irrigation canals and around the small houses on the outskirts of the city. The citizens ran away with shouts of terror, and hid wherever they could. Some gates were locked shut, some were left ajar.

Alexander knew that his plan of catching Persepolis by surprise had been successful. Nobody had suspected the swift arrival of large Macedonian troops. That was why he had not created a battle or troop alignment plan. He let the detachment chiefs and lokhagosi take the initiative instead. He himself rode to the treasury with the stronger getaerosi and Thessalians, arriving before its guards could do anything about hiding the silver, gold, jewels, crimson pigment and incense.

While the infantry engaged the weak Persian city guards among the cherry and peach orchards, the mud, sweat and dust-covered horsemen dashed toward the palaces which stood atop the tall platforms.

Light white columns covered in thin grooves, forty elbows each, stood like a forest, concealing the mysterious dwelling of Persian rulers. In the north corner of the palace platform, the staircase leading to the Gates of Xerxes was being defended by archers and a detachment of elite royal guards: the "Immortals" in their glittering gilded armor. The majority of these brave warriors had died at Gaugamela, and some of them had gone north with Darius. Those left in Persepolis could only provide brief resistance to the fierce push of the best Macedonian cavalry.

Before the palace servants knew what was happening, the Macedonian riders were in the courtyard, having blown through the unlocked Gates of Xerxes, and their enormous statues of winged bulls.

Raging horses thundered up the enormous northern staircase which led from the platform through the portico of twelve round columns, into the apadana, the Reception Hall. This was a square space, two hundred elbows high, its tall roof supported by massive square columns arranged in rows around the entire hall, similar to other giant halls of Persepolis palaces.

Having dismounted, Alexander remained at the cool apadana. Ptolemy, Hephaestion and Philotas ran off, leading their soldiers through the palace halls in search of the treasury and scattering terrified palace servants. They reached the treasury, which stood separately in the eastern section of the palace, through a triple pylon and a southern entrance facing the valley. The famous gazaphilakia was there, among the "Hundred Pillar" halls and "Ninety-Nine Pillar" halls, as well as in the tangled corridors of the eastern corner of the palace platform.

The Macedonians held the last brief battle in a narrow passageway between the treasury and the southern palace. During that time, the hero of the Persian Gates battle, Crateros, managed to capture the guards' barracks. Those were located near the treasury, behind the hundred pillar Throne Hall. A few minutes later, the royal treasurers knelt before Alexander and handed him the fanciful keys with which to open the treasury rooms. Afterwards, the treasury was sealed and placed under guard, having passed into the ownership of the great commander.

Exhausted to the limit, and having already entrusted the horses to the palace servants, the Macedonians collapsed where they stood. The soldiers had no energy left even for pillaging.

Unlike at Susa, Alexander had no wish to hurt the local population, despite the fact that Persepolis had not surrendered and did not send out ambassadors to greet him. This last had been justified by the suddenness of the Macedonian attack. They had burst so unexpectedly into the city that it had been too late for the people to decide anything.

Leontiscus and Crateros rode around the city squares and main streets, placing guards everywhere. This was not a frivolous precaution, considering that the city could still be hiding large detachments of enemy soldiers. Sleeping Macedonians were everywhere, lying on the streets and in the gardens, snoring on rugs, blankets and mats taken from the citizens.

Thais rode into this sleeping kingdom in the evening, having waited in a suburban garden with a group of guards. As agreed, she arrived at the western staircase where servants labored hard to wash off the blood which covered the white steps. Bodies of palace defenders had already been removed, but the sharp tang of blood still hung in the sunset stillness.

Thais spent that night in the house of a fugitive wealthy nobleman, where terrified male and female slaves were ready to fulfill the foreigner's every wish. She was tired and blackened by the sun and dust, and seemed menacing to them despite her beauty and small stature. Their fear was amplified by the expressive gestures of both Leontiscus and Ptolemy, who ensured that Thais was well settled before they vanished. The slaves were even more terrified by a group of riders who settled to rest in the garden and placed their horses not only in the empty stables but also in the house.

Having said good night to the Macedonian captains, Thais felt very alone before the entire crowd of servants. They had been abandoned by their owners, yet still dutifully protected their possessions. Thais' first order of business was to request a bath. Once she was told that the bath was ready, she stuck a dagger into the belt of her short chiton and went into a small round room. There she was met by an old female slave, a Greek from Ionia, who spoke in a dialect Thais knew. Moved by a meeting with the first free Helenian woman in many years, who had arrived at the heart of Persia along with an undefeated army of fearsome conquerors, the old woman took Thais under her wing in a motherly fashion. After the bath, the old Greek carefully rubbed down the hetaera's entire body and rubbed some kind of smelly brown ointment into her rough, scratched knees. She explained that the precious medicine was more valuable than silver. It was collected in the desert mountains beyond Persepolis where it appeared in smudges on bare rocks.

"Perhaps it is the flammable green oil?" Thais asked.

"No, Mistress. The burning oil is aplenty to the east and north, on the shores of the Girkanian Sea. But this is a rare gift of Gaea with the power to heal all things, especially wounds. You'll see. All your scratches will be gone tomorrow."

"Thank you. Prepare this ointment for tomorrow to heal the wounds of my friends," Thais said, referring to Ptolemy and the old lokhagos. They had both received light wounds during the clash near the gates.

The slave nodded her agreement as she wrapped Thais in rare cloth to keep her warm after the massage. She called two more maids with ivory combs to brush out the Athenians black hair, glossy after the bath. Thais felt nothing. She was already asleep, her head tossed back, her small mouth slightly open.

As soon as the two maids were finished, the old slave covered the young Helenian with a blanket as tenderly as if she were her own daughter.

The next day Alexander, clean and fresh, looking like a young Helenian god in his golden armor, received kshattra, an envoy of Parsa and his associates. All of this was held in the same hall that had only recently been occupied by the ill-fated "king of kings". The Persians brought lists of all the valuables in the city, and thanked the great conqueror for not pillaging Persepolis. Alexander smiled mysteriously, exchanging amused glances with his captains. They all knew the only thing that had kept the soldiers from pillaging the legendary capital was the incredible fatigue that had caught up with them just as they reached their goal. Now that the first excitement had passed, it took nothing to keep order among them. Now Alexander really did issue an order not to touch anything in the city.

The Macedonians seemed to have cracked during that last dash. Now they gazed indifferently upon the unprecedented luxury of palaces and the wealth of priests and nobles.

Old veterans, exhausted by the marches and terrible battles, cried from happiness as they gazed upon their divine leader finally sitting on the throne of Persian rulers. The war was over, the goal had been reached. They only missed their fallen comrades, who hadn't lived to see such glory.

Alexander believed that now that he had conquered Asia, he could go east to the edge of the world, but he kept his plans secret even from his closest friends. The inevitable campaign to chase after Darius was still ahead of them because until the king of Persia was eliminated, Alexander could not assume the role of a ruler, despite compliance of the people. There was always the risk of a sudden strike if Darius managed to gather sufficient troops.

As soon as spring came to the northern mountains, it would be time to give chase and also move the royal residence to Ecbatana. This was located five thousand stadiums north of Persepolis. Higher in the mountains was the cool summer capital of Akhimenides and also a fortified city, completely unlike the arrogantly open Persepolis. Alexander decided to transfer the treasures from all three gazaphilakias: Susa, Persepolis, and Babylon, to Ecbatana. He also ordered Parmenius' giant train to be diverted there, because he intended to make Ecbatana and Babylon his two capitals, and the former would also become a camp for the preparation of the next campaign.

Eris appeared suddenly, having beaten even the supplemental infantry troops. She brought a letter from Hesiona, who had gone to Ecbatana with Nearchus. He had decided to wait for Alexander there and rest from the great labor of building fleets. Nearchus promised to find a house for Thais there as well. Ptolemy strongly advised the Athenian to settle in Ecbatana for the duration of the eastern campaign, but the hetaera did not hurry, as she hadn't yet fully recovered from the murderous ride to Persepolis.

The black priestess arrived on Salmaakh, and now accompanied Thais in her excursions around the city with two old friends, Lykophon and lokhagos. They had been assigned again to protect the beautiful Athenian. Za-Asht reluctantly parted with the young Thessalian and was taken to Ecbatana by Hesiona so that she could set up a home for Thais.

The Athenian and her companions wandered the huge palace halls, staircases and portals, surprised at how little wear they found on the steps, the sharp corners of door and window frames, and the gaps between square columns. The palaces of Persepolis, the huge halls for receptions and royal ceremonies had been attended by very few people and looked like new, even though the earliest structures had been built almost two centuries ago. Here, at the foot of the mountains of Mercy, the rulers of Persia had built a special city. It was not to serve gods or celebrate country, but solely to glorify themselves.

The giant, winged bulls with human faces and childishly round cheeks were considered to be portraits of kings, exuding health and power. The splendid bas-reliefs of lions at the bottom of the northern staircase glorified the courage of king hunters. In addition to the winged gods and lions, the bas-reliefs portrayed the rows of soldiers in long uncomfortable garments, walking in small mincing steps. They also showed slaves and tax collectors, sometimes with carriages and camels, lined up in endless lines to bow before the "king of kings" on the throne. Thais tried counting the figures on one side of the staircase, reached a hundred and fifty and gave up.

She was struck by the overabundance of columns in the giant palace rooms. There were fifty, ninety or even a hundred of them in throne rooms. It was like a forest, in which people wandered and lost direction. Thais didn't know whether this had been done on purpose or because the builders did not know of another way to support the roof.

She, the daughter of Hellas, was used to plenty of life and space in the temples and public buildings of Athens and thought these reception halls would have looked a lot more majestic had they not been so crowded by columns. The heavy stone pillars in the temples of Egypt served a different goal, creating the atmosphere of mystery, twilight and separation from the world, which could not be said about the tall white palaces of Persepolis.

Thais made another discovery: there wasn't a single woman's portrait among the great multitude of statues. The purposeful absence of the entire half of humankind appeared arrogant to the Athenian. Akin to other countries where Thais had observed the oppression of women, the Persian state was bound to fall into ignorance and breed nothing but cowards. From this, the hetaera gained a better understanding of the amazing victories won by Alexander's smaller army. The wrath of goddesses, those keepers of destinies, procreation, joy and health, was inevitable for such a country. The king of Persians and his closest associates, now dashing about somewhere in the north, were now taking the full brunt of the retribution for the excessive glorification of men.

Persepolis was not a city in the same sense as how the Helenians, Macedonians and Finikians used the word. It was not a collection of temples, like Delphi, Ethes or Hierapolis. Instead, Persepolis was created as a place where the rulers of the Akhimenide dynasty attended to the matters of state and accepted signs of respect. That was why only the homes of the nobles and houses for visitors surrounded the platforms of white palaces. These were circled from the south by a wide half-circle of cabins for the craftsmen, gardeners and other slaves, and from the north by stables and fruit gardens. The strange city, so splendid and defenseless, arrogant and dazzling, abandoned by the Persian nobles and wealthy citizens, was now quickly filling up with people. The curious, the fortune hunters, the leftovers of mercenary troops, and the messengers from distant southern and eastern countries arrived from who knew where, wishing to see the great and divine conqueror, Alexander, young and beautiful as a Helenian god.

The Macedonian king did not mind the gathering. His main forces were gathered here as well, getting ready for a celebration Alexander had promised they would have before marching to the north.

Thais almost didn't see Ptolemy and Leontiscus. Alexander's associates were busy from dawn till late night and had no time for rest or entertainment. From time to time messengers came to Thais' house bringing a gift of some sort: a rare piece of jewelry, a carved ivory chest, a pearl necklace or a diadem. One time Ptolemy sent a sad slave girl from Edom, who was skilled at bread baking, as well as an entire sack of gold. Thais accepted the slave, but gave the gold to the lokhagos to give out to the Thessalian horsemen. Ptolemy was angered by her doing that, and sent no news after that until he was dispatched to her with a request from Alexander.

The king invited the Athenian to discuss an urgent matter. He received her and Ptolemy on the south terrace, surrounded by a solid white-pink wall of blooming almond trees. Thais had not seen Alexander since the crossing of Arrack and found him changed. The unnatural glint in his eyes was gone; they had turned deep and reacquired their distant gaze. His face, once thin from superhuman strain, had regained its color and youthful smoothness of skin. His movements were slightly lazy, as those of a sated lion. Alexander greeted the hetaera happily, sat her next to him and ordered sweets prepared by local chefs from nuts, dates, honey and buffalo butter.

The Athenian placed her fingers on the king's broad wrist and smiled questioningly, but Alexander remained silent.

"I am dying of curiosity," the hetaera exclaimed suddenly. "What do you need me for? Tell me, don't torture me."

The king abandoned his serious demeanor. At that moment Ptolemy was reminded of the way Alexander used to be when they'd been childhood friends.

"You know my dream of the queen of Amazons. You yourself tried to kill it in Egypt."

"I killed nothing," Thais said indignantly. "I only told the truth."

"I know. But sometimes one wants to realize a dream, if only in a fairy tale, or a song, or in a theatrical performance."

"I am beginning to understand," Thais said slowly.

"Only you, a rider, an actress, and a woman as lovely as a goddess, are capable of fulfilling my wish."

"To see the queen of Amazons at your side? In a theatrical performance? What for?"

"You have guessed. But it will not be at a theater, no. You shall ride with me through the crowds of revelers gathered here for the celebration. It will start a rumor that the queen of Amazons came to me to become my subject and my wife. A legend will be born that everyone will believe. A hundred thousand witnesses will spread the news through all of Asia.

"And then? What will happen to the queen?"

"She will go to her domain at Thermodont. And you, Thais, will come to my feast at the palace as a guest."

The hetaera snorted. "I agree. But where will I get other Amazons to accompany me?"

"Find two. You won't need more. You'll be riding with me."

"Very well, I'll take my Eris. She'll be my army captain. Her menacing looks will convince anyone."

"Thank you. Ptolemy, order the best craftsmen to make a golden helmet for Thais …"

Thais interrupted, saying enthusiastically, " …and a silver one for Eris …and round shields with images of snakes and hawks …and bows with quivers and arrows …and short spears …and small swords with golden hilts. Oh, and also a nice leopard hide!"

"Did you hear that, Ptolemy?" Alexander said, pleased with her answer.

"Of course. But what are we to do about the armor? It cannot be made as quickly. And it cannot be simply found for women. If the armor does not fit precisely right, they will look as if they are playing dress-up."

"That is not a problem," Thais said. "We shall ride in the nude, like true Amazons, wearing only the belts for swords and quivers."

"Splendid!" Alexander exclaimed, hugging and kissing Thais.

The Athenian and Eris and a hundred Thessalian horsemen, the escort of the future "queen of Amazons", went to the royal baths near one of the large lakes, ten parsangs south of Persepolis. The swift Araks flowed into it. The silt brought by the spring floods had already settled, and the blue mirror of the lake had regained its pristine clarity.

The white structures of a small palace, the shoreside verandahs, staircases descending all the way to the water, and the distant shores vanishing in the blue midday haze were completely deserted. This place could be a dwelling of a goddess or a god. Here the manmade structures were built in harmony with the surrounding nature, the same way as in Thais' native Hellas. The builders of palaces and temples of Egypt, Babylon and Persia all tried to separate themselves from nature. But this was an exception. At this quiet lake, Thais felt calm and peaceful for the first time in years. It was as if she were dissolving in the pure mountain air, the sunshine, the barely audible splashing of waves, and the rustling of sprawling pine trees.

The two women chose a square gazebo. The staircase leading to the water was surrounded by a tall railing, completely hiding them from the curious. Thais lay on the marble in the sun at the edge of water, evening out her coppery tan, while Eris sat on the steps, thoughtfully gazing at the water and listening to the wind.

When the heat receded, an old servant came to visit them, riding in a light boat made of white wood and bringing fresh fruit. He was a slave from the distant Caducei and he took Thais sailing on the lake. A long time before, the old Caducean served a Greek mercenary and had learned Coyne. In simple and descriptive words he told her legends about lakes, about the beautiful peri, the nymphs of fire, love, and wisdom who dwelled in the surrounding mountains. He also told her about the mean and gloomy genies, the male deities of desert chasms who served the peri.

The boat glided slowly over the transparent waters, the oar splashing in a regular rhythm. As she listened to the old man's quiet voice, Thais dreamed with her eyes open. The carefree, airy beauties with flashes of fire in their light garments slid over the water, undulating seductively in flight. They beckoned to the outcroppings of bare rocks, guarding the forbidden dwellings of the desert spirits. Thais, too, wanted to become a peri, neither a human being nor a goddess, free of troubles, love affairs, discourse and competition occupying both people and Olympian gods alike.

Returning from her dreams, Thais ran her hands over her muscular, smooth, earthly body, feeling sad and amused at the same time. She sighed, then dove into the cool depths of the lake, inaccessible to the fiery beauties.

Six days passed quickly, and the eve of the celebration finally arrived. Having talked to the Thessalians, the Athenian decided to appear in the city in the evening. The mad horde burst into the city with shouts and whistles, striking their shields, accompanied by clanking weapons and harnesses, hoofbeats and neighing. They all rushed to the northeast edge of the city and to a large house which had been prepared in advance.

Rumors about the arrival of the queen of Amazons had spread through the city instantly. Hundreds of people were struck by the noisy intrusion and had told everyone about the event. Having mistaken the Thessalians for Amazons, they counted nearly a thousand menacing, female riders carrying throwing knives in their teeth.

After that, nobody saw a single Thermodont woman until the divine conqueror of "king of kings", the new ruler of Asia, Alexander himself rode out to the crowded square near the southern palaces, accompanied by his captains. The huge and beautiful Macedonian's golden armor and helmet, molded into the shape of a lion's head, shone brightly in the sun. Golden reins contrasted the black hide of his mighty horse, Bucefal, who was almost as famous as his rider.

The queen of Amazons, also in golden armor, rode to Alexander's left, a place of high honor. People watched Alexander and his divinely beautiful companion with bated breath. The Amazon, in her pure and disdainful nudity, sat atop an incredibly beautiful horse, reddish chestnut, with a long black tail and mane, braided with golden threads. The pacer, small and agile, looked as small as a lizard next to the huge Bucefal. The Amazon queen's copper-skinned body was circled by a belt of golden squares with a short sword. Her back was covered by a leopard skin, upon which rested her bow and arrows, framed by two long blond braids which fell from under the glittering helmet. The queen's face was framed by a wide helmet strap, which, combined with a low brim, gave her a warlike and uncompromising look. On her left arm, above her elbow, the Amazon carried a shield with the image of Circe's golden hawk in the center.

Another Amazon rode a step behind the queen on a charcoal gray mare. The woman was dark-skinned, wore a silver helmet and carried silver weapons. A silver snake coiled in the center of her shield, and her wild, dark blue eyes peered from under the helmet, eternally watchful and ruthless. A short silver spear was clutched in her right hand. Her horse, bowed and danced, swishing her silver braided tail.

Alexander, with his officers and Amazons, rode slowly through the crowds toward the southern edge of Persepolis. There, on a smooth stretch of the valley, tents and seats were constructed for the guests, as well as a space for athletic competitions and a stage for actors and dancers. It was incredible how quickly magicians, famous musicians and gymnasts had managed to get here for the celebration.

At the intersection of two large streets, the wealthy Persians could be recognized by their colorful garments and the absence of women. Wealthy female citizens, wrapped in light scarves, huddled against walls and fences, while female slaves almost threw themselves under the hooves, pushing men aside. Persian nobles openly admired the splendid horses and the majestic royal retinue.

"Look!" a tall, warlike man exclaimed, addressing a friend whose features betrayed a touch of Indian blood. "I thought the legend about Amazons was false. I thought they would have to be as crooked in the legs as the Massaget women, from horseback riding since childhood."

"But now you see that the Amazon's seat …"

"Is completely different."

"Yes, their calves are not wrapped around the horse, but lie on the horse's back, with their knees bent and heels resting on the spine."

The half-Indian froze, gazing after the queen of Amazons who rode with Alexander into another district, where the street was even wider and more crowded.

"En aristera! To the left!"

The sudden, piercing yell of the dark-skinned Amazon startled everyone. The queen instantly covered herself with her shield. A heavy knife, thrown with great force, thudded loudly against it. The black Amazon's horse dashed to the left, parting the crowds. Before anyone could grab the attacker, he had already collapsed on the ground with the spear thrust deeply behind the left collarbone. It was a strike from which there was no possible recovery. Thais recognized the training of Kibela's temple.

After a moment, the enraged getaerosi burst into the crowd, crushing everyone in the way. They surrounded a group of spectators near the dead attacker and led them down a side street. Two of them tried to jump over the rope and were killed on the spot. The queen's face showed no trace of fright. She smiled carelessly at Alexander. The king spoke a few words to

Ptolemy, who turned his horse and rode after the getaerosi.

Despite the attack, the glorious parade didn't slow down even for a bit. Beyond the city limits, rows upon rows of soldiers greeted the king with thunderous shouts. Argiroaspides in the front rows struck their ringing silver shields. Drums rumbled. The black Amazon's horse started dancing, striking her hooves in rhythm with the drums and bowing to the left and right. Armfuls of blue, pink and yellow flowers flew under the horses' feet. Both Amazons were showered by flowers. They laughed and shielded themselves from the fragrant bunches, causing even greater delight among the revelers.

Ptolemy caught up with Alexander not far from the improvised theater. "The black-skinned one has an exceedingly firm and swift hand," he said unhappily, addressing the king.

"Did you manage to find the reason for the attack?" Alexander asked. "Who and why needed to kill beauty, a thing that is harmless during war and carries no cause for revenge?"

"These people who live at the edge of the desert despise women. They have no sense of beauty and, having acquired an idea, are ready to kill, regardless of consequences and the thought of attacking like cowards."

"What harm was the queen of Amazons?"

"They said that the one who threw the knife was a relative of some beauty who was designated to become your wife."

"Without asking me," Alexander said and chuckled.

"They say some people know special magic and that nobody can resist the charms of their women."

Alexander said disdainfully, "And seeing the splendor of the queen of Amazons they decided to kill her even at the cost of life?"

"They value life poorly. The only thing of value is service to their gods," Ptolemy said, looking unusually dismayed.

"Give orders to kill everyone who helped the assassin, and marry his beauty off to one of the stablemen serving the getaerosi!"

Alexander dismounted and caught "the queen of Amazons" as she hopped off Boanergos. Taking her hand, he led her to the highest row of benches under a tent of precious crimson cloth, taken from the stores of the East palace.

The sun was setting behind the hills when Alexander finally left the celebration. They rode in a row: Thais, still in her Amazon guise, Ptolemy, Hephaestion and Crateros. The other captains rode a few steps behind and a double row of armored getaerosi protected them on each side.

Hephaestion said something quiet to Crateros, who listened, then suddenly burst into laughter. Thais glanced at him, surprised by the unusual merriment coming from the normally serious Crateros.

"They were remembering the end of the performance," Ptolemy explained.

Yes, Thais too remembered the incredible snake dance. It was performed by a tall, slender and unusually agile Nubian woman and a pale buxom Babylonian. It seemed as if the black body of a snake coiled around the white girl. The black "snake" seemed to rise from behind her "victim", resting her head on her shoulder, or springing from the ground, sliding between the Babylonian's legs.

"Are you talking about the snake dance?" Thais asked.

"Not at all. Can such delicate art get through to Crateros? No, he was recalling a group of Babylonian acrobats, performing the pantomime of love."

"What was good about that?" the hetaera wondered. "It was disgusting. The girls were beautiful, yes, but the men -"

"But how artful they were in their poses. Even the servants of Cotytto wouldn't think of such things."

"Were you also delighted by that performance?" Thais asked Ptolemy.

"Do you know me so badly? Or are you pretending?"

Thais squinted mischievously, fixing a chain connecting her "borrowed" braid behind her back.

"No man can watch this with anything but indignation, though a eunuch might enjoy it," Ptolemy said, sounding angry.

"I wonder why? I, for example, am angry because the sacred service to Aphrodite and Kibela, the mystery known only to the goddess and the lovers who can rise to her level, was displayed for show, humiliating people to the level of beasts and creating primitive emotions and degradation of beauty. It is a despicable violation of the gods' bequest," Thais said indignantly.

"I understand that well. But I also feel as if I've been robbed," Ptolemy said, and smiled.

"Ah, you wanted to trade places with those acrobats," Thais guessed.

"Why not? Not on stage, of course. But if a beautiful woman is being held and caressed in front of me, I feel offended. I cannot take such a sight."

Alexander listened to the conversation with interest, nodding his approval. "I want to ask you a question," he said to Thais.

"Yes, Majesty."

Alexander gestured her to ride closer.

"Would you like to be the queen of Amazons in reality?" Alexander asked quietly.

"For you, yes. For me, no. You cannot continue a fairy tale you have invented."

"That is true. How do you know?"

"A fantasy can only be realized through a woman. And you could not be with me for longer than a day before you left."

"You took all of me just as furiously as I took you."

"The priestess of Kibela said that beauty and death are inseparable. I did not understand her then, but now …"

"What now?"

"And now the kisses of the great Alexander are with me, and have been since that night at the Euphrates. I am riding with you, and the legend of your love is realized for the moment. It is not your love for me, but for the queen of Amazons. And the queen is gone." Thais urged Boanergos into the darkness, ignoring Ptolemy's warning shout.

At home, in the light of three lanterns, slave girls were hurriedly brushing out Thais' hair. It had to be pulled up under the helmet in the morning in order to turn her into the blond Amazon. The tangled mass of wavy strands barely gave in to the slippery ivory combs. The Athenian tapped her foot impatiently, looking at the brightly lit platform of the palace through a crack in the curtain. Alexander's guests had already gathered. This was the last night before the army's departure to the north.

Thais managed to be ready by the time Leontiscus arrived to accompany the hetaera to the feast. The Thessalian gazed in astonishment at her modest, maidenly outfit. A short, translucent white ecsomida did not conceal a single line of her body. It left bare her left shoulder, left breast and strong legs in silver sandals with long straps. Thais braided her black hair into two thick plaits which hung to her knees. She wore no jewelry except for simple gold hoop earrings and a narrow diadem with large gold topazes.

The contrast to "the queen of Amazons" was so striking that Leontiscus couldn't help staring at the

Athenian. She was barely taller than his shoulder, yet he could not shake off the feeling that he was looking up at her.

Eris accompanied her mistress and hid somewhere in a niche, determined to wait till dawn and the end of the feast.

In addition to his friends, the army officers, the select getaerosi historians and philosophers, Alexander invited eight people from the noblest Persian families.

Strangely, no other women except Thais were invited into the throne room of Xerxes, where all the commanders of the victorious army were now assembled.

The platform, with its huge white palaces, loomed like a mountain and stood thirty elbows high under the stars of the early southern night. Beams of light from the flames danced in the bronze pails of burning oil which burst through the zigzagging terrace railing.

As she ascended the broad white staircase of a hundred steps, Thais felt excitement growing in her chest. The rush carried a touch of anguish and desperation as well, as she would feel before performing a sacred dance. To the east, in the light of a starry, moonless sky, she saw the wall of mountains, and felt as if a curtain fell away before her mind's eye. She was transported to Hellas, filled with golden sunshine and pines, heard the bubbling and splashing of pure brooks in the steep, moss-covered chasms. She could see the white pink and bronze statues of nude goddesses, gods and heroes, wild foursomes of rearing horses frozen in sculptural groups, bright colored frescoes and paintings in the galleries, pinacotecs and homes. In her mind she walked barefoot over the warm dust of rocky paths, descending to the blue sea. She dove into the waves as she would rush into her mother's arms, to join the gentle Nereids being carried to the fragrant colorful shores. They were the women of the sea, companions to Thetis, and Poseidon's raging horses, their manes of foam fluttering in the roar of the wind and thunder of waves.

"Thais, wake up." Leontiscus gently touched her bare shoulder.

The Athenian's mind suddenly returned to the platform of the Persepolis palaces, overshadowed by the huge winged bulls of Xerxes' pavilion. Startled, she realized she had stood here for a few minutes, dreaming, until the patient Thessalian reminded her that everyone was waiting at Xerxes' Hundred Column hall.

Thais passed through a structure adjacent to the gates with four pillars and three entrances, twenty-five elbows each. She walked by the exit to her left that led to the apadana and Darius' palaces. She headed along a path outside of the wall, heading toward the northeastern part of the platform where Xerxes' palaces and the treasury stood. She was not concerned that her pure white outfit would be stained by the soot from the huge flaming basins on either side of her. The night was quiet, columns of black smoke rose vertically, and the soot did not fly in every direction. Leontiscus followed a path made of sparkling lime, continuing through an unfinished, four-columned pavilion in a courtyard in front of Xerxes' palace. A wide portico with sixteen slender columns was also lit by pails. Here they used sheep fat, without scent or soot, used by the Persians to light the indoors.

Thais entered the soft half-light of the giant hall and paused near one of a hundred columns. They were proportionately slender, but looked as crowded as palm trees in a grove. The west corner of the hall, brightly lit and set with tables, was filled with a noisy crowd of servants and musicians, obscuring the guests. A group of female flutists had settled between the columns. Other musicians were set up at the end of a row of tables, near the outermost line of columns. Behind them, heavy curtains fluttered over tall windows. Thais inhaled deeply, lifted her head and stepped into the light of many lanterns and torches attached to the walls. Greetings and applause burst like an explosion when Alexander's inebriated companions saw her. She stood motionless for a few moments, as if offering everyone the opportunity to admire her without arrogance, which always required the humiliation and negation of other people. Thais appeared before the revelers with a splendid feeling of inner peace and dignity, which gives one the ability to not be afraid of denigration and to not overcome shyness with haughtiness.

Alexander's guests were over-sated and spoiled by the availability of women. A huge number of captives, slave girls, musicians-auletridae, widows of slaughtered Persians. Women of any age, nation, skin color and taste had inevitably ruined the attitude toward a woman as something precious, an attitude cultivated in Hellas and adopted by Macedonians.

Thais, however, was a famous hetaera and much more unattainable than all the other women surrounding the Macedonian army. She paused in front of the lanterns to fix her unruly hair, lit up through her delicate chiton, then smiled and walked slowly toward the foot of Xerxes' throne, where the great army commander sat.

Her walk combined the celebration of feminine beauty, enjoyment of her own agility and the fluid lines of her figure, celebrated by a poet in a hymn about Calliroa[31]. Graceful ripples seemed to flow from her shoulders to her feet, as if sluicing down the firm, polished stone of her body and "singing in motion" like the waves in Calliroa's spring.

The Persians, who had never seen Thais before, realized immediately that they were witnessing a

---

31 Calliroa – she of the beautiful stream is a legendary spring nymph.

treasure of Hellas. Many generations of people dedicated to health and the difficult labor of land-rearing along the barren seashores, living in harmony with nature, had created a splendid human image. They did not know that Thais also carried a share of even more impressive blood, ancient and strong blood of the people of seagoing Crete, the relatives and contemporaries of the forefathers of India.

Thais sat at Alexander's feet, next to Ptolemy. The feast had been interrupted by her arrival, and now continued on. A messenger delivered a letter informing Alexander that the money captured in Susa, Pasargadae and Persepolis had been safely delivered to Ecbatana.

According to the preliminary count, Alexander now had over a hundred and fifty thousand talents at his disposal. All of Hellas couldn't dream of such wealth. If all this treasure were transferred to Hellas, Macedonia and Ionia, it would devalue all fortunes and bankrupt all wealthy citizens. Alexander decided to keep his loot behind the seven walls of Ecbatana.

There was more good news. Spies reported that Darius had been unable to gather a large army. Two thousand mercenaries and three or four thousand light cavalry presented no threat to Alexander's victorious army. Finishing off the enemy and getting rid of the former "king of kings" for good was now a relatively simple task.

Intoxicated by the unprecedented victories, delighted by the giant haul of loot, the multitude of slaves and the sheer size of the country now at their feet, the young soldiers and middle-aged veterans of the Macedonian army raised their goblets, endlessly praising the great Alexander, boasting of their victories and shedding tears for their fallen comrades.

The twenty-six year old hero, ruler of Egypt, Finikia, Syria, Minor and Greater Asia, was drunk with more than wine. He was inebriated by his glory, his success, and even more with his plans for the future.

He gazed upon his raucous friends with love, resting his mighty arms upon the gold armrests of the throne. It was decorated with blue enamel, the throne of the menacing conqueror of Hellas. Alexander leaned toward Thais with a carefree smile and asked the meaning of her simple outfit.

"Did you not understand? I have only just buried -"

"Who? What are you talking about?"

"The queen of Amazons and her love," the Athenian whispered.

Alexander frowned and sat back in his seat. Ptolemy thought the king was displeased and, in an attempt to interrupt the conversation, asked Thais to dance.

"There is no room. I would rather sing," the hetaera replied.

"Sing! Sing! Thais shall sing!" everyone shouted.

The noise subsided, and those who were most rambunctious were subdued by their neighbors. Thais borrowed a seven string sitar with bells from one of the musicians and started singing, in a measured hexameter, an old anthem about the first Persian war. She sang about the scorched Athens and the oath to serve nothing but war until the last of the Persians was tossed into the sea. Thais sang the raging melody with such vicious temperament that many guests jumped up from their seats, stomping their feet in rhythm with the song, and tossing precious goblets against the columns.

Soon the entire hall thundered with the war hymn. Alexander himself rose from the throne to participate. With the last appeal to remember the viciousness of their enemies, and especially the envoy Mardonius, Thais tossed the sitar to the musicians and sat down, covering her face with her hands. Alexander lifted her by the elbow so that she was even with his face. After he kissed her, he addressed the guests. "How shall we reward the beautiful Thais?"

Interrupting each other, the army officers started offering various gifts, ranging from a goblet filled with silver to a war elephant.

Thais raised her hand and addressed Alexander loudly. "You know I never ask for gifts or rewards. But if you wish, allow me to make a speech and do not be angry if you don't like it."

"Speech! Speech! Thais, speech!" the soldiers yelled in unison.

Alexander nodded merrily, drank some undiluted wine and settled back onto the throne. Leontiscus and Hephaestion cleared a spot on the table, but Thais refused.

"A man must not put his feet where he eats," she said. "It is a habit of barbarians. Give me a bench."

Obliging hands immediately placed a heavy bench, decorated with ivory, in front of her. Thais jumped onto it and clapped her hands for attention. She hardly needed to do that, as all eyes were riveted to her.

The hetaera started by thanking Alexander for inviting her, and Ptolemy and Leontiscus for aiding her along the journey, as well as for the magnificent horse. That horse had not only made it possible for her to travel ten thousand stadiums through Syria and Finikia to Babylon, but also allowed her to be the only Helenian woman to participate in the five thousand stadium march to Persepolis.

"This city," Thais continued, "is heart and soul of Persia. To my great surprise, aside from treasure and splendid palaces, there are no temples here, no gathering places for scientists or philosophers, no theaters, no gymnasiums. There are no statues or paintings glorifying beauty or heroic deeds of gods in human guise and godlike heroes. There is nothing here except the arrogant, fat-faced royal bulls accepting gifts and processions of humble subjects. There are multitudes of columns forty elbows tall on a platform thirty elbows tall. All that just to elevate the rulers by humiliating the subjects.

"Is that why the crippled Helenians, Ionians, Macedonians and Frakians were brought to labor here? Is that why Xerxes and his vicious envoy brought blood and death to Hellas, twice burned down my native Athens, and enslaved thousands upon thousands of skilled artists of our country? I am here alone with you, victorious heroes who crushed the might of evil rulers. I serve the goddess of beauty and know that there is no crime worse than raising one's hand at beauty created by others. But what if it is used to serve evil powers? Then it is only a deception, for there is no beauty without kindness and light."

Thais held out her arms as if beseeching the entire assembly. The soldiers hummed approvingly, but with menace. The hetaera straightened.

"You are leaving north tomorrow, leaving untouched the dwelling of tyranny you crushed. Am I the only one to carry the fire of Athens in my heart? And what of the torment of enslaved Helenians that lasts till this day, and the tears shed by mothers even though it's been eighty years? Does divine Alexander truly find pleasure in sitting on the throne of the destroyer of Hellas, like a servant who snuck into his master's room?"

The Athenian's voice, high and ringing, struck hard. Alexander jumped from his seat as if stung. The others froze.

Alexander stared at Thais silently, his head tipped forward as if expecting to be struck. Then he raised his face slowly to hers.

"What do you want then, Athenian?" the king asked. His tone was akin to a lion's roar, making his seasoned warriors shudder.

Thais realized the great impact of the king over people, the magical power of his voice that ordered enormous crowds. Gathering all her willpower, she lifted her enormous, luminous eyes to meet Alexander's and held out her hand.

"Fire!" she shouted.

Alexander grabbed her around the waist, pulled her off the bench and led her to the wall.

"Take it," he said. He picked up a torch and handed it to the hetaera, then took another.

Thais stepped back in a respectful bow. "I should not be the first. The one whose divine mind and strength has brought us here must begin."

Alexander turned and pulled Thais along the walls with him. Their two torches instantly set fire to window drapes, rugs and silk pulls, as well as to light wood trellises for flowers.

The insanity of destruction overcame Alexander's comrades. The soldiers grabbed torches, mingling screams of delight with war cries, and scattered around the palaces, burning everything, shattering the lanterns and overturning pails of burning fat and oil.

Within a few minutes, the hall of Xerxes, the empty treasury and the other premises were engulfed in flames. Apadana caught up as well, after fire spread to the residential palaces of Darius and Xerxes at the southwest corner of the platform.

It was no longer possible to remain there. Alexander, still holding Thais' hand, ran down the northern staircase until they reached the city square. There he stood, surrounded by his officers, entranced by the titanic flames rising into the black sky. Roof and ceiling supports that had sustained for hundreds of years in dry heat, burst into flames as if they'd been dipped in oil. Silver sheets covering the roof melted, falling in rivers of liquid metal onto staircases and platform tiles, then solidified into hot metal discs and bounced into the dust of the city square. Flames whistled and roared louder than the screams of local citizens who all crowded at the edge of the square, too afraid to come closer.

The starry sky seemed to have gone out. Nobody had ever seen a blacker night than the one surrounding the blinding heat of the gigantic fire. People gazed upon it with a superstitious dread, as if it hadn't been started by the hands of Alexander and the small Athenian woman, but by the powers of the underworld and Titans, who were trapped there and now burst to the surface of Gaea. Citizens of Persepolis fell to their knees anticipating greater perils. As expected, Alexander and his officers made no attempt to restrain their soldiers who took the fire as a signal to pillage. The crowd of shocked citizens scattered, hoping to save some of their possessions from the enraged Macedonians.

Supports crashed with deafening noise, throwing upward vortices of sparks. Alexander shuddered, came back to reality and finally let go of Thais' hand, which had grown numb in the king's strong palm. He leveled a careful gaze at the hetaera, the way he had after her speech, then yelled, "Leave."

Thais raised an arm in front of her face, as if defending herself.

"No," the king said firmly. "Not forever. I shall call you."

"No, you shall not," Thais replied.

"How can you know?"

"You know your weaknesses, you overcome them, and that gives you strength and power over people."

"Are women my weakness then? Nobody has ever said that to me."

"It is not surprising. Your heart is not about women, but about the divine insanity of reaching for all things unattainable. There is nothing in the world more elusive than feminine beauty. And you flee from this hopeless struggle, to which poets and artists are doomed. Beauty slips away, like the horizon. You have chosen your horizon and there you shall go."

"And when I return?"

"Only Moiras[32] knows that. Geliaine, great king."

"I ask you to stay here for now. I am leaving Black Cleitus behind, as he is sick and would like …"

"I understand."

"But be careful. Do not go out without guards. The news of she who burned down Persepolis will spread faster and wider than the fairytale about the Amazons."

Thais did not reply, only turned and walked slowly into the darkness. Eris followed silently a few steps behind, keeping a watchful eye.

---

32 Goddesses of fate.

Chapter Twelve. The Heirs of Crete

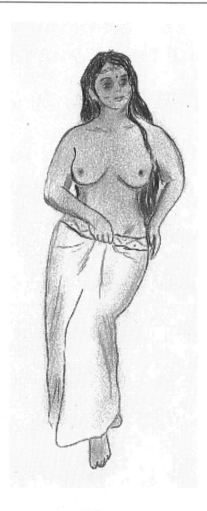

Mountain wind, cool even at summer's dazzling midday, picked up the parchment lying in front of

Thais. She pressed it back down with the golden hilt of her dagger. The mental image of her friend faded, then vanished somewhere in the scorched valley that spread to the east from the seven walls of Ecbatana.

After two years of silence, Hesiona had sent a long letter. Nearchus' faithful lover had been forced to go through a lot in order to be with her beloved. One could only envy the Cretan who found such love and patience in the Theban. Unfortunately, Alexander's grand plans required a large fleet. The ships were built at the Euphrates delta and at the Tigris. The second site was run by Nearchus' new assistant, half-Cretan, half-Finikian Onesikrit.

Cedars, black pine, oaks and elms were floated down the Euphrates and Tigris to Nearchus' docks. Hesiona wrote in a typical Theban epic style, describing her wanderings between Babylon and small shipbuilding towns, various palm oases, lonely temples and poor fishing villages lost among the reeds. Flies, the bane of Babylon and Susa that hovered in black swarms over markets, homes and even in the temples, looked harmless in comparison to the billions of stinging bloodsuckers that gathered in clouds above the still waters. Fortunately, the frequent winds brought on some relief. People spent the rest of the time surrounded by smoke, and Hesiona assured her friend that she was now completely smoked through and indestructible as an Egyptian mummy.

Thais looked around and sighed. Flies were never a problem in the clear air of Ecbatana. Hesiona would have been happier in this city that resembled her native, destroyed Thebes.

A child's footsteps rang loudly over the marble tiles of the high terrace. Ptolemy's son looked more like his mother than his father. The strategist had convinced Thais to enter into an official marriage with him as soon as the Macedonians returned from their chase after Darius.

A crippled Thessalian appeared at the end of the terrace, limping and grumbling. He had stayed with Thais in Ecbatana as a housekeeper and a stable master after the Thessalian riders and the rest of the Helenian soldiers were allowed to go home. Now Roykos also looked after the boy, who needed a man's hand and a warrior's skill. After he'd gone east with Alexander, the captain of riders, Leontiscus, had not returned. Thais did not like to think about that. The wound was still too fresh.

The boy was begging for permission to ride Boanergos. Roykos was convinced that they should wait until a smaller horse from beyond the mountains of Iberia, one who had been sent by Ptolemy, was completely tame. Thais made peace between the two by promising to take her son riding in the evening. It was a habit she observed religiously in order to stay in shape in case of a sudden departure.

Little Leontiscus hopped down the broad steps toward a pavilion of rough gray stone, Eris' favorite sanctuary. No one dared violate her seclusion during those hours, when the former black priestess sat and dreamed about the unknown with her eyes open. Thais' son was allowed to run up to the pavilion and call out to Eris, inviting her to wrestle or to race. His mother frequently participated in the wild scrambling, delighting in the rush around the wide yard in front of the house.

Za-Asht went to Thessaly with her Lykophon. She was replaced by Okiale, a sad, kind and shy girl from northern Syria. As far as Okiale was concerned, there was nothing above little Leontiscus. She spoiled the boy beyond belief, not listening even to Eris, of whom she was terrified. The only child was surrounded by childless women, and couldn't help but be a favorite. Especially because he was just as lively, smart and pretty as Thais. The main danger lay with the cook, who was always eager to overfeed the boy somewhere in a secluded corner.

Only now had Thais come to appreciate the meaning of the tradition common in all of Hellas: to give one's son to be fostered with relatives who had many children. That way, the boys formed groups and learned under the guidance of experienced instructors. In any case, they were to be away from their mother's household, especially if it were a wealthy household with multitudes of slave girls and servants. The Spartans believed that children could only grow into soldiers if they were brought up separately from their families, living in special military dormitories. The more enlightened Athenians, Boeotians and Thessalians used the military upbringing in combination with the necessary education.

As she observed her growing son, seeing how he possessed the energy and liveliness of both his parents, Thais couldn't wait for Ptolemy to return and arrange for the boy's upbringing among other boys of the same age and skilled teachers. For some reason, it never occurred to her that Ptolemy could die in the unknown faraway, at the edge of the Earth, at the Roof of the World.

The immeasurably courageous, modest and romantic Thessalian, Leontiscus, was gone from her life. He had died from a wound on the third day after the battle, wearing a smile as was expected from a Helenian. He called Hephaestion and left Thais his last greeting and all his possessions, which he had left in Ecbatana, including great quantities of gold and jewels. A year later Thais ordered the men to locate the relatives of the cavalry captain. They lived in a village near Phtia and the Athenian sent them everything except a few mementos.

Leontiscus had died during a brutal battle against the Scythians at Alexandria Eskhata, the Most Distant One, beyond Sogdiana and the River of Sands. His body now rested under a heavy stone slab in the fortress city of Alexandria Eskhata, nicknamed "Nymphe Tanaton", the "Bride of Death" by the Macedonian soldiers. The arrows of the Scythian riders, too swift for the heavy Macedonian cavalry who were armed with both long swords and powerful bows, took many victims.

Even Alexander limped for a long time after that from an arrow that had pierced his tibia on that day. He managed his anger through displaying mad courage, dashing at the enemy ahead of everyone else. As a result he received such a strike on the head from a slingshot rock that his vision faltered for twelve days, and he could not think with the same divine clarity as he had before.

The last battles against the Scythians broke him. The king returned from Alexandria Eskhata on a stretcher after reaching a peace agreement with the incredible tribes from the steppes which stretched far into the cold land of darkness beyond the Sea of Birds, Thanais and the Black Sea. Several centuries later, a beautiful city was built over the ruins of Alexandria Eskhata, and would be called "Tirozi Chakhon", the "Bride of Peace".

More than once, Thais recalled Leontiscus' story about the Massaget who had been executed by Alexander after the battle of Gaugamela. The young tribe leader had turned out to be a prophet. The fighting methods of which he told Alexander were used by the Scythians, and ultimately stopped the undefeated army's movement to the east. Alexander turned south, moving upstream along the River of Sands, headed toward the giant, ice-covered ridges of the Roof of the World and Parapamizes, which had glimmered on the horizon since the beginning of the campaign almost three years before.

Ptolemy was courageous and careful, insightful, but not fond of showing off. He knew his own value but was not prone to bragging. He had gradually risen above the other six of Alexander's closest associates, becoming known as the most reliable and cautious one. He kept a journal of the campaign and proved to be a talented writer in his letters to Thais. His wife felt that nothing could possibly happen to this intelligent warrior, whose fate was taking him toward dazzling heights. Only the proximity of the superhuman Alexander left him in the shadow.

Thais returned to reading Hesiona's letter.

The Theban asked her to come to Babylon and stay at the house bought for her by Nearchus before his departure. Alexander had asked him to assist the other sailor, Onesikrit, who was Nearchus' assistant at navigation and map reading. Nearchus had gone to Bactriana with a group of shipbuilders so they could participate in the march beyond India. They were going to the limits of the world at the edge of the ocean which could not be reached from across the steppes. The river Indus flowed beyond the colossal mountains of Parapamizes and Gindukush, connecting with the Nile somewhere in the west. The edge of the dry land was only a few thousand stadiums to the south.

Nearchus had been forced to say goodbye to Hesiona for a long time. "And just imagine ..." Thais could hear Hesiona's laughter in her mind. "The latest news from Nearchus is that my brave sailor was appointed to command the Agrian cavalry in addition to his countrymen, the Cretan archers, of which there are not many left."

"I should probably quit hoping for Ptolemy's speedy return and take care of my son's education on my own," Thais thought and quickly read through the remainder of the letter. Hesiona wrote about a big theater being constructed in Babylon. In order to speed up the delivery of construction materials, Alexander had ordered them to demolish the Etemenanki tower, thus committing an act of barbarism unheard of for a true Helenian. It was also unwarranted, despite the fact that the tower had been damaged by time.

The statue of Alexander which had been created by Lysippus now stood in a courtyard of a temple. Priests of a new cult prayed to it. Having placed the letter under her dagger, Thais sat for awhile in contemplation, listening to the wind beat against the coarse foliage of the trees which threw shade over the terrace. She then straightened, rung a silver disk to call a slave in an eastern fashion, and ordered the slave to bring her the writing set.

"Year one of the hundred and thirteenth Olympiad. Rejoice, Hesiona!

"I think you ought to come to Ecbatana and wait here for the army's return from the Indian campaign. I have lived in this city for three years now. Once in the winter, snow fell for several minutes. It reminded me of my native Athens, where we get severe winters and at least once a year snow stays on the ground for a day. You have already noticed the similarity with your Thebes. And the air here, at higher levels, is similar to the luminous, delicate and life-giving air of our Hellas, the breath of Olympus and the beating of the wings of sacred birds.

"Everywhere in Asia, with the exception of the three blessed cities of Ionia: Khios, Clazomene and Ethos, the sun is heavy and blinding. It oppresses the mind and emotions, and dust covers the horizon. Even in Egypt the light is too strong, and the air doesn't sparkle or shimmer with the magical glow in which all objects are so clear, and women and statues appear so alluring that every Helenian becomes an artist. It is time for you to rest from the humid heat and flies of Babylon. I am afraid for Alexander, Ptolemy, Hephaestion and all our people, who spent these three years in battles and marches beyond the borders of Persia from the Sea of Birds, in the steppes and mountains, where winter carries snowy winds and cold never heard of in Hellas. The resistance of Bactrians, Sogdians and especially Scythians have exceeded Alexander's imagination and the abilities of his army. The army of experienced veterans melts away as they struggle further east, and the people of the defeated countries who now comprise almost a half of the army are much less reliable.

"Elevated through his unprecedented victories, Alexander, the divine pharaoh of Egypt, who is already being worshipped in the ancient cities of the Mother of People, Mesopotamia, has become intolerant of any contradiction. In the past he was assured of his wisdom and strength and was capable of listening to the arguments of his comrades. Now he finds it humiliating to the dignity of a great king and conqueror. Sadly, the Asians turned out to be artful flatterers, ready for all manner of humiliation. My teacher in Egypt once said that the worst poison, even for the wisest and strongest of men, is the constant edification of themselves and their deeds. Alexander has taken a full cup of this poison and has become capable of things previously incompatible with his truly great personality.

"You must already know of the murder of the brave, albeit stupid and vain Philotas, the leader of the getaerosi and of Alexander's personal guard. Having killed Philotas, Alexander immediately dispatched assassins to Ecbatana, ruled by his old and experienced warrior Parmenius, who was also killed before he even heard of his son's execution. I believe the accusations of an assassination plot against Alexander were invented by the obliging advisers in order to justify the killings.

"This instance of injustice was followed by others. I don't think you have heard about the branchides massacre. When our army faced great difficulties and much danger while they crossed the swift and free flowing Ocsos (also known as the River of the Sea), they met with a huge crowd of dirty, bedraggled and wild people. They carried green branches (thus, their name branchides), danced and screamed with joy in nearly unrecognizable Coyne. These were the descendants, grandchildren and great-grandchildren of Helenian captives, whom Xerxes had taken deep into Persia to construction sites on its eastern borders. Alexander rode off to the side, from where he surveyed the savage vagrants. Suddenly he became enraged and ordered every single one of them killed. The pitiful crowd had no time to scatter.

"At the beginning of the campaign, when they marched through woods and plains at the edge of the Sea of Birds rich in game, Alexander hunted lions, tigers and bears, and encouraged his comrades to go up against the mighty animals with nothing but short spears. Ptolemy was the only one who did not participate in the savage sport, calmly ignoring the mockery from Alexander himself. However, when Crateros was bitten by a bear, Alexander stopped the hunt ..."

Thais was tired of writing. She called Roykos and ordered her servants to prepare the horses: Boanergos for herself and Salmaakh for Eris. She had to bring Eris because the black priestess refused to let her mistress go riding without her protection.

"We will have to part at some point," Thais had reproached her. "We cannot die at the same moment."

"Yes we can," Eris replied calmly. "I shall follow you." She touched the knot of hair at the back of her head.

"And what if you die first?" the Athenian asked.

"I shall wait for you on the shore of the River of Death. We shall descend into the kingdom of Hades hand in hand. I have already asked the Great Mother to let me wait for you in the fields of asphodels."

Thais gazed upon this strange woman, this slave, this goddess who had descended to the mortal world to protect her. Her smooth, firm face did not wear the expression of blood thirst or a deadly threat to the enemies, as Thais had imagined in the past. It was filled with faith in something unknown to the free-thinking Athenian, the victory over fear and pain, akin to the virginal priestesses of Artemis in Ethes, who set forth the legend of the Amazons. But they plunged into sacred rage of the maenadae, fighting with the fierceness of wild cats. Eris' typical expression was such that it should have been adopted by Athenian sculptors for the statue of Leanna, instead of portraying the symbolic lioness with her tongue cut off. Eris' restrained behavior was merely a reflection of her inner focus and seriousness, captured in the direct gaze of her clear blue eyes, the slight tension in her eyebrows, and the even, slightly metallic sound of her voice. Only the darkness of her skin, hair and lips reminded one of the fact that she was a daughter of the Night, possessing of knowledge of Gaea-Kibela.

Helenians have always admired those Olympic champions who overcame their opponents using a quality rare in mere mortals: divine calm, the virtue of gods. A poet once said that "they spent their lives keeping delicious calm, the first of their great achievements. There is nothing beyond this virtue, enhancing every passing day ..."

Olympic calm was Eris' distinctive feature as well, and it gave a peculiar depth to her every gesture and word. Even now, Thais watched with pleasure as Eris sat firmly on the prancing, temperamental Salmaakh. The Syrian slave girl handed over Leontiscus as if he were a fragile Miletan vase, while he wiggled and squealed with delight. Both women rode down paved streets, choosing short and steep descents and ignoring the admiring gazes of pedestrians. Thais and Eris had long since become used to them. Just as Thais and Egesikhora in the past, this pair could not help but draw attention. Young men in particular were left breathless as they gazed after the beautiful riders.

After a wild dash around a racing field, deserted and abandoned after the Persian carriage races were forgotten, Thais came home pacified. Once she had washed off the dust and put her tired son to bed, she returned to her letter in a different mood.

"Alexander," she wrote, "continues to distance himself from his soldiers and even his military advisers, philosophers, geographers and mechanics.

"The great Macedonian carried out a deed that surpasses those of mythical heroes Hercules, Theseus and Dionysus. Hellas was always closer to the east than to the dark and savage west. It was as if it reached out to the ancient arts and great knowledge accumulated in vanished kingdoms across the Ionia that sat at the edge of Asia, and across the legendary Crete. Alexander opened the gates to the east wide open. A flood of enterprising Helenians poured over the lands that were now either free or emptied by war: craftsmen, merchants, artists and teachers.

"The Macedonians, with their war spoils of money and slaves, received large estates and settled in places with warmer climate and better soil than their mountainous homeland. New cities required food, lumber and stone for new construction. The soldiers lived well and quickly became wealthy. The conquered lands turned out to be so vast that Hellas started feeling a lack of people, similar to how Sparta had felt after its men had hired themselves out as mercenaries. That was what caused their country to decline completely in its final effort to fight Alexander. The entire land of Hellas could become deserted, as its people rush to Asia and become scattered among the masses of its native population and the limitless valleys and mountains. If things go that way, what sort of Hellas will we come back to?"

Thais pondered, tickling her chin with her stylus as she did so.

"Alexander and all the Macedonians became coarse through the difficult war," the Athenian continued. "The mutual relationships between the subordinates and their superiors are now more strained than ever. The overly humble obedience of the new associates made the army leader even more susceptible. The old dream of homonoya, the intellectual equality of all people, was forgotten.

"The divinity of the great Macedonian was now established by methods more appropriate for a leader of a savage tribe than for the ruler of the world. With the prompting of his Persian advisers, Alexander decided to introduce the ritual requiring people to throw themselves on the ground before him, but ran into strong opposition from his old comrades. At first, when the captains and soldiers from Alexander's inner circle saw their leader seated on a golden throne, wearing a long Persian garment and a tall tiara, they laughed. They asked Alexander what sort of a masquerade or game he was playing at.

"Athenian philosopher Callisthenes believed in Alexander's divinity at first and even started writing Anabasis, a history of his glorious campaigns. Now he became the first to state that deification had never taken place during a hero's life, even if he were the son of a god. Not with Hercules and his great heroics; not with Dionysus, who carried out the first march into India. Both were only deified after they died. In his earthly life Dionysus was a Theban, and Hercules was an Argevan. Deification of a living man, even a son of the gods, was against the spirit of Hellenism and was no more than barbarism.

"'Alexander is not a god,' the philosopher stated publicly. 'He is not a son of Zeus from a mortal woman. He is the most courageous of the men of courage, he is the most intelligent of the most talented army leaders. But only his deeds, divine in their meaning, can make him a glorious hero and elevate him to a demigod.'

"Alexander bore a grudge against Callisthenes. The philosopher was supported by the Macedonian veterans, but had no influential friends. In the end, he and a few young men from the king's guards were convicted for a conspiracy to murder Alexander as well as for some other crimes. The young men were stoned by Alexander's captains. Callisthenes was chained, put into a cage and, according to the latest rumors, hung in Bactriana.

"Alexander did, however, get rid of the humiliating ritual. Before the army retreated from the River of Sands to Marakanda, Alexander drank a lot, trying to alleviate his suffering from the headache caused by the head wound from a stone. In a fit of rage he killed Black Cleitus, the brother of Lanisa, Alexander's nurse in Pella. Black Cleitus, the faithful, if slightly dim, giant who had saved his life twice.

"After surviving fits of deep depression and guilt, Alexander went against the cloudy fortress of Bactriana. There he married Roxanne, the daughter of a Bactrian nobleman who had been captured as a war slave. Ptolemy wrote that the marriage did not soften Alexander's outbursts of rage which occurred more and more frequently. Even his closest friends were forced to take great care in their dealings with the king.

"At the beginning of their march across the eastern plains, Alexander replaced his lion head helmet with another, this time decorated with the wings of a large bird. Local priests assured the king that he was possessed by Simurg, the spirit of high hills who descended to earth in the shape of a gryphon to help people in their troubles.

"However, I do not know how much Alexander helped the inhabitants of the eastern plains."

Thais interrupted the sentence, chuckled quietly and added, "You see, I have fallen under Ptolemy's influence. The wise warrior likes to predict troubles and list all former tragedies, even though it never interferes with his courage and happy temper. He is too happy, when it comes to women. In this he equals Alexander's passion for new discoveries. However, you already knew that. A long time ago in Egypt you foretold that he would have many women but only one goddess. Now this 'goddess' is his wife. Now what?"

"Enough. I am tired of writing and you will get tired of reading. Come here to Ecbatana and you and I shall have plenty of time to talk, ride and dance. There are many poets, philosophers, artists, musicians and performers here. Lysippus is here too, with his apprentices, as well as the Eubian Stemlos famous for his horse sculptures, and the famous singer Aminomena. There are many wonderful people. Travelers from distant countries like India and Iberia are arriving as well, and all wait for Alexander.

"Come over. You will be better off here than alone in Babylon. Let us not suffer too much for our husbands. Aside from battle- and campaign-related hardships, they have their own share of happiness. Ptolemy wrote about vast valleys covered with fragrant sylphius, of the breathtaking views of gigantic snow mountains with rows upon rows, peak upon peak, blocking the way to the south and east. He writes of mountain lakes of magical blue, as deep as the skies. Of the unimaginable spaces where flat hills, crowned with strange statues of flat-face and broad-hipped women, rise in an endless line, like sea waves between Crete and Egypt. It is possible that above all, he delights in the feeling of everyday changes, the expectation of wonders and the approaching end of dry land.

"Ptolemy writes that the closer they get to India, the more trees they see that are similar to those we have in Hellas. Firs and pines in the mountains beyond Parapamizes are exactly the same as in the ones that grow in the mountains of Macedonia, and sometimes it feels to him like he is home again. There is no explanation to this."

Thais finished the letter and sealed it. To ensure it departed as soon as possible, she ordered it to be taken to the house of the city overseer and treasurer Garpal, who had replaced the murdered Parmenius. Four thousand and five hundred stadiums was the distance between Ecbatana and Babylon, but angareyon, the state mail, would deliver the letter in only six days.

Ptolemy had made Thais promise that she would not use skilled secretaries to write their letters. These people could betray all their secrets. But writing this letter had tired Thais. She went down to the swimming pool near the staircase, to which Ptolemy had connected a water line from a mountain spring so it remained cool even in the summer. She dove into the seashell-like enclosure with a joyous yelp, cutting through the greenish water. Having heard the shout, Eris ran in too. She splash around, then rubbed down her copper-skinned mistress with a thick towel.

Eris had barely had a chance to cover Thais with a towel before a messenger from Lysippus arrived. The great sculptor was inviting Thais and, for some reason, Eris to visit him the next morning.

Thais handed the letter to the black priestess, saying, "You are invited, too. Someone wants to make a statue of you. It's about time. I was wondering about other sculptors who saw you at least once. Although this is strange, because Lysippus and his students have little interest in the beauty of women. They prefer to portray men, battle scenes, and horses."

Eris pushed away the Athenian's hand with the letter. "You are forgetting that I cannot read your language, Mistress. And has the honorable Lysippus forgotten that I am obligated to go with you?"

"You do always accompany me, that is true. But if Lysippus mentions you in the invitation, it means there is something he wants with you specifically. What is it? A sculptor puts sculpting above all things. We Helenians value a man's perfection, his harmonious development, both physical and spiritual. We call it callocagatia. We also value a man's portrayal by various arts. That is why our cities and temples are filled with countless statues and paintings, and more are created each year. Would you like for someone to make a statue of a goddess or a nymph based on you?"

"No. Or rather, I do not care. But if that is your wish …"

"Of course it is my wish. Keep that in mind if you receive an offer. And don't rub me so hard. I am not a statue."

"You are better than all the statues in the world, Mistress."

"How many have you seen? And where?"

"Many. I traveled a lot as a girl in the entourage of the high priestess."

"I didn't know anything about that."

The black priestess allowed a smile to light her face for a moment.

Alexander had ordered an enormous studio to be constructed for Lysippus near the palace of a former Persian nobleman which had been given to the sculptor as his new home. The rooms, shielded by thick walls of red stone, were always cool and had to be heated during winter. Dry cedar logs with fragrant bits if thyme, lavender, rosemary or myrrh burned in semicircular niches.

Lysippus received his guests on the veranda under a tall roof supported by palm tree pillars and surrounded by a wall of pink granite. The veranda served both as a studio and as a classroom for the apprentices, who came from Hellas, Ionia, Cyprus and even Egypt, where artists began borrowing the methods of their former students, the Helenians. These in turn had begun studying in Egypt nearly seven centuries prior.

As usual, there were others present: several philosophers, wealthy art patrons, poets who sought to find inspiration in enlightened conversations, and travelers from distant countries, who had heard about the wide open home of the famous artist.

Lysippus, the Athenian's old friend and an Orphic of high initiation, put his arm around Thais' shoulders. He beckoned Eris, who stood near the entrance, and silently pointed at a broad bench where two of his students sat. Eris flashed her eyes at them and sat down at the edge, as far as she could from the merry young men. They sent admiring and meaningful gazes and gestures her way, but it was all in vain. They might as well have tried to attract the attention of one of the statues decorating the studio, home and garden of Lysippus.

"Come, Athenian. I shall introduce you to my old friend and your compatriot, sculptor Cleophrades. He despises war and does not make statues of kings or army leaders. He only sculpts women, which is why he is not as famous as he deserves to be. Besides, he knows you."

Thais was about to object, but choked on her own words when she saw the sculptor. The man's harsh blue eyes bulged slightly, like those of Athena herself. The scarred face, under a thick gray beard, brought back the memory of a brief meeting near Theseyon, on the way to the hill of Nymphs.

"I promised to see you some years later," Cleophrades said in his deep voice. "Very well, two Olympiads have passed, and I now see not a girl, but a woman at the height of her strength and beauty. You must be about twenty-six," the sculptor said, looking Thais over unceremoniously. "Have you given birth?"

"Yes," Thais found herself replying obediently. "Once."

"Not enough. Two would have been better. A woman of your strength and health would only benefit from that."

"Gneziotes apamphoyn," Lysippus said in the Attic dialect, pointing at Thais. She blushed from the direct gaze of one artist and the direct words of the other.

"Yes, you are right," the stern Cleophrades agreed. "Purity of origin down both lines, father's and mother's. You shall be my model, Athenian. You were destined for me. I have waited patiently for your maturity," he said, leveling an imperious gaze at Thais.

Thais paused, then nodded.

"Yet again you pick that which will not bring you wealth," Lysippus mused. "Thais is too seductive for a goddess, too small and agile for a cora, and not menacing enough for a female warrior. She is a woman, and not a standard established in Helenian art over the centuries."

"I think you are both right and not right, great master. When you created your Apoxiomenes, the image of an athlete, you bravely departed from the standard set by Polycleitus, and even more so by Doriphorus. And I understand why. Doriphorus' standard was that of a mighty Spartan, a warrior created by Lacedemonians over millennia of parental selection, the killing of the weak, and the harshest development of strength and stamina. Huge chests and incredibly thick stomach muscles, especially the obliques. Such man can run for many stadiums in heavy armor, carry a massive shield into battle as well as a spear longer than that of any other warrior, and survive being run over by a heavy cart. Until the invention of heavy bows and slingshots, Spartans defeated all enemies without exception."

"You understood me well, Cleophrades, although you are a sculptor of women. My Apoxiomenes is lighter and more agile. Now, however, everything has changed again. More soldiers fight on horseback, and infantry no longer fight one to one, but in hundreds of soldiers, forged into one machine by discipline and the ability to fight side by side. The times of Doriphorus and Apoxiomenes are over."

"Not entirely, Lysippus," Thais said. "Think of Alexander's guards who earned the title of 'Silver Shields'. They required heavy armor, swift step, and strong strike."

"You are correct, Athenian. But that is a special part of the army, akin to battle elephants, and not the majority of soldiers."

"Battle elephants. What a comparison," Thais said. She laughed, paused, then added, "Still, I knew one Spartan. He could have been a model for Doriphorus."

"Of course such men still exist," Lysippus agreed. "They became a rarity because they are no longer needed. Too much is required to create them, and it takes a long time. The army requires more people now and as quickly as possible."

"We speak of men," Cleophrades rumbled. "Was that why we invited Thais?"

"Yes," Lysippus said, then caught himself. "Thais, help us. We started a dispute about a new statue with our guests." The sculptor pointed at a group of four men with thick beards and strange head wraps, who stood separately from the regular visitors. "They are Indian sculptors, and we disagree in the key criteria of feminine beauty. They reject the outstanding charm of the statue by Agesander, and believe that the modern fashionable sculptures represent a wrong trend. Is that so?" He turned to the Indian and one of them, apparently an interpreter, quickly said something in a lovely fluid language.

One of the guests, the one with the thickest beard, nodded energetically and said through the interpreter, "Our impression is that the Helenian artists no longer love women. They love men more."

"That is an odd impression." Lysippus shrugged, while Cleophrades grinned broadly and with a hint of menace.

"I don't know anything," Thais said. "Who is Agesander, and what is this statue?"

"He is a new sculptor and a great master," Lysippus explained. "His statue of Aphrodite for a temple in Melos[33] became famous among other sculptors, although I find her more similar to Hera."

"The model was not a Helenian woman, but more likely a Syrian. These women have beautiful breasts and shoulders, but lack waist and have a flat flabby bottom. Their legs are always disproportionately thin," Cleophrades said.

"Agesander had skillfully draped all that," Diophosus said, who was also a sculptor and Thais' acquaintance.

"But he failed to hide the awkward lower body," Lysippus objected. "And a poorly developed lower belly."

"I do not understand all the praises," Cleophrades said calmly. "I do not deny Agesander's skill and have no envy of his great ability, I only dislike his choice of model. Does his goddess have a Helenian face? He gave her a classic profile, but the bones of her head appear fragile and narrow, as is common for a Syrian or any other woman from the eastern shores. Had no one noticed how closely set her eyes were and how narrow her jaw?"

"What is so bad about that?" Stemlos asked with a chuckle.

---

33 Aphrodite of Melos by Agesander is what will later become known around the world as Venus de Milo.

"It is bad even for your horses," Cleophrades retorted. "Remember Bucefal's broad forehead. And for us Helenians, ancient Cretans, and Egyptians, the favorite image is Europa. You can translate this ancient name as you wish: euryopis, wide-eyed or europis, wide-faced, and it is more likely to be both. Europa's bones are still carried around in a huge myrtle wreath during the Ellotia celebration on Crete. We artists should pay more attention to our women and foremothers, instead of flaunting the foreign models. They are quite lovely, but ours are more beautiful."

"Good health to you, Cleophrades," Lysippus exclaimed. "One of the many nicknames of my friend Thais is 'wide-eyed one'. Have you noticed how similar she is to Athena Parthenos by Phidias? You know the one. She was the model for several copies. She wore a crown and had eyes made of chrysolite."

Much to the surprise of all present, the Indians started bowing with their hands folded and exclaiming something in approval.

"Good for you, euryopis," Lysippus said. He smiled at Thais, then glanced at Eris and added, "We asked you here to serve as a model for our debate. You and Eris will have to pose nude. We want to see in you the combination of the ancient Cretan and our Helenian blood. Eris too combines two lines: ancient Nubian and another one, possibly Libyan." He pointed at the broad heavy stool for modeling. Thais obligingly dropped her clothes into the arms of the patient Eris. A sigh of admiration rushed through the studio. Everyone here adored feminine beauty and valued it as the greatest natural treasure.

"Morphe teliteres goetis! Oh, the enchanting, thrilling feminine form," one of the young poets exclaimed.

Cleophrades froze, his left palm pressed to his temple, his eyes leveled on the copper tanned figure. Thais stood as easily as if she were alone with her mirror and not on a stand before a group of strangers. Calm certainty in her own perfection and in the fact that she inspired nothing but admiration among the artists, surrounded the young woman with an almost tangible aura of the immortal gods.

"Have you found what you were looking for?" Lysippus asked.

"Yes," Cleophrades almost shouted.

The Indians were startled and looked with surprise at this Helenian, suddenly consumed by inspiration.

"This is the most ancient image of a woman," Lysippus said triumphantly. "Strong, not very tall, broad-hipped, round-faced and wide-eyed. Is she not beautiful? Who can object to that?" he asked his students.

Leptines, a sculptor from Ethes, said this was the exact image created by the artists of Ionia two centuries ago. The artists Exekias and Psyacs, for example.

"It is as if they copied her face and body," the sculptor said, pointing at Thais.

"I cannot find a reason for this," Lysippus said. "But only two sculptural standards became fashionable over the last century. One imitates the unrivaled coras of Acropolis and recreates a tall woman with a powerful chest, widely spaced breasts, broad shoulders and stomach muscles akin to male athletes. They are not agile and do not require strong development of rear muscles, which is why they are flatter in the back. The other standard, introduced by Polycleitus, Cresilaus or perhaps even Phradionus, is a broad-shouldered, narrow-hipped, small-breasted woman with no waist, who looks more like a boy and also has an undeveloped behind. Such are female runners, Amazons and female Olympians created by these artists. You, Ephesian, know about the statues created for the temple of Artemis in your city by the sculptors I just named a hundred or more years ago."

"They ruined the image of Artemis and the Amazons," Leptines exclaimed. "Enchanted by teenage youths, they attempted to find the image of a boy in a woman. And why would a man need a boy instead of a woman? The harsh and simple life of my ancestors, who escaped from the Dorian invaders to come to the shores of Asia Minor, created stout, muscular, agile women of small height. They and Carian and Phrygian women, who went to the north and made it to the river Thermodont, founded the city of the Amazons. They served Artemis with a motto: no obedience to any man."

"What you tell is so interesting, sculptor," Thais exclaimed. "Then I am a woman created for a harsh life?"

"You are from a pure bloodline of those who lead a harsh life," Leptines replied.

"Ephesian, you took us away from the main conversation, though your story is interesting," Lysippus interrupted, then pointed at a second stool next to Thais. "Eris, stand here."

The black priestess looked at her mistress questioningly. "Go ahead, Eris, and do not be embarrassed. These are not regular people, these are artists. And we are not just women to them, but the embodiments of goddesses, nymphs, or muses, all things that enlighten a poet. We elevate his dreams into the vastness of the world, sea and sky. Don't resist if they touch you. They need to know which muscles are concealed under the skin in order to portray the body correctly."

"I understand, Mistress. But why are there only men here? Are there no female sculptors?"

"You ask a deep question. I shall ask Lysippus. I think it is that we do not possess the same love and desire toward a female image as men do. And we have not yet matured to realization of beauty outside of our personal relations. Perhaps there are women sculptors among the followers of Sappho of Lesbos."

Eris climbed onto the second stool, dark as Egyptian bronze. She did not possess that self-assured, coquettish supremacy that overflowed in Thais, but had the even greater serenity of a goddess, indifferent to earthly fuss, whose youthful liveliness was the only thing separating her from a harsh or even tragic destiny.

"Bombaks!" Leptines exclaimed in astonishment. "They look alike."

"I expected as much," Lysippus said. "Similar purpose of their bodies and the equal level of harmonious development led to inevitable likeness. But let us take these features separately, in order to understand Agesander and his predecessors, who turned the fashion of Helenian sculpture toward foreign images and models. You, Cleophrades, shall correct me or add to my statements, as I am not a great connoisseur of feminine beauty. So shall you, Leptines, because while you are young, you clearly understand the true language of the body.

"We must not repeat a common mistake of the Helenian artists, which the sculptors and painters of Egypt and Crete managed to avoid. It is particularly important to remember that when you attempt to create a composite image, its purpose is to convey beauty to the entire people, not just to fulfill an order from one customer. If that is done, the image will be created to serve only two people: the client and the sculptor himself. When gods bestow the gift of vision and recreation upon an artist, and give him a tender, sensitive soul, they often take away some of his manliness."

Lysippus hesitated, noticing that his listeners were flushed and frowning.

"I do not wish to accuse artists of lacking in manhood compared to an average person. I refer of that

Herculean courage which exists in a wrathful soul, filling heroes and other remarkable people. Compared to them, you are fragile."

"What is so bad about that?" Leptines said impatiently, interrupting his teacher.

"Nothing. But the demands are the same both from a hero and from a great artist, if he dreams of creating a truly great work of art. Lack of courage leads us toward errors in selection of a model and an image of a woman. We are discussing women, after all, and that is most important. Frequently the artist chooses a model and creates a sculpture of a maiden or a goddess with large facial features, very manlike, broad-shouldered and tall. A hero will never pick a woman like that, nor would a strong courageous man who is a leader to his people. A hero requires a woman filled with feminine power, capable of being his wife and companion and of bearing strong offspring. Such lovers accompanied artists from the ancient times, for the artists themselves were also warriors, farmers and hunters.

"Watch and listen." He turned toward the models, gesturing with his hands. "They are both of small, nearly identical, height, as appropriate for a Kharita. Thais is," Lysippus squinted an exacting eye, "three elbows and three palystas, Eris is taller by half a palysta. That is shorter than the modern standard, based on Persian and Finikian women.

"The second important feature is a combination of a small waist with rounded hips, forming uninterrupted lines of an amphora without a single chink. This has been celebrated by our poets since the ancient times and was once valued greatly by our sculptors. Nowadays, from Polycleitus to the newly-fashionable Agesander, women's stomach muscles are portrayed to be the same as men's, but the hips are forgotten. It is a serious mistake. Look here." He approached Thais and ran his hands over her hips. "The wide pelvis of a mother demands balance. How? By developing the muscles that are weak in a man, and less necessary of course. Instead of a thick layer of upper abdominal muscles, a well-built woman has deeply set muscles, here," Lysippus pressed into Thais' side, causing her to half-sigh, half-groan.

Lysippus went over to Eris and placed his hands, pale from working with wet clay, over her dark skin.

"See? She too has a very strong muscle that hides behind the oblique abdominal one. It spreads like a broad leaf from here, from the lower ribs to the pelvic bones and the pubic bone. Along its center line is another muscle in the shape of a pyramid. See how well it is outlined under the smooth skin?

"These muscles support the lower part of the stomach and press it between the convex front side of the hip, near the groin. This is also a result of their constant development. Remember this well, because this illustrates the proportions contrary to those of Agesander's statue, whose stomach protrudes too much at the bottom. As I understand it, the delightful convexity of the hips is caused by exercising the muscles that lift the leg forward. But that is not enough."

"She," said the sculptor, going back to Thais, "has very strong, deep-set muscles that pull the leg up to the pelvis. Neither the Creto-Helenian or the Nubian women have a single flaw in the line where the leg connects to the pelvis. That is not an accident either. Some people possess this gift of the Kharitas since birth. The outline of Thais' hips is even more pronounced from exercising the rear muscles that go up: this one in the middle, between the two big ones and some other ones that cannot be felt, but that lift up the layer of the top muscles. They all connect the pelvis and the hip, turn the leg, lift it back and to the side, as well as straighten the body. I would call those muscles "dancing muscles", and those that press the legs together "riding muscles".

"Remember, women must develop their deep muscles just as much as the men must develop their surface muscles. Keep that in mind, when you create an image that is beautiful, healthy and harmonious, strong without coarseness, as the daughters of Hellas should be. And not only those of Hellas, but those of the entire Ecumene. Agility without the loss of the power of Eros, and motherhood. That is an ideal and a standard removed as far from Agesander's Melos statue as it is from the runners and Amazons by Polycleitus.

"A woman is not a delicate youth. She is his opposite, and stronger than him. Women of many nations have dances with undulations of the waist and rocking of the hips. These movements are natural for them, as they exercise the deep-set muscles, create a flexible waist and polish the internal organs of her womb, where a child is conceived and grown. Where such dances do not exist, or where they are forbidden, I have heard childbearing is painful and the offspring are weaker."

The great sculptor finished his speech and stepped away, pleased. There was applause from his students who had listened intently and now expressed their overwhelming agreement.

Cleophrades rose from his seat and went to stand between Thais and Eris.

"No one could say it more clearly and wisely than you. I want to add only one thing, perhaps because I find Agesander's Aphrodite to be an interpretation contrary to my own. Look. Here before you stand two beautiful women of different origins. The great Lysippus pointed out immediately how alike they are, as they were created by the gods according to one standard.

"But he forgot to mention one more feature that is important in the definition of beauty. Their breasts sit high, are both wide at the bottom and more rounded than those of Agesander's model. His Aphrodite, despite the maturity of her body, has slightly sharpened breasts, as those of a young woman, and at the same time their centers are at least one dactyl lower than those of Thais and Eris. That is not a mistake of the artist, but a blind following of the model. Syrian women are often proportioned such."

"You are right, Cleophrades, I memorized Agesander's creation less well than you, and I agree with you," Lysippus replied.

Both the great sculptor of Hellas and his friend, a nearly unknown creator of a few statues of women, would have been saddened if they could see into the future. Then they would discover that thousands of years later the improper representation of the feminine body by Agesander would be mistaken by artists for a true standard of Helenian beauty.

"Do you wish to add something, Leptines?" Lysippus asked.

The Ephesian sculptor nodded, then held out a hand, asking for silence. "You said nothing about the rear portion of the body."

"There is nothing drastically different there compared to Agesander, or rather to the statue that inspired our debate," Lysippus said with a frown.

"No. But there is, great master. You yourself spoke about the lowered and flat buttocks of Agesander's Syrian model. As you can see, our model is sphayropigeon, round-bottomed." He drew in the air, following Thais' outline but not daring to touch her.

"Yes, of course. The reason is the same: the development of dancing muscles that bend the body backward and forward. Their greatest convexity is shifted higher and protrudes more, forming a pronounced roundness. The Milos statue is flat in the upper back, and the models of Polycleitus and Cresilaus are flat-backed as well. Looking at those models you can see clearly that they would never excel at dancing balarita or even eumelea. And our guests can perform even the most difficult of dances, is that not so, Thais?"

"Why ask the 'fourth Kharita'?" Leptines exclaimed, then pointed at Eris. "What about her?"

"Eris, would you please show them something from the Great Mother's dances?" Thais said. "They need to see."

"Why?"

"To understand feminine strength and beauty, and to create images of goddesses that would captivate the imaginations of those not fortunate enough to see you in real life."

"Very well, Mistress."

Eris pulled out the dagger from her hair and handed it to Thais. Leptines tried to take a closer look at the weapon, but Eris glared at him so savagely that he pulled his hand away. She did however, reluctantly allow Lysippus to take the dagger and the great artist froze at the sight of the ancient treasure.

The narrow blade, made of the hardest black bronze and decorated with parallel golden grooves, was topped by a hilt made of electron in the shape of letter tau of delicate craftsmanship. The top horizontal bar of the hilt was slightly bent and had gryphon heads on each side. It was molded in one piece with the cylindrical handle slightly thicker in the middle, and carved with circular grooves. On the outside, the handle was decorated with three round black agates set between the grooves. Near the blade the handle split in two, hugging the base of the blade with two taloned gryphon paws. The weapon had been created by masters who had died many centuries before. It was worth a great deal of money, but all black priestesses were armed with the identical daggers.

Thais took the blade away from Lysippus, and Eris let out a sigh of relief. Turning toward Thais, she asked her to sing the morning anthem of the Mother of Gods.

"Start slowly, Mistress, and speed up the rhythm after each half-verse."

"In the early spring I walk among white asphodel flowers," Thais began. "The sun rises higher, shadow of the night slips away …"

Eris lifted her arms above her head, folding her hands in a peculiar way, with palms turned up. She started slowly bending backwards with her eyes fixed on her chest. When the dark tips of her breasts, as wide as the steppe hills, rose vertically as if pointing at the zenith, Eris turned her head to the right. Tapping the rhythm with her right foot, she started turning right to left, raising and stretching out her leg for balance. The dazzling, almost bluish whites of her eyes were visible in thin strips between her half-closed eyelids, and her mouth formed a menacing, toothy smile.

Thais increased the tempo of the song. Never changing her pose, Eris spun first one way, then the other, switching her feet imperceptibly.

Lysippus pointed at her, obviously pleased. Who else could have done this?

Thais clapped her hands, stopping Eris, who straightened in one movement and froze on the spot.

The fragment of the dance impressed the Indian artists. The eldest of them bowed and held out his arms. Eris hesitated. The man pulled out a jewel which glittered over his forehead in his turban, and held it out to Eris, saying something in his own language. Eris looked at her mistress for direction. Thais glanced at the interpreter.

"Our great master presents the only thing he has of value as a sign of his utmost admiration for the perfection of the soul, body and dance. These are all three components that make a chitrini," the interpreter said.

"You see, Eris? You must take this gift. One cannot decline such a sign of respect. The foreigner recognized perfection of the soul in you. What did the Indian say? Chitrini? What is that?" Thais asked.

"Let us ask the honorable guest to explain," Lysippus chimed in.

The elderly Indian asked for a board, covered with a layer of alabaster. Such pieces were used by artists for large sketches. The interpreter stepped forward, bowed, then raised his hands and folded them in front of his forehead. This was a sign of readiness, meaning he was prepare to serve the guest and the host.

"Worshiping a woman and her beauty is greater among our people, it seems," the Indian began. "And the power of beauty is stronger in our country. We think that when a man and a woman come together in love, it increases the spirituality of both and improves their Psyche, the soul of any offspring they conceive. The greatest of gods don't only obey the charms of the heavenly beauties, the apsaras, or hetaerae, as you call them, but also use them as powerful weapons. The main heavenly hetaera, Urvashi was designated to seduce the wise men when they achieved too high a level of perfection and power compared to the gods. Physical love in our country is elevated not only to serve beauty and the mysteries of nature, as in Hellas, but also to serve the gods, as it was among the ancestors of Indian people on Crete, in Asia and in Finikia.

"The scores of gods and goddesses include a multitude of celestial beauties of sunlight, including surasundari or apsaras, Urvashi's helpers. One of their chief missions is to inspire artists to create beautiful things and to bring comprehension and comfort to all people. The celestial maidens bring their own image to us artists, and thus are called chitrini, from the word chitra, which is a painting, a statue, or a verbal poetic description. Imbued with the magical power of art and the ability to create the miracle of beauty, chitrini bring us all under the same law. He who cannot fulfill his task loses his power and becomes blind to the invisible, becoming a mere craftsman."

"This is very close to the Orphic teaching of the muses," Lysippus whispered to Thais. "There is a reason why, according to legend, Orpheus brought his knowledge from India."

"Or from Crete," the Athenian replied quietly.

"One of the main secrets of the artists' skill," the Indian continued, "is the inexhaustible wealth of colors and forms in the world. The soul of any man will always get an answer to his call, if he calls. The mystery will only increase his curiosity. But there are main forms and main gods. Their embodiment is the most difficult task and requires a heroic deed from the artist. His creation, however, lives longer than mountains and rivers on the face of the Earth, akin to the eternal life of the celestial world.

"That is why the entire multitude of chitrini possesses common features shared by them all. This feminine image was described by a poet fifteen hundred years ago."

The Indian held out his arms and started reciting in another dialect, apparently quoting something. The interpreter looked around helplessly. Then another Indian started translating into a more common language he knew.

"This woman is a joyous dancer, a courageous lover, an agile and strong chitrini. She is of small height with a slender waist and curved hips, with a strong straight neck, with small hands and feet. Her shoulders are straight and more narrow than her hips, her breasts are firm and set high and close, because they are wide at the base. Her face is round, her nose is small and straight. Her eyes are large, eyebrows narrow, hair darker than Indian nights. Her only scent is the smell of honey. Her ears are small and set high." The Indian caught his breath. "And now look at them," he said suddenly, pointing at Thais and Eris. "The poet inspired by gods who died so long ago described them both. Do we need any more proof of the immortal beauty of chitrini?"

The Helenians gave loud exclamations of delight. Lysippus, who sent for a chest to be brought from another room, approached the speaker, carefully carrying a statuette made of ivory and gold.

"This is a gift to you, Indian, to confirm what you said," Lysippus said, then lifted the sculpture in his palm.

Time had damaged the statuette of a semi-nude woman slightly around her face, headdress and right arm. With her left hand, the woman was pulling up the broad floor length skirt that flowed in waves. Deep gores appeared lower down the middle, in the shape of the letter mu. Her loose, wide sash sat at a slant, revealing almost all of her stomach, tiny waist and the top part of her curvy hips. Large, round breasts sat high and close but seemed too well-developed for the narrow torso and shoulders. Her face, though damaged by time, still held its round shape and a steadfast gaze of long widely set eyes.

"Chitrini?" Lysippus asked, smiling.

"Chitrini!" the Indian said, then nodded. "Where from?"

"From the island of Crete. Connoisseurs believe she is one thousand five hundred years old. That means she is a contemporary of your poet. Take it."

"For me?" the Indian asked, stepping back in reverent awe.

"For you. Take it to your country where beliefs, standards of art and attitude toward women are so close to the great lost art of Crete."

The Indian said something to his companions and they began chattering loudly and excitedly, raising his arms like Athenians at Agora.

"Today is a true holiday for us at your house, oh wise teacher," the eldest Indian said. "We have long since heard of your fame as the most incorruptible and greatest artist of Hellas, who came to Asia with Alexander. We have now seen that there is far more glory in the depth and generosity of your knowledge, and we have met not one, but two surasundari–chitrini at your home. But this last gift is particularly special. Even with all of your wisdom you may not know of a legend, that there once was a land in the west which was wiped out by terrible earthquakes and underwater volcano eruptions."

"I know this legend, and she does too," Lysippus said, pointing at Thais. "And so do those of my students who have read Creteus and Timeus by Plato. There once was a rich and powerful seafaring country in the west. Its capital, the City of Waters, perished from the wrath of Poseidon and Gaea. Egyptian priests, from whom Plato learned this legend, did not give the precise location of that country, which was called Atlantis. Followers of Plato believe Atlantis to have been located to the west of the Pillars of Hercules in the great ocean. Creteus, unfortunately, remained unfinished, and we do not know what else the great scholar might have wanted to tell us."

"Then you know the rest. Our legend states that the seafaring country was in your sea. Its position, description and time coincide with those of the island of Crete. The time of demise, not of the country itself, but of its wisdom and the best of its people, took place eleven centuries ago."

"Right at the time of the fall of the Cretan state after the terrible eruption and flood," Lysippus said, addressing Thais.

"Some of the most skillful and knowledgeable people of Crete survived the disaster and subsequent capture by people who attacked Crete the moment its might was crushed and its fleet was gone. They escaped to the east, to their new motherland of Licaonia and Cilicia, as well as Phrygia. But they found the places for possible settlements were already occupied, so they continued their journey.

"The legend says nothing of how they could have reached the river Indus, where they founded their city. They found people there who were distantly related to them: the Dravidians, and taught them arts. Whether they traveled across the land through Parthia, Bactria and the mountains or whether they managed to sail down the Euphrates and make it into the delta of the Indus from the sea using their seafaring skills, the legend doesn't say. Now you can see that your gift is sacred, for it brings to us a creation of an artist whose people founded the art of our country. I haven't enough words to thank you, Lysippus."

The Indians bowed in unison before the somewhat overwhelmed great sculptor. Then the eldest Indian approached Thais and Eris, now both dazzlingly beautiful in sunny yellow and dark blue ecsomidae. The eldest took the women's hands and pressed them to his forehead, speaking mysterious words that sounded like a prayer or an incantation.

Then the four Indian guests covered the statuette with a snow white cloth and carried it home with reverence. Eris stood with her eyes downcast, her skin looking even darker from the flush. Lysippus looked after them and spread his hands.

"I agree with the Indian master, that days of meetings and conversations such as these are rare," he said.

"I wish I could see him again," Thais said.

"You will soon meet a traveler from an even more distant and ancient Middle empire, who had only just arrived to Ecbatana."

"Can I invite him to my house?"

"No, it may not be appropriate among his people. You'd better come here. I shall arrange it so there is no big gathering and we can talk freely. I am certain that you and I will both hear many new things."

Thais clapped her hands with delight and tenderly kissed her friend, who had replaced her Memphis teacher. However, the news came in a completely different form from what Thais had expected.

The day after she met Cleophrades, Thais received a visitor. It was one of the participants of the gathering at Lysippus' house. He was an art patron, a wealthy young Lydian who multiplied his fortune by slave and livestock trade. He arrived accompanied by a secretary and a strong slave, who carried a heavy leather sack.

"You will not deny my request, Mistress Thais," he began directly, fanning himself with a perfumed purple handkerchief.

The Athenian instantly disliked the tone of half-request, half-statement carelessly uttered by the Lydian's handsome lips. She did not like him, either. Still, by the rules of hospitality she asked what his request was.

"Sell me your slave," the Lydian said insistently. "She is more beautiful than anyone I have ever seen, and thousands have passed through my hands."

Thais leaned against the railing of the verandah, no longer hiding her disdainful smile.

"You mustn't laugh at me, Mistress. I know the value of a good thing and brought you two talants," he said, then pointed at his mighty slave who was sweating under the weight of the sack of gold. "It is an unprecedented price for a dark-skinned slave, but I am not used to being denied. Having seen her, I was consumed by unconquerable desire."

"Aside from the fact that nothing in this house is for sale," Thais said calmly, "or the fact that Eris is not a slave, this woman is not for you nor for any mere mortal."

"But I am not a mere mortal," the Lydian said imperiously. "I understand a thing or two about love. And if she is not a slave then who is she?"

"A goddess," Thais replied seriously.

The Lydian laughed. "A goddess serving you? That is too much even for such a famous and beautiful hetaera as yourself."

Thais straightened. "It is time for you to leave, guest. In Athens those who cannot watch their tongue, and do not know the rules of proper conduct, are tossed down the stairs."

"And my people tend to remember what is said, and obtain what they desire by any means. The prize justifies the means," the man said ominously, but Thais ran up to the upper balcony, no longer listening to him.

A day later, when Eris and Okiale went to the market, the Lydian connoisseur of women stopped Eris and attempted to seduce her away with various promises. Eris continued on without listening to him. The enraged slave trader grabbed her shoulder, then froze when he was faced with the blade of a dagger.

Eris laughed when she told her mistress about the failed admirer, and the Athenian laughed along with her. Unfortunately, both young women turned out to be lacking in insight. They did not realize the extent of the intense and petty anger of the Asian traders in living merchandise.

A new caravan arrived from Bactria. Thais was dressing up to go see the chief and find out the latest war news. Much to her vexation, she realized she was out of the dark crimson paint made of Cyprus seashells, and used for tinting nipples and toes. Eris volunteered to run to the market. Only a horseman could make it faster than she, and even then he would have gotten stuck in the market stampede. Thais agreed.

Eris was gone a lot longer than expected. The Athenian became worried and sent a swift-footed girl, Roykos stepdaughter, to find out what had happened. The girl rushed back, out of breath, pale and with her sash missing. She told Thais that Eris was tied up and surrounded by a crowd of men who were about to kill her.

Thais had long since sensed a shadow hanging over Eris, and now the trouble had come. Roykos had already taken out Boanergos and Salmaakh and armed himself with a shield and a spear. Thais hopped onto Salmaakh. They dashed down the steep narrow street at breakneck speed, the way Eris always went. Thais was not mistaken in the path she chose. She saw a small crowd in a wide semi-portico, a niche within a tall wall. The crowd surrounded five huge slaves who were holding Eris. Her arms were twisted mercilessly behind her back, her neck was pushed back by a thick rope, and one of the slaves was trying to catch her feet. The Lydian who had visited Thais was sprawled in the dust at Eris' feet with his stomach cut open. Thais instantly knew what to do.

"E-e-e-e-eh!" she screamed right over Salmaakh's ear.

The mare went mad and rushed at the people, bucking and biting. The stunned slaves let go of Eris' arms. At the same moment Thais cut the rope with her left hand, and Salmaakh's front hooves landed on the back of the man trying to tie Eris' feet.

Roykos also took active part. One of the slaves who had held Eris' arms crashed on the ground from a hard hit with the shield right in the face. Another one jumped aside and grabbed his knife, but the old warrior raised his spear. By then, people were running in from everywhere, yelling and screaming. Thais held out a hand to Eris and turned the rearing mare. The black priestess hopped easily behind Thais and the horse carried the two women out of the crowd. Roykos would have covered their retreat, had it been necessary, but the slaves didn't dare follow Thais and Eris because the sympathies of the crowd were entirely on the side of the women.

Thais ordered Roykos to tell the people who surrounded the wounded man not to touch him until help arrived, and to get him the most famous doctor in Ecbatana.

The Athenian rushed home, examined Eris, then ordered her to go bathe in the pool. She put medicinal lotion over the many scratches in Eris' dense and supple dark skin. Eris, who was extremely pleased that her sacred dagger was safe, told her mistress about her adventure.

The Lydian with five strong slaves had waited for Eris, having spied on her during prior trips. They grabbed her so that she couldn't break free, and started dragging her under the portico. The Lydian knocked and the door at the back of the portico opened. Apparently, they intended to drag Eris inside and tie her up. Unfortunately for them, the Lydian was too quick to celebrate and decided to rip off the black priestess' clothes right there and then.

"In the case of rape we carry this in our sandals," Eris said, and lifted her right foot. There was a small roll of leather on the sole, in front of the strap that went between the toes. Shifting her big toe to the side, Eris tapped her toes on the floor, and a razor-sharp blade that looked like a leopard claw popped out of the leather roll. One swipe of such a terrible talon could inflict a huge wound. The Lydian's exposed intestines were a good example of that.

Thais finished tending to Eris, gave her some poppy broth and put her do bed despite the protests. Roykos arrived with a note from the doctor, who had already been informed of what had taken place.

"I sewed up the scoundrel's stomach with a coarse thread," Alkander wrote. "He'll live if his fat doesn't interfere."

The day after the attack, Thais asked for Eris. Her slave stood, unusually serious and solemn. Lysippus and Cleophrades sat in the comfortable armchairs of Babylonian craftsmanship with the look of judges. By the fluttering of her nostrils, Thais noticed the hidden concern of the black priestess.

"I hereby testify before the two respected and well-known citizens above the age of thirty," the Athenian recited the established formula, "that this woman named Eris is not my slave, but is a free person. She is not obligated to anyone in her actions and is her own mistress."

Eris trembled. The whites of her eyes looked enormous on her bronze face.

Cleophrades, being the elder, rose. He hid a grin in his grizzled dark beard.

"We should examine you to establish the absence of any markings or brands. But there is no need for that, as we have all seen you without clothing as recently as five days ago. I suggest we sign." He leaned over the document that had been prepared in advance, and scratched his sign with the long-lasting ink made of walnuts. Lysippus signed as well, then he and Thais approached a frozen Eris. With his strong sculptor's fingers, Lysippus opened and removed the silver bracelet above her left elbow.

"You are sending me away, Mistress?" Eris asked sadly, her breath coming out in gasps.

"No, not at all. It's just that you will not be seen as my slave anymore. We have had enough of this masquerade. Hesiona, as you know, considered herself to be my slave, too. She was also a priestess, like you, only serving a different goddess. And now, as you know, the Daughter of a Snake is my best friend, replacing my beautiful Egesikhora."

"Who am I going to replace?"

"You don't have to replace anyone. You are your own person."

"And I can live here with you?"

"As long as you wish. You have become a near and dear person to me," the Athenian said. She put her arms around Eris' neck and kissed her, feeling the trembling of the black priestess' body.

Two large teardrops rolled down her dark cheeks, her shoulders relaxed, and a sigh escaped her lips. Then came a smile as brief and beautiful as lightning.

"And here I thought it was my death hour," Eris said simply.

"How so?"

"I would have killed myself to wait for you at the shore of the River."

"I realized your mistake," Cleophrades said, "and I was watching you so I would be able to interfere in time."

"Is there any difference whether it's sooner or later?" Eris asked with a shrug.

"There is a difference. You would have realized later what you hadn't understood now, and would have subjected Thais and both of us to much grief from your silly ingratitude."

Eris gazed at the sculptor, then knelt before him and lifted his hand to her lips. Cleophrades picked her up, kissed her cheeks and made her sit in a chair next to him, as was appropriate for a free woman.

Thais rose and nodded to Eris. "I'll be right back," she said and left the room.

"Tell us about yourself, Eris," Lysippus said. "You must be a daughter of famous parents, and of good ancestry down both male and female lines. Such perfection, callocagatia, can only be acquired over a long course of generations. It is different from talent."

"I cannot tell you anything, great sculptor. I do not know anything and can only vaguely remember some other country. I was taken to the temple of the Mother of Gods when I was very small."

"Pity. I really wish to know. We would have undoubtedly confirmed what we already know about our famous beauties: Aspasia, Lais, Frina, Thais and Egesikhora."

Thais came back, carrying a white ecsomida with blue trim. "Put this on. Don't be shy. Don't forget, they are artists."

"I have known that they were different since our first visit," Eris replied, nevertheless hiding behind her mistress as she changed.

Thais did Eris' hair and added a beautiful gold diadem. Instead of the simple sandals, albeit with fighting claws, the Athenian told her to put on the holiday ones. These were made of silver leather. The main strap was tied in two bows in silver clasps to three strips of leather. They hugged the heel as well as a wide bracelet with bells around the ankle. The effect was stunning. The artists started slapping their hips with appreciation.

"She is an Ethiopian princess," Lysippus exclaimed.

"I will say to you the same thing I said to that rage-obsessed Lydian. She is not a princess, she is a goddess," Thais said.

The great sculptor studied the Athenian, trying to figure out whether she was joking or serious. When he could not decide, he said just in case, "Will the goddess consent to be a model for my favorite student?"

"That is a primary duty of goddesses and muses," Thais replied.

Chapter Thirteen. Keoss Ritual

The Lydian scoundrel who had attempted to steal Eris did survive. Three weeks later, he showed up at Lysippus' house complaining about Thais, and showing the ugly scar that sliced through his body. Thais decided it was necessary to convey all to the city chief. The Lydian was exiled and prohibited from ever showing up in Ecbatana, Susa or Babylon.

Thais' life in Ecbatana took on a monotonous rhythm after Cleophrades started sculpting her and Ehephilos started sculpting Eris. Both of them had to rise at first light. The sculptors, much like Lysippus himself, preferred morning hours. The women appeared as soon as the sun rose from beyond the eastern hills, and the clouds above the giant granite ridge turned pink, scattering before the power of Helios. Ehephilos didn't rush, proceeding slowly and not working Eris overly hard. Cleophrades, however, worked as zealously as if he were consumed with sacred madness. The pose he chose was difficult even for someone as physically well-developed as Thais.

Lysippus, who had set aside a section of his verandah for the sculptors, frequently showed up to rescue his friend.

Ptolemy sent surprisingly little news. He stopped writing long letters and sent only quick word of himself twice, sending it through sick and wounded officers when they returned to the capital of Persia. All was well. Both detachments of the army – one led by Hephaestion and the other by Alexander – took different paths to cross the icy mountain ridges of terrible height, where one could never get warm and suffered from sleeping sickness. Now the troops were descending toward the long awaited Indus.

One time, Lysippus invited Thais into his apartments. There, behind a carefully hidden door, was an absida with a tall, crack-like window that reminded Thais of the Temple of Neit in Memphis. A narrow beam of the midday sun fell onto a tile of pure white marble, reflecting a column of light at Lysippus. He looked stern and solemn. The light over his head gave the sculptor the look of a priest holding some secret knowledge.

"Our great divine teacher Orpheus discovered ovomanthy, or divination by the egg. Sometimes one can see the future hidden in the yolk and white of a bird's egg. Only those who have been initiated and know how to find the signs, then decipher them using multi-level mathematical calculation, can predict the future. Different birds have different purposes.

"In order to find out what I wish to know, I need an egg of a long-living and high-flying bird. A condor would be best. Here it is," said the sculptor. He unwrapped a bundle of fleece to reveal a large gray egg. "And to help it, there is a second one from a mountain raven."

Lysippus skillfully sliced the condor egg with a sharp dagger and allowed its contents to spread over the marble. He poured the raven's egg over a black lacquered tile. Peering carefully at both and correlating what he saw, he whispered something, then made mysterious markings on the edges of the marble slab. Not daring to move, Thais observed what was taking place, though she didn't understand anything of what she was seeing.

Lysippus started calculating and summarizing. Thais, who was enjoying the respite from the many difficult posing sessions with the ruthless Cleophrades, did not notice that the sunbeam had shifted to the left and off the marble slab. Lysippus rose abruptly and wiped sweat from his large, balding brow.

"The Indian campaign is destined to fail."

"What? Did everyone perish?" Thais started, not immediately comprehending the words spoken by the sculptor.

"There are no indications of that and there cannot be any. The flow of destiny is not beneficial and the space they plan to cross is unconquerable."

"But Alexander has maps, skilled geographers, cryptii and navigators. Everything he could get from Helenian science and the guidance of the great Aristotle."

"Aristotle turned out to be blind and deaf not only toward the ancient wisdom of Asia, but also to the Helenian's own science. Although this often happens when one becomes admired and successful on his path. He forgets that he is but a student, following one of many roads of discovery. He forgets the necessity of keeping his eyes open, preserving the ancient knowledge in his memory and combining it with the new."

"What did he forget, for example?"

"Democritus and Anaximander of Millet, the Pythagoreans, and Plato, who taught in agreement with our Orphic legends that Earth is a hemisphere, or even a sphere. That is why all maps of flat Earth, calculated by Hecateus are incorrect. Eudox of Knid, who lived in Egypt, calculated the size of the Gaea globe by observing the star Canopus and discovered it to be 330 thousand stadiums in circumference. These wise men wrote that the distance to the stars is incomprehensibly large for a human mind, and that there are dark stars as well as other inhabited lands, like our Gaea. In addition to the planets we already know about, there are many distant ones, and we cannot see them with naked eye, just as not everyone sees the sickle of the planet of Morning, dedicated to your goddess."

Thais looked around in alarm, as if afraid to see one of the enraged Olympians behind her back. "How could Democritus know about the planets invisible to him?"

"I think from the teachers who possessed the knowledge of the ancient people. At one Babylonian temple I was shown a small tower with a copper dome that could rotate on a thick axle. The dome was inset with a window made of convex glass of splendidly polished transparent mountain crystal. This round window, three podes in diameter, had been called the "Eye of the World" by the Chaldeans since the ancient times. Through it the priests managed to see four tiny stars in the night sky, near the biggest planet. They also saw a greenish planet beyond the gloomy Chronos. I saw it, too."

"And Aristotle knew nothing of this?"

"I cannot tell you whether he dismissed it or simply did not know. The former is worse, for it is criminal for a philosopher. He himself writes that Earth is a sphere, but he left Alexander ignorant."

"What else does Alexander's teacher not know?"

"You ask a question that is unacceptable for an Orphic, who believes in the limitlessness of the world and knowledge."

"Forgive me, teacher. I am ignorant and do my best to partake from the spring of your knowledge."

"Aristotle should know," Lysippus said more gently, "that several centuries ago the Finikians followed the order of the Pharaoh Neho, and sailed around the shores of Libya. Having spent two years on this heroic undertaking, they proved that Libya is an island of the size surpassing all imagination. They did not find the edge of the world, nor did they find gods or spirits, but the sun started doing strange things in the sky. It rose straight above their heads at noon, but then tilted to the side, although the sailors were still headed south. Then the sun started rising on their right instead of their left."

"I do not understand what that means."

"It means that first they went around Libya and turned north while following its shores. The change of the noonday location of the sun toward the south or north during their voyage speaks of that, which has long since been known to the Orphics and priests of India and Babylon, who used a wheel as the symbol of the world."

"But Earth looks like a wheel on the maps by Hecateus, too."

"A flat wheel. The Orphics know that this wheel is, in fact, a sphere, and Indians have long since considered Earth to be a globe."

"But if that is so, then Alexander is trying to reach the edges of the world, not knowing its true shape and size. Then Aristotle …"

"Thousands of pseudo-prophets have deceived thousands of kings, certain of the truth of their pitiful knowledge."

"They ought to be killed."

"Are you that bloodthirsty?"

"You know I am not. But those who preach false knowledge, not knowing the truth, will bring about terrible disasters. Especially if they are followed by such mighty conquerors and kings as Alexander."

"So far Aristotle has caused no disaster to Alexander. On the contrary. Having convinced him of the closeness of the edges of the world, he has made him reach for that goal with all his might. Alexander has a share of madness from his maenad mother, and he has invested it in his divine power and the abilities of an army leader."

"What will happen when the truth comes out? Will Alexander forgive him for his ignorance in geography?"

"Some of it has already come out. There was a reason why Alexander went to India using the route of Dionysus. Perhaps he found out about the Middle Empire."

"You said you wanted to show me a man who came from there. When?"

"Very well. Tomorrow. But now you must go to Cleophrades or else he will smash my entire collection of Egyptian statuettes. I was careless and left it at the workshop."

While he waited for her, the Athenian sculptor dashed around the verandah as if he were a leopard. Thais' punishment was being forced to pose till evening. Eris, who had long since been free of her obligations, had to wait a long time for her in Lysippus' garden.

"Tell me, Mistress," Eris asked on their way home. "What makes you serve as a model so obligingly? It tires you more than any other occupation and uses so much of your time. Do they pay a lot of money?" She looked doubtful. "I do not think that Cleophrades is rich."

Thais shook her head. "You see, Eris, every person has his or her own duties that correspond to whatever gifts the fate bestowed. The greater the gift, the greater the duty. A king must care about his citizens and about the development of his country. An artist must create that which brings joy to others, a poet ..."

"I understand," Eris interrupted. "I was taught also that if I possess greater beauty than that of my friends, then my service must be greater and more difficult as well."

"You have answered your own question. We were gifted by Aphrodite. We must serve people or else the divine gift will vanish before we fulfill our destiny. There are many sculptors and artists who would have paid a handful of gold to us for each hour of posing, but I shall be an obliging model to Cleophrades without a single obol. What about you?"

"Ehephilos asked me and I refused because I understand that I serve the Great Mother and, as you know, one cannot take money for that. Although sometimes I wish I had a lot of money."

Thais was surprised. "What for?"

"To make you a present. The most expensive and beautiful one I could find."

"You have long since done that," Thais said, chuckling, "having given yourself to me."

"Not at all. You bought me, or rather exchanged me when I was sentence."

"Do you not understand, priestess of the Highest Goddess, the Queen of Earth and Fertility? How I found and kept you is an accident. Any slave girl could have been obtained that way. But you did not become a slave girl. Instead you become someone completely different, unique and unlike any other. And that was when I found you again, and you found me."

"I am happy that you understand that, Thais," Eris said, addressing her by name for the first time in all the years of their life together.

There were days when Cleophrades was simply a man. On those days he was a true Athenian: gregarious, merry, hungry for news. He was definitely that way on the day in which he met a guest from the distant East, a yellow-skinned man with eyes that were even more narrow and slanted than those of the dwellers of Central Asia. The features of his face were delicate, and looked somewhat like a mask carved out of pear wood. His clothing, threadbare and faded, was made of especially thick and heavy material. It was most likely silk, which was both rare and expensive on the shores of Asia Minor and Finikia. A loose blouse hung limply over his thin body and his wide pants. The pants were cut in a similar way to barbaric fashion, much different from the tight Scythian leggings. Deep wrinkles betrayed both the traveler's age and his fatigue from the innumerable hardships of his journey. Dark eyes observed everything carefully and with obvious intelligence. He was so attentive it almost made the speaker uncomfortable.

Thais could not remember his complex name with its unusual intonations. The guest spoke the old-fashioned Persian fairly well, though he raised his voice in a funny way and swallowed the "rho" sound. A scholarly Persian friend of Lysippus easily managed the duties of an interpreter. Fortunately, both Lysippus and Thais knew some Persian as well.

The traveler assured them that it had been eight years since he'd left his native country. He had crossed monstrous expanses of mountains, valleys, deserts and forests, all inhabited by different people. According to his calculations, he had walked, ridden and sailed a distance three times greater than that covered by Alexander when he voyaged from Ecbatana to Alexandria Eskhata.

Thais and Lysippus exchanged glances.

"If I understand the honored traveler correctly, he states that the inhabited land, Ecumene, stretches much further beyond Alexandria Eskhata than it is marked on the map by Hecateus. On that map there are only twenty thousand uninhabited stadiums to Cape Tamar, where the enormous wall of snowy mountains reaches the shore of the Eastern ocean."

The guest's face betrayed a hidden smile. "My Heavenly Empire, or Middle Empire, as we call it, lies twenty thousand stadiums to the east of the River of Sands, using your measure."

"What do you know of the Eastern ocean?"

"Our empire reaches its shores and my compatriots fish in its waters. We do not know how large the ocean is or what lies beyond it. But there are sixty thousand stadiums from here to its shores."

Lysippus opened his mouth, not even attempting to hide his surprise, and Thais felt a cold shiver run down her spine. Only yesterday Lysippus had told her about the vast expanses of Libya spread to the south, and today the strange, yellow-faced man spoke of unimaginably huge and inhabited lands, Ecumene, with unquestionable sincerity. Ever since her childhood, the journey Dionysus had taken to India had always been a deed Thais viewed as that of a mighty god. Now it appeared small compared to what had been accomplished by this frail man of average height, with wrinkle-covered yellow face, who came from lands far beyond the imaginary dwelling of gods.

Thais' heart filled with deep pity for Alexander. He was fighting through scores of enemies with superhuman heroism and was still separated from his goal by a distance twice greater than that which he had covered so far. The student of a great philosopher had no idea he was being led by an ignorant blind man. Lysippus' ovomanthy filled Thais with certainty that even if he followed the Indian route, the limits of

Ecumene would turn out to be much farther away than those shown on Helenian maps.

The world was turning out to be much more complex and vast than Alexander's companions and philosophers had ever thought. How could she communicate that to Alexander? He no longer wished to listen even to his own cryptii, who had discovered a great desert and long mountain ranges to the east of the Roof of the World. Had it not been for the savagely warlike Scythians he would have gone further to the east, beyond Alexandria Eskhata, which was the city nicknamed 'Bride of Death' where Leontiscus had fallen. Thais knew it was not possible to take away Alexander's dream to be the first mortal to reach the edges of the world. But where were those edges? Judging by the traveler with unpronounceable name, millions of yellow-faced dwellers of the Heavenly Empire along the Eastern ocean already possessed far greater knowledge and art than what they termed common barbarians.

Such were the Athenian's thoughts as she watched the guest. She watched him fold his delicate hands and settle comfortably in a deep Persian armchair as if to rest. He gladly accepted an invitation to stay at Lysippus' house before continuing on to Babylon, where he hoped to get to know the capital of wise men and mages of western Asia. After then he hoped to meet Alexander.

During the few days during which the traveler stayed with Lysippus, Thais discovered many things she would have considered a fairy tale in her home country. The yellow-faced traveler taught her that the Heavenly Empire was born during times as ancient as those of the origins of Egypt, Crete and Mesopotamia. He spoke of a precise calendar created two thousand years before the construction of the Parthenon. According to him, the state had been founded two thousand years prior to the establishment of that calendar. He spoke of skilled craftsmen and artists, of astronomers who made maps of the sky, and of mechanics who created complex water powered devices. He told her of unusually tall bridges, temple towers of iron, china and bronze, of palaces erected atop manmade hills, and artificial lakes dug by thousands of slaves.

The wise men of the Heavenly Empire had even created a device which could predict earthquakes and where they were to take place. The traveler described in detail places where nature had been made more beautiful by human hands, like the mountains crowned by temples whose wide staircases of thousands of steps were surrounded by ancient trees. He spoke of roads made of blue-glazed bricks which led to sacred places, and alleys of tall, white-barked pines, every tree the identical height and age, stretching for hundreds of stadiums.

The son of the Heavenly Empire spoke of skilled doctors who healed patients by sticking tiny gold needles into affected areas. He amazed the Helenians with his story of two glass and metal mirrors at the emperor's palace which could help a doctor see through a person and find places impacted by illness inside the body. Thais, who earned the traveler's respect with her insatiable curiosity and intelligent questions, received from him a gift of a small china cup. It was decorated with a wonderful blue pattern of reeds and birds in flight, wrapped in a length of dazzling gold silk.

The Athenian hurried to thank the slant-eyed scholar by presenting him with a saucer made of black china. He had never seen anything like it, despite the many countries through which he had traveled. With the perceptiveness of a caring woman, Thais pressed the traveler to take a cedar box filled with gold staters which had been recently minted with Alexander's profile, based on the model by Lysippus. The scholar was clearly limited in his means, and possibly even hopeful of asking for Alexander's help, and he was deeply touched by the gift. Following Thais' example, Lysippus also gave him a substantial sum with which to complete his journey. Now the yellow-faced traveler could afford to go to Babylon and wait for Alexander even if it took two or three years.

Then he gave to Thais a pair of earrings of astonishing craftsmanship, which she thought were most likely the last thing of value he had managed to keep over his long journey. The earrings were made of transparent pale green stone of uncommon strength and consisted of rings and miniature balls, one inside the other. The amazing piece of art had been carved out of a solid piece without the integrity of the stone being broken. The earrings dangled from gold hooks, jingling delicately and sounding like the echo of a distant wind over dry reeds. Tiny rosettes enclosed within the balls were made of faceted pieces of stone which were called "tiger's eye" in the distant empire. They shimmered through the slits in the stone with a mysterious, moon-like light. The incredible artistry of that country's stone carvers surpassed everything the Helenians had ever seen. It only convinced them further of the truth of the traveler's story. The Athenians took time to marvel at the creation, but Thais was afraid to wear such a rarity too often.

The yellow-faced man surprised Lysippus and Thais by telling them a legend about the birth of the first creatures. He said they had come from an egg, dropped by the God of the Sky Tian' into the Great Waters. Thais was very interested in the story because this legend closely resembled the Orphic teachings about the beginning of all beginnings.

Guan-Yin, the mother of mercy and knowledge, was equal in power to the male deities of Sky and Thunder. She was also similar to the Great Mother of Crete and Asia Minor.

In the end, the traveler saddened Thais with his conviction that all things in the world have two beginnings: Yang and Yin. All things of light, day and heaven were associated with the male beginning called Yang, while all things of darkness, night and earth were associated with the female beginning called Yin. Yin was obliged to obey Yang, for only then would life flow toward light and heaven.

Thais shook her head with disdain, then told the yellow-faced man that his empire would always exist at a lower level of spiritual development than those countries in which the female beginning was recognized as that of benevolence and creation. Besides, countries where the female population was oppressed had never been known for their valor or courage in war or their struggle against enemies. Enslavement of women was inevitably followed by the birth of men with souls of slaves.

Lysippus gently reminded the enraged Athenian of some of the names of Kibela, the great female goddess. For instance, he said, there was the Ruler of the Lower Abyss and Queen of Earth, which were consistent with the aspect of Yin. Thais retorted that the Great Mother had many guises. The problem was not in them, but in the consequences of societal structure which had been created by men attempting to establish their supremacy.

Much to the Athenian's surprise, the yellow-faced man suddenly slumped. The piercing lights in his narrow eyes faded with sadness. He admitted that despite all the might of his country, the skill of the artists, and the hard work of the people, the Heavenly Empire was torn by civil wars and frequent external attacks from battle-skilled nomadic tribes.

The cruelty of their rulers made life intolerable. They distanced themselves from the lives of their people and were indifferent to disasters such as poor crops, floods and droughts. If they'd possessed more courage, this man and his compatriots would have long since revolted, overthrown the evil rulers, and eliminated cruel laws. The man lamented that all they needed was a little courage so they could escape from the country where they lived in crowded, suffering poverty, subject to injustice because of overpopulation. They needed at least as much valour as the weakest soldier in Alexander's army. Through this admission, the Helenians realized that the legendary empire, while bearing a proud name, was no better than any other country ruled by tyranny.

Thais was completely undone by another of the traveler's confessions. He told them he had been inspired by a legend about paradise. The legend said he should go west, to a land inhabited by Dragons of Wisdom and located within a circle of tall mountains somewhere in the center of Asia. He had crossed Central Asia and all of its rocky deserts and come to Mesopotamia, where western legends placed another paradise of perfect happiness. But he had found nothing like that which the legend had said existed. Instead, he discovered it was simply a fairy tale invented by European scholars in order to take their people out of slavery in Egypt and lead them to the east.

The yellow-faced man consoled himself with the truth that he might not have found paradise, but he had discovered a wisdom which was much different from the mindset of his native people.

Thais was reluctant to part from the traveler. The Athenian's irresistible charm broke some of his reluctance, but he refused to draw any maps or mark any distances until he met with Alexander.

He confided in her that instead of paradise and Dragons of Wisdom, he had met kind, welcoming people. They lived in stone structures on the slopes of tall mountains at the origins of the greatest river of the Heavenly Empire, the River Blue. These people considered themselves to be followers of a great Indian wise man. The wise man taught them to always follow the middle way between two extremes, between good and evil, between light and dark. He advised this because he said all things in the world change with time. What was good today could become bad tomorrow, and evil could turn good overnight. The traveler wanted to stay with them and become their student, but they sent him further to the west, where nobody knew of the great countries of the east. They said there he would find a man who had power enough to unite East and West by using the wisdom of both. The traveler was to see that man, the great conqueror Alexander, and tell him of the paths and countries beyond the Roof of the World. But he was only to share this knowledge if Alexander turned out to be as wise and perceptive as they had heard.

"And what if he is not?" Lysippus asked quickly.

"Then I am not to tell him anything," the traveler said evenly.

"They could find out by force," the sculptor insisted.

The yellow-faced man chuckled disdainfully. "The road is long, the distances are tremendous, mountains and deserts carry no water and are swept by terrible winds. A small error in directions would only be discovered years later, but it would lead them astray by thousands of stadiums, toward their deaths." He suddenly erupted into a broken, squealing laugh.

A huge caravan arrived in Ecbatana, dispatched by Alexander from the tallest range of Parapamizes. The mountains, their surfaces glittering with ice, stood twice as tall as Olympus and even more majestic. Much to their delight, when the Macedonian army, or rather the part of it led by Alexander and Ptolemy, reached the foot, they ran into ivy-covered hills. Among them lay the city of Nyssa.

In Alexander's opinion, both the ivy and the name of the city proved that Dionysus had stopped here at the end of his journey to India. The local tribes weren't dark but had a slightly coppery skin color. They did not look like the surrounding tribes and undoubtedly had arrived from the west. The Macedonians were struck by the sight of numerous herds of thriving livestock, especially the bulls, which were spotted, long-horned and enormous. The king immediately sent a caravan of these bulls to Macedonia.

When the caravan arrived at Ecbatana, three quarters of the animals were still intact. Thais ran to inspect the bulls, moved more by them than she had been by a letter from Ptolemy. She had to force herself to walk away from the splendid animals. They would rest for two months at a mountain pasture near Ecbatana before the next march to Tyre, followed by a sea voyage to Alexander's homeland.

The bulls looked much like the famous Cretan breed used during the sacred games. According to the legend told by the Indian sculptor, the settlers from the west could possibly have been Cretan. Lysippus agreed with that interpretation. Myths about Dionysus were as ancient as Crete itself. The great artist added that the journey of Dionysus to India was nothing more than the exodus of people who managed to escape from Crete. The Athenian jumped in delight and kissed Lysippus for this interesting idea.

Afterwards, she went home to read Ptolemy's letter. His missives from Sogda and Bactriana were filled with accumulated irritation and fatigue. This last letter, however, reminded her of the old Ptolemy. The army leader, who had become the head of Alexander's advisers, had no illusions. He anticipated much work ahead, but also the approaching end of the campaign.

Indeed, after celebrations at Nyssa and a lightning fast raid on the fortress of Aornos, they passed the three-peaked mountain, Mera. The mountain was located near the boundaries of Ecumene, according to the calculations of geographers and navigators, and descended into Svat. A messenger arrived, informing them that Hephaestion had been successful in getting his cavalry and infantry, as well as the supply carts supervised by Crateros, to the shores of the Indus. As usual, Hephaestion began constructing a bridge to cross the river. It was not wide in that area and, in both Aristotle's and Alexander's opinion, led to the East Ocean. Nearchus and the Agrian cavalry rushed there as well. They brought skilled Finikian, Ionian and Cypriot shipbuilders in order to construct ships for the trip to the east.

Alexander's plan was simple. Having crossed the Indus, the army would march two to three thousand stadiums over dry land, uninhabited all the way to the ocean shores, while Nearchus' fleet prepared to transport everyone back to the west by sea, to the Nile and to Alexandria on the shores of the Inner Sea.

"Expect us not from the east but from the west," Ptolemy wrote. "We shall arrive at Tyre, then take the 'royal road' through Damascus into Babylon. We will need no more than six months to accomplish this, although interruptions along the way are possible. If Aphrodite is merciful, go to Babylon to meet us eight months after receiving this letter. This will be the end of Asian campaigns for good. Forever. After that, we shall only wage war around the Inner Sea, conquering Libya, Carthage, and Italian cities. Everything to the Pillars of Hercules.

"New cavalry detachments from the Persian aristocracy as well as splendid horsemen-archers from Sogdiana and Bactriana have agreed to sail with us to Egypt. We managed to pull together a cavalry no worse than the brave Thessalians. Your admirers, the Argiroaspides, have become so few after the battles with Scythians and Bactrians that they were made a part of Alexander's personal guard, joining Agema and the getaerosi. Only the infantry, the veteran phalanx, is still the same. The army, having grown to a hundred thousand people, is now half cavalry. The importance of infantry, once the most important factor in battle, has been reduced. The indestructible wall of shields and long spears that used to crush even the most daring enemy became too vulnerable here, among the endless plains and mountain labyrinths. It was subject to long distance shooting attacks from horseback archers, who were as swift as the wind."

Over a year and a half, Alexander had managed to restructure the army to suit the war conditions in Asia.

New officers became prominent, Seleucus among them. He was a man of enormous height and superior strength even to the Black Cleitus, but much merrier and smarter than the unfortunate brother of Lanisa.

Ptolemy wrote that as they moved further into India, the mountains became taller and they ran into more snow and glacier ice at the inhospitable ranges. The rivers, half-covered with enormous boulders, became swifter. Through these increasing difficulties Alexander saw a sign of the approaching end of the campaign. The end of the world should be obstructed precisely so, making it inaccessible to mere mortals. Beyond these obstacles, demigods dwelled in gardens filled with trees of Eternal Wisdom, along the shores of the Waters of Life, the resting place of the sun. These waters gave immortality to gods and titans. Could the titans have been the original dwellers of the world's boundaries?

Aristotle dispatched special messengers with new considerations for his student. Of course Alexander had had no time to read them during the difficult march up the slopes of Parapamizes and Bactria. He now pondered the writings of the great philosopher and shared his doubts with Ptolemy. In the past, Aristotle had encouraged the king's push to the east, to meet the carriage of Helios; however, in his latest writings he warned Alexander against blind faith in ancient myths, of which the son of Olympias was so fond. Aristotle wrote that Alexander was unlikely to meet supernatural creatures, for none of the serious travelers have ever met godlike people or manlike gods in any of known Ecumene.

Alexander only chuckled. For him, the traces of Dionysus discovered in Nyssa were more convincing than the sophistry of the old scholar.

In his letter, Ptolemy reminded Thais of the meeting in Babylon and asked that she not bring their son into the hot climate. He promised to tell her many interesting things about countries that had never been seen, not even by mythical heroes.

Even at this point he had traveled further than Dionysus. The voyage of Argonauts to Colchis, according to Nearchus' calculations, was three times shorter than the distance the army had covered over dry land. And the army had crossed over much greater obstacles and met against much greater enemy resistance.

Ptolemy was writing from the valley of Svat. There, he said, "morning fog sparkled in millions of pearls over the groves of low trees, covered with dark pink blossoms. The emerald water over swift river rushes over purple rocks. Its shores, covered with bright blue flowers that spread in a wide border to the gentle slopes, were overgrown with trees of incredible size that we have never seen in Hellas. They are only comparable to the cedars of Finikia and Cilicia. But those trees spread out, and these grow straight up, raising their dark green tips half a stadium high. Here, as before, the firs and pines are much like those in Macedonia, and my heart was sick with yearning for my native mountains."

Thais regretted that she could not participate in the amazing journey, but quickly consoled herself, realizing how difficult it would have been for Ptolemy to protect her during the march. It had been difficult even for the tough men of remarkable strength. Her faithful Thessalians and the dear Leontiscus were no longer there to come to her rescue.

Ptolemy wrote about Roxanne, who accompanied the king. She was the wife of the great army leader, the divine Alexander. The entire army was at her service and should she become pregnant from the king, any soldier would give his life to guard the heir to the undefeated ruler of Asia.

Who was Thais? A hetaera, whose love Alexander both desired and feared, publicly rejecting her. She was a wife to Ptolemy, but after how many lovers of this collector of beauty? Even the merry tone of the letter made her think that Ptolemy had found many beautiful girls in Bactria and in the valley of the Indus. She was sure he had also collected a nice loot of precious stones. Of course she would get some of the latter, but quite would it be given in compensation for the former?

No, Ptolemy knew of her indifference. He was sometimes hurt by it. However, it was also convenient for him.

Before the bulls of Dionysus left the pastures of Ecbatana, Hesiona arrived. She had heard nothing of Nearchus and read Ptolemy's letter anxiously. It was clear that the Cretan fleet leader was back to his preferred role of navigator, map expert and shipbuilder.

The "Daughter of a Snake" had recovered from the hardships of life with her restless sea-goer and looked as pretty as ever in her pink Babylonian dress. Thais invited her to visit Lysippus, but Hesiona preferred to spend the morning hours, while the sculptors were busy with their models, at home playing with Leontiscus.

Now there was one more childless female admirer of her son, and that was most displeasing to the Athenian. Nearchus did not want children, believing he could not provide enough reliability for them; a sailor's fate was much too uncertain. To Hesiona's question of what he thought of her, Nearchus smiled slightly and told her that she was sufficiently intelligent, beautiful and rich to take care of herself in the case of his demise. Hesiona tried to explain to the Cretan that, aside from being provided for, she needed many other things from him which she did not want from anyone else in the world. The fleet leader told the Theban that she was quite free, but that he would be glad if she waited for his return because, much to his surprise, he had never found a woman better than her.

"Did you look?" Hesiona asked.

"We all like to take chances," he said with a shrug.

Gradually, the Theban realized that her intended was as obsessed with the dreams of the hidden Ocean as was his childhood friend, Alexander. Alexander never felt at peace without Nearchus. He always tried to find something for Nearchus to do that was near him, calling himself the chief navigator of his army. As a result, Hesiona was left alone in a big house for so long that she considered divorcing her famous husband. He seemed to have dissolved in the unreachable distance.

The "Daughter of a Snake" asked how Thais managed to bear Ptolemy's even longer absences. Her friend replied that she didn't need Ptolemy as much as Hesiona needed Nearchus.

"I am presently impatient for his return," Thais said, "because of his son. Leontiscus must be separated from this house before you and your like spoil him irrevocably."

"You shall miss him," Hesiona exclaimed.

"No more and no less than any Helenian mother. I'll bear myself a girl to brighten things up. She will be with me for eighteen years and by then I shall be finished with my wanderings and ready to take care of the house."

"Ptolemy's house?"

"Unlikely. The older he and I get, the younger will his lovers be. It will be difficult for me to tolerate dazzling youth near me when I have nothing left with which to compete against her, except for my good name and position. When all that is left are the name and position, one's old life is over and it is time to begin another one."

"What other one?"

"How am I to know? Ask me about it in fifteen years."

Hesiona laughed and agreed, having no idea that fate had prepared amazing but different paths for them both. They would soon separate forever.

The friends rode their old horses and bought another horse for Eris, a spotless Parthenian stallion as black as night. Eris had become a respectable rider and could manage a strong horse. In the evening they rode into the mountains, up the slopes overgrown with wormwood and thyme, passing rare outcroppings of dense dark stone which had been smoothed by the wind. Letting the horses graze, the three women chose a large, flat boulder which had absorbed sunlight all day and spread out on it, feeling the welcoming warmth on their skin. A cool wind flowing through the rocky valley carried the scent of gum from the woods above, mixed with the fresh and sharp smell of the grasses. An enormous snow-covered peak obstructed the sun from the west, and the gentle warmth from the rock was quite pleasing. Sometimes the first faint stars appeared in the twilight sky, and brias, the desert owl, called out several times before the riders returned to the city.

Each of them behaved differently during these silent mountain vigils. Eris sat hugging her knees and resting her chin on them, observing the jagged mountain range and the shimmering, pearly mist of the distant plain. Hesiona pulled herself to the edge of a drop overhanging the valley and lay on her stomach, observing the play of water in a creek at the bottom of the crevasse. She watched for mountain goats and for chipmunks who popped out of their burrows and whistled to their neighbors. Thais settled on her back with her arms spread and watched the sky with its few slow clouds and mighty gryphs. Observation of the sky hypnotized her.

Hesiona quietly watched Thais, whom she considered to be the best of women, and was astonished by the constant change of expressions on her face, though her body remained completely still. As she gazed at the sky, Thais suddenly smiled, then transformed into a picture of deep sadness, or even dared the fates with an expression of menacing stubbornness. It was all done with a barely perceptible movement of her lips, eyelids, eyebrows and the nostrils of her nose, which was as straight as if it had been smoothed along a carver's ruler, with a Cretan dip at the bridge that softened the heavy, classic Helenian profile. Watching Thais reminded Hesiona of the mysterious art of the Egyptians, who managed to communicate a change in mood even though their statues were made of hard polished stone.

Once, when Thais appeared more sad and thoughtful than usual, the Theban asked, "Do you still love him?"

"Who?" Thais asked, not turning her head.

"Alexander. Was he not your greatest love?"

Thais sighed deeply. "Lysippus once told me that a skilled sculptor can use the same outlines to create flesh as mighty and heavy as a rock, and can imbue his creation with incredible power of inner flame and desire. In the same image ... almost."

"I did not quite understand you. I became a bit savage among swamps and sailors," Hesiona said with a smile.

The Athenian turned serious. "If a man wishes to follow gods, his love must be as free as theirs. Not like an irresistible force that crushes and tears us apart. Strangely, the more it possesses its victims, the weaker they are before it. The more enslaved they are by their feelings, the more poets glorify these pitiful people who are ready to commit any humiliation and lowly deed. They would lie, kill, steal, break a vow ... Why is that? Is that the wish of the light-bearing. silver-footed Aphrodite?"

"I understand. You have no hope, have you?"

"I have long since known that. Now you know too. Then why must I weep under the star that cannot be taken from the sky? It follows its predestined path. And you follow yours."

They visited symposiums, adopted enthusiastically by the Persians, who followed the artists' example. Only Eris flatly refused to go. She was disgusted by the sight of people who ate and drank too much.

Thais also admitted to Hesiona her aversion toward gluttons. She had been sensitive toward any expression of crudeness ever since she was a child, and presently lost all tolerance for it. Loud laughter, shallow jokes, uncontrolled eating and drinking, hungry glances that used to glide over her without bothering her, now irritated her. The Athenian decided this attitude meant she was growing old. Spirited discussions heated with wine, poetic improvisations and love dances felt more and more like nonsense. She could hardly believe that she and the golden-haired Spartan used to be called the queens of symposiums.

"It is not old age, my beautiful friend," Lysippus said in response to the Athenian's question He pinched her lightly on her smooth cheek. "Call it wisdom. Or call it maturity, if the first term seems too formal. Each year you will move further away from the games of your youth. The circle of your interests will become broader and your expectations of yourself and others will go deeper. You must be more demanding of yourself first, then toward others, or else you shall turn into a haughty aristocrat with an impoverished heart and mind. And you will die. Not physically, of course. With your health, you may live a long time. But you will die spiritually and walk around as your own outer shell, which would truly be a corpse. You are likely unaware of how many such living corpses trample the face of Gaea. They are deprived of conscience, honor, dignity and kindness. These are all things that form the basis of a man's soul and are awakened, strengthened and upheld by artists, philosophers and poets. But these people get in the way of the living while looking exactly like them. Except they are insatiable in the most basic and simplest of desires: food, drink, women, the power over others. And they seek to satisfy themselves by all means. Have you heard of the Hecate's companions?"

"The Lamias or Mormos or whatever they are called? Those who travel with her at night and drink the blood of passersby at the crossroads? Vampires?"

"That is primitive symbolism. In the secret knowledge, the creatures of Underworld that drink living blood are those insatiable living dead, ready to take everything possible from their countries, communities, people – their own and those of others. They are the ones that beat and overwork their slaves to death just to get more gold, silver, houses, spears, and new slaves. The more they take, the greedier they become, reveling in the labor and sweat of people subservient to them."

"You speak of terrible things, teacher." Thais shrugged as if from cold. "Now I will look at everyone more carefully."

"Then my words have reached their goal."

"What is to be done with such living dead?"

"They ought to be killed, of course, stripping them of their false living appearance," Lysippus said after a pause. "The trouble is that only rare people can recognize them, and those who have reached such a spiritual level are no longer capable of killing. I think the final elimination of the vampires is a matter of distant future; when homonoya, the intellectual equality among people, is established the number of those rare people will increase many fold."

Thais went to the studio, sad and thoughtful. Cleophrades was waiting for her near the clay version of the statue. During the last few days, the sculptor had been delaying the completion of his work, letting her go early or suddenly pausing as if he forgot about his model and thought about something else. Today he did not sign to her impatiently to get onto the posing cube as he usually did. Instead, he stopped her with an outstretched arm.

"Tell me, Athenian. Are you fond of money?" Cleophrades asked with gloomy shyness.

Thais was surprised and saddened by this question "Why do you ask me this?"

"Wait," he said, looking away. "I cannot speak. I can only work with my hands."

Thais frowned. "Not just with your hands, but also with your head and heart," she objected. "So tell me, why did you speak of money?"

"You see, you are as wealthy as Frina, but Frina was insanely wasteful. In contrast, you live modestly, despite your income and your position as the wife of Alexander's first advisor."

"Now you speak more clearly," she said, and sighed with relief. "And here is my answer. Money is not a goal, but an opportunity. If you treat it like a power that gives you various opportunities, then you shall value money but it will not enslave you. That is why I disdain miserly people, but I am also disgusted by stupid spending. Money means much work from a lot of people and tossing it away is the same as tossing away bread. One can bring upon himself the wrath of gods and become empty and dead, as Lysippus says."

Cleophrades listened, frowned and suddenly made a decision. "I shall tell you what prompted this thought. I decided to cast the statue from silver, but what I saved up is not enough. I don't have time to wait and save more. I will be sixty in Hekatombeon."

"Why do you wish to use such expensive metal?"

"I could reply to you like a young man by asking are you not worthy of it? But I shall give you a different answer. This is the best work of my life, and the best model. This would fulfill my dream to complete my life journey in a worthy manner. I could ask Lysippus. But I already owe him too much. And besides, this creator of athletes and horsemen only recognizes bronze and, I shudder to say, uses the Thelmes alloy[34]."

"How much silver do you need?"

"I am planning to use not the pure metal but an alloy including fourteen parts of red Cyprus copper. Such silver does not stain and does not become fogged, as we say, with the dusty dew. It holds polish as well as the dark stone of Egypt. I need twelve talants of pure silver to cast, and all I have is a little more than four and a half. A huge difference."

"So you need seven and a half talants? Very well. I shall send for it tomorrow and will dispatch eight talants to you the day after tomorrow, just in case."

Cleophrades froze, gazed at his model at length, then took her face in his hands and kissed her on the forehead.

"You do not know the value of your good deed. This isn't just tremendous treasure, it is ... You will understand after Hekatombeon. You will have to pose a bit more after casting, while I work on minting. That

---

[34] An alloy of poorly purified copper and silver impurities – primarily zinc.

is nearly the most important part of the work," he said, finishing in his usual brisk, businesslike tone. "But it is quick. I am myself in a great hurry."

Thais did not understand the meaning of Cleophrades' last words. The Athenian sculptor and Ehephilos finished their work almost simultaneously, the young Ionian wrapping up about ten days sooner. Cleophrades invited Thais and Eris to come late to Lysippus' house and spend the end of the night till morning. To ensure nothing happened to them at such late hour, several friends showed up to accompany them.

The late half moon shone over the pale gray cobblestones, giving them a bluish tinge. Like a heavenly road stretched between dark walls and rustling garden foliage.

At the door they were welcomed by Ehephilos and Cleophrades, dressed in light-colored holiday garments. They crowned their models with wreaths of fragrant yellow flowers that seemed to glimmer in the moonlight as if emitting their own light. Each took his model by the hand and led her into the dark unlit house, leaving their companions in the garden. Before they stepped into the moonlit verandah, welcoming them with its wide-open curtains, Cleophrades ordered Thais to close her eyes. Holding her by the shoulders, he placed the Athenian in the proper spot, then allowed her to look.

Ehephilos did the same with Eris.

Thais cried out with amazement, and Eris sighed deeply and loudly.

Before them, the nude Aphrodite Anadiomena with Thais' head and body stood on the toes of one foot. Her other foot was bent behind her in a light run, rising from porous silver that resembled foam. The uplifted face and the arms outstretched toward the sky combined the upward movement and the gentle, love-filled embrace of the entire world.

The shimmer of moonlight on polished silver gave the goddess miraculous transparency. Foam-born, woven from starlight, she appeared on the shore of Cyprus, emerging from the sea to raise the eyes of mortal toward stars and beauty of their lovers, pulling them away from the monotonous necessity of Gaea and the dark power of the underworld, Kibela. The aura of spiritual and physical purity possessed by Thais was vastly multiplied in the goddess, and surrounded her with a soft glow. Thais, who was a Helenian and had grown up surrounded by sculptures of people, gods and goddesses, hetaerae and heroes, without whom Hellas would have been unimaginable, had never before seen a statue with such power of enchantment.

Next to her, half a step behind, Artemis Acsiopena was cast from dark, almost black bronze. She held out her left arm as if moving aside an invisible curtain, reaching with her right hand for the dagger hidden in the knot of hair at the back of her head. Moonbeams reflecting on her indomitable face emphasized the unstoppable movement of her entire body, which was appropriate for the goddess of retribution.

Thais sniffed, unable to contain her emotions. This quiet sound told Cleophrades of the success of his creation better than any words. Only then did Thais notice Lysippus. He sat in an armchair nearby, his eyes squinted and his hands folded. The great sculptor was silent, watching both women, and finally nodded with satisfaction.

"Rejoice, Cleophrades and Ehephilos! Two great creations appear to celebrate Hellas here, thousands of stadiums away from our homeland. You, Athenian, surpassed everything you created before. And you, apprentice, have become equal to some of the greatest artists. I am pleased that both goddesses are not novelties and not built to suit the fickle taste of current generation. They are examples of the original beauty, so difficult for the artists to achieve and so necessary for the proper understanding of life. Let us sit and be quiet as we wait for dawn."

Thais, captivated by both statues, did not notice that the moon had set. The outlines of both sculptures changed in the predawn twilight. Acsiopena seemed to have stepped further back into the shadows and Anadiomena dissolved in the air.

With stunning suddenness, the rosy eyes of Eos flashed from behind the mountain range with the appearance of the bright dawn, and one more miracle took place. Crimson light played over the polished silver body of Anadiomena and the goddess lost the starry weightlessness of the moonlit night. She appeared before the enraptured spectators in all her light-filled, nearly tangible might.

Competing with her in power and in beauty of clear and powerful outlines, Artemis the Avenger no longer appeared to be a menacing black shadow. She stood like a warrior approaching her goal without rage or anger. Each line of Ehephilos' statue was sharper than those of the sculpture by Cleophrades, embodying inevitability. The power of the rising Anadiomena resonated with the reddish black embodiment of fate. Both sides of existence – the beauty of a dream and the merciless responsibility for one's actions – stood together so overwhelmingly that Lysippus shook his head. He said the two goddesses should be displayed separately, otherwise they would cause confusion and contradictory emotions.

Thais silently took off her wreath, put it onto Cleophrades and knelt in front of the sculptor. The moved Athenian lifted her up and kissed her. Eris followed her friend's example, but she did not kneel before her much younger sculptor. Instead, she clutched him in a firm embrace and kissed him fully on the lips. The kiss lasted a long time. For the first time, the Athenian saw the unapproachable priestess as a woman and realized that those who sought higher bliss in the temple of the Mother of Gods did not risk and give their lives in vain. When it was Thais' turn to kiss Ehephilos, the sculptor barely responded to the touch of her lips, busy as he was in trying to contain his breath and his madly beating heart.

Lysippus offered to continue the "ritual of the gratitude of muses", as he referred to Thais' and Eris' actions, at the table. There the black Khios wine with the scent of rose petals was already prepared. This was a rarity even for the "glory of Helenian arts". There was also an oynohoya vessel, filled with water from freshly melted snow. Everyone lifted the precious glass goblet to the glory, health and joy of the two sculptors, Cleophrades and Ehephilos, as well as to the master of masters, Lysippus. The artists responded with praise to their models.

"The day before yesterday an artist from Hellas told me about a new painting by Apelles, the Ionian, at the temple on the island of Cos," Lysippus said. "It too shows Aphrodite Anadiomena. The painting is already famous. It is hard to judge by description. Painting and sculpture can only be compared by the level of their impact upon people."

"Perhaps it is because I am a sculptor," Cleophrades said. "But I feel that your portrait of Alexander is deeper and stronger than his painted portrait by Apelles. In the past, in the last century, Apollodorus of Athens and Parrasius of Ethes could express beauty beyond many sculptures with a mere outline. Our great artist Nikias helped Praxiteles by painting marble with hot wax paints and giving it a miraculous semblance to a living body. You love bronze and you don't need Nikias; however, one cannot help but admit that a union between a painter and a sculptor is truly great for marble."

"Paintings by Nikias are great on their own," Lysippus said. "His Andromeda is a true Helenian, death-defying courage combined with her youthful desire to live, although according to the legend she is an Ethiopian princess, like Eris. This silver Anadiomena may well turn out to be better both in workmanship and in the beauty of the model. As far as Artemis is concerned, there is nothing like her in Hellas and has never been. Not even in the temple at Ethes, where artists have been competing to create the best image of Artemis for four centuries. There are seventy of her statues there. Of course they did not possess the modern skill in the ancient times."

"I know of a splendid Artemis at Leros," Cleophrades said. "I think it has the same idea as the one by Ehephilos, although it is a century older."

"What is she like?" Eris asked, her voice tight with a tinge of jealousy.

"She is not like you. She is a maiden who has yet to know a man but is already blossoming with the first feminine beauty. She is filled with the fire of sensations and her breasts nearly burst from insatiable desire. She leans forward with her arm outstretched, like your Artemis, but before a huge Cretan bull. The monster, stubborn yet already overcome, is beginning to kneel before her."

"According to an ancient legend, the Cretan bull is defeated by a woman," Thais said. "I wish I could see a sculpture of that."

"You would sooner see the battle at Granic," Lysippus said with a laugh, implying the tremendous group of twenty-five horsemen he couldn't seem to finish, much to the displeasure of Alexander, who wished to erect it in Trojan Alexandria.

"I hesitated at length, whether to show Eris my Artemis with the dagger fully exposed," Ehephilos said thoughtfully.

"You did well not to show it. A muse can carry a sword, but only to defend, never attack," Lysippus said.

"Acsiopena, much like the black priestess of Kibela, attacks when she punishes," Thais objected. "You know, teacher, only here in Persia and in Egypt, where an artist is recognized as a master of elevating royalty, did I realize true meaning of beauty. There is no spiritual elevation without it. People must be lifted beyond the usual level of everyday life. An artist, by creating beauty, gives comfort in a memorial, poeticizes the past in a monument, expands heart and soul in the images of gods, women and heroes. One must not distort beauty, or else it would stop giving strength, consolation and spiritual fortitude. Beauty is fleeting, our touch with it is all too brief, and that is why, as we grieve the loss of it, we gain deeper understanding and appreciation of beauty yet to come, and look for it that much harder. That is why the sadness of songs, paintings and tomb memorials is so lovely."

"You have surpassed yourself, Thais," Lysippus exclaimed. "Wisdom speaks through your lips. Art cannot disgust and corrupt or else it would stop being art as we Helenians understand it. Art either rejoices in the splendor of beauty or grieves for the loss of it. It can only be so."

These words by the great sculptor would forever remain with the four that met dawn at his house.

Thais was sorry Hesiona could not have been there, but after having thought about it she realized the little celebration had to include only the artists, their models and the main patron of the endeavor. Hesiona saw the statues the following day and burst into tears with delight and a strange anxiety. She remained pensive all day and only managed to sort out her emotions in the evening, when the two friends were settling for the night in Thais' room. This was where they often stayed when they wanted to talk.

"Having seen such harmonious and inspiring creations, I suddenly felt fear for their fate. It is as uncertain as the future of any of us. Our lives are so short, but these goddesses must exist forever, traveling thorough future centuries, as we do through light wind. And Cleophrades ..." Hesiona fell silent.

"What about Cleophrades?" Thais asked anxiously.

"He made your statue out of silver instead of bronze. There is no question about the splendor of such material. But silver is valuable by itself. It is money. Something you can use to pay for land, house, livestock, and slaves. Only a powerful polis or ruler can allow twelve talants to sit without use. And think of all the greedy scum that don't believe in our gods? They wouldn't hesitate to chop off Anadiomena's arm and take it to a merchant, like a piece of dead metal."

"You have alarmed me," Thais admitted. "I really hadn't thought of the uncertain destiny of not only people, but entire states. During the few years of Alexander's campaigns we have seen old order fall apart and thousands of people lose their place in life. Fates, tastes, moods, attitude toward the world, possessions and each other – everything is feeble and changeable. What would you suggest?"

"I do not know. Should Cleophrades give or sell her to some famous temple, I would be much more at rest than if she went to some art patron, even if he were as wealthy as Midas."

"I shall talk to Cleophrades," Thais decided.

Some time passed before the Athenian had a chance to fulfill her intentions.

The sculptor showed Anadiomena to anyone who wished to see her. Visitors came to Lysippus' garden where the statue was placed in one of the pavilions, and admired her at length, unable to pull away. Then Anadiomena was transferred back into the house, and Cleophrades disappeared. He returned in Hekatombeon, when even Ecbatana became hot, and the snow cap on the southwest ridge turned into a narrow strip resembling a cloud.

"I beg you," Thais said to him as soon as they met, "to tell me what you want to do with Anadiomena."

Cleophrades gazed upon her at length. A sad, almost tender smile rested upon his usually stern and glum face.

"If the world was arranged according to dreams and myths, then I would be the one begging, not you. But unlike with Pygmalion, in addition to the silver goddess, a live Thais is before me. And everything is too late."

"What is too late?"

"Both Anadiomena and Thais. Still, I do have a request for you. My friends are holding a symposium in my honor. You must be there. Then we shall settle the matter of the statue. It contains not only your beauty but also your silver. I cannot manage it singlehandedly."

"Why then and not now?"

"It's too early."

"If you intend to torment me with riddles," the Athenian said, slightly put out, "then you have succeeded in this unworthy mission. When is the symposium?"

"At hebdomeros. Bring Eris, too. Although, I hardly need to say that, since you are practically inseparable. And also Nearchus' wife."

"The seventh day of the first decade? The day after tomorrow?"

Cleophrades nodded silently, then raised his hand and vanished into the back of Lysippus' great house.

The symposium began in the early evening. It was set in the garden and included nearly sixty people of various ages. They were almost exclusively Helenians, settled at narrow tables in the shade of great sycamores. Among the attendees there were only five women: Thais, Hesiona, Eris, and two new Ionian models of Lysippus, who assumed hosting the party in the old bachelor's house. Thais knew one of them well. She was short with a long neck, a merry round face, and constantly smiling, plump lips. She resembled a cora in Delphi, at the entrance to the Scythian treasury of the Apollo's temple. The other woman was a complete opposite of the first one, indicating the host's broad tastes. She was tall with long, slanted eyes on an elongated face, and a mouth with its tips pointing upward like the moon. She had joined Lysippus' household only recently, and everyone grew to like her for her slow, graceful movements, modest demeanor and beautiful garments of dark crimson cloth.

Thais chose to wear a shocking yellow ecsomida. Eris wore a sky blue one, while Hesiona showed up in a strange, draping garment of bright blue and gray, a south Mesopotamian costume. The seductive quintet took their places to the left of the host while Cleophrades and other sculptors: Ehephilos, Leptines, Diosphos, and Stemlos settled on the right. There was more black Khios wine, as well as rose Knid wine, diluted with ice cold water. The gathering was becoming rambunctious.

Thais found the verboseness of the speakers rather unusual. One after the other they stepped forth and, instead of toasting, spoke about Cleophrades' deeds, his military heroics, and his sculptures, praising him without superfluous flattery. On his request, the new model sang strange, sad songs in a low, resonating voice, and Hesiona performed a hymn to Dindimena.

"I could ask you to sing in the nude, as is customary for hymns, as their name indicates," Cleophrades said, thanking the Theban. "But let the dances be our hymns to physical beauty, of which I ask Thais and Eris. That is my final request."

"Why your final one, Cleophrades?" the unsuspecting Athenian asked.

"Only you and your friends do not know of the true purpose of this symposium. I shall answer you with Menander's verses. 'There is a beautiful custom among the Keossians, Phania: he who does not live well must not live poorly, either.'"

Thais shuddered and paled. "You are not from Keoss, Cleophrades. You are an Athenian."

"I am from Keoss. Attica is my second homeland. And my island is really not that far from Sunion, where the famous temple with seven columns is raised to the sky over the sheer marble drops eight hundred elbows tall. Since childhood, it became for me a symbol of spiritual heights reached by the creators of the art of Attica. When I came to Sunion, I saw the spear and the crest on the helm of Athena Promakhos. The bronze Maiden twenty elbows tall stood on a huge pedestal at the Acropolis between Propyleus and Erekhteyon. I sailed to her call and saw her, proud and strong, with slender neck and high, prominent breasts. That was the image of a woman that enchanted me forever. And that was how I became an Athenian. None of it matters anymore. The future will meet the past, and that is why you must dance for me."

Thais, obedient model that she was, improvised complex dances of the highest skill level, in which a woman's body transformed and granted a dream after dream, a legend after legend. In the end, Thais was exhausted.

"As I watched you," Cleophrades said, "I was reminded of your Athenian nickname. You are not only a Fourth Kharita, but you were also called Euryale, or Storm. Let Eris take your place."

At Cleophrades' sign, Eris danced as she had before the Indian artists. When the black priestess froze in the last pose and Ehephilos wrapped a light cape around her body, Cleophrades rose, holding a large golden goblet.

"I have turned sixty years old, and I cannot do more than my last Anadiomena. I cannot love women, I cannot enjoy travel, sea-bathing, good food or loud singing. Ahead of me is a spiritually deprived, miserable life. We Keossians have long since forbidden that a man should live that way, for he must only live in a worthy fashion. I thank you, my friends, who came to honor me in my last hour. Rejoice, rejoice all, and you, splendid Thais. How I would have wanted to love you. Forgive me, but I cannot. Lysippus will take care of the statue. I gave it to him. And let me embrace you, my godlike friend."

Lysippus put his arms around the sculptor, not hiding the tears in his eyes.

Cleophrades stepped back and raised his goblet. At the same time, all others raised their cups, filled with life-giving wine. So did Thais. Only Hesiona remained motionless, observing the scene with horror in her wide eyes. Eris watched the Athenian's every movement in admiration and shock.

Tipping his head back, Cleophrades downed the poison, faltered, then straightened out, leaning against Lysippus' shoulder. The goblet rang as it fell on the ground. The other guests drank their cups and threw them as well, shattering glass, china and clay. The pieces would be placed under the tombstone.

"Haire! Easy sailing across the river. Our memories are with you, Cleophrades!" everyone exclaimed.

The sculptor, his face gray and his lips trembling, made one last tremendous effort. He smiled broadly, gazed into the darkness of Hades before him, and collapsed.

At that moment, or so it seemed to Thais, the sun vanished behind the mountain range. Light summer twilight fell upon the silent group of people.

There were two physicians among the guests. They examined Cleophrades and placed him on a stretcher.

The others placed a wreath on his head, crowning him as a victor in a competition. Had he not walked victoriously along the difficult path of his life? In the light of torches and the moon, the sculptor was carried to the Helenian and Macedonian cemetery.

High above the city in a juniper grove, low trees shed their bronze-like needles over a few graves. The Athenian sculptor had asked in advance that he be buried rather than arranging a funeral pyre. The grave had already been prepared and was covered with a temporary slab until the friends of the late sculptor, other sculptors, could design and build another tombstone.

The participants of the sad ceremony returned to Lysippus' house after the cemetery, where they held a midnight memorial feast. Night drew to a close.

Shocked and tired, Thais remembered another dawn, a dawn when she had admired the power of the artist who had just departed to the kingdom of Hades. As if guessing her thoughts, Lysippus invited her, Eris and Ehephilos, as well as a few other friends, into a workroom lit by alabaster lanterns.

"You heard from Cleophrades that he left Anadiomena to me," Lysippus said, addressing Thais. "Even before that he told me of your generous donation to complete the statue. Thus, you and I are co-owners of Anadiomena and Cleophrades' heirs. Tell me, what would you prefer: to keep the statue, let me keep it or entrust me to sell it? Its value is tremendous, not even considering the material. I cannot pay you back your share. You can probably pay me back mine, but I think that this statue ought not to be owned by you or any person who understands that the miracle of art and the goddess cannot be held in singular possession."

"You are right as always, teacher. Allow me to surrender my share, as you call it, and leave the statue with you."

"My generous Thais," Lysippus exclaimed with pleasure. "Perhaps there will be no need of your generosity. I admit that I once spoke with Alexander about Cleophrades' intention to sculpt you and ..."

Thais' heart beat faster and she sighed.

"He said," Lysippus continued, "that if, in my opinion, the statue is successful, he would be the first contender for it. I asked him why he wouldn't simply order it. He looked at me as if I had asked an inappropriate question. I suppose you would not mind if I sell Anadiomena to Alexander. He will send it to Hellas, perhaps to Athens or to Cythera."

Thais lowered her lashes and tipped her head, then asked, with her gaze still lowered. "What will Ehephilos do with his Acsiopena?"

The young sculptor frowned. "I shall keep Acsiopena until Eris agrees to be mine."

"One does not discuss such things in front of everyone, as if I were a market whore," Eris replied indignantly. "The Great Mother requires nighttime for her mysteries. Those who dare violate her rules become akin to beasts, not knowing that love is sacred and requires preparation of body and soul. Have you Helenians forgotten the orders of the Mother of Abyss, Kibela?"

Thais looked at the black priestess in amazement. What made her pronounce such a tirade? Having guessed, she smiled and her sad eyes twinkled merrily.

"Ehephilos - or should we call you Eriphilos[35]? Were you not an artist, I would have used all my power to keep you from this mad pursuit that could mean your death. Even to you, the creator of Acsiopena, I say beware, beware and beware again. You will not gain happiness, but will discover Eros available only to a few people, but at the cost of their lives."

---

35 Eriphilos is a seer who traveled to Troy with the Greek army, despite the fact that he knew he would die there.

"What do you speak of, Mistress?" Eris exclaimed, wheeling towards her. "Are you encouraging him?"

"Why not? It's about time you shed the darkness that descended upon you at the temple of Kibela. Whether you want it or not, part of you has already been consumed by the statue."

"Do you suggest that I serve a man?"

"Not at all. The man will serve you. Look at him. He can barely resist the urge to wrap his arms around your legs."

"I cannot violate my vow and abandon you."

"It is entirely up to you and him how to reach an understanding. And if not, then you had better kill him and put him out of his misery."

"I agree, Mistress Thais," Ehephilos exclaimed.

"Do not rush to celebrate," Eris interrupted sternly. "Nothing happened yet."

"It will," Thais said with certainty then apologized to Lysippus, who observed this "family scene" curiously.

Arguments aside, a few days later Artemis Acsiopena left Lysippus' home, bought for an enormous sum – not by a Helenian, but by one of the Indian artists that visited Lysippus. He purchased the statue for an ancient temple of strange faith called Eridu. It was located at the Euphrates delta, near the most ancient city in Mesopotamia. The sculptor saw a particularly good omen in the similarity between the name of the temple and that of his love.

What happened between him and Eris remained forever under the cover of night. Thais, who was naturally observant, noticed that that night, Eris' swift movements became a bit smoother and her blue eyes sometimes lost their cold steely glint.

A couple of months after the sale of the statue, Ehephilos came to Thais, looking utterly miserable. He begged her to take a walk in the garden with him. Not far from the stone wall where the stream from the pool flowed across a small pit, the sculptor jumped into waist-high water, ignoring his clean and pressed clothes. Ehephilos knelt, reached into the pit and raised his folded hands. Large rubies, emeralds, sapphires, sardonyxes, gold and silver bracelets, belts and a golden goblet with turquoise glittered in the sun.

Having figured out what the matter was, Thais burst out laughing and advised the young sculptor to pick up his gifts, gather them into a sack, take them home and not give Eris any more jewelry. She would not accept anything unless it came from Thais herself.

"Why is that?"

"She and I are tied together in life and death by our mutual salvation. If you really want to, you can give her sandals with silver straps. It's the only article of clothing she cannot resist. And not only from you, but from anyone who wants to make her a present."

The new Olympiad started after the death of the Athenian artist. Time flew swiftly, approaching the date set by Ptolemy. Winter nights in Ecbatana grew cooler. Thais spent long evenings in conversation with Lysippus and his learned friends.

There was no fresh news from Alexander or his comrades. There were neither caravans with loot nor carts with the sick and wounded. Perhaps the great conqueror had truly managed to realize his dream and go beyond the limits of Ecumene, to the forbidden boundary of the world?

Hesiona was worried. Thais started considering life without Ptolemy, in case he did not wish to return from the Gardens of Wisdom, having tasted the Water of Life. At four years old, Leontiscus already boldly rode a small horse delivered from Iberia, from the Sea of Birds, and competed with his mother at swimming in a lake. Leontiscus, who couldn't yet read, already spoke three languages: Attic, Macedonian, and Aramaic. Thais did not want to part from her son. But she had to fulfill Ptolemy's request and leave him behind under the watchful eye of the Macedonian veteran Roykos, his wife, and the Syrian slave girl who was utterly devoted to the boy. In the month of Gamelion,

Thais left Ecbatana. Lysippus traveled with her to meet his patron and main client, as did Ehephilos, who allegedly went to see his Acsiopena, as Lysippus had promised them a trip to Eridu. He received quite a few leusa dregma dracontos – dragon glares, as Thais called them, flashed at him by Eris. The sculptor bore them valiantly.

Babylon met them with huge crowds of people, noisy markets, sounds of unimaginable languages and a mix of strange costumes. Ambassadors from various countries were waiting for Alexander, but there was still no news from him. Worse yet, there were rumors of his demise – first in the waters of the Indus, then somewhere in the mountains. Alexander's envoy in Babylon was ordered to capture anyone who spread these rumors and bring them in for interrogation in order to discover the source of their information, under the threat of flogging or even death. The connections pointed to foreign merchants or politicians who wished to cause panic and somehow use it to their advantage.

Thais realized that the wait could be long and decided to rent the same house in the New City, on the other bank of the Euphrates, near the Lugalgira gates, where she lived before. Much to her astonishment, when she went to look, she did not find her former home there. Only the garden, the old wooden pier and the path remained unchanged. The house had been replaced with a beautiful pavilion tiled in translucent pink marble, with pillars of bright blue stone and gold surrounding the rectangular pool with clear fresh water. All this belonged to Alexander and was guarded by two savage-looking Scythians, who unceremoniously chased Thais away. An enraged Eris offered to kill them right there and then, but the Athenian, touched by this proof of Alexander's love, ordered Eris in no uncertain terms to do nothing. In the end, all Ecbatana visitors settled at Hesiona's house, much to Ehephilos' joy. The city was overfilled.

Thais discovered other news in Babylon. The huge theater of Dionysus, of which she had heard from Hesiona, remained unfinished. Its construction materials, which were the remains of the Etemenanki tower, had been bought by the priests of the Marduk temple. Alexander had allowed its restoration against the advice of his old seer, Aristander. The old man had predicted great personal peril for the king should the sinister temple be revived; however, Alexander wished to increase his influence with the help of priests of various religions, and hadn't listened.

Chapter Fourteen. Wisdom of Eridu

Warm Babylonian winter came to an end, summer drew near with its threat of heat. As there was still no news from Alexander, Lysippus decided they should all take a trip to Eridu. The sculptor joked that Euryale and Eris were going to Eridu with Ehephilos. The four friends sailed down the Euphrates, but Hesiona stayed home to wait for Nearchus. She swore this was going to be the last time she waited. The next time, she would leave him forever.

In the south the river split into many streams and flows, forming an enormous swamp almost five hundred stadiums long. Only the most experienced navigators could find the main section of the river within that labyrinth of reeds and sea grass, since it deflected to the west where sticky clay and salt flats guarded the eastern edge of the Syrian Desert. They sailed nearly fifty parsangs, or fifteen hundred stadiums, in three days without a single docking. Then the Euphrates flowed in one broad stream, heading east. After another twenty-five parsangs, the river curved around an elevated rocky plain from the north. The plain had been the location of the oldest cities in Mesopotamia. Swamps and salt flats stretched all the way to the left bank, from the east and northeast. The endless spread of quiet water, swamps and reeds, inhabited by wild boars, reached the Tigris and went on for another thousand stadiums.

On the fifth day of their voyage, they docked at an ancient, half-destroyed pier with a staircase of huge stone slabs climbing the right bank. From there, a wide road drowning in hot dust took them to the ruins of an impossibly ancient city, then further southwest to a small town atop a flat hill. Majestic ruins, a few ramshackle newer structures, and a large inn surrounded three splendid temples. Two of them, or rather the one that was damaged the least, reminded Thais of the main building of Kibela's sanctuary as well as similar structures of both Babylon and Susa. The third temple bore traces of multiple restorative efforts and as a result had peculiar architecture. Its foundation rested upon a platform with rounded corners and brick siding. In its center, a wide staircase led toward a portico with three pillars under a heavy, pyramid-shaped roof. Beyond that rose an incredibly tall round tower with several sloping levels.

Informed about the arrival of the guests, priests and servants met the Ecbatanians at the platform, bowing to them with dignity and humility. Most of them were dark-skinned, much like Thais' Indian friends who had visited her in Ecbatana.

After the ceremonial greeting, the guests were taken to a side wing which was designated for rest and overnight shelter, and served nuts, dates, honey, rye cakes and milk. The travelers bathed and took time to enjoy their meal.

Eventually, a tall priest entered and sat down on a bench, pointedly avoiding physical contact with the visitors. He was dressed in white and his thick beard covered his face almost to the eyes. From the corner of her eye, Thais saw Lysippus make a sign in the air and point at her with his eyes. The priest rose, clearly moved, and Lysippus drew another oval in the air. The priest, apparently affected by this sign language, made a welcoming gesture and led Thais and Lysippus through a tall, narrow passage, then into an inner room of the tower. Two more priests joined them along the way. One was a dark-skinned man with broad shoulders who appeared to have tremendous strength. The other wore a colorful garment and a blunt, narrow beard beneath a mane of curls. The latter turned out to be an interpreter. After exchanging some information, both priests expressed their desire to offer their knowledge to the Helenians. That was when Thais realized that initiated Orphics had access to the temple's mysteries.

As if wishing to prove this to be true, Lysippus and Thais were taken down the longest passageway, its wall ornamented by vertical rows of tightly stretched silver strings of various lengths. The tall priest walked, touching various groups of strings as he went, and the strings responded with a lovely, long moaning sound, echoing along the stone passage.

"This sound lives inside every person, connecting generations," the priest explained. "Through centuries, flying into the unknown future. If you understand this symbol there is no need to explain the other one." The priest pointed at the deep trenches running across the passage, covered with boards which had been painted with images of animals and mythical monsters. Thais interpreted this as separation between generations, filled with darkness and ignorance, driving human beings to animal state. She wasn't too shy to ask the Indians. The priest smiled kindly.

"The first drops of rain do not saturate the earth but they are first signs of a plentiful rain," the second dark-skinned priest said. "You too are drops. Let us retire for conversation to a place of inviolate seclusion."

The round hall was lit by strange torches which shed neither smoke nor soot, set on the ledges around square half-columns. Large cushions of soft, thin leather were scattered over the rugs. The room was furnished with two octagonal tables and hard stools of dark wood, which the two priests occupied. Heavy fragrant smoke from two bronze incense burners settled around the hall like blue fog.

Thais noticed colorful images of animals between the columns: tigers, rhinoceri, wild bulls. Images of elephants were most ubiquitous. The giant animals were known in Mesopotamia and sometimes brought to Babylon, but were never portrayed in the local temples, palaces or on the gates, akin the Gates of Ishtar.

"What would you like to choose as the subject of our conversation?" the dark-skinned priest asked.

"During the many years of our friendship, my pupil has asked me questions I could not answer. Perhaps you, who possess thousands of years of wisdom, would be so kind as to enlighten us both," the great artist said modestly.

"Knowledge, akin to good," the elder priest replied, "must not be scattered about haphazardly. Akin to wealth or military power, knowledge in the wrong hands serves to elevate one people and humiliate others. In addition, and this is very important, great discoveries - like the fact that the Sun is a sphere circled by planets, and the Earth is also a sphere that hangs in space - these can destroy faith in those gods that are only created by human imagination. A wise man's knowledge will not destroy his faith in the grandeur of the world or the coherence of its laws, sensed so well by poets and artists. A fool, on the other hand, would lose any faith whatsoever and fall into a black pit of senseless animal existence. Fortunately, an ignorant man's stupidity saves the careless truth seekers. They are simply not believed or they are laughed at, as happened with your philosopher Anaxagoras. He was the first Helenian to teach that the Sun was a fiery globe. Because of this 'amusing misdirection', even his great notion of nus, the universal intelligence, which overlaps with our philosophy, had no noticeable influence upon Helenians. Even earlier than that, you had another giant of thought, Anaximander. He taught that man is a result of a long line of transformations of animals, starting with a primordial fishlike creature. He also realized the vastness of space and inhabited worlds. There was Alcmeon, the physician and student of Pythagoras, who discovered two centuries ago that the brain was the organ of intelligence and the receptor of the senses. He also discovered that planets followed circular orbits. He also was ridiculed. But the Orphic teaching, Indian in spirit, was either taken from us Indians or from our common ancestors, which is why you are free in your possession of wisdom without the foolish conceit."

"You mentioned ridicule," Thais said indecisively. "We have a god named Mom, a creature of Night and the abyss of Tartar, who denies everything and laughs at everything, violating even the calm of the Olympian gods. I have seen people here for whom ridicule and destruction of all things ancient, great, and beautiful constitute the meaning of life. They also ridicule Eros, inventing base pantomimes and reducing the divine passion to the level of beastly lust. In their eyes I am simply a whore who ought to be stoned."

"I agree with you regarding the harm brought on by ignorant ridicule," the tall Indian replied. "But we think that the reason for it is not the existence of some specific god. Small people dwelling between the mighty states of Egypt and Mesopotamia have always lived in degradation. People who have no power compensate for the humiliation by ridiculing those who subdued them. Among the minor people, life is uncertain and swift. There is nothing permanent and there is no time to establish faith and philosophy."

"I would add to this the similarity to monkeys," the elder priest said. "There are many of them in our country, and some are considered sacred. However, monkeys are the idlest of all animals. Living in safety among the trees, in groves with plenty of fruit, monkeys do not need to spend time or effort in feeding themselves as do other animals, like a tiger who persistently hunts his prey, an elephant or bull forced to eat lots of grass to sustain their enormous bodies. Other animals value time and do not waste it on trifles. But the lazy monkeys quickly satisfy their appetite and seek entertainment in foolish tricks. They toss nuts to hit a tiger in the eye, defecate on an elephant's head, then make fun of them as they giggle from a safe height, They sense their own insignificance and uselessness and take it out on other worthy animals."

Helenians started to laugh, but the Indian was serious. Lysippus and Thais grew silent.

It was long since evening, but the conversation continued until well after midnight. Thais realized she had a need to spend several days here. She didn't think she would ever get another opportunity to discover the wisdom of the ancient country.

Eris sat in her usual pose, her legs curled up as she waited for Thais. The Athenian collapsed onto the cushions in exhaustion and fell into a sleep filled with fantastic images of unknown gods.

Over the next few days Thais found out about the twelve Nidanas or "Reasons for Being". Each of them was considered a consequence of a previous one, and the cause of the following one. The Great Nature or the life-giving power, Shakhty, was not all that different from the Great Mother of pre-Hellenic beliefs, having a dominant female deity. The sixth sign of the zodiac was Kagna, or the Virgin. She represented Shakhty, the Power of Nature, or Mahamaia, the Great Illusion and indicated that the primal forces must correspond to the number six and stand in the following sequence:

1. Parashakhty: the highest power of warmth and light that gives life to all things on Earth.
2. Djnanishakhty: the power of the mind and wise knowledge. It is two sided. The first is Smiriti, or memory. This is a huge power capable of bringing ancient notions and future expectations to life. The other side is foresight, the ability to see through the curtain of Maia into Time, which is one in all three of its aspects: past, present and future, and is much more complex than the time passed with the beating of one's heart.
3. Ichchashakhty: the willpower, the currents flowing through the body and concentrated on the fulfillment of desires.
4. Kriashakhty, or the power of thought: which is material, and can have physical impact with its energy.
5. Kundalinishakhty: the life principle of all of Nature. This power undulates like a snake and combines two great contradictions of attraction and repulsion, which is why it is also called a serpent. Kundalini balances out the inner and outer aspects of life. Its forward movement

inside a person gives him the power of Kama-Eros and leads to transformation.
6. Matrikashakhty: the power of speech, music, signs and letters.

Of this entire list of primal forces, the Helenians liked Kundalinishakhty the best. It was a notion close to them both, as they were spiritual artists and poets, able to relate to the dialectic teachings of Heraclitus of Ethes, Anaxagoras and Antiphontus.

Lysippus noted that the philosophers of Hebrew people considered the snake a power of evil that destroyed the happiness of the first people.

Both Indians smiled, and the elder priest said, "Our sacred book Aitarea calls your Gaea-Earth Sarporajini, or the queen of serpents, the mother of all moving things, for a serpent is a symbol of movement in the struggle between opposing forces. According to our myths, there used to be a race of snakelike people, or Nags, who numbered no more than a thousand. The people who inhabit the Earth now are the fifth race, created under the symbols of Bull and Cow. The bull is sacred in your land in the west, and the cow is sacred in ours. From the Nags my people have inherited the ability to rule over the poisonous snakes of India. Here, at our temple, there is a priestess of Nag who performs the ritual kiss of the sacred serpent. No mortal, not even one of the highest caste, can perform this ritual and remain alive."

Thais, burning with curiosity, made the elder priest promise her a demonstration of the terrible ritual.

Much in the Indians' stories remained unclear to Thais and Lysippus. The enormous extent of time, tracked by them from the creation of the world, went entirely against the calculations of the Egyptian, Finikian, Hebrew and Pythagorean scholars. The Hebrews had the shortest count of only six thousand years. According to the Indian data, the first real people appeared on Earth eighteen million, six hundred, sixteen thousand, five hundred and sixteen years ago. With the same frightening precision, the Indians had calculated the length of the dark and menacing period of troubles in the history of mankind, which started after the great battle in India two thousand, seven hundred, seventy years prior, when the best of people perished. This era or, as they called it, Kali-Yuga, was to last another four hundred, twenty-nine thousand years.

"Other scholars believe it to be much shorter," the tall Indian said. "Only a bit over five thousand years."

Lysippus and Thais exchanged glances. Such enormous discrepancy contradicted the precision of the enormous numbers. Noting the Helenians' confusion, the Indians continued to tell them about the precise calculations developed by their mathematicians. In the book of "solar science", the time was segmented in a way with which the Helenians were not familiar. One hour equaled twenty-four Helenian minutes, and one minute or vikala was twenty-four seconds. The time was further fragmented by a factor of sixty, all the way down to a kashta: an unimaginably brief moment of one three hundred millionth of a second.

To Lysippus' question, what was the use in numbers that could be neither measured nor imagined, the Indian replied that the human mind had two stages of consciousness. At the higher stage, called buddhi, a person was capable of comprehending such small measures and understanding the structure of the world made up of the smallest particles and central forces that were eternal and undefeatably strong, despite their being mere points of energy.

The Helenians learned about the great physician Jivak, who lived three hundred years before and possessed a stone that could show a body's internal organs. They also learned of another healer who protected people from smallpox by making a small scratch and rubbing into it some blood from a person who had survived the disease.

"Then why don't physicians use this method today?" Thais exclaimed. "You speak of it as something half-forgotten."

The elder priest gazed at her silently while the younger cried out with indignation. "You must not say such things, beautiful initiated one! All this and many other things constitute a mystery locked in ancient books. If it is forgotten, then such is the will of gods and Karma. When we, the priests of the highest caste, discover that a person of a lower caste has overheard the reading of the sacred books, we pour molten lead into his ears."

"Then how do you carry out the distribution of the knowledge?" Thais asked acidly. "You have only just spoken of the perils of ignorance."

"We care not about the distribution, but about preservation of the knowledge among those who are meant to possess it," the tall priest replied.

"Among one caste? And what of the others? Are they to be kept ignorant?"

"Yes. To fulfill their destiny. If they do it well they will be born into a higher caste in their next life."

"Knowledge preserved by a small group will invariably grow weaker and become forgotten," Lysippus interrupted. "Closed circles that are castes are only good for breeding animals, not people. The Spartans tried creating a breed of warriors, and even succeeded at it. But all things in life change faster than people can anticipate. The life of war put the Lacedemonians at the brink of extinction."

"We have not one, but many castes, as is necessary for human existence," the Indian objected.

"Still, I find the Helenian approach toward people more consistent. In your sacred books and philosophic writings, you place humans at the same level as gods;

however, in reality you breed them like livestock and keep them ignorant," Lysippus said firmly.

"Do Helenians not acknowledge the nobility of one's origins?" the elder priest asked, frowning.

"They do. But there is one basic difference. We believe that a nobleman can be born anywhere and that he deserves any knowledge, art and skill he wishes to learn and use. If he finds an equally good mate, the noble line of their descendants would be equally welcome in an Athenian palace as they would be in a house of a Chalhidian farmer. Good and bad can originate anywhere. It is common to believe that particularly outstanding individuals are born of gods and goddesses."

"But you have slaves whom you do not consider human, and humiliate to the level of animals," the Indian exclaimed.

Thais wanted to object, but Lysippus stopped her by gently squeezing her hand. He rose and left the Athenian alone with the Indians, then followed the familiar path to his room. He returned with a large chest made of purple amaranth wood with ornate golden corners. Having placed it carefully on the octagonal table, the sculptor opened the clasp. He revealed a strange mechanism: a combination of gears and levers of various sizes. Silver rings were marked with letters and symbols.

The Indians leaned over the chest, obviously interested.

"A follower of Pythagoreans, Heraclitus of Pont, who was close to Aristotle, discovered that the globe of Gaea revolves around itself, akin to a top, and that its axis is tipped with respect to the plane traveled by the Sun and its planets. This mechanism was built to calculate the movement of planets, without which navigation and prediction of the future could not exist. Here is someone's mind that established itself one time, having designed this mechanism, to be followed by the other's hands and the tables inscribed on the cover. People who use it are free from long calculations and have time for higher pursuits."

The stunned priests grew quiet. Lysippus took advantage of their dismay and said, "We Helenians, instead of punishing the seekers of knowledge with molten lead, open wide the porticos and gardens of our academies and schools of philosophy. We are catching up with you who started comprehending the world several thousands of years earlier."

"That is because there are so few of you and you are forced to preserve your students in order to ensure the passage of the torch of knowledge. But there are so many of us. If we shout out our knowledge in a town square it will be instantly distorted by the ignorant and turned against true scholars. In Kriashakhty and Kundalini we have discovered secrets of personal strength and we carefully guard the technique of its learning and usage. It would cause great trouble if this knowledge were to end up with a person of imperfect Karma."

This is when Thais discovered the law of Karma, or retribution. Karma made Nemesis, daughter of the Night and the Helenian goddess of fair punishment, look naïve, small and weak.

In the colossal cosmic mechanism, whose workings were at the basis of the world, all things – gods, people and animals – were subject to Karma. They must all live out their errors, imperfections and particularly their crimes in a series of incarnations, their fate growing better or worse depending on their personal and social behavior. Lying and deceit, especially captured in books, constituted terrible crimes because they resulted in harmful consequences for many people and could take thousands of years to eliminate. Destruction of beauty was also considered to be one of the worst crimes. When someone forbade something to someone else, he took upon himself the Karma of his subject, whatever it might be.

"Then by keeping knowledge from the lower castes, you take their ignorance upon yourselves? That of millions of people?" Thais asked suddenly.

The elder priest reeled back and the tall Indian's eyes flashed in anger.

"It is no worse than you Helenians for not letting your slaves study," the elder Indian replied. "There are so few of you who are free, and so many of them. Their numbers grow greater each day. That is why your world will soon perish, despite your great conquests."

Lysippus had to stop the Athenian once again when she wanted to disagree. Thais paced herself, reasoning that each faith had its weaknesses. Attacking them might have been appropriate in a public dispute, but not in a peaceful conversation. Instead of arguing further, the Athenian finally dared ask a question that had tormented her for a long time.

"My teacher, the great artist Lysippus, reproached me cruelly for one misdeed and even distanced himself from me for an entire year. Beauty is the only thing that ties people to life and makes them both value it and struggle against its challenges, diseases and dangers. People who destroy, distort or ridicule beauty must not live. They must be destroyed like rabid dogs for they are the carriers of incurable disease. Artists are like wizards who bring beauty to life, but are also held more responsible than those who are blind, because they can see. That was what Lysippus told me three years ago."

"Your teacher is entirely correct and in complete agreement with the law of Karma," the dark-skinned priest said.

"Thus when I destroyed the beautiful palaces of Persepolis, I destined myself to terrible punishments in this and future lives?" Thais asked sadly.

"Are you that woman?" the Indians asked, gazing at their guest curiously.

After a long silence, the elder priest spoke. And his words, pronounced with much gravity and certainty, gave comfort to the Athenian. "Those who wish to rule build traps for gullible people, and for the rest of us because we yearn for miracles and all things unusual. Those who want to control people's minds construct traps by playing numbers, symbols and formulas, spheres and sounds, giving them semblance to the keys of knowledge. Those who wish to control emotions the way tyrants and politicians do, especially emotions of the mob, build enormous palaces that humble people and take over their emotions. A man who wanders into such a trap loses his individuality and dignity. The palaces of Portipora, as we call Persepolis, served as just such traps. You correctly guessed as much and served as the weapon of Karma, as the evil contained in a punishment sometimes serves the good. I would acquit you of Lysippus' charges."

"I realized that myself and forgave her," the sculptor agreed.

"And didn't explain to me?" Thais reproached.

"I realized it not with my mind, but with my feelings. Only our teachers from India who know Karma were able to put it into words for us," Lysippus bowed, pressing his hands to his forehead after the Asian fashion.

The priests bowed even lower in response.

Thais returned to her room earlier than usual that day.

Eris moved a small table with food toward her, waited for the Athenian to satisfy her hunger then beckoned to follow her, smiling only with her eyes. Moving in silence, she led Thais to a staircase that served as transition from the front section of the temple to the main tower. Artemis Acsiopena stood framed by two staircases on a wide pedestal in front of a deep, unlit niche. Rays of light fell from small side windows high above and crossed in front of the statue, making the darkness behind her appear deeper. Bronze glistened as if Artemis had only just emerged from the darkness of the night, following the tracks of some criminal. Ehephilos was sitting at the foot of the pedestal with his eyes raised to his creation in prayer. He was so deep in thought that he didn't move and didn't sense the women's arrival. Thais and Eris stepped back quietly and returned to their room.

"You destroyed him, khalkeokordios, you copper heart," the Athenian said angrily, as she glared at the black priestess. "Now he will not be able to continue sculpting."

"He is destroying himself," Eris said indifferently. "He feels as if he must sculpt me, like a statue, according to his desires."

"Then why did you let him …"

"In gratitude for the art and for the glorious dream about me."

"But a great artist cannot drag himself after you like a slave."

"He cannot," Eris agreed.

"Then what are his options?"

Eris shrugged. "I am not asking for love."

"No, but you inspire it. You are akin to a sword undercutting men's lives."

"What do you wish me to do, Mistress?" Eris asked, using her former subservient tone. The Athenian read sad determination in the blue eyes.

Thais held her and whispered a few gentle words. Eris huddled against her like a younger sister, losing her goddess-like serenity for a moment. Thais patted her head and smoothed down the thick mane of her hair, then went to Lysippus.

The great sculptor became seriously concerned with the fate of his best pupil and took Thais to see the priests.

"You spoke of knowledge as salvation," he began, once the four of them were settled in the round hall. "According to you, the suffering that exists in the world would have decreased many fold had people spent more time pondering troubles that originated from ignorance. This very accurate statement coexists for you with inhumane laws of the mystery of knowledge. However, in addition to one's mind, there are also one's feelings. What do you know of them? How can one conquer Eros? We are losing a great sculptor, the one who created the statue purchased by your temple."

"If you mean the goddess of the night Ratri, she is not for the temple. She is only kept here before being sent forth to India."

"We consider her the goddess of the moon, health and women, equal to Aphrodite," Thais said.

"Our goddess of love and beauty, Lakshmi, is only one light side of the deity. The dark side is the goddess of destruction and death, the punishing Kali. Before, in the ancient times, when each deity was both benevolent and menacing, they were combined in the image of the night goddess Ratri, whom I serve," the dark-skinned priest said.

"How can you worship only the female goddess if your gods send heavenly beauties to crush the might of scholars?" Lysippus asked. "In that respect, your religion appears evolved to me, for it places men on equal footing with gods, but it also appears primitive, because its deities use beauty as a weapon of unworthy seduction."

"I do not see anything unworthy in such seduction," the priest said, smiling. "After all, it is not a mere yakshini, a demon of lust, who carries it out, but a celestial beauty imbued with arts and high intelligence, much like her," he said, glancing at Thais.

Mischief long contained suddenly took over Thais, and she directed a long, passionate gaze at the priest.

"What was I talking about?" the priest muttered, then rubbed his forehead, trying to remember. "Ah yes. There are two ways toward perfection and enlightenment, both of them secret. One is asceticism, a complete denial of all desires, a path of deep thought connecting the lower consciousness with the higher one. First and foremost it requires elimination of the merest thought of that which you call Eros. That is where a woman with her power is an enemy."

"As in the Hebrew faith where she is the reason of the original sin, destruction of paradise and other troubles."

"No, not like that. Besides, you apparently do not know the depth of their religion, which secretly follows Babylonian wisdom. You do not know Cabala. We do not have a personal god at the height of philosophy of the sacred Upanishads. There is only Parabrahman, the reality of all-encompassing Cosmos. In a similar way, there is no personal menacing Jehovah in Cabala, but there is Eyn-Soph, the endless and limitless existence. The absolute Truth appears in the form of a nude woman named Sephira. Together with the male beginning Hokma, wisdom, and female mind Bina, Sephira forms a threesome, or the crown of Kater, the head of Truth. Women are allowed into sanctuaries. The Kadeshim maidens are sacred in their nudity and dedicated to god, akin to our temple dancers, Finikian and Babylonian women, to say nothing of your priestesses of Aphrodite, Rhea and Demeter. There are many similarities between ancient faiths, originating from the same place and headed in the same direction."

"Then why do the Jewish priests shout at us, calling us idol-worshipers and hating our laws and notions?"

"There are Eulokhian writings of high wisdom. There are also writings about an all-powerful god occupied only with the affairs of men, like a supreme ruler of Earth. Those writings were composed five hundred years later. The purpose of the latter religion is preservation of an ancient but small nation surrounded by enemies. In it you will find first of all the notion of sin, with which you Helenian and we Indians are equally unfamiliar. The sole purpose of love for procreation is considered to be one's sacred duty among our people. Since the ancient times our women were never separated from men, and have always been equally free. That is what our sacred Vedas tell us. How can we consider impure a passion that is as natural as life itself, in whose fires future generations are born?"

"Then why do your gods keep scholars from rising into the higher world? Why do they send apsaras, the heavenly hetaerae, to interfere with them?" Thais asked, and pointed up, making both priests smile.

"We call it the higher world not because it is located somewhere up above, but because of its nature compared to our world," the dark-skinned priest said. "I have already started telling you about the two different paths one must follow to achieve perfection. Again, the first path is that of clarity of thought, the elimination of all physical desires, including one's desire to live. But the ancient dark-skinned people of India, from whom I originate, developed a different path. It is a philosophy that is the origin of all Indian learning, and is particularly useful during the modern era of ignorance, jealousy and anger, called Kali-Yuga. It contains the deepest knowledge and the most powerful ability to control the powers of the human body. It is called Tantra. Briefly, its essence is that a man must experience all of life's primary desires to their fullest in order to live through them and become free of them in the briefest time."

"Are you a follower of Tantra?" Thais asked.

The priest nodded.

"And are you now free of all temptations and desires?" she asked, giving the priest such an expressive look that all muscles of his powerful body became strained.

He took a full breath and continued. "Tantra does not deny desire, especially Eros. Rather it recognizes it as a moving power of life and an opportunity for spiritual elevation. We never deny others in this elevation, remembering the story of Brahma."

The Indian told them a charming legend about the love of a heavenly apsara to Brahma, the main god of the Indian trinity. Occupied with observation and enlightenment, he did not respond to her call. Then the apsara cursed him, predicting that he would receive less respect from the faithful than all other gods. Brahma went to the other god of the trinity Vishnu and the latter explained to him that a grave sin had been committed. In order to correct it, he would have to become the apsara's lover and carry out thirty other acts of purification, because a woman is the greatest treasure and the working hands of Nature-Shakhty. A man denying a woman's passion, no matter who she was, commits a grave sin. That was why the followers of Tantra worshiped Shakhty and were greatly advanced in Eros.

"Both men and women?"

"Indeed," the priest replied. "Action is vital. Desire alone is not enough. In order to reach the great spiritual elevation that frees one from one's brief primitive desires, those who carry out the ritual, both he and she - or at least one of them - must undergo long preparation of body and all senses."

"We also go through a long training," Thais noted.

"I do not know what it is like," the dark-skinned priest said. "If you watch the serpent's kiss you will realize the power of our Tantric ways for yourself."

"When can I see it?" Thais asked impatiently.

"As soon as now."

"May I send for my friend?"

Thais, Lysippus and Eris descended down a narrow staircase into a large cellar under the tower. The interpreter remained upstairs. The Helenians knew the Persian language tolerably well, and the Indians spoke it fluently.

In a spacious square room, brightly lit by the smokeless Indian torches, they were greeted by two pale-faced and one dark-skinned, short and stocky young woman of about thirty, who looked much like the elder priest.

"My sister," he said, guessing his guests' thoughts. "She is our Nagini, the ruler of serpents."

"Is she initiated into Tantra?" Thais asked.

"She would die without," the priest replied sternly. "She will not only carry out the ritual, but all the required preparations. Sit."

They settled onto a cool stone bench near a wall. A fourth girl appeared, carrying a large, flat bowl filled with warm scented milk and a handful of fragrant herbs. The ruler of serpents shed her clothes, then rubbed down her entire bronze colored body with the herbs soaked in the milk. She pinned up her hair and put on a soft leather apron that covered her from collarbone to knees.

Never looking at the visitors and keeping her expression calm and serious, the ruler of serpents approached the heavy metal door carrying a golden cup filled with milk. At her sign, a grate was lowered, separating her from her assistants and guests.

The girls started playing instruments similar to flutes. One played the quiet, melodious main theme while the other punctuated it with a rhythm of whistling sounds. The short dark-skinned priestess started singing in a high-pitched voice, making a sharp vibrating whistle in place of a refrain. She opened the door and spread out her arms, still holding the cup. The black emptiness of a cave loomed behind the door, though a gap glowed faintly at the other end of it, indicating a narrow passage to daylight. For some time the priestess sang, accompanied by the flutes. Or rather it seemed like a long time to Thais, who was waiting for something terrible to happen.

Suddenly the dark-skinned woman leaned forward and placed the cup beyond the threshold of the door. The flutists stopped playing. Everyone could clearly hear the rustling of a heavy body sliding over a stone floor. A wide, flat head peeked out from the darkness of the cave. Two clear eyes tinged with crimson looked over everyone carefully, as Thais had imagined they would. The head with square scales, similar to a soldier's chest armor, briefly dipped into the milk and the priestess called with a melodious, whistling sound.

A giant male serpent slipped into the cellar. He was twenty elbows in length with a greenish black back which became deep olive on the sides. The usually brave Athenian felt a chill run down her spine. She sought and found Eris' hand, who responded with an anxious squeeze of her fingers.

The serpent coiled himself up, directing his pitiless and fearless gaze at the priestess, who bowed to him respectfully. Continuing to sing, she raised her arms high above her head with her palms folded together. She raised onto her tiptoes, then started rocking from side to side, flexing her sides, her legs pressed firmly together, maintaining incredible balance. The rocking movement increased in frequency. The enormous serpent matched it as he slithered and coiled on the floor, raising his head until it was level with the priestess' head. Only then did Thais notice three ribbons braided into the woman's hair, each of them armed with rows of polished, glittering needles. The serpent rocked in rhythm with the priestess, approaching slowly.

Suddenly she held out her right hand and patted the monster's head, dashing with fantastic swiftness away from the opened maw that struck at the spot where her face has been only a fraction of a second prior.

The rocking and singing continued. The priestess moved her feet with the skill and control of a dancer as she approached the serpent. Having reached the right moment, she took his head into her hands, kissed it, then darted away again. The serpent struck with the barely perceptible speed, but each time the ruler of serpents guessed his intentions exactly and moved away even faster. Three times the young woman kissed the serpent's head, evading his bite with incomprehensible ease, or offering him the edge of her apron, into which he sunk his long, poisonous fangs.

Finally, the irritated serpent rose up in a spiral, struck at the woman, missed and froze, then rocked and aimed again. The priestess bent her back, clapped her hands and in one lightning fast movement pressed her lips to the serpent's mouth. The snake struck at that second, but this time he did not stop. He chased after the priestess, but incredibly, she managed to evade him, slipping through the narrow door behind the grate, which had been opened and shut by a fourth assistant in advance.

The clang of metal, the thud of the serpent's body and the angry beast's hissing reverberated along Thais' nerves like a force of nature.

"What happens now?" she exclaimed in the Attic dialect, causing the Indians to glance at her with surprise.

Lysippus translated and the elder priest chuckled. "Nothing. We shall leave, the torches will be put out, and Nag will return to his cave. There is a platform where he can warm himself in the sun. The door will be shut while he is out there."

"Is he very poisonous?" Thais asked.

"Come closer to my sister," the priest replied.

Respectfully, and not without trepidation the Athenian approached the woman, who stood without anxiety or arrogance, regarding the Helenians. Sensing a strong smell which resembled that of a crushed corn lily leaf, Thais saw that the snake ruler's apron was covered in yellow green liquid which dripped slowly to the floor.

"Poison," the priest said. "With each strike, Nag prepares to bite and sprays it from his teeth."

"Is this poison very strong?" Lysippus asked.

"This is one of the largest and most poisonous snakes in India. It can kill a horse or an elephant in one minute. A man or a tiger can live longer, up to two minutes, using your time scale. This poison is enough to kill thirty people."

"Is he tame at all?" Eris asked.

"Nag cannot be tamed. The creature knows no gratitude, attachment, fear or anxiety. He is devoid of nearly all feelings typical for a creature with warm blood, and is like the worst kind of people in that respect. Only the incredible skill of our Nagini saves her from death, which waits for her at each moment."

"Then why does she do this?" Thais glanced at the priestess, who was carefully rolling up the poison-covered apron. She looked like an ancient bronze statue with the strong outlines of a woman used to hard labor on the farm.

"Each one of us needs to test himself in the art, especially if it is dangerous and unknown to other people. In addition, the power of the Tantric training gives her reliable protection."

"If Tantra can influence feelings, heart and body so strongly, can you cure the young artist of the overbearing and hopeless love for my friend?"

"Artists reside in the middle, between the ascetics and the followers of Tantra. Poetic thought does not fear temptation because its position is rooted in love, which is desire, and desire is a hope for continued life. True poetry discards all falsehoods and in that is akin to asceticism, but it also burns in the fire of Eros toward a lover or a Muse. This dual ability of an artist makes the cure difficult. But we shall try."

"What is the essence of the healing process?"

"Each thought has an outward expression if one's attention is strongly focused upon it. Persistent desire causes the necessary result."

"Do you mean satep-sa? Hypnosis?"

"That too. However, it is more important to emphasize his yearning for Khado-Lilith, hidden in the heart of each man. Just like you Helenians, we have a legend of several races of people who preceded the current one. Helenians believe in races of the golden, silver and copper ages, which proves the common origins of such myths. There is one essential difference. We consider prior races to be more heavenly in origin, while you consider them more earthbound than contemporary people and therefore less evolved."

"You are incorrect, priest," Lysippus interrupted. "Are the titans and titanides inferior to the living people? Prometheus and his followers sacrificed themselves to save people from ignorance."

" … And ended up only increasing their suffering with increased responsibility, having given them a dream of free will, but not elevated them from the darkness of limited life," the tall priest added.

"According to our myths, Chronos devours his children from Rhea-Gaea. Uranus also slaughters them. In other words, Time and Heaven wipe their fruits from the face of Earth. Does the legend mean that Earth, Nature or Shakhty are incapable of creating truly godlike people?"

"It means that humankind must ultimately recreate itself, evolving in knowledge and self-perfection. Our sacred texts speak of prior races of creatures who were spirits. I will not speak of the first three, as they are distant from us. Immediately preceding us was the fourth race with beautiful women of heavenly origin.

Hebrew mythology does not acknowledge the series of various races but only includes once-created pairs of people, identical to modern humans. However, they too have a legend that the first of men, Adam, had another wife before his human wife, Eve. Her name was Lilith. The legend made her into a harmful demon, beautiful but constantly causing harm to Eve until God sent three angels who exiled Lilith to the desert.

"Indian Liliths are different. They too can fly through the air, but they are endlessly kind toward people. The queen of these forewomen we call Khado. Then she was called Sangie Khado, and her beauty surpassed all imagination. Unlike the apsaras, Khado did not possess intelligence. They only had emotions. The dream of a beautiful human body and inhuman power of Eros lives among us as the memory of these Liliths."

"I heard from the eastern people the legend of peri, the heavenly beauties born of fire. They also fly through the air and descend to their chosen mortal lovers," Thais said, remembering her stay at the lakes near Persepolis.

"Undoubtedly it too is an echo of the memory of Lilith," the elder priest said, paying increasingly greater attention to Thais. "Our task is to awaken this memory in the artist's heart, guide it, and let the particularly skilled sacred dancers do the rest, displacing in the heart of the artist his deadly passion toward a model not wishing to unite her fate with his."

"I have seen a real Lilith of the ancient Mesopotamians near the Euphrates." Thais told them about the small sanctuary along the mountain path with the image of a winged woman in the niche over the altar. "I think of all the ancient female images, that goddess had the most perfect body. May I peek at your skilled dancers?"

The elder priest smiled indulgently, struck a small bronze disk and nodded at the interpreter, ordering him to leave the room. The Babylonian smoothed down his beard and rushed out. Apparently, the chosen temple dancers did not appear before just anyone. Eris suddenly remembered something and rushed off as well.

Two girls appeared from behind a hidden door between the statues of two elephants. The dancers wore identical metallic jewelry on their dark smooth bodies including wide, slanting gold sashes, necklaces, anklets, large round earrings and tiaras with glittering rubies in their short coarse hair. Their faces were as motionless as masks. With their narrow, slanting eyes, short noses and wide, full mouths, the two looked like twins. The peculiar build of their bodies was also much alike. They had narrow shoulders, slender arms, small pert breasts and thin torsos. This nearly maidenly fragility was in sharp contrast to the lower portion of the body. They were massive, with wide, thick hips and muscular legs, falling just short of giving the impression of brute force. From explanations made by the elder priest, the Helenians derived that these girls were from the distant eastern mountains beyond the River of Sands. They embodied most clearly the duality of people with their ethereally light upper bodies and massive lower halves, filled with earthy power.

Thais questioned whether they could dance. "Women of small height are always more agile than those akin to coras and imperious statues. I know nothing of these people from the distant eastern mountains and steppes that were never reached by Alexander's scouts."

After a brief order, one of the girls sat on the floor with her legs crossed and started rhythmically clapping her hands, her glittering bracelets ringing loudly. The other girl started dancing with the kind of expressiveness that only came from talent refined by years of training. Unlike the dances of the West, the legs took little part in the movement, but arms, head and torso performed astonishingly graceful undulations, and fingers opened akin to flowers.

Thais burst into applause. The dancers stopped, then vanished after a sign from the priest.

"They are so singular, these girls," Thais said. "But I do not understand their allure. There is no harmony, no likeness to the Kharitas."

"Ah, I understand," Lysippus suddenly said. "You see, a man knows that these women combine two opposing powers of Eros."

"Do you agree, teacher?" Thais doubted it. "Then why do you always follow perfection in your art?"

"In the art of beauty, yes," Lysippus replied. "But the laws of Eros are different."

"I think I understand," Thais said with a shrug. "Do you think Ehephilos feels the same way?"

"I think these slant-eyed girls will cure him," Lysippus smiled.

"Do you think Cleophrades would have liked them too? He worked so hard on the Anadiomena, having picked me. Why?"

"I cannot speak for he who has crossed the River of Forgetfulness. I think you are not Lilith, but what they call their celestial hetaerae: apsara. Only a few who are capable can possess you and take everything you have to give. For everyone else there are the endlessly forgiving, mad and passionate Liliths. Any one of us can be chosen by them. The knowledge of Lilith's generosity toward all men troubles our hearts and draws us irresistibly with the memory of past centuries."

"And who is Eris in your opinion?"

"She is certainly not Lilith. She is ruthless to weakness and intolerant of inability. Ehephilos became infatuated with the embodiment of an image. Unfortunately for him, the image and the model turned out to be one and the same."

"Cleophrades spoke of his infatuation with me."

"It was worse for him than for Ehephilos. At least Ehephilos is young."

"According to you I can no longer be loved? Thank you, my friend."

"Do not attempt to reproach me for attempting to sort out your mood. You know that anyone would fall at your feet if you wished it so. This priest who had learned and overcame it all is struck by you. How easy it is for someone such as you. Just a few glances and poses. That is too bad, for you cannot respond to him as Lilith. A feeling worthy of an apsara sits in you like a tip of a spear. I suppose you were Alexander's lover and gave him all power of Eros."

Thais blushed. "What of Ptolemy?"

"You bore him a son. That means his Eros for you is stronger than yours for him, otherwise there would have been a daughter."

"And what if it were equal?"

"Then I don't know. It could have turned out either way. Come. Our hosts are politely waiting for us to depart."

They thanked the priests, repeated their request for Ehephilos and walked through the dark temple to their rooms. Four torches burning near the door marked how much time was left till dawn.

"Thank you, Lysippus. When you are with me, I am not afraid to do something stupid," Thais said. "Your wisdom -"

"Wisdom, Athenian, brings little pleasure to its owner. There are few wise people. Wisdom comes gradually to those who are not susceptible to flattery and are capable of dismissing lies. Years pass and you suddenly discover in yourself the absence of old desires and realization of your place in life. Self-limitation comes, care in your actions, foresight of consequences, all of which makes you wise. It is not happiness in your poetic notion, not at all. People recover from anxiety and anger by singing and dancing, knowing nothing about their essence. One must not pontificate much on the subject of gods and people, for silence is a true language of wisdom. Open hearts understand it well. It is even less wise to speak truths to people who prefer miracles and shortcuts that do not exist. All there is, is a gradual ascent. But here is what I can tell you with certainty, as the greatest wisdom: adoration is the fastest way to ruin the one it is directed at."

"Do you mean adoration of a woman?"

"Not at all. That is a natural celebration of beauty and Eros. I speak of the groveling before kings and army leaders who hold people's fates in their hands, be it for a long time or for a moment. It does not matter."

"Are you thinking about Alexander?"

"Imagine for a moment being a man admired by millions of people. All different kinds of people: truthful ones and liars, noble and subservient souls, courageous men and cowards. Truly, one must possess divine power not to break down and betray one's own dreams."

"To betray one's destiny?"

"He who betrays his country is considered deserving of death by all people. But do people not see those who betray their own soul? After all, such traitors no longer possess truthfulness. Such a person cannot be relied on for anything. He will go from bad to worse and his inner evil will grow. Many speak of my honesty. I really do try to be that way invariably, never telling secrets and never trying to find out that which others do not wish to tell me. A great crime grows from a chain of small errors and misdeeds, and great dignity worthy of gods is born of countless acts of restraint and control over one's self."

"So you think …"

"Evaluate only yourself. That is difficult. When it comes to judging outstanding and especially great people, rely on time and people. Doing the right thing is not enough. One must also recognize when they ought to be done. We cannot board a boat that has already passed by or the one that has yet to arrive. Knowing what to do is only half the matter, the other half is to know the right time to do the deed. There is an appropriate time for all things, but most people miss it."

"Did Alexander miss his time?"

"No, I suspect that he did what he did too early. But once again you make me judge that which occupies you most. Go to bed."

Thais obeyed. She told Eris how the priests of the Eridu temple had taken upon themselves the task of striking the mad love for her from Ehephilos' heart. The black priestess showed neither joy nor sadness for this. Thais tried to imagine what it was like for her. If it had been Thais, she would have been at least a little bit saddened by the loss by an unloved, but still remarkable and devoted admirer. But all Eris could think of was Nagini, the ruler of snakes. Her impenetrable soul was struck by the terrible ritual with the huge poisonous snake, of which she'd never heard before. Thais was also overwhelmed. The moment she closed her eyes before going to sleep, she clearly saw the young Indian woman and the colossal snake in a deadly dance, like a bronze sculptural group.

A few days had passed since their arrival at Eridu when a hot western wind swept in. Thais slept poorly during the hot nights. The wind from the Syrian desert rustled and whistled with irritating monotony through countless gaps and windows in the temple ceiling, bringing with it relaxation of body and depression of soul. It continued to blow the next day, never strengthening, never weakening. The Athenian was overcome by melancholy. Her existence seemed aimless to her. She was filled with the memories of those who were gone, the deeply hidden love, the long wait for Ptolemy, the role of a mistress of a big house and a guardian of shared riches that were essentially war loot. She could increase the wealth, but what for? She could ... She could do many things but she kept returning to the question: what for? Did the surges of strong emotion make her tired of the usual enthusiasm with which she tackled every task? Perhaps she grew old and could no longer be on fire as before, riding at breakneck speed, being moved to tears at the sight of beauty, listening to stories and songs with bated breath?

Eris became much like her mistress. The two of them spent their days sprawled naked on leather cushions, resting their chins on their crossed arms and silently staring at the wall, which was decorated with patterns of blue paint.

Lysippus was hiding somewhere in the bowels of the temple, and Ehephilos was taken away so they could "beat the love out of him", his teacher said, somewhat crassly.

A few days passed. Or perhaps an entire month? The regular flow of time no longer existed for Thais. Many things connected with the past, present and future lost their meanings. All this became serenely mixed in Thais' newly balanced heart, without grief or enthusiasm, expectation or joy, piercing memories or regrets of things that could not be.

Lysippus reappeared one day, chuckling at something. He found them reclining lazily, side by side, snacking on cakes with cream with great gusto. Peering at them carefully, the sculptor found no change except dimples on their cheeks and true Olympian calm.

"Why are you laughing, teacher?" Thais asked indifferently.

"Healed!" Lysippus laughed openly.

"Who is healed? We are?"

"You have nothing to be healed from. Ehephilos. He decided to stay at Eridu."

Thais became interested and rose on one elbow. Eris glanced at Lysippus.

"He wants to stay at Eridu and make statues of these whatever they are, the slant-eyed Liliths."

"Then he really is healed," Thais said, laughing. "But you are losing a student, Lysippus."

"He is not lost for the art and that is the main thing," the sculptor replied. "By the way, they want to buy the Anadiomena by Cleophrades. They offer double its weight in gold, which is now more valuable than silver. One stater, which was worth two drachma, is now worth a four drachma owl. Many Helenian merchants are going bankrupt."

"Then sell it," Thais said calmly.

Lysippus stared at Thais in amazement. "What of Alexander's wish?"

"I think when Alexander returns, he will have too much on his hands to think about the Anadiomena. Remember the enormous number of people waiting for him in Babylon. And in addition to people there are mountains of papers, petitions and reports from his gigantic empire. Especially if he also adds India to it."

"He won't," Lysippus said with certainty.

"I have no idea how much the Anadiomena is worth."

"A lot. They probably will not give as much as my teacher Polycleitus' Diadumenus was paid. The entire world knows that it was bought for one hundred talents, and that was in the olden days when money was worth more. The Anadiomena is so beautiful that, including the value of silver, she will sell for no less than thirty talents."

"That is a huge price. What do sculptors charge in general?" Thais asked in amazement.

"For models and classic subjects a good sculptor takes two thousand drachmas, for statues and bas-reliefs it can be up to ten thousand."

"But that is only a talant and a half."

"Can one compare the exceptional creation by Cleophrades to good but ordinary work?" the sculptor objected. "Should we hold back with the Anadiomena then?"

"Let us wait," Thais agreed, thinking of something else. Lysippus was surprised by the absence of strong emotion the mention of Alexander used to cause.

The Athenian picked up a silver bell given to her by the elder priest and shook it. He appeared a few minutes later and stopped in the doorway. Thais invited him to sit down and inquired about the health of his younger associate.

"He is gravely ill. He is not fit to perform the high Tantric rituals with her," he said, nodding toward Eris.

"I have a big favor to ask, priest. It is time for us to leave the temple, and I wish to test myself one more time."

"Speak."

"I wish to receive a kiss of the snake, like your ruler of serpents."

"She is mad. You made her into manolis, a maenadae consumed by insanity!" Lysippus exclaimed, yelling so loudly the priest looked at him with reproach.

"You feel capable of performing this terrible ritual?" the Indian asked seriously.

"Yes," Thais said with certainty and the careless courage Lysippus remembered from long before.

"You are killing her," the sculptor told the priest. "You are a murderer if you allow this."

The priest shook his head. "There is a reason she has this desire. One must measure his strengths before carrying out life's tasks, for life is an art and not cunning. It is for open eyes and hearts. It is possible that she will perish. Then such is her predetermined Karma, to stop her life at this age. If she does not perish, the trial will multiply her strength. So it shall be."

"Me, too." Eris stood next to Thais.

"You may come too. I had no doubt of your wish."

Lysippus, speechless with terror and indignation.

Thais and Eris descended into the dungeon. The ruler of snakes undressed them and took off all their jewelry, then rubbed them down with milk and corn lily and put aprons on them. The naturally musical Athenian took but a few minutes to learn the simple tune. Eros took more time, but as they were both dancers they captured the rhythm right away.

The ruler of snakes summoned her monster and Thais went in first for the deadly game. When the serpent rose, tipping its scaled head forward, Thais heard whispering in a strange language, pressed her lips to the monster's nose, and backed away swiftly. The serpent dashed after her, spilling poison all over her apron, but Thais was already out of his reach, albeit shivering from the experience.

The serpent was given some milk, and Eris stepped forth. The black priestess decided not to wait and as soon as the serpent rose on his tail, she smooched him loudly on the nose and pulled away, not getting a single drop of poison on herself. The ruler of snakes cried out in surprise and the enraged monster threw himself after her. The Indian woman escaped his fangs, splashed milk into his face from the second cup in her hands, shoved Thais and Eris behind the grate and sighed with relief.

Thais kissed her and gave her an expensive bracelet. The same evening the elder priest gave Eris an incredibly rare necklace made of the fangs of the largest snakes ever captured in the Indian jungle. Thais also received a valuable gift: a necklace made of talons of black gryphs, set in gold and strung on a chain.

"This is an attribute of a guardian of secret paths leading to the east, beyond the mountains," the priest explained.

"What about mine?" Eris asked.

"As appropriate, yours is a symbol of courage, stamina and giving," the Indian replied. looking at the black priestess with much greater respect than before.

In addition, the elder priest gave Thais a goblet of transparent chalcedony with the snake dance carved on it.

Chapter Fifteen. Unfulfilled Dream

A horseman on a sweaty horse rushed in from the Euphrates. Hesiona was waiting at the ancient pier, along with a thirty oar boat, the privilege of being the wife of the fleet commander.

A short note had stated, "There is news from Nearchus and Alexander. The army is coming back. I am here to get you."

That was enough for Lysippus, Thais and Eris. They got ready as quickly as possible and departed after a long farewell with their Indian hosts. The priests presented everyone with enormous wreaths of blue flowers.

Ehephilos climbed on the overhang of the portico and waived at the cloud of dust raised by the horses' receding hooves.

The Helenians rode several parsangs on their tough and slender local horses without stopping.

From the distance they saw a long, reddish-brown vessel resting on the glassy waters and a linen tent erected on the tiles of the pier. The Theban rushed to meet Thais.

"They didn't reach the limits of the Ecumene in India," she ranted excitedly. "The army revolted at the fifth river and refused to go further. That was when my Nearchus discovered that the Indus flows from the mountains that were far away from the sources of the Nile, not to the east but to the south, into the ocean. The Indus delta lies in the direction of the sun. Enormous expanses of land and sea separate these two rivers, so vast that no one could ever imagine -"

Lysippus put a hand on Thais' shoulder to calm her down. She was startled by the wise man's touch.

"Alexander was badly wounded while attacking a fortress, and was rescued by your Ptolemy, who was nicknamed Soter, or Savior, after that. They fought against many elephants. Bucephal perished. Then they descended down to the Indus. The army marched across the desert while Nearchus sailed along the shores of India for eighty days. He nearly starved to death while Alexander was dying of thirst in the desert. Then Alexander waited for him for a long time at the designated spot and dispatched the messengers to Persepolis from there -"

The Theban had spilled all this at once. Now she paused finally to draw breath.

Lysippus playfully shook Hesiona by the shoulders. "Please stop. Otherwise you will suffocate and we won't find out what happened next. The wife of the great fleet leader like Nearchus ought to narrate the news in a more orderly manner. Who told you all this?"

"Deynomachus, one of Nearchus' associates. He became sick and was sent to Persepolis with the caravan then went to Babylon to wait for Nearchus."

"Then where is Nearchus himself?"

"He is leading the fleet to Babylon and seeking out a convenient route to Arabia and Libya along the way."

"Another trip!" Thais exclaimed.

"Yes. Alexander himself wants to go by sea as he no longer trusts maps or descriptions of the dry land that deceived him so cruelly in Bactria and in India."

"Then what did Deynomachus tell you?"

"Everything. He brought along a lokhagos, one of those who traveled with Alexander across Hedrosia[36]. They spent two days and two nights talking about the incredible trials of their journey. Then I left them at my house to sleep and rest and I rushed here. Oh, I memorized every detail. You know I have a good memory," Hesiona added, noticing Thais' glance.

"If such is the case," the sculptor decided, "then let us follow the example of Deynomachus. We shall sail and you shall tell us the story, but not at nights. There is plenty of time."

The Daughter of the Snake was not exaggerating her abilities, and Thais found out more about the Indian campaign than she would have from Ptolemy's letters. Ptolemy had become Alexander's chief associate after Hephaestion, who was a chiliarchus, or kings direct replacement. There was no position above that. And Ptolemy was still the great army leader's closest friend.

After they crossed the Indus using a floating bridge built by Hephaestion's detachment, the Macedonian army entered friendly territory. The Indians hailed Alexander as the king of kings of the West. At the same time, the aristocracy, referred to as "the higher castes", considered Macedonians to be barbaric and nicknamed them "a bunch of farm boys" because they were primarily interested in livestock.

In the capital of this country, Taxil, Alexander arranged a splendid celebration and started preparing the next river crossing into the hostile kingdom of the

---

36 Modern northwest Pakistan and southeast border of India

Pauravs. That river, named Hydaspes (Jhelum) by the geographers, was the site of the most brutal battle Alexander's army had experienced since Gaugamela. The clash was even more dangerous than at Gaugamela because at some point Alexander had completely lost control over his troops.

The Hydaspes swelled and flooded after endless rains. Its silt-covered shores turned into a swamp. The Indian army, headed by King Porus himself, waited on the east bank. Alexander hoped to easily overcome the Indians' resistance, but made a big mistake. The best detachments of the Macedonian army, led by Ptolemy, Hephaestion, Kenos and Seleucus, had crossed the river, but Crateros and his reserves remained on the west bank. The Macedonians were met by two rows of battle elephants spaced at sixty elbows from each other. Between them walked archers with enormous bows that could only be shot by setting one end on the ground. The arrows of these bows penetrated armor and shields, like little catapults.

At first the Indians overran the Macedonians. The new Bactrian and Sogdian archers on horseback, led by Alexander, fought desperately while sinking in mud. Agrians and hypaspists dashed to their help but the elephants kept stubbornly pressing the Macedonians against the muddy bank, and Crateros with his reserve troops were still nowhere to be seen. It turned out that he had positioned himself behind a split in the river and, having found himself on an island, was forced to cross again.

Suddenly Bucephal collapsed from under Alexander. He was not wounded, but the old war horse's heart could not stand the entire day of fighting through the thick mud. Alexander took a fresh horse and sent forth his still-courageous phalanx – only six thousand people – against the elephants. The brave veterans went into battle against the huge beasts roaring the war cry "Enialos, Enialos!". They forced the elephants to turn around and trample their own troops, completely crumpling and scattering the lines of the excellent Indian cavalry. The Macedonians chased after them like demons, striking the elephants with their long sarissas. The reserve cavalry of King Porus struck from the side. The phalanx could have lost a large part of its soldiers there, but Alexander forced the infantry to line up and close their shields, tossing the cavalry back. Reserve troops led by Krateros had finally arrived at that point. The Indians fled and the reserves gave chase.

Alexander's main military force could not move from exhaustion.

After that day in Targelion of the third year of one hundred thirteen Olympiad, the Macedonian army appeared to snap. While they were still at the Indus, the soldiers reluctantly agreed to cross it, having found out about Nearchus' discovery. The terrible battle at the Hydaspes, the monstrous elephants, and great military ability of the Indian army had completely depressed the Macedonians, especially after Alexander's earlier assurances that India was laid out, wide open before them.

The great conqueror treated the defeated king of the Pauravs with great mercy. He left him on the throne and did his best to secure his friendship.

Among the picturesque hills above the Hydaspes, just beyond the site of the battle, Hephaestion started building two new cities, following Alexander's orders. The two were named Nikea, or Victory, and Bucephalia, in memory of the great war horse who was buried there.

Even before the battle, Nearchus proposed to Alexander that he build a large fleet and transport the army down the Indus. The king had opposed this suggestion at first, then gave his permission so that he could sail east. There he hoped to reach the legendary river Ganges, flowing near the boundaries of the world.

Nearchus disregarded his ruler's orders and, with the help of the Finikians, in addition to light, thirty-oar boats that could be easily dragged from one river to the next, constructed several heavy, flat-bottomed vessels based on his own drawings. Those ships would later save the entire army.

Alexander continued his push into the east with the same zeal as always. He crossed one river after another, working his way through battles in a hilly country inhabited by the Aratts, brave Indian tribes who lived without kings. The Macedonians had to fight over thirty-eight fortified towns and settlements before they crossed the rivers Akesinas (Chenab) and Hydraot (Ravi). During the battle at the fortress of Sangala, Alexander's army lost twelve hundred people.

The army reached the fifth river, Hyphasys (Bias), and Alexander continued moving east, traveling along the impossibly tall mountains which were visible from as far away as a thousand stadiums. The ridges marched in steps toward the hilly country, providing no change in their surroundings. Nothing indicated that they might be nearing any type of boundary. All of upper India was behind them, but no one knew what lay ahead. Not even the most experienced cryptii knew the local language, so they could not find out anything about the way forward.

Now the fifth river flowed before them, as swift and cold as those they had crossed before. The same hills stretched beyond, wrapped in blue mist and the greenery of thick woods. The army stopped.

Porus told his conqueror about the land of Magadha beyond the Hyphasys, whose king had two hundred thousand infantry soldiers, twenty thousand horsemen and three thousand elephants. Officer Chandragupta, who had been imprisoned there and escaped, confirmed Porus' words. In the southwest there was a land of the mighty Aparajit, undefeated tribes who owned many particularly large battle elephants.

Nothing was said of the boundaries of the world or of the giant ocean. All at once the Macedonian soldiers realized that further travel was pointless. It was obvious the land, inhabited by skilled warriors, could not be taken by surprise. India was so vast that Alexander's entire army could be scattered and lost there, their bones buried among the endless hills. The loot no longer attracted the exhausted army. Their infallible and unbeatable leader had gone too far in his search for the Great Ocean. He had led them to a land which he did not know how to conquer. His luck had almost run out at the Hydaspes. There the army had been saved by the selfless courage of the phalanx and the shield-bearers. But the veterans no longer possessed their former daring. They had been broken by the terrible battle and the endless war. Once they refused to obey, the army insisted. The march ahead made no sense. They had to return home while they still had the energy to cross all that space.

Alexander was beside himself. He insisted that the end of their journey was near. The Ganges was close and the ocean was just beyond. Then they would all sail home, past India to Egypt.

During a war council with Alexander, Kenos, a Hydaspes battle hero, represented the army. He said that the information collected by the cryptii was being held secret from the soldiers, and that the Ganges was not close at all. In fact it was three thousand stadiums away. There was no ocean beyond the Ganges, only endless mountain ranges. Couldn't Alexander see how few Macedonians and Helenians were left in the army? Did he not keep track of the numbers of killed, wounded, and deceased from illnesses, or the ones left to stay in the new cities he had built? Those who were still alive and able were worn out. They were like horses who'd been ridden too far and too long.

At a sign from Kenos, seven tall Macedonians stood before the king. They were naked, wearing only their helms, showing their many scars and sores from old and still-bleeding wounds. They shouted,

"Alexander, do not make us go forth against our will. We are not the same as we were before. If we are forced, we will become even worse. We can no longer support you. Can you see this, or have your eyes lost their sight?"

The great leader became enraged. He tore at his own clothes, intending to show these "weaklings" his own scars and wounds, of which he had more than any of the soldiers. But he restrained himself and retired to his tent, taking no food. Finally he sent a messenger to the soldiers, telling them he would obey the will of the gods.

It had been a long time since the army had watched the old seer Aristander with such anxiety. Now they watched in silence as he cut open the sacrificial sheep on the shore of the Hyphasys. Before Aristander could pronounce the menacing foretelling, Ptolemy, Seleucus, Kenos and all other officers standing nearby saw clear signs of failure and death. They could not cross the river.

When Alexander ordered the army to turn back, the soldiers' loud cheers showed how their patience was at its limit. Alexander ordered twelve stone columns to be erected on the bank of the Hyphasys, marking the end of his Indian campaign. The army returned to the rain-flooded Nikea on the Hydaspes, where the fleet was being constructed. Tragically, Kenos died of exhaustion upon arrival, having served a great service to his comrades before his death.

From that point Alexander's army sailed down the river. Most of the light rowboats perished on the rocks and in whitewater. Nearchus' broadsided ships navigated the swollen Hydaspes and the Indus with much more success. Nearchus offered to build more ships of that kind but Alexander refused.

Having lost his dream of reaching the East Ocean, Alexander's mind was now on his long-abandoned empire, and he hurried home.

The cavalry followed the Indus shore. Hephaestion's detachment traveled along one bank. Another detachment, led by Crateros, traveled along the opposite bank, as the two commanders always argued with each other. The infantry traveled on ships with Alexander and Ptolemy.

From time to time there were skirmishes with brave tribes fiercely defending their lands from Macedonians. Alexander seemed to have become possessed by a demon. He was bent on eliminating all signs of resistance in the countries where his army traveled. There were senseless killings. Macedonians no longer needed large numbers of slaves, and had they kept the tribe members instead of killing them, they would have had to either deliver them to the markets or feed them. Both of those options did little but stall the army's progress.

In the land of Mali, at the edge of the great Tar desert, the natives' courage exceeded that of other tribes. There the Macedonian army was delayed at a well-construction and fearlessly defended fortress for a long time.

Enraged by the resistance, Alexander stormed the wall himself. As soon as he reached the top, the ladder broke. Alexander had no choice but to jump off the wall and land inside the fortress. Only two people were with him: Peuketos and Leonnatus, his personal shield bearer, who carried after him the black shield of Achilles he had picked up at Troy.

Alexander owed him his life. During the attack, an arrow struck Alexander through one lung and he collapsed. Peuketos was also wounded and fell to his knees. Leonnatus, who was also bleeding, covered them both with the sacred shield of the Trojan war hero and, fighting as mightily as Hercules, held back their enemies until the Macedonians finally broke into the fortress, mad with fury. Within minutes all defenders of the fortress were slaughtered. The king was carried to his ship, an arrow still protruding from his chest.

"Wait!" Thais interrupted. Hesiona stopped speaking. "Where was Ptolemy, and why is he the Soter and not Peuketos or Leonnatus?"

"I don't know. Deynomachus didn't know either. Perhaps Ptolemy managed to get to Alexander the quickest with sufficient number of soldiers to save everyone. The soldiers consistently call him the Savior and no one else. They must know better."

"What happened next?" Lysippus asked.

When Alexander was brought to the ship, nobody dared touch the arrow in his chest. They thought the king was dying.

Perdicca, his most experienced officer, ordered them to roll Alexander onto his side. He broke off the tip of the arrow with his strong fingers then pulled out the arrow. He bound the wound tightly and told the king to drink water with wine and yarrow leaf. When physicians arrived, the bleeding had stopped. Alexander became fully conscious, wakened by the soldiers' screams and shouts. The army demanded to see the king, dead or alive. Alexander ordered that he be carried to the shore under a tent so that people could see him.

When the ship docked at a convenient spot, a long-term camp was established. They ensured it was built as far as possible from the smoking ruins of the fortress with its piles of corpses. Alexander was pale as death, yet used one last, herculean effort to mount a horse, despite his friends' cautioning him. He managed to reach his tent on his own, riding through his overjoyed army. That last strain exhausted his strength. For many days he lay suffering with the pain in his punctured lung, indifferent to everything.

Meanwhile Nearchus engaged all soldiers with any kind of carpentry skills to help him build more ships. He was able to find thousands of assistants among the Macedonians and the seashore dwellers.

The Macedonian camp attracted not only adventurers, merchants and women, but also scientists, philosophers, artists and performers. A new year had begun, the first year of the one hundred fourteenth Olympiad.

The army slowly traveled down the Indus. Alexander's extraordinary life force overcame yet another dangerous wound that would have been deadly for most people. Still sick, he spent much time conversing with Indian philosophers. Helenians called them gymnosophists, nude scholars, because it was their custom to constantly walk around wearing hardly any clothes, emphasizing the absence of earthly desires.

With much bitterness, Alexander realised that he crossed one river after another, depleting the patience of his army in vain. It turned out that the Hydaspes joined the Akesinas and the Hydraot, and later the Hyphasys. It eventually fell into a large left arm of the Indus, Laradzos (Satledge), four thousand stadiums below the Indus crossing which had been constructed by Hephaestion. Had Alexander not pushed so stubbornly to the east across the foothills of the huge mountain ranges, but instead descended to the south after the Indus crossing, the entire great Indian plain would have been open to Alexander's army.

But it was all over. Alexander no longer wished to go anywhere but Persia and the western sea. At the Laradzos he founded another Alexandria which he called Opiana. It was said that while he was there, the king secretly visited an impossibly ancient temple in the ruins of a huge city, a thousand stadiums below the merging of the Indus and the Laradzos. The priest of the temple told Alexander a great mystery, and Alexander never brought up India again. Not even to his closest friends. This news traveled among the soldiers like the wind, making them much better informed than their officers wished.

As they slowly sailed down the Indus, the Macedonians acquainted themselves with the country, whose giant dimensions they now had time to comprehend. It was good that they had put a stop to Alexander's insane urge to rush headlong into the depths of India. Only now did they remember Ktesius, a Helenian physician who had served at the court of Artaxerxes and composed a description of India as a large country.

One of the Indians, gymnosophist Kalinas, had decided to accompany Alexander, warning the king about dangers and discouraging the officers from unnecessary attacks on nearby cities.

When Hesiona paused to catch her breath, Lysippus poured her some wine diluted with a quantity of spring water. Thais was deep in thought, as if she were still in India, then asked, "Where was Roxanne?"

"She was with Alexander the entire time. She had a separate tent and sailed on a separate ship. On land she traveled by elephant, as was appropriate for a great queen."

"How does one ride an elephant?"

"I don't know. We can ask when we get to Babylon."

"Continue, please."

In the month of Skyrophorion, Alexander had reached the Indus delta, six thousand stadiums below the convergence of all the tributaries. It looked much like the delta of the Nile. Not only Macedonians, but all the experienced sailors became frightened when he saw the giant waves rushing up the river, raising the water level by twenty to thirty elbows. But they were able to make sense of it once they reached the ocean. The tides there reached levels that were uncommon at the Inner Sea.

Approximately five hundred stadiums from the ocean, above the river delta, Hephaestion started building the Patala port. At the same time, in the month of Hekatombeon, Alexander and Nearchus sailed far into the ocean, five hundred stadiums away from the shore. There he made a sacrifice to Poseidon and tossed a golden goblet into the waves.

Hesiona continued, her hands shaping the story as beautifully as her words. "A month later Alexander traveled further west along the seashore across the deserts of Hedrosia and Karmania. He traveled light with only the infantry and a part of the cavalry. He had already dispatched Crateros with all the carts, families, loot, elephants and livestock along a comparatively easy route across Arahosia and Drangiana[37]. Crateros was accompanied by Seleucus, who, after the Hydaspes battle, forever gave his heart to the elephants and was collecting them as enthusiastically as Ptolemy did jewels ..." Hesiona paused and glanced nervously at her friend.

" ...And women," Thais said calmly. "Continue."

For the first time the Theban realized how indifferent her friend was to Ptolemy's romantic adventures.

Crateros founded yet another Alexandria on the river Arahotos and continued slowly to their designated meeting spot in Karmania on the river Amanis, which fell into the deep sea bay of Harmosia.

Alexander traveled with the caravan in order to set up several provision caches for Nearchus along the seashore. The Cretan left Patala with the entire fleet

---

37 Desert regions of Pakistan, south Afghanistan and southeast Iran.

two months later, in Maymakterion, after the change in the winds from summer to winter.

At first Alexander had wanted to entrust the fleet to Onesikrit. Nearchus was against that, pointing out the carelessness and well-known deceitfulness of his assistant. As much as Alexander wanted to travel together with Nearchus, he had to agree with the fleet commander's arguments. Alexander made it his primary mission to document the shoreline and the sea route connecting India and Persia. That was why he decided to lead the caravan himself across the deserts. The march turned out to be nearly the hardest one of all that had been experienced by the Macedonian army. At first the army was joined by great numbers of civilians: merchants, craftsmen, women. They all perished of hunger and thirst, although the majority of them drowned.

"Yes, drowned," Hesiona repeated, noticing her listeners' confusion. "When the army camped in a dry valley among the hills. A thunderstorm took place somewhere in the mountains and gave start to a mighty stream that instantly crashed onto the unsuspecting people. The soldiers were used to sudden attacks and escaped by climbing the hills, but the rest perished."

Even at night the gray sand and rocks of the Hedrosia desert radiated heat, imbued with the strong scent of myrtle trees. It was as if a thousand incense burners filled the air with the precious myrrh of Arabia. Large white flowers covered the impassable thickets of low, stocky trees covered with thorns. These were followed by waterless sands.

The journey became more and more difficult. They had to save food, and water supplies nearly ran out. Uncontrollable soldiers looted some of the carts which carried provisions for Nearchus. Only one cache could be set up. In search of water, they were forced to turn into the depths of the country and both the navigators and cryptii became confused. As a result, they had to travel back to the sea, determine their direction and head straight north.

They finally arrived at the city of Pura on the same river where the three portions of the army were set to meet. They rested and continued to travel down the river to the city of Hulaskira in Harmosia.

Crateros arrived on time with his army, women and elephants. His detachment, having traveled a longer route, did exceptionally well. He had no losses among people or animals and no significant delays along the way. Crateros was a passionate hunter and had allowed himself a few forays away from his main route, remembering Alexander's request to look for the terrible beast "man eater". The animal had been mentioned in Ktesius' descriptions of India. Those descriptions were wrought with many improbable stories but included evidence from many witnesses. The Persians were clearly terrified by the beast and called it martichorus, or swallower of people. Its huge size, terrible maw, hard scaly armor and spike-covered tail made the beast sound like something between a crocodile and a behemoth. Crateros himself had heard these stories, but similar to the borius of the Libyan desert, no one could point out its exact dwelling, and Crateros' search turned out to be in vain.

There was no news of Nearchus. Alexander waited patiently, refusing to believe that the Cretan was dead, and not wishing to go on without his friend. From time to time he dispatched carriages and riders to the river delta and to the bay, but no one had heard of the fleet. Three months passed, autumn ended and the month of Gamelion began. One day the spies' carriages returned bearing five emaciated vagrants, among whom Alexander recognized Nearchus and Archias. The king hugged the Cretan, amazed that he had managed to make it there and remain alive after losing the fleet. Now it was Nearchus' turn to be surprised. The fleet was fine, he said. They lost only five ships out of eighty. The ships were waiting in the river delta. He had rushed to the meeting point in order to get provisions for the starving sailors. Alexander was overcome with joy.

Nearchus, clean and rubbed down with fragrant oils, was given a gold necklace and wreath, then headed a celebratory procession. The most beautiful girls, nude save for garlands of flowers, danced around him and sang, glorifying his victory over the sea. It was a grand victory indeed. Eight thousand stadiums along a wild deserted shore, inhabited only by the ichtiophages, the fish-eaters who only ate cured fish, mollusks and crabs which they baked in the sun. Helonophages, or turtle-eaters, were only marginally better, as they avoided raw food. They tossed out the precious turtle armor as if it were garbage. Nearchus ordered the men to gather as many as possible.

All along their voyage they saw not a single city or temple, though they occasionally saw cabins built from the enormous bones of sea monsters. The sailors got to see the monsters in their living state and said the huge black beasts tossed up whistling fountains of water.

Nearchus kept a detailed journal of the distances they crossed, landmarks and observations of the phases of the moon.

Before Nearchus, these seas had been traversed by the envoy of Darius the First Skilak, whose journey was successful. However, the Cretan did not trust Skilak. Having visited the Indus, Skilak described it as a river flowing to the east. How many troubles and losses could have been avoided had Alexander known from the beginning about the Persian Gulf and the true direction of the Indus? Aristotle himself believed that the origins of the Indus and the Nile were located in the same country because elephants lived both in India and in Libya, but not in any other country. Considering Skilak to be a liar, Nearchus set out on his voyage with great reservations. However, this time, Skilak's information turned out to be correct.

Halfway through their voyage, the ships reached Astola, the island of Nereids, who were mermaids from the Finikian legends. The brave Finikians didn't dare approach the enchanted place. However, Nearchus' ship had a Helenian crew, and everyone wanted to explore the island and meet the beautiful sea maidens. The Cretan ordered them to drop anchor some distance from the shore and went to meet the mermaids on a boat. Much to the disappointment of Nearchus, Archias, Deynomachus and their companions, the island was bare and completely deserted. There was nothing but two half-ruined cabins made of bones and bits of turtle shells, evidence of helonophages' temporary stay on the island. Another tale of distant seas was put to rest.

Onesikrit swore that the island really was inhabited by the Nereids, but the gods turned people's eyes away from the sacred land, leading the fleet to a completely different place. Nearchus, calm and skeptical, chuckled into his long, wild beard as he listened to these fanciful tales.

Onesikrit had nearly played a fateful role in the fate of the fleet. When they saw the prominent cape of Arabia[38], he had insisted on docking there. Nearchus ordered them to turn in the opposite direction and enter the Harmosia bay[39]. From the Harmosia bay and the Amanis delta, Nearchus decided to lead the fleet to the delta of the Euphrates, then to Babylon, examining the shoreline of Arabia that came close to the shores of Karmania, right next to the bay. Alexander wanted to sail around Arabia and find a route to Ethiopia; however, he agreed with Nearchus that a mission like that would require a different fleet made up of large

---

38 Modern Oman
39 Ormuz gulf

ships that could carry great stores of water, provisions, and wood for repair. One of the main difficulties along the way from India was the absence of good wood required for fixing damage to the ships. Thankfully, after the Pleiades had set, the weather near the shoreline that month was calm. Had the voyage taken place during the stormy months, many more ships would have been lost.

Alexander's army was split into three parts again. Hephaestion led the army, the caravan and the elephants along the shoreline to Pasaragdes and Susa. Alexander and the cavalry rode in the same direction through Persepolis. Eventually they would all be in Susa.

"My Nearchus will be sailing by on his way to Babylon. I would very much like to meet him here, which is why I am in such a rush," Hesiona said, finishing her long story.

The Theban's hopes were not to pass. They arrived at Babylon long before Nearchus, and stayed at Hesiona's for two weeks. The city was in a frenzy over the news of Alexander's return, and the streets were filled with crowds of newcomers arriving from everywhere. For the first time Thais saw the slender Libyans with the skin the color of dark copper. The Athenian looked pale next to these dwellers of Lydian steppes, despite her coppery tan. The Etruscans from the Italian shores were an unprecedented sight: powerful, stocky people of average height with sharply-outlined profiles of Egyptian type. Lysippus had read historic books by Timeus and Teopompus and had heard stories of travelers of how the Etruscan's wives enjoyed incredible freedom even compared to the Spartans. They were stunningly beautiful and took great care of their bodies, frequently appearing in the nude. During meals they sat next to their husbands and other men and carried themselves with unheard-of liberty. Men often shared the love of women between them: such was their custom.

"If such are the Etruscan customs, then they do not have hetaerae and I would not have been popular with them," Thais said half-jokingly.

"They really do not have hetaerae," Lysippus agreed, then added thoughtfully. "All their women are hetaerae, or rather they are the same as our women were in the ancient times. We did not need hetaerae because women were true companions of men."

"Our compatriots are unlikely to agree with you," the Athenian said, laughing. "Presently I am more interested in elephants than the Etruscans. A caravan of fifty of these animals arrived yesterday. Although," she said, sounding puzzled, "it is strange to call an elephant an animal. They are something else entirely."

"They really are," Lysippus agreed.

"They'll listen to you, after all. You know how to order, teacher."

The Athenian's sweet tone made the sculptor suspicious. "What do you want from me, restless child?" he asked.

"I have never ridden an elephant. How do they do it? You can't just sit astride such a huge thing."

"The battle elephants are ridden in a little gazebo saddle. The same goes for the everyday riding, except the walls are lower and have large side cutouts. I watched them from the distance. I have never ridden an elephant either."

Thais hopped up and put her arms around the artist's neck. "Let's go. We'll take Hesiona and Eris. We'll only travel one or two parsangs."

Lysippus agreed. They chose the biggest elephant, one with long tusks and hostile eyes. A yellow fringe danced around his forehead and around the roof of the colorfully painted gazebo saddle. Thais settled triumphantly on a cross bench with Eris, facing Lysippus. Hesiona stayed home, having flatly refused to participate. The caretaker made the giant rise, and the elephant started down the road. His thick skin slipped and moved oddly over his ribs, making the gazebo tilt, rock and dive. Thais and Eris found the rhythm of the elephant's walk, but Lysippus was barely able to stay on his bench. He wiped sweat continuously from his brow and cursed the overly long promenade. Being unfamiliar with the inconveniences of riding an elephant and also being unaccustomed to it, they had chosen a too-distant destination for their ride. The great sculptor bore it bravely, like a true Helenian, but in the end was only too glad to climb off the elephant, grunting and stretching as he did so.

"I don't envy Roxanne," Thais said, jumping straight down from the gazebo.

Hesiona was waiting for them. "Amazing news!" she shouted from the doorway. "Garpal escaped with a mass of gold from the king's treasury!"

Garpal was Alexander's designated treasurer in Ecbatana. He had recently arrived in Babylon in order to meet his ruler.

"Where did he go, and what for?" Lysippus exclaimed.

"To Hellas, to Cassander, with a detachment of Helenian mercenaries left behind in Babylon."

"What about Alexander?" Thais asked.

Hesiona flapped her hand dismissively. "He probably doesn't know yet. More news: in Susa, Alexander decided to get married and also to marry all his officers to Asian women. The king himself took Darius' eldest daughter, who was named Stateira, like her mother. Crateros became related to Alexander by marrying Roxanne's sister. Hephaestion married Dripetis, Darius' daughter and a sister of his former wife. Seleucus took Apama, the daughter of the late envoy Spitamenus. Ptolemy married Sirita, who was nicknamed Atacama, the Persian princess from Darius' family. Nearchus was supposed to have a bride, too, the daughter of Barsina of Damascus and Mentor; however, he is still at sea and will not be able to attend the celebration. As far as I know my Cretan, he'll dodge this marriage. Eighty officers and getaerosi are marrying girls of noble origins, and ten thousand Macedonian soldiers are entering lawful marriage with their slave girls, who are Persians, Bactrians, and Sogdians. There will be a celebration worthy of the feast of the titans, with three thousand actors, musicians and dancers."

"Alexander wishes to create stronger ties between Macedonia, Hellas and Asia," Lysippus said thoughtfully. "But must he be in such a hurry? They will marry and abandon these wives. The king is in a great rush. Thousands and thousands of unattended matters are waiting for him in Babylon."

"I have to go home to Ecbatana. My son is missing me," Thais said suddenly. "I shall leave the day after tomorrow if I can pack that fast. This place will become very hot soon."

"Will you not stop by Susa?" Hesiona asked.

"No. The direct route through Garmal and the Sacred Fires is shorter and more convenient. You will stay here to wait for Nearchus. I know that, which is why I am not even asking. But what about our teacher?"

"I shall wait for Alexander here, though at first he probably won't have time either for me or for the arts," Lysippus replied.

A few hours before the departure, a messenger on horseback found Thais through Hesiona and the city overseer. He brought her a sealed letter from Ptolemy, who begged her not to be angry at him for the mandatory marriage with the Persian girl. He assured her that Alexander had forced them all to the speedy marriages and that they had done it only for the king's sake. With his usual conviction, Ptolemy spoke of this marriage as a simple, meaningless favor to Alexander.

He promised to tell Thais some kind of a secret that would be important for them both, once they met. Ptolemy mentioned the uncommonly lovely precious stones he had collected for her, but kept the words casual, because he knew what her reaction would be had he tried to bribe her openly.

Thais took a pin, stuck the letter to the table, cut it into small pieces with a sharp dagger, and scattered them in the wind.

She said a sweet but brief goodbye to Hesiona and Lysippus, not knowing that she was seeing them for the last time. Her small party traveled through the Ishtar gates and vanished down the northern road.

Thais spent the fateful third year of the hundred and fourteenth Olympiad in Ecbatana. Thais remembered every month of it well, down to the dark days of Targelion, during which Alexander died by a strange coincidence. The terrible battle of Hydaspes which had broken the spirits of the Macedonian army had also taken place at the end of Targelion, the third year of the prior Olympiad. Perhaps Aristander could have warned him, had the old man still been alive. But no. Alexander had long since stopped listening to him.

Some time passed before Ptolemy appeared in town. At first Thais enjoyed her grown Leontiscus, who became deeply attached to his mother. But then she felt lonely without the company of Lysippus.

One time she ascended to the cemetery in the hills and gazed for a long time upon the dazzling white tile on Cleophrades' tomb. The wind moved the lacy shadow of juniper over it, making it look like script. Kneeling in the searing silence, she remembered the splendid inscription on the tomb of Anacreontus.

"Anacreontus' tomb! Beneath it the swan of Teoss is asleep, and the passion of fiery youth is asleep." Thais found herself composing the verses of the epitaph she had decided to carve on this blank white tile. It was already partially covered with ivy, the favorite graveside plants of Helenians. "Here lies Cleophrades," she said aloud, "the sculptor of Athens, who molded the beauty of the feminine body with the eternal light of the goddess."

After the new year, in the midst of summer heat, Hephaestion came to Ecbatana and brought a letter from Ptolemy, as well as an enormous quantity of jewels. Thais was also given an unexpected gift from Alexander: a gold statuette of a woman that looked like Thais, dressed like a maenadae. She was the companion of Dionysus, and was covered in ivy from head to waist with a few tendrils descending below her waist. Thais was delighted by the workmanship of the sculpture, but understood its meaning only after she saw the king one last time.

Hephaestion visited the Athenian at her house and told her about their adventures during the campaign. Thais peered at the merry giant's long-familiar face with anxiety, finding in him traces of immeasurable fatigue and a strange emptiness. Sometimes Hephaestion's gaze rested on something invisible and life itself seemed to leave his eyes.

In honor of Alexander's closest friend and chiliarchus, the citizens of Ecbatana organized a great celebration. Judging by the number of actors, it almost equaled the marriage celebration in Susa.

Tragically, Thais' foreboding came true. At the beginning of the celebration, Hephaestion became ill with a strong fever, and felt increasingly worse. As soon as the news reached Babylon, Alexander took the best horses and rushed to Ecbatana with Ptolemy and the most famous physicians. But it was too late. One of the pillars of Alexander's empire, the king's closest friend, the life-loving giant who easily bore the unimaginable difficulties of marches and battles, died in Puanepsion on the seventh day of his sickness, in the third year of the hundred and fourteenth Olympiad.

No one had ever before seen the great leader in such deep grief. Not even when he killed Black Cleitus. Alexander drank alone night after night, then spent his days consulting with an architect from Athens. The architect's name was Stasicrates and he was known for his majestic structures.

Stasicrates constructed a giant burial pyre for Hephaestion, shaped like a temple of cedar and sandalwood, using great quantities of frankincense and myrrh. The flame, which reminded Thais of the fire of Persepolis, swallowed the hero's body. The wake was attended by several thousands of people. After seven days of drinking following the wake, Alexander went to the northern mountains to conquer Cassites. They wer, a mountain tribe who were not afraid of the king, whose name alone caused other armies to scatter.

He was accompanied by Ptolemy, the last of his close friends aside from Nearchus. Ptolemy was now the chief caretaker of the empire. Depressed after the death of his friend, his face swollen from the nightly feasts in which he had to participate, Ptolemy came to Thais before their departure and spoke to her at length. He told her the terrible secret he kept for ten years, since the time Alexander had visited the Ammon oracle in an oasis in the midst of Libyan desert. At the time, Ptolemy had bribed a junior attendant of the oracle with a talant of gold so he could eavesdrop on the oracle's foretelling. That is how he knew Alexander was told he would die at a young age, not much older than thirty years.

"He is now thirty-two, and if ..." Ptolemy didn't dare pronounce the terrible word. "Then his great conquered kingdom shall fall apart and vanish from existence because Alexander alone can rule it without exhausting himself with the great multitude of tasks." He frowned. "You are not listening to me."

"Yes, I am. I have only just realized why Alexander was so desperate, in such a rush to get to the edges of the world, to the shores of the East Ocean. He knew about the prophecy and carried it inside, like a poisoned dagger over naked skin."

"You are probably right. But it doesn't matter anymore. If Ammon's foretelling is correct, then I will be the first one to advocate the split of the empire. I will only ask for Egypt. It is off to the side and near the Inner Sea, which is what I need. Will you come with me and be the queen of Egypt?"

Thais blinked at him. "What if the prophecy is not true?"

"Then everything will go as it is now. Alexander will sail with Nearchus and I shall stay in Babylon as his envoy and chief strategist of Asia. But you didn't answer my important question."

"What about Sirita?"

"I swear by the hammer of Hephaestus, you know the answer for yourself. You are only asking me out of mischief. The Persian girl will stay in Persia, I shall marry her off to one of the envoys of the eastern borders. But be careful trying my patience. I can take you whenever I want, wherever I want, tied and under strong guard."

Thais rose and approached Ptolemy, still not giving him a direct answer.

"You spent too much time making war in Scythia and India and have forgotten what your wife is like. My dear army man, women like me cannot be taken by force. We either die by killing ourselves, or kill those who allow themselves such use of force. You are not a Helenian, but a Macedonian, who has grown wild in war marches, grabbing helpless women like any other loot at your feet."

Ptolemy flushed crimson and grabbed for her with predatory curved fingers, then remembered himself and jerked his hand away, as if burned by fire. He nodded.

"Let it be so. You are right. I really have gotten used to women's unquestionable obedience."

"It is well that you took away your hand, Ptolemy. Had you grabbed me, I am not sure, but I believe Alexander's chief officer might have been carried out of here as a lifeless body."

He scowled. "Your black demon, Eris. She and you would have been tortured and executed."

"Ah, so Eris is a demon now, and not a generous protector? Learn to control yourself when your wishes are not fulfilled, otherwise you shall never become a real king, Ptolemy. I am not certain about the execution as long as Alexander is alive. Besides," she said lightly, "there is always poison."

Ptolemy became ashamed for the first time. He mumbled something about going through a long war filled with endless killing and rape, and being used to instant and unquestioning obedience, then repeated his question about Egypt.

Thais softened and held out her small, firm hand.

"If you will learn to understand me again, then I agree. Only there cannot be either a second or third queen during my rule. What would you want me for, disobedient and unfaithful?"

"I would be happy with your absolute honesty. To speak nothing about your beauty, intelligence, knowledge, ability to interact with people, and understanding of the arts. I could not find a better queen for the ancient country where people's tastes are established and unmistakable, and where they can easily tell the real thing from a trifle."

"And what if the wild Amazon or a careless Nereid comes back to life in me?"

"You shall take care of that yourself. So. Do you agree?"

Thais nodded after a brief pause.

"May we seal our agreement with a kiss?"

The Athenian agreed.

Despite it being winter time, Alexander's cavalry went into the mountains. They stayed much longer than was necessary for the conquering of the Cassites, scattered through Parthia and Girkania. Was Alexander planning to visit the Sea of Birds again?

Thais was thinking of other things. The tired conqueror, devastated by the loss of his best friend, was exhausted by a mountain of hateful tasks related to governing the empire. In these matters his habit of lightning fast decisions did not help, but rather hurt him. He simply did not wish to go back to Babylon.

Bad news arrived from Hellas. The fugitive treasurer, Garpal, and Cassander declared Alexander mad and possessed by a manic egotism; however, the army leader's fame was far too great to be slandered thus. The return of all statues from Asia, taken out by previous conquerors, was considered to be his greatest deed in Hellas. Alexander was worshiped like a contemporary Hercules. Garpal the traitor came to a bad end. He was executed.

Architect Stasicrates told something entirely different. He proposed to Alexander that he do something entirely unheard-of. He suggested he create a statue of him six hundred elbows tall, by carving it out of the mountain Athos in Khalkidhiki. Alexander only laughed and said that the giant pyramids of Egypt told nothing of the rulers who had built them. Great size did not equal great glory.

The people of Hellas were even more impressed by the arrival of the Macedonian veterans, led by Crateros. They were set free and given both honors and great rewards by Alexander. The phalanx and the Agrian cavalry ceased to exist. All Helenian mercenaries who had been left behind in the new fortresses and Alexandrias were also able to return home.

Hephaestion's ashes were temporarily placed in a mausoleum of snow white limestone on a hill near

Ecbatana. The place had a view of the eastern valley, overgrown by silvery grass. Thais grew fond of visiting the peaceful place with Eris.

She remembered the story Hephaestion had told her not long before his illness, about the incredible deed by the Indian wise man, gymnosophist Kalinas. Kalinas had come to Alexander and declared his decision to leave the boundaries of the land. The king did not understand at first and offered him a unit of strong guards. The old man explained that he was feeling poorly and did not wish to live any longer, but that he was far away from his homeland and could not reach it in time. On the Indian's request, soldiers built a large bonfire. Alexander, thinking the man wanted to make a sacrificial offering, gave Kalinas a horse and five gold goblets. The wise man gave the presents to those who built the bonfire, climbed on top and ordered it to be set on fire from all sides. Then the old man lay down, remaining completely motionless amidst the smoke and flames.

Alexander, struck by such courage, ordered trumpets to play and had all the elephants give the gymnosophist a royal sendoff with their roar. The soldiers did not recover from Kalinas' death for a long time. They felt they'd lost someone who had protected the army along the way. Hephaestion considered the Indian's death to be a great heroic deed, worthy of example. He wanted to find the same kind of courage in himself and without a doubt had told Alexander about it. The giant pyre was the king's response to his friend's words. The deserted hill that had bustled with construction activity only a month prior was cleaned and set to order. Flowers and shrubs were planted around the mausoleum.

For Thais, this was a good place for her to think about the upcoming changes in her life. Ptolemy had yet to arrange anything for their son. He'd sworn to find the best gymnastics and military teachers immediately after he returned to Babylon with Alexander, since he was unable to leave him alone.

One day in Elafebolion, a month of remarkably lovely weather, Thais arrived at the tomb and saw a small party approaching. They stopped about five stadiums from the mausoleum. Two of them separated from the rest and slowly rode toward the hill. They were tall and wore glittering helms, one riding a black horse and the other a dappled gray one.

Thais' heart beat faster. She recognized Alexander and Ptolemy. In honor of his Bucephal, the king always picked black horses. Six Persian youths designated by Ptolemy to be her guards jumped up in alarm and ran out from under a lonely elm where they'd waited for their charge. Thais calmed them down, explaining who the men were. The soldiers did not mount, but lined up in the distance, bowing their heads with respect.

The king gazed in amazement upon Thais and Eris, standing on the white steps of the temporary mausoleum. The two women were dressed in identical pale blue ecsomida, like two statuettes of Corinthian and Egyptian bronze. He dismounted and quickly approached Thais, holding out both hands to her.

"I am glad to find you here, honoring the memory of a friend," Alexander said. He was smiling, but his eyes were sad. "I wished to speak with you before returning to Babylon."

"Whenever you want, King. Even now."

"Alas, now there are too many people waiting for me, impatient to rest after a march. I shall set a meeting here and let you know. Will you allow me that, Ptolemy? After all, your wife is my friend."

"She is not asking permission." Ptolemy laughed. "Why do you ask, all-powerful King?"

"A king must observe tradition even more closely than the last of his subjects," Alexander said, sounding somber. "For how else am I to inspire respect toward law and the sense of good measure?"

Ptolemy flushed slightly under his dark tan. With his reputation as a wise man of state he did not like to make even the smallest mistake.

Four days later a messenger arrived and told her Alexander was waiting for her at Hephaestion's tomb. Thais twirled in front of the mirror, choosing a lavender ecsomida cut just above the knees. She wore the earrings from the Heavenly Empire, the gift from the yellow-faced man. After thinking about it, she also added the necklace from the talons of the black gryph, the memento from the Eridu temple. Only a firm demand from Thais forced Eris to stay home, which meant she was permitted to accompany the Athenian no further than the city walls. Boanergos, now a mature twelve year old stallion, scattered the measured hoofbeats of a pacer as swiftly as before.

Alexander sat on the top step of the mausoleum without armor, helm or weapons, wearing only the leg coverings he did not like to remove. He rarely took them off because they hid the scars of terrible wounds on his legs.

He took the pacer's reins and caught Thais as she was dismounting, gently tossing her up into the air. The smart horse walked away without command and hid in the shade of the elm. Alexander peered at the Athenian, seeing her for the first time after a long separation, ran his fingers over the talon necklace and touched a tinkling carved earring. Thais explained the meaning of the gryph's talon, the sign of the Guardian of Secret Paths, and told him how she came to have it.

Alexander listened as his gaze glided over her figure, clearly outlined through the transparent ecsomida.

"Are you still wearing the chain belt?" he asked, noticing the glint of gold. "Still with the xi?"

"There cannot be another one. Impossible," Thais replied quietly. "I wanted to thank you, King. For the house in the New City, near the Lugalgira gate."

"I use it to escape sometimes," the king said, chuckling sadly. "But I cannot stay long."

"Why not?"

"There are too many matters of state. Also ..." Alexander suddenly switched, dropping the dispirited manner of speaking he had adopted recently. His voice became energetic. "Sometimes I wish to throw myself into the fire of Eros. To feel like a young man again. In you I have found the divine madness which also inhabits my soul, akin to the underground fire. You cracked the stone walls and let it out. What man can resist such force?"

"In order to awaken it, one requires a force in response, as a salamander requires fire," Thais said. "And there is not one, except you."

"Yes, when I was the way I met you in Memphis. No. That was in the middle of the Euphrates." He sighed. "That man is far away now," Alexander said, subsiding.

Thais looked at the king's beautiful face, discovering unfamiliar traces of tired and disdainful cruelty. These were unsuitable for Alexander's prior image, that of a dreamer and the bravest of the brave warriors. Such people could never be either disdainful or cruel. His low forehead seemed more rounded from the pronounced eyebrow ridges. His large, straight nose was emphasized by the sharp creases near his mouth, of which the full lips had already started to stretch over his strong round chin. Deep vertical lines cut through the once gentle outlines of his cheeks. Despite the conditions he had survived, his skin remained as smooth as before, reminding her of the young age of the great king. In Sparta, Alexander would have reached the age of a grown man only two and a half years ago.

"Are you very tired, my king?" Thais asked, filling the question with all the tenderness of which she was capable, as if the great conqueror and ruler had suddenly become a boy not much older than her Leontiscus.

Alexander lowered his head in silent agreement.

"Does the urge for the boundaries of Ecumene still burn in you?" the Athenian asked quietly. "Perhaps you've chosen the wrong path."

"There is no other one. One cannot go to the east of Asia, or south or north without meeting armed detachments or entire armies. They would annihilate you or make you a slave, whether you have five hundred companions or five. It does not matter. Only having gathered a large force can one penetrate the wall of hostile people of different languages and different faiths, understanding nothing about my goal. You can see for yourself that I had to overturn enormous kingdoms and crush countless enemies. But only two years later, Chandragupta has already taken away a part of the conquered land from me in India and kicked out my envoys. No, I cannot reach the boundaries of Ecumene by land. Now I shall try it by sea."

"Perhaps if you traveled alone, like the yellow-faced dweller of the East, you could get further in."

"Perhaps. But there are too many dangers along the way, and each one can be deadly. And it would require too much time. Traveling on foot is too slow. No, I was right when I took the path of force. The sizes of Ecumene calculated by the greatest scientists of Hellas are incorrect. It is far greater, but that is their mistake and not mine."

"Will you travel again, then, into the unknown?"

"I am tired not of traveling, but of the cares of the huge state. They crashed upon me like a river during a flood."

"Can you not divide these cares by trusting them to your faithful associates?" Thais asked.

"I believed at first that I was surrounded by the worthiest men, that together we formed the top of a spear capable of penetrating anything. For the first time, the Spartan stamina became a standard for tens of thousands of my soldiers. The honor of that accomplishment goes to my father, Philip. He was the one who gathered and trained an army of such courage and endurance that the quality of individual warriors had approached that of the Lacedemonians. With these select thirty-five thousand, I deflected and crushed a force far greater in number but worse in the quality of people. All went well while our goal was shared, the enemy was powerful, and we were not burdened by the colossal war loot. Unity wears off, as does physical strength. Like rust eats through iron, the flattery of one's associates, the crowds of loose women and merchants, priests and philosophers, relatives and false friends eat through the purity of heart and self-restraint.

"Those people who are harder than an eagle's talon and were not worn out during the ten years of war and rule in the conquered countries, are few. Only a handful in the entire Great Empire. And I am losing them one after another as I lost the incomparable hero Hephaestion. I became enemies with some, sometimes for a good reason as they did not understand me, and sometimes unjustly, as I did not understand them. But the worst thing was the further we went, the greater became the difference in our goals. I could no longer think of homonoya, the equality between all people, as I could not find it among my closest friends and associates. The main poison in the hearts of all people is the idiotic arrogance of origin, tribe and religion. I am helpless to fight it. Such is the end of the Asian campaign. I, the ruler of half the world, wash my hands of it, feeling like a traveler at the beginning of his path. You are right. I would have been happier walking alone as a free traveler in tattered clothes, relying on the mercy of gods and that of any armed passerby."

Thais pulled the Macedonian's lion-like head to her, caressing it gently, like a mother. She could hear his anxious breathing as it screeched through his arrow-punctured lung. His powerful arms, once divinely calm and still, shook with a nervous shudder.

"Do you want to be my queen?" Alexander asked. He straightened and asked with his usual abruptness.

Thais was startled. "One of the wives of the king of kings? No!"

"You wish to be the first among all or the only one," the Macedonian said, chuckling unkindly.

"You always misunderstand me, my king," Thais replied calmly. "And you will not understand me until we are together forever. I do not need to be either exceptional or free of competition. But I must have the right to protect you, sometimes against your immediate desires or the will of your friends and associates. Otherwise you cannot rely on me at a difficult time of betrayal or sickness."

"Then you want …"

"I want nothing. I am simply explaining. Too late. These things ought to have been discussed much sooner."

"I am still young. Nothing is too late for me."

"Need I tell you, ruler of people, that a true queen cannot be appointed or confined to your bed. The efforts of both are required here so that others may see and feel it. Many years are needed to become a queen and you don't even have a year at your disposal."

"Yes. I am sailing with Nearchus to seek the route to Ethiopia. Ninety ships are ready and being loaded at the docks of Babylon and the Euphrates Alexandria."

"Will you take me to the ocean with you? Not as a queen, just as a companion?"

Alexander replied glumly after a pause. "No. The paths of war are uncertain and the demands of the tumultuous shores of the waterless deserts are great. You are precious. Wait for me in Babylon."

"As Ptolemy's wife?"

"I shall appoint Ptolemy chiliarchus to replace Hephaestion. He shall rule the empire in my absence."

Thais stood up, gazing at the king tenderly, sadness in her eyes. Alexander rose too. The awkward silence was broken by the approaching hoofbeats of a galloping horse. A rider from Persian nobility, the new getaerosi, lifted a rolled letter above his head. Alexander made a permissive gesture and the messenger dismounted and approached, holding the scroll in front of his lowered face.

"Forgive me. I'll read this." the king said, unrolling the vellum. Thais noticed a few lines written in a bold script.

Alexander turned to Thais with a crooked smile. "I must hurry back to Babylon. Nearchus has returned from his research mission to Arabia and we can set sail. Seleucus approaches with a large caravan of elephants and Peucestus is bringing young soldiers from Ariana."

Thais whistled through her teeth like an Athenian boy. Boanergos raised his head, perked his ears and trotted to his mistress after a repeated command. Alexander gestured to his Scythian groom.

"Before we part, explain to me, King," the Athenian said, taking the pacer's reins. "Explain the meaning of your gift which was brought to me by Hephaestion."

"It was my dream at Nyssa, where I saw the ivy and the Cretan bulls. You know the army of Dionysus consisted only of maenadae. I dreamed of you as a maenadae, nude and powerfully alluring, wrapped in ivy. The glittering scepter of Dionysus pointed at you. I ordered a sculptor from Susa to make an image of you as a maenadae from my dream and my memory."

"I thank you for it with all of my heart, as well as for the house at Lugalgira."

Thais boldly wrapped her arms around the king's neck and froze in his arms for a moment. Then she paled, pulled away and mounted the pacer. Alexander took a step toward her, holding out his hand and seemed to stumble against her firm gaze.

"Destiny and I gave you a chance thrice. First in Memphis, then at the Euphrates and the third time in Persepolis. Fate does not offer favors four times and neither do I. Geliaine, great king, ton eona. Forever, as Plato said."

Thais urged the pacer forward, her head lowered. Large tears rolled from under her long eyelashes and fell onto the horse's black mane. Alexander rode next to her, very quiet. One stadium behind them, the king's guards rode in the cloud of dust. Alexander lowered his bare head, his broad shoulders sagged and his arm hung limply. Thais had never seen the divine victor look that way. He was the image of a man who had exhausted his strength and had no hope. Even Cleophrades looked stronger and tougher during his last Keoss feast. What would happen when Alexander returned to the matters of the great empire in Babylon?

"In the name of Aphrodite and everything that draws us to each other, Alexander, my king, leave Babylon immediately. Do not linger another day. Swear it," she said. She took his hand and squeezed it firmly.

Alexander looked into her huge gray eyes and replied tenderly and sincerely. "I swear by the Styx, my Ayphra, my luminous one."

Thais hit Boanergos with her heels and he quickly passed the king and his slow-riding guard. The Athenian flew through the gates of Ecbatana like the wind, galloped down the streets to the house. There she tossed the reins to a servant, ran across the garden to Eris' gazebo, and locked herself in till evening.

Two months later, during the last days of Targelion, the news of Alexander's sudden death crashed like a mountain rockfall.

In less than ten days, a messenger brought Thais two letters at once. One was from Ptolemy and the other from Hesiona. The Theban described in detail the king's last two days of life. Impossibly fatigued, he gathered his officers to distribute the ships. Together with Nearchus he gave instructions, attempting to comprehend every detail of preparation of the giant fleet.

Tortured by insomnia, he went swimming in the Euphrates at night. Eventually, the king became feverish and left his usual residence in the palace of Nebuchadnezzar, moving instead to his house with a shaded pool in the New City. He did not wish to see anyone except Nearchus. He swam as he was burning up, but the fever became worse. He still could not sleep.

Alexander ordered a sacrifice to the twelve Olympians and Aesculapius. When he spoke with Nearchus, he insisted they set sail in two days. The Cretan had never seen his divine friend in such an unnatural state of anxiety. Alexander spoke constantly of the ocean and gave orders, sometimes repeating himself and becoming confused. In the morning, when his fever subsided, Alexander ordered that he be carried to the palace in the Old City in order to make the sacrifice. He was so weak at that point he could barely speak.

The great leader fought death till the last moment. A few hours before his passing, he wished to say farewell to his friends and his army. Holding back tears, the young getaerosi and warriors from the royal guard passed silently by the bed. Alexander managed to find it in him to greet each one by raising his right arm and sometimes lifting his head. He was conscious till the last minute.

The army officers, who were now called diadochs and Alexander's heirs, gathered to hold an emergency council. Their first order of business was to have the hero's body, covered in scars from terrible wounds, carefully washed and preserved in a mix of fragrant resins, strong wine and honey. Smiths and minters were already making a gold sarcophagus.

Thais could not read any further. Her vision blurred with tears. Long-contained grief had finally burst forth. Falling face down on the bed, the Athenian wept, having torn her clothes and let down her hair according to the old custom.

Alexander, the greatest hero of Macedonia, Hellas and Ionia, descended into the darkness of Hades at the age of a mere thirty-two years and eight months. Thais' heart ached with the notion that prior to his death, exhausted and lonely, he might have been thinking about her, while swimming in the Euphrates or secluding himself in the house on that side of the river at the Lugalgira gates.

With another flood of tears, Thais thought of the king's great loneliness. Everyone around him constantly demanded wise decisions, gold, protection, and love, never realizing his endless fatigue. Never watching him with knowing and understanding eyes and heart. Perhaps that was why he'd sought comfort in the ghosts of the past. If that were the case, had she been with him during those last few hours, she would have been able to recognize the signs of approaching peril. She would have. Alexander wanted to fulfill the promise he gave Thais: to get out of Babylon with Nearchus' fleet.

The Athenian wept so bitterly that Eris became frightened for the first time during their life together and ran to get a physician. Thais refused to see him, but obeyed her friend and drank some kind of thick and bitter brown potion that plunged her into long and dreamless sleep.

It was four days later before Thais found it in herself to emerge from the dark room and take care of the usual occupations of a mother and a head of the household. After a few more days she felt brave enough to read Ptolemy's letter.

He wrote that everything had taken place as he'd predicted. During the council of the diadochs he was the first to suggest the division of the empire and negotiated Egypt for himself. Perdicca was appointed to replace Alexander and become the chief strategist of Asia. He was also entrusted with protecting Roxanne, who was seven months pregnant by the king. Antipatros became army chief in Hellas and Macedonia and the chief strategist of all countries west of Ionia. The leader of getaerosi, Seleucus got Babylonia and India. The one-eyed Antigonus received Asia Minor with the exception of Ionia and Frakia, which went to Lysimachus. Nearchus did not want anything but the fleet, which he received and prepared to sail to Arabia without Alexander.

Ptolemy reminded Thais of her promise to accompany him to Egypt. He would have to wait for Roxanne to give birth. If there were a son, everything would stay the same. If a daughter were born the council would select a new king.

Such was the new incredible change in Thais' life. Roxanne had a son, Alexander the Fourth, and Ptolemy urgently called the Athenian to Babylon. With the select troops who were loyal to him, he took the sarcophagus with Alexander's body and hurried to Egypt.

Since then Thais had remained in Memphis as the queen of the legendary Land of the Nile that was sacred to all Helenians.

And here was the Nile itself, splashing quietly against the steps of the Neit temple.

Chapter Sixteen. The Queen of Memphis

"You shall rule in Memphis and I shall stay in Alexandria," Ptolemy said, arguing with Thais.

For the first time, they were on the brink of a divorce. She reproached him for breaking his vow not to take another wife after Sirita, who he abandoned in Babylon. Now that he was an acknowledged king of Egypt, he'd fallen in love with Berenice and married her secretly, setting her as the queen in Alexandria. And before that there was Eurydice, who bore him a son after he took her by force in Ionia and brought her to Persia.

For the first time, Ptolemy did not yield to Thais' demands. In ten years of victorious campaigns with

Alexander's army, during which cities were crushed and thousands were subject to rape and violence, he had become accustomed to going through hundreds of women without giving it a single thought.

"One more, one less. Is it really worth talking about?" Ptolemy thought naïvely. He was preoccupied by other things. He had recently realized that his efforts to transform Egypt by introducing the spirit of Hellas along with Alexander's genius had been in vain.

"This boulder of ancient beliefs, customs and ways of life, akin to a rock made of black Elephantine granite," he explained to Thais, speaking as intelligently and convincingly as always. "It cannot be changed any other way but by breaking it into pieces. But that would not be wise. When you destroy something, you cannot immediately replace the old with the new, for the country is left without law and tradition and transforms into a gathering of barbaric scoundrels. I shall begin with Alexandria and turn it into a city open to the entire world, open to all teachings and faiths, to philosophers of all schools. First and foremost it will be open for trade between Asia and the Inner Sea. Alexandria, where I keep in the gold sarcophagus the body of the great Alexander, my childhood friend and half-brother, shall become the most beautiful city in Ecumene. The lighthouse on Pharos will become more famous than the Etemenanki tower. I shall also build a Museum for the philosopher. I have already collected more scrolls and books at the Library than in any city of Hellas. I gave an order to the captains of all ships arriving to the Alexandria bay to inform me of the new works of art, scientific discoveries and famous books. I have enough gold to buy a lot. Had it not been for the war ..."

Ptolemy frowned and Thais patted his shoulder compassionately. She knew about the unending war among the diadochs, Alexander's heirs. The chief strategist of Asia, Alexander's old comrade Perdicca, was appointed by the diadochs' council to rule the kingdom until Roxanne's son grew up. He then attacked Ptolemy to take Egypt as well. His own officers killed Perdicca as soon as he reached the Delta, and the army was transferred to Ptolemy.

"I shall fight for Egypt, for Cyprus, and perhaps for Hellas, but in order to carry out all these plans I must live in Alexandria. That is where I invite everyone with the strong spirit of enterprise, everyone who is able to look ahead and work hard, who is talented and intelligent. I invited the Hebrews from Babylon, Syria, and Judea to live freely and carry out trade in Alexandria. I place many hopes on these stern and capable people to multiply the riches and make the city blossom, as I do with your compatriots, who are quick in making decisions and in carrying them out.

"It is true that Athenians are sometimes brave beyond their powers, but they like to take risks and face the danger calmly. I can wage war and argue. There is no one to fight and nothing to argue about in the depths of Egypt. Everything has been built millennia ago, and some of it is already forgotten and covered with sand. Memphis loves you and you understand Egyptians, their different faiths and mystical teachings. You are initiated into their secret rituals. Be the queen of Memphis, where we were both crowned to rule. Help me here and I swear the inviolate oath of the Styx waters that I shall not call another woman a queen as long as you are with me."

"As long as I am with you," Thais repeated slowly, agreeing with the arguments of her wise husband.

And so she remained in Memphis alone, unless you counted the little Irenion, or Irana, as Thais called her in Doric dialect. Her daughter's name reminded her of Persia, and the girl herself was growing increasingly like Ptolemy. Leontiscus was in Alexandria with his father. The boy expressed the same deep love of the sea as permeated Thais' entire being, even as she was forced to live away from its gentle waves and sparkling blue expanse as if by a cruel joke of fate.

The people of Memphis honored their queen more for her kind eyes and striking beauty than for any real power, which was in fact held by Ptolemy's envoy. Thais never tried to be an imposing ruler, having taken upon herself palace celebrations, receptions for the ambassadors and temple ceremonies. All this was wearisome for the lively Athenian. The Egyptian traditions required the queen to sit motionless for hours atop an uncomfortable throne, wearing heavy jewelry. Thais tried to make her receptions and participation in the celebrations as brief as possible.

She had to limit her riding outings to evening twilight and dawn hours. The Egyptians could not imagine their queen galloping on horseback instead of riding slowly and solemnly in a gilded carriage. Salmaakh met her end there, and they purchased a similar gray Libyan mare for Eris. Boanergos was approaching the age of twenty, and while was no longer as playful, he was still light and swift on his feet, jealously not letting any horse pass him. The beautiful pacer, purchased from the queen of Amazons according to rumors, always attracted attention in Memphis. That did not help keep their riding secret.

In the evenings Thais liked to sit on the steps of the Neit temple facing the Nile, watching the dark, mighty river as it rolled toward her native Inner Sea, waiting for the reflections of stars to sparkle in the river. These evening visits became her favorite kind of rest. Of all the mandatory signs of power, she left only the gold tiara in the shape of a snake, the sacred uraeus that descended, upon her forehead.

Eris sat one step lower, glancing at two shy Egyptian girls from noble families who carried a fan and a mirror. It was their duty to accompany the queen everywhere. Cool wind sometimes fluttered in from the river and the Egyptian girls, completely nude save for the colorful beaded necklaces and sashes, shivered and clutched at each other. Eris silently signed to them, pointing at a large coverlet of the finest wool. The girls smiled gratefully, wrapped it around themselves, and left their queen to sit in peace.

The Neit temple, where she had been initiated into the Orphic teachings and began studying the wisdom of Asia, had long since become a home for Thais. The temple priests remembered the Delos philosopher well, as they did her prior visits to the temple, and were not surprised when nine years later she revisited the temple in all the splendor of the beautiful queen of Egypt.

Since then, Thais had sometimes secluded herself in her former room between the thick pylon walls, and had become friends with the high priest of the goddess. The friendship between the young queen and the old temple servant began with the Athenian's attempt to discover the fate of Hesiona and Nearchus. Fulfilling the wish of their late king and friend, as they promised just before his death, Nearchus had inherited the entire fleet and sailed around Arabia in order to continue the route to Egypt and Nubia across the Eritrean Sea.

After two years passed with no news of Nearchus, Thais decided that, no matter how big Arabia was, the sailors had to have reached their goal and sent word. She had heard about the trips taken by Egyptians to Punt across the Eritrean Sea in the days when Hellas had not even existed. So she began looking for knowledgeable people. It turned out to be a short search. The high priest of the Neit temple had access to secret archives where records and maps of the voyages to the distant eastern shore of Libya were kept. The Egyptians had traveled there two thousand years prior, searching for gold, ivory, incense, slaves and rare animals.

Thais' most vivid memory was of visiting the archive somewhere in the ancient temple underground, near the small pyramid. There she had seen four attendants or priests with emaciated faces of fanatic ascetics, dressed head to toe in the green robes of Distant Land Scholars. They had accompanied the queen and the Neit priest, who served as an interpreter for the ancient sacred language. The green ascetics either knew no other language or did not wish to speak any other way.

Fragile sheets of brown vellum covered with mysterious lines, hieroglyphs and markings shaped like flying birds were unrolled before Thais.

"You said that shortly before the death of the great Alexander, Nearchus arrived at Babylon with new discoveries, did you not?" the Neit priest asked.

"His assistant, Archias, confirmed that the sea from the Euphrates delta was but a gulf between India and Arabia," Thais said. "And Gireon stated that the southern coast of Arabia stretched infinitely far southwest."

The Neit priest translated to the archive keepers, and their eyes flashed. One said something in a low voice and knocked the largest sheet, unrolling it on a stone tile with his knuckles.

"We do not know about the gulf," Thais' companion translated. "But here is the shore of Arabia, going to the west and southwest. Here it ends in a kind of angle, turning northwest through the narrow gates of the sea you call Eritrean. That sea has been traveled back and forth by our seamen. Its length has been measured to be five hundred skhens or parsangs from the Gates to the Neho canal. Two months of sailing, gods willing."

"Then shouldn't Nearchus have been in Egypt a long time ago?" Thais asked. "All ninety ships of his fleet could not have perished."

"Queen, Your Majesty judges correctly."

"What could have happened then?"

The Neit priest translated her question. The archive keepers mumbled words as mysterious as chants, poked their dark, thin fingers into various spots on the dusty map and finally reached an agreement.

"The land scholars say that the fleet leader did not make it into the Eritrean Sea," the Neit priest said with authority.

"That could not have happened to Nearchus, the most skilled of sailors. He has the best navigators from Finikia, Egypt and Cyprus."

"It could happen in that area. If Your Majesty would please look here ... This is the southern shore of Arabia, stretching in the direction of India to the east and north for several hundred skhens. From the sound it is opposed by the huge cape of Nubia, or Libya as you call it. The Cape of Fragrances[40] protrudes into the Great Ocean like a horn. Our sailors traveled around it, facing great dangers on their way to Punt. It reaches halfway across the edge of Arabia. Then look here, Queen. Nearchus' fleet was sailing along the shore to the southwest. Terrible storms often take place there. They bring sand and dust from the deserts of Arabia, obscuring the sea for many skhens. Nearchus could have gotten caught in such a storm when his fleet was across from the Cape of Fragrances. The shore of Arabia curves to the south near the round bay with the Cape of Pearls. Right across from that spot, the Horn of Nubia approaches as closely as eighty skhens. Imagine now, that a strong sandstorm carried the fleet to the south. The ships could have accidentally crossed the gap between Arabia and Nubia. Further, from the east side of the Horn, the shore travels south, curving more and more to the west. What would a fleet leader do, who was initially traveling southwest along Arabia?"

"He would continue sailing along the shore of Libya, thinking he is sailing by Arabia," Thais replied without hesitation.

---

40 Somalia peninsula.

"Indeed. See? The shore to the south from the Cape of Fragrances goes southwest to the Punt for five hundred skhens. Further along it turns southeast, and that is where the fleet leader would discover his mistake."

"Then what?"

"I cannot tell you that, for I do not know Nearchus. He may turn back. If he is strong and brave, he would go forward and around, as Finikians have done when ordered by the great Neho."

"The Cretan is stubborn and strong," Thais said sadly. "Besides, Alexander himself dreamed of sending ships around Libya, having heard nothing of Neho."

"Then expect the fleet in three years, as it happened with the Finikians," the priest replied. "Two years have already passed."

Five more years passed, and it became obvious that Nearchus' fleet had vanished without trace in the vastness of the sea. Along with him, the Daughter of the Snake had gone forever from Thais' life. Eris was all that was left to her.

The unavoidable losses followed one after another. She hadn't heard from Lysippus in a long time. He sent word once that he'd sold the Anadiomena to Seleucus, who traded her to the Indians for elephants. Lysippus did not know how many elephants they offered, but twenty-five talents, added to the twelve talents that made up the value of the silver, added to two hundred twenty thousand drachmas, which was an enormous sum. She wrote to her teacher, asking him to use the money for the school of sculptors in Carius, which he had dreamed of starting for a long time, but she never received an answer. Something must have happened to the great sculptor. Or had the endless war over Alexander's inheritance in Ionia and Mesopotamia interfered with the letter?

Thais had a vague premonition that her teacher was gone, and it was correct. After his departure to

Hellas, where he met with Cassander who had supposedly ordered a statue, Lysippus fell ill and died shortly after. Following tradition, his heir, the eldest son Euticratus, opened the great sculptor's secret chest. Lysippus had a rule. He placed one piece of gold into the chest after selling a statue. Euticratus counted fifteen hundred pieces, which made obvious the sculptor's giant legacy. Thais would have been even more astonished had she known that not a single one of Lysippus' fifteen hundred statues ever reached the heirs of Helenian art. Only a few of them became known to the future generations, thanks to the Roman marble copies from Lysippus' bronze originals. Had she known that, Thais would have realized how little hope there was for preserving her silver statue, even though the bronze was more likely to be used for weapons of war by the future ignorant conquerors of Hellas, Asia Minor and Egypt.

Many people descended into the Amelet stream, the river of Rescue from Cares in the kingdom of Hades. So many changes, impressions, and so much turmoil took place over ten years. They swirled by like a storm from the moment Thais left Athens for Egypt and returned as queen.

Now, there were very few changes in her life. Time flowed slowly, like the Nile during winter. Was that the case for all who reigned without ruling? With the queens, whose husbands remained the true rulers? Thais realized Roxanne must have felt the same way with Alexander and probably felt even worse now that he was gone. Little Alexander, who was born two months after the death of the great army leader, was guarded like a talisman and a symbol of power – first, by Antipatros, the chief strategist of Hellas and Macedonia, and now, after his death, by Antigonus the One-eyed.

Aristotle died too, outliving his great student by only one year. Lyceum in Athens was now run by the scholar of plants, Theophrastus. There, serious students still walked among the splendid pine trees and chestnuts, having been allowed to obtain secret knowledge. The Athenians came in the evenings to listen to philosophic talks. In Ecbatana, Lysippus had told her about the birth of the new movement of stoics, who stated that all people were equal citizens of the world. They founded the first true system of evaluating one's behavior not based on one's faith in divine word, but on the importance of one's life to the society.

The priest interrupted her thoughts. "Would Your Majesty like to learn anything else?"

Thais was startled from her thoughts. They were approaching the Neit temple, where a worried Eris paced gracefully up and down the broad staircase.

"Tell me, Father, why did they show me the secret drawings of land and sea, but did not do it for Alexander or even for Nearchus?"

"We were not asked, and knowledge only goes to those who seek it. You are one of us, you are harmless and not powerful, because you do not seek power. A great genius, an army leader, or a ruler, regardless of his origins, has yet to bring happiness to people. The greater he is, the greater the trouble. People usually follow laws that are thousands of years old, having grown from the healthy experience of generations. They are connected by the necessity of life, faith and service to gods and power. A great man places himself above all things commonly human, destroying the foundations of existence, and making the eternal mistake of reducing his deeds to nothing thus plunging him into the abyss of Darkness. Godlike people only bring happiness when they have no power. People like philosophers, healers, poets or artists."

"Do you believe Alexander only brought suffering and misfortune?"

"His deeds have yet to be weighed on the scales of time, and the gods of destiny have yet to count the black and white sides of his life. My mind is too small to comprehend the enormity of his accomplishments. Initially he was given beauty and physical strength, a brave heart and a clear, all-encompassing mind, as well as knowledge. Then he obtained military strength: tough hearts and tempered bodies of Macedonian and Helenian soldiers. He wanted to multiply his knowledge but multiplied his wealth instead, having taken at once that which was stored over the centuries by a large people in a large country. Due to his youth, he gave away the treasures thoughtlessly, being neither greedy nor wasteful himself. He gave it into hands that were as unworthy as before. Except the prior owners kept it in their own country, and the new ones, having received it easily, spent it on trifles across strange countries, having enriched greedy and calculating merchants and sold for pennies the ancient works of art and tens of thousands of enslaved people. And so Alexander's forces fractured and lost any sense of purpose. The natural resistance of the people fighting against the intrusion into their native lands, brought forth savagery, cruel and bloody violence, the killing of the innocents that was offensive to the gods. Instead of studying the land and establishing peace, learning the common traits among the customs, beliefs and goals that unite all people of the world, endless circles of future power struggle emerged along with intrigue and misfortune. And here we are today, several years after the split of the empire. There is still bloodshed and war going on in Hellas, Ionia, Mesopotamia and on the islands of the Green Sea."

"Then why did it happen that way and not differently, Father?" Thais asked.

"It could not have been different, if he who has power, gold, and the will to alter fates of countries and people, does not understand that each part of his might has a reverse side. This reverse side will inevitably be presented to him by fate unless he is careful. For gold, the result is humiliation, envy, and struggle for wealth in the name of wealth. For power it is cruelty, violence, and murder. For will it is persistence in the use of power and gold and blindness."

"What can protect us from these evil forces?"

"Love, my daughter. All three of these powerful levers must be used with love and in the name of love toward people."

"Does not love have a reverse side?"

"Alas, but on a different, more personal level. Relationships between people can bring forth the desire to humiliate others, torture and drown them in mud. Light-filled hearts do not have this, but a member of the mob who has been beaten and humiliated either personally or through his ancestors and relations, can be subject to this."

"You did not tell me how to guard against this, Father."

"Always keep to the middle and keep an eye on the edges."

"Oh, I know. My teacher told me the same thing. Apparently wisdom universally arrives to the same conclusion."

"Have you read the inscription at the front of this temple?"

"I cannot read the sacred language and ancient writings of Egypt."

"Meden agan. Nothing superfluous. Moderation is the noblest thing. Ubris, or obnoxious arrogance, is the worst. Know the depths of your heart."

"The same is inscribed on the temple of Apollo in Delphi."

"That confirms what you said about universal wisdom."

"Then the face of higher wisdom turns toward people always and everywhere, bypassing the gods?"

"That is so, but be careful speaking such truths to the faithful of all kinds, both the childishly naïve ones and the fierce fanatics. Truth and kindness shine like torches, lighting the way for those lost in the dark. But one carrying a torch can stumble into a shed of oil that goes up in flames from the slightest spark."

Thais studied the old priest, then suddenly asked, "Tell me, are you not surprised that the Queen of Egypt does not read Egyptian?"

"No. Do you think many queens knew the sacred language? If so, you are mistaken. You have surpassed many, not just in beauty but also in the knowledge of different faiths. Faith is the soul of the people. It gives origin to customs, laws and people's behavior. You sing at the ceremony of the Mirror of Isis like a true Egyptian, dance the sacred Scarf Dance like a Finikian, ride a horse like a Libyan, and swim like a Nereid of the Green Sea. This draws to you everyone who inhabits the Black Land."

"How do you know?"

The old man chuckled.

"Tell me, Father, if I want to know more about the distant lands of Libya and Nubia, will you help me?"

"I shall," the old priest agreed without hesitation.

Thais started gathering all geographic information, descriptions of rare animals, gems and plants gathered in Egypt over four thousand years. Most discoveries had been made thirty and twenty centuries before by the envoys of the pharaohs of Upper Egypt, who chose Sienna and Elephantine as their residences. These brave and proud people called themselves "chief caravan leaders of the South" and "rulers of all that is and is not". The young queen particularly liked those titles. The "rulers" mapped a route on land into the depths of the mysterious continent, of which Helenians did not have a clear idea. Not even after Herodotus, although the seafarers of Crete knew more than he did.

The priest and the queen became friends. The people of Memphis came to know that Queen Thais liked to be alone in the evenings, so they never violated her solitude. The Athenian immersed herself into memories during the uncommonly quiet Nile evenings, when the twilight clothed all earthly things in transparent fabric without color or shadow. Thais stopped dreaming and frequently thought about the past. Perhaps it was the sign of approaching old age, with no more visions of the future, longing for things that could not be and desire for a new turn in life.

The observant Athenian could not help but notice the sharp division in the life of the Egyptian people and their rulers. Hellas was different because even during the age of tyranny people and their rulers stood together with common rituals, habits, and duties to the gods and spiritual life.

Egyptian people led their own existence, pitiful and colorless. The rulers made up a small group of the privileged, whose existence had no purpose or sense even to themselves, save for the struggle for power and wealth. When Ptolemy became king, matters did not change – at least not in the heart of Egypt. What was she for then, the Queen of Memphis? Was she to contribute to a bunch of parasites? After her initial enjoyment of the outward side of power faded, Thais began feeling ashamed of it all. She now understood why the monuments and temples fell to ruin, and pride and glory of the illustrious past were being covered with sand. The people, having lost their interest in life, and the nobles who did not understand the meaning of ancient beauty and did not care about anything but small private matters, certainly could not protect the great multitude of architectural and art treasures of Egypt which had accumulated over millennia.

Troubling thoughts tormented Thais. She secluded herself in the upper hall of the palace with its blue ceiling and pillars of black wood, with heavy drapes of pale gray fabric hanging between them, reminding her of the grooved columns of Persepolis palaces.

Harsh daylight reflected the blue ceiling in two enormous metallic mirrors. Thais stood before them, holding a round hand mirror with a handle in the shape of a lioness, and examined herself from head to toe.

Her strong body had lost the daring exaltation of youth, but remained flawless even now that Thais was over thirty-seven years of age and her two children were growing up. It had become stronger, broader, and acquired more pronounced curves but, much like her face, it had withstood life's trials. Years added some firmness to the outline of her lips and cheeks, but the neck, which is the weakest feature of any woman as she ages, still supported her head proudly, like a marble column skillfully colored by Nikias.

Mischief and a wild desire to do something forbidden still rose in Thais, making her head spin as much as it had during the distant Athenian days. She called Eris and the two of them slipped away from their guards and rode to the dessert. There they stripped off their clothes and galloped around wildly like two naked Amazons, singing Libyan battle hymns until the horses were covered in foam. Then they returned to the palace slowly and properly.

In order to make escape easier from the courtiers and the palace guards, Thais started keeping horses at the house of an old Nubian at the southern edge of the city.

Such rides and swimming in a pond protected from crocodiles were rare. Tired after some long Egyptian ceremony, Thais would spend time playing with her daughter, then spend her evening at the steps of the Neit temple.

The Egyptian girls slept peacefully, wrapped in a blanket. Eris rested her chin on her knees and froze with her eyes wide open. She could acquire a state akin to sleep without sacrificing her watchfulness.

Nikturos, the Nighttime Guardian, shone in the twilight with sinister leaden light, reminding Thais of her first visit to Egypt, when she had been captured to be sacrificed to Sebek and rescued by Menedem, the warrior of herculean courage.

Thais had considered erecting a monument to Egesikhora and Menedem here in Memphis, from where the river carried their ashes to the native seas. Then she changed her mind. The tombstone would have stood alien among thousands of monuments of other feelings and rituals of other faiths. Sculptures of Egesikhora and Menedem would have been as lonely as she was. And when Thais was gone, who would take care of the cenotaph? This was not Hellas, after all, where the beauty of sculptures was something with which people grew. There, it would not occur to anyone to harm a statue.

While the muse lovers in Memphis, especially Helenians, still remembered the gold-haired Spartan, who would know of Menedem, one of thousands of Laconian mercenaries? Thais set aside the idea of the monument. Instead, a beautiful marble frieze was carved in Alexandria and sent to Egesikhora's and Menedem's homeland. The appearance of the Night Guardian awoke the grief for those who were gone and vague anxiety in Thais' heart ...

A pleasant bit of news awaited her at the palace. Ptolemy had sent a gorgeous Frakian slave experienced in taking care of horses, and new tack for Boanergos made with stunning workmanship, decorated with red gold to match his color. As before, Ptolemy felt guilty before Thais and made unexpected and luxurious gifts.

In the morning the Athenian ordered the groom to saddle the pacer to show off his new tack. The slave brought out the black-maned horse in his sparkling harness with a skillfully minted piece over his forehead portraying two fighting panthers. Thais patted her equine favorite and kissed his warm nose between the sensitive nostrils. Boanergos neighed gently and rubbed his head against his mistress' bare shoulder, digging the ground impatiently and chomping at the bit.

Just as Thais was getting ready to mount, Irana's nanny ran in, screaming that the girl was sick. Tossing the reins to the handsome groom, the Athenian ran back to the palace and found her daughter sick in bed. The girl had run off into the garden and eaten green Persian apples after the nanny had given her some almond cookies.

The palace physician quickly got rid of the stomach ache. Having rubbed down and consoled her daughter, Thais remembered that the pacer was still waiting for her. She hoped he hadn't lost his patience and broken the fence. Would Eris remember to exercise the horse?

The maid she dispatched to the stables rushed in, accompanied by an old stable-hand. She fell to her knees before the queen and cried out that Boanergos had been poisoned and Eris had vanished with her horse.

The Athenian grabbed the old stableman by the shoulder. The thin fabric of his tunic crackled from the pull.

"I am not at fault, Majesty," the old man said with dignity. "The horse was poisoned by whoever made the golden tack. Sun of Egypt, go and see for yourself."

Thais remembered herself, dashed down the stairs and ran to the stables. She was dressed in a short ecsomida for riding instead of a long royal garment and managed to outrun everyone.

Boanergos lay on his left side, having stretched out his legs with his perfect black hooves. A strand of thick mane covered a glassy eye. A sinister shade of blue was spreading in the corner of his lips, stretched by convulsions.

Thais imagined that her faithful horse was looking at her with reproach, expecting her to rescue him. The Queen of Egypt fell to her knees in tears and reached out with both arms to lift the massive head. A strong yank from behind her kept her from touching the pacer. Thais turned around angrily, swift as a panther, and met Eris' dark gaze. Her friend was breathing heavily. Behind her a guard was holding the reins of her sweaty horse.

"Don't touch. The entire tack might be poisoned. The accursed slave handled it in gloves and I was stupid enough to imagine he was doing so to avoid staining the sparkling gold. Had you ridden out right away ... The Great Goddess is watching over you."

"Where is the scoundrel? Where is that murderer?"

"I noticed something wrong when he became anxious about your delay, glanced this way and that, and when Boanergos suddenly fell to his knees he ran away. I ran to the horse at first and did not call the guards right away. The disgusting creature managed to get away. They are looking for him."

Thais straightened out and wiped her tears. "I do not understand the sense in poisoning Boanergos and not me."

"That would be more difficult. Many people are responsible for your water and food."

"But what did my poor pacer have to do with this?"

"The poison had delayed action. You would have had just enough time to ride out and put some distance between you and the city. Boanergos would have fallen there."

"Do you think there was an ambush?"

Instead of answering, Eris took Thais' hand and led her to the gates. A circle of soldiers separated, their heads bowed, and Thais saw the bodies of two strangers - the Delta residents, judging by their clothes. Their distorted faces and swollen mouths indicated the cause of their deaths.

"Here is proof. We would have both dismounted to take care of the horse and these two had long daggers. I rode to our favorite spot behind the red obelisk with a group of soldiers. We surrounded them, but these hyenas managed to take poison. Whoever sent them was skilled in such matters and supplied everything to cover up the tracks. They knew the time and place of our rides. And here we thought we were riding in seclusion."

"But you do not think that …"

"Of course not. The courageous warrior, just ruler and lover of women, he is not capable of this. No, I sense the hand of someone experienced in court intrigues,. Possibly a woman."

Thais shuddered and clenched her fists. "Let us go to Boanergos."

Soldiers and stable-hands stood around the pacer, waiting for instructions.

"Put on gloves and take off the tack," Thais ordered. She turned to Eris. "If only I had time to think," she said bitterly. "Whoever sent this gift was careless. Do such people always consider themselves smarter than others?"

"What if it's proof to someone who feels he deserves a favor?" Eris asked.

"My wise goddess," the Athenian exclaimed, putting her arms around the black priestess. "Then this was probably not her either?"

Eris nodded in agreement.

"Not her, but someone who would benefit from her being a queen. 'Benefit' is a terrible word when it comes from someone who has power over others. So many underhanded deeds are done for that reason."

Thais made a decision. She turned to the men. "Wrap the tack in canvas, dip it in hot wax and sew it into thick leather. I shall apply my seal. Take my Boanergos to the red obelisk. Make him a grave at the edge of the plateau overlooking the valley. Call the stone carvers working on a new pylon for the Neit temple., I wish to speak with them. I also want to see the royal sculptor, Hab-Au."

Thais consulted with the craftsmen till evening, until she decided to erect a vertical slab at Boanergos' tomb with a bold outline of the pacer running toward the rising sun. The sculptor insisted he be permitted to portray the queen and all her sacred names. Thais forbade it and ordered only one inscription in Greek: "Boanergos, horse of Thais."

At the same time she asked Eris to gather all her favorite things, jewelry and clothes. She ordered all mementos from India and Mesopotamia to be placed in a separate treasury, entrusting the matter to the faithful Roykos. The Thessalian's family now consisted of seven people, including his second Finikian wife. Thais had long since picked up on the Macedonians' and Helenians' attraction toward the Finikian and slant-eyed Scythian women from the distant eastern mountains. Both made splendid wives: faithful, strong and caring hostesses.

Roykos' eldest son, who was learned in sciences, became a treasurer in Thais' house. He was ordered to count and gather all liquid cash, gold and valuables, of which there was much.

Having finished with business, Thais settled in an ivory chair.

"What are you thinking about, Mistress queen?" Eris said with uncommon gentleness, running her fingers through Thais' unraveled black braids.

Thais was silent.

"Has a queen ever abandoned her kingdom and left the country she ruled?" Eris asked. "Would that be a weakness, unsuitable for the elevated state and destiny?"

"If the queen does not rule then her position is imaginary," Thais replied, matching her tone. "Would it not be smarter to let someone else have this position? Someone who would not be imaginary?"

"In Memphis?"

"In Alexandria. There will be no more queens here, only the envoy who is already running everything. However, it is too soon to speak of it. I want to go to Ptolemy and discuss the circumstances with him."

"It has not been long since the king expressed his highest appreciation for your contribution here. The information you gathered about Nubia, Punt and Libya in general became a foundation for studying the geography of the entire country at the Alexandrian Museum. He also praised the boatmen of Queen Thais …"

The black priestess spoke of the groups of young people hired by Thais to serve in heavily populated areas along the Nile. Many small children living near the enormous river drowned or were killed by the crocodiles. Swift, light boats with green flags now sailed along the shores, always ready to assist children and animals. Thais was fond of both and they reciprocated with utmost trust.

Eris thought she heard a rustling among the garden shrubs. Putting out the lantern she peeked down.

A dark, windless night enveloped the small palace, which had been chosen by Thais to be her residence in the garden district of Memphis. Leaves did not move, dogs did not bark, only bats dashed around. Both friends could hear their barely audible peeps. Being able to hear the bats was a measurement of age among Helenians and Egyptians. When someone stopped hearing the bats, he turned the corner toward old age.

"I shall go and check the gallery," Eris whispered. "I am worried about that handsome slave who managed to escape."

"He wouldn't dare. Not after his accomplices perished," Thais objected.

"Possibly. Still, I'd like to check. Do not put on the light." Eris dissolved in the darkness.

The upper rooms of the palace were aligned along a gallery connected to the open veranda on the east and north sides of the house. The gallery was separated from the veranda by the sliding papyrus hangings, and from the rooms by blue translucent drapes stretched tightly between wood posts. Luminaries were lit along the northern gallery, lighting Thais' dark room with a semblance of moonlight.

Suddenly, a clear silhouette of a nearly nude man carrying a short stick appeared against the drapes. Thais rose noiselessly, reaching out for something suitable for defense, and picked up an onyx vase that weighed nearly a talant. A second shadow, Eris, appeared behind the first, pulling out her terrible dagger. The first shadow paused and listened. Thais approached slowly, raising the vase above her head. Eris paused as well. The man with the stick stood still, then whistled almost as quietly as a bat. A third shadow with a long knife appeared behind Eris.

All that followed took place almost instantaneously. The first man pulled out a knife from his loincloth and sliced through the drapes. The third shadow, seeing Thais, made a dull warning sound to his accomplice, but the latter had no time to turn around as he received a dagger through his left shoulder.

Thais shouted, "Look out!"

The black priestess turned around and the second assassin attacked her. The Athenian threw the onyx vase at the Frakian's familiar face as hard as she could. The murderer managed to throw his knife at the same time Thais threw the vase, and Eris fell at the feet of her victim in a pool of blood.

Guards and nearly all of her palace servants rushed in, having heard the queen's screams. Fortunately, after Ptolemy's insistence, the staff included a skilled physician.

A dozen luminaries were lit. Thais forbade taking Eris to her room. She was placed on the queen's bed. The first assassin was dead, but the second was still alive and tried to get up to his knees. Thais pulled out Eris' sacred dagger and rose it above him, but stopped.

"Shake him," she ordered the soldiers. "Perhaps he will regain his senses. Pour water on him. Get my interpreter."

The interpreter ran in. He spoke eight languages. Forgetting about him, the Athenian fell before her friend's bed while the physician worked quickly on the other side, trying to stop the bleeding. She took Eris' clammy hand and pressed it against her own cheek.

The black priestess' eyelids moved, her seemingly unseeing blue eyes opened, then filled with the light of consciousness. A smile touched her gray lips.

"Like a Helenian," Eris whispered, barely audible.

The queen's bitter scream made everyone in the room fall to their knees.

"Eris, my beloved friend, do not go! Do not leave me alone!"

Only then did she fully realize how precious to her was this melayna aymi ero, kai kale – black, but beautiful through and through, as Eris' friends called her. Eris was more dear than anything in the world, more dear than life itself, for life appeared impossible to Thais without the divinely strong, calm and intelligent friend.

All of the queen's associates respected Eris, despite her outward solemnity. She liked good people and good things, although she never insisted on gaining the friendship of the former or the possession of the latter. She had no false pride and never wished to humiliate others or demand special attention or honors for herself.

Unyielding simplicity, complete absence of unworthy desires and envy gave her strength to get through any challenge. Eris understood from the first glance the innate loveliness of events and objects that most people miss. Her incredible beauty had stopped being a weapon since she'd left the temple of Kibela-Gaea. While poets celebrated her and artists went to great lengths to get her as a model, the Athenian was often surprised how few people understood true meaning and the power of Eris' beautiful image. Compared to Thais, she appeared more mature. As if she possessed a deeper understanding of matters and things than other people. At times of merriment, Eris equaled the Athenian, who was still a girl at heart, fond of crazy and mischievous tricks.

This divine friend, sent to Thais by the Great Mother or Aphrodite, was departing from her into the dark kingdom. Thais felt as if her heart were also dying, that the shadows of the dead was gathering: Menedem, Egesikhora, Leontiscus, Alexander ...

Holding back sobs, Thais whispered a prayer to the three all-powerful goddesses, begging them to bring Eris back. As if in response to her plea, the blue eyes opened again, filled with the warm light of life.

"Do not, grieve, my friend, I shall wait."

Even in her perilous condition, Eris did not forget her promise to wait for Thais in Hades, in the fields of asphodels along the River, to cross it hand in hand with her friend.

Thais could no longer contain the desperate surge of grief. Roykos decided to send for the high priest of Neit, afraid that the queen would die of shock.

The old priest walked in, catching his breath, but never losing his majestic posture. He leaned over the unconscious Eris, took her hand and held it at length. He then touched the queen's shoulder. Thais lifted her grief-twisted face and met the calm, sad gaze of her friend.

"I think she will live," the priest said. Thais caught her breath, unable to speak a word. "I sent for our physicians to help your Helenian. I recall your mentioning the substance from the mountains near Persepolis. Do you still have it?"

"Yes, yes. I'll get it right away." Thais rushed for the chest where she kept the fantastic medicines of Mesopotamia, India and Bactriana.

The priest found a dark brown clamp which resembled tree resin, and handed it to the newly-arrived, middle-aged Egyptians wearing simple white robs. Modest but self-assured, they discussed something with the palace physician, crushed a piece of the medicine into some milk, and, unclenching Eris' teeth, made her drink it. Her wound was covered with a bunch of bluish herb with a strong strange scent, and it was firmly bound.

"Now Your Majesty must drink this," the priest said, handing Thais half a cup of a drink that looked like transparent, slightly glowing water. "Otherwise the shock you had sustained today may cost you dearly. Wounds of the heart must be treated immediately, for the consequences are distant and uncertain."

Thais took the cup, remembered something and set it aside.

"I thank you. I have one more thing to take care of. Call the interpreter. What can you tell me?" she asked the pale Finikian waiting for her at the gallery.

"Very little, Queen. The son of hyena only uttered a few words in Frakian. From them, we understood that four assassins were dispatched, which means we got them all. He spoke a name. I wrote it down for fear of a fateful mistake. Here," the interpreter handed a writing slate to Thais.

"It is a male name, sounds Ionian," the Athenian said after a pause.

"Your Majesty is correct," the interpreter said, then bowed.

"Where is the assassin?"

"The son of hyena went mad with pain. We killed him to stop the torture, unsuitable for a living being."

"You did well. I thank you."

Returning to the room, Thais listened to Eris' weak, even breath and addressed the old priest. "Now give me the medicine, my friend. I shall visit you soon, once Eris is out of danger, to ask important advice."

"I shall expect Your Majesty." The old man bowed. "And I shall be sad to part with you."

Thais shuddered, took the cup and downed it at once. One of the Egyptian healers, the Helenian physician, Roykos and his first wife stood watch at Eris' bed. Assured that Eris would be watched, Thais settled nearby on an additional bed that was brought in for her. Glittering spots flowed before her eyes as the Egyptian potion swiftly acted.

Three days later, Eris was able to sit up in bed. Smiling weakly, she said she had never been that close to the threshold of Hades. Strangely, she said death from loss of blood could be pleasant.

"You simply lose your strength and dissolve in the nothing. Had it not been for you, I would not have wanted to come back," Eris said, sighing.

"Are you unhappy with me?" the Athenian reproached her gently.

"Do not think that. It is just that the older you become, the more sadness you know from the understanding of life and its unstoppable flow. Once you take the step toward the Great Mother, you do not wish to return. Had it not been for you, I would not have."

Thais kissed her friend tenderly and her eyes filled with tears again. Eris wiped them off and told Thais she was sleepy.

The next day Thais wanted to go to the Neit temple on foot, but yielded to the black priestess and rode properly in a carriage under fans, accompanied by thirty horsemen. Six huge Nubians accompanied her up the stairs, keeping their hands on their swords and fighting sticks and peering around. Thais smiled inwardly. After eliminating the four assassins, there was no immediate danger, although she had ordered strong guards to remain around Eris' room.

Everything inside her was singing with joy. Eris was alive, fully able and recovering swiftly. Compared to her own mood, the high priest of Neit appeared thin, aged and sad to her.

"What is wrong, my friend?" Thais asked. "Perhaps you needs a healer's assistance? Or my brown medicine?"

"Hold on to the medicine. It has the great healing power of Gaea's sap, flowing from her stone breast. No. I am well. But I am sad because you decided to leave us."

"You will not judge me for this decision, will you? I made it final after Eris' wound. She and I are connected in both life and death. I cannot risk a friend who is always ready to offer her body to an assassin's strike in place of mine. I lost two beloved people here in Memphis and I would have died had I lost this one."

The old priest told the Athenian of an ancient prophecy about the last Queen of Memphis. The prophecy overlapped incredibly with her own sensibilities. He added the people's legends about Queen Thais. They said she came from another country, became an Egyptian and was able to absorb the spirit of the Black Land to a degree that the priests of Sais, who kept count of true kings of Egypt, decided to include her in their list by giving her an Egyptian name.

"What is it?"

"That is a secret. Ask them. You can stop by Sais on your way to Alexandria."

"I do not deserve this," Thais objected sadly. "Couldn't the Egyptians see that I only played a role someone handed down to me?"

"If an actress plays a role and awakens in people the memory of their past, noble feelings of the present and thoughts of the future, is she not a messenger of gods and a hand of destiny?"

"Then she is obligated to continue, even at the price of her life."

"No. All things predetermined end. The role ends when the forces of the dark western deserts threaten the theater itself. The spectacle will end tragically, causing fear and putting out the newly-born aspirations."

The Queen of Memphis suddenly knelt at the feet of the old Egyptian. "Thank you, my friend," she said. "Allow me to call you Father, for who else but a father could be a spiritual teacher of ignorant people? I am fortunate. Here, in your temple Memphis, I studied with the wise man from Delos, then with Lysippus and now, in my loneliness, I have found you here. Allow me to make a large sacrifice to Neit. I can also give a hundred bulls to Artemis for saving my friend."

"Only at the lowest level do people require bloody sacrifices to pacify the gods and destiny. That is because they place their gods at the same level as themselves or even with beasts of prey. It is a heritage of dark ages, a custom of barbarian hunters. Do not do this. It is better to give the money to some worthy cause. I shall accept a bloodless sacrifice so I may continue teaching true ways to young seekers of truth."

"What about Neit? Would a few people educated in true knowledge be more dear to the goddess than senseless animals roaring under the knife and drowning in blood?"

"Then why do we carry on with these rituals and sacrifices?"

The old man smiled weakly, glanced around and, once assured of the absence of strangers, said, "Stupid and self-centered philosophers of other faiths had often asked questions they considered blasphemous. If your god is so powerful, then why does he allow people to be stupid? If he is all-knowing, then why does he need temples, priests and rituals?"

"And the answer is?" Thais asked anxiously.

"A god occupied by people's affairs and acting like a human only exists in the imagination of people whose imagination runs shallow. He is needed at their level of faith, as one needs a place for concentration and prayer, as one needs the intermediaries, the priests. Millions of people still demand religion. Otherwise they lose all faith and, therefore their moral rules, without which states and cities cannot exist. That is why, while people are still ignorant, we protect ancient faiths, even after having rid ourselves of superstition and fallacy. Very few, even among wise rulers, know that people's morality, their upbringing in dignity and respect of their elders, labor and beauty are more important for the fate of people and countries. They are more important than siege machines, elephants, armored soldiers and multi-oar ships. All this falls when people's morality and upbringing diminishes. People great and small plunge themselves into drinking and savage revelry. Faith, honor and dignity drown in wine, the love of one's homeland and traditions of the forefathers fade away. Many kingdoms of Mesopotamia and Persia perished that way. The doom of Egypt approaches, as well as that of Hellas, Carthage, and the still-young Rome, menacing with its legions. The most important things upon which a man stands are not weapons or war, but morality and laws of behavior among one's own people and others."

"You said Hellas too, Father."

"Yes, Majesty. I am aware you are Helenian, but have you not noticed that the lower the morality and dignity among the people, the more the people try to prove their superiority over others by humiliating them? Even such great scholars as Aristotle have excelled in this lowly business. The poison had penetrated that far."

"Alexander had always opposed Aristotle," Thais objected.

"And I thank him for that. Do not rush to grieve. Even now the savage separation between people is giving way to the ideas of equality and unification."

"I know about the stoics, Father."

"There are more ancient teachers. You shall remember them when you have time to ponder."

"And our beautiful gods ..." the Athenian said.

The priest raised a hand in warning. "I am not touching your Olympians, who were alien to us before, although lately the beliefs of Hellas and Egypt have been converging in common deities. You must not touch them either. Understanding requires many years of thinking and working through old feelings. Hastiness would only lead to one thing: the loss of faith in a man's life and future. Be careful."

Thais kissed the old priest's hand and returned to the waiting carriage.

Preparations for her journey went unnoticed. Still, rumors spread about the queen's impending journey to her husband in Alexandria. Roykos' family, well established in Memphis, was leaving with Thais. They were leaving without regret because the head of the family and his first wife could not part with the mistress, and the Finikian was dying to get to the sea. Irana's nanny was coming too. She was a young, half-Helenian, half-Libyan who was sufficiently educated for the family. She was not a slave, but had become attached to the little girl and had eyes for Roykos' eldest son.

Prior to their departure, Thais took the still-weak Eris on a boat ride among the blooming lotuses. The boat glided noiselessly across a wide lake, rustling as it cut through copses of blue flowers and large thick leaves.

Once upon a time lotuses had bloomed here as she'd taken a boat ride with Menedem. Was her royal privilege: the luxurious gilded boat, the striped tent, the well-trained Nubian oarsmen better or more enjoyable? Never.

Young people always yearn for a more elevated status, unaware of the price they will pay. They have no idea that youth will eventually come to an end and the time will come when they would be willing to give up all they had acquired so they could return to the happy hours of their outwardly simple, but spiritually deep life and emotions of youth. Perhaps power and wealth would blind them and make them forget the past. That seemed to happen to many people. Just as well, if that made them happy. Presently there was no greater joy than to watch Eris' thin face livened by the surrounding beauty, and to listen to the happy chatter of little Irana. Thais' farewell to Egypt would remain beautiful in her memory.

Thais opted to leave at an early hour, to avoid too much notice, and kept the time of her departure secret. Regardless, a huge crowd of Memphis citizens showed up to see Thais off. They were genuinely sad and invited her to come back soon. Hundreds of wreaths made of sacred lotus flew into the water and onto the deck of her ship. Lotus was only allowed to be picked for such exceptional occasions.

The ship undocked quietly, water splashed, and houses, temples and pyramids sailed away. Thais would never see the strange ancient city again, though she had given it so much of her soul and so many years of her life. She would never come back to the philosophers' retreat, the Neit temple. It was ton eona again. Forever.

Chapter Seventeen.
Aphrodite Ambologera

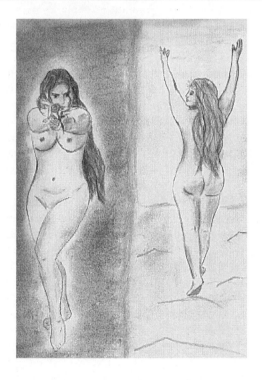

Alexandria impressed Thais with the speed with which it was growing. In the few years she'd spent in Memphis, the city had become larger than the ancient capital of Egypt. It had also acquired a beautiful pier filled with lively and noisy crowds every evening. Many ships were docked at the bay, and the foundation of the gigantic lighthouse at Pharos towered in the distance.

The city was not Egyptian. Thais did find many similarities with Athens, possibly intentional. There was even a wall similar to Ceramic which separated the Amaphontus district from the shanties of Racotis. It too was inscribed with invitations to famous hetaerae, much like in Athens, Corinth and Clazomene. Ptolemy constructed the Museum and the Library more rapidly than had did the other structures, and the two towered over the roofs, attracting the eye with the whiteness of their stone and the majestic simplicity of architecture. Palms, cedars, cypresses and sycamores rose in the gardens and around houses, rosebushes filled the slopes of the elevated portion of the city.

The most beautiful thing was the dazzling blue sea. Fatigue from the monotony of the past few years and anxiety for the uncertain future dissolved in the vastness of its waves. Thais would never part from the sea again.

Holding back her desire to dive into the greenish water near the shore, she walked away from the sea, heading toward the hill with Alexander's tomb. Thais took off all symbols of royal distinction, and yet passersby still turned to look at the small woman with the unusually smooth and clear face. Her regular features were surprising even here in the land where chiseled, beautiful faces of ancient people of the East and Hellas were commonplace. Something in the way she walked, her coppery tan, the depth of her enormous eyes and the figure outlined through the chiton of the finest Egyptian linen caused strangers to follow her with their eyes. Roykos limped a few steps behind her, shoulder to shoulder with his eldest son, armed and watchful, having sworn to Eris that he would keep an eye on Thais.

Much as she had several years ago, the Athenian approached the manmade hill of sea pebbles, held together with lime and tiled with gray Siena granite. The guard consisted of decearchos and one lokhagos, and was located in a portico made of massive slabs. The bronze doors could withstand a strike of the mightiest siege machine. During the previous visit, Ptolemy had shown Thais a clever mechanism built to protect the tomb. One only had to knock out specific supports and a mass of pebbles would crash down from above, concealing the tomb. It would only take one night to pour in lime and egg solution and cover it up with stone tiles prepared in advance.

Thais showed the lokhagos a signet ring with the royal seal and he bowed to her. Ten soldiers opened the bronze doors and lit the lanterns. The familiar golden sarcophagus decorated with bas-reliefs stood in the center of the tomb. As before, her heart filled with sadness. She took the jug of black wine and a vessel of precious oil brought by Roykos, made an offering to the shadow of the great army leader, then paused in a strange kind of stasis akin to sleep.

She heard the rustling of wings of swiftly flying birds, she heard the splashing of waves and dull thunder as if from the distant hoofbeats of a thousand horses. In these ghostly sounds, Thais imagined she could hear Alexander's powerful voice in her heart, saying a single word: "Return."

Return where? To the native shores of Hellas, to Memphis? Or here to Alexandria? The gold of the sarcophagus responded coolly to her touch and she found she could not focus on the past. She glanced one last time at the golden figures of the bas-reliefs, left and descended the hill, never looking black. The feeling of freedom she had first experienced at the Eridu temple had firmly established itself in her mind. She had completed the last thing that that filled her with a sense of incompleteness.

Thais returned to the white house under the cedars. She had received the house from Ptolemy after she had refused to stay at the palace. In full royal regalia, Thais and Eris rode in a carriage toward Ptolemy's majestic palace. The first thing Thais demanded was a face to face meeting. The king, who was preparing a grand welcome and a feast for her, obliged reluctantly. However, when a Nubian slave brought in and opened the leather package with the gold tack, Ptolemy forgot his displeasure.

"This is a gift delivered to me in your name by a young Frakian slave," Thais said.

"I never sent it, although I do enjoy things with such exceptional workmanship."

"And these two fighting panthers tell you nothing?"

Ptolemy, sensing Thais' seriousness, still tried to laugh it off. "Perhaps it was sent by one of your countless admirers."

"Perhaps. Maybe one who wished me dead."

Ptolemy jumped up in anger.

Thais continued. "Order this to be taken to the learned physicians of the Museum to determine the nature of the poison from which Boanergos fell. It was because of this that my own life was pushed to the edge of the Tartar. I would have been there a long time ago, had it not been for her," the Athenian said, pointing at Eris.

"In my name?" Ptolemy roared. His mighty voice resonated through the entire palace. Soldiers ran in, their weapons clanging.

"Do not be angry in vain. Neither Eris nor I suspected you for a moment. But this was sent by a man from your inner circle, there is no doubt about it."

"It cannot be!"

"Think about it. Look at the panthers, my wise Ptolemy. One more thing: you appointed Berenice's son as your heir, and not your eldest son, Ptolemy the Lightning. And not my Leontiscus. I thank you for doing that. The boy will not die at the hands of assassins. But Lightning Ptolemy's mother is now gone to the kingdom of Hades, and I am still alive and ruling."

"Berenice?" Ptolemy's voice broke, as if he had received a mortal wound.

"No," Thais said with certainty, bringing him back to life. She handed him a tablet bearing the name. "Here."

Ptolemy shrugged.

"Ask Berenice. I think she will recognize the name, although she may not be associated with this ghastly deed."

Ptolemy left in a rage and returned in a few minutes, dragging the disheveled Berenice, who must have been getting ready for the feast. Her delicate face was deathly pale and twisted with fear, and her black eyes darted between Thais and her husband.

"Do you know him?" Ptolemy snatched the fateful tablet from Thais.

Berenice read it and fell at his feet. "My cousin on my mother's side. But I swear by the Styx and the gloom of Amenti -"

"Do not swear, Majesty." Berenice froze, hearing the way Thais uttered the title. "We know of your innocence."

The Athenian pulled up Berenice and the latter, while taller, suddenly seemed small before the Queen of Memphis.

"I shall order the rascal apprehended at once," Ptolemy shouted and struck a metal disk.

"You shouldn't. He was certain to escape as soon as he received word about the failure of his attempt. But you must remember him, Majesty," Thais said almost menacingly. She stepped away from Berenice, sending away the servants with an imperious gesture. "I am calling off the feast. Today I shall speak alone with my husband."

Ptolemy did not dare disagree.

They talked till dawn, having settled Eris in one of the adjoining rooms. No one knew of what the king and the queen spoke. At dawn, Thais placed the sacred uraeus before Ptolemy, took off the colorful royal beads and Egyptian garments, and put on her favorite yellow ecsomida and the gryph talon necklace.

A view of the limitless sea, tinged with the rosy gaze of Eos, greeted them from the enormous palace terrace.

Ptolemy himself brought crimson wine from the Cretan vineyards and poured two delicate goblets, carved from mountain crystal during the rule of the first pharaohs of Egypt.

"Geliaine, Majesty! May the gods of Hellas, Egypt and Asia protect you in all your glorious deeds as a builder and collector." Thais raised her goblet, splashed in the direction of the sea and drank.

"When you say that you are tearing away a portion of my heart," Ptolemy said. "I am pained to part with you."

Smiling mischievously, the Athenian tapped the wine vessel, which had been made of the horn of an Indian unicorn beast of fantastic value. "Do you drink only from this one, being afraid of poison?"

Ptolemy blushed slightly and did not answer.

"You have come of age. It is time to choose only one queen. And you have done so. What is there to be sorry about?"

"The glorious past is unforgettable, when I accompanied Alexander. You were with us in Mesopotamia."

"It is unforgettable but you cannot live in the past. When will the ship be ready?"

"I ordered a sturdy ship to be prepared along with a strong guard. You may sail in two or three days, only tell the navigator where to go."

"To Cyprus, to Pathos."

"I thought you were returning to Athens."

"Conquered by the late Antipatros, with Munikhia locked up by Macedonians, and with the fresh grave of Demosthenes who poisoned himself? No, until you,

Cassander, Seleucus and Lysimachus end the war against Antigonus, I am not going there. I am sure you are aware that Cassander's officer in Argos burned five hundred people alive, and in response Antigonus' strategist completely decimated the sacred Corinth?"

"Such is war."

"It is a war of savages. Both soldiers and officers must be barbarians if they allow themselves to do in Hellas what foreign invaders did not dare. If things continue this way, I do not expect anything good for Hellas."

Ptolemy watched Thais and listened carefully to her.

"You speak the same way as the new philosophers who recently appeared at the Museum. They call themselves stoics."

"I know of them. They are attempting to find the new kind of morality, originating from the equality of all people. Best of luck to them."

"There will be no luck! Roman state grows in the west, ready to reduce the entire world to slavery. For some reason they particularly despise the Hebrews. Romans imitate Helenians in the arts, but in their essence they are malevolent. They rely solely on military force and are cruel toward children, women and animals. Instead of theaters they have enormous circuses where they slaughter animals and each other to amuse a roaring mob."

"Are they skilled at bloody sacrifices?" Thais asked.

"Yes. How did you know?"

"I know of a prophecy. Countries like Hellas, Rome, and Carthage, where people offer bloody sacrifices, placing their gods at the same level as beasts of prey, are headed toward swift demise, the destruction of all they have created, and the complete disappearance of these people."

"I must tell this to my philosophers. Would you like to meet with them at the Museum?"

"No. I have little time. I would like to see Leontiscus."

"He is sailing near the shores of Libya, but I had guessed your wish yesterday and sent a fast ship."

"The advantage of being a king's son. I thank you once more for your decision to make him a simple sailor and not an heir, an envoy or some other kind of ruler. He is much like me and is not suited for that role."

"You gave him your Cretan blood and the limitless love of the sea. What do you wish for Irenion?"

"I want her fostered with Pentanassa, a friend of mine from an ancient family, whose names are inscribed on the monuments of Cyprus. I want to make her into a good wife. She possesses your common sense, caution in all matters and, I think, your foresight. The separation of Alexander's empire and your choice of Egypt still serve as the best examples of your wisdom as a statesman."

"I chose Egypt for another reason. Here I am a king of a multitude of strange people and create a new state as I see fit, selecting the most suitable people to bring to power. Those whose wellbeing is connected with my rule will serve to protect me at the time of trouble. There will be no more insufferable envy, backstabbing, squabbling or competition between powerful but ignorant people from ancient families, of the kind that kept Hellas from blossoming as it could have, with such great people. Its best citizens were always subject to slander and shame. The nobles expressed their gratitude toward the most outstanding people by executing them, sending them into exile, betraying and imprisoning them. Remember Pericles, Phidias, Socrates, Plato, Themistocles, Demosthenes. One more cup to our farewell." Ptolemy raised the crystal goblet and suddenly stopped. "I have nothing to reproach you for after all these years, except one thing. Would you like to know what it is?"

Thais nodded.

"How could you allow the silver Anadiomena to be sold away? Did you not know how much I love you, and the beauty of women, and everything connected with you?"

"I did not allow anything. Such was its destiny. Lysippus intended the statue for Alexander, but at first the king had no time. Then he was gone. At that point, you had no time for sculptures. But I am glad that the Anadiomena went to India. They have a special attitude toward feminine beauty, and with the current state of affairs in Hellas I am not at all certain about the safety of a statue made of silver, even if it were placed in a temple."

"Very well, you are right. I retract my criticism. Incidentally, when Seleucus was hiding out here, he told me about his plans for another Indian campaign. I advised him to reconsider and give up his part of India to Chandragupta. He said he would if the latter gave him five hundred elephants."

"He is sweet, that giant and collector of giants."

"He is not that sweet from the male standpoint. Elephants are a powerful military force, fairly mobile and better than a phalanx or heavy cavalry. There is a reason why Seleucus is collecting elephants for his army. He and I are friends, but will his heir be friends with my heirs? In order to counterbalance his elephants, I will have to acquire some of my own. India is inaccessible to me, which is why I will have to get elephants from Libya. That is where the information you collected about southern routes is particularly valuable, especially that of the voyages to the Punt. I have already ordered ships to be prepared so that we may sail across the Eritrean Sea to the Cape of Fragrances and beyond, from where Egyptians brought various rare animals. Libyan elephants are different from those in India. They have bigger ears, huge tusks and sloping backs, and are more savage and difficult to tame. However, they are even better for waging war because they are mean-spirited and courageous. Are the twists of fate not amusing? You helped Seleucus to get his elephants with your statue and helped me even more to discover where to get them. I thank you again."

"It is daytime," Thais reminded the king. "Berenice must be in agony by now, and it is time for me to go."

Ptolemy and Thais poured some wine for the gods, embraced and kissed like brother and sister. The Athenian woke up Eris, who had fallen asleep to the soothing splash of a fountain. They walked to their house, still inspiring as much delight in the passersby as they had many years before. No one would have given the forty-year-old Thais and thirty-five-year-old black priestess more than fifty years between the two of them.

"If only you know how easy it is to move in the ecsomida," Thais exclaimed. "And I don't have to watch my gestures, words or facial expressions for fear of alarming my subjects. I do not have any more subjects and owe nothing. I can sing, even though I haven't done it in such a long time I may have lost my voice."

"You will always have one subject," Eris said, laughing. She bowed in a subservient Asian fashion.

The Athenian stopped and looked at her friend. Eris raised her eyebrows in puzzlement.

"You have reminded me of one important bit of business. I almost forgot."

"What business?"

"You'll see. I know it is useless teasing you with riddles. It is just that I haven't finished thinking it over yet."

Tired after being up all night, Thais gladly succumbed to a bath and powerful Ionian massage. She slept all day till evening and spent half the night on the terrace, pondering her meeting with her son. Leontiscus was almost fifteen years old, close to the age of an epheb.

Thais decided to combine the meeting with her son and the meeting with the sea. They would go to Pharos, where Nearchus had shown her Cretan ruins surrounded by brush and sand. There she used to dive among the splashing waves and crying seagulls near the deserted shore. This time she would take Eris with her. She was uncertain about her friend's attitude toward the sea. It would be sad if she treated it differently from how Thais herself treated it. Many people were alarmed by the sea, made sick or were simply frightened by it.

The Athenian worried in vain. The day turned out to be a true celebration for her. The swanlike white boat cut through the blue waves which gently rocked the small vessel. Leontiscus was as slender as his mother, with the same gray eyes and copper tan as Thais, and with fuzz already growing over his upper lip. The boy watched her with delighted eyes all the way to the northern shore of Pharos. A portion of the shoreline was already dressed in carefully fitted stone, set atop the giant boulders of the old Cretan bay. Leaving the boat near the western dock, Thais, along with Leontiscus and Eris, walked to the distant edge of the pier. Water splashed near the steep wall. Imitating Alexander, she poured a mix of wine and fragrant oil into the sea and told Leontiscus to toss a gold medallion as far as possible.

"And now let us surrender to Thetis," she yelled happily.

Leontiscus was unashamed of nudity, much like his mother. The boy undressed and dove in. Rolling waves shattered into small swift splashes as they reached the island.

"Come on, Mother!" Leontiscus called, swimming powerfully into the sea, where the waves came slower and more menacing, bubbling up in heavy walls. A pod of dolphins showed their sharp fins and black backs as they approached the swimmers. Holding her breath, Thais slipped into the dense water. Finally! She even forgot about Eris for a few moments.

"Eris, dear, swim here," Thais shouted, and was startled by the lightning speed with which the black priestess dove into the sea. The Athenian knew that Eris swam, though reluctantly, without the overwhelming joy Thais herself experienced in the water. But there was Eris with her battle cry, "Euryale! Euryale and Eris!" She swam fast enough to catch up with Leontiscus and was not at all afraid of the dull menacing hum with which the waves rose and fell in the open sea.

"Holy Mother of Gods! It is so easy to swim in this dense water. There is no darkness of the swamp, as you would see in a river or a lake. The sea holds you up," Eris said happily.

Wind flew in from the east, put out the glittering mirrors on the slopes of the waves, and pressed down the sharp peaks of foam. Thais felt as if invisible Nereids surrounded them, slapping them lightly over neck and shoulders, playfully splashing their faces and smoothing them over with gentle hands. She told Leontiscus about it, and was again surprised by the boy's gaze. It followed her carefully and constantly.

Eris soon became tired, as she had not yet fully restored her strength. Thais and Leontiscus dove endlessly, descending into the depths, swimming and tumbling like the dolphins that raced side by side with them, peering with their small friendly eyes and smiling with their black and white mouths.

Mother and son finally became tired and climbed onto the smooth granite tiles. Eris doused her friend with fresh water, washed off the salt and helped brush out her black braids. Leontiscus dried himself off, then approached his mother shyly and settled at her feet, putting his arms around her strong knees.

"Tell me the truth, Mother. Are you a goddess?"

Meeting the pleading gaze of his clear gray eyes, Thais shook her head in denial.

"But you are not a mere mortal, are you? You are a Nereid or a nymph who descended to my father. I heard the servants whispering about it at the palace. Do not deny my question, Mother, tell me. I only want to know."

The boy's arms, strengthened from working with oars and sails, tightened around his mother's knees. His earnest faith made Thais' heart falter and she remembered Alexander. A single hint dropped by his mother had given him the necessary confidence. At the same time, her usual truthfulness stood against the deception.

"You are right, my boy," Eris said suddenly. "Your mother is not a mere mortal, but she is not a goddess, either."

"I knew it. You are one of the daughters of Thetis from a mortal man. And this sash with the star that you wear. Is that a mark of the curse of mortality? Like Hyppolita's sash?"

"Yes. I am not immortal - and I do not possess the goddess power to give you miraculous strength or invincibility in battle," the Athenian rushed to add. "But I have given you the love of the sea. Thetis will always be merciful to you."

"Mother, dear Mother! That is why you are so inhumanly beautiful. Being your son is such joy! I thank you," Leontiscus covered Thais' knees and hands with kisses.

She pulled him up and patted his curly dark hair. "Go get dressed. It is time to go!"

The boy's face filled with sadness. "Can you not take me with you? We would be so happy together!"

"I cannot, Leontiscus," Thais said, feeling a lump in her throat. "You must be with your father, not your mother. You are a man, a sailor. Conquer the sea to bring joy, not demise to people. Thetis and I shall always be with you."

Leontiscus turned away and went to retrieve his clothes. A moment longer, and he would have seen his mother cry.

Their seaside expedition seemed to have caused Leontiscus to grow up. On their way back he held his head higher, his face bearing the distinctive Cretan features. As the boat approached the dock, the boy touched his mother's arm and whispered, pointing at Eris. "Is she also?"

"Even more than I am," Thais replied in a whisper.

Leontiscus took the black priestess' hand, pressed it to his forehead and his cheek and kissed the palm. Astonished, Eris kissed both his cheeks, a favor she had never bestowed upon anyone. Thais thought how good it would have been for the boy to have a friend like that nearby.

Not being a goddess, she could not have known, that five years later Ptolemy would be utterly defeated during the great sea battle of Salamis, near the Famagusta Bay at the eastern shore of Cyprus, and that Leontiscus would be taken prisoner. Fortunately, the noble victor and the Athenian favorite, Demetrius Poliorcetus, would soon return the son to his father and would be, in turn, defeated by him shortly after. The monument honoring Demetrius' victory, the statue of the winged Nika at the Samotrakia island, would delight people the world over for thousands of years.

The sea, as if celebrating the return of its daughter, carried Thais' ship Circe swiftly and calmly to the northeast, from Alexandria toward the island of Cyprus. The Athenian thought about her prior sea voyages. Each one had been blessed by particularly good weather. How could she not believe in the mercy of Thetis?

"They say there are fifty Egyptian skhens from Pathos to Cyprus," said the captain, who was the most experienced navigator from Astypalaya. "But I measured more – two thousand and eighty stadiums."

"How can you measure the sea?" Eris asked in astonishment.

"There are several methods, but I use the simplest one," the captain said. He squinted, peering into the distance. "The weather is good and the sea is calm, so you can see for yourself."

The captain ordered two middle-aged sailors to come on deck, one with an enormous bow and a coil of thin rope, and the other with a sea clepsydra that was known for being exceptionally steady. Held by a wide sash, the sailor with the bow hung over the water, his feet planted against the ship's side. He shot an arrow with the length of rope marked by brightly colored fish bladders. The first two times the rope settled poorly, but on the third try it flew in a straight line. As soon as the ship's bow reached the starting point of the rope, the navigator struck a copper gong and the second sailor started the clepsydra. The second strike sounded when the ship's stern passed the end of the rope.

"Drop count?" the navigator shouted.

"Thirty-one," was the answer.

"See," the captain explained to Eris. "The rope is half a stadium long and lays straight thanks to the skill of my sailors. The ship ran its length in thirty-one heartbeats or the drops of clepsydra. One must make a correction for waves and the deflection of the rope. I would say our Circe is doing approximately sixty stadiums per hour. This is a good speed under medium sails and without oars. One must make many measurements in order to calculate the distance correctly. You can calculate how much time it would take to reach Pathos, but do it silently. Do not anger the Old Man of the Sea."

The navigator picked the time when ethesies, summer winds blowing toward Egypt, changed direction for a brief time and caused the waves to travel from the northwest. The sea grew darker, taking on the color of Khios wine, with Poseidon's white-maned horses rushing across its dusky vastness. The strong wind tore the foam off the waves, carrying the glittering bubbles across the cloudless sky. Every Helenian was used to seeing the sea in that state, and the strength of the wind did not bother the seamen. They knew it would weaken by evening and there would be no terrible storm.

Thais and Eris settled at the bow and sang all kinds of songs, accompanying themselves on systra and sitar. They sang sad and melodious Helenian tunes, long and mournful Persian ones, abrupt and dissonant Finikian and Egyptian ones. They sang the songs of Libyan pirates accompanied by wild shouts and whistles, much to the delight of the sailors and the ire of the navigator, because they caused the seamen to lose their concentration.

Thais secluded herself for games and conversations with her daughter in a spot between the second deck level at the stern and the side of the ship, protected from wind and waves by reed baskets. During one such heart to heart conversation the little Irana stunned Thais by telling her about the dream she had had of becoming a hetaera. With the childish naïveté, Irana spoke of rich presents the hetaerae receive, of feasts with music and dancing, of being worshiped by men.

The more her mother frowned and the broader Eris smiled, the more eloquently the girl attempted to prove her point. She plunged into glorifying men's kisses and tender embraces.

An enraged Thais realized whose words the girl was repeating, but held back her anger and explained patiently to her daughter that she had been told nothing but fairy tales. In real life, no matter what one did, especially for a woman, nothing happened easily or effortlessly.

"We women are not given that many paths by the gods," she told her daughter quietly, smoothing her straight brown hair and looking into her serious brown eyes. "That is why each path must be selected thoroughly. One must know and weigh each of her abilities granted by the gods, and the possibilities for improvement.

"The path of hetaera is one of the most difficult ones out there. It is akin to the path of an artist, a musician or an architect. What man would be so stupid as to become a musician without a sense of pitch? Young girls often think that the youthful charm, melodious laughter and graceful walk are sufficient for achieving success. That is not true. After a year or two she would end up leading a lowly existence in drunken trysts with crass, beast-like strangers in the slums. Even if you possess a perfect body, a beautiful face, splendid hair and some ability as a singer and a dancer, all that is only sufficient for a slave actress, who is often subject to beatings by the theater owner.

"In order to become an outstanding hetaera, in addition to beauty and grace you must possess an outstanding memory, read in three dialects, love and know history, remember the foundations of philosophic teachings. Then you would be able to talk with poets and philosophers as an equal and elevate yourself above less educated men. And even that is not enough. You must have flawless taste in clothes, understand the art of sculpture and painting, perhaps even draw or sculpt yourself. You must be able to understand people's character from the first glance, rule men without forcing them, and be a hostess of symposiums. You also must be an athlete in a sport in which you can compete with men. For instance, I am considered a good rider and an even better swimmer. I can hold my own against any man. I am not even talking about possessing the stamina of a Spartan, the wine tolerance of a barbarian, or the health of a Cretan bull.

"If you, possessing the beginnings of all of the above, go through the Corinth school from the age of six to thirteen, those years would be watered by the tears of insults, trials, hard work and punishment. If you completed that, then you would become a truly famous hetaera. That is, if you are fortunate. If you do not become sick, and if your beauty does not fade prematurely."

Thais reclined in the wicker armchair and closed her eyes as if tired by the memories. Irana grew silent, snuggled up to her mother and said, "I understand, Mother. I do not wish to be a hetaera anymore."

"You are clever and cautious, daughter of a king, famous for his careful wisdom. Go take a nap. It's growing hot. And send your nanny over."

As soon as the girl left, Thais jumped up and paced up and down the deck. Eris embraced her, being familiar with her friend's moods.

"Nothing has happened, it's just that the nanny is ready for marriage and tells the nonsense that fills her head to Irana."

"I must not have spent enough time with my daughter, if -"

"Then it is your fault and not the nanny's." Eris smiled.

Thais stomped her foot and laughed. "You are right. But I'll show her a hetaera's glorious life."

"Isn't it a bit too late to flaunt your royal ire? This too is your fault, to be honest."

"How is this my fault, oh goddess of justice?"

"You missed that the nanny is a grown woman. It is time, or else she will waste herself away in empty yearnings, and her firm breasts will sag without love. Whose fault is it? It is the fault of she who is older and wiser. She lives with you, and you must be a mother to her."

"These educated girls from good families are nothing but trouble. They read too much."

"She has probably read some of your own adventures. Many books have been written about Alexander and his associates."

The nanny rushed in. She was a buxom girl with dreamy dark eyes and long eyelashes.

"Call Roykos! Tell him to bring a piece of rope."

The old Thessalian showed up and looked at Thais expectantly.

"Undress!" the Athenian ordered the nanny, who stared at her mistress in amazement.

Eris, hiding a smile, tugged on the clasps of the girl's chiton. Like a true Helenian, she wore nothing but outer clothing. Thais touched the girl's breast, shook her head and asked, "Did you use the juice of cikuta? How long?"

"A year and seven months in Puanepsion," the nanny mumbled.

"Crazy girl! You should have asked me. Now they will remain rock hard."

"So be it," the girl said boldly.

"Is the juice of cikuta that miraculous?" Eris inquired.

Thais nodded. "If one's breasts are small it makes them grow and firms them up forever. But one must use strict moderation and our silly girl here has overdone it, I think."

"Your fault again," Eris said sternly. "A mistress must sometimes be a mother."

"Yes, my fair friend, you are correct," Thais said, critically examining the nanny's voluptuous body.

"Majesty ... Mistress ... I do not know what ..."

"Oh yes, you do," Thais interrupted, trying to maintain the necessary sternness in her voice. "You are infatuated by love and want to be a hetaera, and fill my little girl's head with your nonsense."

"Mistress, I only told her what I'd read."

"You lie. You have added your own fantasies as well. I shall fulfill them. Go to the sailors' quarters as you are. You shall please them till the end of our voyage. This will be the start of your service to Aphrodite. The seamen are lonely for women. Their kisses are firm, their bodies are strong and their arms are tireless. What more can you wish for?"

"Majesty!"

"I forbade you to mention my title. Forget it."

"Mistress, have mercy! I did not think ... did not want ..."

"You do not want to serve Aphrodite by giving your maidenhead to the ship's crew? Then you must have confused my daughter out of malice. Your words were deceitful and you must be sacrificed to the Old Man of the Sea."

Thais ordered the Thessalian with a discreet wink. "Roykos! Tie her arms and legs and toss her into the sea."

"Uncle Roykos! You wouldn't!" the girl screamed.

"Yes I will. Hold out your hands," the old soldier replied, giving her a frightening grimace.

The girl fell at Thais' feet, shaking and crying.

"Enough. Game over." Thais suddenly laughed. "Get up. Now you shall think ten times before telling something to Irana."

"Oh, Mistress, were you joking? You are not angry?"

"I am angry! But I cannot stand to torture you any longer. Or him," she said, pointing at the corner of the deck where Roykos' eldest son stood as pale as chalk, ready to rush to the rescue.

"May I go?" the girl asked as she leaned to pick up her chiton.

"Go! Here is something to remember." Thais slapped the nanny's behind so hard the imprints of her fingers flushed red on her skin, and the girl squealed.

Eris gave her another smack and a shove. The girl rushed to the quarters designated for women.

"Well, don't just stand there," Thais said to Roykos' son. "Be a man. Go console her."

The young man vanished in an instant.

"You struck her to tears," Eris reproached.

"I don't know about that," Thais replied, blowing on her fingers. "What a sturdy girl. And now, my dear Eris, let us take care of you."

"You rule today, oh lioness," Eris joked, glancing at her friend with a touch of alarm.

"You shall be the one to turn into a lioness," Thais promised and took her friend to her own quarters which had direct access to the bridge instead of the stern, as did the room designated for the other women.

"Stand in front of me and hold the mirror. No, not like that. Turn it toward yourself. Close your eyes."

Eris obeyed, knowing Thais' fondness for unexpected and amusing tricks.

Thais took out a carefully hidden box of ornate silver and uncovered a diadem in the shape of two snakes woven from green gold wire. The reptiles' heads were broad, akin to the serpent at the Eridu temple. They crisscrossed and each held a sardonyx bead in its mouth, striped black and white. The Athenian placed the diadem on Eris' head. It fit perfectly, which was not surprising considering it was made in three days by the best jewelers of Alexandria based on Thais' design. Instead of a traditional diadem or stephane, the piece looked like the crown of an Ethiopian princess.

"Now look."

Eris could not suppress an exclamation of surprise.

Thais beamed, pleased with herself. "I had them make the eyes out of sapphires to match yours, instead of rubies like on the amulets of Hebrew beauties," Thais said. The diadem did indeed go well with her friend's black hair and dark bronze skin.

"Is this for me? What for?"

"I thought about it while we were still in Alexandria but did not tell you. We are traveling to the lands where people with your skin color arrive either as slaves or as high royalty. So in order to keep from being mistaken for a slave, you shall wear a piece of jewelry suitable only for those of elevated status. Remember it and walk like a princess. As for your barbaric necklace made of the poison snake teeth ..."

"I will not take it off. It is a sign of distinction more precious than any other."

"Very well, but wear this over it," Thais took a sky blue beryl necklace from the box and fastened it around Eris' neck.

"You are giving me the gift of the high priestess of Kibela?" Eris exclaimed.

"As long as you wear it, no one will question your status. This truly is a royal gift."

They finally approached Cyprus. The Athenian pressed her hands to her chest, a sign of particular anxiety. The ship was approaching a native corner of the Inner Sea, still remote but similar to other islands of Hellas. After so many years spent in other countries, it was time to reunite with her homeland. The peak of Trident Olympus, which was usually hidden in the clouds, revealed itself clearly above the blue mist of forest-covered mountains. On Thais' orders, the captain did not take the ship to the crowded Pathos, but went around the Northern cape and entered the Golden Lagoon, where the Athenian's friends owned some property.

Luminous air and turquoise waters of the lagoon which cut into the purple hills like an amphitheater made Thais feel as if she were back in Attica. The stone pier ran adjacent to the white road leading up the mountain, whose terraces housed small homes painted with pink clay and overshadowed by cypresses, sycamores and sprawling pines. A pure stream fell from above, flowing into a flat pool on the shore and scattering into small droplets. Beyond the houses were bands of the dark greenery of myrtles, covered with white flowers, a sign of the hottest portion of summer. The incomparable aroma of the seashore on a sunny summer day awoke childhood memories of her life spent in a small Attica village under the gentle watch of her parents. Thais sent the ship back with a note of gratitude to Ptolemy and immersed herself into her childhood.

Every day she took Irana, her nanny, and Eris to the west side of the bay, protected by a long cape that slithered into the sea like a dragon's spine. They swam till they dropped, climbed the rocks, chewed their favorite sweet brown figs and shot at each other using their hard, metallic-looking seeds.

Thais' friends turned out to have an entire gaggle of girls aged eight to twelve, their own daughters and nieces as well as the children of their servants and slaves. Following old traditions they all played together. They ran around playing tag, wove wreaths, and danced with abandon, wrapped in flower garlands under the hot sun, or completely nude under the bright moon. They dove into the sea trying to find a corner with intact bunches of blood red coral missed by professional coral gatherers. At full moon they competed to see who would swim the farthest along the silver moon path, carrying a goblet in one hand to make an offering to Thetis, Poseidon and Hecate.

Sometimes Thais and Eris went riding on the small but stout Cyprus horses who were good in the mountains. After the death of Boanergos, the Athenian had no wish to buy her own horse. Sometimes, as they used to do in Ecbatana with Hesiona, they climbed the mountains on foot. They followed the steep paths, picked a large overhanging plateau which seemed to float in the air, and settled there.

Eris was intoxicated by height. With her eyes flashing and her head tipped back, the black priestess sang strange songs in a language even she did not know, memorized at the temple during her early childhood, or perhaps even earlier in her now-forgotten country. The sad melody went on without beginning or end, suddenly exploding in verses filled with passion and rage, rising into the clear sky like a call for justice. Eris' nostrils trembled, her teeth flashed and her eyes darkened savagely. Everything in Thais wanted to respond to this yearning. The mystical song made her want to stand on the edge of the outcropping, spread her arms and throw herself down into the dark greenery of the woods that looked like a mossy coverlet from above.

Thais was not afraid of heights, but still marveled at Eris' self-control as she stood with her back toward the abyss and casually pointed something out.

Armed with spears, they went on longer trips. Thais wanted her friend to experience in its entirety the enchantment of the woods and mountains of Cyprus, so similar to her beloved Hellas.

For the first time, Eris saw the groves of sprawling pines with long needles, oaks with dark round filigree leaves and red bark, mixed with enormous chestnuts, walnuts and lindens. She was amazed by the forests of tall junipers with their strong scent akin to the cypresses, and the gloomy dark thickets of a different species of juniper with yet another fragrance.

Thais herself was experiencing for the first time the groves of tall cedar trees that were different from those on the Finikian shore. These were slender with short, greenish blue needles. More cedar woods sprawled over the mountain ridges, marching to the east and south among the silence and gloom of the endless colonnades. Below them, crystal clear springs flowed from under rocks, and elm trees grew like thick round hats of greenery supported by twisted charcoal gray trunks.

Thais loved the rocky, sun-drenched plateaus covered with dark bushes of Finikian juniper and fragrant rosemary, crawling stems of thyme and silver bunches of wormwood. The air was filled with warm aromas of a multitude of fragrant plants. The sun seemed to pour itself into one's veins as it reflected off the white outcroppings of marble that popped up at lower heights.

Eris settled on her back. Her dreamy blue eyes met the blue of the sky. She said she was not at all surprised that Hellas had so many artists and beautiful women, and why everyone she met was a connoisseur of beauty one way or another. The nature was a glowing and uplifting world of clearly outlined forms, inviting thoughts, words and deeds. At the same time, these dry and rocky shores, poor in fresh water, did not encourage easy living. Instead, they demanded constant labor, skilled farming and courageous seamanship. This life did not pamper the people living it, but did not consume all of their time with a search for sustenance and protection from natural disasters. Had it not been for the anger, the war and the constant threat of slavery … Even in such a beautiful part of the Ecumene, people had failed to create a life filled with divine serenity and wisdom.

Eris rolled over onto her stomach and gazed at the distant woods or the blue sparkling of the sea. She thought of the countless slaves who had created this beauty: the splendid white temples, porticos, galleries and staircases, piers and windbreakers. What was the purpose of this beauty? Did it soften people's temperaments? Did it reduce violence and cruelty? Did it create more people like Thais and Lysippus who were just and humane? What was life's direction? No one knew, and to receive an answer to that question would mean gaining an understanding of where Hellas, Egypt and other countries were going. Was it toward the better, toward the flourishing and justice, or toward cruelty and death?

Thais was occupied by different thoughts. For the first time she was free of duties and obligations of her elevated rank. She was uninterested in the fact that people admired her, and did not need the constant exercise for distant travel. The Athenian gave herself up to observation for which she always had an inclination. Everything around her felt like home. Her body absorbed the luminous sky, the scents and dry heat of earth and the menacing blue expanse of the sea.

Thais wanted to live like that for years, not depending on anyone and not owing anyone. But summer passed, as did the rainy and windy winter, and the white clusters of asphodels rose again along the roads and paths. The Athenian's lively mind and body demanded activity, new impressions, and perhaps love.

One hundred seventeenth Olympiad was coming to an end, and Thais had fully experienced the meaning of the word ametocleitos as applied to fate: merciless, inevitable and irrevocable. Her Egyptian mirror now reflected silver strands in her thick black hair. Thais noticed the first wrinkles on her smooth body which was still akin to a polished Ethes statuette. They had not been there before and ought not to have been there now. Even her impeccably young body had given in to the pressure of time. The Athenian had never realized how much she would be wounded by this discovery. She set aside the mirror and secluded herself among the laurels to grieve alone and come to terms with the inevitable.

Eris found her there when she brought an urgent letter from Ptolemy. Everything had unfolded as Thais foresaw back in Babylon, when she had explained to Eris the uncertain fate of royal children.

Cassander arrested Alexander's mother, Olympias and accused her of treason. He also captured Alexander's widow Roxanne and his twelve year old son, Alexander the Fourth, the heir of Macedonia, Hellas and Asia. The cruel tyrant ordered the great king's mother and the former high priestess of Pella to be stoned and his widow and son executed. The soldiers did not dare raise their hands against Alexander's own flesh, so Cassander himself tied up the mother and son and drowned them. All of Hellas, all diadochs, and all of Alexander's soldiers who were still living were outraged by the disgusting deed. But, as it often happened, the culprit went unpunished. None of those with power or military force rose against him. For Cassander's crimes were not limited to the slaughter of Alexander's family. The tyrant of Macedonia had carried out many more atrocities.

Eris bitterly regretted that she was not living in Macedonia and had no access to Cassander's inner circle. She would have killed him without delay, she said, although she had no doubt that gods would eventually punish the scoundrel. Her prophecy about Cassander's approaching end turned out to be correct.

The news of the despicable crime resonated deeply with Thais. It caused a spiritual crisis, perhaps because it coincided with the realization of her departing youth. It was now Eris' turn to entertain her by taking her to secret female dances in the moonlight in honor of Hecate, and gathering colorful pigments to the east from the Golden Bay, where green and blue malachite and azurite veins came to the surface of the mountain slopes in bright and pure hues.

In the fall Thais decided she'd spent enough time in country seclusion and decided to go to Pathos. The bustling city was a trade center for copper, cedar and particularly the special fibers for lamp wicks that did not burn away. It was famous the world over for its temple of Aphrodite Anadiomena. There, at Pathos, the goddess appeared from sea foam and starlight, which was why she bore the nickname of Patia or Cypredae, which meant 'born at Cyprus'.

The sacred road led from the temple to a section of the shore separated from the rest of the bay by a wall. Nine marble columns honoring Aphrodite's nine qualities framed the open portico of the pier, which was made of cube-shaped slabs of dense dark stone brought from the Trident Olympus. Two steps led to a water-covered landing made of the same stone. Transparent green waves rolled in from the sea and scattered at the sand bank. Long strips of white foam twirled fancifully over the smooth surface of the landing. Based on these curlicues, the priestesses of the goddess tried to divine the future, for according to the most ancient legends, this was the same spot where the gold-footed Aphrodite, the joy of people and gods, had emerged from the sea.

The beauties of the island: women from noble families, hetaerae, and daughters of farmers and shepherds bathed here after praying at the temple, believing the goddess would bestow upon them a fraction of her irresistible power of attraction. On the fifth day of each week, which was dedicated to Aphrodite, the place was crowded by curious bachelors in search of brides, artists with drawing paraphernalia, and sailors from ships arriving from all Helenian islands, from Finikia, Ionia, Egypt, Sicily and even from Carthage.

After some hesitation, Thais decided to participate in the ritual. Eris examined her friend and assured her that she still looked well enough to bathe during the date. Thais objected and went bathing at night, an hour before midnight, the time dedicated to Eros. Full moon shone over the knee-deep water at the first step, when both friends, having offered a bloodless sacrifice at the temple, entered the sea.

Focused and solemn, Thais stood in the moonlit sea, small waves splashing around and caressing her shoulders as if Thetis were trying to console her. Following a sudden urge, the Athenian raised her arms to the sky, whispering, "Foam-born, here I am at the place where you appeared in the world. Give me a sign. Tell me what to do next. A brief time shall pass and I will no longer bring joy to people or experience their power and yearning for beauty. I will no longer be able to serve you. Life is short. By the time you gather bits of knowledge and realize how to live, you are no longer able to go on. I beg you, oh gold-footed one, show me the way or kill me. Add gentle death to all your prior priceless gifts so that your divine will would see me across the River."

Thais stood for a long time, watching the dark glimmering mirror of the sea, sometimes lifting her head to peer into the delicately-veiled sky. There was no sign or word surrounding Thais, nothing but the whispering of waves.

Delighted shouts, the ringing of small tambourines, and splashing of water startled the two women. They found themselves surrounded by young girls and men, drawing them in a merry dance to the second step of the landing where water was above their shoulders. Not letting the two friends cover up with capes after emerging from the sea, the young people, who were artists and poets as well as their models and lovers, wrapped Thais and Eris in garlands of white flowers that shone like silver in the moonlight. Ignoring their protests, they took them to a symposium as guests of honor.

Thais managed to get their clothes and appeared at the feast fully dressed, much to the disappointment of the sculptors, who had heard a lot about the beautiful bodies of the Athenian and the Ethiopian princess.

During the symposium, Thais secretly observed who attracted more admiring glances. What it she, with her simple hairdo with three silver ribbons, wearing a gryph talon necklace and laughing openly and merrily, or was it Eris, always imperious, with her proudly raised head wearing a crown of menacing serpents, and the necklace of blue beryls sparkling against the dark skin of her long neck.

"They are looking at Eris more. No, at me. No, at Eris." Failing to establish supremacy, Thais became absorbed in singing and dancing. This was the first real symposium of Helenian poets and artists she had attended in many years. Even Eris succumbed to the atmosphere of merriment and youthful love, earning insane admiration of the guests with her dancing.

The Athenian's involvement did not last long. Thais settled off to the side, resting her face on one hand, and watched the young people with pleasure while sensing a strange sort of alienation at the same time.

Several times she caught the careful gaze of her host, a tall Ionian with much gray in his thick mane of wavy hair. It was as if he were trying to understand and weigh all that was happening in Thais' heart. His wife, formerly a famous singer, led the symposium like an experienced hetaera. Following a barely noticeable sign from her husband, she stepped between the tables into the middle of the hall. She whispered to the musicians, they took the first few chords of the halting accompaniment, and the hostess' voice rose amid the silence like a bird freed from its cage.

Thais shivered as the melody reached her heart. This was the song of the Great Threshold that rose inevitably in the path of each man and woman, in the middle of all roads of life. It was erected by Chronos after a number of years, designated by Ananka-Destiny. For the more fortunate ones, the Threshold was merely a small rise. Peaceful farmers stepped over it without noticing. Old warriors did not see the Threshold in their last battle. But people with changeful, event-filled lives, the creators of beauty, travelers and seekers of new lands, they often ran into a kind of wall, with the future beyond that was dark even for the most perceptive. They either chose not to cross the Great Threshold and wait for the end of their days by its side, or they threw themselves bravely into the unknown future, leaving everything behind: love and hate, happiness and peril.

The singer sang in Aeolian dialect, addressing Thais as if perceiving her as someone who had arrived at the Threshold and stood before it in noble and fearless contemplation.

The song struck a chord with the young ones as well, despite the fact they were still far from the Threshold of Destiny. Its shadow subdued the passionate joy of the symposium, providing a sign to end the celebration. The guests vanished into the night in pairs and groups. Luminaries between the portico of the entrance and the feasting hall were put out. Thais and Eris rose, thanking their hosts.

"You are guests of our city," the master of the house said. "You would do us an honor if you agreed to rest here, under our roof. The inn is far away from the Sacred Road, and it is late."

"Worthy host, you do not even know who we are," the Athenian replied. "And we arrived without invitation. We were brought here by your friends. They were sweet and we did not wish to offend them."

"You are wrong to think that citizens of Pathos do not know Thais," the host said with a chuckle. "Even if we'd never heard of you, your beauty and conduct at the symposium would have been sufficient. The visit to my house by you and your royal friend is a holiday. Please make it last by staying overnight."

Thais stayed with nary an inkling of a great change in her destiny. It would transpire after her visit to the house on the shore of Cypredae.

The next day, while swimming with the wife and daughters of the host, the Athenian learned of the sanctuary of Aphrodite Ambologera. Until then, she and many other Athenians had believed that the incarnation of Aphrodite Averting Old Age was but one of symbols of the many-faced goddess. Perhaps it was the youngest of her images, akin to the statues of a barely-blossoming girl made of transparent pink Rhodes marble. It was much loved by sculptors and forbidden at temples by the strict censors of old tradition.

Here on Cyprus, Aphrodite's birthplace, there was an ancient temple of Ambologera Averting Old Age. It was visited by the goddess' favorites, men and women who were approaching the Great Threshold of the Mother. They made offerings, listened to prophecies, selected a new path and went home either encouraged, or with their heads lowered in sadness, seeing nothing but the dust of the road under their sandals.

The temple of Aphrodite Ambologera was located three days away on foot from Pathos, at the border of an ancient Finikian colony at the southeast of the island. It was said that the temple had been built by Helenians and Finikians together, as they both worshiped the Averter of Old Age. Thais set her mind on visiting it.

"This will not bring you serenity or happiness," Eris said with certainty, warning her friend.

Thais replied that she presently did not possess either of the two, and would not until she found another path. "Do you not feel that way yourself?"

"No. I never parted from sorrow, and thus never lost the guiding light in my life," Eris replied mysteriously.

The Athenian did not listen. Accompanied by her new friends, they rode up a twisting stone road, ascending into the mountains through pine groves and dark cedar woods. After the silence and the dry resin-scented air at the southern slope of the mountain range, the travelers emerged onto a vast plateau. Bluish rocks protruded through the surface among silvery grasses rippling in the wind. A peak towered ahead, split in half by a wide road with the temple at the top. The entrance to the valley had once been marked by structures that were presently in ruins. All that was left were broad, even levels, surrounded by enormous stone slabs and covered with trees. Walnuts, chestnuts and sycamores that were centuries old stood in their crimson autumn attire, followed by two giant cedars whose clear outlines formed a kind of gate and whose sprawling horizontal branches were so thick they screened away small rocks that fell from above.

An alley, framed by flaming gold trees, led deep into the valley. A sense of incredible light and serenity descended upon Thais. Other visitors grew quiet and spoke in whispers, trying not to interrupt the rustling of autumn leaves and the bubbling of a spring that flowed along the bottom of the valley, pouring over the edges of terraced pools in small cascades among the flat, moss-covered stones.

Mountains rose in the gaps among trees, covered with the moss of centuries and wrapped in a mysterious enchantment of ages past.

Further into the valley the rows of dark cypresses intersected with crimson pyramid poplars. The smell of heated autumn foliage and needles was simultaneously fresh, bitter and dry without any tinge of road dust. Behind them the valley broadened and spread in a pool of evening sunlight, filled with peace and warmth. Reddening crowns of oaks, elms and maples foamed among the spread of flat pine tops.

The temple of Aphrodite Ambologera resembled a fortress. The walls of gray stone protruded into the gorge, closing off the mountain peak from the west. The façade of the sanctuary with its colonnade faced the east, soaring above the plateau. It was planted generously with grapes and fruit trees. Their Pathos friends asked them to wait, then struck a bronze sheet hanging on a short chain three times and stepped through a dark narrow entrance. They soon returned with two priestesses of unquestionably high rank. They examined Thais and Eris sternly and seriously, then one of them, who was dressed in a pale gray garment, suddenly smiled. She placed her hands on their shoulders and nodded lightly to their hosts, then led the two women into the temple.

The usual silent rituals followed: evening fasting, cleansing and nighttime watch on the floor at the sanctuary's door.

At dawn the high priestess appeared, ordered them each to eat an apple and take off their clothes, then led the two friends to the Goddess Averting Old Age, Aphrodite Ambologera. Neither the Athenian nor the black priestess had ever seen the likes of this temple. A triangular skylight in the roof directed the bright glow of the sky towards two walls the color of helianthus petals which converged ahead in the direction of the east.

Upon the walls, bronze nails held up enormous sheets of wood at least ten elbows wide, cut from whole tree trunks. Only thousand year old trees like Lebanese cedars could possess such girth. Two goddesses were painted on them in pure mineral colors used for eternal frescoes by an artist who must have been a greater genius than Apelles himself.

The left painting, in hot shades of red earth and flaming sunset, portrayed a woman at the height of earthly fertility and health. Her full lips, breasts and hips were so filled with desire, they seemed ready to burst from wild broiling passion, pouring forth the dark blood of the Great Mother, the Queen of the Abyss. Her hands reached toward the viewer with an irresistible yearning and held a dark rose, which was a symbol of feminine essence, and a square vessel with a star with which Thais was familiar.

"Lilith," Thais said, barely moving her lips, unable to take her eyes off the painting.

"No," Eris replied. "Lilith is kind. This one is death."

The priestess raised her eyebrows when she heard them, and pointed at the right wall with agitation. The Athenian sighed in relief as she saw the embodiment of her dream.

The blue color scheme blended together the sea, the sky and the low horizon. Against this backdrop the goddess' body assumed a pearly tinge of early dawn, when large stars still shone above and the opal sea splashed against rose-colored sand. Urania walked, barely touching the ground with her bare toes, reaching up to the morning sky, wind and clouds. The face of the goddess half-turned over her shoulder, looked both into the distance and at the viewer, promising comfort with the gaze of her eyes. These were gray, like Thais'. Light shone over her forehead and between her eyebrows, emphasizing, rather than competing with, the light in her eyes.

A time-blackened incense-burner fumed on a low altar before each painting.

"Were you told of the two faces of Ambologera?" the priestess asked.

"Yes," Thais and Eris replied in unison, remembering their evening conversation with the temple's philosopher.

"Neither the Olympian gods nor the Great Mother herself can avert the aging of a mortal body. All things in the world are subject to the flow of time. But there is a choice. It is before you. You may burn in the last fire of serving Aphrodite. Or you may transfer this fire to the all-encompassing love, leading toward heaven, serving Urania in tireless care about the happiness of those young and old. Place something that is not necessarily valuable but that is most precious to each of you before the goddess of your choice."

Without hesitation Thais approached Urania, unclasped the chain sash with a single star given to her by Alexander and placed it on the altar.

Eris remained motionless. The priestess of Ambologera gazed at her in surprise.

"Is there no middle path?" Eris asked.

"There is," the priestess said. She smiled and clapped her hands three times.

Heavy panes of the wall between the paintings opened slowly. A semicircular balcony overlooked a peaceful valley with vineyards, olive trees and a field of wheat. Men and women worked hard that cool morning, growing the fruits of Gaea-Demeter. There were quite a few elderly people, gray-haired men and women in heavy garments and dark head coverings.

"Peaceful labor in the quiet and serenity of the last years of life is a noble end of a farmer," the priestess said.

"Then there is a fourth way," Eris said.

"Why did you come to Ambologera?" the priestess asked, spreading her arms as if to stop Eris from going back to the sanctuary.

The black priestess, majestic, proud and solemn, appeared more imposing than ever to Thais. Her blue eyes gazed at the priestess with elevated confidence, but without daunting or mocking, and the priestess calmed down.

"Why do I need the insult of another faith?" Eris asked. "You showed three paths and all three are for lonely men and women. A person leaves the community of others only after death. There must be a way of serving people not just by means of personal perfection, but by direct action to their benefit."

"Then you did not understand the depth of the symbols you saw. The middle path gives people food to sustain them, for a farmer always has more to feed an artist and a poet and thus increases the beauty of the world. The path of Urania is for a wise and gentle woman. It can only be expressed through love and care for others. That is what a woman must always do to achieve joy in her heart. That is why Urania is an ideal woman and that is why Plato considered her to be the most important for the future of humankind."

"And forgot about the perils and screams of slaves who give their lives to serve like beasts of burden so that Urania's admirers could pour their love over their equally elevated fellows." Eris replied angrily, causing the Athenian to stare at her friend in amazement.

"No!" Eris exclaimed, leaning forward like her statue of Acsiopena. "Heavenly Love and celestial peace are not possible over the corpses of the defeated or the backs of slaves. You, people of the west, who reached the heights of philosophy and flaunting your freedom, do not see the essential error in all your reasoning. You imagine power only through murder and sacrifice. Those who are more skilled in murder are stronger and, consequently, right. Such are your gods, your heroes and you. This is a curse of the Great Mother you shall bear to the end as long as the people of the west exist. That is why the second image of Ambologera, Urania, is a lie for poets and failed lovers."

"What of the other image?" the stunned priestess asked hoarsely.

"The goddess of Dark Eros? There is truth in her, and I used to serve her with all the passion of youthful faith. It is a good path for those filled with animal power."

"Or those who have yet to comprehend Urania," Thais interjected.

"Thousands of years ago, the Great Mother appeared to people in the same two images – those of destruction and creation, death and eternity. Except eternity is not available to us, and we must not deceive ourselves and each other with that symbol of our heart's yearning. It is but a way to conceal the cruel truth of the Great Mother. We all know, and this knowledge runs deep inside us, that eternal forces of nature are always ready to destroy. And we create in our dreams – exalted and pure, or lowly and dark – a multitude of gods and goddesses to protect us from the forces of the Great Mother, as one would try to hide from a storm behind a delicate curtain. The weak plead for miracles, like the beggars for money, instead of taking action and clearing their path by their own power and will. The burden of a free and fearless man is great and sad. And if he does not attempt to load it off onto a god or a mythical hero, but carries it himself, he becomes truly godlike, worthy of heaven and stars."

The overwhelmed priestess of Ambologera covered her face with her hands.

"There is also eternal reincarnation," Thais dared, uncovering the Orphic mystery.

"With the payment for the past when there is nothing you can do to correct it?" Eris continued. "I was taught the notion of Karma at Eridu and I came to believe in it. That is why the fourth path is so difficult for me. I could kill everyone who brings suffering to others, and who use falsehoods to lead people into the abyss of cruelty, and who teach them to kill and destroy supposedly for the benefit of humankind. I believe there will be time, when there are more people like me, and each would kill at least ten scoundrels. The river of human generations will become cleaner with each century until it turns unto a crystal clear stream. I am ready to devote my life to this, but I need a teacher. And not the kind of teacher that only gives orders. Then I would be a mere assassin, like all fanatics. I need a teacher to show me what is right and what is wrong, what is light and what is darkness, and leave the last decision to me. Can there not be a path like that? And I need a teacher who can tell a dead soul from a living one, and who knows who is unworthy of living on this earth another hour. In order for a human being to undertake the difficult duty of retribution, he must possess the divine precision of aim. Only the highest consciousness, reinforced by a wise teacher, can avoid that which always happens when force is used blindly. A healthy tree is cut, leaving a rotten one behind. Precious seedlings of future heroes are killed, allowing more room for human weeds to flourish."

The priestess of Ambologera dared not look up under Eris' burning gaze. Thais approached and embraced her friend, feeling each of her muscles trembling.

"I have no answer for you, even having sampled the ancient wisdom of Eridu," the Athenian said sadly. "Perhaps you and those like you will become weapons of Karma without being burdened by responsibility. I know little and am not very intelligent. But I feel that with people like you there would be much less grief and poison in the Ecumene."

"I do not know where you came from, sun-scorched woman," the priestess of Ambologera finally said. "Or who placed words into your mouth, to which I do not know an answer. Perhaps you are a messenger of the new people sent to us from the future, or perhaps you are the last of those who were left in the past. Your notions about Urania are incorrect and distasteful. Your friend will tell you that one in the position of power can do much for the sake of Heavenly Love."

"I see you have never risen high enough." Thais smiled. "A female ruler is more helpless than others. And this is not only because she is held back by the rules of behavior, guidelines and rituals of religion, or limited by the royal inaccessibility. She is overseen by advisers telling her what is beneficial and what is not. That is, they tell her what is beneficial for power, beneficial for accumulation of wealth, beneficial for war. Nothing is ever said about what is beneficial for the heart, your own and those of other people. You said that a woman must work for her heart. I was a queen and succeeded very little at that. I could not even save my own child from exclusively male upbringing that turns a young man into a weapon of war instead of a servant of Urania."

Thais remembered Leontiscus and his boyish faith in beautiful Nereids, and her eyes filled with tears.

Eris said quietly, "We are used to thinking about gods as jealous creatures who would destroy perfection in people and their creations. Would a true admirer of beauty be capable of such a thing? Does that mean that a man is beyond gods? Of course not. The fact that gods were invented and had the worst human traits bestowed upon them, reflects the entire wrongness and unworthiness of our life, in which fate, of which we are weapons, takes the good ones away and protects the bad ones. We must correct this on our own, and if we cannot save the good ones we can at the least eliminate human scum, not letting them live any longer or better."

The priestess of Ambologera stood dismayed between the two incredible women she'd met for the first time, who were so different and so alike in their inner greatness. She bowed before them, which she had never done for anyone, and said modestly, "You do not require my advice or Ambologera's health. Please get dressed and go downstairs. I shall ask for a wise man, a friend of our philosopher. He arrived recently from Ionian and has been telling us strange things about Alexarches, Cassander's brother."

"Brother of a ruthless killer? What good can one expect from a man like that?" Thais asked sharply.

"Still, I think both of you need to learn about Uranopolis, the City of Heaven, the place for people like you."

And the two friends discovered something unheard of, that had never happened anywhere in the Ecumene, not captured in the inscriptions carved in stone, in legends or in historic records. Alexarches, the son of Antipatros and the younger brother of Cassander, the ruler of Macedonia, had received a plot of land in Khalkidhiki, at the isthmus behind Athos mountain, where Xerxes had been ordered to construct a canal once upon a time. There Alexarches founded the city of Uranopolis, thirty stadiums in circumference. Being a scholar of linguistics, Alexarches invented a special language for his citizens. He refused to be addressed as a king and assumed only the title of the High Councilor in the Council of Philosophers who were in charge of the city. His own brother, who once declared Alexander mad, now said the same about Alexarches. Alexarches then abandoned construction in Khalkidhiki and transferred Uranopolis to Pamphilia[41]. He took with him the descendants of the Pelasges who resided near Athos. They were joined by freedom-loving Ephesians, Clazomenes and Carians.

Citizens of Uranopolis were all like brothers and sisters, equal in their rights. They proudly called themselves Uranides, or Children of Heaven. They worshiped the Maid of Heaven, Aphrodite Urania, in the same way Athenians worshiped Athena, and minted her image on their coins. Other gods of the citizens were sun, moon and stars and were also portrayed on the coins along with the more upstanding citizens. Alexarches dreamed of spreading the idea of

---

[41] A portion of west Taurus and Ichel at the southern coast of Turkey.

brotherhood among people under the protection of Urania, the united love, to all of the Ecumene. First and foremost he wished to eliminate the difference between languages and religions. He wrote letters to Cassander and other rulers in the language invented for the City of Heaven. The wise man saw two of these letters, but no one could decipher them.

What she learned overturned all of Thais' intentions.

What she dreamed of during the sleepless nights in Athens, in Egypt, in Babylon, and in Ecbatana, had come true. She felt the warm breath of the Lykean mountains. Love that did not serve jealous deities, that did not slavishly follow armies, was becoming a foundation of the city-state of Aphrodite, the daughter of Heaven, the highest deity of wisdom and hope.

She now had a goal, a place to apply her ability in inspiring artists and poets, as well as her own thoughts of reaching Urania. And this goal was so close, across the sea and to the north of the golden Bay, a mere thousand stadiums away. She was grateful to Ambologera. Without her, she would never have found out about the existence of the city from her magical dream.

A few months later, having gathered all her treasures and left Irana to be brought up on Cyprus, Thais and her inseparable friend were aboard a ship, rushing toward the broad Adalian Bay. Lykean mountains rose from beyond the horizon like heavy stone domes, covered with dazzling white snow, like a promise of purity. The ship slowly sailed around a sharp rock and they saw a small blue port with a delta of a swift river at the back. On its western shore the structures of Uranopolis, standing behind a low wall, were turning pink in the rays of the rising sun. Cypresses and sycamores rose along the streets and around the façades of modest homes. The central square was occupied by the recently finished building of the Council of Heaven, which sparkled with freshly cut white lime and a plinth of bluish stone visible from afar.

The ship docked. Thais glanced at the less than mighty walls, straight streets and a low sloping hill of Acropolis. She saw a whirlwind of visions of enormous seven and nine walled cities of Persia and Finikian coast, the cities of Egypt, protected by scorching deserts that fell before the conquerors and were pillaged and deserted. The white magnificence of Persepolis, turned into blackened ruins by her own hands.

Uranopolis suddenly seemed like a fragile altar of humankind's heavenly dream, set precariously at the edge of the hostile world. A premonition of doom squeezed Thais' heart with a cruel hand and when she glanced at Eris, she recognized the same anxiety in her friend's face. The City of Heaven could not exist long, but the Athenian felt no doubt or desire to seek a safe place on Cyprus, in Alexandria, or in one of the more secluded corners of Hellas.

The City of Heaven was her dream and the meaning of her future life. If it vanished, what would remain of her, unless she gave all of herself to serve the Children of Heaven? Responding to her thoughts, Eris squeezed her hand firmly and nudged her toward the gangplank.

Thais and Eris descended onto the pier. Sailors, supervised by Roykos, carried heavy bundles and boxes with valuable offerings to the mission of Alexarches and Urania.

Epilogue

Such was the end of the incredible life of Thais of Athens. The darkness of Hades and the abyss of centuries past swallowed her up along with the first City of Love and Heaven.

Creation of the glorious dream could not have existed for long among the mighty and savage kings or army leaders, or priests of false faith, greed and deception.

The tiny island of the budding new morality in the sea of ignorance, Uranopolis, was soon wiped from the face of Gaea by a horde of experienced conquerors.

The two friends vanished along with the city. Did they manage to escape enslavement, sailing to other, still peaceful isles? Or did they give themselves to Thetis, pursued by invading soldiers? Did Eris send her Thais to the underworld with the firm hand of a black priestess and follow her immediately? One could invent any ending to correspond to his own dream. One thing is certain: neither Thais nor Eris became slaves of those who destroyed Uranopolis and ended their good service to people.

About the Author

Ivan Yefremov (1908 – 1972) was a Soviet writer and paleontologist. In addition to introducing a new paleontological field taphonomy – the study of fossilization patterns, Yefremov has written a series of novels and short stories, including science fiction, historic fiction, adventure and drama.

Yefremov is frequently ridiculed for his enthusiasm and faith in the viability of a communist society, as described in his best known science fiction novel *Andromeda Nebula*. It is not widely known that his more mature works such as *The Hour of the Bull* and *The Razor Blade*, had the writer either hindered or blacklisted by two Soviet administrations in a row (three if you count Stalin's, during which Yefremov started and abandoned some of his writing projects, for fear of persecution), as Yefremov's interpretation of a fair and balanced society deviated sharply from the government propaganda of the time.

To Yefremov's fans, including scientists, astronauts, writers, and artists, he is known for his thorough scientific analysis, study of art and history, emphasis on physical and intellectual balance and strong female characters.

About the Translator

Maria K. is a pen name of Maria Igorevna Kuroshchepova – a first-generation Russian-Ukrainian immigrant. An engineer by education, an analyst by trade, as well as a writer, photographer, artist and amateur model, Maria brings her talent for weaving an engaging narrative to stories of life, fashion and style advice, book and movie reviews, and common-sense and to-the-point essays on politics and economy.

Acknowledgments

Huge thanks to my husband Gerry Seymour who had to put up with months of questions like, "Where in the world is Harmosia?!" and "Any idea where I might find a picture of a battle elephant?"

I bow before my incredible editor Genevieve Graham-Sawchyn, who took upon herself to untangle the grammatical mess that is an enormous work of literature written by a Russian and translated by another (albeit bi-lingual) Russian.

I am grateful to my sisters and brothers in writing for providing feedback on the illustrations and unedited snippets from the book I shared with them, and for cheering me on all the way.

Other works by Maria K.

A Child in Translation

A deeply personal autobiographic narrative about growing up in Soviet Ukraine that delivers a vivid picture of life in a part of the world most outsiders have never thought about. Please meet Maria from the Ukraine. She came to the West as an alien, bringing with her a childhood yet to be defined by translation.

Available in print and e-format.

Stories for Anastasia

It's Raining Cats and Dogs!
How do you entertain a child who has spent a lot of time in hospitals? You come up with some marvelous stories! And author Maria K. certainly has done that.

In *Stories for Anastasia*, Maria, who comes from a long line of storytellers, provides a charming collection of essays written to entertain her young niece, who needed activities to keep the child busy while she recuperated.

The essays are nonfiction and are written in a humorous style. They illustrate that you can find fun and excitement in everyday events.

Welcome to Maria's household, where the occupants include some book-crazy, martial arts-trained technology geeks, some homeless animals, and a very old house just begging for attention.

Available in print and e-format.

Made in the USA
Lexington, KY
09 January 2014